D0226137

The Complete Guide to the TOEFL® Test

iBT EDITION

BRUCE ROGERS

TOEFL® iBT is a registered trademark of the Educational Testing Service (ETS), Princeton, New Jersey, USA. The test questions and all other testing information in this text are provided in their entirety by Heinle ELT. No endorsement of this publication by ETS should be inferred.

HEINLE
CENGAGE Learning™

Australia • Canada • Mexico • Singapore • Spain • United Kingdom • United States

HEINLE
CENGAGE Learning

The Complete Guide to the TOEFL® Test, iBT Edition

BRUCE ROGERS

Publisher, Academic ESL: James W. Brown

Executive Editor, Dictionaries & Adult ESL:
Sherrise Roehr

Director of Product Development:
Anita Raducanu

Associate Development Editor: Jennifer
Meldrum

Director of Product Marketing: Amy Mabley

Senior Field Marketing Manager:
Donna Lee Kennedy

International Marketing Manager: Ian Martin

Assistant Marketing Manager: Heather Soberg

Senior Print Buyer: Mary Beth Hennebury

Development Editor: Charlotte Sturdy

Production Editor: Chrystie Hopkins

Project Manager: Merrill Peterson

Production Services: Matrix Productions

Compositor: Parkwood Composition Service

Cover Designer: Studio Montage

Library of Congress Control Number: 2005936075

ISBN 13: 978-1-4130-2303-9

ISBN 10: 1-4130-2303-7

Heinle
20 Channel Center
Boston, MA 02210
USA

Cengage Learning is a leading provider of customized learning solutions with office locations around the globe, including Singapore, the United Kingdom, Australia, Mexico, Brazil, and Japan. Locate your local office at:
international.cengage.com/region

Cengage Learning products are represented in Canada by Nelson-Education, Ltd.

Visit Heinle online at **elt.heinle.com**
Visit our corporate website at **cengage.com**

Credits appear on page 818, which constitutes a continuation of the copyright page.

Printed in the U.S.A.
5 6 7 8 9 10 — 10

Contents

PREFACE

TO THE STUDENT

If you are preparing for the TOEFL® (Test of English as a Foreign Language) iBT, you are not alone. About a million people all over the world take the test every year. A high score on this test is an essential step in being admitted to undergraduate or graduate programs in the United States and Canada. But preparing for this test can be a difficult, frustrating experience. Perhaps you haven't taken many standardized tests such as the TOEFL test. Perhaps you're not familiar with the format, or you're not sure how to focus your studies. Maybe you've taken the test before but were not satisfied with your scores.

And now the TOEFL iBT (iBT = Internet-Based Test) is a much more communicative test. What new skills are required? What tactics are needed for top scores? How can you best practice for this version of the test?

You need a guide. That's why this book was written—to guide people preparing for this important test so that they can earn the highest scores possible.

The Complete Guide to the TOEFL® Test, iBT Edition is the most complete, accurate, and up-to-date preparation book available. It is based on years of experience teaching preparation classes in the United States and abroad. It is simply written and clearly organized and is suitable for any intermediate to advanced English language student.

This book offers a step-by-step program designed to make you feel confident and well prepared when you sit down in front of the computer on the day of the test. It teaches you the test-taking techniques and helps you polish the language skills you need to do well on all four sections of the test, including the Speaking Section, which, for many students, is the greatest challenge of the TOEFL iBT. And *The Guide* is an efficient way to prepare for the TOEFL iBT. By concentrating only on the points that are actually tested on the TOEFL test, it lets you make the most of your preparation time and never wastes your time.

ABOUT THIS EDITION: WHAT'S NEW?

This edition of *The Complete Guide to the TOEFL® Test, iBT Edition,* like the TOEFL iBT itself, has been completely updated. It reflects the changes made in the format, the items, and the basic philosophy of the revised exam.

On the TOEFL iBT, the first section of the test, Reading, features longer readings and new question types. In the first section of this book, Guide to Reading, you'll work with extended readings similar to those on the test and learn about new item types. One new type of question, for example, asks you to complete an outline or summary of the reading. These questions require you to have a "global" (general) understanding of readings rather than an understanding of individual facts in the reading. There are questions that ask you *why* an author wrote some part of the passage or *how* the author communicates ideas. There are questions that ask you to recognize paraphrases of complex sentences. In the first section of the book, you will find explanations and exercises that help you develop the skills you need to answer these new question types.

In the Listening Section of the test, the lectures and conversations have gotten longer and more involved as well. However, note taking is now permitted. There are also some new question types in Listening. The second section of the book, Guide to Listening, offers tips and help with note taking as well as experience with answering all types of questions about the lectures. Another new feature of the test is the "authentic language" used by the speakers. On past forms of the test, the speakers sounded like actors reading from a book. On the TOEFL iBT, the speakers sound more natural, like real professors giving classroom lectures or real students discussing campus situations. The new Audio Program for this Guide reflects these changes, and the lectures and conversations have the same feel as those used on the actual test.

The Speaking Section of the TOEFL iBT is all new, and so is the Guide to Speaking in this book. There are two types of Speaking Tasks on the exam. Independent Speaking Tasks ask the test-taker to use his or her own knowledge and background as the topic of two short responses. The four Integrated Speaking Tasks require the test-taker to listen to information from a lecture or conversation and (for two of the tasks) from a reading. Many test-takers find the Speaking Section—especially the Integrated Tasks—the most challenging section of the test. One reason is simply that test-takers have little experience with this type of task. The new Guide to Speaking in this book provides extensive practice and hints for scoring well on this section.

The Writing Section, like the Speaking Section, has an "independent" and an "integrated" component. The Independent Task is similar to the essay section on previous versions of the test. It draws upon the test-taker's own experiences and background knowledge. The new Integrated Task is based on a lecture and a reading with contrasting ideas. The Guide to Writing in this book has been expanded and a new section on the Integrated Task has been added to prepare you for this part of the test.

Another new feature of this text is the Communicative Activities provided at the end of each section to give you and your classmates more speaking and writing practice.

ORGANIZATION OF THIS BOOK

Getting Started   Two sections introduce you to the book and the test:

▶ **Question and Answers about the TOEFL® iBT** This section provides you with basic information about the design of the Internet-based test and helps you understand the revised scoring system.

▶ **Ten Keys to Better Scores on the TOEFL® iBT** This section presents the "secrets" of being a good test-taker: arranging your preparation time, using the process of elimination to make the best guess on multiple-choice items, coping with test anxiety, pacing yourself during the test, and other important techniques.

Main Sections   The main part of this textbook is divided into four sections reflecting the four parts of the exam: Reading, Listening, Speaking, and Writing. Each of these four parts consists of the following:

▶ **An introduction** to each test section with basic strategies.

▶ **A preview test** to give you a feel for each part of the test and to provide a basis for understanding the lessons.

▶ **Lessons** that break down the knowledge and skills that you need into comprehensible "bites" of information. Each of the twenty-eight lessons in this book contains sample items from the preview tests that illustrate exactly how the point brought up in that lesson is tested on the TOEFL iBT. Furthermore, each lesson contains one or more exercises that practice the relevant points.

▶ **Review tests** that go over the points discussed in the lessons. These tests put together the points practiced in isolation in the lessons.

▶ **Tutorials** (found near the end of each section) covering important testing points that require more time to master than points brought up in the lessons.

▶ **Communicative activities** (found near the end of each section) that are designed to encourage classroom communication.

Guide to Reading   Each of the eight lessons in this section covers one of the main types of questions that appear in the Reading Section of the TOEFL iBT and is designed to give you extensive practice reading passages and answering these questions. The tutorial for this section helps you build your vocabulary.

Guide to Listening   Each of the six lessons in this section concentrates on one of the main types of questions asked about the conversations and lectures. There is extensive practice for listening, taking notes, and answering questions. The tutorial for this section is about note taking.

Guide to Speaking   This section is divided into two parts, one covering the Independent Tasks and one covering the Integrated Tasks. Each of the six lessons focuses on one of the six types of Speaking Tasks and provides exercises to help you plan and deliver the responses. The tutorial for this section helps you improve your pronunciation.

Guide to Writing   This section is divided into two parts as well: Integrated Writing and Independent Writing. The eight lessons in this part of the book guide you through the process of planning, writing, and editing the two writing responses. The tutorial for this section helps you improve your written grammar.

Two Complete Practice Tests   Taking realistic practice tests is one of the best ways to get ready for the TOEFL® test. You can take these tests in the book or on the accompanying CD-ROM.

Audio Program   The audio component provides all the material needed for the exercises and tests. It is available on either audio CD or audio cassettes. (The audio program is sold separately.)

Answer Key and Audioscript   Answers and explanations for questions and a script for the Audio Program are provided. This resource is also available online at elt.heinle.com/toefl.

CD-ROM   The computer CD-ROM includes four complete practice tests: the two tests from this book and two additional practice tests.

To the Teacher

The TOEFL iBT puts a lot of emphasis on communicative skills, and as much as you can, you should put the same emphasis on interaction in the classroom. In the past, a lot of TOEFL test preparation involved coaching students for the Structure Section of the test, but the TOEFL iBT does not directly test grammar. No matter which of the four parts of the test you are preparing for, be sure to have students work in pairs or small groups and encourage lively give-and-take discussion.

Students who feel perfectly comfortable taking long multiple-choice tests may feel more challenged by some of the communicative tasks they are given on this test. It is recommended that in every class you do some practice for the Speaking Tasks. You might, for example, begin with two or three students giving one-minute timed, impromptu talks. These can be "integrated" tasks based on summaries of newspaper articles or news stories from television or radio, or they can be "independent" tasks based on students' own experience. Make sure everyone gets a chance to talk, and get the rest of the class involved in asking the speaker questions about the presentations.

At least once a week it is useful to work on one or more of the Communicative Activities. These are designed to get students involved in talking and working together by playing games, having discussions, or working on projects. There are ten or more activities for each of the four sections of the test.

A good way to begin the course is by taking one of the two practice tests. This familiarizes students with the test and shows them what to expect when they take the actual exam.

You can work through the lessons starting at the first lesson, or you can begin with the section in which your students seemed to have the most problems on the first practice test.

It is certainly important to give your students exposure to computers, especially for the Writing Section. However, the computer skills required to take the test are relatively basic and the focus should be on applying language skills and using test-taking strategies, not developing computer proficiency.

Following are the amounts of time suggested to cover each section of *The Guide*. These times are approximate and will vary from class to class.

Getting Started	1 to 2 hours
Guide to Reading	20 to 24 hours
Guide to Listening	14 to 18 hours
Guide to Speaking	12 to 16 hours
Guide to Writing	12 to 16 hours
Practice Tests	8 to 10 hours

What if you don't have time to cover everything in *The Guide?* Don't worry! *The Complete Guide to the TOEFL® Test, iBT Edition* was designed so that you can skip parts of the exercises and lessons and still improve your students' scores.

I welcome your thoughts, comments, questions, and suggestions. Please feel free to contact me via e-mail: Bruce_Rogers_CGT@mail.com

ABOUT THE AUTHOR

Bruce Rogers has taught test preparation and English as a Second/Foreign Language courses since 1979. He has taught in the United States, Indonesia, Vietnam, Korea, and the Czech Republic. He is also the author of Heinle's *The Complete Guide to the TOEIC® Test* and *The Introductory Guide to the TOEIC® Test.* He lives in Boulder, Colorado, USA.

Acknowledgments

I would like to thank all of the English-language professionals who provided their comments and suggestions during the development of *The Complete Guide to the TOEFL® Test, iBT Edition* as well as earlier editions.

Thanks to the students of Front Range Community College and Cambridge Center for Adult Education who allowed me to use their writing and speaking samples and to the professors at the University of Colorado who allowed me to sit in on their lectures. Thanks to Kevin Keating, University of Arizona, for suggesting some of the Communication Activities.

Special thanks to Jody Stern, Charlotte Sturdy, Linda Grant, Chrystie Hopkins, Merrill Peterson, Jennifer Meldrum, and Anita Raducanu for their expert help and advice.

Heinle ELT would like to thank the following reviewers for their contributions.

Joshua Atherton
University of Texas
Arlington, TX

Consuelo Fernandes Barbosa Ivo
Centro Cultural Brasil Estados Unidos
Campinas, Brazil

Valéria Benévolo França
Cultura Inglesa Rio Brasilia
Botafogo, Brazil

Dorina Garza Leonard
Instituto Tecnológico de Monterrey
Monterrey, Mexico

Claudia Hernandez
Colegio Patria de Juarez
Mexico City, Mexico

Eduardo Ipac
Centro Cultural Brasil Estados Unidos
Campinas, Brazil

Ruo-chiang Jao
Merica Language Institute
Yeonghce City, Taiwan

Rangho Jung
EG Language School
Seoul, Korea

Maria Aurora Patiño Leal
Instituto Tecnológico de Monterrey
Monterrey, Mexico

Dr. Carolyn Prager
Spanish American Institute
New York, NY

Dr. Karen Russikoff
California State Polytechnic University
Pomona, CA

Joan Sears
Texas Tech University
Lubbock, TX

Barbara Smith-Palinkas
University of South Florida
Tampa, FL

Kwang-Ja Son
Moonjin Media
Seoul, Korea

Robert Richmond Stroupe
Soka University
Tokyo, Japan

Graciela Tamez
Instituto Tecnológico de Monterrey
Monterrey, Mexico

Grant Trew
Nova Group
Osaka, Japan

Gabriela Ulloa
Instituto Tecnológico de Monterrey
Monterrey, Mexico

Hilda Zacour
Instituto Miguel Angel, Mexico
DF, Mexico

GETTING STARTED

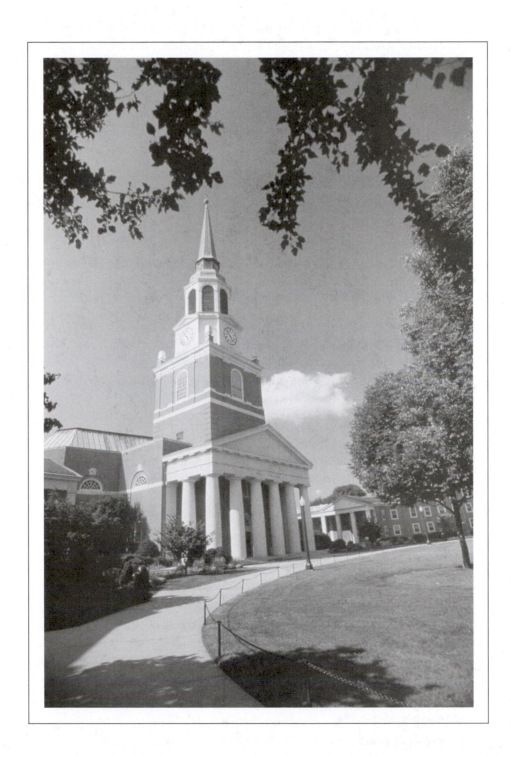

QUESTIONS AND ANSWERS ABOUT THE TOEFL® iBT

Q: What is the TOEFL Test?

A: TOEFL stands for *Test of English as a Foreign Language.* It is a test designed to measure the English-language ability of people who do not speak English as their first language and who plan to study at colleges and universities in North America.

Educational Testing Service (ETS) of Princeton, New Jersey, prepares and administers the TOEFL test. This organization produces many other standardized tests, such as the Test of English for International Communication (TOEIC), the Scholastic Aptitude Test (SAT), and the Graduate Record Exam (GRE).

Although there are other standardized tests of English, the TOEFL test is by far the most important in North America; ETS has offered this exam since 1965. Each year, almost a million people take the TOEFL test at testing centers all over the world. About 5,000 colleges, universities, and other institutions in the United States and Canada either require students from non-English-speaking countries to supply TOEFL test scores as part of their application process or accept TOEFL test scores as evidence of a person's proficiency in English.

Q: And what is the TOEFL iBT?

A: For more than thirty years, the TOEFL test was given as a paper-and-pencil, multiple-choice test. In 1998, a computer-based version of the test became available in many parts of the world. The newest generation of the test, the TOEFL iBT (Internet-based test), was introduced during the 2005–2006 academic year.

As the name implies, the test is delivered over the Internet. Test-takers work on the tests at individual computer stations at official testing centers. The test is offered only on scheduled testing dates.

The TOEFL iBT is significantly different from the computer-based version of the test.

Q: Different? How is the TOEFL iBT different?

A: For one thing, the basic way in which the TOEFL iBT tests English is different. The new test emphasizes a test-taker's ability to *communicate* in an academic setting. For that reason, a Speaking Section has been added and the Writing Section has been expanded.

Specifically, the TOEFL iBT differs from the previous version in the following ways:

▶ There is a new Speaking Section that tests your ability to communicate orally. You record responses that are scored by raters at ETS.

▶ You are allowed to take notes during all parts of the test.

▶ There are "integrated" tasks that require you to combine your speaking and writing skills with your reading and listening skills.

▶ Grammar skills are tested indirectly, especially in the Speaking and Writing Sections. There is no separate grammar section.

▶ There are some new types of questions in Reading and Listening.

▶ The lectures and conversations that you hear on the audio portions of the test are "authentic English." In other words, the language that you hear is more natural, more like the language used in the "real world." It contains the pauses, repetitions, self-corrections, and "umms" and "uhs" that you would expect to hear in a real lecture or conversation.

▶ The test is *not* "computer adaptive" (unlike the previous computer-based version). In other words, if you answer a question correctly, the next item is not more difficult, and if you answer a question incorrectly, the next question is not easier. All test-takers see the same question during each administration of the test.

▶ There is a new scoring system.

Q: Why did the test change?

A: One reason is that, over the last thirty years, most language teachers have changed the way they teach. The emphasis is no longer on analyzing and learning individual grammar points or memorizing vocabulary. The emphasis is on communicating in the target language in a meaningful way. That's why the new version of the TOEFL test measures your ability to communicate orally and in writing.

Another reason for the changes is that university admissions officers wanted more information about incoming students. Can they read and understand materials in textbooks? Understand and take notes on lectures? Hold conversations with teachers, administrators, and other students? Write papers involving a number of sources? The new test indicates whether candidates have these skills.

Q: Is the TOEFL iBT more difficult than previous versions?

A: The Reading and Listening Sections and the Independent Writing Task have changed only a little, and you will probably not find them more difficult than similar sections in earlier versions of the test. However, the Integrated Writing Task and the Speaking Section may seem challenging because you do not have much experience with this kind of task. With the practice that you get in *The Complete Guide to the TOEFL, iBT Edition,* you should feel much more comfortable and confident when you actually take the test.

Q: What format does TOEFL iBT follow? How long does it take to complete?

A: The Internet-based test is divided into four sections: Reading, Listening, Speaking, and Writing, each with its own time limit. The four sections are always given in the same order. The first two sections, Reading and Listening, are mostly multiple-choice questions, while the Speaking Section requires you to give short oral presentations and the Writing Section requires you to write short essays.

The entire test takes from three and a half to four hours.

TOEFL® iBT Format

1. Reading
3 readings (about 600 to 700 words per reading)
39 questions (12 to 14 per reading; mainly multiple-choice)
60 minutes

2. Listening
2 conversations
4 lectures/discussions
34 questions (5 per conversation, 6 per lecture; mainly multiple-choice)
About 50 minutes

Mandatory break: **10 minutes**

3. Speaking
2 Independent Tasks (based on your own knowledge and experience)
4 Integrated Tasks (based on short readings and/or lectures)
About 20 minutes

4. Writing
1 Independent Task (based on your own knowledge and experience)
1 Integrated Task (based on a short reading and a lecture)
50 minutes

Total time: 3-1/2 to 4 hours

The actual numbers in the chart above may vary from test to test. In the Reading Section, there may be four or five readings and from 36–70 questions. The Reading Section may vary in length from 60 to 100 minutes. In the Listening Section, there may be additional conversations or lectures and from 34–50 questions. The Listening Section may last from about 50 minutes to about 90 minutes.

Q: How does the scoring system for the TOEFL iBT work?
A: You will receive a Section Score for each of the four skill areas and a Total Score.

Reading	0 to 30
Listening	0 to 30
Speaking	0 to 30
Writing	0 to 30
Total Score	0 to 120

In addition to the numerical score, ETS will send a score "descriptor," a short written description of what English-language skills a typical person at your score level has or does not have.

In the following chart, you can compare total scores on the TOEFL iBT with scores that are approximately equivalent to scores on the computer-based test (TOEFL CBT) and the paper-based test (TOEFL PBT).

Total Score		
TOEFL® iBT	TOEFL® CBT	TOEFL® PBT
120	300	677
115	280	650
110	270	637
105	260	620
100	250	600
95	240	587
90	230	570
85	223	563
80	213	550
75	203	537
70	193	523
65	183	513
60	170	497
55	157	480
50	143	463
45	133	450
40	120	433
35	107	417
30	93	397
25	80	377
20	63	350
15	50	327
10	37	317
5	20	310
0	0	310

Q: What is a passing score on the TOEFL test?
A: There isn't any. Each university—and in some cases, each school or department—has its own standards for admission, so you should check the requirements for the universities that you are interested in. (These are generally available online.) Most undergraduate programs require scores between 65 and 80, and most graduate programs ask for scores between 70 and 100. In recent years, there has been a tendency for universities to raise their minimum TOEFL test requirements. Of course, the higher your score, the better your chances of admission.

Q: How and when will I receive my test scores?
A: You can obtain your scores online about fifteen business days after you take the test. You will also receive a written notification of your scores by mail shortly after that. The admissions offices of universities that you designate can also receive your scores online or by mail.

Q: How do I register for the TOEFL iBT?
A: You can register online at http://www.toefl.org. You may also register by phone or by mail.

Q: What computer skills do I need to take the TOEFL iBT?

A: The computer skills required are very basic ones. You really only need to know how to point to items on the screen and click on your choice with a mouse, as well as how to scroll up and down through a document. For writing, you also need basic word-processing skills.

Q: What do I do if I need help?

A: There is a Help button on the task bar for each section, but this button will only give you the directions for that part of the test. It will not give you any hints to help you answer questions or solve any technical problems. Clicking on Help is basically a waste of your time.

If you have a problem with your computer or need some other kind of help, raise your hand and a test administrator will come to you.

Q: Where is the TOEFL iBT given?

A: It is administered at a network of testing centers that include universities, binational institutes, and ETS field offices all over the world. When you register for the test, you will be assigned the closest test center. Most test centers will offer the TOEFL iBT thirty to forty times a year, depending on the size of the center.

On a given day, ETS will give a different version of each TOEFL test in each of the twenty-four time zones of the world. This prevents a person who takes the test in one time zone from giving information about the test to people in other time zones.

Q: Can I choose whether to take the TOEFL iBT or earlier versions of the test?

A: No. Once the Internet-based test has been phased in, you will no longer have the option of taking the computer-based or the paper-based test.

Q: How much will the Internet-based test cost?

A: The TOEFL iBT will initially cost US$140.00.

Q: What should I bring with me to the exam site?

A: You should bring your passport or other ID with you. You will have to check all other personal materials before you enter the testing room.

Don't bring any reference books, such as dictionaries or textbooks, or any electronic devices, such as translators, cellular phones, or calculators. You are not permitted to smoke, eat, or drink in the test center. You do not have to bring pencils or paper. (You will get a pen and a booklet of blank paper for note taking.)

Q: How can I get more information about the TOEFL test?

A: You can contact ETS via e-mail or get updated information about the test from the ETS TOEFL iBT home page: http://www.toefl.org.

Ten Keys to Better Scores on the TOEFL® iBT

⊶ #1: Increase your general knowledge of English.

There are two types of knowledge that will lead to better scores on the TOEFL iBT:

▶ A knowledge of the tactics and techniques used by smart test-takers
▶ A general command of English

Following a step-by-step preparation program for the TOEFL iBT such as the one in *The Guide* will familiarize you with the test itself and with the tactics you need to raise your scores. The practice tests that are part of this program will help you polish your test-taking techniques.

But no matter how many test-taking tips you learn, you won't do well without a solid foundation of English-language study. The best way to increase your general knowledge of English is to use English as much as possible.

If you have the opportunity, taking English-language classes is an invaluable way to prepare for the test. In the past, students would sometimes say, "I can't go to English class today; I have to prepare for the TOEFL test!" This is no longer a good excuse. The TOEFL iBT tests a greater range of English-language skills, and any English class you take will help you prepare for the test. General English classes are now a form of TOEFL test preparation, and TOEFL test preparation classes will now teach more general English.

Conversation classes and presentation-skills classes will help you prepare for the Speaking Section of the test. Of course, reading classes can help you prepare for the Reading Section, listening classes for the Listening Section, and writing (composition) classes for the Writing Section. Although there is no special grammar section on the TOEFL iBT, structure (grammar) classes will be useful for both Writing and Speaking. Academic skills classes can help you with note taking, reading and writing tips, and test-taking skills.

Non-language classes taught in English (business or biology, for example) are also a useful way to improve all of your skills. The TOEFL iBT was designed, after all, to measure your ability to do well in this type of class.

You can also improve your English outside of the classroom. Reading English-language books, magazines, and newspapers can improve your reading skills and build your vocabulary. So can visits to English-language Web sites. Going to lectures and movies, watching TV, and listening to news on the radio are ways to improve your listening skills. If you are living in an English-speaking country, take advantage of this fact and talk to the people around you as much and as often as you can. If possible, join a "conversation partners" program. If you are living in a non-English-speaking country, try to find people—native or non-native speakers—that you can have conversations with.

One important job is to systematically build your vocabulary. An improved vocabulary will help you on every section of the test. You should keep a personal vocabulary list in a notebook, on index cards, or on a computer. When you come across an unfamiliar word, look it up and record the word and its definition.

⚙ #2: LEARN AS MUCH ABOUT THE TEST AS POSSIBLE.

It's important to have up-to-date information about the test. ETS has said there may be minor changes in the format of the Internet-based test in the future.

You can get a lot of information about the test from the *TOEFL® Information Bulletin* for the current testing year. You can download it from the TOEFL Web site (www.ets.org/toefl). Paper versions of the bulletin are available at many language schools or international student offices.

There is a lot of other information and practice available on the TOEFL® Web site. You can join the "TOEFL® Practice Online Community" (for free) to get the latest information about the test and to take an official practice test and get daily study tips. There is also a discussion board on which you can read messages from other people who are preparing for the test and you can post your own questions and tips.

⚙ #3: MAKE THE MOST OF YOUR PREPARATION TIME.

You need to train for the TOEFL test just as you would train for any important competitive event. Naturally, the sooner you begin training, the better, but no matter when you begin, you need to get the most out of your preparation time.

One good way to organize your preparation time is to make a time management chart. Draw up an hour-by-hour schedule of your activities. Block out those times when you are busy with classes, work, or other responsibilities. Then pencil in times for TOEFL test preparation. You'll remember more if you schedule a few hours every day or several times weekly than if you schedule all your study time for long blocks on weekends.

One good method of studying for the TOEFL test (or almost anything!) is the "30-5-5" Method:

▶ Study for thirty minutes.
▶ Take a five-minute break.
▶ When you return, spend five minutes reviewing what you studied before and previewing what you will study next.

⚙ #4: BE IN GOOD PHYSICAL CONDITION WHEN YOU TAKE THE TEST.

Of course, you should eat healthful foods and get some exercise during the time you are preparing for the test. The most important concern, however, is that you not become exhausted during your preparation time. If you aren't getting enough sleep, you need to reduce your study time or cut back on some other activity. This is especially important during the last few days before the exam.

⟊— #5: Get some computer practice.

If possible, take at least one of the practice tests on the enclosed CD-ROM. These tests closely simulate the actual test. Also, try to take the test that is available on the ETS Web site.

The computer skills that you need for the Reading and the Listening Sections are very basic: scrolling, pointing, and clicking.

The most difficult skill is the ability to word-process (type) your two essays for the Writing Section. If you are not accustomed to working on an English-language keyboard, you should get as much typing practice as possible to improve your speed and accuracy.

You also will have to record your responses for the six Speaking Tasks by talking into a microphone. Talking into a computer microphone may be a new experience for you. Get as much practice doing this as possible. (In the About Speaking section of this book, on pages 401–402, there is information about how you can use a computer to record your voice and play it back if you have a microphone.)

⟊— #6: Become familiar with the format and directions.

You should have a clear "map" of the TOEFL iBT in your mind and know what is coming next. You can familiarize yourself with the basic design of the test by looking over the chart in the Questions and Answers section (p. xiv) and by taking practice tests.

The directions for each part of the test will always be the same, and so will the examples. If you are familiar with the directions from using this book, you can immediately click on the Dismiss Directions button and save yourself a little time during the test.

⟊— #7: Organize the last few days before the exam carefully.

Don't try to "cram" (study intensively) during the last few days before you take the test. Last-minute studying probably won't help your score and will leave you tired. You need to be alert for the test. The night before the test, don't study at all. Find your passport and other documents you will need. Then go to a movie, take a long walk, or do something else to take your mind off the test. Go to sleep when you usually do.

On the day of the test, wear comfortable clothing because you will be sitting in the same position for a long time. If you are testing in the morning, have breakfast before the test. If other people from your class or study group are taking the test on the same day, you can have breakfast together and give one another some last-minute encouragement. Give yourself plenty of time to get to the testing center. If you have to rush, that will only add to your stress.

○━ #8: USE TIME WISELY DURING THE TEST.

In the Reading and Listening Sections, there is no time limit on individual items. However, there are time limits for the sections (60 to 100 minutes for Reading and about 50 to 90 minutes for Listening). These time limits are fairly generous, but you still need to be careful to give yourself a chance to answer all the questions. You need to find a balance between speed and accuracy. Work steadily. Never let yourself get stuck on an item. If you are unable to decide on an answer, guess and go on.

In the Speaking and Writing Sections, there are time limits for each of the tasks. You need to practice these tasks so that you can complete your responses in the amount of time you are given.

For all four parts of the test, the most important timing tools you have are the on-screen clocks. Glance at these now and then to see how much time you have left. However, don't become obsessed with checking the clock.

○━ #9: FOR MULTIPLE-CHOICE ITEMS, USE THE PROCESS OF ELIMINATION TO MAKE YOUR BEST GUESS.

Unlike some standardized exams, the TOEFL iBT doesn't have a penalty for guessing on the multiple-choice sections (Reading and Listening). In other words, incorrect answers aren't subtracted from your scores. Even if you have no idea which answer is correct, you should guess because you have a one-in-four chance of guessing correctly. However, whenever possible, try to avoid guessing blindly. It's better to make an educated guess. To do this, use the process of elimination.

The process of elimination is a simple concept. For each multiple-choice question, there is one correct answer (or two on some Listening items). There are also a number of incorrect answers, called *distracters*. They are called distracters because their purpose is to distract your attention from the correct answer. You need to try to eliminate distracters. If you can eliminate one, your chances of guessing correctly are one in three, and if you can eliminate two, your chances improve to one in two. (And if you can eliminate three, you've got the correct answer!) Often, one or even two distracters are fairly easy to eliminate.

What if you eliminate one or two choices but can't decide which of the remaining choices is correct? If you have a hunch (a feeling) that one choice is better than the others, choose it. If not, pick any remaining choice and go on.

Remember, in the Reading and Listening sections, you should *never* leave any items unanswered. *Always* guess. (The Reading Section has a Review Feature that lets you check very quickly what items you left unanswered. You should use this feature just before the end of the Reading Section.)

○━ #10: LEARN TO FIGHT TEST ANXIETY.

The TOEFL iBT and similar tests (such as SAT, ACT, GRE, and GMAT) are often called "high-stakes tests." This means that a lot depends on these tests. They can have a major influence on your plans for your education and career. A little nervousness is normal. If you were going to participate in a big athletic contest or give an important business presentation, you would feel the same way.

There is an idiom in English that describes this nervous feeling quite well: "butterflies in the stomach." These "butterflies" will mostly fly away once the test starts. And a little nervousness can actually help by making you more alert and focused. However, too much nervousness can slow you down and cause you to make mistakes.

If you begin to feel extremely anxious during the test, try taking a very short break—a "ten-second vacation." Close your eyes or look away from the monitor, take your hand off the mouse, and lean back in your chair. Take a few deep breaths, shake out your hands, roll your head on your neck, and relax. Then get right back to work. (Don't use this technique while you are listening to a lecture or giving a speaking response.)

A positive, confident attitude toward the exam can help you overcome anxiety. Think of the TOEFL test not as a test of your knowledge or of you as a person but as an intellectual challenge, a puzzle to be solved.

GUIDE TO READING

About Reading

The Reading Comprehension Section of TOEFL iBT is always the first section of the test. You will usually see three passages, but sometimes there will be four or five. After each passage, there are twelve to fourteen questions. The first section of TOEFL iBT tests your ability to read and answer questions about passages (readings). It contains three passages, and after each passage are from twelve to fourteen questions for a total of 39 questions. The passages are generally from 600 to 700 words long. You have 60 minutes in which to finish this section.

If there are three passages, you will have 60 minutes.
If there are four passages, you will have 80 minutes.
If there are five passages, you will have 100 minutes.

When you take the Reading Section on the computer, the passages appear on the right side of the screen and the questions appear on the left.

Skills that are tested in this section include the abilities to

- scan for details
- use context clues to understand the meaning of vocabulary
- draw inferences
- recognize coherence
- understand how the author explains certain points
- understand why the author uses certain examples or mentions certain details
- recognize restatements (paraphrases) and sentence simplifications
- distinguish between important ideas and minor ones
- analyze and categorize information in order to complete summaries and charts

You can skip answers and come back to them later. You can come back and change your answers at any time during the Reading testing period. If you want, you can take notes about the passages while you are reading.

The Passages

The passages are very similar to the type of material that you would find in an introductory undergraduate university textbook.

The passages cover a wide range of topics, but in general can be classified as follows:

1. Science and technology, including astronomy, geology, chemistry, mathematics, physics, biology, medicine, and engineering
2. History, government, geography, and culture
3. Art, including literature, painting, sculpture, dance, drama, and architecture
4. Social science, including anthropology, economics, psychology, urban studies, and sociology
5. Biography and autobiography

Some passages might be classified in more than one way. For example, a biography might be about the life of a historical figure, an artist, or a scientist.

Most of the context for the readings is North American (U.S. or sometimes Canadian). However, you may also see some international contexts, especially from English-speaking countries such as the United Kingdom, Australia, and New Zealand.

The passages are mainly *expository*. In other words, they explain something. However, some passages may be *narrative* (telling the story of an event or a person) or *persuasive* (arguing in favor of or against some point or issue). Passages may employ various patterns of organization and development: cause and effect, comparison and contrast, definition, classification, and analysis.

The vocabulary used in the Reading Section is sophisticated but not unrealistically difficult. Some specialized vocabulary is "glossed"—in other words, it is marked with a blue underline, and you can get a definition by clicking on the word or phrase. If there are words that you don't know that are not glossed, sometimes you can guess the meaning from the context of the sentence. And remember that it is not necessary to understand every word in the passage in order to answer the questions correctly.

THE QUESTIONS

Multiple-Choice Questions

Most of the questions in the Reading Section are multiple-choice questions. There are eight main types as shown in the following chart. The chart also shows you in which lesson in *The Guide* you will find more information and practice for this question type.

Standard Multiple-Choice Reading Questions				
Type of question	Explanation	Example	Probable number per test	Lesson
Factual questions (detail questions)	These ask you to locate and identify specific information in the passage.	According to the information in paragraph _____, where did . . . According to the passage, why did . . . Which of the following is true, according to the author?	7 to 10	1
Negative factual questions	These ask which of the answer choices is *not* true, according to information in the passage, or is *not* mentioned in the passage.	According to the information in paragraph _____, which of the following is NOT . . . The author mentions all of the following in the passage EXCEPT . . .	1 to 4	1

continued

Type of question	Explanation	Example	Probable number per test	Lesson
Vocabulary questions	These ask you to identify the meaning of a word or phrase used in the passage.	The word _____ in the passage is closest in meaning to	6 to 10	2
Inference questions	These ask you to draw conclusions based on information in the passage.	From the information in paragraph _____, it can be inferred that . . . In paragraph _____, the author suggests that . . .	3 to 6	3
Questions about the author's purpose	These ask you why the author uses a certain word, detail, or example in a passage.	Why does the author mention _____ in paragraph _____? Why does the author give details about _____?	2 to 3	4
Questions about the author's methods	These ask you to describe how the author explains or accomplishes something in the passage.	How does the author explain the concept of _____ in paragraph _____?	2 to 3	4
Questions about the author's attitude	These ask you how the author feels about a certain issue, idea, or person that is mentioned in the passage.	What is the author's opinion of _____? Which of the following most accurately reflects the author's opinion of _____?	1 to 2	4
Sentence restatement/ simplification questions	These ask which choice best restates and summarizes the information in a sentence from the passage.	Which of the following sentences best expresses the essential information in the sentence below? (Incorrect answer choices omit important information or change the meaning of the original sentence in an important way.)	2 to 3	5
Reference questions	These ask what word a pronoun or other reference word refers to.	The word _____ in the passage refers to . . .	3 to 4	6

Other Reading Questions

The last two questions in each set of questions have special directions.

Sentence Addition Questions

The second-to-last question in each set of questions will generally be a sentence addition question. This type of question gives you a sentence that is *not* in the passage and asks you to put it into the passage. Four black squares appear between sentences of the paragraph. You must click on one of these squares to put the new sentence into the correct place in the paragraph.

There is more information and practice about sentence addition questions in Lesson 7.

Complete-the-Summary and Complete-the-Chart Questions

The last question in each set of questions will be either a complete-the-summary or a complete-the-chart question. Complete-the-summary questions are worth two points and complete-the-chart questions are worth three or four points. (All the other questions in the Reading Section are worth only one point.) You can get partial credit if you answer some parts of these questions correctly.

For complete-the-summary questions you are given six answer choices and you must choose three of these to create a summary of the passage. Incorrect choices are only minor ideas or they are not mentioned in the passage.

For complete-the-chart questions, you are given a number of answer choices and you must put them in the proper category in a chart. The answer choices will be some important characteristic or example, and the categories will be major concepts described in the passage. You have to decide which of the answer choices is related to which category and place it in the correct place in the chart. Some of these questions have seven possible answers and five blanks in the chart. These are worth three points. Some questions have nine possible answers and seven blanks in the chart, and these are worth four points.

There is more information and practice about complete-the-summary and complete-the-chart questions in Lesson 8.

SPECIAL FEATURES

The Reading Section of the TOEFL iBT includes the following helpful features.

Titles

Passages in the Reading Section of the TOEFL iBT have titles. The titles help you get a quick, overall idea of what the passage is about.

Illustrations, Maps, Charts, Drawings, and Pictures

On the TOEFL iBT, maps, charts, drawings, and photographs may be used to clarify points made in the passage and to make the passages seem more like authentic textbook material.

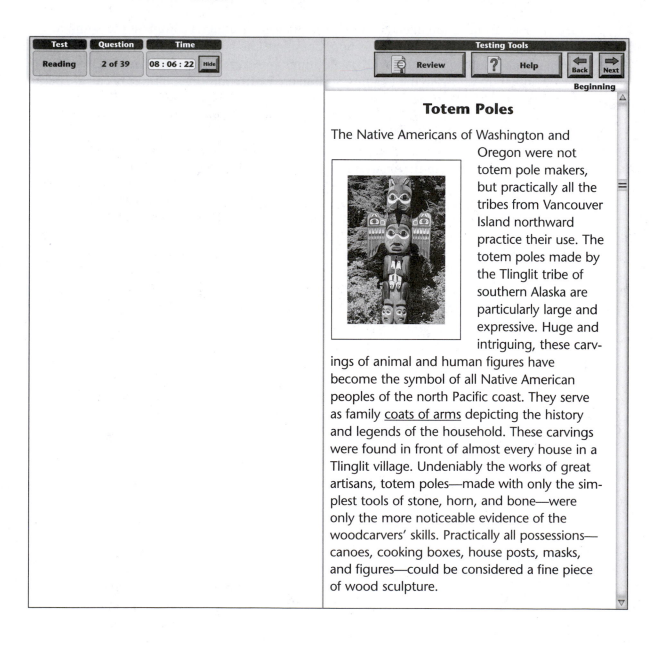

Test	Question	Time		Testing Tools
Reading	2 of 39	08 : 06 : 22 Hide		Review Help Back Next

Beginning

Totem Poles

The Native Americans of Washington and Oregon were not totem pole makers, but practically all the tribes from Vancouver Island northward practice their use. The totem poles made by the Tlinglit tribe of southern Alaska are particularly large and expressive. Huge and intriguing, these carvings of animal and human figures have become the symbol of all Native American peoples of the north Pacific coast. They serve as family <u>coats of arms</u> depicting the history and legends of the household. These carvings were found in front of almost every house in a Tlinglit village. Undeniably the works of great artisans, totem poles—made with only the simplest tools of stone, horn, and bone—were only the more noticeable evidence of the woodcarvers' skills. Practically all possessions— canoes, cooking boxes, house posts, masks, and figures—could be considered a fine piece of wood sculpture.

Glossed Vocabulary

If the passage contains difficult idioms, topic-specific vocabulary (words that are usually used only to talk about the topic), or vocabulary that might be unfamiliar to a test-taker, this vocabulary will be *glossed*. These words or phrase will be underlined in blue. If you click on the underlined vocabulary, you will get a short definition. There will probably not be more than two or three glossed expressions per passage.

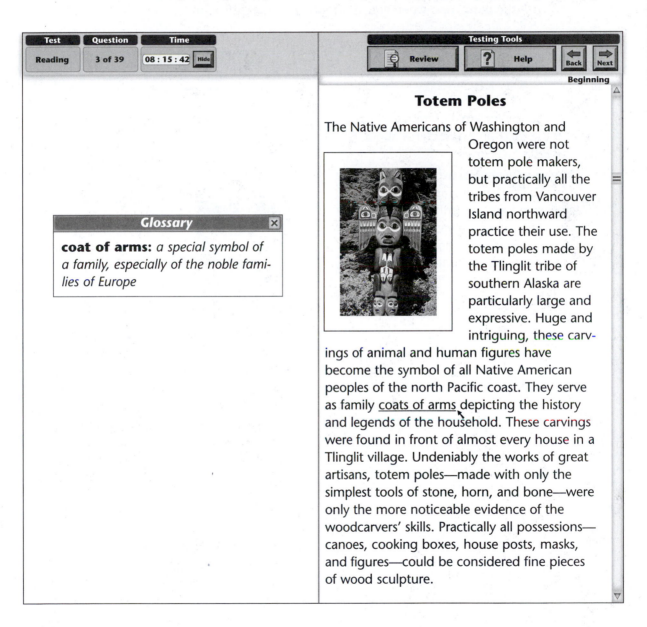

Test	Question	Time		Testing Tools			
Reading	3 of 39	08 : 15 : 42 Hide		Review	Help	Back	Next

Beginning

Glossary

coat of arms: *a special symbol of a family, especially of the noble families of Europe*

Totem Poles

The Native Americans of Washington and Oregon were not totem pole makers, but practically all the tribes from Vancouver Island northward practice their use. The totem poles made by the Tlinglit tribe of southern Alaska are particularly large and expressive. Huge and intriguing, these carvings of animal and human figures have become the symbol of all Native American peoples of the north Pacific coast. They serve as family coats of arms depicting the history and legends of the household. These carvings were found in front of almost every house in a Tlinglit village. Undeniably the works of great artisans, totem poles—made with only the simplest tools of stone, horn, and bone—were only the more noticeable evidence of the woodcarvers' skills. Practically all possessions—canoes, cooking boxes, house posts, masks, and figures—could be considered fine pieces of wood sculpture.

Highlights and Paragraph Markers

Arrows and highlighted text will help you find parts of the passage and specific words or sentences that are asked about. Most questions tell you the number of the paragraph where the information to answer a question comes from. These paragraphs are not numbered in the TOEFL iBT (although they *are* numbered in this book). Instead, they are marked with an arrow (➔) that appears at the beginning of the paragraph when you are working on that question.

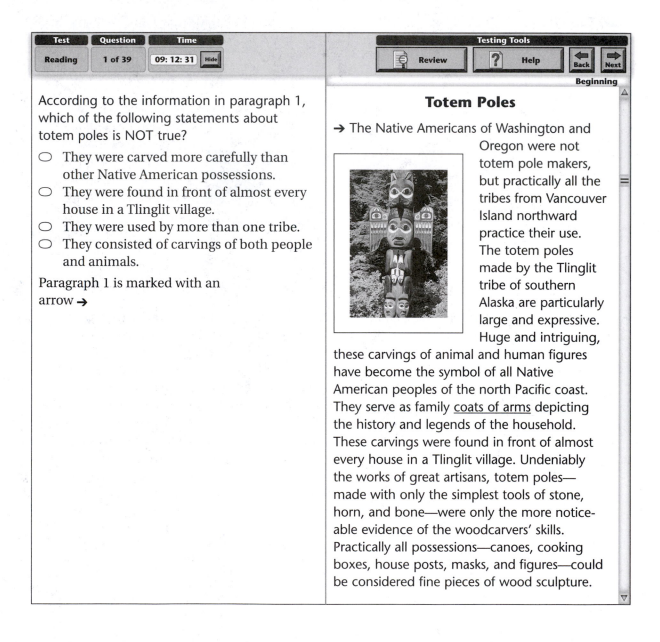

Test	Question	Time		Testing Tools
Reading	1 of 39	09: 12: 31 Hide		Review Help Back Next

Beginning

According to the information in paragraph 1, which of the following statements about totem poles is NOT true?

○ They were carved more carefully than other Native American possessions.
○ They were found in front of almost every house in a Tlinglit village.
○ They were used by more than one tribe.
○ They consisted of carvings of both people and animals.

Paragraph 1 is marked with an arrow ➔

Totem Poles

➔ The Native Americans of Washington and Oregon were not totem pole makers, but practically all the tribes from Vancouver Island northward practice their use. The totem poles made by the Tlinglit tribe of southern Alaska are particularly large and expressive. Huge and intriguing, these carvings of animal and human figures have become the symbol of all Native American peoples of the north Pacific coast. They serve as family <u>coats of arms</u> depicting the history and legends of the household. These carvings were found in front of almost every house in a Tlinglit village. Undeniably the works of great artisans, totem poles—made with only the simplest tools of stone, horn, and bone—were only the more noticeable evidence of the woodcarvers' skills. Practically all possessions—canoes, cooking boxes, house posts, masks, and figures—could be considered fine pieces of wood sculpture.

Words that you are asked about (especially in vocabulary and reference questions) are marked with a highlight.

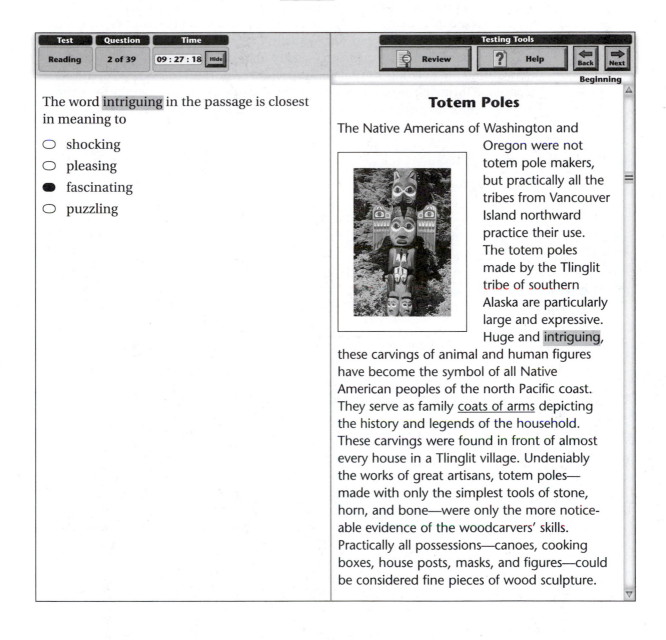

| Test | Question | Time | | | Testing Tools | |
| Reading | 2 of 39 | 09 : 27 : 18 Hide | | Review | ? Help | Back Next |

Beginning

The word intriguing in the passage is closest in meaning to

○ shocking

○ pleasing

● fascinating

○ puzzling

Totem Poles

The Native Americans of Washington and Oregon were not totem pole makers, but practically all the tribes from Vancouver Island northward practice their use. The totem poles made by the Tlinglit tribe of southern Alaska are particularly large and expressive. Huge and intriguing, these carvings of animal and human figures have become the symbol of all Native American peoples of the north Pacific coast. They serve as family coats of arms depicting the history and legends of the household. These carvings were found in front of almost every house in a Tlinglit village. Undeniably the works of great artisans, totem poles—made with only the simplest tools of stone, horn, and bone—were only the more noticeable evidence of the woodcarvers' skills. Practically all possessions—canoes, cooking boxes, house posts, masks, and figures—could be considered fine pieces of wood sculpture.

READING

Review Feature

This is one of the most useful features of the Internet-Based Test. You operate the review feature by clicking on the button marked Review on the toolbar. This allows you to see a list of all the questions (actually, the first line of each of the questions) to see if you answered the question or skipped it. You can use this feature at any time during the Reading Section. It is especially important to use this when you have gone through the test and reached the final question. You can then use the review feature to quickly locate the questions that you did not answer.

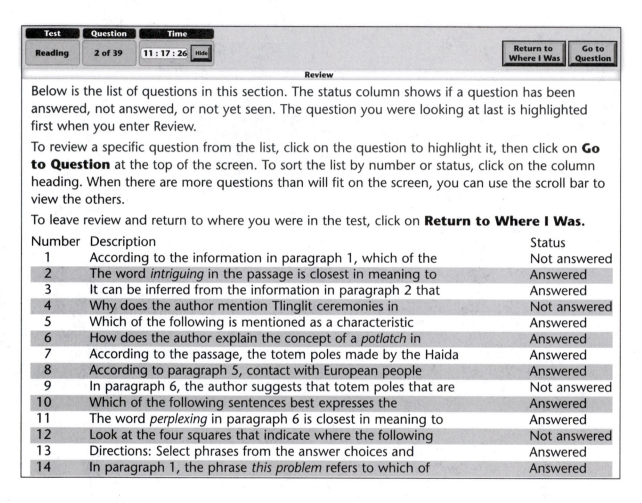

Test	Question	Time		Return to Where I Was	Go to Question
Reading	2 of 39	11 : 17 : 26 [Hide]			

Review

Below is the list of questions in this section. The status column shows if a question has been answered, not answered, or not yet seen. The question you were looking at last is highlighted first when you enter Review.

To review a specific question from the list, click on the question to highlight it, then click on **Go to Question** at the top of the screen. To sort the list by number or status, click on the column heading. When there are more questions than will fit on the screen, you can use the scroll bar to view the others.

To leave review and return to where you were in the test, click on **Return to Where I Was.**

Number	Description	Status
1	According to the information in paragraph 1, which of the	Not answered
2	The word *intriguing* in the passage is closest in meaning to	Answered
3	It can be inferred from the information in paragraph 2 that	Answered
4	Why does the author mention Tlinglit ceremonies in	Not answered
5	Which of the following is mentioned as a characteristic	Answered
6	How does the author explain the concept of a *potlatch* in	Answered
7	According to the passage, the totem poles made by the Haida	Answered
8	According to paragraph 5, contact with European people	Answered
9	In paragraph 6, the author suggests that totem poles that are	Not answered
10	Which of the following sentences best expresses the	Answered
11	The word *perplexing* in paragraph 6 is closest in meaning to	Answered
12	Look at the four squares that indicate where the following	Not answered
13	Directions: Select phrases from the answer choices and	Answered
14	In paragraph 1, the phrase *this problem* refers to which of	Answered

If you want to review a question from the test, click on the question to highlight it, and then click on the phrase Go to Question. You may scroll down to see other questions.

If you want to leave the review and return to the place where you were working in the test, click on Return to Where I Was.

How to Approach the Passages and Questions

You do not read a newspaper and a textbook in the same way. How you read depends on what you are reading and why you are reading it. When taking the Reading Section of the test, your purpose is simple. It is not to enjoy or even understand the reading perfectly. You don't need to comprehend every word or every detail. Your goal is simply to correctly answer as many questions as you possibly can.

Here are the steps you should follow to get as many correct answers as possible:

1. First, look at the title and quickly scroll through the passage to get an idea of what the passage is generally about. Then quickly click through the questions. You don't have to read the answer choices at this time; just look at the questions and try to fix them in you mind.

2. Now read the passage at a comfortable speed. After you have read the first screen, scroll through the passage at a steady pace. Word-by-word reading slows you down and interferes with your comprehension. Try to read in units of thought, phrase by phrase rather than word by word.

3. During your first reading, don't worry about understanding or remembering details. You can come back and look for that kind of information later if needed.

4. Next, answer each question one by one. If you believe you know the answer, answer that question right away. If you find the question difficult, skip the question for now. You can later use the review feature to easily locate the questions that you skipped.

Important: It's better to leave difficult questions blank than to answer them immediately because the review feature only tells you if you answered the question or not. It doesn't tell you that you had trouble with a question.

When answering any multiple-choice question on the test (in the Reading and Listening sections), you should use the process of elimination to ensure that you make the best guess. (See page xx for more information about using the process of elimination.)

Finding Information in the Passages

The highlighted words and paragraph markers make it easier for you to find the information you need for many questions.

It will also help if you remember that most of the questions in each set follow the order of the passage. The information needed to answer the first question will come somewhere near the beginning of the passage. The answer for the next question will be found *below* that point in the passage. For example, if question 1 is a vocabulary question about a word in paragraph 1, the answer for question 2 will be found lower down in paragraph 1 or in the next paragraph or two. In general, you will be scrolling *downward* as you look for information to answer questions.

Vocabulary and reference questions, especially, can help you pinpoint information for other types of questions. Let's say that question 2 is a vocabulary question.

The computer will highlight the word that is asked about. Then let's say that question 5 is a reference question. Again the computer will highlight a word. This tells us that the information you need to answer questions 3 and 4 will be found somewhere between the two words that are highlighted.

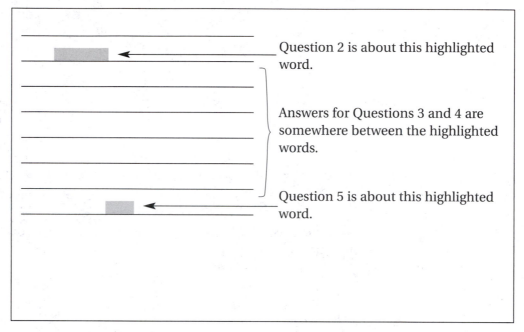

To answer some questions—especially complete-the-summary and complete-the-chart questions—you will have to search through the entire passage to find the information that you need.

TIMING

There are usually only three passages on the TOEFL iBT. Each passage is from 600 to 700 words long. If you read and work at an average speed, you should have no trouble finishing within the sixty-minute time limit. (If there are more than three passages, you will have more time to work on them.)

There is a countdown clock on the screen that tells you how much time remains in which to finish this section. There is also an indicator that tells you which question you are working on (17 of 39, for example). You can use these features to see if your timing is on target.

Note: *There is also an indicator at the top of the screen that tells you that you are working on the Reading Section—but you should already know that!*

The last questions in each set of questions—complete-the-summary and complete-the-chart questions—will take an extra amount of time. You need to budget more time for these questions.

Since there are three passages, you need to read each passage and answer the questions about them in a little less than twenty minutes. (You need to leave yourself a little time at the end of this section to use the review feature to go back and answer questions that you skipped). When you take the Preview Test, see if you can comfortably finish the two passages in forty minutes. If not, you need to work on increasing your speed.

There is no penalty for incorrect guesses. If you are taking the actual test and find that you are not able to complete this section in time, you need to make sure that you have answered every question even if you have to guess. However, when possible, you should not guess blindly. If you have only a short time remaining (less than five minutes), you should first answer any remaining vocabulary or reference questions because those go quickly. Then you should quickly skim any part of the passages that you have not read and answer any other questions. If you can't find the information that you need to answer the questions, choose the answer choice that seems most reasonable to you. Only in the last minute or so should you guess blindly.

TAKING THE TEST ON THE COMPUTER

Only the simplest computer skills are needed for this part of the test: clicking and scrolling.

Marking Answers

When you first begin the Reading Section, you will see directions. Since you will already be familiar with the directions, you should immediately click on the Dismiss Directions button and begin the test.

Important Note: *You must scroll through the entire passage and then click Next before you see the questions and can begin answering them.*

When you have finished reading the directions, click on the button below.

Dismiss Directions.

This section tests your ability to comprehend academic reading passages. It consists of three reading passages and a set of questions about each of them. All of the questions are worth one point except for the last question in each set. Special directions for the last question will tell you how many points it is worth.

You have 60 minutes to complete this section of the test.

In the passages, some words or phrases are underlined. Definitions or explanations for these words are provided at the end of the passage. On the actual test, these words will be underlined in blue and you can click on them to get the definition or explanation.

As soon as you have finished one question, you may move on to the next one. (On the actual test, you click on Next to move to the next question.) You may skip questions and come back to them later, and you can change your answers if you wish. (On the actual test, you click on Back to return to a previous question.)

To answer a multiple-choice question, simply click on the oval of the choice that you want and the oval will turn black. If you want to change your answer, click on the oval of another choice. Or, if you want to leave that question blank for now, click on that question again and the oval will appear unmarked.

Helpful tip: You don't even need to click on an oval—you can click anywhere on the answer choice. This is faster because the answer choice is a bigger target.

To answer a sentence addition question, simply click on the black square where you think the sentence should be placed. Clicking on the square again makes the sentence disappear; clicking another square moves it to that position.

To answer a complete-the-summary or a complete-the-chart question, you click on the answer choice and then on the blank in the summary or chart where you want to put it. Clicking a second time makes the choice disappear from the blank, and clicking another blank moves it there.

Navigating through the Passage

The passages are too long to fit on the screen at one time. To move up and down through the passage, use the standard scroll bar that separates the passage on the left from the current question on the right.

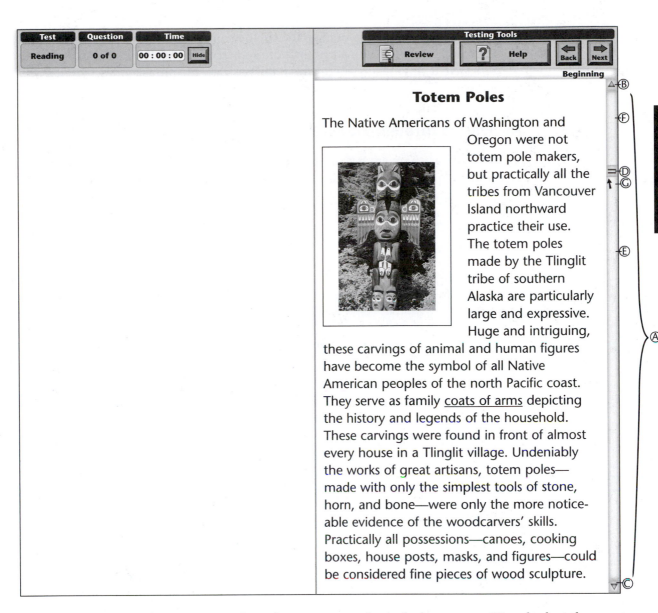

There are a number of ways to move through the passage. First, look at the scroll bar. It is labeled A.

▶ If you click once on the up or down arrows (labeled B and C), the text will move up or down one line on the screen. This may be the most convenient way to scroll when you are looking for specific information in a paragraph.

▶ You can also click on an up or down arrow and hold it down. As long as you hold down the arrow, the text will move quickly up or down.

▶ Using your mouse, you can position your cursor (G) on the slider (D) and move through the passage as quickly or as slowly as you like by "pushing" the slider up or down with the cursor.

▶ You can also click on the empty space (E) below the slider to move to a lower part of the passage, or on the space above the slider (F) to move upward through the passage.

▶ When you are at the top of the passage, the word *Beginning* will appear over the scroll bar. When you are at the bottom of the passage, you will see the word *Finished.* If you are anywhere else in the passage, the phrase *More Available* will appear.

Navigating through the Section

On the tool bar, there are two arrows marked Back and Next. When you finish answering a question, simply click Next to move to the following question. If you want to return to the question you just finished, click Back. You can use these buttons to move as far back as you want, from question to question and from passage to passage.

Of course, you can also use the review feature to locate and go to a specific question.

Tactics for Reading

- As with all sections of the test, be familiar with the directions. When the directions appear, click on the Dismiss Directions button right away.

- First look over the passage quickly, then look over the questions about the passage (*not* the answer choices, just the questions). Try to hold these questions in your mind or take some quick notes as you look them over.

- Read the passage at a comfortable rate, looking especially for information that the questions ask about. If it is helpful, take notes as you read.

- Answer the questions, referring back to the passage as necessary.

- Skip questions that you find difficult. Go back to these by means of the review feature after answering the last question on the test.

- If there are some questions that you think you can answer correctly, but you still have some doubts about them, keep track of the numbers of these questions on your notepaper. If you have enough time, go back to these questions after you've answered the questions that you skipped.

- Don't spend too much time on any one question or passage.

- Leave yourself time to use the review feature at the end of this section.

- If you haven't finished when only a few minutes remain, skim quickly though any part of the passages that you haven't read. Then answer any vocabulary or reference questions that you haven't completed yet. After that, read the remaining questions. If you can't find the answer in the passage quickly, pick the answer choice that seems most logical to you.

- When there is only about a minute left, make sure that you have answered all the questions even if you have to guess.

- Even if you finish all the questions and checked the ones you found difficult, don't stop working on this section before the time runs out. Keep checking your work until the sixty minutes are up.

READING PREVIEW TEST
DIRECTIONS

This section tests your ability to comprehend academic reading passages. It consists of two reading passages and a set of questions about both of them. (On the actual test, there will be three passages.) All of the questions are worth one point except for the last question in both sets. Special directions for the last question will tell you how many points it is worth.

You have forty minutes to complete this section of the test. (On the actual test you will have sixty minutes.)

In the passages, some words or phrases are underlined. Definitions or explanations for these words are provided at the end of the passage. On the actual test, these words will be underlined in blue and you can click on them to get the definition or explanation.

As soon as you have finished one question, you may move on to the next one. (On the actual test, you will click on Next to move to the next question.) You may skip questions and come back to them later, and you can change your answers if you wish. (On the actual test, you will click on Back to return to a previous question.)

As soon as you have read these directions, go on to the first passage.

Biological Barriers and Pathways

1   Virtually all living things have some way of getting from here to there. Animals may walk, swim, or fly. Plants and their seeds drift on wind or water or are carried by animals. Therefore, it is reasonable to expect that, in time, all species might spread to every place on Earth where favorable conditions occur. Indeed, there *are* some cosmopolitan species. A good example is the housefly, found almost everywhere on Earth. However, such broad distribution is the rare exception. Just as barbed wire fences prevent cattle from leaving their pasture, biological barriers prevent the dispersal of many species.

2   What constitutes barriers depends on the species and its method of dispersal. Some are physical barriers. For land animals, bodies of water, chains of mountains, or deserts are effective. For example, the American bison spread throughout the open grasslands of North America, but in the southern part of the continent there are deserts, so the bison could not spread there. For aquatic creatures, strong currents, differences in salinity, or land areas may serve as barriers.

3   Some barriers involve competition with other species. A dandelion seed may be carried by the wind to bare ground, and, if environmental factors are right, it may germinate. There is not much chance, however, that any individual seedling will survive. Most places that are suitable for the growth of dandelions are already occupied by other types of plants that are well adapted to the area. The dandelion seedling must compete with these plants for space, water, light, and nutrients. Facing such stiff competition, the chances of survival are slim.

4   For animals, some barriers are behavioral. The blue spotted salamander lives only on mountain slopes in the southern Appalachian Highlands. Although these creatures could survive in the river valleys, they never venture there. Birds that fly long distances often remain in very limited areas. Kirkland's warblers are found only in a few places in Michigan in the summer and fly to the Bahamas in winter. No physical barriers restrict the warblers to these two locations, yet they never spread beyond these boundaries. Brazil's Amazon River serves as a northern or southern boundary for many species of birds. They could freely fly over the river, but they seldom do.

5   There are three types of natural pathways through which organisms can overcome barriers. One type is called a *corridor*. A corridor consists of a single type of habitat that passes through various other types of habitat. North America's Rocky Mountains, which stretch from Alaska to northern Mexico, is an example. Various types of trees, such as the Engelmann spruce, can be found not only at the northern end of the corridor in Alaska but also at higher elevations along the entire length of this corridor.

6   A second type of natural pathway is known as a *filter route*. A filter route consists of a series of habitats that are different from one another but are similar enough to permit organisms to gradually adapt to new conditions as they spread from habitat to habitat. The greatest difference between a corridor and a filter route is that a corridor consists of one type of habitat, while a filter consists of several similar types.

7   The third type of natural pathway is called a _sweepstakes_ route. This is dispersal caused by the chance combination of favorable conditions. Bird watchers

are familiar with "accidentals," which are birds that appear in places far from their native areas. Sometimes they may find a habitat with favorable conditions and "colonize" it. Gardeners are familiar with "volunteers," cultivated plants that grow in their gardens although they never planted the seeds for these plants. Besides birds and plants, insects, fish, and mammals also colonize new areas. Sweepstakes routes are unlike either corridors or filter routes in that organisms that travel these routes would not be able to spend their entire lives in the habitats that they pass through.

8   Some organisms cross barriers with the intentional or unintentional help of humans, a process called *invasion.* An example is the New Zealand mud snail, which was accidentally brought to North America when trout from New Zealand were imported to a fish hatchery in the United States. It has caused extensive environmental damage in streams and rivers. In the invasive species' native environments, there are typically predators, parasites, and competitors that keep their numbers down, but in their new habitat, natural checks are left behind, giving the invaders an advantage over native species. Invasive species may spread so quickly that they threaten commercial, agricultural, or recreational activities.

Glossary

salamander: *a type of amphibian animal resembling a lizard*

sweepstakes: *a game of chance; a lottery*

---

1 of 26   The word cosmopolitan in the passage is closest in meaning to

- ○ worldwide
- ○ useful
- ○ well-known
- ○ ancient

2 of 26   How does the author explain the concept of biological barriers in paragraph 1?

- ○ By providing several examples of biological barriers
- ○ By describing the process by which barriers are formed
- ○ By comparing biological barriers with a familiar man-made barrier
- ○ By explaining how houseflies have been affected by biological barriers

3 of 26   What does the author suggest about American bison in paragraph 2?

- ○ They spread to North America from South America.
- ○ A body of water stopped them from spreading south.
- ○ They require open grasslands to survive.
- ○ They originally lived in deserts.

4 of 26   According to the passage, very few dandelion seedlings survive because of

- ○ the danger of strong winds
- ○ competition from other dandelions
- ○ the lack of a suitable habitat
- ○ competition from other species

5 of 26   In this passage, the author does NOT provide a specific example of

    ◯ a bird that is affected by behavioral barriers
    ◯ an aquatic animal that is blocked by physical barriers
    ◯ a land animal that is affected by behavioral barriers
    ◯ a tree that has spread by means of a corridor

6 of 26   The word slim in this passage is closest in meaning to

    ◯ unknown
    ◯ impossible
    ◯ remarkable
    ◯ unlikely

7 of 26   The phrase these two locations in paragraph 4 refers to

    ◯ Michigan and the Appalachian Highlands
    ◯ Brazil and the Bahamas
    ◯ the Appalachian Highlands and Brazil
    ◯ the Bahamas and a few places in Michigan

8 of 26   Why does the author mention the Amazon River in paragraph 4?

    ◯ To give an example of an important physical barrier
    ◯ To point out that many migrating birds fly across it
    ◯ To provide an example of a behavioral barrier
    ◯ To describe a barrier that affects aquatic animals

9 of 26   According to paragraph 6, how does the author distinguish a filter route from a corridor?

    ◯ A corridor consists of one habitat for its entire length, but a filter route consists of more than one.
    ◯ Organisms cannot live all of their lives in some parts of a filter route, but they can in a corridor.
    ◯ The distance from one end of a filter route to the other end is longer than the distance from one end of a corridor to the other.
    ◯ Plants spread through a corridor, while animals spread through a filter route.

10 of 26   In paragraph 8, the author gives New Zealand mud snails as an example of

    ◯ an invasive species that was unintentionally transported to another habitat
    ◯ a native species that has been damaged by an invasive species
    ◯ an invasive species that was intentionally brought to a new environment
    ◯ an animal that spread by means of a sweepstakes route

11 of 26   Which of the following sentences best expresses the essential information in the sentence below? (Incorrect answer choices omit important information or change the meaning of the original sentence in an important way.)

In the invasive species' native environments, there are typically predators, parasites, and competitors that keep their numbers down, but in their new habitat, natural checks are left behind, giving the invaders an advantage over native species.

○ Invasive species are organisms that leave their native environments behind and move to a new environment.

○ Native species are at a disadvantage compared to invasive species because they face environmental dangers that invasive species have left behind.

○ The greatest danger from invasive species is that they may spread parasites among native species.

○ In a new environment, predators, parasites, and competitors prevent invasive species from spreading faster than native species.

12 of 26 Look at the four squares [■] that indicate where the following sentence could be added to the passage.

> **They may be blown off course by storms or may be escaping population pressures in their home areas.**

The third type of natural pathway is called a *sweepstakes route.* This is dispersal caused by the chance combination of favorable conditions. ■ Bird watchers are familiar with "accidentals," which are birds that appear in places far from their native areas. ■ Sometimes they may find a habitat with favorable conditions and "colonize" it.■ Gardeners are familiar with "volunteers," cultivated plants that grow in their gardens although they never planted the seeds for these plants. ■ Besides birds and plants, insects, fish, and mammals also colonize new areas. Sweepstakes routes are unlike either corridors or filter routes in that organisms that travel these routes would not be able to spend their entire lives in the habitats that they pass through.

Circle the square [■] that indicates the best place to add the sentence.

13 of 26 DIRECTIONS: Below is an introductory sentence for a brief summary of the passage. Complete the summary by writing the letters of **three** of the answer choices that express the most important ideas of the passage. Some of the answer choices are incorrect because they express ideas that are not given in the passage or because they express only details from the passage.

Biological barriers prevent organisms from spreading to all habitats where conditions are suitable.

- _____
- _____
- _____

Answer Choices

A. Organisms that spread by means of sweepstakes routes include species of birds called *accidentals* that appear in places far from their homes.

B. Biological barriers can be the result of physical features, climate, competition, and behavior.

C. Organisms can cross barriers by means of three types of natural pathways: corridors, filter routes, and sweepstakes routes.

D. Behavioral barriers do not prevent the spread of species from place to place as effectively as physical barriers.

E. Humans may accidentally or intentionally bring some species across natural barriers, and these species may have certain advantages over native species.

F. American bison spread throughout the grasslands of North America.

Mysteries of Easter Island

Test	Question	Time		Testing Tools		
Reading	1 of 39	02:32:42 Hide		Review	Help	Back Next

Beginning

1   Easter Island is an isolated island in the Pacific between Chile and Tahiti. The island is roughly triangular and covers only 64 square miles (165 square kilometers). Because of its immense statues, Easter Island has long been the subject of curiosity.

2   There are 887 carved stone statues, called Moai, on Easter Island (not all complete). It is not known exactly what significance the Moai had to the Easter Islanders, but they were obsessed with building these statues. Some statues are as tall as 33 feet (11 meters) and weigh as much as 165 tons (167 metric tons). All portray a human head and sometimes an upper body. They are all carved from stone taken from a volcano on the island. Some are topped with a red "hat" called a *pukao,* made from a different type of stone, and a few have white coral eyes. The statues were moved on a network of roads on rollers made of palm logs and were then placed on stone bases called *ahu.* Most were built between 800 and 1500 A.D.

3   By the eighteenth century, the population had grown too large for the small island. At its peak, it was around 12,000. The only crop—sweet potatoes—could no longer feed the population. The palm forests had been cut down to provide rollers for the statues and to make way for roads. In 1722, when the first westerner, Admiral Jacob Roggeveen, visited the island, he wrote that there were hundreds of statues standing. When Captain Cook visited in 1774, he reported that only nine statues were still standing. Obviously, something dramatic had occurred during those years.

4   Any commentary about Easter Island would be incomplete without mentioning the theories of the Norwegian explorer and scientist Thor Heyerdahl, who came to the island in the 1950's. Heyerdahl learned that there had been two groups of islanders: the Hanau Momoko and Hanau Eepe—names once mistranslated as "Short Ears" and "Long Ears." The Hanau Momoko were dark-haired, the Hanau Eepe mostly red-haired. The Hanau Eepe used heavy earrings to extend the length of their ears. Heyerdahl theorized that the Hanau Momoko were Polynesians from other Pacific islands, but that the Hanau Eepe came later in rafts from South America. He believed that the Hanau Momoko became the servants of the Hanau Eepe, who forced them to build the statues. Because the Hanau Eepe were the masters, the statues resembled them. Heyerdahl said that the red "hats" of the statues actually represented the red hair of the Hanau Eepe. He also pointed out that the ears of the statues resembled those of the Hanau Eepe. According to Heyerdahl's theory, the Hanau Momoko eventually rose up in revolt, overturning most of the statues and killing off all but a few Hanau Eepe.

5   Heyerdahl gave other evidence for the South American origin of the Hanau Eepe. The stonework of the stone platforms called *ahu* was incredibly intricate, unlike any made by other Pacific Islanders. However, the Inca people of South America were famous for intricate stonework. Another piece of evidence Heyerdahl presented was the fact that the staple food of the Easter Islanders, the sweet potato, is not found in Polynesia. He believed that it came with the Hanau Eepe from South America.

6   DNA testing has proven that all Easter Islanders were in fact descended from Polynesians. The current theory is that the Hanau Momoko and Hanau Eepe were two of perhaps twelve clans of islanders, all of whom built statues. The "statue toppling wars" broke out among the clans as the island became overpopulated. When one group won a victory over another, they toppled their enemies' statues. Archaeologists say that the resemblance between the stonework of the Easter Islanders and that of the Inca is coincidental. As for the sweet potato, most scientists now believe that sweet potato seeds came to the island in the stomachs of sea birds.

7   Mysteries about the Moai of Easter Island certainly remain, but current archaeological research has made one lesson clear: overpopulation and overuse of resources such as occurred on Easter Island can lead to the downfall of thriving societies.

Glossary

clans: *social units larger than families but smaller than tribes*

toppling: *knocking over; overturning*

14 of 26   The word immense in paragraph 1 is closest in meaning to

⃝ large

⃝ strange

⃝ ancient

⃝ ruined

15 of 26   According to the information in paragraph 2, which of the following type of Moai is the LEAST common?

⃝ Those that are carved from volcanic stone

⃝ Those with red stone "hats"

⃝ Those with white coral eyes

⃝ Those that portray a human head

16 of 26   Which of the following best explains the term *ahu* in paragraph 2?

⃝ Platforms made of stone

⃝ Red stone "hats"

⃝ Rollers made from palm logs

⃝ Specially constructed roads

17 of 26   What does the author refer to with the phrase something dramatic in paragraph 3?

⃝ The arrival of westerners

⃝ The toppling of the statues

⃝ The destruction of the forests

⃝ The building of the statues

18 of 26   Which of these statements best reflects the author's opinion of the theories of Thor Heyerdahl?

⃝ They are important but incorrect.

⃝ They are strange but true.

⃝ They are valid but incomplete.

⃝ They are outdated but useful.

19 of 26   In paragraph 4, the author says that the terms *Hanau Momoko* and *Hanau Eepe*

⃝ mean "Dark-Haired" and "Red-Haired" in the language of the Easter Islanders

⃝ originally come from the language of the Inca

⃝ have never been accurately translated into English

⃝ do not really mean "Short Ears" and "Long Ears" in the language of the Easter Islanders

20 of 26   What can be inferred from the information in paragraph 4 about the ears of the Easter Island statues?

⃝ They were broken off in the statue-toppling wars.

⃝ They were not made of the same kind of stone as the other parts of the statues.

⃝ They were long like those of the Hanau Eepe.

⃝ They were not made of stone but of wood from palm trees.

21 of 26   The word intricate in paragraph 5 is closest in meaning to

○ heavy
○ complex
○ colorful
○ breakable

22 of 26   According to modern theory, how did sweet potato seeds come to Easter Island?

○ They were brought from South America.
○ They were washed up by the waves.
○ They were brought by westerners in 1722.
○ They were transported by sea birds.

23 of 26   The main point of paragraph 7 is to

○ argue that more research is needed
○ point out certain dangers that can destroy societies
○ summarize recent research
○ explain why some mysteries will never be solved

24 of 26   The word thriving in paragraph 7 is closest in meaning to

○ isolated
○ divided
○ successful
○ remarkable

25 of 26   Look at the four squares [■] that indicate where the following sentence could be added to the passage.

> **After all, they say, the statues themselves show that the islanders were skilled stone workers.**

DNA testing has proven that all Easter Islanders were in fact descended from Polynesians. ■ The current theory is that the Hanau Momoko and Hanau Eepe were two of perhaps twelve clans of islanders, all of whom built statues. ■ The "statue *toppling* wars" broke out among the clans as the island became over-populated. When one group won a victory over another, they toppled their enemies' statues. ■ Archaeologists say that the resemblance between the expert stonework of the Easter Islanders and that of the Inca is coincidental. ■ As for the sweet potato, most scientists believe that sweet potato seeds came to the island in the stomachs of sea birds.

Circle the square [■] that indicates the best place to add the sentence.

26 of 26   DIRECTIONS: Select phrases from the answer choices and match them to the group of people to which they relate, according to the theories of Thor Heyerdahl. TWO answer choices will not be used. ***This question is worth 4 points.***

Answer Choices	Hanau Momoko
A. Extended the length of their ears by wearing heavy earrings	• _____
B. Were the first to arrive on Easter Island	• _____
C. Were one of twelve groups on the island that died out because of overpopulation	• _____
D. Did the actual work of building the statues	*Hanau Eepe*
E. Brought sweet potatoes to Easter Island	• _____
F. Provided the physical models for the statues on Easter Island.	• _____
G. Learned how to build the statues from other Pacific Islanders	• _____
H. Were almost all killed during a revolution	• _____
I. Knocked over most of the statues	

This is the end of the Reading Preview Test.

LESSON 1
FACTUAL AND NEGATIVE FACTUAL QUESTIONS

(A) Factual Questions

Factual questions ask about explicit facts and details given in the passage. They often contain one of the *wh-* words or phrases: *who, what, when, where, why,* and so on.

Factual questions often begin with the phrase *According to:*

According to the passage, . . .

According to the author, ...

According to the theories of _____,

According to the information in paragraph 3, . . .

Factual questions sometimes begin with this phrase:

What does the author say about . . . ?

When you see these phrases, you know that the information needed for an answer is directly stated somewhere in the passage (unlike answers for inference questions).

Scanning

To **scan** is to read quickly to find certain information. To answer factual questions, you must scan the passage or paragraph to locate and identify information that the question asks about. (The question often gives the number of the paragraph where the information is found and marks it with an arrow, which makes your job easier!) If you are not sure from your first reading where in the passage or paragraph to look for specific answers, use the following techniques:

▶ Focus on one or two key words from the question. These might be dates, names, or other nouns—something that will be easy to find as you scan. Lock these words in your mind.

▶ Scan the passage as you scroll down looking for these words or their synonyms. Look only for these words. Do *not* try to read every word of the passage.

▶ Remember that questions generally follow the order of the passage. Therefore, you will usually scroll *down* from the last question that you answered, not up.

▶ When you find the key words in the passage, carefully read the sentence where they occur. You may have to read the sentences preceding or following that sentence as well.

▶ Compare the information that you read with the answer choices.

Correct answers for factual questions seldom use exactly the same words that the passage uses. They often contain synonyms and have different grammatical structures.

There will generally be two or three factual questions about each of the three passages.

Here is part of a passage from the Preview Reading Test and a factual question about it.

Sample

5   Heyerdahl gave other evidence for the South American origin of the Hanau Eepe. The stonework of the stone platforms called *ahu* was incredibly intricate, unlike any made by other Pacific Islanders. However, the Inca people of South America were famous for intricate stonework. Another piece of evidence Heyerdahl presented was the fact that the staple food of the Easter Islanders, the sweet potato, is not found in Polynesia. He believed that it came with the Hanau Eepe from South America.

6   DNA testing has proven that all Easter Islanders were in fact descended from Polynesians. The current theory is that the Hanau Momoko and Hanau Eepe were two of perhaps twelve clans of islanders, all of whom built statues. The "statue toppling wars" broke out among the clans as the island became over-populated. When one group won a victory over another, they toppled their enemies' statues. Archaeologists say that the resemblance between the stonework of the Easter Islanders and that of the Inca is coincidental. As for the sweet potato, most scientists now believe that sweet potato seeds came to the island in the stomachs of sea birds.

According to modern theory, how did sweet potato seeds come to Easter Island?

- ○ They were brought from South America.
- ○ They were washed up by the waves.
- ○ They were brought by westerners in 1722.
- ○ They were transported by sea birds.

The key words that you would probably focus on in this question are *sweet potato seeds*. The answer for the question comes in the last sentence of paragraph 6, which says "most scientists now believe that sweet potato seeds were brought to the island in the stomachs of sea birds."

Note that sweet potatoes are also mentioned in paragraph 5, which says that Heyerdahl thought that the sweet potatoes came from South America, but most modern scientists do not believe this. Notice also that the correct answer choice is not written using exactly the same words as the information in paragraph 6.

(B) Negative Factual Questions

Negative factual questions ask you to determine which of the four answer choices is not given in the passage. These questions contain the words *not, except,* or *least,* and these words always appear in *uppercase* (capital) letters.

> According to the passage, all of the following are true EXCEPT . . .
>
> Which of the following is NOT mentioned in the passage?
>
> Which of the following is LEAST likely?

To answer this kind of question, you need to scan the passage to find answers that *are* correct or that *are* mentioned in the passage. The correct answer, of course, is the one that does not appear or is mentioned in another context. Sometimes, the three incorrect choices are clustered in one or two sentences. Sometimes they are scattered throughout the passage and will take you more time to find.

Negative factual questions take more time to answer than most of the other types of questions. You may want to skip these questions and come back to them later by using the Review feature.

Here's a part of one of the passages from the Reading Preview Test and a negative factual question about it.

Sample

2   What constitutes barriers depends on the species and its method of dispersal. Some are physical barriers. For land animals, bodies of water, chains of mountains, or deserts are effective. For example, the American bison spread throughout the open grasslands of North America, but in the southern part of the continent there are deserts, so the bison could not spread there. For aquatic creatures, strong currents, differences in salinity, or land areas may serve as barriers.

3   Some barriers involve competition with other species. A dandelion seed may be carried by the wind to bare ground, and, if environmental factors are right, it may germinate. There is not much chance, however, that any individual seedling will survive. Most places that are suitable for the growth of dandelions are already occupied by other plants that are well adapted to the area. The dandelion seedling must compete with these plants for space, water, light, and nutrients. Facing such stiff competition, the chances of survival are slim.

4   For animals, some barriers are behavioral. The blue spotted salamander lives only on mountain slopes in the southern Appalachian Highlands. Although these creatures could survive in the river valleys, they never venture there. Birds that fly long distances often remain in very limited areas. Kirkland's warblers are found only in a few places in Michigan in the summer and fly to the Bahamas in winter. No physical barriers restrict the warblers to these two locations, yet they never spread beyond these boundaries. Brazil's Amazon River serves as a northern or southern boundary for many species of birds. They could freely fly over the river, but they seldom do.

5   There are three types of natural pathways by which organisms can overcome barriers. One type is called a *corridor*. A corridor consists of a single type of
habitat that passes through various other types of habitat. North America's
Rocky Mountains, which stretch from Alaska to northern Mexico, is an example.
Various types of trees, such as the Engelmann spruce, can be found not only at
the northern end of the corridor in Alaska but also at higher elevations along the
entire length of this corridor.

In this passage, the author does NOT provide a specific example of
○ a bird that is affected by behavioral barriers
○ an aquatic animal that is blocked by physical barriers
○ a land animal that is affected by behavioral barriers
○ a tree that has spread by means of a corridor

The author does provide an example of a bird that is affected by behavioral
barriers in paragraph 4 (the Kirkland warbler) and, in the same paragraph, of a land
animal that is affected by behavioral barriers (the blue spotted salamander). In
paragraph 5, the author gives an example of a tree that has spread by means of a
corridor (the Engelmann spruce). The author mentions that aquatic animals are
blocked by physical barriers, but does not give a specific example of any of these
animals.

EXERCISE 1.1

FOCUS: Scanning short passages to find and identify answers for factual questions
and negative factual questions.

DIRECTIONS: First, read the questions about each of the passages. Then locate the
sentence in the passage that provides the information needed to answer the question. For the negative factual questions, find the sentence that probably contains
the three incorrect choices. Underline the sentence and write the number of the
question that it answers next to the sentence. Don't worry about answering
the questions themselves; concentrate on finding the information in the
passage. The first one is done as an example.

Passage 1

1   The first known dentist to practice in the North American colonies was William
Dinly, who came to Plymouth Colony from England in 1630. According to
① legend, he became lost in a snowstorm while riding to see a patient and was
never seen again. In most colonial settlements, however, dentistry was a rare
and unusual practice. In emergencies, barbers, jewelers, and blacksmiths all
probably extracted teeth.

2   One of the first native-born dentists was Paul Revere, the famous silversmith
and patriot. Revere, who began practicing in Boston in 1768, made false teeth
from African ivory. One of his patients was the Revolutionary War general Joseph

Warren. When the general died at the battle of Breeds Hill, Revere identified him by examining his teeth. This was the first known case of identification by means of dental records. Today, of course, dental records are commonly used as a means of identification.

3   By the early nineteenth century, most communities in the United States had one or more dentists, although not all of them had much training. In 1840, dentistry became a true profession. That's when the first dental school was opened in Baltimore, Maryland. The course lasted sixteen weeks. There were only five students in the first class, and only two of these graduated. This school has recently been restored as a museum of dental history.

4   The most common cure for toothaches was simply to pull out the offending tooth. Many dentists advertised "painless" extraction methods in the newspapers of the times. "Negative Spray" and "Vitalized Air" were two methods of reducing pain. It is not known today how these mysterious processes worked, but it is unlikely that they worked very well. In 1844, dentist Horace Wills had patients inhale the gas nitrous oxide just before having a tooth pulled. The tooth could then be painlessly removed. Nitrous oxide mixed with oxygen is still used today to reduce pain during dental procedures. Two years later, in 1846, the dentist William Morton gave a public demonstration of the effects of ether, which could be used as anesthesia not only during dental operations but for surgeries of all kinds.

5   Another important development in dentistry was the discovery of X rays in 1895. X rays allow dentists to look inside teeth to discover defects. Early decay, impacted teeth, abscesses, and bone loss are all things that dental X rays reveal.

6   The first dental drills appeared in the 1870's. They were powered by foot pedals like the sewing machines of the time. Drills were given electric power in the late 1890's. These power drills, which were at first called "dental engines," could be used for more than drilling cavities. They could also be used to shape and polish teeth. Quieter, faster drilling equipment aimed at reducing the discomfort of drilling was developed by John V. Borden in the 1950's. These drills work at high speeds to reduce the pressure and vibration caused by older drills, and are cooled by air or water to reduce the pain caused by the heat that drilling produces.

1. What story is told about the first dentist in the North American colonies?
2. People in which of the following occupations probably did NOT practice emergency dentistry?
3. What material did Paul Revere use to make artificial teeth?
4. How many students graduated in the first class to study dentistry in the United States?
5. How is the building that housed the first dental school in the United States used at present?
6. According to the passage, what were "Negative Spray" and "Vitalized Air"?
7. In what year did William Morton demonstrate ether?
8. Which of the following is NOT one of the problems that X rays can indicate?

9. What were "dental engines"?

10. How did the dental drills that were developed in the 1950's reduce heat and pain?

Passage 2

1   A deer's antlers grow from knob-like bones on the deer's skull. Antlers are made of bone, not horn, and are live, growing tissue. They have a constant blood and nerve supply. Deer use their antlers to fight for mates during the breeding season or to gain leadership of a herd. Among most species, only the bucks (male deer) have antlers, but both male and female caribou and reindeer (which are domesticated caribou) have antlers. Musk deer and Chinese water deer do not have antlers at all.

2   Unlike animals with horns, such as cattle and bison, deer lose their antlers every year. Those that live in mild or cold climates lose their antlers in the winter, after the breeding season. New ones begin to grow out in the early spring. Deer that live in tropical climates may lose their antlers and grow new ones at any time of year.

3   New antlers are soft and tender. Thin skin grows over the antlers as they develop. The short, fine hair on the skin looks like velvet. When the antlers stop growing, in early fall, this velvety skin dries up. Deer scrape their antlers against trees and shrubs to rub the skin off, an activity called a buck rub. The full-grown antlers are hard and strong. The antlers fall off several months later.

4   Young male deer—called button bucks—develop only small bumps for antlers during their first winter of life. For the next few years, the deer's antlers are small and straight. As deer mature, their antlers grow larger and form intricate branches. However, contrary to popular belief, it is not possible to accurately determine ages of deer by counting their "points" (the branches of their antlers). The size and shape of a buck's antlers depend on diet and general health as well as on genetic factors.

5   Deer antlers can grow up to one inch (2.5 centimeters) in a single day. That is the fastest growth rate in the animal kingdom. Scientists doing cancer research are studying deer antlers to try to learn how they can grow so rapidly. They hope that if they can answer that question, they may learn how cancer cells grow so quickly.

11. According to the passage, what are a deer's antlers made of?

12. The author says that the main purpose of a deer's antlers is to . . .

13. How are reindeer and caribou different from other types of deer?

14. When do deer that live in temperate climates lose their antlers?

15. What does the hair on a deer's antler resemble?

16. What is meant by the term *buck rub*?

17. What do a two-year-old deer's antlers look like?

18. The appearance of a deer's antlers does NOT depend on . . .

19. How much can a deer's antlers grow in one day?

20. Why are some scientists studying the antlers of deer?

Passage 3

1   Henry Schoolcraft was a pioneer in the study of Native American cultures. He studied chemistry and geology at Middlebury College in Vermont. As a young man, he managed his family's glassmaking business, and his first book was a treatise on glassmaking. However, when the family business failed he decided to head west to explore unknown territory and write about it in hopes of making a profit.

2   In 1803, the United States purchased the Louisiana Territory from France. President Thomas Jefferson immediately authorized the exploration of the vast territory. Meriwether Lewis and William Clark were chosen to find a pathway to the Pacific Ocean. Steven Long was sent to explore the Rocky Mountain region. Zebulon Pike went to the Southwest. Henry Schoolcraft was chosen to lead an expedition to the Ozark Mountain region of Missouri. In his book *Journal*, Schoolcraft wrote about the minerals, the plants, the animals, and the people, both Native Americans and white frontiersmen, of the Ozarks.

3   Later, Schoolcraft became the chief naturalist for an exploration party that went to the upper Mississippi River Valley and the Great Lakes district. He became a negotiator with the Native Americans of the area and was appointed Indian Agent to the Ojibwa tribe. He married the daughter of an Ojibwa man and a white woman. He learned to speak the Ojibwa language. With the help of his wife, he collected a great deal of authentic folklore of the Ojibwa and other tribes. He wrote many books on Native Americans and their history and culture. The famous American poet Henry Longfellow based his epic poem *Hiawatha* in part on the writings of Schoolcraft.

4   Schoolcraft has his critics, who point out that Schoolcraft's research was incomplete and sometimes inaccurate. He lived in a romantic age. There is no doubt that he changed his materials to make them more appealing to his readers. He invented some of his stories completely, and he mixed the traditions of the Ojibwa with those of other tribes. Despite his failings, he did succeed in bringing the culture of Native Americans to the attention of the public.

5   Schoolcraft's work contrasted sharply with that of the ethnographers who
worked in the last decade of the nineteenth century and the first decade of the
twentieth. Their aim was to achieve complete accuracy in creating a record
of Native American life, which at that time appeared to be in danger of completely vanishing within a few decades. Unlike Schoolcraft, they tended to take
notes in the original language. With the development of the phonograph, it
became possible to preserve not just words but also the tone and emphasis of
oral delivery.

Glossary

naturalist: *a scientist that studies nature*

epic poem: *a long poem that tells a story*

ethnographers: *scientists that study groups of people*

21. What was the subject of Schoolcraft's first book?
22. What event made Schoolcraft decide to become an explorer?
23. Which of these explorers was sent by Jefferson to the Southwest?
24. Which of the following did Schoolcraft probably NOT write about in his
    Journal?
25. What was Schoolcraft's role in the expedition to the upper Mississippi Valley?
26. Who assisted Schoolcraft in collecting information about Native Americans?
27. How did Schoolcraft influence Henry Longfellow?
28. According to the passage, Schoolcraft changed some of his materials in
    order to . . .
29. What was the main goal of the ethnographers mentioned in the passage?
30. What tool was available to the ethnographers but not to Schoolcraft?

EXERCISE 1.2

FOCUS: Answering factual and negative factual questions about reading passages.

DIRECTIONS: Read the following passages and the questions about them. Decide
which of the choices best answers the question, and mark the answer.

Passage 1

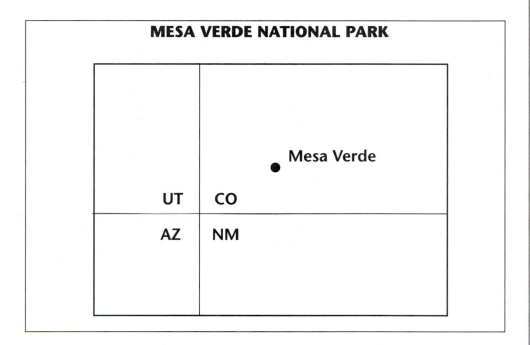

1   <u>Mesa Verde</u> is the center of the prehistoric Anasazi culture. It is located in the high plateau lands near Four Corners in the U.S. Southwest, where Colorado, Utah, New Mexico, and Arizona come together. The climate in this region is dry, but at the bottom of deeply cut canyons, seeps, springs, and tiny streams can be found. These provided the water for the Anasazi crops of corn, beans, squash, tobacco, and cotton. Farming was the main business of these people, but the Anasazi domesticated the wild turkey, hunted deer, rabbits, and mountain sheep, and gathered wild plants.

2   For a thousand years the Anasazi lived at Mesa Verde. These Native Americans were not related to the Navajos, who came to the area long after the Anasazi. However, because no one knows what the Anasazi actually called themselves, they are commonly called by their Navajo name, which means "the ancient ones" in the Navajo language.

3   The first Anasazi people, who are called the Basket Makers by archaeologists, came to the area around 550. This formerly nomadic group began to live a more settled life. They built underground dwellings called pit houses. These were clustered into small villages, mostly on top of mesas but occasionally on ledges on the walls of the cliffs that formed the Mesa.

4   In the next 300 years, the Anasazi made rapid technological progress, including the refinement of basket making, pottery making, jewelry making, leather working, and weaving. A Stone Age people, the Anasazi did not use metal, but they skillfully shaped stone, bone, and wood into a variety of tools for grinding, cutting, scraping, and polishing. About 750, they began building

houses above ground. At first these houses were made of poles and mud, but later they were made of sandstone. This period of development is known as the Early Pueblo Period.

5   The Great Pueblo Period (1100–1300) was Mesa Verde's classic age. The population grew to about 5,000. The Anasazis' level of technology continued to rise. Around 1200, there was another major population shift. The Anasazi moved from the mesa tops to the ledges on the steep sides of cliffs where some of their ancestors had lived centuries earlier.

6   On these ledges, the Anasazi built two- and three-story dwellings made of sandstone blocks held together with mortar made of mud. There were no doors on the first floors, and people had to use ladders to get into the buildings. Rooms averaged about six feet by nine feet (two meters by three meters). They were plastered on the inside and decorated with painted symbols. Smaller, isolated rooms were used for crop storage. The largest village (Cliff Palace) had 217 rooms. All the villages had underground chambers called kivas. Men held tribal councils there and also used them for secret religious ceremonies and clan meetings. Winding paths, ladders, and steps cut in the stone led from the villages to the valley below. One might surmise that these settlements were built on the cliffs for protection, but the Anasazi had no known enemies, and there is no sign of warfare.

7   A bigger mystery is why the Anasazi occupied their villages for such a short time. By 1300 Mesa Verde was deserted. It is generally thought that the Anasazi abandoned their settlements because of a prolonged drought, overpopulation, crop failure, or some combination of these. They probably moved southward and were incorporated into the pueblo villages that the Spanish explorers encountered two hundred years later. Their descendants may still live in the Southwest.

Glossary

Mesa Verde: *Spanish phrase meaning* green table *(In English, a* mesa *is a flat-topped, table-shaped mountain.)*

1. The passage does NOT mention that the Anasazi hunted
   - ○ sheep
   - ○ turkeys
   - ○ deer
   - ○ rabbit

2. The most important activity for the Anasazi was
   - ○ growing crops
   - ○ hunting wild animals
   - ○ raising domestic animals
   - ○ gathering wild plants

3. The name that the Anasazi used for themselves
   - ○ means "Basket Maker" in the language of the Navajo
   - ○ was given to them by archaeologists
   - ○ is unknown today
   - ○ means "Ancient Ones" in the Anasazis' own language

4. How long did the Early Pueblo Period last?
   - ○ 200 years
   - ○ 300 years
   - ○ 550 years
   - ○ 1,000 years

5. During the Early Pueblo period, the Anasazi did NOT make
   - ○ pots
   - ○ leather goods
   - ○ metal tools
   - ○ jewelry

6. When did the Anasazi first begin to build houses from stone?
   - ○ Before they came to Mesa Verde
   - ○ During the Early Pueblo Period
   - ○ Between 850 and 1100
   - ○ During the Great Pueblo Period

7. Where did the Anasazi move during the Great Pueblo Period?
   - ○ To pueblo villages in the south
   - ○ Onto the tops of the mesa
   - ○ Onto the floors of the canyon
   - ○ To settlements on the ledges of cliff walls

READING

8. During the Great Pueblo Period, Anasazi houses were mainly made of
   - ○ wood
   - ○ mud
   - ○ stone
   - ○ plaster

9. According to the passage, the Anasazi entered their buildings
   - ○ by means of ladders
   - ○ from underground chambers
   - ○ by means of stone stairways
   - ○ through doors on the first floor

10. According to the passage, *kivas* were used for all of the following purposes EXCEPT
    - ○ clan meetings
    - ○ food storage
    - ○ religious ceremonies
    - ○ tribal councils

11. According to the passage, the LEAST likely reason that the Anasazi abandoned Mesa Verde was
    - ○ drought
    - ○ overpopulation
    - ○ war
    - ○ crop failure

Passage 2

1   The dulcimer is a musical instrument that basically consists of a wooden box with strings stretched across it. The name *dulcimer* is derived from the Latin word *dulcis* (sweet) and the Greek word *melos* (song). In one form or another, dulcimers have been around since ancient times. Their earliest ancestor was a Persian instrument called the santir. Dulcimer-like instruments were played throughout the Middle East and North Africa and were brought by Arab musicians to Spain. From Spain, the instrument spread throughout Europe and eventually to North America.

2   Today there are two main types of dulcimers played in the United States: the hammered dulcimer and the Appalachian, or mountain, dulcimer. The hammered dulcimer is shaped like a trapezoid and is played by striking the strings with small wooden hammers called mallets. On the hammered dulcimer, there are sets of two, three, or four strings, called courses, which are struck at one time to sound each note. There are from twelve to twenty-two courses on a standard hammered dulcimer. The hammered dulcimer is usually categorized as belonging to the zither family of string instruments, although some musicologists challenge this classification.

3   The Appalachian dulcimer's immediate ancestors include the German schei-
tholt, the French epinette, and perhaps the Swedish hummel. It is classified
as a member of the lute family of instruments. Appalachian dulcimers are
painstakingly crafted by artisans, mainly in the mountain areas of West Virginia,
Kentucky, Tennessee, and Virginia. They have three strings—the melody, middle,
and bass string. Sometimes a second melody string is added. This instrument is
played by plucking the strings with the fingers or with quills. They are shaped
like teardrops or hourglasses. Heart-shaped holes in the sounding boards are traditional. Most performers play the instrument while seated with the instruments
in their laps, but others wear them around their necks like guitars or place them
on tables in front of them. Before the 1960's, the Appalachian dulcimer had a
limited appeal. It was usually associated with dance music and with "hillbilly"
music. However, the instrument was popularized by musicians such as Jean
Richie and Richard Fariña during the folk music revival of the 1960's and is
today featured in many types of music.

Glossary

hillbilly: *a person from the rural mountainous regions of the southeastern U.S.*

12. The author says that the word *dulcimer*
    - ○ means "wooden box"
    - ○ was not used until the 1960's
    - ○ means "sweet song" in Persian
    - ○ comes from two languages

13. What is the greatest number of notes that could be played on a standard hammered dulcimer?
    - ○ Three
    - ○ Four
    - ○ Twelve
    - ○ Twenty-two

14. According to the passage, experts do NOT all agree that the
    - ○ Appalachian dulcimer is a member of the lute family
    - ○ hammered dulcimer should be classified as a string instrument
    - ○ hammered dulcimer is a member of the zither family
    - ○ Appalachian dulcimer had a limited appeal before 1960

15. Which of these instruments could NOT be considered an ancestor of the Appalachian dulcimer?
    ○ The zither
    ○ The epinette
    ○ The santir
    ○ The scheitholt

16. According to the passage, how many strings does the Appalachian dulcimer have?
    ○ One or two
    ○ Three or four
    ○ Four or five
    ○ Six or more

17. According to the passage, most musicians play the Appalachian dulcimer
    ○ while sitting down
    ○ with the instrument around their necks
    ○ while standing next to tables
    ○ with wooden hammers

18. According to the passage, Jean Richie and Richard Fariña are known for
    ○ playing dance music and "hillbilly" music
    ○ designing and building Appalachian dulcimers
    ○ helping to bring more attention to dulcimers
    ○ beginning the folk music revival of the 1960's

Passage 3

1 Humanitarian Dorothea Dix was born in the tiny village of Hampden, Maine, in 1802. An avid reader and fast learner, she was taken in by her grandmother, who lived in Boston, and was educated there. When only nineteen years old, she established the Dix Mansion School for girls in Boston. There was no lack of students, and the school provided a good source of income for her and her two

brothers, whom she had brought to Boston to live with her. She also wrote and published the first of many books for children in 1824. In 1836, however, her health failed. She suffered most of her life from "lung trouble" (probably <u>tuberculosis</u>) and depression. She was forced to stop teaching and had to close her school.

2 Later that same year, having partially recovered, Dix set off for Italy to rest and recover her health in the warm Italian sunshine. She never made it to Italy, however. By the time her ship arrived in England, she was too ill to continue. She was taken care of by a kind British friend, William Rathbone. During her time in England, she became friends with Samuel Tuke, who directed the York Retreat for the Mentally Disordered. From Tuke, she learned new, more humane methods for taking care of the mentally ill.

3 Returning to the United States, Dix volunteered to teach classes at a prison for women in Cambridge, Massachusetts. Over the objections of the jailer, she went to the lower level of the jail where the mentally ill were housed. She was shocked to see that they were treated far worse even than ordinary criminals and were forced to live in filthy, miserable, brutal conditions. She vowed to spend the rest of her life improving conditions for the mentally ill.

4 For the next eighteen months, Dix toured Massachusetts prisons, poor-houses, and local jails where other mental patients were confined. She reported on the terrible conditions that she found to the Massachusetts legislature, which soon passed laws to improve conditions. After that, she turned her attention to neighboring New England states and then to the West and South. She traveled thousands of miles by train, coach, carriage, and riverboat, systematically gathering facts in order to convince those in power.

5 When the Civil War broke out in 1861, Dix was nearly sixty years old. However, she volunteered to form the Army Nursing Corps. At first, military authorities, who were not accustomed to female nurses, were skeptical, but she convinced them that women could perform this work acceptably. She recruited over 3,000 women and raised money for medical supplies for the troops. Under her leadership, army nursing care greatly improved.

6 After the war, Dix returned to her life's work and resumed her travels. She saw special hospitals for the mental ill built in fifteen states. She asked the federal government to use the income from public lands to help poor mental patients, and although both houses of Congress approved this bill, President Pierce vetoed it. Even though this plan failed, Dix was able to arouse concern for the problem of mental illness all over the United States as well as in Canada and Europe. Dix's success was due to her independent and thorough research, her gentle but persistent manner, and her ability to convince powerful and wealthy patrons to help her.

Glossary

tuberculosis: *a communicable disease of the lungs*

19. The Dix Mansion school closed because Dix
    ○ was in poor health
    ○ could not attract enough students
    ○ decided to travel to Europe
    ○ had to take care of her brothers

20. Who taught Dix new ideas about caring for the mentally ill?
    ○ Her grandmother
    ○ William Rathbone
    ○ Samuel Tuke
    ○ A jailer at a prison in Cambridge

21. Why did Dorothea Dix first go to the women's prison in Cambridge, Massachusetts?
    ○ She was sent there by the Massachusetts legislature.
    ○ She wanted to do research on prison conditions.
    ○ She was hired to be the jailer.
    ○ She was teaching a class there.

22. Where was Dorothea Dix first able to bring about reforms in the treatment of the mentally ill?
    ○ England
    ○ Massachusetts
    ○ The southern part of the U.S.
    ○ Maine

23. What does the author say about the military authorities in paragraph 5?
    ○ They were not used to women nurses.
    ○ They asked Dix to become superintendent.
    ○ They improved army nursing care during the war.
    ○ They did not allow Dix to recruit nurses herself.

24. Dix was NOT successful in her attempt to
    ○ publish books for children
    ○ arouse concern for the mentally ill
    ○ obtain income from public lands
    ○ become superintendent of nurses

25. What was Dix's "life work" as mentioned in paragraph 6?
    ○ Helping prisoners
    ○ Writing about her travels
    ○ Improving conditions for the mentally ill
    ○ Redefining the profession of nursing

26. Which of the following is NOT given as one of the reasons for Dix's success?
    ○ Her research was independent and methodical.
    ○ She attracted rich, influential sponsors to her cause.
    ○ Although she had a gentle manner, she didn't give up.
    ○ Her personal wealth allowed her to finance projects herself.

Passage 4

1   Ambient divers do not go underwater in submersible vehicles, such as a diving bell, a bathysphere, or in a pressure-resistant suit. They are divers who are exposed to the pressure and temperature of the surrounding (*ambient*) water. Of all types of diving, the oldest and simplest is free diving. Some free divers may use no equipment at all, but many use a face mask, foot fins, and a snorkel. Under the surface, free divers must hold their breath. Most free divers can only descend 30 feet (10 meters) beneath the surface, but some expert divers can go as deep as 100 feet (33 meters).

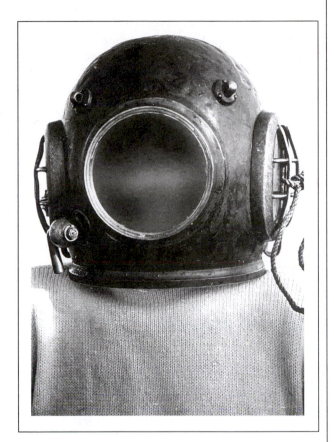

2   SCUBA diving provides greater range than free diving. The word SCUBA stands for Self-Contained Underwater Breathing Apparatus. SCUBA divers wear metal tanks with compressed air or other breathing gases. When using open-circuit equipment, a SCUBA diver simply breathes air from the tank through a hose and releases the exhaled air into the water. A closed-circuit breathing device, called a rebreather, filters out carbon dioxide and other harmful gases and automatically adds oxygen. This enables the diver to breathe the same air over and over. SCUBA divers usually use foot fins to help them swim underwater. They may wear only swimsuits (skin diving), or they may wear rubber wetsuits to help protect them from cold water.

3   SCUBA diving has been practiced since the nineteenth century, but it was not until 1942 that SCUBA diving became simple and safe. That was the year that Jacques-Yves Cousteau, a French naval officer, and Emile Gagnan, an engineer for a natural gas company, redesigned the regulator from an automobile engine so that it could be used to automatically regulate the flow of air to a diver. Cousteau and Gagnan attached the new regulator to hoses, a mouthpiece, and a pair of compressed air tanks and called this equipment the Aqualung. Aqualungs were soon being sold in dive shops around the world, and SCUBA diving became a popular sport.

4   In surface-supplied diving, divers wear helmets and waterproof canvas suits. Today, sophisticated plastic helmets have replaced the heavy copper ones used in the past. Surface-supplied divers get their air from a hose connected to air compressors on a pier or on a boat. Surface-supplied divers can go deeper and stay submerged longer than any other type of ambient diver. Unlike scuba divers, many of whom are sports divers, almost all surface-supplied divers work on tasks such as underwater construction and salvage operations.

Glossary

snorkel: *a long breathing tube that a diver holds in his or her mouth*

27. Ambient divers are ones who
   ○ can descend to great depths
   ○ wear pressure-resistant suits
   ○ use no equipment
   ○ are exposed to the surrounding water

28. According to the passage, a free diver may use any of the following EXCEPT
   ○ a rebreather
   ○ a snorkel
   ○ foot fins
   ○ a mask

29. According to the passage, the maximum depth for expert free divers is
   ○ 10 feet (3.3 meters)
   ○ 30 feet (10 meters)
   ○ 100 feet (33.3 meters)
   ○ 300 feet (100 meters)

30. In paragraph 2, what distinction does the author make between open-circuit SCUBA divers and closed-circuit SCUBA divers?
   ○ Closed-circuit divers use air from a tank, but open-circuit divers do not.
   ○ Closed-circuit divers breathe the same air again and again, but open-circuit divers do not.
   ○ Closed-circuit divers wear wetsuits, but open-circuit divers wear only swimsuits.
   ○ Closed-circuit divers use compressed air, but open-circuit divers use other breathing gases.

31. In paragraph 3, the author discusses how Cousteau and Gagnan
   ○ developed safer and simpler SCUBA equipment
   ○ designed a new regulator for automobile engines
   ○ adapted equipment from the natural gas industry for use by divers
   ○ invented new tactics for military divers

32. Today, surface-supplied divers' helmets are made from
    ○ copper
    ○ canvas
    ○ plastic
    ○ glass

33. Which of the following statements about surface-supplied divers is NOT true?
    ○ They can dive deepest of all ambient divers.
    ○ They can dive only from boats.
    ○ They can stay underwater the longest of all ambient divers.
    ○ They generally dive for work, not for recreation.

Passage 5

1   In 1862, in the midst of the Civil War, President Lincoln signed the Morrill Act. The measure was named for Congressman (later Senator) Justin S. Morrill of Vermont. Popularly called the Land Grant Act, it provided each state with thousands of acres of federally owned land. Each state received 30,000 acres (10,033 hectares) for each senator (all states have two senators) and 30,000 acres for each representative in Congress (the number of representatives depends on the population of the state). The bill required that the land be sold, the proceeds invested, and the income used to create and maintain colleges around the nation to teach agriculture and engineering.

2   The Morrill Act introduced two radical ideas to education: that higher education should be practical, and that it should be available to the working classes, not just to the wealthy. Before land-grant universities, college was basically for a select few, and the curriculum stressed "classical" subjects such as Latin, rhetoric, and mathematics. The Morrill Act promoted the idea that working-class students could attend a quality college to learn to grow corn or build bridges.

3   Although not all states used the money as the Morrill Act specified, some thirty states did establish new universities. Universities that trace their roots to the Morrill Act include Purdue, Rutgers, the University of Illinois, Texas A & M, the University of California, Ohio State, and Cornell. Eighteen states gave their money to existing state universities. A few states gave their money to private colleges. For example, Massachusetts used much of its funds to endow the Massachusetts Institute of Technology. One state changed its mind. Yale University, a private school, was chosen to be funded in Connecticut, but farmers protested, and the legislature moved the assets to the University of Connecticut.

4   It is not surprising that the Morrill Act emphasized agriculture. At the time it went into effect, over 80% of U.S. citizens lived in rural areas. In 1887, the Hatch Act established agricultural research centers at land-grant schools. This led to improvements in fertilizers, seeds, pesticides, livestock breeding, and disease control. Another bill, the Smith-Lever Act of 1914, provided for agricultural extension agents. These agents, who are based at land-grant schools, work directly with farmers to advise them about the latest farming techniques.

5   Gradually, most land-grant universities moved away from the narrow functions that were first assigned to them. Eventually they came to offer a full range of academic offerings, from anthropology to zoology. There are today 105 land-grant institutions in all fifty states and in the District of Columbia, Guam, Puerto Rico, and the Virgin Islands. About one in five college students in the United States attends land-grant schools.

34. According to the passage, when the Morrill Act was signed, its sponsor was
    ○ a general
    ○ a senator
    ○ a congressman
    ○ an engineer

35. What did the Morrill Act say about the land that was given to the states?
    ○ It had to be used by farmers.
    ○ Universities had to be built on it.
    ○ It had to be sold.
    ○ Each state could decide what to do with it.

36. According to the passage, the amount of land that each state received depended on
    ○ the physical size of the state
    ○ the number of senators and representatives
    ○ the number of college students who lived there
    ○ the condition of existing colleges

37. One of the "radical ideas about education" introduced by the Morrill Act was that
    ○ Latin and other classical subjects should be taught in college
    ○ students should learn subjects such as farming by actually working on farms
    ○ colleges should be more selective in their choice of students
    ○ useful subjects such as agriculture and engineering should be taught in colleges

38. According to the passage, the greatest number of states spent the money that they received from the Morrill Act on
    ○ giving money to private universities
    ○ establishing new departments at existing universities
    ○ creating new universities
    ○ rebuilding schools that had been damaged in the Civil War

39. Which of these states funded a private college?
    ○ Connecticut
    ○ Massachusetts
    ○ Illinois
    ○ California

40. Who objected to the way that the Connecticut legislature initially decided to spend its funds?
    - ○ Farmers
    - ○ Students
    - ○ Senators
    - ○ Teachers

41. According to the passage, one effect of the Hatch Act was to
    - ○ create more land-grant schools
    - ○ provide advisors for farmers
    - ○ strengthen engineering programs
    - ○ establish agricultural research stations

42. Today, most land-grant colleges
    - ○ no longer offer courses in agriculture and engineering
    - ○ offer a wider variety of courses
    - ○ now emphasize research more than teaching
    - ○ no longer have an important role in U.S. education

43. How many land-grant schools are in operation at present?
    - ○ 5
    - ○ 20
    - ○ 50
    - ○ 105

Vocabulary questions ask about the meaning of words or phrases in the passage. You have to decide which of four words or phrases is closest in meaning to the word from the passage. Most vocabulary questions ask about single words (usually nouns, verbs, or adjectives). Some ask about phrases involving several words. There will generally be two to four vocabulary questions about each of the three passages (six to ten per Reading Section).

You can often use other words in the same sentence or in nearby sentences as clues to get an idea of the meaning of the expression you are being asked about. These surrounding words are called the **context.**

- **Synonyms**

The first state to institute compulsory education was Massachusetts, which made it mandatory for students to attend school twelve weeks a year.

The word *mandatory* is a synonym for the word *compulsory.* If it is *mandatory* to attend school twelve weeks a year, then *compulsory* education must mean "mandatory," "required," "necessary."

- **Examples**

Many gardeners use some kind of mulch, such as chopped leaves, peat moss, grass clippings, pine needles, or wood chips, in order to stop the growth of weeds and to hold in water.

From all the examples given, it is clear that *mulch* means "material from plants."

- **Contrast**

In the 1820's, the Southern states supported improvements in the national transportation system, but the Northern states balked.

Because the Southern states *supported* improvements, and because a word is used that indicates contrast between the first part of the sentence and the second part (*but*), then the word *balked* must have a meaning that is basically the opposite of *supported.* In other words, the Northern states must have "refused to support" improvements, or "been against" improvements.

- **Word Analysis**

A tiger standing in tall grass is almost invisible because of its striped markings.

The prefix *in-* often means "not." The root *-vis-* means "see." The suffix *-ible* means "able to be." Even if you are not familiar with the word *invisible,* you could probably guess that it means "not able to be seen."

■ **General Context**

In a desert, vegetation is so scanty that it is incapable of supporting any large human population.

As is generally known, deserts contain little vegetation, so clearly the word *scanty* must mean "scarce" or "barely sufficient."

You can use any of these techniques to help you answer vocabulary questions about the passages.

These are the steps that you should follow when you answer vocabulary questions:

1. Look at the highlighted word or phrase and the four answer choices. If you are familiar with the word, guess which answer is correct, but don't click on the answer yet.

2. Read the sentence in which the word appears. (The word will be highlighted so it will be easy to find.) See if context clues in the sentence or in the sentences before or after help you guess the correct meaning.

3. If context clues do not help you guess the meaning of the word, use word analysis. In other words, see if the prefix, root, or suffix can help you understand the word.

4. If you still are not sure which answer is correct, read the sentence to yourself with each of the four answer choices in place. Does one seem more logical, given the context of the sentence, than the other three? If not, do any seem illogical? If so, you can eliminate those.

5. If you are still not sure, make the best guess that you can and go on. If you have time, come back to this question later.

Here is part of a passage from the Reading Preview Test and a vocabulary question about it.

Sample

Virtually all living things have some way of getting from here to there. Animals may walk, swim, or fly. Plants and their seeds drift on wind or water or are carried by animals. Therefore, it is reasonable to expect that, in time, all species might spread to every place on Earth where favorable conditions occur. Indeed, there *are* some cosmopolitan species. A good example is the housefly, found almost everywhere on Earth. However, such broad distribution is the rare exception. Just as barbed wire fences prevent cattle from leaving their pasture, biological barriers prevent the dispersal of many species.

The word cosmopolitan in the passage is closest in meaning to
- ○ worldwide
- ○ useful
- ○ well-known
- ○ ancient

There are two clues to help you find the meaning of the highlighted word. The first is in the preceding sentence, where the author says "all species might spread *to every place on Earth* where favorable conditions occur." The author then says that there really are some of these *cosmopolitan* species—species that spread everywhere in the world. Then, in the following sentence, the author gives the example of the housefly, which is found "almost everywhere on Earth," again indicating that a *cosmopolitan* species must be one that lives all over the world. This information should help you choose *worldwide* as being closest in meaning to *cosmopolitan*. Notice that if you put the three incorrect answer choices—*useful, well-known,* and *ancient*—into the passage in place of *cosmopolitan,* the sentence does not make sense in the passage.

At the end of the Reading Section of this book, there is a special tutorial called "Vocabulary Building." This section contains lists of words that may appear in vocabulary questions and that are useful to learn to develop your academic vocabulary. The exercises will help you practice using context to guess the meaning of words.

EXERCISE 2.1

FOCUS: Using context to guess the meaning of words in short passages.

DIRECTIONS: Read the passages and then guess the meaning of the highlighted expressions in the passage. Write one or two synonyms or a definition on the lines next to the expressions. The first item is done for you.

Passage 1

Everyday life in the British Colonies of North America may seem glamorous, especially as reflected in antique shops. But judged by today's standards, it was quite a drab and harsh existence. For most people, the labor was hard and constant from morning to dusk.

Rudimentary comforts now taken for granted were lacking. Public buildings were often not heated at all. Drafty homes were heated only by inefficient fireplaces. There was no running water or indoor plumbing. The faint light of candles and whale oil lamps provided inadequate illumination. There was no sanitation service to dispose of refuse; instead, it was consumed by long-snouted hogs that were allowed to roam the streets freely.

1. drab _____uninteresting, dull_____

2. constant _____

3. dusk _____

4. rudimentary _____

5. faint _____

6. refuse _____

7. roam _____

Passage 2

When Charles W. Eliot took over as president of Harvard in 1869, he broke with the traditional curriculum. The usual course of studies at U.S. universities at the time emphasized classical languages, mathematics, rhetoric, and ethics. Eliot pioneered a system under which most required courses were dropped in favor of elective courses. The university increased its offerings and stressed physical and social sciences, the fine arts, and modern languages. Soon other universities all over the United States were following Harvard's lead.

---

8. took over _____

9. curriculum _____

10. elective _____

11. stressed _____

Passage 3

1 The Pleiades, named after the Seven Sisters of Greek mythology, is a cluster of stars in the constellation Taurus. It is among the nearest to Earth of all star clusters, probably the best known, and certainly the most beautiful. The cluster has been known to humans since antiquity, and is mentioned in Homer's *Odyssey*. It appears as a dipper-shaped group of stars high overhead on autumn evenings. It is so young (only a few million years old) that many of its stars appear to be surrounded by a blue mist. This luminous haze is actually starlight from the hot blue stars that dominate the cluster reflecting off the interstellar dust and debris that was left over after the stars were formed. Our own sun's stellar neighborhood probably looked much like this just after its formation.

2 Despite its name, the cluster is actually composed of about 250 stars, only a handful of which are visible with the naked eye. The seven brightest are named for the Seven Sisters of Greek mythology: Asterope, Electra, Maia, Taygete, Celaeno, Alcyone, and Merope. Six of these are considerably brighter than the seventh one, Merope. According to one myth, Merope is dimmer than her sisters because she is mourning a lost lover.

12. cluster _____

13. mist _____

14. luminous _____

15. debris _____

16. a handful _____

17. mourning _____

Passage 4

Interior designers may claim that a solitary goldfish displayed in a glass bowl makes a striking minimalist fashion statement, but according to a team of British researchers, goldfish learn from each other and are better off in groups than alone. In one experiment, two groups of goldfish were released into a large aquarium separated by a transparent panel. On one side, fish food was hidden in various locations. The fish on that side foraged for the food while the fish on the other side of the clear panel watched. When released into the feeding area, these observant fish hunted for the food exactly in the proper locations. Other experiments showed that fish raised in a group are less fearful than fish raised alone. And not only are they less skittish, but they are also better at eluding enemies in the event of actual attack.

18. solitary _____

19. striking _____

20. transparent _____

21. foraged _____

22. skittish _____

23. eluding _____

Passage 5

Although business partnerships enjoy certain advantages over sole proprietor-ships, there are drawbacks as well. One problem that partnerships face is the fact that each general partner is liable for the debts of any other partner. Moreover, he or she is responsible for lawsuits resulting from any partner's mal-practice. Interpersonal conflicts may also plague partnerships. All partnerships, from law firms to rock bands, face the problem of personal disagreements. Another problem is the difficulty of dissolving partnerships. It is usually much easier to dissolve a sole proprietorship than it is to terminate a partnership. Generally, a partner who wants to leave a partnership must find someone—either an existing partner or an outsider that is acceptable to the remaining partners—to buy his or her interest in the firm.

24. drawbacks _____

25. liable _____

26. conflicts _____

27. plague _____

28. terminate _____

Passage 6

1   Some 2,400 years ago, the Greek philosophers Democritus and Leucippus first proposed the idea of the atom. They suggested that if you slice an item, such as a loaf of bread, in half, and then in half again and again until you could cut it no longer, then you would reach the ultimate building block. They called it an atom.

2   Today we know that an atom is even more infinitesimal than that. To grasp the scale of the atom, look at the dot over the letter *i*. Magnify this dot a million times through an electron microscope and you will see an array of a million ink molecules. If you could somehow blow up this image a million times, you would see the fuzzy image of the largest atoms. And as tiny as atoms are, they are composed of still tinier subatomic particles.

---

29. slice _____

30. ultimate _____

31. infinitesimal _____

32. grasp _____

33. blow up _____

34. fuzzy _____

EXERCISE 2.2

FOCUS: Answering multiple-choice vocabulary questions in short passages.

DIRECTIONS: Read the passages and then answer the questions about the vocabulary in the passages by marking the oval next to the correct answer.

Passage 1

1   The Civil War created feverish manufacturing activity to supply critical material, especially in the Northern states. When the fighting was over, the stage was set for dramatic economic growth. Wartime taxes on production had vanished, and the few taxes that remained leaned heavily on real estate, not on business. The population flow from farm to city increased, and the labor force that it provided was buttressed by millions of recent immigrants. These newcomers were willing to work for low wages in the mills of the North and on the railroads of the Midwest and West.

2   The federal government's position towards economic expansion was nothing if not accommodating. The government established tariff barriers, provided loans and grants to build a transcontinental railroad, and assumed a studied position of nonintervention in private enterprise. The <u>Social Darwinism</u> of British philosopher Herbert Spencer and American economist William Graham Summer prevailed. The theory was that business, if left to its own devices, would eliminate the weak and nurture the strong. As business expanded, the rivalry heated up. In the 1880's, five railroads operating between New York and Chicago vied for passengers and freight traffic, and two more were under construction. As a result of the rivalry, the fare between the cities decreased at one point to one dollar. Petroleum companies likewise competed savagely with each other, and many of them failed.

Glossary

Social Darwinism: *The belief that the strongest individual or business will survive and rule weaker people or businesses.*

1. The word feverish in the passage is closest in meaning to
   ○ sickly and slow
   ○ extremely rapid
   ○ very dangerous
   ○ unexpected

2. Which of the following is closest in meaning to the word critical in the passage?
   ○ industrial
   ○ serious
   ○ crucial
   ○ impressive

3. The phrase the stage was set in the passage is closest in meaning to which of the following?
   ○ The game was over.
   ○ The progress continued.
   ○ The foundation was laid.
   ○ The direction was clear.

4. The phrase real estate in the passage is closest in meaning to
   ○ tools and machines
   ○ personal income
   ○ new enterprises
   ○ land and buildings

5. Which of the following is closest in meaning to the word buttressed in the passage?
   ○ supplemented
   ○ concerned
   ○ restructured
   ○ enlightened

6. The word closest in meaning to accommodating in the passage is
   ○ persistent
   ○ indifferent
   ○ balanced
   ○ helpful

7. The word prevailed in the passage is closest in meaning to
   ○ influenced
   ○ succeeded
   ○ premiered
   ○ evolved

8. The phrase left to its own devices in the passage is closest in meaning to
   ○ forced to do additional work
   ○ allowed to do as it pleased
   ○ made to change its plans
   ○ encouraged to produce more

9. Which of the following is closest in meaning to the word nurture in the passage?
   ○ take care of
   ○ pay attention to
   ○ feel sorry for
   ○ watch out for

10. The phrase vied for in the passage is closest in meaning to
    ○ competed for
    ○ gained
    ○ searched for
    ○ restricted

11. Which of the following could best be substituted for the word savagely in the passage?
    ○ fiercely
    ○ suddenly
    ○ surprisingly
    ○ genuinely

Passage 2

1 All birds have feathers, and feathers are peculiar to birds. No other major group of animals is so easy to categorize. All birds have wings, too, but there are other winged creatures, such as bats and certain insects.

2 Many adaptations are found in both feathers and wings. Feathers form the soft down of goose and ducks, the showy plumes of ostriches and egrets, and the strong flight feathers of eagles and condors. Wings vary from the short, broad ones of chickens, which seldom fly, to the long, slim ones of albatrosses, which spend almost all their lives soaring on air currents. In penguins, wings

have been modified into flippers and feathers into a waterproof covering. In kiwis, the wings are almost impossible to detect.

3   Yet diversity among birds is not as striking as it is among mammals. The difference between a hummingbird and an emu is great, but hardly as dramatic as that between a bat and a whale. It is variations in details rather than in fundamental patterns that have been important in the adaptation of birds to many kinds of ecosystems.

Glossary

down: *soft, short feathers found under the outer feathers of water birds that keep these birds warm*

12. In the passage, the phrase peculiar to is closest in meaning to
    ○ necessary for
    ○ important to
    ○ symbolic of
    ○ unique to

13. The word categorize in the passage is closest in meaning to
    ○ appreciate
    ○ comprehend
    ○ classify
    ○ visualize

14. The word showy in the passage is closest in meaning to
    ○ ornamental
    ○ powerful
    ○ pale
    ○ graceful

15. Which of the following is closest in meaning to the word detect in the passage?
    ○ utilize
    ○ observe
    ○ extend
    ○ describe

16. In the passage, the word diversity is closest in meaning to
    ○ function
    ○ heredity
    ○ specialty
    ○ variety

17. The word hardly in the passage is closest in meaning to
    ○ definitely
    ○ not nearly
    ○ possibly
    ○ not softly

18. Which of the following could best be substituted for the word fundamental in the passage?

○ basic
○ shifting
○ predictable
○ complicated

Passage 3

1   Manufactured in the tranquil New England town of Concord, New Hampshire, the famous Concord Coach came to symbolize the Old West. Its rugged body and a suspension system made of leather straps could handle the hard jolts from rough roads. A journalist describing a railroad shipment of thirty coaches bound for Wells, Fargo and Company wrote, "They are superbly decorated … the bodies red and the running parts yellow. Each door is painted, mostly with landscapes, and no two coaches are exactly alike."

2   Wells, Fargo and Company was founded in 1852 to provide mail and banking services for the gold camps of California and later won a monopoly on express services west of the Mississippi. A Wells, Fargo Concord Coach carried nine to fourteen passengers as well as baggage and mail. The accommodations were by no means plush. However, while conditions may have been primitive and service not always prompt, the stagecoach was still the fastest method of travel through much of the Far West.

---

19. The word tranquil in the passage is closest in meaning to

○ busy
○ industrial
○ peaceful
○ tiny

20. The word symbolize in the passage is closest in meaning to
    - ○ fulfill
    - ○ represent
    - ○ deny
    - ○ transform

21. Which of the following is closest in meaning to the word rugged in the passage?
    - ○ streamlined
    - ○ roomy
    - ○ sturdy
    - ○ primitive

22. In the passage, the word jolts is closest in meaning to
    - ○ shocks
    - ○ injuries
    - ○ signs
    - ○ accidents

23. The phrase bound for in the passage in closest in meaning to
    - ○ belonged to
    - ○ headed for
    - ○ built by
    - ○ owned by

24. In the passage, the word superbly is closest in meaning to
    - ○ occasionally
    - ○ surprisingly
    - ○ professionally
    - ○ wonderfully

25. In the passage, the word plush is closest in meaning to
    - ○ inexpensive
    - ○ clean
    - ○ convenient
    - ○ luxurious

26. The word or phrase closest in meaning to prompt in the passage is
    - ○ polite
    - ○ on time
    - ○ available
    - ○ at risk

Passage 4

1 To the Hopi people of Arizona, the institutions of family and religion are of paramount importance. The Hopi believe in a harmonious existence that makes the self-sacrificing individual the ideal. The Hopi individual is trained from birth to feel that his or her highest responsibility is to and for the Peaceful People—the Hopi's own term for themselves. Fighting, bullying, and attempting to surpass others bring an automatic rebuke from the community.

2 Implicit in the Hopi view is an original and integrated theory of the universe. With this they organize their society in such a way as to obtain a measure of security from a hazardous environment made up of foes, famines, and plagues. They conceive of the universe—humans, animals, plants, and supernatural spirits—as an orderly system functioning under rules known only to them. These rules govern their behavior, emotions, and thoughts in a prescribed way.

27. The word paramount in the passage is closest in meaning to

○ greatest
○ differing
○ equal
○ decreasing

28. Which of the following is closest in meaning to the word harmonious in the passage?

○ cooperative
○ hostile
○ philosophical
○ exclusive

29. The word bullying in the passage is closest in meaning to

○ lying
○ organizing
○ entertaining
○ tormenting

30. In the passage, the word rebuke is closest in meaning to

○ prestige
○ reaction
○ criticism
○ compliment

31. Which of the following could best be substituted for the word hazardous in the passage?

○ dangerous
○ random
○ familiar
○ changing

32. The word foes in the passage is closest in meaning to
    ○ fears
    ○ needs
    ○ failures
    ○ enemies

33. The word prescribed in the passage is closest in meaning to
    ○ illogical
    ○ set
    ○ unbearable
    ○ harsh

Passage 5

1   Canadian researchers have discovered a set of genes that determine the lifespan of the common nematode. This finding sheds new light on the aging process that may allow science to eventually delay the inexorable process of aging.

2   By manipulating the newly discovered genes, the team at McGill University in Montreal was able to increase the lifespan of the nematode fivefold. Altering the genes apparently caused the metabolism of the worms to operate at a more leisurely pace. This caused the DNA effects thought to bring about aging to accumulate at a reduced rate. Of course the causes of aging in humans are more involved than those in nematodes. However, researchers are confident that these discoveries will provide invaluable clues about this hitherto mysterious process.

34. The word determine in the passage is closest in meaning to
    ○ control
    ○ maintain
    ○ shorten
    ○ explain

35. Which of the following is closest in meaning to the phrase sheds new light on in the passage?
    ○ contradicts what is know about
    ○ emphasizes the importance of
    ○ provides more information about
    ○ calls more attention to

36. The word inexorable in the passage is closest in meaning to
    ○ cruel
    ○ essential
    ○ unstoppable
    ○ incomprehensible

37. What is meant by the word manipulating in the passage?
    - ○ discovering
    - ○ understanding
    - ○ modifying
    - ○ destroying

38. The phrase more leisurely in the passage is closest in meaning to
    - ○ slower
    - ○ more predictable
    - ○ more efficient
    - ○ harder

39. The word involved in the passage is closest in meaning to
    - ○ serious
    - ○ well known
    - ○ easily observed
    - ○ complicated

40. Which of the following is closest in meaning to the word clues in the passage?
    - ○ plans
    - ○ hints
    - ○ secrets
    - ○ discoveries

41. The word hitherto in the passage is closest in meaning to
    - ○ universally
    - ○ almost
    - ○ previously
    - ○ somewhat

LESSON 3
INFERENCE QUESTIONS

Some of the questions about the Reading passages require you to make **inferences.** The answers to these questions are not directly provided in the passage—you have to "read between the lines" to answer them.

Inference questions can be written in a number of ways. Many times the questions contain some form of the words *infer* or *imply.*

▶ Which of the following can be inferred from the passage?

▶ It can be inferred from the information in paragraph _____ that . . .

▶ In paragraph _____, the author implies that . . .

▶ Which of the following does the passage imply?

▶ Which of the following would be the most reasonable guess about _____?

▶ The author suggests that . . .

▶ It is probable that . . .

▶ It can be concluded from the information in paragraph _____ that . . .

Here is a section of one of the passages in the Reading Preview Test and an inference question about it.

Sample

What constitutes barriers depends on the species and its method of dispersal. Some are physical barriers. For land animals, bodies of water, chains of mountains, or deserts are effective. For example, the American bison spread throughout the open grasslands of North America, but in the southern part of the continent there are deserts, so the bison could not spread there. For aquatic creatures, strong currents, differences in salinity, or land areas may serve as barriers.

What does the author suggest about American bison?
○ They spread to North America from South America.
○ A body of water stopped them from spreading south.
○ They require open grasslands to survive.
○ They originally lived in deserts.

In this paragraph, the author gives the American bison as an example of land animals that are blocked by physical barriers. The passage tells us that the American bison spread through the open grasslands of North America, but could not spread to the south because of a desert. Therefore, bison must need open grasslands to survive. This idea is not directly stated anywhere in the passage, but it can be inferred.

EXERCISE 3.1

FOCUS: Identifying valid inferences based on sentences or short passages.

DIRECTIONS: Read each sentence or short passage and mark the answer choice that is a valid inference based on the information that you read.

1. If a metalworker from 3,000 years ago could somehow travel forward in time, he would recognize virtually every step of the lost-wax process that today is used to cast titanium for jet engines.

_____ A. Titanium has been forged for thousands of years.
_____ B. The lost-wax method of casting metal is very old.
_____ C. Metalworking has changed very little in 3,000 years.

2. When apple growers talk about new varieties of apples, they don't mean something developed last month, last year, or even in the last decade.

_____ A. Apple growers have not developed any new varieties in recent decades.
_____ B. Some varieties of apples can be developed in a short time, but others take a long time.
_____ C. New varieties of apples take a long time to develop.

3. High levels of serum cholesterol used to be thought of as a problem only for adults.

_____ A. High levels of serum cholesterol are no longer a problem for adults.
_____ B. Only children have a problem with high levels of serum cholesterol.
_____ C. High serum cholesterol affects both adults and children.

4. Alpha Centauri, one of the closest stars to Earth, is just 4.3 light years away. It can be seen only from the Southern Hemisphere. However, the closest star (other than our own Sun, of course) is a tiny red star, Proxima Centauri, which is not visible without a telescope.

_____ A. Proxima Centauri is the closest star to Earth.
_____ B. Alpha Centauri is invisible from Earth without a telescope.
_____ C. Proxima Centauri is closer than 4.3 light years from the Earth.

5. Compared with the rest of its brain, the visual area of a turtle's brain is quite small, since turtles, like all other reptiles, depend mainly on senses other than sight.

_____ A. No reptile uses sight as its primary sense.
_____ B. Animals that depend on sight all have larger visual areas in their brain than turtles do.
_____ C. The visual area of other reptiles' brains is smaller than that of turtles.

6. An old but still useful proverb says, "Beware of oak, it draws the stroke." In general, trees with deep roots that tap into groundwater attract more lightning than do trees with shallow, dry roots. Oaks are fifty times more likely to be struck than beeches. Pines are not as safe as beeches but are still much safer than oaks.

_____ A. The roots of oaks are fifty times deeper than those of beeches.
_____ B. Pines' roots are deeper than beeches', but not as deep as those of oaks.
_____ C. The deeper the root, the safer the tree.

7. Illegible handwriting does not indicate weakness of character, as even a quick glance at the penmanship of Franklin D. Roosevelt or John F. Kennedy reveals.

_____ A. Roosevelt and Kennedy both had handwriting that was difficult to read.
_____ B. Roosevelt's handwriting was more illegible than that of Kennedy.
_____ C. The author believes both Roosevelt and Kennedy had weak characters.

8. Jack London spent only a year prospecting for gold in Alaska. However, nearly half of his forty books are set there.

_____ A. London was successful in his search for gold in Alaska.
_____ B. Although London worked in Alaska for only a short time, he wrote almost twenty books while he lived there.
_____ C. London's experiences in Alaska had a strong influence on his writing.

9. Most fish take on the coloration of their natural surroundings to a certain degree. It's not surprising, therefore, that fish inhabiting the warm, shallow waters around tropical reefs are colored all the brilliant hues of the rainbow.

_____ A. Tropical fish are unlike other fish because they take on the coloration of their environment.
_____ B. Tropical reefs are brightly colored environments.
_____ C. Tropical fish are brightly colored because they inhabit warm waters.

10. Although sheep herding is an older and more beloved occupation, shepherds never caught the attention of filmmakers the way cowboys did.

_____ A. There have been more films about cowboys than about shepherds.
_____ B. Films about shepherds are older and more beloved than films about cowboys.
_____ C. Cowboys are generally younger than shepherds.

11. The Okefenokee Swamp is a fascinating realm that both confirms and contradicts popular notions of a swamp. Along with huge cypresses, dangerous quagmires, and dim waterways, the Okefenokee has sandy pine islands, sunlit prairies, and clear lakes.

_____ A. Although most swamps are not very interesting, the Okefenokee is an exception.
_____ B. The Okefenokee has features that are not commonly associated with swamps.
_____ C. Unlike most swamps, the Okefenokee does not have huge cypresses, dangerous quagmires, or dim waterways.

12. Thomas Jefferson preferred the Roman style of architecture, as seen in the buildings at the University of Virginia, to the English style favored by Charles Bullfinch.

_____ A. The architecture of the University of Virginia was influenced by the Roman style.
_____ B. Bullfinch was an English architect.
_____ C. Jefferson preferred to build in the English style of architecture.

13. In all cultures, gestures are used as a form of communication, but the same gestures may have very different meanings in different cultures.

_____ A. No two cultures use the same gestures.
_____ B. One gesture almost never has the same meaning in two cultures.
_____ C. A person from one culture may misunderstand the gestures used by a person from another.

14. Even spiders that do not build webs from silk use it for a variety of purposes, such as constructing egg sacs and nursery tents.

_____ A. All spiders build webs.
_____ B. Spiders that build webs don't build egg sacs or nursery tents.
_____ C. Silk is used by all spiders.

15. In theory, a good screwdriver should last a lifetime, but it seldom does, usually because it is used as a substitute for other tools.

_____ A. Using a screwdriver for purposes other than those for which it was intended can shorten its life.
_____ B. All screwdrivers, if they are really good, last a lifetime.
_____ C. If you want a screwdriver to last a lifetime, use other tools to substitute for it.

EXERCISE 3.2

FOCUS: Answering inference questions based on passages.

DIRECTIONS: Read the following passages and the inference questions about them. Mark the choice that best answers each question.

Passage 1

1   Pigeons have been taught to recognize human facial expressions, upsetting long-held beliefs that only humans have evolved the sophisticated nervous systems needed to perform such a feat. In recent experiments at the University of Iowa, eight trained pigeons were shown photographs of people displaying emotions of happiness, anger, surprise, and disgust. The birds learned to distinguish between these expressions. Not only that, but they were able to correctly identify the same expressions on photographs of unfamiliar faces. Their achievement does not suggest, of course, that the pigeons had any idea what the human expressions meant.

2   Some psychologists had theorized that, because facial expression is vital to human communication, humans have developed special nervous systems capable of recognizing subtle differences between expressions. Now the pigeons have cast doubt on that idea.

READING

3   In fact, the ability to recognize facial expressions of emotion is not necessarily innate even in human babies, but may have to be learned in much the same way that pigeons learn. In experiments conducted several years ago at the University of Iowa, it was found that pigeons organize images of things into many of the same logical categories that humans do.

4   None of these results would come as any surprise to Charles Darwin, who long ago wrote about the continuity of mental development from animals to humans.

1. From the information in paragraph 1, it can be inferred that pigeons
   - ○ show more emotions than people thought they could
   - ○ can understand the human emotions of happiness, anger, surprise, and disgust
   - ○ can identify only the expressions of people that they are familiar with
   - ○ have more sophisticated nervous systems than was once thought

2. The author probably believes that the psychologists mentioned in paragraph 2
   - ○ will need to revise their theory
   - ○ no longer believe that expressions are important in human communication
   - ○ have conducted their own experiments with pigeons
   - ○ no longer think that the pigeons have cast doubt on their theories

3. In paragraph 3, the author suggests that, at birth, human babies
   - ○ have nervous systems capable of recognizing subtle expressions
   - ○ can learn from pigeons
   - ○ are not able to recognize familiar faces
   - ○ may not be able to identify basic emotions through facial expressions

4. What can be inferred about the experiments that were conducted several years ago at the University of Iowa?
   - ○ They were completely contradicted by more recent experiments.
   - ○ They supported the idea that pigeons and humans share certain mental abilities.
   - ○ They were conducted by scientists on human babies.
   - ○ They proved that animals other than pigeons could recognize human expressions.

5. If Charles Darwin could have seen the results of this experiment, his most probable reaction would have been one of
   - ○ rejection
   - ○ surprise
   - ○ agreement
   - ○ amusement

Passage 2

1 The Titus-Bode Law predicted that there would be a fifth planet between Mars and Jupiter. In 1800, a group of astronomers nicknamed the "celestial police" was organized to search for the missing planet. Before the plan could be put in effect, another astronomer, G. Piazzi, discovered 1 Ceres, the largest asteroid, in this position in space on New Year's Day, 1801. While trying to locate Ceres again, the astronomer H. Olbers discovered 2 Pallas in 1802. J. Harding discovered 3 Juno in 1804. H. Olbers also discovered 4 Vesta, the brightest asteroid, in 1807. It was not until 1836 that a fifth asteroid, 5 Astrea, was added to the list. At first, many nineteenth-century astronomers did not find asteroids of much interest. One even called them "the <u>vermin</u> of the sky." In 1891, Max Wolf pioneered the use of astrophotography to detect asteroids. Then Wolf went on to discover 248 asteroids, beginning with 323 Bruscia. At present, around 150,000 asteroids have been discovered. Most are spotted today by automated systems that pair telescopes with computers.

2 Asteroids vary in size from Ceres, with a diameter of 570 miles, to tiny bodies that are only the size of pebbles. Only the four largest—Ceres, Palas, Vesta, and Juno—are spherical. Most are elongated or irregular. Asteroids are not uniformly distributed through space. Many occur in clusters called groups, or in even tighter clusters called families. Families of asteroids with similar characteristics, indicating a common origin, are called Hiruzama asteroids.

3 H. Olbers advanced the theory that asteroids are the remnants of a large planet that exploded. Other astronomers suggested that the asteroids were originally moons of Jupiter that broke away and then disintegrated. The most commonly accepted theory among astronomers today is that they occupy a place in the solar system where a sizeable planet could have formed but was prevented from doing so by the disruptive gravity field of nearby Jupiter. Originally, perhaps, there were only a few dozen asteroids. These were eventually fragmented by mutual collisions to produce the present population of asteroids.

4 When new asteroids are discovered, they are given a temporary six-character name. The first four numbers correspond to the year of discovery. The first of the two letters corresponds to the half-month period in which the asteroid was discovered, and the second to the sequence in which the asteroid was discovered in that half-month. For example, the asteroid 2006 AC was the third asteroid (C) to be discovered in the first half of January (A) in 2006. After the orbit of an asteroid has been calculated, asteroids receive a number that corresponds to the order of discovery (currently from 1 Ceres to 95959 Covadonga). The first several hundred asteroids were named for female characters from mythology. (Ceres, for example, is the Roman goddess of the harvest.) Even after these names were used up, the convention of giving asteroids female names continued up until 334 Chicago. A person who discovers an asteroid may submit a name to the International Astronomical Union. Some are named for places or for things. Some are named to honor famous scientists, painters, writers, or even pop stars, such as musicians and actors. Some are named after colleagues, family members, and even pets. Discoverers may not, however, name asteroids after themselves. Of the 150,000 known asteroids, only about 10% have names.

5   Most asteroids are found in the Main Asteroid Belt between Mars and Jupiter. Some have highly eccentric orbits, such as 3200 Phaeton, which swings close to the Sun. Some asteroids, called Near Earth Asteroids (NEAs), pass close to Earth. It is feared that one day an asteroid may hit Earth and cause a great deal of damage. In fact, most scientists believe that a collision between an asteroid and the earth made dinosaurs extinct.

6   In July of 2002, without warning, a medium-sized asteroid called 2002 MN passed relatively close to Earth. It was not observed until three days after it had passed. This was the closest an asteroid had come to Earth since 1994 XM. That asteroid missed the Earth by only 64,000 miles. However, the one in 2002 was much larger than 1994 XN and potentially much more destructive. Other near misses involved 1989 FC and 433 Eros in 1975. While there are programs to watch for Near Earth Asteroids, 2002 MN proved that these programs are not completely effective. Some people believe that there should be a much larger worldwide program to detect and possibly destroy asteroids that are heading towards our planet.

Glossary

vermin: *small, unwanted, destructive animals, usually insects or mammals such as rats*

6. It can be inferred from the information in paragraph 1 that the Titus-Bode Law deals with which of the following?
   - ○ The size of planets
   - ○ The position of planets around the Sun
   - ○ The speed of bodies in space
   - ○ The existence of asteroids

7. What does the author imply about G. Piazzi in paragraph 1?
   - ○ He was not trained as an astronomer.
   - ○ He worked closely with H. Olbers.
   - ○ He was not a member of the "celestial police."
   - ○ He discovered the four largest asteroids.

8. It can be inferred from the information in paragraph 1 that H. Olbers
   - ○ was not looking for 2 Pallas when he found it
   - ○ discovered the largest asteroid
   - ○ discovered many asteroids a few years after finding 4 Vesta
   - ○ worked closely with J. Harding

9. The author implies that the nineteenth-century astronomers mentioned in paragraph 1 believed that
   - ○ astronomers should work on projects other than asteroids
   - ○ astrophotography was a valuable tool
   - ○ more time should be spent searching for asteroids
   - ○ asteroids were dangerous because they might strike Earth

10. It can be inferred from the information in paragraph 2 that asteroids in a family
    ○ always have a common origin
    ○ are closer together than those in a group
    ○ all have the same shape
    ○ are brighter than those in a group

11. What does the author imply about the three theories that he explains in paragraph 3?
    ○ They are all valid theories.
    ○ The first two theories are no longer considered valid.
    ○ All three theories have been proven to be false.
    ○ The third theory is older than the first two.

12. What can be inferred from the information in the paragraph about the asteroid named 2002 MN?
    ○ It has a temporary name.
    ○ It was the two-thousandth and second asteroid to be discovered.
    ○ Its discoverer's first name began with M and last name began with N.
    ○ It was discovered in January of 2002.

13. What can be inferred from the information in the paragraph about the asteroid named 433 Eros?
    ○ It is named for a female character from mythology.
    ○ It was discovered in 433 A.D.
    ○ Its orbit has never been calculated.
    ○ It was the four-hundred and thirty-third asteroid to be discovered.

14. It can be inferred that the first 333 asteroids to be discovered
    ○ all had feminine names
    ○ were all named for mythological characters
    ○ all were given the names of historical persons
    ○ were all named for their discoverers

15. Which of the following can be inferred from the information in paragraph 6?
    ○ Smaller asteroids move faster than medium-sized asteroids.
    ○ Large asteroids are easy to detect if they approach the earth.
    ○ The bigger the asteroid, the more destructive it might be.
    ○ Even if a large asteroid misses the Earth, it might cause damage.

Passage 3

1   Probably the world's most famous geyser is Old Faithful, located in the Upper Geyser Basin in Yellowstone National Park in Wyoming. There are over 300 geysers in the Basin, the largest concentration of geysers in the world, and over 700 in Yellowstone Park. Before the earthquake of 1959, Old Faithful's eruptions came almost like clockwork, every 60 to 65 minutes. Since that earthquake, eruptions have been as few as 30 minutes apart or as long as 120 minutes apart.

2   An eruption of Old Faithful is a spectacular sight, one which has been drawing tourists to Yellowstone since the 1870's. The geyser usually gives a warning: a short burst of steam. Then a graceful jet of steam and boiling water rises up to 180 feet (60 meters) in the air, unfurling in the sunlight with the colors of the rainbow playing across it. Each eruption lasts from one and a half to five minutes. When it erupts, it sprays up to 8,400 gallons (32,000 liters) of water in the air.

3   The eruption is only the visible part of the spectacle. In order for a geyser to erupt, there are four necessary conditions that must exist. First, there must be an abundant supply of water. Old Faithful is supplied with water from groundwater and rainfall, but other geysers in Yellowstone are partly supplied from creeks and rivers.

4   Second, there must be a heat source. All geyser fields are located over recently active volcanic areas. In the Upper Geyser Basin, a steady supply of heat is provided by hot spots of molten lava as little as two miles (5 kilometers) below the surface. When water trickles down to the hot spots, it heats up.

5   However, the water would never be ejected from the geysers with such tremendous force if it were not for geyserite, a material that is mainly composed of the mineral silicon dioxide. The presence of geyserite is the third necessary condition. Geyserite is dissolved from the rocks and deposited on the walls of the geyser's plumbing system and around the surface of the geyser. These deposits make the plumbing system pressure-tight. This allows the water to be carried all the way to the surface rather than leaking out into the loose rock, sand, and soil that surrounds the plumbing system.

READING

6 The final condition is a special underground plumbing system. Geysers have various types of plumbing systems, but all have a narrow spot, a constriction point near the surface. The water in this narrow spot acts like a valve or a lid that allows pressure to build up in the water below, causing the eruption. A geological feature that has water, geyserite, and heat but no special plumbing will be a hot spring, not a geyser. Geologists studying Old Faithful theorized that it had a relatively simple plumbing system composed of an underground reservoir connected to the surface by a long, narrow tube that grows even narrower near the surface. In 1992, a probe equipped with a video camera and heat sensors was lowered into the geyser and confirmed the existence of a constriction, a narrow shaft, and a cavern about the size of a large automobile 45 feet (15 meters) beneath the surface.

7 As water fills Old Faithful's plumbing system, it is heated in the reservoir like water in a teakettle. But while water in a kettle rises because of <u>convection</u>, the water in the tube and the constriction above prevents free circulation. Therefore, the water in the upper tube is cooler than the water at the bottom. The weight of the water puts pressure on the water below, raising the boiling point of the water in the reservoir. Eventually, enough pressure builds to push water past the constriction point and out of the mouth of the geyser. The pressure drops as the water is released, and a sudden, violent boiling takes place through the length of the tube. A tremendous amount of steam is produced and the water roars out of the geyser in a superheated mass. This is the eruption, and it continues until the reservoir is emptied or the steam runs out.

8 There are two main types of geyser. A columnar geyser (also called a cone geyser) such as Old Faithful shoots a fairly narrow jet of water from a formation of geyserite that looks like a miniature volcano. A fountain geyser has an open pool at the surface that fills with water before or during the eruption. When a fountain geyser erupts, water sprays in all directions but does not reach the height of the jet from a columnar geyser.

Glossary

convection: *the movement of gases or liquids caused by heat*

16. The author implies in paragraph 1 that the earthquake of 1959 made Old Faithful geyser erupt
    - ○ more violently
    - ○ less regularly
    - ○ more often
    - ○ less spectacularly

17. It can be inferred from the information in paragraph 1 that
    - ○ there are some geysers in Yellowstone Park that are not in Upper Geyser Basin
    - ○ geysers are always found in groups, never individually
    - ○ some of the geysers in Upper Geyser Basin are not actually in Yellowstone Park
    - ○ the most spectacular geysers are not located in Yellowstone Park

18. What can be inferred about the material geyserite?
    - ◯ Water does not pass through it easily.
    - ◯ It is found in geysers, but not in any other formations.
    - ◯ Yellowstone Park is the only place where it is found.
    - ◯ It is found only deep in the Earth.

19. The passage implies that Old Faithful would not erupt at all if
    - ◯ there had not been an earthquake in 1959
    - ◯ the plumbing system were not surrounded by loose rock, sand, and soil
    - ◯ the level of the streams and rivers in Yellowstone Park suddenly dropped
    - ◯ there were not a narrow point in its plumbing system

20. We can infer from paragraph 6 that, compared to Old Faithful, many other geysers
    - ◯ are more famous
    - ◯ shoot water much higher in the air
    - ◯ have more complicated plumbing systems
    - ◯ have much smaller reservoirs

21. The author implies that the probe that was lowered into Old Faithful in 1992
    - ◯ showed that it was very difficult to investigate geysers
    - ◯ confirmed that the geologists' theory about Old Faithful was correct
    - ◯ indicated that Old Faithful's plumbing system was more complex than had been believed
    - ◯ made some very surprising discoveries

22. It can be inferred that the author compares the geyserite formation at the mouth of Old Faithful with a volcano because of the formation's
    - ◯ shape
    - ◯ age
    - ◯ size
    - ◯ power

23. It can be concluded that Old Faithful does NOT have
    - ◯ a source of heat
    - ◯ a narrow tube
    - ◯ a cone at its mouth
    - ◯ an open pool at the surface

Passage 4

1 Airports have not always been called airports. At first they were called "flying fields," and were simply level, grassy fields. Some airports, such as Dallas's Love Field and Louisville's Standiford Field, still retain the word *field* in their names. Most of these early airports had hangars for servicing and storing planes, and in some cases observation stands for watching the air shows that were popular in the early 1900's. Some of these airfields also housed the earliest airplane factories.

2   During World War I, many military airports were built in Europe. Afterwards, commercial airlines shared these fields with the military. The field at Le Bourget, near Paris, was the first to have a building dedicated to commercial air travel. This building was called an "airway station" and, like others in Europe and North America, resembled a train station. Early airplane interiors resembled the interior of railroad cars. These were efforts to assure passengers that there was really nothing strange about air travel.

3   Coastal airports of the 1920's and 1930's could accommodate both land-planes, for short-range domestic flights, and seaplanes ("flying boats") for international flights. LaGuardia Airport near New York City had both a marine terminal and a landplane terminal. The design of the marine terminal was compared to the Parthenon in Greece and the landplane terminal, built on two levels, adopted the best of train-station design.

4   As planes became heavier and carried more passengers and baggage, it became necessary to pave the runways so that the planes would not sink into muddy fields. And as planes became larger, the major design problem became scale—how to allow adequate space on the ground while permitting convenient and rapid movement of passengers.

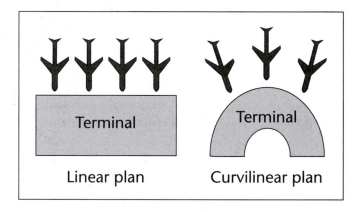

5   Most terminal designs take one of five approaches. The simplest one is the linear plan. Terminal buildings that follow the linear approach may be straight or curved. Passengers board aircraft parked next to the terminal. This approach works well for small airports that need to provide boarding areas for only a few aircraft at one time. Curved terminal buildings offer no major advantages over straight buildings. The first curved terminal was Tempelhof Airport near Berlin. The design was adopted to accommodate the fence of a nearby cemetery rather than for any functional reason. However, the curved design became a model for other airports.

6   The pier plan evolved during the 1950's when piers (concourses) were added to the linear airport design. Passengers are processed in the central terminal and are then routed down long piers to their gates. At first, passengers boarded the plane by walking from the gate and then climbing a moveable staircase into the plane. Later, passengers could walk directly from the boarding area onto the plane through a jetway, a moveable covered corridor. The pier plan allows many planes to park next to the buildings. However, it creates long walking distances for passengers. People-movers such as moving sidewalks and electric carts can make these distances more tolerable. Chicago's O'Hare, Amsterdam's Schiphol, and London's Gatwick follow this general plan.

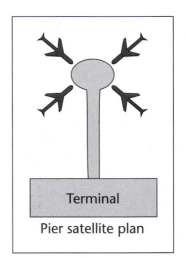

Pier satellite plan

7   In the satellite plan, a central terminal is connected to numerous concourses that lead to satellite terminals where aircraft are parked in a cluster. This approach also involves long walks, particularly if a passenger must transfer from one "satellite" to another. Monorails and electric trains can reduce these distances. Terminal I at Paris's Charles de Gaulle consists of a single round terminal surrounded by seven satellites. One drawback of this design it that it is difficult for an airport to expand without disrupting operations.

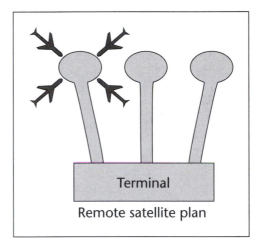

Remote satellite plan

8   In the transporter plan, some system of transport is used to move passengers from the terminal to the aircraft or to a remote satellite. If buses are used, passengers must climb a moveable stairway. If mobile lounges are used, they can link directly to the aircraft; passengers never have to go outside. This system allows for easier airport expansion. Washington Dulles is an example of an airport following the transporter plan.

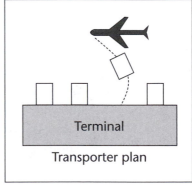

Transporter plan

9   Air travel can be a stressful experience. In recent years, designers have added details to make airports more pleasant. Britain's Sanstead airport, Japan's Kansai airport, the renovated Ronald Reagan Airport in Washington, and Denver International Airport all feature large open areas with light filtering through the walls and roof to create attractive public spaces.

24. In paragraph 1, the author suggests that Standiford Field and Love Field
    - ○ have been in operation for many years
    - ○ were sites of famous air shows
    - ○ were always called "airports"
    - ○ were sites of aircraft factories

25. From the information in paragraph 2, it can be inferred that in the early days of air travel, passengers
    - ○ preferred to travel by plane rather than by train
    - ○ traveled to airports on trains
    - ○ were accustomed to train travel
    - ○ refused to use airports that were shared with the military

26. In paragraph 3, the author suggests that seaplanes
    - ○ were not as safe as landplanes
    - ○ were used only for domestic flights
    - ○ could fly farther than landplanes
    - ○ were not as convenient as boats

27. It can be inferred from the passage that both Le Bourget and the LaGuardia landplane terminals
    - ○ were influenced by the design of railway stations
    - ○ resembled the Parthenon in Greece
    - ○ were built by the same architect
    - ○ were built on two levels

28. It can be inferred from the passage that scale would not be a problem in airport design if
    - ○ airports were larger
    - ○ aircraft did not need so much room to maneuver on the ground
    - ○ other forms of transportation were more efficient
    - ○ airplanes could fly faster

29. The linear plan of airport design would probably be best at
    - ○ a busy airport
    - ○ an airport used by many small airplanes
    - ○ an airport with only a few arrivals and departures
    - ○ an airport that serves a large city

30. Information in paragraph 5 suggests that the Tempelhof Airport near Berlin was
    - ○ not intended to be a model for other airport terminals
    - ○ built long before the nearby fence was built
    - ○ a great improvement on straight linear terminals
    - ○ designed to solve several functional problems

31. The passage implies that the term *satellite plan* is used to describe some airports because
    ○ these airports are located far from a city just as a satellite is located far from a planet
    ○ satellites will someday be launched and tracked from these sites
    ○ airports that make use of this plan utilize data from satellites
    ○ small terminals circle the main terminal like satellites around a planet

32. In paragraph 7, the author suggests that monorails and electric trains carry people to satellite terminals mainly from
    ○ airplanes
    ○ the central terminal
    ○ the center of nearby cities
    ○ other satellite terminals

33. It can be inferred from the information in paragraph 8 that mobile lounges would be preferable to buses when
    ○ passengers are in a hurry
    ○ flights have been delayed
    ○ the weather is bad
    ○ passengers need to save money

34. The author suggests that making airports more attractive will
    ○ make airports more efficient
    ○ cost a great deal of money
    ○ not solve any real problems
    ○ help passengers feel relaxed

Passage 5

1   In 1877, an unfamiliar type of weed appeared in Bon Homme County, South Dakota, and began spreading across the northern Great Plains. The plant, called tumbleweed, has green stems, intricate branches, a nearly round shape, and long leaves with sharp points on the end. Mice, bighorn sheep, and pronghorn antelope feed on it. The branches are soft and green when young but woody and gray when mature. Unlike other plants, the tumbleweed does not spend its entire life rooted to the soil. In the fall, a layer of cells in the stem weakens and the plant breaks off from its roots and rolls across the fields in the wind. The tumbleweed doesn't depend on wind, birds, or mammals to disperse its seeds. As this woody sphere rolls along, it drops its numerous seeds (up to 250,000 per plant). The seeds are unusual in that they lack any kind of a stored food reserve. Instead, each seed is a coiled, embryonic plant wrapped in a thin membrane.

2   Within ten years, tumbleweeds had invaded twelve western states and four western Canadian provinces, thriving in regions too dry for other plants. The sharp tips of the leaves penetrated heavy leather gloves as well as the legs of horses. It obstructed irrigation canals. It built up in great numbers against fences in such dense masses that it formed wind breaks and eventually the fences were destroyed. Farmers and ranchers viewed the weed with alarm. One legislator in North Dakota even proposed building a fence around the entire state to keep tumbleweeds out.

3   To present-day Americans, the tumbleweed symbolizes the Old West. Tumbleweeds are mentioned in the books of Zane Grey. Western musicians sing sad ballads about tumbleweeds. They share scenes with cowboys and covered wagons in old western movies such as those made by director John Ford. The image of tumbleweeds blowing down the main street of a deserted western town evokes ideas of desolation and loneliness. Yet the tumbleweed is actually a comparatively recent newcomer.

4   Although most settlers found the appearance of this weed unusual, one group of immigrants did not find it at all unfamiliar. The tumbleweed, it turns out, was a native of southern Russia, where it was known as the Tartar thistle. It was probably unintentionally brought into the United States by these immigrants in bags of flax seeds.

5   It was agriculture that enabled the tumbleweed to spread so quickly. In the U.S. Midwest, the tall prairie grasses would have made it impossible for tumbleweeds to roll any great distance. Tumbleweeds thrive in ploughed fields, especially if it is sandy. Archaeologists have found tumbleweed seeds in the oldest agricultural sites in the world. Without agriculture, tumbleweed can live only in areas that are naturally open and bare.

6   Frontier settlers gave the plant various names: saltwort, Russian cactus, buckbush, and wind witch. Botanists at the U.S. Department of Agriculture preferred Russian thistle as the plant's common name. However, these botanists had a much harder time agreeing on the plant's scientific name. Generally, botanists compare a plant to published accounts of similar plants or to samples kept as specimens. Unfortunately, no book described the weed and no samples existed in <u>herbaria</u> in the United States. The U.S. botanists did not realize that the plant had been catalogued and classified years before, in 1810, by Robert Brown of the British Museum. He discovered it in Australia, where it was probably also brought by accident. However, Brown didn't get credit for his discovery for 170 years.

7   Since 1945, pesticides have been able to keep tumbleweeds under control for the most part, but they still cause problems sometimes, especially during dry, windy years. And one interesting use for tumbleweeds has been discovered: young tumbleweeds are able to remove radioactive materials from the soil faster than any other plants.

Glossary

herbaria: *scientific collections of dried plants*

35. Which of the following can be inferred about tumbleweeds?
    - ○ They have strong stems and roots.
    - ○ They require a lot of care.
    - ○ They reproduce efficiently.
    - ○ They provide food for people and domestic animals.

36. Information in paragraph 1 implies that most of the world's plants
    - ○ have more than 250,000 seeds
    - ○ do not depend on wind, birds, or mammals to disperse their seeds
    - ○ have seeds with coiled, embryonic plants wrapped in a thin membrane
    - ○ have seeds with stored food reserves

37. In paragraph 3 the passage suggests that most present-day Americans
    - ○ consider the tumbleweed beneficial
    - ○ don't know when the tumbleweed came to North America
    - ○ have never heard of tumbleweeds
    - ○ think that tumbleweeds are newcomers to the United States

38. It can be inferred from the information in paragraph 3 that the books of Zane Grey
    - ○ tell the story of the invasion of tumbleweeds
    - ○ are about the Old West
    - ○ are biological descriptions of tumbleweeds
    - ○ were written before tumbleweeds came to the United States

39. It is probable that the group of immigrants mentioned in paragraph 4
    - ○ was from southern Russia
    - ○ deliberately brought tumbleweed seeds to the United States
    - ○ had lived in South Dakota for many years
    - ○ was from Australia

40. It can be inferred from paragraph 5 that tumbleweeds spread best in
    - ○ cold, wet climates
    - ○ farmers' fields that are full of mature plants
    - ○ dry, bare, sandy areas
    - ○ areas with tall prairie plants

41. It can be inferred from the information in paragraph 6 that the botanists at the U.S. Department of Agriculture
    ○ consulted the work of Robert Brown
    ○ gave the names saltwort, Russian cactus, buckbush, and wind witch to the tumbleweed
    ○ could not decide on a common name for the tumbleweed
    ○ found it difficult to classify the plant scientifically

42. Paragraph 7 suggests that tumbleweeds would be most useful after
    ○ a large prairie fire
    ○ an oil spill
    ○ an accident at a nuclear energy plant
    ○ an earthquake

LESSON 4
PURPOSE, METHOD, AND OPINION QUESTIONS

Some questions in the Reading Section ask *why* an author does something in a passage (a **purpose question**), *how* an author does something in a passage (a **method question**), or *what an author thinks about* something in the passage (an **opinion question**).

(A) Purpose Questions

Purpose questions ask *why* the author of a passage (or someone that the author quotes) uses a certain piece of information in the passage. ETS calls this kind of question a "rhetorical purpose" question. This kind of question really asks you about the *development* of the passage. In other words, it asks you why an author makes a point or why the author supports and strengthens a point in a certain way. The question may ask you why the author . . .

- mentions a specific piece of information
- uses a certain example
- refers to a study
- uses a certain sequence or order of events
- makes a comparison
- quotes a person or a document
- uses a particular word or phrase

Purpose questions may also ask you the importance of a sentence or paragraph to the passage.

Here are some examples of purpose questions:

▶ Why does the author mention _____ in paragraph __?
▶ Why does the author give an example of _____?
▶ _____ in paragraph __ is given as an example of . . .
▶ The author refers to _____ to indicate that . . .
▶ The author quotes _____ to show that . . .
▶ The phrase _____ in paragraph __ is used to illustrate the effect of . . .
▶ Why do the scientists mentioned in paragraph __ say that . . . .
▶ Why does the author provide details about _____ in paragraph __?
▶ The author gives statistics about _____ in paragraph __ because . . .
▶ Why does the author first discuss _____ and then discuss _____?
▶ The author's main purpose in paragraph __ is to . . .

Here is a section of one of the passages in the Reading Preview Test and an example of a purpose question about it.

Sample

For animals, some barriers are behavioral. The blue spotted salamander lives only on mountain slopes in the southern Appalachian Highlands. Although these creatures could survive in the river valleys, they never venture there. Birds that fly long distances often remain in very limited areas. Kirkland's warblers are found only in a few places in Michigan in the summer and fly to the Bahamas in winter. No physical barriers restrict the warblers to these two locations, yet they never spread beyond these boundaries. Brazil's Amazon River serves as a northern or southern boundary for many species of birds. They could freely fly over the river, but they seldom do.

Why does the author mention the Amazon River in paragraph 4?

○ To give an example of an important physical barrier
○ To point out that many migrating birds fly across it
○ To provide an example of a behavioral barrier
○ To describe a barrier that affects aquatic animals

The topic of this section of the passage is behavioral borders. The author first gives two examples of animals that are affected by behavioral barriers. The author then provides an example of a behavioral boundary, so the third choice is the best. The Amazon is clearly a behavioral boundary, not a physical one, because the author says, "They (the birds) could freely fly over the river, but they seldom do."

To answer purpose questions correctly, you must think like the author. Imagine that you have written the passage. Why would you use this example, word, statistic, etc.?

Probably there will be three or four of these questions in each Reading Section.

(B) Method Questions

Method questions ask *how* the author of a passage (or someone that the author quotes) explains something or accomplishes something in the passage. Again, these questions are really about the development of the passage. How does the author strengthen or clarify a point that he or she has made?

The question may ask how the author . . .

- explains a concept
- supports an idea or a theme or an argument
- clarifies an idea
- introduces a topic
- gives an example
- shows the importance of a person, development, or idea

Here are some examples of method questions:

▶ In paragraph __, the author explains the concept of _____ by . . .

▶ How does the author explain the idea of _____ in paragraph __?

▶ How do some scientists explain _____?

▶ The author illustrates the idea of _____ by . . .

▶ The author shows the significance of _____ by . . .

Following is a section of one of the passages in the Reading Preview Test and an example of a method question about it.

Sample

Virtually all living things have some way of getting from here to there. Animals may walk, swim, or fly. Plants and their seeds drift on wind or water or are carried by animals. Therefore, it is reasonable to expect that, in time, all species might spread to every place on Earth where favorable conditions occur. Indeed, there *are* some cosmopolitan species. A good example is the housefly, found almost everywhere on Earth. However, such broad distribution is the rare exception. Just as barbed wire fences prevent cattle from leaving their pasture, biological barriers prevent the dispersal of many species.

How does the author explain the concept of biological barriers in paragraph 1?
- ○ By providing several examples of biological barriers
- ○ By describing the process by which barriers are formed
- ○ By comparing biological barriers with familiar manmade barriers
- ○ By explaining how houseflies have been affected by biological barriers

The author explains the concept of biological barriers by giving an *analogy.* In other words, the author compares two things or ideas in order to clarify one of them. The author of this passage wants to clarify the idea of biological barriers. He compares a familiar type of barrier—farmers' barbed wire fences that prevent cattle from leaving their fields—to the less familiar concept of biological barriers that block the dispersal of species. The author does *not* give any examples of biological species (although he does give an example of an organism that is not blocked by barriers: the housefly). He does *not* describe how barriers are formed, and he does *not* explain how houseflies have been affected by biological barriers. (In fact, the housefly has not been greatly affected by barriers at all.)

There will probably be one or two method questions in each Reading Section.

(C) Opinion Questions

These questions ask you what the author (or someone the author quotes, such as an expert in the field) thinks about some issue or idea. The author's opinion is usually not stated directly. You have to infer what the author thinks by the language and the ideas that he or she presents in the passage.

Here are some examples of opinion questions:

▶ Which of the following statements best expresses the author's opinion of _____?

▶ In paragraph __, the author expresses the opinion that . . . .

▶ The author of this passage probably believes that . . .

▶ What is the author's opinion of _____?

Here is a section of one of the passages in the Reading Preview Test and an example of an opinion question about it.

4   Any commentary about Easter Island would be incomplete without mentioning the theories of the Norwegian explorer and scientist Thor Heyerdahl, who came to the island in the 1950's. Heyerdahl learned that there had been two groups of islanders: the Hanau Momoko and Hanau Eepe—names once mistranslated as "Short Ears" and "Long Ears." The Hanau Mamoko were dark-haired, the Hanau Eepe mostly red-haired. The Hanau Eepe used heavy earrings to extend the length of their ears. Heyerdahl theorized that the Hanau Momoko were Polynesians from other Pacific islands, but that the Hanau Eepe came later in rafts from South America. He believed that the Hanau Momoko became the servants of the Hanau Eepe, who forced them to build the statues. Because the Hanau Eepe were the masters, the statues resembled them. Heyerdahl said that the red "hats" of the statues actually represented the red hair of the Hanau Eepe. He also pointed out that the ears of the statues resembled those of the Hanau Eepe. According to Heyerdahl's theory, the Hanau Momoko eventually rose up in revolt, overturning most of the statues and killing off all but a few Hanau Eepe.

5   Heyerdahl gave other evidence for the South American origin of the Hanau Eepe. The stonework of the stone platforms called *ahu* was incredibly intricate, unlike any made by other Pacific Islanders. However, the Inca people of South America were famous for intricate stonework. Another piece of evidence Heyerdahl presented was the fact that the staple food of the Easter Islanders, the sweet potato, is not found in Polynesia. He believed that it came with the Hanau Eepe from South America.

6   DNA testing has proven that all Easter Islanders were in fact descended from Polynesians. The current theory is that the Hanau Momoko and Hanau Eepe were two of perhaps twelve clans of islanders, all of whom built statues. The "statue toppling wars" broke out among the clans as the island became overpopulated. When one group won a victory over another, they toppled their enemies' statues. Archaeologists say that the resemblance between the stonework of the Easter Islanders and that of the Inca is coincidental. As for the sweet potato, most scientists now believe that sweet potato seeds came to the island in the stomachs of sea birds.

Which of these statements best reflects the author's opinion of the theories of Thor Heyerdahl?

○ They are important but incorrect.
○ They are strange but true.
○ They are valid but incomplete.
○ They are outdated but useful.

Only the first answer choice summarizes the author's opinion of Thor Heyerdahl's theories. In paragraph 4, the author says, "Any commentary about Easter Island would be incomplete without mentioning the theories of the Norwegian explorer and scientist Thor Heyerdahl. . . ." Clearly, the author believes that Heyerdahl is an important expert on Easter Island because anything written about Easter Island is incomplete if it does not examine these ideas. He also says that an important part of Heyerdahl's theory is that one group of Easter Islanders—the Hanau Eepe—came from South America. However, in paragraph 6, the author says that DNA testing has shown that all Easter Islanders come from Polynesia. So, while the theory is important, it is incorrect. In the second answer choice, the word *true* tells us that this choice is incorrect, and in the third choice, the word *valid* does the same. While Heyerdahl's theories may be outdated (last answer choice) there is no reason to think that they are useful. Again, you need to think like the author to answer opinion questions.

You will probably see one or two opinion questions per Reading Section.

EXERCISE 4.1

FOCUS: Recognizing correct and incorrect answer choices for purpose, method, and opinion questions.

DIRECTIONS: Read the passages. Then mark the statements about the passage True (T) or False (F).

Passage 1

1   Optics is a branch of physics that describes the behavior and properties of light. Among many other things, optics deals with microscopes, telescopes, eyeglasses, mirrors, prisms, cameras, rainbows, and sunsets. Optics explains reflections, refraction, diffraction, dispersion, and polarization. Optics usually describes the behavior of visible light, infrared light, and ultraviolet light. Since light is an electromagnetic wave, optical scientists sometimes study phenomena such as X rays, microwaves, and radio waves that share some of the properties of light.

2   However, as a field, optics is usually regarded as largely separate from physics. It has its own journals, societies, and conferences. The purely scientific aspects of the field are called optical physics. The applied technology aspects are called optical engineering. Applications of optical engineering related to lighting systems are called illumination engineering.

3   Because of the wide application of the science of light, optics tends to be very cross-disciplinary. Optical scientists may work with other physicists, but they may also work with electrical engineers, medical researchers, astronomers, biologists, and others.

T / F   1. In paragraph 1, the author explains the idea of optics in part by explaining what optical scientists work on and study.

T / F   2. The author mentions X rays, microwaves, and radio waves as examples of phenomena that are NOT studied by optical scientists.

T / F   3. In the author's opinion, optical scientists should be considered part of the community of physicists, not separate from it.

T / F   4. The author mentions optical engineering as an example of a purely scientific application of optics.

Passage 2

1   The British historian Arnold Toynbee developed the "challenge and response" theory of history. In his monumental ten-volume work, *A Study of History* (published between 1919 and 1925), Toynbee compares the rise and fall of 26 major civilizations and examines why some civilizations fail and others succeed. He says that all civilizations start out as a small village or tribe, or, in the case of the Mongol empire, as just three individuals who had survived the destruction of their community. Toynbee concludes that, to be successful, civilizations must face challenges, such as a harsh climate, divisive groups, or foreign invasion. If the challenge is too great, the civilization will fail. However, if the civilization reorganizes and responds in a creative way, it will not only survive but prosper. The challenge is like the irritating grain of sand that forms the pearl inside the oyster. An example is China at the end of the glorious Tang dynasty in the eighth century. The Chinese of that time were plagued by foreign invasions, misrule, economic problems, and rebellions. The empire was fragmented into smaller kingdoms. However, in the tenth century, during the Song dynasty, the Chinese went on to overcome their problems, reunite their country, and re-establish a civilization ruled over by a dynasty of powerful emperors and their palace officials, the mandarins.

2   Toynbee's theory had an influence on Oswald Spengler's monumental book *The Decline of the West*. Toynbee's theory is also sometimes applied by some psychologists to individual people and by some business writers and consultants to businesses. However, as a theory of history, it is no longer considered current. In the late 1950's, Toynbee's reputation was popped like a soap bubble by Hugh Trevor-Roper's devastating article titled "Toynbee's Philosophy of <u>Mish-Mash</u>."

Glossary

mish-mash: *a confusing combination of things or ideas*

T / F 　 5. The author mentions the three individuals in paragraph 1 as an example of a small group that eventually creates a civilization.

T / F 　 6. In paragraph 1, the author compares a hardship that a civilization faces to a grain of sand that causes an oyster to produce a pearl.

T / F 　 7. The author explains the "challenge and response" theory by comparing the civilization of China and another civilization.

T / F 　 8. The author mentions foreign invasions, misrule, economic problems, and rebellions as examples of challenges.

T / F 　 9. The book *The Decline of the West* is given as an example of a book that influenced Arnold Toynbee.

T / F 　 10. The author says that "Toynbee's reputation was popped like a soap bubble" to indicate that Toynbee's reputation was completely destroyed by the article.

T / F 　 11. In the author's opinion, Toynbee's idea is still as important to an understanding of history now as it was when it was first introduced.

Passage 3

1　Isadora Duncan was a daring, dynamic innovator in dance. While she was not very successful in teaching her highly personal style of dance, she taught a whole generation of dancers to trust their own forms of expression. Inspired by the art of Greece, she usually danced barefoot in a loose, flowing Greek <u>tunic</u>. She found further inspiration in nature, using dance movements to mirror the waves of the sea and passing clouds.

2   Isadora Duncan was born in San Francisco in 1877. She gave her first performance in 1899. Early failures gave way to triumphant performances in Budapest, London, and Berlin. She lived most of her life in Europe, establishing dancing schools for children. She died in a freak accident in 1927, her long scarf being caught in the wheel of an open sports car in which she was riding.

Glossary

tunic: *a loose-fitting garment worn by both men and women*

T / F   12. The author thinks Duncan was more successful at teaching her personal style of dance than she was as at dancing.

T / F   13. The author mentions the waves of the sea and passing clouds because these provided inspiration for Duncan's dance.

T / F   14. Budapest, London, and Berlin are given as cities where Duncan experienced early failures.

T / F   15. In paragraph 1, the author discusses Duncan's style of dance, and in paragraph 2 gives her life history.

Passage 4

In the western third of North America, the convoluted folds of the earth's surface and its fractured geologic structure tend to absorb the seismic energy of an earthquake. An earthquake measuring 8.25 on the Richter scale struck San Francisco in 1906. It caused severe damage to the city, but by the time the seismic energy had traveled some 400 miles down the West Coast to Los Angeles, its force had faded to nothing. But in the eastern two-thirds of the continent, the same energy travels much more easily. The earthquake that struck New Madrid, Missouri in 1811, estimated at 8.0 on the Richter scale, did minor damage in Washington, D.C., about 800 miles away, and was even felt as far away as Boston and Toronto.

Glossary

Richter scale: *a scale that measures the strength of an earthquake*

T / F   16. The author mentions the San Francisco earthquake first because it occurred before the New Madrid earthquake.

T / F   17. The author probably uses San Francisco and Los Angeles as examples because they are the same distance apart as New Madrid and Washington, D.C.

T / F   18. The author probably uses the New Madrid earthquake as an example because it was stronger than the San Francisco earthquake.

T / F   19. The author probably uses the New Madrid earthquake as an example because it occurred in the eastern two-thirds of North America.

T / F   20. Boston and Toronto are mentioned in the passage because they are even farther from New Madrid than Washington, D.C.

Passage 5

1   What is a business leader? Is it the same as a manager? There is certainly an overlap between these two roles, but as the business author Bernard Bass wrote, "Some managers do not lead, and some leaders do not manage." There are some personality traits and behaviors that are characteristic of a leader, and some that are characteristic of a manager. For example, leaders are committed to innovation and tend to look to the future for threats and opportunities. Managers try to maintain the <u>status quo</u> and concern themselves with solving problems in the present.

2   Leadership and management are both important to a business organization. Once an organization is established, managers go about maintaining the system, assuming that the organization will always be the same. Management keeps the organization going. However, the environment in which an organization operates is always <u>in flux</u>. There are changes in consumer tastes, technology, cultural trends, and historic events. If the organization is entirely in the management mode, it may not spot these trends because managers tend to look inward. However, if the organization is in the leadership mode, it will track these changes and shape the organization to face new challenges and keep the organization relevant.

3   Here's a classic example: In the 1950's and 60's, North American auto makers built large, heavy, powerful cars with <u>gas-guzzling</u> engines because that was what consumers wanted. The oil crisis of the early 1970's, however, shifted consumer attitudes towards lighter, smaller cars with more fuel-efficient engines. Being in management mode, the "Big Three"—the three major North American auto makers—were very slow to recognize this trend and continued to manufacture the kind of cars that they had made for years. Meanwhile, European and especially Japanese automakers had been making economical cars for years. During this period, the Big Three lost a great deal of market share to international automakers.

Glossary

status quo: *a Latin phrase that means "the current situation"*

in flux: *changing, fluid*

gas-guzzling: *using a great deal of gasoline*

T / F   21. The author clarifies the concept of leadership by contrasting it with that of management.

T / F   22. It is the opinion of Bernard Bass that all managers can become leaders.

T / F   23. The author uses the term *management mode* to mean that an organization is not looking outward.

T / F   24. In paragraph 3, the author gives the example of a failure of leadership among the Big Three.

Passage 6

1   The scale on a thermometer is continuous—it is not divided into a part called "cold" and another part called "warm"—yet the nerves in our skin are divided this way. Nerves experience sensations of warmth, cold, and, at one tempera- ture, neither warmth nor cold. This point, called the *level of adaptation,* is rather like the number zero in the number system. Anything above this point feels warm, anything below cool.

2   That this level of adaptation varies according to what temperature our skin is used to can be demonstrated with a simple activity. Fill one bowl or bucket with ice water, one with hot water (not too hot!), and one with water at room temperature. Then place your right hand in the hot water and your left hand in the ice water and leave them there for a few moments. Now plunge both hands into the water at room temperature. To the left hand, the water feels warm; to the right hand, it feels cold. This is because the level of adaptation has become different for either hand.

T / F   25. The author discusses the scale on a thermometer and the nerves of our skin to show how similar they really are.

T / F   26. The author explains the concept of the level of adaptation in part by comparing it to a familiar mathematical concept.

T / F   27. The author clarifies the idea that the level of adaptation varies by suggesting that the reader perform a simple experiment.

Passage 7

Every scientific discipline tends to develop its own special language because it finds ordinary words inadequate, and psychology is no different. The purpose of this special jargon is not to mystify non-psychologists; rather, it allows psychologists to accurately describe the phenomena they are discussing and to communicate with each other effectively. Some of this terminology—*cognitive dissonance, second-order conditioning, obsessive-compulsive reaction*—is unique to psychology and to closely related professions. Some is shared by all the social sciences and even physical sciences. When psychologists speak of a dependent variable in an experiment, they mean the same thing as a chemist does. Of course, some psychological terminology consists of everyday words such as *emotion, motivation, intelligence, ego,* and *anxiety,* but psychologists use these words somewhat differently. For example, a non-psychologist may use the word *anxiety* to mean nervousness or fear, but most psychologists reserve the term to describe a condition produced when one fears events over which one has no control.

Glossary

jargon: *the specialized language used by people in the same field*

T / F   28. The author explains the special language of psychology in part by giving the reasons why it exists.

T / F   29. In the author's opinion, the jargon used by psychologists is confusing and unnecessary.

T / F   30. The author mentions a chemist to show how different the terminology of social science and physical science is.

T / F   31. The word *anxiety* is given as an example of a word that has a more specialized meaning to psychologists than it does to non-psychologists.

EXERCISE 4.2

FOCUS: Answering multiple choice purpose, method, and attitude questions about longer passages.

DIRECTIONS: Read the passages. Then mark the answer choice that best answers the question.

Passage 1

1 Computer games were designed and played as long ago as the 1950's. The first known game was *Tennis for Two* (1958), designed by William Higginbotham. Another early game was Steve Russell's *Spacewar!* (1961). These games never became very popular. It was not until the 1970's and 80's, when computer arcade games were introduced, that computer games attracted millions of game-players. The first to make a splash was *Pong* (Atari, 1972). It was designed by Nolan Bushnell and Alan Alcorn. The game play was extremely simple. Two players bounced a moving ball back and forth between their two electronic "paddles." Bushnell placed the first game machine in a local gas station. When he returned in a few days, the machine was so full of coins that it could no longer operate. *Pong* became an instant success and it helped create the arcade game industry. Other blockbuster games such as *Space Invaders* (Bally/Midway,

1978), *Asteroids* (Atari, 1979), and *Donkey Kong* (Nintendo, 1981) followed. Perhaps the most popular arcade game ever, *Pac Man* (Bally/Midway, 1980) was based on an ancient Japanese folk tale. Some of these arcade games, and other games that were not seen in arcades, were available for play on personal computers. It can even be said that computer games helped popularize the idea of owning a home computer and shaped the way computers were made. Steve Jobs and Steve Wozniak (who had met while designing games for Atari) designed the Apple II, the first popular personal computer, so that it could be used to play computer games at home.

2   Today, there are four main types of devices that computer games can be played on. Personal computers, consoles, handheld consoles, and arcade machines are all common platforms. Personal computer (PC) games are designed to be played on standard home computers. Often no special controls are needed—the game can be played with a keyboard or mouse—but some games are played with a <u>joy stick</u>. Video feedback is received by the user through the computer monitor and audio feedback through speakers or headphones. Players can buy PC games at the store—usually stored on CD ROMs—or download them from the Internet. Players of PC games can also play against live opponents on the Internet.

3   Console games are often referred to as video games. They are played in a specially made computer called a console. PlayStation (SONY), GameCube (Nintendo), and XBOX (Microsoft) are the three most famous types of consoles. Players interact with the game through a controller: a handheld device with buttons, analog sticks, or pads. Games are generally stored on cartridges or sometimes on disks. Games are available for sale at many types of stores and for rent at video rental stores.

4   Handheld consoles are portable, battery-powered consoles that can be played anywhere. The most famous is the Game Boy, first released in 1989. The tiny screen, audio speakers, and controls are all part of one unit. Like console games, handheld console games are usually stored on cartridges.

5   Arcade games are played on a device composed of a video screen, a coin box, specially designed computer hardware, and a set of controls. Controls include the classic joy stick and buttons, light guns, and pads on the ground that detect pressure. These machines are located in public places and players must pay to play them.

6   Some computer games can also be played on devices that are not primarily designed for game-playing. A good example of this type of device is the cell phone. Many games are now available for more than one platform. Some games, such as *Mario Brothers* (1983), which was first developed as an arcade game, have been "ported" (modified) to work on all four platforms. Today, games for personal computers and for consoles are routinely launched on the same day. This is possible because of the increased computing capabilities of consoles. They can now handle games that were formerly only playable on personal computers. In fact, in a recent year, console games outsold personal computer games by about 380%.

7   Although there are exceptions, such as in South Korea, retail sales of computer games have been down in recent years. In the three biggest markets—the U.S., the U.K., and Japan—sales peaked in the late 1990's and have been declining ever since. However, this doesn't mean that fewer people are playing computer games. Today, many games are "shareware" that can be downloaded from the Internet for free. These games pay for themselves by advertising or other means.

Glossary

joy stick: *a control device used to play games on computers. Joy sticks can be used to operate vehicles, fire guns, etc.*

1. The author uses the expression "make a splash" in paragraph 1 to indicate that the game *Pong*
   - ○ failed when it first appeared
   - ○ had a big impact
   - ○ was technologically advanced
   - ○ was difficult to play

2. The author mentions Steve Jobs and Steve Wozniak in paragraph 1 because they
   - ○ built a popular computer that could be used to play games
   - ○ developed many famous computer games
   - ○ designed hardware for arcade games and console games
   - ○ founded and owned the Atari company

3. The author classifies computer games primarily by
   - ○ the type of platform they are played on
   - ○ their popularity
   - ○ the content of the games
   - ○ the type of people who enjoy them

4. Why does the author mention cartridges in paragraph 4?
   - ○ This is the only way to store games.
   - ○ This is one similarity between handheld consoles and some console games.
   - ○ They are used only on handheld consoles.
   - ○ They are used in some countries but not in others.

5. *Mario Brothers* is given in paragraph 6 as an example of a computer game that
   - ○ is no longer available
   - ○ was released as a console game and a PC game on the same day
   - ○ can be played on any kind of platform
   - ○ was developed as a PC game but later became an arcade game

6. The author mentions cell phones in paragraph 6 because
   - ⃝ they are a type of game platform that was not discussed in previous paragraphs
   - ⃝ cell phones and computer games were developed at about the same time
   - ⃝ computer game platforms are used only for entertainment, but cell phones have more important uses
   - ⃝ there are many similarities between cell phone design and game platform design

7. The author mentions South Korea in paragraph 7 because
   - ⃝ PC games are still more popular than console games there
   - ⃝ the popularity of computer games began to decline there in the mid 1990's
   - ⃝ several popular computer games were developed there
   - ⃝ the market for computer games there has not behaved as it has in the biggest markets

---

Passage 2

1 Blood is a complex fluid composed of several types of cells suspended in plasma, the straw-colored, liquid portion of the blood. Disc-shaped red blood cells make up the majority of blood cells. Hemoglobin in the red blood cells picks up oxygen in the blood and delivers it to the tissues of the body. These cells carry carbon dioxide from the body's cells to the lungs and deliver it to the tissues of the body. These cells then carry carbon dioxide from the body's cells to the lungs.

2 Think of it as a railroad hauling freight. The cargo (oxygen) is loaded into a railroad car (hemoglobin). Then the locomotive (a red blood cell) carries the cars where they are needed. After unloading, the train returns with a different cargo (carbon dioxide) and the process starts all over again.

3 Blood cells are made up of two components. The hemoglobin is in solution inside the cell. The cell is surrounded by a membrane that holds in the hemoglobin. A rough analogy would be a toy balloon. The plastic would be the membrane, and the hemoglobin the air inside it. The blood types that most of us know—A, B, O, and AB—are properties of the membrane. The hemoglobin of a person with type A blood is identical to the hemoglobin of a person with type B, O, or AB blood. A balloon may be yellow, red, blue, or green, but the air inside it is the same.

4 Hemoglobin is the part of the cell that traps the oxygen and carbon dioxide. It contains a compound called poryphyrin that consists of a carbon-based ring with four nitrogen atoms facing a central hole. The nitrogen bonds to an iron atom, and the iron then captures one molecule of oxygen or carbon dioxide.

---

8. The author explains how the blood carries oxygen and carbon dioxide by
   - ⃝ comparing the process to a train carrying freight
   - ⃝ giving examples of how the body uses oxygen
   - ⃝ analyzing the composition of plasma
   - ⃝ comparing blood and other fluids

9. The author compares blood types to

- ○ the air inside balloons
- ○ the color of a balloon
- ○ the material a balloon is made of
- ○ the string attached to a balloon

Passage 3

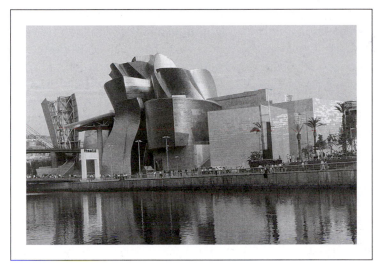

1   The 1960's saw a rising dissatisfaction with the modernist movement in architecture, especially in North America, where its failings were exposed in two influential books, Jane Jacobs's *The Death and Life of Great American Cities* in 1961 and Robert Venturi's *Complexity and Contradiction in Architecture* in 1966. Jacobs highlighted the destruction of the richness and variety of America that occurred as a result of the urban renewal programs sponsored by the federal government. She went on to say that these historic buildings were being replaced by massive, impersonal buildings. Venturi implied that modernist structures were without meaning because they lacked the complexity and intimacy of historical buildings. Both writers called for a new style of architecture.

2   By the early 1980's, post-modernism had become the dominant style, particularly for public buildings in the United States. Post-modernism evolved from modernism and yet it is a contradiction of that style. In fact, post-modernists have little in common with one another in terms of style or theory. They are united mainly in their opposition to the modernist style. One quality that is common to many post-modernist buildings is characterized by what architect Peter Jencks calls "double coding," a mixture of two styles: modern mixed with tradition, contemporary with historical, functional with decorative, and familiar with newly invented. These characteristics can be seen in Robert Venturi's bold designs for the Brant-Johnson House (1975) in Vail, Colorado, which mixes contemporary and Italian Renaissance styles. Similar characteristics are clear in the work of Venturi's disciple Michael Graves. Graves's Portland Building (1982) in

Portland, Oregon, and his Humana Tower (1986) in Louisville, Kentucky, have the bulk of skyscrapers but incorporate historical souvenirs such as colonnades, belvederes, keystones, and decorative sculpture. Likewise, Robert Stern's Observatory Hill Dining Hall (1984) at the University of Virginia in Charlottesville, Virginia, combines the red brick and white wood of Thomas Jefferson's original plan for university buildings with modern building forms and walls with large windows. Chinese-American architect I. M. Pei's design for an addition to the Louvre Museum in Paris (1989) included a glass pyramid, referring to the Egyptian art in the Louvre and the fact that French emperor Napoleon Bonaparte played a major role in making Egypt a subject of study in the early 1800's.

3   Another major tendency in post-modern architecture is the emphasis on decoration, which modernism eliminated. This can be seen in the works of Phillip Johnson, who was once a champion of modernism but became an out-spoken advocate of post-modernism. He wrapped the AT&T building (1984), which is now the SONY Building, in New York City, in pinkish granite and topped it with a tower that looks like an enormous piece of <u>Chippendale</u> furni-ture. Some architects turned entire buildings into sculptures. Frank Gehry's monumental Guggenheim Museum in Bilbao, Spain (1997), resembles an enormous abstract sculpture made of glass and titanium steel.

Glossary

Chippendale: *an ornate style of furniture first developed in Britain in the eighteenth century*

10. Which of these statements best expresses the opinion of Jane Jacobs and Robert Venturi as given in paragraph 1?

   ○ Post-modern buildings are massive and impersonal.
   ○ Modernist architecture is rich and varied.
   ○ The federal government should increase its urban renewal efforts.
   ○ Modernism should be replaced by some other style of architecture.

11. The primary purpose of the second paragraph is to

   ○ explain "double coding" and give examples of various combinations of styles
   ○ describe several features of skyscrapers
   ○ discuss how Pei's pyramid refers to Napoleon Bonaparte and his study of Egyptian culture
   ○ show how post-modernism evolved from modernism

12. The author probably uses the word *souvenirs* in paragraph 2 because
    - ○ tourists often visit the Portland Building and the Humana Building and buy souvenirs
    - ○ the Portland Building and the Humana Building now exist only in people's memories
    - ○ some features of the Portland Building and the Humana Building remind people of the past
    - ○ the Portland Building and the Humana Building house important museums

13. The author presents details about the AT&T (now the SONY) building in New York City to show that it
    - ○ resembles an abstract sculpture
    - ○ influenced post-modern furniture design
    - ○ was built when Johnson was a modernist architect
    - ○ has ornamental architectural features

Passage 4

1   A few languages have only one class of nouns and treat all nouns the same way, but most languages have different classes of nouns. One common way to classify nouns is by gender. In Indo-European languages, genders typically include feminine, masculine, and neuter. Latin has all three of these, but in many of its modern descendants, such as Spanish and French, the neuter gender has all but disappeared. However, a few words in French, especially pronouns with no clear gender, such as *cela* (this), are considered neuter by some grammarians.

2   English is one language that uses natural gender (also called logical gender). Gender depends on biology. *Mother* is feminine, *father* is masculine, and *chair* is neuter. There are, however, a few oddities. Ships are sometimes referred to as *she,* and so are nations. Animals can be neuter or follow natural gender:
    "This is my dog Suzy. *She's* really smart."
    "I saw a tiger at the zoo. *It* was really beautiful."

3   Other languages use grammatical gender. Languages that have only two genders, such as Arabic, Spanish, French, and Urdu, all use grammatical gender. So do some languages, such as German, Russian, and Greek, which have masculine, feminine, and neuter nouns. Sometimes grammatical gender is logical, especially for nouns that refer to people. In Spanish, for example, *hijo* (son) is masculine and *hija* (daughter) is feminine. However, while the assignment of gender to certain nouns seems obvious to a native speaker of these languages, it seems arbitrary and confusing to non-native speakers. Why is *chaise* (chair) feminine in French but *banc* (bench) masculine? Why, in German, is *Fels* (rock) masculine, *Fenster* (window) neuter, and *Tür* (door) feminine? And noun gender varies by culture. In French, *soleil* (sun) is masculine, while *lune* (moon) is feminine. The reverse is true in German: *Sonne* (sun) is feminine, but *Mond* (moon) is masculine.

4   In some languages, such as modern Greek, it is impossible to predict the gender of a noun by the form of the noun. Gender must simply be memorized. In other languages, it *is* possible, or at least it is sometimes possible. In Latin, most singular nouns that end in *a* are feminine, most singular nouns that end in *us* are masculine, and most nouns that end in *um* are neuter. There are, however, exceptions, such as *agricola* (farmer), which is masculine, and *ulmus* (elm tree), which is feminine. For some languages, there are complicated and often incomplete rules that relate form to gender. This is true in German. It may be useful to learn the rule that nouns that end in *lein* and *chen* (meaning young or small) are all neuter. The noun *Mädchen* (little girl) is, rather unexpectedly, neuter. However, is it worth learning that, of the 107 single-syllable nouns ending in a nasal sound plus another consonant, 70% are masculine? A student may end up learning more rules than nouns.

5   Besides gender, there are many other classes of nouns. According to the linguist Carl Meinhof, the Bantu language family has a total of 22 noun classes. No single language in this family expresses all of them, but Sesotho has 18 and Swahili has 15. Tamil—spoken in Sri Lanka—divides nouns into rational versus nonrational. In Ojibwa (a Native American language), there is a distinction between animate and inanimate nouns. The names of all living things, as well as sacred things and things connected to the earth, belong to the animate class. Still, the assignment is somewhat arbitrary, as the word for *raspberry* is animate but the word for *strawberry* is inanimate. Fula (an African language) distinguishes between liquids and solids, and Indonesian distinguishes between things that can be folded and things that can't be. In Dyibal, an Australian Aboriginal language, the four classes of noun are (1) all animate objects except for women; (2) women, water, and fire; (3) edible fruits and vegetables; and (4) everything else. Zande, an African language, has classes that include heavenly objects (moon, rainbow), metal objects (ring, hammer), and edible plants (pea, sweet potato). The Alambiak language, spoken in Papua New Guinea, has a class that includes tall, long, or slender objects, such as arrows, fish, and snakes, and one that includes short, squat, or round things, such as turtles, houses, and shields.

14. The author probably does NOT give an example of a language with one noun class because
    - ○ all languages have noun classes
    - ○ the passage does not discuss these languages
    - ○ these languages are no longer spoken
    - ○ the examples would be confusing

15. The grammarians mentioned in paragraph 1 believe that the French word *cela*
    - ○ can be either feminine or masculine
    - ○ is not really a pronoun
    - ○ is neither masculine nor feminine
    - ○ should not be considered neuter

16. The *oddities* that the author mentions in paragraph 2
    - ○ are exceptions to the general gender rules in English
    - ○ prove that English follows grammatical gender
    - ○ always follow natural gender
    - ○ show that natural gender is always logical

17. Which of these statements probably best expresses the author's opinion of rules about the gender of nouns in German?
    - ○ They are more important for native speakers of German than for non-native learners.
    - ○ It is more important for students to learn these rules than to memorize nouns.
    - ○ The only rule that students must know is the one about nouns that end in *lein* and *chen*.
    - ○ Some of them are confusing and are probably not very useful.

18. The main point of paragraph 5 is to discuss
    - ○ noun classes other than gender
    - ○ the work of linguist Carl Meinhof
    - ○ noun classes in the Bantu language family
    - ○ gender in non-Western languages

19. The author gives Tamil as an example of a language that
    - ○ distinguishes between animate and inanimate
    - ○ has 22 noun classes
    - ○ distinguishes between thinking and nonthinking
    - ○ has a class for all nouns that don't fit into other classes

20. How does the author show that the way Ojibwa assigns nouns to a noun class is somewhat arbitrary?
    - ○ By pointing out that sacred things are considered animate
    - ○ By explaining that two types of fruit belong to the same class
    - ○ By showing that two very similar items belong to different classes
    - ○ By suggesting that raspberries and strawberries are connected to the earth

21. The author gives *turtles, houses,* and *shields* as examples of
    - ○ three separate noun classes
    - ○ short, round, or squat things
    - ○ things that Alambiak speakers consider inanimate
    - ○ Alambiak nouns that are difficult to classify

Passage 5

1 The sea has been rising relative to the land for hundreds of years, geologists say, but the rise has accelerated over the last few decades. The Atlantic and Pacific coasts of the United States have eroded an average of two to three feet (0.6 to 1.0 meter), the Gulf Coast even faster. In places the erosion has even been more dramatic. Highland Light, the oldest lighthouse on Cape Cod, was 400 feet (135 meters) from the sea when it was built in 1797. Now it is only about 100 feet

(35 meters) from the ocean. Just in the last ten years, a series of harsh winter storms has eaten up over forty feet (10.3 meters) of the beach in front of the lighthouse.

2   The United States has over 19,000 miles (33,600 kilometers) of beaches, and nearly half of the population of the United States lives within 50 miles (80 kilometers) of the coast. Some estimates claim that between 80% and 90% of the U.S. coastline is eroding. And the problem is not confined to the United States. Egypt, Thailand, India, the U.K., Australia, and Japan—almost every country that has a coastline—share this problem.

3   During storms, the action of heavy waves carries sand into the sea and leaves it on the ocean floor. During calm periods, erosion reverses. Sand is slowly moved landward by the action of gentler waves. In recent times, however, the buildup of sand has not kept pace with erosion. In many places, sand has been replaced by sediment.

Lately, the leading cause of the increased rate of beach erosion has been global warming. Greenhouse gases such as carbon dioxide and methane are generated by human activities such as the burning of fossil fuels. These gases are accumulating in the atmosphere, trapping in the sun's heat. Forests are being cut down, leaving fewer trees to remove carbon dioxide from the air. Global warming has likely increased the frequency of severe storms that tear sand from beaches. Average temperatures are likely to rise higher in the near future, melting glaciers and polar ice caps, causing the levels of the sea to rise, and making coastal erosion even worse.

4   Clearly, something must be done. Too many people live and vacation in Miami Beach, Atlantic City, Malibu, Galveston, and Honolulu to simply allow roads, houses, and resorts to fall into the sea. Many engineers maintain that the best way to protect coasts is to build protective structures such as sea walls and breakwaters to protect beaches from the ravages of storms. These structures have been tried in a number of places along the U.S. coastline and in other countries, notably Japan.

5   The problem with defensive structures is that they often don't work. One study, in fact, has shown that these structures accelerate the erosion of beaches. Not only that, they can be unsightly, destroying the natural beauty of beaches. The states of Maine, North Carolina, and South Carolina have banned the building of these structures.

Some communities have tried another solution: beach replenishment (also called beach nourishment). These programs simply replace lost sand with sand from deeper parts of the ocean or, in the case of some California beaches, with sand brought in by trucks from the desert. These programs are costly. It costs over US$1 million to replenish one mile (1.61 kilometers) of beach. Again, however, this method of preserving beaches is of dubious value. Another study has shown that only 10% of replenished beaches have lasted more than five years. In some locations, the supply of suitable sand is limited. And the quality of the sand used for replenishment is seldom as high as the sand that it replaces.

Glossary

Cape Cod: *a peninsula stretching eastward from the coast of southern Massachusetts; it is a favorite place for vacationers*

22. It can be inferred that the author of this passage
    - opposes the use of both protective structures and beach replenishment
    - believes beach replenishment would be more effective than protective structures
    - opposes any actions to prevent beach erosion
    - denies that beach erosion is a serious problem

23. The author illustrates the problem of beach erosion in part by
    - using Highland Light as a dramatic example of how severe beach erosion can be
    - exploring the economic cost of beach erosion on one seaside community
    - comparing the situation at Highland Light with similar places in other countries
    - saying that the situation on Cape Cod is typical for most seaside communities

24. The author probably mentions the fact that nearly half of the population of the United States lives within fifty miles (eighty kilometers) of the coast to show that
    - patterns of population distribution in the United States are changing
    - beach erosion affects a vast number of people in the United States
    - the problem in the United States is more severe than it is in many other countries
    - beach erosion is not a concern for more than half of the population of the United States

25. The author explains global warming by
    - giving its causes and showing how it affects beach erosion
    - comparing and contrasting it with other causes of beach erosion
    - giving examples of ways to reduce its impact
    - evaluating how it may actually reduce beach erosion

26. The author mentions Japan in paragraph 4 because Japan has
    - banned the use of protective structures
    - ignored the problem of beach erosion
    - tried beach replenishment programs
    - built seawalls and breakwaters

27. The author cites the two studies in the passage in order to
    - suggest that the sea is not rising as fast as was originally believed
    - strengthen the engineers' claim that protective structures and beach replenishment are necessary
    - propose two new solutions to the problem of beach erosion
    - support his own position about protective structures and beach replenishment

READING

Lesson 5
Sentence Restatement Questions

You will see two or three **sentence restatement questions** in the Reading Section. This type of question presents a sentence from the passage and then asks you to choose the sentence that best restates or summarizes the information in the original sentence. The correct choice will not look like the original sentence. It will use different grammar and different vocabulary, substituting synonyms for words in the original sentence.

The special directions that are given for these questions tell you that you have to select the choice that has the **essential** information that is in the original sentence. The directions also tell you that incorrect choices **omit important information** from the original sentence or **change the meaning** of the original sentence. To find correct choices, you must identify the sentence that summarizes or simplifies the information in the sentence from the passage. In other words, a choice that eliminates details and examples from the original sentence may be a correct answer as long as it does not leave out important information.

Look at the following section from one of the passages in the Reading Preview Test and the restatement question about it.

Sample

Some organisms cross barriers with the intentional or unintentional help of humans, a process called *invasion*. An example is the New Zealand mud snail, which was accidentally brought to North America when trout from New Zealand were imported to a fish hatchery in the United States. It has caused extensive environmental damage in streams and rivers. **In the invasive species' native environments, there are typically predators, parasites, and competitors that keep their numbers down, but in their new environment, natural checks are left behind, giving the invaders an advantage over native species.** Invasive species may spread so quickly that they threaten commercial, agricultural, or recreational activities.

Which of the following sentences best expresses the essential information in the sentence in **bold**? (Incorrect answer choices omit important information or change the meaning of the original sentence in an important way.)

- ○ Invasive species are organisms that leave their native environments behind and move to a new environment.
- ○ Native species are at a disadvantage compared to invasive species because they face environmental dangers that invasive species have left behind.
- ○ The greatest danger from invasive species is that they may spread parasites among native species.
- ○ In a new environment, predators, parasites, and competitors prevent invasive species from spreading as fast as native species.

The first choice expresses part of the idea (that invasive species leave their native environment behind) but it does *not* include an important idea from the original sentence: Invasive species have an advantage over native species because they have left the dangers found in their home environments behind them.

The second choice is correct. This choice gives the main ideas of the original sentence: Invasive species have an advantage over native species because they have left the dangers (the "natural checks") of their home environment behind. However, native species *do* have to deal with natural checks. This correct choice does not give the examples mentioned in the original sentence: predators, parasites, and competitors. There are also differences in grammar and vocabulary between this choice and the original. However, this choice best restates and summarizes the original sentence.

The third choice changes the meaning of the original sentence in an important way. This choice says that invasive species are dangerous because they spread parasites among native plants. However, the original sentence says that invasive species are at an advantage because they have left dangerous parasites behind.

The fourth choice also significantly changes the meaning of the original. This choice says that predators, parasites, and competitors prevent invasive species from increasing their numbers as fast as they would in their home environments. In fact, it is the lack of these dangers in the new environment that gives them an advantage over native species.

When you answer sentence restatement questions, ask yourself, "What is the important idea or ideas in the sentence?" (there may be two or three). Then read the four choices. If the choice changes the meaning of the original, or does not express the main idea(s) completely, it is not the right choice.

Remember: The right choice has **the same meaning** as the original sentence, but it may simplify and summarize the original sentence. It may *not* omit important information.

EXERCISE 5.1

FOCUS: Recognizing correct and incorrect choices for sentence restatement questions.

DIRECTIONS: Read the original sentence, and then read the sentence below it. Mark the answer **I** if the second sentence is an incomplete restatement of the original sentence, **X** if the second sentence is incorrect according to the original sentence, and **C** if it is a correct restatement or simplification of the original sentence.

1. Ranging from the size of sparrows to the size of small airplanes, the pterosaurs ruled the skies during the Jurassic period, but today there are no reptiles capable of flight.

_____ Pterosaurs, which ranged in size from small to large, were flying lizards that lived during the Jurassic period.

2. The architects of the temples of ancient Rome and Greece worked anonymously, as did the builders of the medieval cathedrals in Europe.

_____ No one today knows the names of the architects of the Roman and Greek temples or of the cathedrals of medieval Europe.

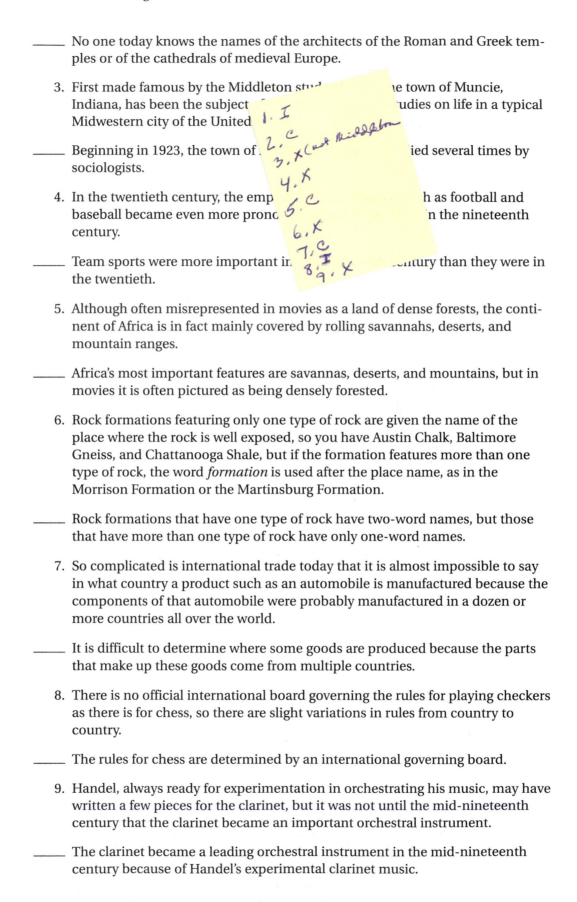

3. First made famous by the Middleton stu_____ _e town of Muncie, Indiana, has been the subject _____ udies on life in a typical Midwestern city of the United _____

_____ Beginning in 1923, the town of _____ ied several times by sociologists.

4. In the twentieth century, the emp_____ h as football and baseball became even more pronc_____ n the nineteenth century.

_____ Team sports were more important in_____ ntury than they were in the twentieth.

5. Although often misrepresented in movies as a land of dense forests, the continent of Africa is in fact mainly covered by rolling savannahs, deserts, and mountain ranges.

_____ Africa's most important features are savannas, deserts, and mountains, but in movies it is often pictured as being densely forested.

6. Rock formations featuring only one type of rock are given the name of the place where the rock is well exposed, so you have Austin Chalk, Baltimore Gneiss, and Chattanooga Shale, but if the formation features more than one type of rock, the word _formation_ is used after the place name, as in the Morrison Formation or the Martinsburg Formation.

_____ Rock formations that have one type of rock have two-word names, but those that have more than one type of rock have only one-word names.

7. So complicated is international trade today that it is almost impossible to say in what country a product such as an automobile is manufactured because the components of that automobile were probably manufactured in a dozen or more countries all over the world.

_____ It is difficult to determine where some goods are produced because the parts that make up these goods come from multiple countries.

8. There is no official international board governing the rules for playing checkers as there is for chess, so there are slight variations in rules from country to country.

_____ The rules for chess are determined by an international governing board.

9. Handel, always ready for experimentation in orchestrating his music, may have written a few pieces for the clarinet, but it was not until the mid-nineteenth century that the clarinet became an important orchestral instrument.

_____ The clarinet became a leading orchestral instrument in the mid-nineteenth century because of Handel's experimental clarinet music.

10. No single theory explains inflation, but when put together like the pieces of a jigsaw puzzle, these theories provide a pretty clear picture of why prices go up.

_____ Considered together, various theories can explain inflation, but individual theories are inadequate.

11. Pasta has an advantage over bread as a staple of life in that it can be dried and preserved.

_____ If it is important to save food for later, pasta is better than bread because it can be dried.

12. The painter Thomas Gainsborough rivaled Sir Joshua Reynolds in the quality of his artwork, but not in his social or financial success.

_____ Reynolds was much more successful financially and socially, but Gainsborough was a far more talented painter.

13. Greek literature is no exception to the general rule that poetry develops earlier than literary prose.

_____ The literature of Greece is an example of literature in which literary prose developed before poetry.

14. By studying photographs of deserts taken from space, geologist Farouk El-Baz discovered that sand dunes, like glaciers, move at a steady, predictable rate.

_____ The geologist Farouk El-Baz learned to predict the movement of glaciers by studying photographs taken from space.

15. Around 1915 D. W. Griffith and other directors began to make longer films that provided the same powerful emotional appeal as theatrical melodramas while presenting visual spectacles far beyond what the theater could offer.

_____ Like melodramas, the longer films that were made by D. W. Griffith appealed strongly to the emotions.

16. Contrary to popular belief, there is no validity to the stories one hears of initials carved in a tree by a young boy becoming elevated high above his head when he visits the tree as an old man.

_____ Over time, initials that are carved into a tree will be elevated by the growth of the tree.

EXERCISE 5.2

FOCUS: Answering sentence restatement questions about sentences in the context of short passages.

DIRECTIONS: Read the passage, paying particular attention to the sentence in **bold.** Then decide which of the four choices best expresses the important information of the sentence in the passage. Remember: Choices are incorrect because they do not state all of the important information in the original sentence or because they change the meaning of the original sentence.

Passage 1

A bird's territory may be small or large. Some males claim only their nest and the area right around it, while others, such as hawks, claim immense territories which include their hunting areas. Gulls, penguins, and other waterfowls nest in huge colonies, but even in the biggest colonies, each male and his mate have tiny territories of their own immediately around their nest. Males defend their territories chiefly against other males of the same species. **In some cases, a warning call or a threatening pose may be the only defense that is needed, but in other cases, intruders may refuse to leave peacefully and a battle for the territory takes place.**

1. Which of the following sentences best expresses the essential information in the sentence in **bold?**
   ○ Usually a warning call is all that is required to get the invading bird to leave, but sometimes a threatening pose is also needed.
   ○ If an intruder is threatened by the pose of the bird that occupies the territory, a struggle will take place.
   ○ Sometimes the invader can be frightened away, but sometimes the defender must fight.
   ○ The intruder generally frightens the defender with warning calls and threatening poses.

Passage 2

Psychologist Abraham Maslowe believed that, even though each person is a unique individual, all humans have certain common needs. Maslowe identified these needs and put them in order from the most basic to the highest-level need. This hierarchy of needs has become the basis for many theories of motivation. The five classes of motivation are as follows:

1. Physiological needs (food, water, air, etc.)
2. Safety needs (protection from threats)
3. Love and social needs (feelings of belonging and affection)
4. Self-esteem needs (feelings of self-worth, achievement, and recognition from others)
5. Self-actualization needs (fulfillment of one's ambitions)

   Maslowe believed that individuals try to fulfill the most basic needs first. He suggested that a largely satisfied need—it does not have to be fully satisfied—is no longer a motivator of behavior. People move on to try to satisfy higher-level needs. It follows that for people whose hunger is regularly satisfied, the need for food does not motivate them in the way that it does people who are regularly concerned about the availability of food. **It is also possible, of course, that people are concerned with several of these classes of motivation simultaneously, as would be the case if, on the same day, a person installed a fire safety alarm (satisfying a need for protection) and joined a folk-dancing club (satisfying a need for belonging).**

Glossary

hierarchy: *a group of things, people, or concepts that is arranged according to their rank or importance*

2. Which of the following sentences best restates the information in the sentence in **bold?**

   ○ People may satisfy more than one of Maslowe's categories of needs at the same time.

   ○ Obviously, for some people, installing a fire safety alarm is more important than joining a social club.

   ○ A typical person is more motivated to satisfy a higher-level need, such as the need for belonging, than a lower-level need, such as the need for protection from fire.

   ○ The fact that people can simultaneously satisfy several of these classes of motivation suggests that Maslowe's hierarchy is not a valid theory.

Passage 3

The first Dutch outpost in New Netherlands was established at Fort Orange (now Albany) in 1624. It became a depot of the fur trade. But the most important settlement was built at the southern tip of the island of <u>Manhattan</u>, which commanded the great harbor at the mouth of the Hudson and East Rivers. Peter Minuit, the first governor general of New Netherlands, "purchased" the island from the Canarsie Indians. **However, the Canarsie might be described as tourists from <u>Brooklyn</u>, and Minuit had to make a later payment to the group that actually resided there.** In 1626, engineers from the Netherlands arrived in Manhattan to begin constructing Fort Amsterdam. Within its rectangular walls, permanent houses were built, replacing the thatched dwellings of the original Manhattanites. The fort became the nucleus of the town of New Amsterdam. Soon Manhattan had its first skyline: the solid outline of the fort, the flagstaff flying the Dutch flag, the silhouette of a giant windmill, and the masts of trading ships.

Glossary

Manhattan: *one of the five boroughs (sections) of New York City, Manhattan is today the commercial heart of the city*

Brooklyn: *another borough of New York City, located across the East River from Manhattan*

3. Which of the following sentences best expresses the information in the sentence in **bold?**

○ The Canarsie could be considered "tourists" because they did not actually live in Manhattan.

○ Later, the governor-general had to pay the real residents of Manhattan because the Canarsie had just been visiting.

○ Even in its earliest days, Manhattan benefited greatly from tourism.

○ The Canarsie had to give the payment that they received for the island of Manhattan to another group because the Canarsie lived in a nearby area, not in Manhattan itself.

Passage 4

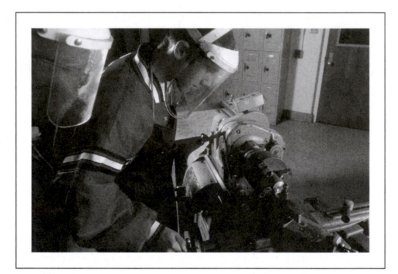

Until the late 1700's, metal could not be turned on a <u>lathe</u> to make it uniformly smooth and round because a machinist could not guide the cutting tool evenly by hand against the turning piece. This problem was solved by the toolmaker David Wilkinson of Pawtucket, Rhode Island. In 1798 he invented a <u>machine tool</u> in which the cutter was clamped onto a moveable slide that could be advanced precisely, by hand crank, parallel to the work. The slide rest lathe, as it came to be called, allowed the machinist to turn large pieces of metal very quickly and precisely. It permitted the manufacture of machine parts that are so uniform that they can be used interchangeably. Many people regard the slide rest lathe as one of the most important developments in the production of machine tools. Woodworking, metalworking, toolmaking, and manufacturing were all revolutionized. Without this tool, mass production would not have been possible. **As it turns out, the great British toolmaker Henry Maudsley had developed what was basically the same mechanism several years**

earlier, but this was unknown to Wilkinson and seems to be a case of "great minds thinking in the same channels," and so should not detract from his accomplishment in any way.

Glossary

lathe: *a tool in which a piece of metal or wood is spun on a horizontal surface while a blade of some kind cuts or shapes it*

machine tool: *a tool used to make other tools*

4. Which of the following sentences is closest in meaning to the sentence in **bold** in the passage above?

○ Maudsley's invention inspired Wilkinson to develop an even more important tool, the slide rest lathe.

○ The great toolmaker Maudsley developed the slide rest lathe earlier than Wilkinson, so Maudsley should get more credit for his accomplishment than Wilkinson.

○ That Maudsley developed the slide rest lathe before Wilkinson was coincidental and should not diminish Wilkinson's accomplishment.

○ Maudsley did not realize that Wilkinson had invented the slide rest lathe earlier; it was simply a case of two great minds thinking in the same way.

Passage 5

There has never been an adult scientist who has been half as curious as almost any child under the age of six. Adults sometimes mistake this superb curiosity about the world as a lack of ability to concentrate because a child's curiosity may leap from topic to topic quickly and unpredictably. **The truth is that children begin to learn at birth, and by the time they begin formal schooling at the age of six, they have already absorbed a fantastic amount of information, perhaps more, fact for fact, than they will learn for the rest of their lives.** Adults can multiply by many times the amount of knowledge children absorb if they learn to appreciate this curiosity while simultaneously encouraging children to learn.

5. Which of the following sentences best expresses the information in the sentence in **bold** in the passage?

○ The first five or six years of school should be considered the most important for children.

○ Before the age of five or six, children probably learn more than they do for the rest of their lives.

○ Children who are in school learn facts faster than preschool children do.

○ Formal schooling may actually cause children to begin learning at a slower rate.

READING

Passage 6

Among mammals, rodents show the greatest variety of nest-building patterns. Beaver dams contain a single-chambered lodge that provides a home for a pair of beavers and their last two litters. **Wood rats, also known as pack rats or trade rats, build nests of twigs and leaves in wooded areas, while in the desert, they build houses of pebbles and cacti.** Laboratory rats and house mice use cloth, paper, or similar material to build bowl-shaped nests. Prairie dogs build virtual underground towns consisting of interconnected burrows. Each burrow contains a multi-chambered living area. One chamber is built high above the bottom of the burrow. This serves as an underground "lifeboat" that traps air for the prairie dogs in case the burrow is flooded.

6. Which of the following sentences best explains what the author means in the sentence in **bold** in the passage above?
   - ○ Wood rats are given their name because they are found only in wooded areas.
   - ○ Wood rats, pack rats, and trade rats all use different materials to build their nests.
   - ○ The houses built by wood rats in forests are larger than those they build in the desert.
   - ○ Wood rats use different materials for nest building depending on what is available.

Passage 7

A sense of humor has long been considered an important character trait. People regularly rank humor as one of the most important traits that they look for when choosing a friend, a roommate, an employee, or a potential spouse. Public speakers are told to begin their speeches with a joke, and sales personnel are told that they will have more success if they can get their clients laughing before they begin their sales pitch. There is medical research to indicate that laughter can reduce stress and even extend life. Clearly, humor is important, but w people spend much time thinking about the topic of humor. There are, wever, a couple of important facts that everyone should know about humor. e is that humor is learned, not inherited. Infants have no sense of humor, but kly learn what is funny from their parents and later from friends and from ooks, television, magazines, and movies. It is, therefore, possible to sharpen your sense of humor, no matter what your age. Another important fact to remember is that humor is highly subjective. What is funny changes from era to era, from country to country, and from group to group. A joke book from the nineteenth century may contain a few funny jokes, but it also contains jokes that leave us scratching our heads and wondering "Why was *that* funny?" Similarly, if you go to a comedy act when you visit another country, you probably won't laugh as hard or as often as the other people in the audience, even if you understand the language perfectly. **This may be in part because you don't understand the cultural references—a joke about a politician that you have never heard of will probably not be very funny—but it is also because there are some basic differences in what people in various countries think is humorous.** Studies have also shown that men and women find different things funny, and so do people of different age groups. All of this indicates that you have to pay attention to your audience when you employ humor. What you find hilarious, someone else may find baffling or even offensive.

7. Which of the following best expresses the information in the sentence in **bold** in the passage?
   - ○ A comedian's joke about a politician that you are unfamiliar with is not funny because this kind of joke depends on an unknown cultural reference.
   - ○ People often do not laugh at jokes told by a comedian from another country partly because they do not know the cultural references and partly because they don't understand the language very well.
   - ○ Jokes that are about politicians are common all over the world, and so can be understood by people no matter where they come from.
   - ○ Even if you understand the cultural references, you may not find a joke funny because of basic differences in humor from culture to culture.

Passage 8

Alice Walker has written books of poetry and short stories, a biography, and several novels. She is probably best known for her novel *The Color Purple,* published in 1982. The book vividly narrates the richness and complexity of black people living in rural Georgia during the 1920's and 1930's. Although the novel was attacked by certain critics when it was first published, it was highly praised by others and won both the American Book Award and the Pulitzer Prize for fiction. It became a best-seller and was made into a successful film by director Steven Spielberg. The novel gets much of its special flavor from its use of the vocabulary, rhythms, and grammar of Black English, as well as from its <u>epistolary style</u>. This style of writing was a narrative structure commonly used by eighteenth-century novelists, such as Jane Austen and Jean-Jacques Rousseau. **Unlike most epistolary novels, which have the effect of distancing the reader from the events described by the letter writer, *The Color Purple* uses the letter form to bring the reader into absolute intimacy with the uneducated but wonderfully observant Celie, the main character of the novel.**

Glossary

epistolary style: *a way of telling a story by means of letters written by one of the characters in the story*

8. Which of the following sentences best restates the information in the sentence in **bold** in the passage?

○ Rather than making events in the novel seem more distant, the letter style in *The Color Purple* brings the reader close to the primary character Celie.

○ The epistolary style generally makes readers feel more distant from the action of the novel, as can be seen in the novel *The Color Purple*.

○ If Celie, the main character in *The Color Purple*, had been more educated, then the events that take place in this book would seem more intimate.

○ Unlike books that are written in the epistolary style, *The Color Purple* brings the reader very close to its main character, Celie, because the author of this book is so wonderfully observant.

Passage 9

1　The system of law in the state of Louisiana is different from that in all the other forty-nine states. If you have ever seen the movie or the play *A Streetcar Named Desire*, you heard the character Stanley Kowalski (played by Marlon Brando in the movie) tell his wife Stella, "We got here in Louisiana what's known as the Napoleonic Code." Stanley was right. The system of law in Louisiana is based on the system first formulated by the French Emperor Napoleon Bonaparte. Napoleon was not only a brilliant general, he was also a capable administrator. He understood that a uniform system of law had to be in place. He therefore took existing law, which was based on ancient Roman law and the thousands of laws passed by the Revolutionary government of France, and codified it. That is, he put all the law into writing so that it could be understood by everyone. When it was adopted in France in 1804, it was considered a very progressive system of law. Colonial Louisiana was never governed under the Napoleonic Code (Louisiana was bought by the United States in 1803) but because of its French traditions, Louisiana adopted the Napoleonic code as its legal system.

2　How do the legal systems of the other forty-nine states differ from that of Louisiana's? They all have laws based on English common law. English common law is a system of law that is based on court precedent. Laws and statutes are interpreted, and the ruling of one judge influences or even controls the ruling of another judge. The Napoleonic Code, on the other hand, takes the civilian law approach. Civilian law is based on scholarly research and the drafting of legal code which is passed into law by the legislative branch. It is then the judge's job to interpret the intent of the legislature rather than follow judicial precedent.

3　**Except for differences in terminology, there is not, in fact, that much practical difference between Louisiana law and the law of the other states, and even those differences are eroding every day, especially in the area of commercial law.** However, in some areas, such as the laws that govern inheritance, the differences are quite striking.

Glossary

A Streetcar Named Desire: *a 1947 play by Tennessee Williams set in the city of New Orleans, Louisiana; it was made into a movie in 1951*

9. Which of the following sentences best restates the information in the **bold** sentence in the passage?

○ The main difference between the legal system of Louisiana and that of other states is in the area of commercial law.

○ There are many important differences between Louisiana law and law in the other forty-nine U.S. states, including differences in legal terminology.

○ Although the two systems use different terminology, Louisiana's legal system and that of the other states are alike and are becoming more so.

○ The terminology of Louisiana's legal system and that of the other states is becoming more and more similar, especially the terminology of commercial law

Passage 10

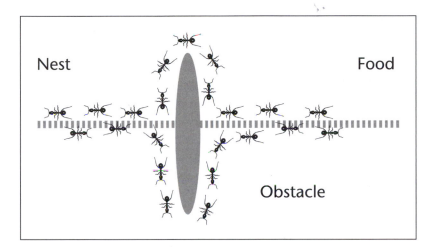

Ants can find the shortest route from a food source to a nest without using the sense of sight. They are also capable of finding a new shortest route when the old path has been blocked by an obstacle such as a pebble or a twig. The primary means that ants use to find and follow the shortest path is a <u>pheromone</u> trail. Ants deposit a certain amount of pheromone while they walk, and other ants can detect this pheromone with their antennae. Ants always follow a direction that is rich in pheromones rather than one that has a lower concentration of pheromones. This is why ants move in a line. When an unexpected obstacle appears and blocks the path of ants on their way to a food source, the ants can no longer follow the accustomed path. The same is true of the ants on the other side of the obstacle that are taking food back to the nest. The ants on both sides have to choose between turning left or right. On average, half the ants go one way, half the other. Those ants that choose, by chance, the shorter path around the obstacle will get back to the original path on the other side of the obstacle sooner than those that take the longer path. **All ants move at the same speed, but it takes more time to go around the longer side of the twig or the pebble than it takes to go around the shorter side, and**

therefore, in the same period of time, the shorter path receives more ant traffic and a higher buildup of pheromones. This concentration of pheromones on the shorter path in turn causes more and more ants to choose that path. Eventually all the ants will choose the shorter route.

Glossary

pheromone: *a chemical that is produced by an animal and serves as a stimulus for other animals of the same species*

10. Which of the following sentences best expresses the information in the sentence in **bold** in the passage?

 ○ Fast ants will travel the long route while slow ants will travel the shorter route, and because there are more slow ants than fast ones, there is a greater amount of pheromones deposited on the shorter route.

 ○ More ants use the shorter route, not because some ants travel faster but because it takes less time, and this results in more pheromones on the shorter path.

 ○ It is the job of certain ants to mark the shorter path around a twig or a pebble with pheromones so that all ants that follow know which path is fastest.

 ○ Ants that travel a longer distance will naturally deposit more pheromones because they spend more time traveling, so most ants will follow the longer route.

LESSON 6
REFERENCE QUESTIONS

Reference questions ask you to look at a highlighted pronoun or other reference word in the passage. You are then given four nouns or noun phrases, usually taken from the paragraph in the passage where the highlighted word is found. You must choose which of these words or phrases (called the **referent**) the highlighted word refers to.

Two things to remember:

- The referent almost always comes *before* the reference word in the passage.
- The referent is *not* always the noun that is closest to the reference word.

Here are some of the reference words you might be asked about:

Personal pronouns/adjectives	he, him, his, she, her, hers, it, its, they, them, their, theirs
Reflexive pronouns	himself, herself, itself, themselves
Relative pronouns/adverbs	who, whose, whom, which, that, where, when
Demonstrative pronouns/adjectives	this, that, these, those (may also be used before nouns or noun phrases: this one, that time, these new ideas, those problems)
Other reference words	some, few, any, none, several, both here, there most, many one, ones another, other, others the former, the latter (some of these words may also be used in phrases: some of these, several examples, both places, most of which, one theory, another process)

To answer reference questions, first look at the passage and read the sentence in which the highlighted word appears and a few of the sentences that come before this sentence. If you can't decide immediately which of the four answers is correct, substitute each of the four choices for the highlighted reference word in the passage. Which one of the four is the most logical substitute?

Here is a part of one of the passages from the Reading Preview Test and a reference question about it:

Sample

4   For animals, some barriers are behavioral. The blue spotted salamander lives only on mountain slopes in the southern Appalachian Highlands. Although these creatures could survive in the river valleys, they never venture there. Birds that fly long distances often remain in very limited areas. Kirkland's warblers are found only in a few places in Michigan in the summer and fly to the Bahamas in winter. No physical barriers restrict the warblers to these two locations, yet they never spread beyond these boundaries. Brazil's Amazon River serves as a northern or southern boundary for many species of birds. They could freely fly over the river, but they seldom do.

The phrase these two locations in the passage refers to

○ Michigan and the Appalachian Highlands
○ Brazil and the Bahamas
○ the Appalachian Highlands and Brazil
○ the Bahamas and a few places in Michigan

By reading the sentence, we see that the phrase these two locations refers to the two places where the Kirkland warbler is restricted, which are "a few places in Michigan in the summer" and "the Bahamas in winter." The first choice gives Michigan as one of the places, but the Appalachian Highlands is mentioned in the passage as the habitat of a type of salamander, not of the Kirkland warbler. The second choice correctly mentions the Bahamas but also gives Brazil. Brazil is given as the location of the Amazon River, which is mentioned as a behavioral boundary for many types of birds, but not for the Kirkland warbler. The third choice incorrectly gives both the Appalachian Highlands and Brazil. Only the fourth choice gives both of the locations that the phrase these two locations refers to.

You will probably see two or three reference questions in the Reading Section. You may find that this is the easiest type of Reading question, but be careful not to answer these questions so quickly that you make mistakes.

EXERCISE 6.1

FOCUS: Finding the referents for pronouns and other expressions in sentences and short passages.

DIRECTIONS: Each of the sentences or short passages has one or more pronoun(s) or other reference words highlighted. Read each one, then write the referent or referents (which may be words or phrases) on the line(s) provided.

1. X rays allow art historians to examine paintings internally without damaging them.

_____

READING

2. Florists often refrigerate cut flowers to protect their fresh appearance.

_____

3. Water is an exception to many of nature's rules because of its unusual properties.

_____

4. The principles used in air conditioning are basically the same as those that are used by the human body to cool itself.

_____

_____

5. Ropes are cords at least .15 inches (3.8 millimeters) in diameter made of three or more strands that are themselves formed of twisted yarn.

_____

_____ ers, and what are called primal cuts of beef into _____ ces are then packaged and sold.

_____

_____ eciduous trees, but they differ greatly in size and

_____

8. Harriet Boyd Hawes greatly expanded the world's knowledge of the ancient Minoans by discovering a number of their archaeological sites on Crete, by supervising their excavation, and by then publishing her findings.

_____

_____

9. In the past, biologists considered mushrooms and other fungi a type of non-green plants. Today, however, these organisms are commonly regarded as a separate kingdom of living things.

_____

10. Using the clock as a model, eighteenth-century inventors developed many other machines based on wheels and gears, some of which were of incredible complexity.

_____

11. The glaciers in Olympia National Park are unusual because they are found at altitudes lower than those at which glaciers are usually found.

_____

_____

1. paintings
4. principles; body
9. mushrooms
11. glaciers; altitude

12. The detailed information in maps is now produced almost entirely from satellite photography rather than by ground surveying or aerial photography because this method is faster, cheaper, and often more accurate.

   _____

13. Even after the Revolutionary War, American importers continued to obtain merchandise from Britain because British merchants understood American tastes, offered attractive prices, and provided them with easy credit.

   _____

14. Yasuo Kuniyashi was born in Japan in 1883 and studied at the Los Angeles School of Art and Design. He also studied and painted in New York City for several years. That's where he gave his first one-person show. In the 1920's, like many artists of the time, Kuniyashi went to Paris. While living there, he was influenced by the works of Chagall and other French artists.

   _____

   _____

   _____

15. The poisonous, plantlike anemone lives in a coral reef. When a small fish ventures near this creature, it is stung and eaten. For some reason, the anemone makes an exception of the clown fish. When the clown fish is in danger from a predator, it dashes among the anemone's tentacles. The clown fish even builds its nest among the anemone's tentacles, where it cannot be raided by other fish.

   _____

   _____

16. William Dean Howells, a contemporary of Mark Twain, wrote a number of books that realistically portrayed life on farms in the midwestern United States. One of his followers, Hamlin Garland, was even more bitter in his criticism of rural life than his mentor.

   _____

   _____

17. While fats have lately acquired a bad image, one should not forget how essential they are. Three basic types of nutrients—fats, carbohydrates, and proteins—provide energy for the body in the form of calories. Of these, fats provide the most efficient means of storing energy. Fats also act as insulation against cold and as cushioning for the internal organs. Without fats, there would be no way to utilize the fat-soluble vitamins A, D, E, and K, which are

essential to human health. Moreover, some contain fatty acids that provide necessary growth factors, strengthen the immune system, and aid in the digestion of other foods.

_____

_____

_____

_____

18. The Wisconsin Dells is a region along the Wisconsin River where swift-running water from melting glaciers cut though soft sandstone. The Winnebago Indians had a name for it—Nee-ah-ke-coonah-er-ah—meaning "the place where dark rushing waters meet," and early French settlers called it "les dalles," meaning "the flat rocks." The strange formations that have been carved out of the rocks there have been delighting tourists since the 1800's. Some are named for objects that they resemble, such as Grand Piano and Chimney Rock, while others have been given colorful names, such as Devil's Elbow, Witches' Gulch, Fat Man's Misery, and Cow in a Milk Bottle.

_____

_____

EXERCISE 6.2

FOCUS: Answering multiple-choice reference questions about longer passages.

DIRECTIONS: Read the following passages and the reference questions about them. Decide which one of the four choices best answers the question and mark that answer.

Passage 1

1   In addition to the various types of deep mining, several types of surface mining may be used when minerals lie relatively close to the surface of the earth. One type is open-pit mining. The first step is to remove the overburden, the layers of rock and dirt lying above the ore, with giant scrapers. The ore is broken up in a series of blasting operations. Power shovels pick up the pieces and load them into trucks or, in some cases, ore trains. These carry it up ramps to ground level. Soft ores are removed by drilling screws, called augers.

2   Another type is called placer mining. Sometimes heavy metals such as gold are found in soil deposited by streams and rivers. The soil is picked up by a power shovel and transferred to a long trough. Water is run through the soil in the trough. This carries soil particles away with it. The metal particles are heavier than the soil particles and sink to the bottom, where they can be recovered.

3   The finishing-off process of mining is called mineral concentration. In this process, the desired substances are removed from the waste in various ways. One technique is to bubble air through a liquid in which ore particles are suspended. Chemicals are added that make the minerals cling to the air bubbles. The bubbles rise to the surface with the mineral particles attached, and they can be skimmed off and saved.

1. The word them in the passage refers to
   ○ power shovels
   ○ layers of rock and dirt
   ○ giant scrapers
   ○ pieces of ore

2. To which of the following does the word These in the passage refer?
   ○ ramps
   ○ trucks or ore trains
   ○ augers
   ○ blasting operations

3. The phrase another type in the passage is a reference to another type of
   ○ deep mining
   ○ ore
   ○ metal
   ○ surface mining

4. The word This in the passage refers to
   ○ a power shovel
   ○ gold
   ○ running water
   ○ a long trough

5. In the passage, the phrase this process refers to
   ○ surface mining
   ○ the depositing of soil particles
   ○ mineral concentration
   ○ placer mining

6. The word they in the passage refers to
   ○ the processes
   ○ the air bubbles
   ○ the chemicals
   ○ the minerals

Passage 2

1   Mount Rainier, the heart of Mount Rainier National Park, is the highest mountain in the state of Washington and in the Cascade Mountain Range. The mountain's summit is broad and rounded. It is 14,410 feet (4,392 meters) above sea level and has an area of about one square mile (2.58 square kilometers). Numerous steam and gas jets occur around the crater, but the volcano has been dormant for many centuries.

2   Mount Rainier has a permanent ice cap and extensive snow fields that give rise to over forty glaciers. These feed swift streams and tumbling waterfalls that race through the glacial valleys. The lower slopes of the mountain are covered with forests. There are alpine meadows between the glaciers and the forests that contain beautiful wild flowers. The Wonderland Trail encircles the entire mountain. Its 90-mile (145-kilometer) length can be hiked in about a week's time. The Nisqually Glacier is probably the ice region that is most often explored by visitors. Not far from there lies Paradise Valley, where hotel accommodations are available.

7. To which of the following does the word It in the passage refer?
   ○ The national park
   ○ The summit of Mount Rainier
   ○ The Cascade Mountain Range
   ○ The state of Washington

8. The word These in the passage refers to
   ○ glaciers
   ○ snow fields
   ○ steam and gas jets
   ○ streams and waterfalls

9. In the passage, the word that refers to

   ○ forests
   ○ wild flowers
   ○ alpine meadows
   ○ glacial valleys

10. What does the word there in the passage refer to?

    ○ Paradise Valley
    ○ Wonderland Trail
    ○ Nisqually Glacier
    ○ Mount Rainier

Passage 3

1 Some people associate migration mainly with birds. Birds do travel vast distances, but mammals also migrate. An example is caribou, reindeer that graze on the grassy slopes of northern Canada. When the weather turns cold, they travel south until spring. Their tracks are so worn into the land that they are clearly visible from the air. Another migrating mammal is the Alaskan fur seal. These seals breed only in the Pribilof Islands in the Bering Sea. The young are born in June and by September are strong enough to go with their mothers on a journey as far as southern California. The males do not journey so far. They swim only to the Gulf of Alaska. In the spring, males and females all return to the islands, and there the cycle begins again. Whales are among the greatest migrators of all. The humpback, fin, and blue whales migrate thousands of miles each year from the polar seas to the tropics. Whales eat huge quantities of tiny plants and animals (called plankton). These are most abundant in cold polar waters. In winter, the whales move to warm waters to breed and give birth to their young.

---

11. The phrase An example in the passage is an example of a

    ○ migratory mammal
    ○ place where mammals migrate
    ○ migratory bird
    ○ person who associates migration with birds

12. The word Their in the passage refers to

    ○ caribou
    ○ tracks
    ○ birds
    ○ grassy slopes

13. The word They in the passage refers to

- ○ female seals
- ○ young seals
- ○ the islands
- ○ male seals

14. The word there in the passage refers to

- ○ the Gulf of Alaska
- ○ the Pribilof Islands
- ○ southern California
- ○ the Pacific Coast of North America

15. The word These in the passage refers to

- ○ three types of whales
- ○ tiny plants and animals
- ○ polar seas
- ○ warm waters

Passage 4

1   Design is the arrangement of materials to produce artistic or functional effects. Design plays a role in visual arts as well as in the creation of commercial products. Designers are concerned with the direction of lines, the size of shapes, and the shading of colors. They arrange these patterns in ways that are satisfying to viewers. Various elements are involved in creating a pleasing design.

2   *Harmony,* or *balance,* can be obtained in a number of ways. It may be either symmetrical (in balance) or asymmetrical (out of balance, but still pleasing to the eye). Or a small area may balance a large area if it has an importance to the eye (because of bright color, for example) which equals that of the larger area.

3   *Contrast* is the opposite of harmony. The colors red and orange harmonize, since orange contains red. A circle and an oval harmonize because both are made up of curved lines. But a short line does not harmonize with a long line. It is in contrast.

4   *Unity* occurs when all the elements in a design combine to form a consistent whole. Unity resembles balance. A design has balance if its masses are balanced, or if its tones and colors harmonize. But unity differs from balance because it implies that balanced elements work together to form harmony in the design as a whole.

16. The word They in the passage refers to

- ○ lines, shapes, and colors
- ○ commercial products
- ○ designers
- ○ visual arts

17. The word that in the passage refers to
   - ○ a color
   - ○ an area
   - ○ importance
   - ○ balance

18. The word both in the passage is a reference to
   - ○ contrast and harmony
   - ○ orange and red
   - ○ a curved line and a straight line
   - ○ an oval and a circle

19. The word It in paragraph 3 refers to
   - ○ a short line
   - ○ the color red
   - ○ a long line
   - ○ contrast

20. The word it in paragraph 4 refers to
   - ○ balance
   - ○ unity
   - ○ a design
   - ○ a consistent whole

Passage 5

1   In most of the earliest books for children, illustrations were an afterthought. But in the Caldecott "toy books" (named after the British illustrator Randolph Caldecott), which first appeared in 1878, they were almost as important as the lines of text, and occupied far more space in the book. One can almost read the story from the dramatic action in the pictures.

2   Since then, thousands of successful picture books have been published in the United States and around the world. In the best, the words and illustrations seem to complement each other perfectly. Often a single person is responsible for both writing and illustrating the book. One of the greatest, and certainly one of the most successful, illustrator-authors was Dr. Seuss, whose real name was Theodor Geisel. His first children's book, *And to Think That I Saw It on Mulberry Street,* hit the market in 1937, and the world of children's literature was changed forever. Seuss's playful drawings were a perfect complement to his engaging stories and unforgettable characters. In 1957, Seuss's *The Cat in the Hat* became the first book in Random House's best-selling series, Beginner Books, written by Seuss and several other authors. These combine outrageous illustrations of people, creatures, and plants, and playful stories written in very simple language. (*The Cat in the Hat,* for example, uses only 250 words, which is an estimate of the number of words that a six-year-old can read.)

3   Dr. Seuss is not the only well-known author-illustrator, of course. There is Max Sendak, who wrote and illustrated *Where the Wild Things Are,* the story of a little boy named Max who becomes king of the fierce (but funny) creatures that live in the Land of the Wild Things. Robert McCloskey produced both the richly textured illustrations and the delightful story of a family of ducks living in downtown Boston, *Make Way for Ducklings.* Some books are produced by a collaborative author-artist team. Author Margaret Wise Brown combined with illustrator Clement Hurd to produce two delightful books loved by very young children, *Goodnight Moon* and *The Runaway Bunny.* Another example is the husband-and-wife team of writer Audrey Wood and illustrator Don Wood, who were responsible for *King Bidgood's in the Bathtub* and *The Napping House.*

4   Wordless and nearly wordless picture books have also become popular. With a little help, three- and four-year-olds can follow the sequence of events, and they can understand the stories suggested in them. The marvel of books with few or no words is that they allow children and their parents the opportunity to tell and retell the same stories over and over in their own words. One of the most charming examples of a wordless book is Jan Omerod's *Sunshine.* Barbara Berger's *Grandfather Twilight* and David Weisner's *Tuesday* are examples of books containing only a few words.

5   U.S. publishers have also drawn on illustrators from other countries whose original, imaginative works have brought their different visions to American children's books. Among them are Leo Lionni from Italy, Feodor Rojankovsky from Russia, and Taro Yashimi from Japan.

21. The word they in the passage refers to
    - ○ the earliest books for children
    - ○ lines of text
    - ○ the Caldecott "toy books"
    - ○ illustrations

22. The phrase the best in the passage refers to the best
    - ○ picture books
    - ○ illustrations
    - ○ authors
    - ○ words

23. In the passage, the word These refers to
    - ○ Dr. Seuss's drawings
    - ○ unforgettable characters
    - ○ successful illustrator-authors
    - ○ the books of the Beginner Book series

24. The word which in the passage refers to
    - ○ 250 words
    - ○ outrageous illustrations
    - ○ *The Cat in the Hat*
    - ○ people, creatures, and plants

25. The word that in the passage refers to
    - ○ the fierce creatures
    - ○ the little boy nam̃ed Max
    - ○ the book *Where the Wild Things Are*
    - ○ the Land of the Wild Things

26. The phrase ___ in the passage refers to an example of
    - ○ a husb___
    - ○ a delig___
    - ○ an auth___
    - ○ a book ___ *e Bathtub*

27. In the passag___
    - ○ three- an___
    - ○ events in___
    - ○ wordless a___
    - ○ stories tha___

28. The word their ___
    - ○ children and ___
    - ○ books with few or no words
    - ○ charming examples
    - ○ the books *Sunshine, Grandfather Twilight,* and *Tuesday*

29. In paragraph 5, the word their refers to
    - ○ U.S. publishers
    - ○ illustrators from other countries
    - ○ original, imaginative works
    - ○ different visions

(Handwritten note, partially covering questions:)
21 D
22 A
23 D
24 A
25 A
26 C
27 C
28 A
29 B

READING

Passage 6

1   Sericulture, or silk production, has a long and colorful history unknown to most people. Archaeological finds show that sericulture dates to at least 2500 B.C., and may be much older. For much of that time, China kept the secret of silk to itself as one of the most zealously guarded secrets in history. Anyone revealing the secret of silkworm culture or trying to smuggle silkworm eggs out of China was punished by death.

2   The key to China's domination of silk production lies with one species native to China: the blind, flightless moth *Bombyx mori*. This insect lays five hundred or more eggs in four or five days and dies soon after. The eggs are like pinpoints— one hundred of them weigh only one gram. From one ounce (28.3 grams) of eggs come about 30,000 worms (the larvae of the moth), which eat a ton of white mulberry leaves and produce twelve pounds (5.4 kilograms) of raw silk. The silkworm of *Bombyx mori* produces smoother, finer, and rounder thread than other silkworms. Over thousands of years, this Chinese moth has evolved into the specialized silk producer that it is today.

3   At one time, silk was reserved exclusively for the use of the Chinese emperor. Gradually, all classes of society began wearing silk. In addition to being used for clothing and decoration, silk came to have industrial uses in China. This is something that happened in the West only in modern times. Silk was used for musical instruments, fishing lines, bowstrings, bonds of all kinds, and even for manufacturing paper. During the Han Dynasty, silk became an absolute value in itself. Farmers paid taxes in both grain and silk. Values were calculated in lengths of silk as they had once been calculated in gold. The importance of silk is even reflected in all the dialects of the Chinese language. For example, of the 5,000 most common characters in the Mandarin alphabet, around 250 have silk as their "key."

4   In spite of their secrecy, the Chinese eventually lost their monopoly on silk production. Sericulture reached Korea around 200 B.C. when immigrants from China arrived there. Sericulture came to India in A.D. 300. In A.D. 440, a prince of Khotan married a Chinese princess. She wore a huge hairpiece, and when she left China, she hid silkworm eggs in it. It was not until A.D. 550 when sericulture came to the West. Silkworms were carried by travelers in hollow tubes of bamboo to Constantinople. This allowed a silk industry to be established in the Middle East and later Italy. However, high-quality Chinese silks still had a market in the West.

5   It was around 300 B.C. when Greeks and Romans first heard rumors of Seres (China), the kingdom of silk. Perhaps the first Romans to actually see silk were the soldiers of Marcus Licinius Crassus, governor of Syria. At the battle of Carrhae, near the Euphrates River, the Romans were startled to see their enemies, the Parthians, had battle flags made of an unknown fabric: silk. Within decades, silk—which Romans believed was harvested from trees—was being worn by the wealthy families of Rome. The silk craze grew over the centuries, and so did the price of silk. A tunic made of the finest Chinese bark (a type of silk) cost as much as 300 denarii—a Roman soldier's salary for one year!

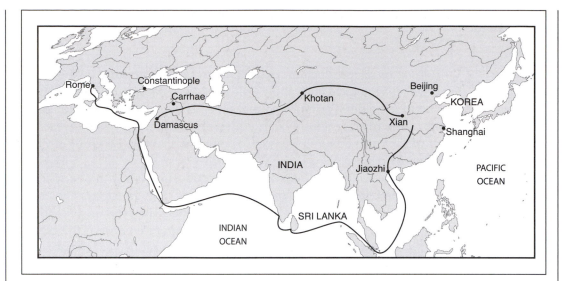

6   Silks were brought to Rome by means of the Silk Road. There were actually two routes, a land route and a sea route. The former stretched from northern China through northern India and then across central Asia to Roman-controlled Damascus. Silks were carried by camel caravans on this route. The latter lay across the Indian Ocean. Silks were brought to Jiaozhi and shipped from the port that is now the city of Haiphong. Via ports in India and Sri Lanka, the silk-carrying ships sailed to Roman-controlled Egypt. The land route, in particular, had immense effects on history, not just on that of Rome and China, but on that of all the lands that it passed through. All sorts of trade goods—silver, gold, jade, spices, porcelain—passed along the route. Ideas traveled the Silk Road too. An important example: the concept of Buddhism was carried from India to China by merchants on the Silk Road. The Silk Road created the first diverse international culture, exposing many peoples to the ideas and riches of both Roman and Chinese cultures.

7   In the last thirty years, world silk production has doubled even though there are artificial fibers that can replace it. China and Japan together manufacture more than 50% of the world's silk. Beginning in the 1970's, the first country that developed sericulture thousands of years ago dramatically increased its silk production and is again the world's leading producer of silk.

Glossary

Khotan: *an independent kingdom on the edge of the Taklamakan Desert in what is today western China*

Constantinople: *the capital of the eastern (Byzantine) Roman Empire (today called Istanbul)*

Parthians: *Central Asian people who ruled an empire centered in today's Iran; the Parthian Empire fought several wars with the Roman Empire*

Jiaozhi: *a Chinese-ruled territory in present-day Vietnam*

30. The word itself in the passage is a reference to
    - ○ sericulture
    - ○ China
    - ○ 2500 B.C.
    - ○ a secret

31. In the passage, the word them refers to
    - ○ eggs
    - ○ silkworms
    - ○ four or five days
    - ○ mulberry leaves

32. The word This in the passage refers to
    - ○ wearing silk clothing
    - ○ reserving silk for the emperor
    - ○ raising silkworms
    - ○ using silk for industrial purposes

33. In the passage, the word they refers to
    - ○ farmers
    - ○ grain and silk
    - ○ values
    - ○ bonds of all kinds

34. The word their in paragraph 3 refers to
    - ○ 5,000 common characters in Mandarin Chinese
    - ○ all the dialects of Chinese
    - ○ the "keys" to the Mandarin characters
    - ○ 250 characters in Mandarin Chinese

35. The word there in the passage refers to
    - ○ China
    - ○ Korea
    - ○ India
    - ○ Khotan

36. The word it in the passage refers to
    - ○ sericulture
    - ○ the princess's hairpiece
    - ○ the Kingdom of Khotan
    - ○ a silkworm egg

37. The word their in paragraph 5 refers to
    - ○ the Parthians
    - ○ the Greeks
    - ○ the Roman soldiers
    - ○ the wealthy families of Rome

38. The phrase The latter in the passage refers to
    ○ the sea route
    ○ silks that were brought across the Indian Ocean
    ○ the land route
    ○ the region known as Jiaozhi

39. The word that in the passage refers to
    ○ the history of Rome and China
    ○ an immense effect
    ○ history
    ○ the Silk Road

40. The phrase An important example in the passage refers to an example of
    ○ an idea that traveled on the Silk Road
    ○ a diverse, international culture
    ○ a concept of Buddhism
    ○ a trade good other than silk

41. The word its in the passage is a reference to
    ○ China
    ○ an increase in silk production
    ○ Japan
    ○ 50% of the world's silk

LESSON 7
SENTENCE ADDITION QUESTIONS

Sentence addition questions tell you to look at a paragraph in the reading passage. In that paragraph, there are four black squares. You are given a sentence that is *not* in the passage and told to add it to the paragraph at one of the four places marked by the black squares. You must decide which of these four squares is the most logical place for the missing sentence. When you click on one of the squares, the sentence will appear at that point in the paragraph.

Sentence addition questions test your understanding of correct sequencing, of paragraph organization, and especially of paragraph **cohesion.** You can think of cohesion as the "glue" that holds the sentences of a paragraph together. There are certain devices that writers use to achieve cohesion. You can sometimes use these devices as clues to help you find the best place to put the "new" sentence. You might see these devices either in the reading passage or in the new sentence.

Devices:

- **Signal Words**

    Scientists have many theories about why the Ice Ages took place. *However,* none of these theories can fully explain why ice sheets formed at certain periods and not at others.

The signal word *However* links these two sentences. It shows that there is a **contrast** between the information in the first sentence and the information in the second.

    Stone tools are more durable than bones. *Therefore,* the tools of early humans are found more frequently than the bones of their makers.

These two sentences are joined by the signal word *Therefore.* This word indicates a **conclusion.** Because the information in the first sentence is true, the information in the second sentence also is true.

    African art first came to the attention of Europeans around 1905 when art critics and artists recognized the dynamic qualities of African sculpture. *Furthermore,* some of the top European artists of the time, such as Picasso and Modigliani, used African art as inspiration for their own work.

These sentences are linked by the signal word *Furthermore.* This signal words indicates **addition.** The first sentence provides you with certain information about a topic (African art), and the second sentence provides you with more information on the same topic.

    If we watch a cell divide under a microscope, what do we see? *First,* the nucleus of the cell begins to look different. The dense material *then* thins out in the middle. *Finally,* a new cell wall forms between the two nuclei. The cell has divided.

The signal words in this paragraph indicate **sequence.** They are used to link sentences that describe a series of events, or as in this paragraph, the steps of a process (cell division).

When people look at cloud formations, they have a tendency to see imaginary shapes. *For example,* they may see faces, animals, maps, household objects, boats, or fairyland figures. *Similarly,* when people view inkblots on a piece of paper, they may see meaningful shapes. Psychologists have long thought that people's responses when they are asked to explain what they see in a set of inkblots reveal a lot about these people's personalities. This concept is the basis for the Rorschach inkblot test, which first appeared in 1921.

For example links the second sentence to the first by providing a specific example (cloud shapes) to illustrate the general concept presented in the first sentence. The key word *similarly* is linked to the first two sentences by comparing similar concepts. (The idea of seeing shapes in clouds is similar to the idea of seeing shapes in inkblots.)

Here is a list of common signal words:

Contrast	however, on the other hand, nevertheless, unlike ____, in contrast
Conclusion	therefore, consequently, thus, hence
Addition	furthermore, in addition, moreover
Sequence	first, after that, afterwards, later, next, then, finally, lastly
Examples	for example, for instance
Similarity	similarly, likewise, like ___

■ Personal Pronouns

Blood travels through the great arteries. *It* then passes into smaller arteries until reaching the capillaries. *They* join to form veins, which carry the blood back to the heart.

The pronoun *It* in the second sentence refers back to the referent *blood* in the first sentence, linking those two sentences. Likewise, the pronoun *they* in the third sentence refers back to *capillaries* in the second and links those two sentences.

■ Demonstratives

A number of methods of improving worker motivation and performance were developed in the 1970's. One of *these* was called Management by Objectives (MBO). *This technique* was designed to improve morale by having workers set their own goals.

The demonstrative pronoun *these* links the second sentence to the first by referring back to the word *methods.* The phrase *This technique* links the third sentence with the second by referring back to the phrase *Management by Objectives.*

■ Synonyms

The earliest remains of ancient animals are those of soft-bodied jellyfish-like animals, worms, and proto-insects. The *fossils* of these creatures show us that, while some animals remained simple, others were becoming increasingly complex.

These two sentences are linked by the word *fossils*, which is a synonym for *remains*.

■ Repetition of Key Words

Hydrilla is an invasive plant imported to Florida from Sri Lanka some fifty years ago to be used as a decorative plant in home aquariums. *Hydrilla* has overgrown more than 40% of the state's rivers and lakes, making life miserable for boaters and often impossible for native wildlife.

The repetition of the key word *hydrilla* links these two sentences.

In addition to these language clues, you can also use content clues. The new sentence might be in contrast to one of the sentences in the passage. The new sentence might give an example of something mentioned in the passage, or it might represent a missing step in a process or a sequence of events.

Remember: There *must* be some kind of key in either the passage or in the new sentence that links the new sentence to either the sentence that comes before the new sentence or the one that comes after it. There must be something—an idea, a word, a phrase—that tells you where to put the new sentence. It's up to you to find the clues!

The third type of natural pathway is called a *sweepstakes route.* This is dispersal caused by the chance combination of favorable conditions. ■ Bird watchers are familiar with "accidentals," birds that appear in places far from their native areas. ■ Sometimes they may find a habitat with favorable conditions and "colonize" it. ■ Gardeners are familiar with "volunteers," cultivated plants that grow in their gardens although they never planted the seeds for these plants. ■ Besides birds and plants, insects, fish, and mammals also colonize new areas. Sweepstakes routes are unlike either corridors or filter routes in that organisms that travel these routes would not be able to spend their entire lives in the habitats that they travel through.

Follow these steps when you answer a sentence addition question:

1. Read the new sentence carefully, then read the sentences in the paragraph that are marked with black squares as well as the sentences immediately before and after the black squares.

2. Look for signal words, personal pronouns, demonstratives, synonyms, and repeated words, first in the new sentence and then in the passage. Do any of these devices link the new sentence to any of the sentences before or after the black squares?

3. If the answer is not clear, look for content clues that could tie the new sentence to the sentence that comes before or after it.

4. Look for places in the passage where the focus seems to shift from one topic to another abruptly, without much transition.

5. You may be able to eliminate certain squares between two sentences because those sentences are closely joined and could not logically be separated.

6. If you still cannot find the answer, just go on to the next question and come back to this question later by means of the Review function.

Here are parts of two passages taken from the Reading Preview Test and sentence addition questions about them.

Sample 1

Look at the four squares [■] that indicate where the following sentence could be added to the passage.

They may be blown off course by storms or may be escaping population pressures in their home areas.

The third type of natural pathway is called a *sweepstakes route.* This is dispersal caused by the chance combination of favorable conditions. ■ Bird watchers are familiar with "accidentals," which are birds that appear in places far from their native areas. ■ Sometimes they may find a habitat with favorable conditions and "colonize" it. ■ Gardeners are familiar with "volunteers," cultivated plants that grow in their gardens although they never planted the seeds for these plants. ■ Besides birds and plants, insects, fish, and mammals also colonize new areas. Sweepstakes routes are unlike either corridors or filter routes in that organisms that travel these routes would not be able to spend their entire lives in the habitats that they pass through.

Circle the square [■] *that indicates the best place to add the sentence.*

Language clues: The personal pronouns *They* and *their* link this sentence to the referent *"accidentals"* in the second sentence.

Content clue: The new sentence explains how the "accidentals" can appear in places far from their native areas. You may have thought that *they* and *their* in the missing sentence refers to "volunteers," but this is not logical. The seeds of plants cannot be blown "off course" because plants do not have a "course" (a chosen direction). They blow wherever the wind takes them. Plants also cannot choose to escape population pressures.

Answer: Choose the second black square.

Sample 2

Look at the four squares [■] that indicate where the following sentence could be added to the passage.

> **After all, they say, the statues themselves show that the islanders were skilled stoneworkers.**

DNA testing has proven that all Easter Islanders were in fact descended from Polynesians. ■ The current theory is that the Hanau Momoko and Hanau Eepe were two of several clans of islanders, all of whom built statues. ■ The "statue toppling wars" broke out among the clans as the island became overpopulated. When one group won a victory over another, they toppled their enemies' statues. ■ Archaeologists say that the resemblance between the expert stonework of the Easter Islanders and that of the Inca is coincidental. ■ As for the sweet potato, most scientists believe that sweet potato seeds came to the island in the stomachs of sea birds.

Circle the square [■] that indicates the best place to add the sentence.

Language clue: The personal pronoun *they* in the new sentence is a link to the referent *Archaeologists* in the previous sentence. The phrase *skilled stone workers* in the new sentence also connects with the phrase *expert stonework* in the previous sentence.

Content clue: The new sentence explains how the resemblance between the stonework of the islanders and the stonework of the Inca could be coincidental.

Answer: Choose the fourth black square.

You will see three sentence addition questions in each Reading Section (one for each passage). The sentence addition question will generally be the second-to-last question in each set of questions (followed by a Summary or Chart Question).

EXERCISE 7.1

FOCUS: Understanding paragraph organization and cohesion and answering sentence addition questions.

DIRECTIONS: Read the new sentence and the passage that follows. Circle the square in the passage to mark the place where the new sentence best fits into the passage.

1. Look at the four squares [■] that indicate where the following sentence could be added to the passage.

> **Early mapmakers, therefore, had little danger of being accused of mistakes even though they were wildly inaccurate.**

Until the nineteenth century, when steamships and transcontinental trains made long-distance travel practical for large numbers of people, only a few adventurers, mainly sailors and traders, ever traveled out of their own countries. ■ In fact, most people never traveled more than a few miles from the place where they were born. ■ "Abroad" was a truly foreign place that the vast majority of people knew very little about indeed. ■ When mapmakers drew maps, imagination was as important as geographic reality. ■ Nowhere is this more evident than in old maps illustrated with mythical creatures and strange humans.

Circle the square [■] that indicates the best place to add the sentence.

2. Look at the four squares [■] that indicate where the following sentence could be added to the passage.

> **In addition, they searched for the elixir of life, a substance that could cure disease and prolong life.**

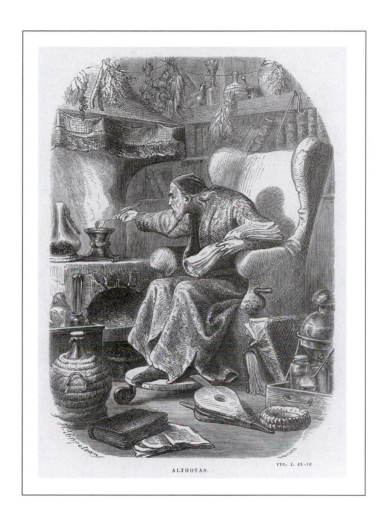

ALTHOTAS.

Throughout the centuries, the dream of medieval alchemists was to discover how to turn lead and other "base" metals into gold. Some alchemists were fakes, but many were learned men with philosophical goals. Their quest was based on the ancient idea that all matter consists of different proportions of just four substances: earth, water, fire, and air. ■ They believed that it was possible to adjust the proportions of the elements that made up lead by chemical means so that it turned into gold, a process that they called *transmutation.* ■ Their experiments were concerned with finding the substance, which they called the *philosopher's stone,* that would cause this astonishing change to take place. ■ They failed to achieve either of their goals. ■ However, their techniques for preparing and studying chemicals helped lay the foundation for the modern science of chemistry.

Circle the square [■] that indicates the best place to add the sentence.

3. Look at the four squares [■] that indicate where the following sentence could be added to the passage.

   When a patch of color is placed on a background that is approximately complementary—say, red on green—both colors appear brighter and more vibrant.

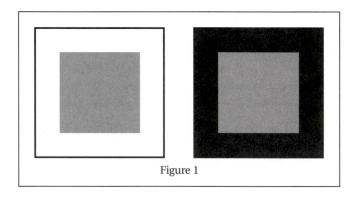

Figure 1

When a small gray square is placed on a larger white square, the small square appears slightly darker than when the same square of gray is placed on a larger black square (see Figure 1). ■ A gray square placed on a colored square—bright blue or yellow, for instance—tends to take on the color of the background. ■ To a viewer, the gray square actually seems to have a blue or yellow tinge. ■ The tinge of color is easier to see if a thin piece of tissue paper is placed over the squares. ■ For this reason, many flags, pennants, and advertising banners are red and green or bright blue and yellow.

Circle the square [■] that indicates the best place to add the sentence.

4. Look at the four squares [■] that indicate where the following sentence could be added to the passage.

   Today all that circuitry and much more can fit into a microprocessor smaller than a postage stamp.

The process of miniaturization began in earnest with the transistor, which was invented in 1947. This was perhaps the most important electronics event of the twentieth century, as it later made possible the integrated circuits and micro-processors that are the basis of modern electronics. The transistor was far smaller than the smallest vacuum tube it replaced and, not needing a <u>filament</u>, it consumed much less power and generated virtually no wasted heat. There was almost no limit to how small the transistor could be made once engineers learned to etch electronic circuits onto a substrate of silicon. ■ In the 1950's the standard radio had five vacuum tubes and dozens of resistors and capacitors, all hardwired and attached to a chassis about the size of a hardbound book. ■ In fact, the limiting factor in making electronic devices smaller is not the size of the electronic components but the human interface. ■ There is no point in making a palm-held computer much smaller unless humans can evolve smaller fingers. ■

_____

Glossary

filament: *a thin piece of metal found inside vacuum tubes and light bulbs. Electricity passing through a filament produces heat and light*

Circle the square [■] that indicates the best place to add the sentence.

5. Look at the four squares [■] that indicate where the following sentence could be added to the passage.

> **However, when the children drew rear views of the adults, the size of the heads was not nearly so exaggerated.**

When drawing human figures, children often make the head too large for the rest of the body. ■ A recent study offers some insight into this common disproportion in children's drawings. ■ As part of the study, researchers asked children between four and seven years old to make several drawings of adults. ■ When they drew frontal views of these subjects, the sizes of the heads was markedly enlarged. ■ The researchers suggest that children draw bigger heads when they know that they must leave room for facial details. Therefore, the distorted head size in children's drawings is a form of planning ahead and not an indication of a poor sense of scale.

Circle the square [■] that indicates the best place to add the sentence.

6. Look at the four squares [■] that indicate where the following sentence could be added to the passage.

> **Confirmation that this phenomenon actually occurs is found in the observed fact that increases in world rainfall typically come about a month after major meteor systems are encountered in space.**

It has been observed that periods of maximum rainfall occur in both the northern and southern hemispheres at about the same time. This phenomenon cannot be adequately explained on a climatological basis, but meteors may offer a plausible explanation. When the earth encounters a swarm of meteors, each meteor striking the upper layers of the atmosphere is vaporized by frictional heat. The resulting debris is a fine smoke or powder. ■ This "stardust" then floats down into the lower atmosphere, where such dust readily serves as nuclei on which ice crystals or raindrops can form. ■ This delay allows time for the dust to settle through the upper atmosphere. ■ Furthermore, proof that meteors actually create dust clouds can be seen in the fact that large meteors sometimes leave visible traces of dust. ■ In a few witnessed cases, dust has remained visible for over an hour. In one extreme case—the great meteor that broke up in the sky over Siberia in 1908—the dust cloud traveled all around the world before disappearing.

Circle the square [■] that indicates the best place to add the sentence.

7. Look at the four squares [■] that indicate where the following sentence could be added to paragraph 1.

> **Each piece of circumstantial evidence, taken singly, may mean little.**

Circumstantial evidence is evidence not drawn from the direct observation of a fact. If, for example, there is evidence that a piece of rock embedded in a wrapped chocolate bar is the same kind of rock found in the vicinity of a candy factory, and that rock of this type is found in few other places, then there is circumstantial evidence to suggest that the stone somehow got into the piece of chocolate during manufacture. ■ It suggests that the candy-maker was negligent even though there is no <u>eyewitness</u> or direct evidence of any kind. ■ Despite a popular tendency to look down on the quality of circumstantial evidence, it is of great usefulness if there is enough of it and if it is properly interpreted. ■ However, a whole chain of circumstances can be as conclusive as direct evidence. ■

Glossary

eyewitness: *a person who actually sees something happen, such as a crime being committed*

Circle the square [■] that indicates the best place to add the sentence.

8. Look at the four squares [■] that indicate where the following sentence could be added to the passage.

> **This, too, is divided into layers.**

The model most generally accepted by geophysicists today envisages Earth as composed of three main concentric spheres. The deep heart of the planet is essentially a huge ball of molten iron, about 4,000 miles (6,400 kilometers) in diameter. The physical properties of this great ball are mostly unknown. The incredible pressure at the core would crush matter into a strange, dense substance unlike any known liquid. ■ Surrounding the molten metal core and reaching almost to the surface is the earth's great inner shell, 2,000 miles (3,200 kilometers) thick, known as the mantle. ■ The mantle seems to be, paradoxically, both rigid and plastic at the same time. ■ Above the mantle lies the thin crust of the earth. ■ Its lower level is a shell of basaltic material similar to the black rock in lava. Topmost of all stand the granite continents. Our great landmasses are, curiously, the lightest of the materials that compose the earth.

READING

Circle the square [■] that indicates the best place to add the sentence.

9. Look at the four squares [■] that indicate where the following sentence could be added to the passage.

> **For example, Harry Turtledove, one of the top writers in this field, has written several books about a world in which the South won the U.S. Civil War and a book about a world in which the Spanish Armada conquered England.**

Alternative history is generally classified as a type of science fiction, but it also bears some resemblance to <u>historical fiction</u>. This type of writing describes an imaginary world that is identical to our own world up to a certain point in history. ■ At that point, the two worlds diverge. ■ Something happens in the imaginary world that never happened in ours, and after that, this world follows a different direction. ■ Some alternative histories suppose that a certain technology had been introduced earlier into the world's history than actually happened. ■ What if the computer had been invented in Victorian times? Many readers find these stories interesting because of the way they stimulate the imagination and get people thinking about the phenomenon of cause and effect in history.

Glossary

historical fiction: *stories that are not true but are based on actual events from the past*

Circle the square [■] that indicates the best place to add the sentence.

10. Look at the four squares [■] that indicate where the following sentence could be added to the passage.

> **The number of shows increased rapidly after the first "Big Top" circus tent was introduced in 1826.**

In the early nineteenth century, the United States was still an overwhelmingly rural nation. ■ Shrewd showmen saw that there was a fortune to be made in taking shows to the people. ■ By 1820 there were some thirty small "mud show" circuses (so named because of the treacherously muddy roads and fields over which their wagons had to travel). ■ This enabled circuses to perform in rain or shine. ■ Like circuses today, early nineteenth-century circuses featured performing elephants, tigers, and lions, bareback riders, acrobats, trapeze and high-wire artists, circus bands, and, of course, clowns. It was not until after the Civil War, however, that circuses became huge three-ring spectacles involving hundreds of performers.

Circle the square [■] that indicates the best place to add the sentence.

11. Look at the four squares [■] that indicate where the following sentence could be added to paragraph 1.

   Butterflies have two pairs of wings and six legs and feed on the nectar of flowers.

12. Look at the four squares [■] that indicate where the following sentence could be added to paragraph 2.

   At first, it is damp and its wings are curled up.

1 When a mammal is young, it looks much like a smaller form of an adult. However, animals that undergo metamorphosis develop quite differently. ■ The young of these animals, which are called larvae, look very little like the mature forms and have a very different way of life. ■ Take the example of butterflies and caterpillars, which are the larval form of butterflies. ■ Caterpillars, on the other hand, are wingless, have many more than six legs, and feed on leaves. ■ To become adults, the larvae must radically change their forms.

2 To accomplish this change, a larva must go through the process of metamorphosis. It does this in the second stage of life, called the pupa stage. When they are ready to pupate, caterpillars settle in sheltered positions. Some spin a <u>cocoon</u> around themselves. The caterpillar then sheds its old skin and grows a protective pupal skin. ■ Inside this skin, the body of the caterpillar gradually transforms itself. ■ The wing buds, which were under the caterpillar's skin, grow into wings. ■ When the change is complete, the pupal skin splits open and the butterfly emerges. ■ Soon it dries out, its wings unfurl, and it flies off. Now it is ready to mate and to lay eggs that will develop into larvae.

Glossary

cocoon: *a silk-like protective covering used by some insects when they change from the pupal form to the adult form.*

Circle the squares [■] that indicate the best places to add the sentences.

13. Look at the four squares [■] that indicate where the following sentence could be added to paragraph 1.

   More recent arrivals no doubt took the same route, crossing on winter ice.

14. Look at the four squares [■] that indicate where the following sentence could be added to paragraph 2.

   The animals magically enlarge this piece of solid land until it becomes the earth.

1 It is believed that the first migrants to come to the New World were hunters who arrived by way of the only link between the hemispheres, the Siberian-Alaskan land bridge. ■ This strip of land remained above water until about 10,000 years ago. ■ These migrants unquestionably brought with them the

skills to make weapons, fur clothing, and shelters against the bitter cold. ■ It seems safe to assume that they also brought myths and folktales from the Old World. ■ But which myths and which folktales?

2   Among myths, the most impressive candidate for Old World origin is the story of the Earth Diver. ■ This is the story of a group of water creatures who take turns diving into the depths of the sea, trying to find a piece of solid land. ■ The duck, the turtle, the muskrat, the seal, the crawfish, or some other animal, depending on who is telling the story, finally succeeds, but it has to dive so deep that by the time it returns to the surface, it is half-drowned or dead. ■ However, in its claws or in its mouth, the other animals find a bit of mud. ■ Not every Native American tribe has a creation myth, but of those that do, the Earth Diver is one of the most common. It is found in all regions of the New World except in the Southwestern United States and the Arctic regions. In the Old World, the story is told in many locations in northern Asia, among some aboriginal Australian groups, and in the South Pacific Islands.

Circle the squares [■] that indicate the best places to add the sentences.

15. Look at the four squares [■] that indicate where the following sentence could be added to paragraph 1.

> **It was an immediate success and spread rapidly, but the original name quickly disappeared.**

16. Look at the four squares [■] that indicate where the following sentence could be added to paragraph 2.

> **They were played at Chestnut Hill, Massachusetts, between British and American players.**

1   ■ Lawn tennis is a comparatively modern modification of the ancient game of court tennis. Major Walter C. Wingfield thought that something like court tennis might be played outdoors on the grass, and in 1873 he introduced his new game under the name *Sphairistike* at a lawn party in Wales. ■ Players and spectators soon began to call the new game "lawn tennis." ■ In 1874 a woman named Mary Outerbridge returned to New York with the basic equipment of the game, which she had obtained from a British Army store in Bermuda. ■ The first game of lawn tennis in the United States was played on the grounds of the Staten Island Cricket and Baseball Club in 1874.

2   The game went on in a haphazard fashion for a number of years. In 1879, standard equipment, rules, and measurements for the court were instituted. ■ A year later, the U.S. Lawn Tennis Association was formed. ■ International matches for the Davis Cup began in 1900. ■ The home team won these first championship matches. ■

Circle the squares [■] that indicate the best places to add the sentences.

17. Look at the four squares [■] that indicate where the following sentence could be added to paragraph 1.

    This process cannot take place without chlorophyll.

18. Look at the four squares [■] that indicate where the following sentence could be added to paragraph 2.

    It prevents nourishment from reaching the leaf and, conversely, prevents sugar created in the leaf from reaching the rest of the tree.

1 Photosynthesis is the process by which plants capture the Sun's energy to convert water and carbon dioxide into sugars to fuel their growth. ■ Chlorophyll is so essential to the life of plants that it forms almost instantly in seedlings when they come in contact with sunlight. ■ A green pigment, chlorophyll is responsible for the green coloring of plants. ■ But what turns the leaves of deciduous plants the brilliant reds and oranges and golds of autumn? ■

2 Trees do not manufacture new, colored pigments for fall. Orange, red, yellow, and other colored pigments are present in leaves throughout the spring and summer. However, they are hidden by the far greater amount of green chlorophyll. When the days grow shorter and the temperatures fall, leaves somehow sense the coming of fall. ■ They form an "abscission layer." ■ This layer is a barrier of tissue at the base of each leaf stalk. ■ Thus, sugar builds up in the leaf, causing the chlorophyll to break down. ■ The orange, red, yellow, and brown pigments now predominate, giving the leaves their vibrant autumn colors.

Circle the squares [■] that indicate the best places to add the sentences.

19. Look at the four squares [■] that indicate where the following sentence could be added to paragraph 1.

    Then he learned that there were prairie dog yips for specific predators.

20. Look at the four squares [■] that indicate where the following sentence could be added to paragraph 2.

    When shown the silhouettes of European ferrets and of Australian dingoes, the prairie dogs made sounds unlike those that they made for any familiar predators.

1 Prairie dogs are among the most sociable wild animals of North America. At one time, they thrived nearly everywhere on the semi-arid lands of the West. Native Americans even used prairie dog colonies as landmarks on the relatively featureless plains. Prairie dogs are members of the squirrel family. They are probably called "dogs" because they make a "yip" noise when they are alarmed that sounds a little like the bark of a small dog. This alarm sound was at one time thought to be a simple warning and expression of fear, meaning something like "Yikes! Watch out!" Biology professor Con Slobodchikoff of Northern Arizona University has been studying the alarm calls of the Gunnison prairie

dog that lives in Arizona for twenty years. He has discovered remarkable levels of complexity in prairie dog calls. ■ First, he discovered that the call for aerial predators, such as eagles or hawks, was different from the call for terrestrial predators or intruders, such as coyotes and humans. ■ For example, there was a distinctive yip for a red-tailed hawk and a different one for a golden eagle. ■ There was one for coyotes, one for foxes, one for domestic dogs, and one for human beings. ■ These sounds were all so distinctive that the differences could be heard with the human ear.

2   By recording prairie dog calls as <u>sonograms</u> and then observing the sonograms on a computer, even more subtle distinctions could be discovered. ■ In one experiment, Professor Slobodchikoff learned that prairie dogs had different sounds for people who wore blue shirts, those who wore yellow shirts, and those who wore green shirts. ■ Even more amazingly, prairie dogs' sounds distinguished between a human who was carrying a gun and one who wasn't. ■ Another experiment showed that prairie dogs could create cries for dangers they had never encountered before. ■

Glossary

sonograms: *"pictures" of sound waves that can be seen on a computer or other instrument*

Circle the squares [■] that indicate the best places to add the sentences.

21. Look at the four squares [■] that indicate where the following sentence could be added to paragraph 1.

> **Motels, in contrast, appealed to motorists, and so they were located along highways, often at the edge of town.**

22. Look at the four squares [■] that indicate where the following sentence could be added to paragraph 2.

> **In fact, their cheap rates attracted travelers without much money.**

1   The first motel (the term comes from a combination of the words *motor* and *hotel*) to appear in the United States was the Motel Inn of San Luis Obispo, California, in 1925. ■ This kind of lodging quickly became popular at a time when more and more people were traveling by car rather than by railroad. ■ Train travelers generally wanted to stay in downtown areas near the railroad stations, and so that's where most hotels were located. ■ When motorists first began traveling long distances by car, they usually stayed at auto camps or tourist courts. ■ These were generally clusters of cabins, often quite crude. Motels, however, were usually single buildings of connected rooms whose doors faced a parking lot or a common area. Typically one would find a "T" or "L" or "U" shaped structure that included rooms, an attached manager's office, and perhaps a small diner. Postwar motels often featured eye-catching neon signs that employed the pop culture themes of the day, ranging from western imagery such as cowboys to "futuristic" images of flying saucers or depictions of atoms.

2   The story of the motel business from the 1920's to about 1960 is one of uninter-
    rupted growth. Motels became common sights on the U.S. highway system that
    predated the <u>Interstate Highway System</u>. ■ They clustered along transconti-
    nental highways, such as Routes 40 and 66, and along the north-south routes
    that ran up and down both the east and west coasts. ■ The motel business was
    one of the few industries that was not hurt by the economic depression of the
    1930's. ■ However, in the 1960's, the Interstate Highway System allowed drivers
    to bypass the smaller roads on which motels were built. ■ At about the same
    time, large motel-hotel chains began to cut into the business of the small,
    family-owned motel.

Glossary

Interstate Highway System: *a national system of high-speed,
long-distance roads connecting major U.S. cities*

Circle the squares [■] that indicate the best places to add the sentences.

LESSON 8
COMPLETING SUMMARIES AND CHARTS

The last question in each set will be either a **complete-the-summary question** or a **complete-the-chart question.** These questions will take you longer than the other questions in the Reading Section. These questions require a general understanding of the entire passage, or at least large parts of it. They are also worth more points than other questions.

The Educational Testing Service refers to these two question types as "reading to learn" questions. That's because to answer these questions, you have to find and connect information from all parts of the passage, as you would when studying material in a textbook. Of course, writing your own summaries and making charts that compare and contrast ideas in an academic textbook can be a useful study technique.

These questions are shown on a full computer screen, but there is an icon on the screen that lets you return to the passage and then come back to the question whenever you want.

(A) Complete-the-Summary Questions

For the complete-the-summary question, you are first given an introductory sentence for a summary. Next, there are spaces in a box for three sentences next to "bullet points" (small black circles).

Then there is a list of six answer choices. You have to decide which three of these six choices are summary sentences—main ideas—for the whole passage. You then click on the sentences that you think are correct and drag them to the three spaces in the box. The answer choices will appear in the box. You do *not* have to put the three sentences into any specific order in the passage. When you finish, you will have "written" a summary of the entire passage.

Incorrect answer choices may be true but are not main ideas in the passage. They are only details or supporting ideas. Choices may also be incorrect because they are not mentioned in the passage. Answer choices may also be incorrect because the information is not accurately presented. Therefore, this type of question requires you to distinguish between major ideas and minor ideas, between information that is present in the passage and information that is not, and between accurate and inaccurate information.

Summary questions are worth two points. You can get partial credit.

---

3 correct choices = 2 points

2 correct choices = 1 point

Fewer than 2 correct choices = 0 points

Here are some tips for completing summaries:

1. First, look for hints in the first paragraph or two about the overall structure of the passage. For example, a sentence in the first part of the passage might say, "There are three main theories about . . ." If you see this kind of "outline" in the passage, then look for signal words or phrases that will introduce these theories: "The first theory . . ." "The next theory . . . ." "The third theory . . . ." These will probably correspond to the three main points of your summary.

2. Unfortunately, there will usually not be an outline of the type mentioned in point 1. Then you will need to study the main idea of each paragraph of the passage and consider the way those main ideas are related. Sometimes, perhaps, two main ideas may be found in a single paragraph, but generally the main ideas of the passage will be developed in one or sometimes more than one paragraph. Look at the paragraphs and try to get a quick idea of what each paragraph is about. Begin by looking at the first sentence or two of each paragraph, because this is the most common position for a topic sentence that presents the paragraph's main idea. Make quick notes about each paragraph on your notepaper. Then look at the answer choices. If there are more paragraphs than answer choices, look for choices that combine the ideas of more than one paragraph. Or you may find that the ideas in some paragraphs are only details and not important enough to be mentioned in a summary.

3. Try to eliminate answer choices that are just details in the passage. These choices usually have a different "feel" to them. They may often be examples of main ideas but not restatements of the major ideas themselves. They are about specific things or concepts rather than about general ideas.

4. Try to eliminate answer choices that do not appear in the passage. These may be about a completely different topic. They may also be about a topic related to the topic of the passage but not mentioned in the passage.

5. Try to eliminate answer choices that don't present the information accurately. They may repeat words from the passage but present it in a way that changes the meaning. They contradict information that is said to be true in the passage.

Here is one of the passages from the Reading Preview Test and an example of a complete-the-summary question about that passage.

Biological Barriers and Pathways

1 Virtually all living things have some way of getting from here to there. Animals may walk, swim, or fly. Plants and their seeds drift on wind or water or are carried by animals. Therefore, it is reasonable to expect that, in time, all species might spread to every place on Earth where favorable conditions occur. Indeed, there are some cosmopolitan species. A good example is the housefly, found almost everywhere on Earth. However, such broad distribution is the rare exception. Just as barbed wire fences prevent cattle from leaving their pasture, biological barriers prevent the dispersal of many species.

2 What constitutes barriers depends on the species and its method of dispersal. Some are physical barriers. For land animals, bodies of water, chains of moun-

tains, or deserts are effective. For example, the American bison spread through-out the open grasslands of North America, but in the southern part of the continent there are deserts, so the bison could not spread there. For aquatic crea-tures, strong currents, differences in salinity, or land areas may serve as barriers.

3   Some barriers involve competition with other species. A dandelion seed may be carried by the wind to bare ground, and, if environmental factors are right, it may germinate. There is not much chance, however, that any individual seedling will survive. Most places that are suitable for the growth of dandelions are already occupied by other types of plants that are well adapted to the area. The dandelion seedling must compete with these plants for space, water, light, and nutrients. Facing such stiff competition, the chances of survival are slim.

4   For animals, some barriers are behavioral. The blue spotted salamander lives only on mountain slopes in the southern Appalachian Highlands. Although these creatures could survive in the river valleys, they never venture there. Birds that fly long distances often remain in very limited areas. Kirkland's warblers are found only in a few places in Michigan in the summer and fly to the Bahamas in winter. No physical barriers restrict the warblers to these two locations, yet they never spread beyond these boundaries. Brazil's Amazon River serves as a northern or southern boundary for many species of birds. They could freely fly over the river, but they seldom do.

5   There are three types of natural pathways through which organisms can overcome barriers. One type is called a *corridor.* A corridor consists of a single type of habitat that passes through various other types of habitat. North America's Rocky Mountains, which stretch from Alaska to northern Mexico, are an example. Various types of trees, such as the Engelmann spruce, can be found not only at the northern end of the corridor in Alaska but also at higher elevations along the entire length of this corridor.

6   A second type of natural pathway is known as a *filter route.* A filter route consists of a series of habitats that are different from one another but are similar enough to permit organisms to gradually adapt to new conditions as they spread from habitat to habitat. The greatest difference between a corridor and a filter route is that a corridor consists of one type of habitat while a filter consists of several similar types.

7   The third type of natural pathway is called a *sweepstakes route.* This is dis-persal caused by the chance combination of favorable conditions. Bird watchers are familiar with "accidentals," which are birds that appear in places far from their native areas. Sometimes they may find a habitat with favorable conditions and "colonize" it. Gardeners are familiar with "volunteers," cultivated plants that grow in their gardens although they never planted the seeds for these plants. Besides birds and plants, insects, fish, and mammals also colonize new areas. Sweepstakes routes are unlike either corridors or filter routes in that organisms that travel these routes would not be able to spend their entire lives in the habitats that they pass through.

8   Some organisms cross barriers with the intentional or unintentional help of humans, a process called *invasion.* An example is the New Zealand mud snail, which was accidentally brought to North America when trout from New Zealand were imported to a fish hatchery in the United States. It has caused extensive environmental damage in streams and rivers. In the invasive species' native environments, there are typically predators, parasites, and competitors

that keep their numbers down, but in their new habitat, natural checks are left behind, giving the invaders an advantage over native species. Invasive species may spread so quickly that they threaten commercial, agricultural, or recreational activities.

DIRECTIONS: Below is an introductory sentence for a brief summary of the passage. Complete the summary by selecting **three** of the answer choices that express the most important ideas of the passage and writing your choices inside the box. Some of the answer choices are incorrect because they express ideas that are not given in the passage or because they express only details from the passage.

Biological barriers prevent organisms from spreading to all habitats where conditions are suitable.

- _____
- _____
- _____

Answer Choices

A. Organisms that spread by means of sweepstakes routes include species of birds called accidentals that appear in places far from their homes.

B. Biological barriers can be the result of physical features, climate, competition, and behavior.

C. Organisms can cross barriers by means of three types of natural pathways: corridors, filter routes, and sweepstakes routes.

D. Behavioral barriers do not prevent the spread of species from place to place as effectively as physical barriers.

E. Humans may accidentally or intentionally bring some species across natural barriers, and these species may have certain advantages over native species.

F. American bison spread throughout the grasslands of North America.

There is no complete outline for the whole passage (although there is a partial outline in paragraph 5). If you were to look at the passage paragraph by paragraph and make notes on the topics of those paragraphs, your notes might look like this:

Paragraph 1: Barriers stop spread of species

Paragraph 2: Physical barriers

Paragraph 3: Barriers involving competition

Paragraph 4: Behavioral barriers

Paragraph 5: Three types of pathways: (1) Corridors

Paragraph 6: (2) Filter route

Paragraph 7: (3) Sweepstakes route

Paragraph 8: Invasion

The information in paragraph 1 is given in the introductory sentence in the question. The main ideas of paragraphs 2, 3, and 4 are combined in choice B. The main ideas of paragraphs 5, 6, and 7 are combined in choice C. The main idea of paragraph 8 is given in choice E (although the word *invasion* does not appear in this choice.)

Choice A mentions "accidentals" as an example of an organism whose appearance represents the sweepstakes route. It is mentioned only as a detail, not as the main idea of the paragraph.

Choice D is about the topic of barriers, but it presents information that is not given in the passage. There is nothing in the passage to suggest that behavioral barriers are not as effective as physical barriers.

Choice F is mentioned in the passage, but it is given as a detail in the discussion of physical barriers. It is not a main idea.

Your best choices, then, are choices B, C, and E.

- Biological barriers can be the result of physical features, climate, competition, and behavior.

- Organisms can cross barriers by means of three natural types of pathways: corridors, filter routes, and sweepstakes routes.

- Humans may accidentally or intentionally bring some species across natural barriers, and these species may have certain advantages over native species.

(B) Complete-the-Chart Questions

The complete-the-chart question consists of a list of answer choices and a simple chart (ETS calls this a "Schematic Table"). You have to place the answer choices into the correct categories to complete an outline of the passage.

The answer choices can be phrases or sentences. In some questions there are seven choices and you must put five into the chart. In some questions there are nine choices and you must put seven into the chart. Correct choices are important characteristics of the different categories.

There will be two or sometimes three categories of information. These categories represent concepts, theories, or divisions in the passage. Often they represent ideas that are compared or contrasted in the passage.

Two of the answer choices *cannot* be placed into the chart. This is because they do not fit properly into any of the categories. This type of question tests your ability to see how information from different parts of the passage fits into logical categories. It also tests your ability to see when points of information are *not* related to general categories.

When you decide which category you want to place an answer choice into, you click first on the choice and then on a space under the category in the chart where you want to put it. You do *not* have to put choices into the category in any special order. As in summary questions, order is not important. When you have finished, you will have created a chart that organizes the information in the passage.

A five-answer chart is worth 3 points and a seven-answer chart is worth 4 points. Partial credit is given.

Seven-answer chart
7 correct choices = 4 points 6 correct choices = 3 points 5 correct choices = 2 points 4 correct choices = 1 point Fewer than 4 correct choices = 0 points
Five-answer chart
5 correct choices = 3 points 4 correct choices = 2 points 3 correct choices = 1 point Fewer than 3 correct choices = 0 points

Here are some tips for answering complete-the-chart questions:

1. First look at the two or three categories of information given in the chart. Be sure that you understand the concepts and the differences between them. If you do not, go back to the passage to familiarize yourself with the categories.

2. Locate the answer choices one by one in the passage. Remember, the choices might be scattered all over the passage, not just in one paragraph. Also remember that the information in the answer choices will not appear the same, word for word, as the information in the passage. Use key words from the choices to help you find the information quickly just as you did when you were answering factual questions (Lesson 1). When you have found information about the answer choice in the passage, read that sentence and the sentences around it.

3. Using your notepaper, take simple notes about each choice. Just write down the letter for the choice and an abbreviation for one of the categories. If you are not able to categorize the choice, write a question mark (?) by the letter of the choice.

4. Now, using your notes, click on the choices that you are sure of and put them in the proper categories. If all the blank spaces in the chart are not full, go back and look at the choices you marked with a question mark. Reread the paragraph and see if you can classify those choices now. If not, guess.

   Here is one of the passages from the Reading Preview Test and an example of a complete-the-chart question about that passage.

Mysteries of Easter Island

1 Easter Island is an isolated island in the Pacific between Chile and Tahiti. The island is roughly triangular and covers only 64 square miles (165 square kilometers). Because of its immense statues, Easter Island has long been the subject of curiosity.

2 There are 887 carved stone statues, called Moai, on Easter Island (not all complete). It is not known exactly what significance the Moai had to the Easter Islanders, but they were obsessed with building these statues. Some statues are as tall as 33 feet (11 meters) and weigh as much as 165 tons (167 metric tons). All portray a human head and sometimes an upper body. They are all carved from stone taken from a volcano on the island. Some are topped with a red "hat" called a *pukao*, made from a different type of stone, and a few have white coral eyes. The statues were moved on a network of roads on rollers made of palm logs and were then placed on stone bases called *ahu*. Most were built between 800 and 1500 A.D.

3 By the eighteenth century, the population had grown too large for the small island. At its peak, it was around 12,000. The only crop—sweet potatoes—could no longer feed the population. The palm forests had been cut down to provide rollers for the statues and to make way for roads. In 1722, when the first westerner, Admiral Jacob Roggeveen, visited the island, he wrote that there were hundreds of statues standing. When Captain Cook visited in 1774, he reported that only nine statues were still standing. Obviously, something dramatic had occurred during those years.

4 Any commentary about Easter Island would be incomplete without mentioning the theories of the Norwegian explorer and scientist Thor Heyerdahl, who came to the island in the 1950's. Heyerdahl learned that there had been two groups of islanders: the Hanau Momoko and Hanau Eepe—names once mistranslated as "Short Ears" and "Long Ears." The Hanau Mamoko were dark-haired, the Hanau Eepe mostly red-haired. The Hanau Eepe used heavy earrings to extend the length of their ears. Heyerdahl theorized that the Hanau Momoko were Polynesians from other Pacific islands, but that the Hanau Eepe came later in rafts from South America. He believed that the Hanau Momoko became the servants of the Hanau Eepe, who forced them to build the statues. Because the Hanau Eepe were the masters, the statues resembled them. Heyerdahl said that the red "hats" of the statues actually represented the red hair of the Hanau Eepe. He also pointed out that the ears of the statues resembled those of the Hanau Eepe. According to Heyerdahl's theory, the Hanau Momoko eventually rose up in revolt, overturning most of the statues and killing off all but a few Hanau Eepe.

5 Heyerdahl gave other evidence for the South American origin of the Hanau Eepe. The stonework of the stone platforms called *ahu* was incredibly intricate, unlike any made by other Pacific Islanders. However, the Inca people of South America were famous for intricate stonework. Another piece of evidence Heyerdahl presented was the fact that the staple food of the Easter Islanders, the sweet potato, is not found in Polynesia. He believed that it came with the Hanau Eepe from South America.

6   DNA testing has proven that all Easter Islanders were in fact descended from Polynesians. The current theory is that the Hanau Momoko and Hanau Eepe were two of perhaps twelve clans of islanders, all of whom built statues. The "statue toppling wars" broke out among the clans as the island became over-populated. When one group won a victory over another, they toppled their enemies' statues. Archaeologists say that the resemblance between the stonework of the Easter Islanders and that of the Inca is coincidental. As for the sweet potato, most scientists now believe that sweet potato seeds came to the island in the stomachs of sea birds.

7   Mysteries about the Moai of Easter Island certainly remain, but current archaeological research has made one lesson clear: overpopulation and overuse of resources such as occurred on Easter Island can lead to the downfall of thriving societies.

DIRECTIONS: Select phrases from the answer choices and match them to the group of people to which they relate, according to the theories of Thor Heyerdahl: Hanau Momoko or Hanau Eepe. Two answer choices will not be used. ***This question is worth 4 points.***

Answer Choices	*Hanau Momoko*
A. Extended the length of their ears by wearing heavy earrings	• _____
	• _____
B. Were the first to arrive on Easter Island	• _____
C. Were one of twelve groups on the island that died out because of overpopulation	
D. Did the actual work of building the statues	*Hanau Eepe*
E. Brought sweet potatoes to Easter Island	• _____
F. Provided the physical models for the statues on Easter Island.	• _____
	• _____
G. Learned how to build the statues from other Pacific Islanders	• _____
H. Were almost all killed off during a revolution	
I. Knocked over most of the statues	

    First look at the categories, Hanau Momoko and Hanau Eepe. Do you understand these? According to the theories of Thor Heyerdahl, there were two groups of people on Easter Island, the Hanau Eepe, the dominant group that came from South America, and the Hanau Momoko, who came from Polynesia and were, until the time of their uprising, the servants of the Hanau Eepe.

    The answer choices give a list of characteristics. We know from looking at the chart that three of these choices will be about the Hanau Momoko and four about the Hanau Eepe. We know that two choices will not be used.

Now look at choice A. Try to find this information in the passage. Use the key words *extended, ears,* and *earrings.* If you look carefully, you will find the sentence that contains this information in paragraph 4: "The Hanau Eepe used heavy earrings to extend the length of their ears." Clearly, this point belongs in the second category. Your first note might look like this: "A. HE."

Information about choice B is also found in paragraph 4: "Heyerdahl theorized that the Hanau Momoko were Polynesians from other Pacific islands, but that the Hanau Eepe came later in rafts from South America." From this sentence we know that choice B belongs in the first category because Heyerdahl believed that the Hanau Eepe came later. Your note for choice B would look like this: "B. HM."

Choice C says that there were several groups that died out. According to Heyerdahl's theory, there were only two groups. There is information about several clans in paragraph 6, but this is part of "current theory," not the theory of Heyerdahl. You might make the following note: "C. ?"

Information about choice D is found in paragraph 4: "He (Heyerdahl) believed that the Hanau Momoko became the servants of the Hanau Eepe and forced them to build the statues." This means that the fourth choice belongs in the first category: "D. HM."

You can find the information about choice E in paragraph 5: "Another piece of evidence Heyerdahl presented was the fact that the staple of the Easter Islanders, the sweet potato, is not found in Polynesia. He believed that it came with the Hanau Eepe from South America." Your note would say "E. HE."

Information about choice F is in paragraph 4: "Because the Hanau Eepe were the masters, the statues resembled them. Heyerdahl said that the red 'hats' of the statues actually represented the red hair of the Hanau Eepe. He also pointed out that the ears of the statues resembled those of the Hanau Eepe." You would write "F. HE."

No matter where you look in the passage, you won't be able to find information about choice G. The passage does not say how either group learned to build statues, so you would write "G. ?"

There is information about choice H in paragraph 4: "According to Heyerdahl's theory, the Hanau Momoko eventually rose up in revolt, overturning many of the statues and killing off all but a few Hanau Eepe." Your note would say "H. HE."

In the same sentence in paragraph 4, the author provides information about choice I: "According to Heyerdahl's theory, the Hanau Momoko eventually rose up in revolt, overturning (toppling) many of the statues and killing off all but a few Hanau Eepe." You would write "I. HM."

Working from your notes, you can quickly complete the chart. Choices B, D, and I should be put under the Hanau Momoko classification. Choices A, E, F, and H should be under the Hanau Eepe classification. Choices C and G should not be used at all.

Hanau Momoko

- B. Were the first to arrive on Easter Island
- D. Did the actual work of building the statues
- I . Knocked over most of the statues

Hanau Eepe

- A. Extended the length of their ears
- E. Brought sweet potatoes to Easter Island
- F. Provided the physical models for the statues on Easter Island
- H. Were almost all killed off during a revolution

EXERCISE **8.1**

FOCUS: Recognizing the most important topics and ideas of paragraphs and answering complete-the-summary questions.

DIRECTIONS: Read each passage. As you are reading, take brief notes on the main topic of each paragraph of the passage in the spaces provided. At the end of each passage, you will find the introductory sentence for a brief summary of the passage. Using your notes, complete the summary. Write the letters of **three** of the answer choices that express the most important ideas of the passage next to the bullet points. Three answer choices will *not* be used. These answer choices are incorrect because they express ideas that are not given in the passage, because they express only details from the passage, or because they contain inaccurate information.

On an actual test, these questions would be worth 2 points each.

Passage 1

1   What is meant by the term *economic resources*? In general, these are all the natural, synthetic, and human resources that go into the production of goods and services. This obviously covers a lot of ground: factories and farms; the tools and machines used in production; transportation and communication facilities; innumerable types of labor; mineral resources. Economic resources can be broken down into two general categories: property resources—land and capital—and human resources—labor and entrepreneurial skills.

2   What does *land* mean to the economist? Much more than to the non-economist. Land refers to all natural resources that are usable in the production process: arable land, forests, mineral and oil deposits, water resources, and so on. What about *capital*? Capital goods, or investment goods, are all the synthetic aids to producing, storing, transporting, and distributing goods and services. Capital goods, or tools, differ from consumer goods in that the latter satisfy wants directly, while the former do so indirectly by facilitating the production of consumer goods. It should be noted that *capital* as defined here does not refer to money. Money alone produces nothing.

3   The term *labor* refers to the physical and mental talents of humans used to produce goods or services (with the exception of one set of human talents, entrepreneurial skills, which will be considered a separate category because of their special significance). Thus the services of a factory worker or an office worker, a ballet dancer, a deep-sea diver, or an astronaut all fall under the heading of labor.

4   All economic resources have one fundamental characteristic in common: they are limited in supply. Certainly the economy of a nation may possess vast amounts of natural resources, capital goods, and labor. However, the supply of these resources is not infinite. A lack of semiskilled and skilled workers, for example, may present a major obstacle to the production process. The same can be said for a shortage of the other factors of production.

Notes on Main Topics:

Paragraph 1 _____

Paragraph 2 _____

Paragraph 3 _____

Paragraph 4 _____

Everything that can be used to produce goods and services is considered an economic resource.

- _____
- _____
- _____

A. Capital does not include the concept of money because money does not directly produce goods or services.
B. No economic resource is unlimited.
C. The work done by a factory worker or an office worker, a ballet dancer, a deep-sea diver, or an astronaut can all be considered labor.
D. Entrepreneurs are vital to the creation and management of economic resources.
E. One form of economic resources is property resources, which include land (natural resources that can be used in production) and capital (tools used in production).
F. Another form of economic resources is human capital, which includes all labor except for entrepreneurial skills.

Passage 2

1   *West Side Story* is a musical tragedy based on William Shakespeare's timeless love story, <u>*Romeo and Juliet*</u>. It is set in the early 1950's, when gang warfare in big cities led to injuries and even death. *West Side Story* transformed the Montagues and the Capulets of Shakespeare's play into rival street gangs, the Jets and the Sharks. The Sharks were newly arrived immigrants to New York from <u>Puerto Rico</u>, the Jets native-born New Yorkers. The play chronicles the rising tension between these gangs and focuses on the story of Maria, a Puerto Rican whose brother Bernardo is the leader of the Sharks, and of Tony, a member of the Jets. As the rival gangs battle in the streets of New York, these two meet and fall in love. The famous balcony scene of the Shakespeare drama takes place on a fire escape of an ugly New York tenement. While trying to stop a fight between the two gangs, Tony inadvertently kills Maria's brother Bernardo and is ultimately killed himself.

2   The talents of a trio of theatrical legends went into the creation of *West Side Story.* Leonard Bernstein, who composed the brilliant score, was a classical composer and the conductor of the New York Philharmonic Symphony. Stephen Sondheim, making his Broadway debut, revealed a remarkable talent for writing lyrics. Among the hit songs of the play are "Tonight," "Maria," "America," "Gee Officer Krupke," and "I Feel Pretty." Jerome Robbins's electrifying choreography broke new ground for musical theater in the 1950. Before *West Side Story,* no one thought that dance could be as integral to a narrative as the music or the lyrics. But the hyper-athletic dances in *West Side Story* are among the most thrilling elements of the play.

3   The play opened in New York City on September 26, 1957, and immediately was a hit with critics and audiences alike. It ran for 734 performances, toured the United States for ten months, and then returned to New York for an additional 246 performances. It won a <u>Tony Award</u> in 1958. It opened to great acclaim in London that same year. The play was revived on the Broadway stage in 1980, 1995, and 2002. It is often performed by school drama departments and community theaters.

4   The classic motion picture *West Side Story* was released in 1961. It was directed by Robert Wise and Jerome Robbins and starred Natalie Wood as Maria and Richard Beymer as Tony. It won ten <u>Academy Awards</u>, including ones for Best Picture and Best Director.

Glossary

Romeo and Juliet: *a play by William Shakespeare set in Verona, Italy and involving rival noble families*

Puerto Rico: *an island in the Caribbean that is inhabited mostly by Spanish-speaking people and administered by the United States*

Tony Awards: *awards given every year for the best play, best director, best actor and actress, and so on*

Academy Awards: *(also called the* Oscars*) awards given every year to the best movie, best director, best actor, best actress, and so on*

Notes on Main Topics:

Paragraph 1 _____

Paragraph 2 _____

Paragraph 3 _____

Paragraph 4 _____

West Side Story is a musical play that retells Shakespeare's Romeo and Juliet.

- _____
- _____
- _____

A.   The play emphasizes music and lyrics more than dance.

B.   The play featured the brilliant work of Leonard Bernstein, Stephen Sondheim, and Jerome Robbins.

C.   The play and later the movie were successful and won many awards.

D.   In the play, Maria, whose brother leads one gang, falls in love with Tony, a member of a rival gang, who is eventually killed.

E.   Jerome Robbins directed the play *West Side Story.*

F.   The balcony scene from the play by Shakespeare takes place on a New York City fire escape in *West Side Story.*

Passage 3

1 Unlike most newborns in the animal kingdom, human infants are born with their eyes wide open and are able to see. However, as any parent knows, babies are not born with full adult visual abilities. Like all parts of a baby's body, it takes years for the eyes, the eye muscles, and the visual cortex of the brain to completely develop.

2 At birth, the eye of a <u>full-term infant</u> is approximately two-thirds the size of that of an adult. Growth is most rapid during the infant's first year and then continues at a rapid but decelerating rate until adolescence. By adolescence the eye is essentially adult size. It should be noted that the visual cortex of the brain itself is also immature at birth. The brain's <u>dendrites</u> are still growing. This immaturity would limit contrast sensitivity and color recognition even if babies' eyes provided perfect information to the brain. Continual visual stimuli and the passage of time will develop the neural connections. The muscles that control the movements of the eye are also immature at birth, and the eyes of many newborns tend to "wander" and cross. However, within a few months, these muscles will learn to work as a team and will be able to control eye-pointing much better.

3 In infants, the sclera (the "white" of the eye) is thin and translucent and often has a bluish tinge. In the baby's first year, this will thicken and become whiter. The cornea (the tissue that lies in front of the iris of the eye) is perfectly clear in full-term babies. In infants born prematurely, there may be a whitish haze in front of the cornea, but this disappears in a month or so. The iris, the colored area surrounding the pupil, is typically lighter than it will be when the child matures. It darkens as the pigmentation of the iris increases in the first year.

4 Research indicates that newborns certainly have some visual abilities. They can detect motion, which is the earliest, most basic perception. Babies glance at moving objects in their first hour of life and track a moving light across their field of vision within the first few hours. Although at birth, infants probably do not have the ability to see colors and cannot distinguish color from grayscale, by two weeks they can see some shades of color. They respond to brightness values in the first month.

5 But newborn vision is limited. Visual ability is made up of many factors: the ability to see and distinguish between colors, to adjust to different distances, to see a single image rather than double images, to orient to moving objects, to see details, and to perceive depth. At four months, all these visual talents mature and start to work in tandem. Just how this happens is not completely clear. For example, how the brain and eye coordinate to process color information remains something of a mystery. But somehow, by the fourth month, babies see the world in vivid color. Studies have indicated that four-month-olds can not only distinguish colors but even have favorites. Most look longer at bright colors such as blue and red than at dull colors such as gray and brown. They prefer patterns such as plaids and stripes to solid colors. Four-month-old babies also

see things farther away. In comparison with the eight-inch distance a newborn handles, a four-month-old can follow a moving object at six to eight feet. The average four-month-old has about 20/80 vision, while a one-month-old has about 20/200. ("Perfect" vision in adults is 20/20.)

Glossary

full-term infant: *a baby that has developed for a full nine months before being born*

dendrites: *the parts of a nerve cell that carry messages from one cell to another*

Notes on Main Topics:

Paragraph 1 _____

Paragraph 2 _____

Paragraph 3 _____

Paragraph 4 _____

Paragraph 5 _____

Human babies can see from birth, but newborn vision is limited.

- _____
- _____
- _____

A. Babies prefer blue and red to gray and brown and plaids and stripes to solid colors.
B. During their first year, babies' eyes grow in size, the visual cortex of the brain and the eye muscles develop, and the various parts of the eye mature.
C. Babies' eyes should be checked by doctors at birth and several times during their first year of life.
D. Newborns can detect motion, distinguish some colors, and react to brightness.
E. At the age of four months, babies' visual abilities begin to work in coordination, and a child of this age has much better vision than a newborn.
F. The average one-month-old baby has about 20/200 vision, but the average four-month-old has 20/80 vision.

Passage 4

1 Clipper ships were the swiftest sailing ships that ever put to sea, and the most beautiful. These "greyhounds of the sea," as they were sometimes called, had their glory days in the 1840's and 1850's. Nearly four hundred of them were built in the shipyards of Boston, New York City, Baltimore, and other Eastern port cities. The master designer of clippers, Donald McKay, built some of the most famous clipper ships at the East Boston Yard. Ships built there, such as the *Lightning* and the *Flying Cloud,* were called Yankee clippers.

2   It was Chinese tea that brought clippers into existence. Tea loses its flavor quickly when stored in the hold of a ship, and merchants were willing to pay top prices for fast delivery. Then came the California Gold Rush of 1849. Gold-seekers from the East Coast were willing to pay almost any price to be rushed to the West Coast by way of Cape Horn. The prices for consumer goods in the gold fields skyrocketed too. A barrel of flour that would sell for five dollars in New York would bring $50 in San Francisco, and a four-month-old penny newspaper would bring a dollar.

3   Before the era of the clippers, most merchant ships were large, slow, and hard to maneuver. Clippers were built for speed, and all other considerations—carrying capacity, cost of operations, durability—were unimportant. A fast ship would bring its owners and captain more profits, and a ship could be paid for in a single trip. The very name *clipper* was given to these ships because the enormous driving power of their sails allowed them to "clip" (move quickly) across the sea. Writer Nicholas Dean called them the "Concordes of the nineteenth century" because the same concept—speed at any cost—brought clippers and Concordes into existence.

4   To give clippers their speed, the clippers' slanted masts, which reached as high as a twenty-story building, carried more sails and more kinds of sails—including topgallants, royal sails, flying jibs, skysails, and moonrakers—than any other type of ship before or since. This huge cloud of canvas sails was controlled by a complicated web of rigging. It took an experienced crew of from twenty-

five to fifty sailors to operate those sails and a hard-driving captain to direct them. The <u>hull</u> of a clipper was long and slender, and the <u>bow</u> was sharp as a knife to cut through the waves. With their sails full of wind, the tall, beautiful clipper ships looked as if they had sailed out of a child's dream.

5   Many remarkable and enduring records were set by clippers. McKay's clipper *Lightning* set a world record by sailing 436 miles (701 kilometers) in a single day, and his *Flying Cloud* sailed from New York, around Cape Horn, and to San Francisco in 82 days. The *James Bains* set the around-the-world record of 133 days. Other clipper records were set by the *Nightingale,* which sailed from Shanghai to London in 89 days, the *Ino,* which made it from Singapore to New York in 81 days, the *Challenge,* which took only 33 days to sail from Hong Kong to San Francisco, and the *Sea Witch,* which sailed from Guangzhou (then called Canton) to New York in 81 days.

6   The British built about 27 "tea clippers," as they called them. Unlike American ships, which were built entirely of wood, British ships were "composites," built with wooden planking over iron frames. The most famous tea clipper was the *Cutty Sark.*

7   Few new clippers were built after 1855, the year when the United States suffered an economic recession. By 1860 the age of the clippers was fading. Gold digging in California was nearly exhausted. American investors found railroad building more profitable than clippers. The Suez Canal cut off so much distance between Europe and Asia that it made the British tea clippers all but obsolete. Most importantly, there was a technological innovation that doomed the clipper, and in fact, the entire age of sail: the development of the steamship.

Glossary

greyhounds: *fast dogs sometimes used for racing*

Concordes: *supersonic passenger planes built by Britain and France. They were extremely fast, but tickets were very expensive.*

hull: *the exterior of a ship*

bow: *the front of a ship*

Notes on Main Topics:

Paragraph 1 _____

Paragraph 2 _____

Paragraph 3 _____

Paragraph 4 _____

Paragraph 5 _____

Paragraph 6 _____

Paragraph 7 _____

There was a need for fast ships because of the trade in Chinese Tea and the California Gold Rush.

- _____
- _____
- _____

A. Everything possible was done to make the clipper ships as fast as possible.
B. Clipper ships, according to one writer, were the Concordes of their era.
C. British clippers used wooden planking over iron frames.
D. The development of the steamship, together with other events, eliminated the need for the clipper ship.
E. Some of the sails that were used on clipper ships had never been used on sailing ships in the past.
F. Many records for speed were broken by clipper ships.

Passage 5

1 Georgia O'Keeffe stands out as one of the most compelling U.S. artists of the twentieth century. For nearly a century, her portrayals of the American land-scape, her still lifes, and her cityscapes have filled canvases with energy and stand in marked contrast to the chaotic images embraced by many of her con-temporaries in the art world. She has had many imitators, but none paint with her intensity, intimacy, and precision.

2 O'Keeffe was born in Sun Prairie, Wisconsin, in 1887. By the time she was in the eighth grade, she had decided that she wanted to become a painter. She took art courses in high school in Wisconsin, and after her family moved, in Williamsburg, Virginia. One teacher, Elizabeth Willis, allowed O'Keeffe to work on her art at her own pace. At times she would work intensely, and at other times she would not work for days. The principal of the school asked Willis if O'Keeffe was lazy. Willis responded, "When the spirit moves Georgia, she can do

more in a day than anyone else can do in a week." After graduating from high school, O'Keeffe attended classes at the Art Institute in Chicago and the Arts Student League in New York City.

3   Discouraged with her progress as an artist, O'Keeffe did not return to the League in the fall of 1908, but moved to Chicago and found work as a commercial artist. During this period Georgia did not pick up a brush, and said that the smell of <u>turpentine</u> made her sick. In 1912 a friend wrote her that a position as an art teacher was open at a college in Texas. She applied and was accepted. Her paintings were first exhibited in 1919 at "291," an experimental art gallery in New York City owned by the photographer and art critic Alfred Stieglitz. The gallery was frequented by some of the most influential artists of the time. Not long after this, O'Keeffe gave up her teaching job and devoted herself entirely to painting. Stieglitz helped O'Keeffe to find buyers for her paintings and galleries that would exhibit her art. They married in 1924.

4   Early in her career, O'Keeffe developed a highly personal, highly refined style. Her early paintings were mostly abstract designs. In the 1920's she produced enigmatic, close-up pictures of flowers and precise cityscapes of New York City. Whether painting mysterious flowers or austere buildings, she captured their beauty by magnifying their shapes and simplifying their details.

5   O'Keeffe's style of painting, and in fact her whole life, changed dramatically during a visit to New Mexico in 1929. She was enchanted by the bright southwestern sunlight, the ancient Spanish architecture, the Native American culture, and the blanched bones of cattle in the desert. She then adopted her characteristic style. Thereafter, she most often painted desert landscapes, often with the whitened skull of a <u>longhorn</u> in the foreground. She used vivid colors that, as one critic put it, "shock the senses." O'Keeffe affectionately referred to northern New Mexico as "the far away," a land of beauty, infinite space, and dazzling light. She began visiting New Mexico once a year for several months at a time. She would drive around on the back roads of New Mexico in a <u>Model A Ford</u>, with the backseat removed to make room for her art supplies. She bought a small ranch called the Ghost Ranch near Santa Fe. When her husband died in 1946, she moved there permanently.

6   In her later years, O'Keeffe became known as the dean of southwestern painters. In 1971 she became aware that her eyesight was failing, but she continued to paint as long as she could. Her illustrated autobiography became a bestseller in 1976. In 1986, she received the medal of the arts from President Ronald Reagan. She died the following year.

Glossary

turpentine: *a material used to thin oil paints before painting with them*

longhorn: *a type of cattle common in the southwestern part of the U.S.*

Model A Ford: *a type of U.S. car made between 1928 and 1931*

Notes on Main Topics:

Paragraph 1 _____

Paragraph 2 _____

Paragraph 3 _____

Paragraph 4 _____

Paragraph 5 _____

Paragraph 6 _____

Georgia O'Keeffe was one of the most important U.S. artists of the twentieth century.

- _____
- _____
- _____

A. Sometimes O'Keeffe worked intensely on her art, and sometimes she didn't work for days.
B. O'Keeffe painted cityscapes and mysterious flowers in her own distinctive style.
C. A visit to New Mexico changed her life and the style and subjects of her paintings.
D. O'Keeffe received an important award from the president of the United States for her artwork.
E. After studying art in school and teaching art, O'Keeffe had a show in New York City and became a full-time painter.
F. Stieglitz was one of the most important photographers of his time.

EXERCISE 8.2

FOCUS: Completing charts ("schematic tables") about passages.

DIRECTIONS: Match the phrases in the answer choices on the left side of the chart to the correct category or concept on the right side of the chart by writing the letter of the choice in the blank next to the bullet point. In each question, two answer choices will not be used.

On an actual exam, five-answer questions are worth three points and seven-answer questions are worth four points.

Passage 1

1 The concepts of analogy and homology are probably easier to exemplify than to define. When the structures of different species are compared, certain features can be described as either analogous or homologous. For example, flight requires certain aeronautical principles of design, yet eagles, bats, and houseflies all have the ability to fly. The wings of these three types of animals all derive from different embryological structures, but they all perform the same function. The flight organs of these three creatures can be said to be analogous. The emphasis in analogy, then, is on function.

2   In contrast, features that arise from the same structures in the embryo but are used in different functions are said to be homologous. A famous example is the forelimb of mammals. Among different species, forelimbs look completely different. They may have changed proportions, fused parts, or lost parts. They have adapted to serve many functions. The forelimbs of a horse are adopted for running, those of a dolphin for swimming, those of a bat for flying, those of a monkey for climbing trees, and those of a mole for digging. However, all come from the same embryological structures and all trace back to the same evolutionary structures: the wings of birds and the forelimbs of mammals all evolved from the fins of fish.

3   As recently as the nineteenth century, some biologists classified animals according to analogy. In 1847 the German biologist Lorenz Oken created a system of classification based on similar functions. In his system, there were four main classes of animals: *intestinal* animals (jellyfish, coral, and anemones); *vascular* animals (clams and snails); *respiratory* animals (insects and worms); and *nerve-and-muscle* animals (fish, birds, and mammals). Using analogy to classify animals is a little like classifying postage stamps according to their color instead of according to their country of origin. Today, of course, classification is based on homology.

Glossary

embryological: *related to an embryo, an organism in its earliest stages of development, before it reaches its distinctive form; among mammals, it refers to unborn animals.*

mole: *a mammal that digs tunnels in the earth*

Answer Choices	Homology
A. Emphasis is put on the function of animal structures.	• _____
B. The emphasis is on appearance, not function.	• _____
C. The current system of classification is based on this concept.	• _____
D. Animal structures have very different functions, but all evolved from the same structure.	Analogy
E. Lorenz Oken's system of classification is based on this concept.	• _____
F. Structures in various animals look very different but are all related to the same structure in the embryos of these animals.	• _____
G. This concept can be applied only to mammals.	

Passage 2

1   Dragons are found in the myths of many cultures and appear in many forms. The name comes from the Greek word *drakon,* meaning "snake." Generally, dragons are portrayed as large, scaly, winged serpents or reptiles with sharp claws.

2   In European myths, dragons are usually carnivorous reptiles with fiery breath. They are generally considered evil and dangerous. European (or Western) dragons are said to live in caves or swamps or on mountaintops, where they often guard treasures. Two of the most famous dragons in European literature are the dragon that <u>St. George</u> killed and the dragon that killed <u>Beowulf</u>. There are also many stories about medieval <u>knights</u> fighting dragons.

3   There are several types of European dragons. The *guivre* has no legs or wings. It is a large serpent with a wedge-shaped head. The *lindworm* has one pair of legs but no wings. The *amphiptere* is basically a flying snake with wings but no legs. The *wyvern*—a particularly bloodthirsty type of dragon—has two legs and two wings and a barbed tail. *Heraldic dragons* have four legs and two wings. Many noble European families chose this dragon as their symbol.

4   The Asian (or Eastern) dragon was also a reptile but often displayed characteristics of other animals, such as camels, deer, lions, eagles, and bulls. Asian dragons have serpentine bodies, do not usually breathe fire, and generally have no wings. Many have a "lion's mane" around their neck and a beard on their chin. They have two antlers coming from their head and two long whiskers coming from their faces. Asian dragons have 117 scales, 81 infused with yang, the principle of good, and 36 infused with yin, the principle of evil. Their favorite food is roasted swallows. Asian dragons symbolize power and unlike European dragons, are generally pictured as good, kind, and intelligent.

5   There are three families of Asian dragons: three-toed, four-toed, and five-toed. Three-toed dragons are native to Japan. Four-toed dragons are from Indonesia or Korea. Some Chinese dragons also have four toes, but the "Imperial dragons" of China have five. Asian dragons come in five colors: blue,

white, black, red, and yellow. Red and black dragons are powerful, but the yellow dragon is the strongest of all. Asian dragons are often pictured with a pearl in their mouths, under their chins, or in their claws. The dragon is thought to draw its strength from this pearl.

6   Many cultures outside of Europe and Asia also have legends of dragons. In fact, it is hard to find a culture that does *not* have a dragon myth. The Piasa ("storm bird") was a dragon known to the Illini, a Native American group that lived by the Mississippi River. It had the head of a bear, large teeth, the antlers of an <u>elk</u>, the scaly body of a fish, and a bear's legs ending in eagle's claws. The tail was fifty feet (15 meters) long and was tipped with a spearhead. It lived in a cave in the cliffs overlooking the river. For many years, the Piasa only hunted buffalos. Then, it captured an Illini warrior and after that, it developed a taste for humans and began attacking villages. The Illini chief Ouatoga used himself as "bait" to lure the beast from its cave. When the dragon stormed out to attack him, his warriors killed it with a shower of arrows. In Ethiopia, there are stories about a four-winged dragon, the Ethiopian Dream Snake. These creatures ate poisonous plants to make their bite and scratches poisonous. They were big enough to kill elephants. Once four of them wove together a raft and sailed to Arabia, where they thought the hunting would be better. Then there is the Rukh of Madagascar, the Anka of Arabia, the Vekher ("wind demon") of Russia, the Demaj of Persia, and the Kukulkan of the Aztecs.

7   The fact that so many cultures have dragon stories in common has led people to wonder if dragons really existed up to the time of the Middle Ages, when they were hunted into extinction. Some people have even wondered if dragons were the last surviving dinosaurs. Scientists, however, have dismissed this theory as highly unlikely since there is no fossil evidence to indicate that any dinosaurs lived past the end of the Mesozoic era, 65 million years ago.

Glossary

St. George: *a fourth-century warrior and saint who, according to a story called "the Golden Legend," killed a dragon*

Beowulf: *a legendary sixth-century Scandinavian king who, according to an eleventh-century poem, killed several monsters but then was killed by a dragon*

knights: *medieval soldiers who wore armor and fought on horseback*

elk: *a large member of the deer family*

Answer Choices	European (Western) Dragons
A. The Piasa and Ethiopian Dream Snake are examples of this type	• _____
B. Are reptilian but also have features of other animals	• _____
C. Can be classified in part according to the number of toes they have	• _____
D. Are generally considered evil and dangerous	• _____
E. Are featured in myths and legends in which they battle humans	Asian (Eastern) Dragons
F. Can be categorized according to the number of wings and legs they have	• _____
G. According to fossil records, lived during the Mesozoic Era	• _____
H. Are generally pictured as meat-eating reptiles that breathe fire	• _____
I. Are generally considered powerful, smart, and benevolent	

Passage 3

1   Luther Burbank and George Washington Carver drastically changed the face of American agriculture, and were close friends besides. They shared the belief that human ingenuity could improve the productivity of nature. However, in their backgrounds and work methods, they could hardly have been more dissimilar.

2   Born in 1849 on a farm near Lancaster, Massachusetts, Burbank was the thirteenth of fifteen children. His formal education stopped just after high school when his father died. He was always an avid reader, however, and was inspired by the works of Charles Darwin. He began raising and selling fruits and vegetables to support his family. He became particularly interested in breeding plants to create hybrids. His first "plant creation" was the Russet Burbank potato, better known as the Idaho potato. This was soon exported to help Ireland recover from the devastating potato famine of 1840–60. After moving to California in 1875, Burbank devised a stream of creations, earning himself the nickname "the plant wizard." One of his less successful creations was a spineless cactus to be used as cattle food, which he hoped would transform deserts into productive cattle lands. However, he successfully developed hundreds of new versions of fruit, vegetables, flowers, and other plants, many of which are the ancestors of the ones grown today. Moreover, he opened the public's eyes to the productive possibilities of plant breeding.

3   George Washington Carver was born a slave in 1864 in Mississippi. He was a curious, intelligent child who became fascinated by plants at an early age. Too poor to afford books, he taught himself about plants by wandering through the fields and forests near his home. Even as a child, he was called "the plant doctor." Carver attended high school in Kansas and studied botany, chemistry, and other subjects at Simpson College in Iowa. He received a master's degree from

Iowa State College. He then accepted an invitation from <u>Booker T. Washington</u> to join the faculty at Tuskegee Institute in Alabama. While Burbank concentrated on developing new types of plants, Carver found new uses for existing plants. In the late nineteenth and early twentieth century, cotton was still "king" of southern agriculture. However, cotton removes nitrogen from soil, and when it is grown year after year, the soil becomes very poor. Through his research he knew that growing peanuts would return nitrogen to the soil and restore its fertility. Therefore, he tried to find new uses for the peanut in order to make peanut farming profitable. He found ways to make soap, cooking oil, shaving cream, glue, paper, and printers' ink from peanuts. He also discovered many new uses for sweet potatoes, soybeans, and pecans, which also restored nitrogen to the soil. By doing so, he helped free southern agriculture from the tyranny of cotton.

4   Burbank's work as a plant breeder was based mainly on instinct. He *did* have remarkable instincts. He always seemed to know which few plants out of the thousands that he grew should be saved for future breeding. Sometimes he might keep just one plant out of ten thousand! Burbank spent most of his work time checking his many acres of plants. However, the value of his contributions was somewhat diminished by his research methods. Although he kept notes and took photographs of his creations, his records were only for his own use. This made it difficult for other scientists to reproduce and contribute to his achievements.

5   Carver, on the other hand, was a thorough, meticulous scientist. He depended more on careful experimentation than on instinct, and he spent more of his time in the laboratory than out in the field. He kept detailed records so that others could duplicate his experiments. He established the George Washington Carver Foundation for Agricultural Research at Tuskegee Institute and encouraged other researchers there to continue his work. In fact, in 1940, he donated his entire life savings of $33,000 to the Institute.

6   Burbank and Carver have one thing in common: there are popular misconceptions about both of them. Most people assume that the city of Burbank, California, was named for Luther Burbank. In fact, it was named for David Burbank, a Los Angeles dentist. And it is widely believed that Carver invented <u>peanut butter</u>. Carver did develop over 400 products from peanuts, but peanut butter is not one of them. Peanut butter was invented by a St. Louis doctor named Ambrose Straub.

Glossary

Charles Darwin: *a British naturalist who formulated the Theory of Evolution*

Booker T. Washington: *a black educator who founded the Tuskegee Institute in Alabama, the first U.S. college for African Americans*

peanut butter: *a spread made from peanuts that is often eaten on bread or crackers*

Answer Choices	Luther Burbank
A. Because of his techniques, made it difficult for researchers who wanted to continue his work	• _____
B. Worked more in the field than in the laboratory	• _____
C. Created alternatives to cotton growing	• _____
D. Was jealous and resentful of the other's success	• _____
E. Focused on creating new types of plants	
F. Kept careful notes about his experiments	George Washington Carver
G. Worked mainly from instinct	• _____
H. Concentrated primarily on finding new uses for familiar plants	• _____
I. Invented peanut butter	• _____

Passage 4

1   Fog is a cloud in contact with or just above the surface of the land or the sea. Fog consists of particles of water or ice suspended in the air. It can be a major environmental hazard. Fog on busy highways can cause chain-reaction accidents involving dozens, or sometimes even hundreds, of cars. Delays and shutdowns at airports can cause economic losses for airlines and inconvenience thousands of travelers. Fog at sea has always been a danger to navigation. Today, with supertankers carrying vast quantities of oil, fog increases the possibility of catastrophic oil spills. Even though planes and ships are equipped with radar that can "see" through fog, accidents are still more common in foggy weather than on clear days.

2   *Radiation fog,* the type of fog most often seen around the world, forms on clear nights when moist air near the ground loses warmth through radiation. This type of fog often occurs in valleys, such as California's San Joaquin Valley, and then spreads outward from the valleys. It is most common in the autumn. Another common type, *advection fog,* results from the movement of warm, wet air over cold ground. It is most common during winter warm-ups and spring thaws. This type of fog occurs along ocean coasts and along the shores of large lakes. It generally forms at night, when the wind is blowing lightly. If the wind blows too hard, it will break the fog up. Advection fogs also form when air associated with a warm ocean current flows across the surface of a cold current. The thick "pea soup" fogs of the Grand Banks, off the coast of Newfoundland, Canada, are largely of this origin, because this is where the cold Labrador Current meets the warm Gulf Stream.

3   Other types of fog are less common. *Steam fog* is the most localized type of fog. Steam fog appears when cold air picks up moisture by moving over warmer water. It is common over seas and over deeper and larger lakes in late autumn and early winter. When it forms over sea, steam fog is also called *sea smoke.* *Upslope fog* is common along high hills and mountains. It forms when winds blow up the side of a hill or mountain, cooling the air. *Frontal fog* occurs when two fronts of different temperatures meet and rain from the warm front falls into

the colder one. *Ice fog* is any kind of fog in which the droplets have frozen into extremely small ice crystals in midair. Generally this requires temperatures well below the freezing point, making it common only in and near the Arctic and Antarctic regions.

4   Although fog can be dangerous, it also has positive environmental effects. For example, advection fog plays an important role in the life of California red-wood trees. Redwood trees have very shallow roots. They depend on water from sources other than water deep underground. What the trees do not get from rain, they get from fog. Advection fog deposits moisture on the tree's needles which then drips to the ground and is absorbed by the roots.

Answer Choices	*Radiation Fog*
A. Involves tiny crystals of ice hanging in the air	• _____
B. Provides water for redwood trees	• _____
C. Often forms in valleys and then spreads outward	
D. Forms in one way over the shore and in another way over the sea	*Advection Fog*
E. Is the most common type of fog	• _____
F. Forms on breezy nights when the weather is warming up	• _____
G. Is also known as *sea smoke*.	• _____

Passage 5

1   Cooperation is the common endeavor of two or more people to perform a task or reach a jointly cherished goal. Like competition and conflict, there are different forms of cooperation, based on group organization and attitudes.

2   In primary cooperation, group and individual fuse. The group consumes nearly all of each individual's life. The rewards of the group's work are shared with every member. There is an interlocking identity of individual, group, and task performed. Means and goals become one because cooperation itself is prized.

3   While primary cooperation is most often characteristic of preliterate soci-eties, secondary cooperation is characteristic of many contemporary societies. In secondary cooperation, individuals devote only part of their lives to the group. Cooperation itself is not a value. Most members of the group feel loyalty, but the welfare of the group is not their first consideration. Members perform tasks so that they can separately enjoy the fruits of their cooperation in the form of salary, prestige, or power. Business firms and athletic teams are examples of secondary cooperation.

4   In tertiary cooperation, or accommodation, latent conflict underlies the shared work. The attitudes of the cooperating parties are purely opportunistic. The organization is loose and fragile. Cooperation ceases when the parties have

achieved some limited mutual goal or when cooperation no longer seems the best method of achieving these goals. One example would be two rival political parties that unite in order to defeat a third party. Another is a criminal who helps the police find another criminal in order to get some favor from the police. This is not, strictly speaking, cooperation at all, and hence the somewhat contradictory term "antagonistic cooperation" is sometimes used for this relationship.

Answer Choices	*Primary Cooperation*
A. If *cooperation* is narrowly defined, this would not be considered cooperation.	• _____
	• _____
B. This is most common among groups that do not read or write.	• _____
C. Members of the cooperating group enjoy the rewards of their cooperation individually.	*Secondary Cooperation*
	• _____
D. This type is further broken down into several types.	• _____
E. Group members value cooperation for its own sake.	
F. This will stop when the cooperating parties reach their goal.	*Tertiary Cooperation*
	• _____
G. Cooperating parties are loyal to the group, but group welfare is not the primary consideration.	• _____
H. The organization and the members join into a single entity.	
I. This type is no longer practiced today.	

READING REVIEW TEST
DIRECTIONS

This section tests your ability to comprehend academic reading passages. It consists of three reading passages (two passages in one set and one passage in the other) and questions about the passages. All of the questions are worth one point except for the last question about each passage. Special directions for the last question will tell you how many points it is worth.

You will have sixty minutes to complete this section of the test.

In the passages, some words or phrases are underlined. Definitions or explanations for these words are provided at the end of the passage. On the actual test, these words will be underlined in blue and you can click on them to get the definition or explanation.

As soon as you have finished one question, you may move on to the next one. (On the actual test, you will click on Next to move to the next question.) You may skip questions and come back to them later, and you can change your answers if you wish. (On the actual test, you will click on Back to return to a previous question.)

As soon as you have read these directions, go on to the first passage.

Noise Pollution

1   The word *noise* is derived from the Latin word *nausea,* meaning "seasickness." Noise is among the most pervasive pollutants today. Noise pollution can broadly be defined as unwanted or offensive sounds that unreasonably intrude into our daily activities. Noises from traffic, jet engines, barking dogs, garbage trucks, construction equipment, factories, lawn mowers, leaf blowers, televisions, <u>boom boxes</u>, and car radios, to name a few, are among the audible litter that is routinely broadcast into the air.

2   One measure of pollution is the danger it poses to health. Noise negatively affects human health and well-being. Problems related to noise include hearing loss, stress, high blood pressure, sleeplessness, fright, distraction, and lost productivity. Noise pollution also contributes to a general reduction in the quality of life and eliminates opportunities for tranquility.

3   A number of factors contribute to problems of growing noise levels. One is increasing population, particularly when it leads to increasing urbanization and urban consolidation, because activities associated with urban living generally lead to increased noise levels. Another is the increasing volume of road, rail, and air traffic. Some people would add to this list a diminishing sense of civility and a growing disrespect for the rights of others.

4   We experience noise in a number of ways. On some occasions, we can be both the cause and the victim of noise, such as when we are operating noisy appliances or equipment. There are also instances when we experience noise generated by others, just as people experience <u>secondhand smoke</u>. In both instances, noise is equally damaging physically. Secondhand noise is generally more troubling, however, because it is put into the environment by others, without our consent.

5   The air into which secondhand noise is emitted and on which it travels is "a commons." It belongs not to an individual person or a group, but to everyone. People, businesses, and organizations, therefore, do not have unlimited rights to broadcast noise as they please, as if the effects of noise were limited only to their private property. Those that disregard the obligation to not interfere with others' use and enjoyment of the commons by producing noise pollution are, in many ways, acting like a bully in a school yard. Although they may do so unknowingly, they disregard the rights of others and claim for themselves rights that are not theirs.

6   Noise pollution differs from other forms of pollution in a number of ways. Noise is transient; once the pollution stops, the environment is free of it. This is not the case with air pollution, for example. We can measure the amount of chemicals and other pollutants introduced into the air. Scientists can estimate how much material can be introduced into the air before harm is done. The same is true of water pollution and soil pollution. Though we can measure individual sounds that may actually damage human hearing, it is difficult to monitor cumulative exposure to noise or to determine just how much noise is too much. The definition of noise pollution itself is highly subjective. To some people the roar of an engine is satisfying or thrilling; to others it is an annoyance. Loud music may be a pleasure or a torment, depending on the listener and the circumstances.

7   The actual loudness of a sound is only one component of the negative effect noise pollution has on human beings. Other factors that have to be considered are the time and place, the duration, the source of the sound, and even the mood of the affected person. Most people would not be bothered by the sound of a 21-gun salute on a special occasion. On the other hand, the thump-thump of music coming from the apartment downstairs at 2 A.M., even if barely audible, might be a major source of stress. The sound of a neighbor's lawn mower may be unobjectionable on a summer afternoon, but if someone is hoping to sleep late on a Saturday morning, the sound of a lawn mower starting up just after sunrise is an irritant.

Glossary

boom boxes: *portable (but still large) radios or CD players*

secondhand smoke: *smoke that comes from someone else's cigarette*

---

1 of 39   The word routinely in the passage is closest in meaning to

○ regularly
○ accidentally
○ recently
○ unfortunately

2 of 39   The phrase this list in the passage refers to a list of

○ types of noise pollution
○ factors that explain why noise pollution is getting worse
○ activities that are associated with life in the city
○ methods of transportation

3 of 39   In paragraph 4, the author implies that secondhand noise pollution

○ is not as damaging physically as noise that one generates oneself
○ damages a person's health as much as secondhand smoke
○ makes people both the cause and the victim of noise pollution
○ is usually more annoying because it is out of one's control

4 of 39   Which of the following is NOT an example of a "commons" as it is defined by the author in paragraph 5?

○ A national park
○ A factory
○ The air over a city
○ The water supply for a city

5 of 39   In paragraph 5, the author explains the concept of interfering with others' use and enjoyment of a commons by

- ○ comparing it to another common negative experience
- ○ pointing out ways in which people, businesses, and organizations sometimes interfere with the rights of others
- ○ explaining that sometimes this interference is intentional and sometimes unintentional
- ○ giving examples of various forms of commons and of ways people interfere with them

6 of 39   The word transient in the passage is closest in meaning to

- ○ irritating
- ○ persistent
- ○ temporary
- ○ immeasurable

7 of 39   Which of the following sentences best expresses the essential information in the sentence below? (Incorrect answer choices omit important information or change the meaning of the original sentence in an important way.)

Though we can measure individual sounds that may actually damage human hearing, it is difficult to monitor cumulative exposure to noise or to determine just how much noise is too much.

- ○ It's hard to monitor cumulative exposure to sound because it is difficult to measure individual sounds.
- ○ The louder the sound, the more difficult it is to measure.
- ○ Individual sounds can be measured, but not the effects of long-term exposure to noise, and it's hard to say what level of sound is safe.
- ○ Individual sounds are not usually very damaging to human hearing, but multiple sounds that occur at the same time can be very harmful.

8 of 39   The word thrilling in the passage is closest in meaning to

- ○ unusual
- ○ exciting
- ○ irritating
- ○ unexpected

9 of 39   Which of the following is NOT one of the components of the negative effects that noise pollution has on people?

- ○ The volume of the sound
- ○ The time when the sound is heard
- ○ The source of the sound
- ○ The combination of one sound and another

10 of 39   In paragraph 7, the author mentions a 21-gun salute as an example of

- ○ a particularly irritating form of noise pollution
- ○ a type of noise pollution that can cause physical damage and fright
- ○ a loud noise that most people tolerate on special occasions
- ○ a noise that is much more annoying than soft music

11 of 39   Look at the four squares (■) that indicate where the following sentence could be added to the passage.

> **On the contrary, they have an obligation to use the commons in ways that are compatible with or do not detract from other uses.**

The air into which secondhand noise is emitted and on which it travels is "a commons." ■ It belongs not to an individual person or a group, but to everyone. ■ People, businesses, and organizations, therefore, do not have unlimited rights to broadcast noise as they please, as if the effects of noise were limited only to their private property. ■ Those that disregard the obligation to not interfere with others' use and enjoyment of the commons by producing noise pollution are, in many ways, acting like a bully in a schoolyard. ■ Although they may do so unknowingly, they disregard the rights of others and claim for themselves rights that are not theirs.

Circle the square (■) that indicates the best place to add the sentence.

12 of 39   DIRECTIONS: Select phrases from the answer choices and match them to the category to which they relate. One answer choice will not be used. **This question is worth 2 points.**

Answer Choices	Noise Pollution
A. After this form of pollution has stopped being created, the environment is no longer damaged by it.	• _____
B. It is simple to determine at what level it becomes dangerous.	• _____
C. Its definition changes from person to person.	• _____
D. It is similar to water pollution in that the level at which it becomes dangerous is known.	*Air Pollution*
E. It can be reduced in a number of ways that are proposed in the passage by the author.	• _____
F. Its effects on a person may vary depending on what kind of mood that person is in.	• _____
G. It has become less of a problem in recent years.	

In A New Light: LEDs

1   At the end of the 1800's, Thomas Edison introduced the incandescent light bulb and changed the world. Remarkably, the incandescent bulb used today has changed little in over a hundred years. An incandescent light consists of a glass bulb filled with an inert gas such as argon. Inside the bulb, electricity passes through a metal filament. Because of resistance, the filament becomes so hot that it glows. Given that 20% of the world's electricity is used to power lights, this represents an enormous amount of wasted energy.

2   In the 1940's a new, more efficient form of lighting, the fluorescent bulb, was introduced. Fluorescents work by passing electrical current through gas in a tube, producing invisible ultraviolet light. A phosphor coating on the inside of the tube then converts the ultraviolet to visible light. Little heat is wasted. Fluorescents have proved popular in offices, factories, and stores, but they never

took over the residential lighting market. The harsh color isn't as pleasing as the warmer glow of incandescent lamps. Besides, they have a tendency to flicker on and off and to produce an annoying buzz.

3   Now, lighting engineers are developing a new form of lighting that is both pleasing to the eyes and energy efficient. This is the light-emitting diode, or LED. LEDs are made up of layers of electron-charged substances. When an electrical current passes through the layers, electrons jump from one layer to another and give off light without producing heat. Different types of materials result in light of different colors. Red, green, and orange LEDs have been used for decades in devices such as digital clocks, calculators, and electronic toys. In the future, however, white-light-emitting diodes (WLEDs) may be used to light homes. Engineers say that they are significantly more efficient than either incandescent or fluorescent lights.

4   Arrays of colored LEDs are beginning to be used in traffic lights and automotive lights. Today, colored light such as a red brake light is created by shining a white incandescent light through a colored plastic filter. This is incredibly inefficient because only the red light that passes through the filter is used. The rest is wasted. Because LEDs actually produce red light, no filter is needed and no light is wasted. LEDs have other practical applications as well. For example, they can be used to light heat-sensitive materials like food or important documents.

5   The next challenge for researchers is to develop an efficient, bright, inexpensive WLED. A few years ago, a Japanese scientist named Shuji Nakamura discovered that, by using layers of gallium nitride, he could create a powerful blue LED. Later, engineers devised two ways to use this blue LED to create a WLED. Red, green, and blue LEDs can be combined, creating a pleasant white light. Another way is to use a chemical coating similar to that inside a fluorescent bulb that converts the blue light to white. Nevertheless, it will still be some time before WLEDs are commonly used in homes. WLEDs are currently only twice as energy efficient as incandescent. They are also very expensive. But researchers believe that they can create WLEDs that are ten times as efficient and one thousand times as long-lasting as incandescent lights, making them cost effective.

6   LEDs may someday have an even greater impact on developing countries than in the developed world. Worldwide, an estimated 2 billion people lack access to electricity. Lighting is usually provided by kerosene lamps. Kerosene is expensive, creates indoor pollution, does not provide very bright light, and worst of all, causes many fires. In India alone, 2.5 million people are killed or injured annually in fires caused by overturned kerosene lamps. A low-energy (1-watt) WLED can provide enough light for a person to read by—more light, in fact, than most kerosene lamps. An entire rural village could be lighted with less energy than that used by a single conventional 100-watt light bulb. Energy to light these efficient LEDs can be provided by batteries that are charged by pedal-driven generators, by hydroelectricity from rivers or streams, by wind-powered generators, or by solar energy. LEDs could revolutionize lighting to the same extent that the cell phone has revolutionized communication in places where land telephone lines are unavailable.

Glossary

kerosene: *a type of fuel made from petroleum that is often used in lamps or heaters*

13 of 39   The word Remarkably in the passage is closest in meaning to

     ○ logically
     ○ generally
     ○ amazingly
     ○ naturally

14 of 39   In paragraph 2, which of the following is NOT mentioned as one of the problems with fluorescent lights?

     ○ The need to replace them often
     ○ An annoying sound
     ○ The harsh quality of the light they produce
     ○ Their tendency to flicker

15 of 39   According to the passage, a red LED is different from a green LED because it

     ○ is made from different materials
     ○ uses a different amount of energy
     ○ uses a red plastic filter, not a green one
     ○ produces less heat

16 of 39   The word they in the passage refers to

     ○ white-light-emitting diodes
     ○ digital clocks, calculators, toys, and similar devices
     ○ engineers
     ○ red, orange, and green LEDs

17 of 39   In paragraph 5, what achievement of Shuji Nakamura does the author mention?

     ○ He discovered the chemical compound gallium nitride.
     ○ He invented the first WLED.
     ○ He found a way to combine blue, green, and yellow LED light.
     ○ He developed a bright blue LED.

18 of 39   It can be inferred from the passage that the most recently developed type of LED is a powerful

     ○ red LED
     ○ white LED
     ○ blue LED
     ○ green LED

19 of 39   In paragraph 5, the author compares one type of WLED with fluorescent light because they both

     ○ use ultraviolet light
     ○ are filled with gas
     ○ employ a chemical coating
     ○ are energy efficient

20 of 39   From the information in paragraph 5, it is clear that WLEDs could be used in homes today if they were

○ not so expensive
○ easier to install
○ twice as efficient as incandescent lights
○ available in various colors

21 of 39   The author gives details about the use of kerosene lights in paragraph 6 in order to

○ explain why people in developing countries prefer kerosene to electrical light
○ show the problems and dangers associated with this form of lighting
○ give an example of a type of lighting that is not as important as it once was
○ demonstrate that kerosene is brighter and easier to use than WLEDs

22 of 39   According to the information in paragraph 6, the electricity to power WLEDs in rural villages would come directly from

○ the energy of the sun
○ batteries
○ water power
○ a human-powered generator

23 of 39   The word conventional in the passage is closest in meaning to

○ inexpensive
○ powerful
○ standard
○ experimental

24 of 39   What opinion about cell phones in the developing world does the author express in paragraph 6?

○ They are an important form of communication, but are still too expensive for many people.
○ They are a much more important technological development than LEDs.
○ They are not as useful as phones that use land lines.
○ They have changed communication in the way LEDs may change lighting.

25 of 39   Look at the four squares [■] that indicate where the following sentence could be added to the passage.

But 95% of the energy goes to produce heat and is basically wasted.

At the end of the 1800's, Thomas Edison introduced the incandescent light bulb and changed the world. Remarkably, the incandescent bulb used today has changed little in over a hundred years. ■ A glass bulb is filled with an inert gas such as argon. Inside the bulb, electricity passes through a metal filament. ■ Because of resistance, the filament becomes so hot that it glows. ■ Given that 20% of the world's electricity is used to power lights, this is an enormous amount of wasted energy. ■

Circle the square [■] that indicates the best place to add the sentence.

DIRECTIONS: Below is an introductory sentence for a brief summary of the passage. Complete the summary by writing the letters of **three** of the answer choices that express the most important ideas of the passage. Some of the answer choices are incorrect because they express ideas that are not given in the passage or because they express only details from the passage.

Incandescent lights and fluorescent lights are two common types of lighting, but incandescents are wasteful and fluorescents are not popular for home use.

- _____
- _____
- _____

Answer Choices

A. There are two ways to create WLEDs, but neither type is commonly used in homes at present.

B. An entire rural village can be lit with LEDs using no more energy than a 100-watt bulb.

C. Color LEDs are in use today, and white LEDs may be used to light homes in the near future.

D. LEDs are much more efficient than incandescent lights but not as efficient as fluorescent lights.

E. The greatest impact of LEDs will probably be in rural areas of the developing world.

F. LEDs, a relatively new form of lighting, are efficient and produce a pleasant light.

The Impressionists

1   In April 1870, an art exhibit opened in Paris featuring famous and priceless works of art. However, at the time, no one knew that these paintings would one day be considered masterpieces. The paintings and the painters were virtually unknown at the time and would remain that way for several years.

2   In the nineteenth century, French art was dominated by the Academy of Fine Arts. Every year the academy held an art show called *Le Salon*. In 1863, the Academy rejected one of the paintings of Édouard Manet. Manet and a group of other independent artists organized their own show, which they called *Salon des Refusés* (Salon of the Rejected), which opened on April 15, 1874. A newspaper critic named Louis Leroy visited the gallery and was not pleased with what he saw. One painting of boats in a harbor at dawn by Claude Monet particularly enraged him. It was called *Impression: Sunset*. Leroy wrote that this piece, and in fact most of the pieces in the show, looked like "impressions"—a term for a preliminary, unfinished sketch made before a painting is done. Leroy's newspaper review was jokingly called "The Exhibition of the Impressionists." Within a few years of Leroy's review, the term *Impressionists* had clearly stuck, not as a term of derision but as a badge of honor, and a new movement was born.

3   The Impressionist movement included the French painters Édouard Manet, Claude Monet, Pierre-Auguste Renoir, Edgar Degas, Paul Cezanne, and the American painter Mary Cassatt. The techniques and standards employed within the Impressionist movement varied widely, and though the artists shared a core of values, the real glue which bound the movement together was its spirit of rebellion and independence.

4   This spirit is clear when you compare Impressionist paintings with traditional French paintings of the time. Traditional painters tended to paint rather serious scenes from history and mythology. Many Impressionist paintings feature pleasant scenes of urban life, celebrating the leisure time that the Industrial Revolution had won for the middle class, as shown in Renoir's luminous painting *Luncheon of the Boating Party.* In that famous painting, the sun filters through the orange-striped awning, bathing everything and everyone at the party in its warm light. Renoir once said that paintings should be ". . . likable, joyous, and pretty." He said, "There are enough unpleasant things in this world. We don't have to paint them as well." It is this joy of life that makes Renoir's paintings so distinctive.

5   The Impressionists delighted in painting landscapes (except for Edgar Degas, who preferred painting indoor scenes, and Mary Cassatt, who mainly painted portraits of mothers and children). Traditional painters, too, painted landscapes, but their landscapes tended to be somber and dark. The Impressionists' landscapes sparkle with light. Impressionists insisted that their works be "true to nature." When they painted landscapes, they carried their paints and canvases outdoors in order to capture the ever-changing light. Traditional painters generally made preliminary sketches outside but worked on the paintings themselves in their studios.

6   "Classic" Impressionist paintings are often easy to spot because of the techniques used by the painters. One of the first "rules" of the Impressionists, that the colors should be dropped pure on the canvas instead of getting mixed on the palette, was respected by only a few of them and for only a couple of years, but most Impressionists mixed their paints as little as possible. They believed that it was better to allow the eye to mix the colors as it viewed them on the canvas. The traditional technique at the time was to make sketches or outlines of the subject before painting them. Generally, Impressionists painted directly onto the canvas without sketches. Impressionists tended to paint with short, thick strokes of paints shaped like commas. While traditional painters paid attention to details, Impressionists valued overall effect. Traditional painters always tried to hide their brush strokes, but Impressionists left brush strokes on the canvas for the world to see. Unlike traditional painters, Impressionists applied one layer of paint on top of the last one without waiting for the paint to dry. These techniques created paintings that seemed strange and unfinished to the general public when they were first painted, but are much loved in our time.

Glossary

palette: *a board with a hole for the thumb on which painters mix their colors*

27 of 39   What point does the author make about the art show that opened on April 15, 1874, at the Salon des Refusés in Paris?

○ It was more popular with visitors and critics than the official show called "Le Salon."
○ It made the painters and paintings shown there instantly successful.
○ Its organizers refused to allow Édouard Manet to display his paintings there.
○ It featured famous paintings and painters before they became well known.

28 of 39   The word virtually in the passage is closest in meaning to the word

○ almost
○ infinitely
○ seemingly
○ forever

29 of 39   According to the author, Louis Leroy used the term "Impressionists" because

○ he understood that these artists did not carefully study their subjects, but only got a quick impression of what they painted
○ he thought that Monet's painting, and all of the paintings at the show, looked like unfinished drawings
○ he believed that giving these artists a group name would help them become famous
○ he thought that the painting *Impression: Sunset* was the best painting at the show

30 of 39   The word derision in the passage is closest in meaning to

○ ridicule
○ sincerity
○ respect
○ sorrow

31 of 39   Which of the following sentences best expresses the essential information in the sentence below? (Incorrect answer choices omit important information or change the meaning of the original sentence in an important way.)

The techniques and standards employed within the Impressionist movement varied widely, and though the artists shared a core of values, the real glue which bound the movement together was its spirit of rebellion and independence.

○ The core of values shared by the Impressionists was the most important connection between them.
○ Although there were artistic differences among the Impressionists, they were united by an independent spirit and shared values.
○ At first the Impressionist movement was held together by a shared set of techniques and standards, but in time they rebelled against these core values.
○ Although the Impressionists' values differed, their techniques and standards helped create a strong, independent spirit.

READING

32 of 39   Renoir's painting *Luncheon of the Boating Party* is given in paragraph 4 as an example of

○ an industrial scene
○ a study of some urban buildings
○ a picture of people enjoying their leisure time
○ a traditional French painting

33 of 39   According to the information in paragraph 5, what did the painters Edgar Degas and Mary Cassatt have in common?

○ They both painted portraits of children and mothers.
○ Neither of them was originally from France.
○ Neither of them was primarily interested in landscapes.
○ They both preferred painting unpleasant scenes.

34 of 39   According to paragraph 5, when traditional painters worked on landscape paintings, they

○ studied the ever-changing light
○ did not make any preliminary sketches
○ never left their studios
○ sketched outdoors but painted indoors

35 of 39   It can be inferred from the information in paragraph 6 that in the author's view, the first "rule" of Impressionism

○ was not really a rule at all
○ was the most important rule of all
○ led Impressionists to mix their colors
○ lasted longer than other rules

36 of 39   The word spot in paragraph 6 is closest in meaning to

○ paint
○ identify
○ admire
○ ignore

37 of 39   The phrase the last one in the passage refers to

○ an artist
○ a painting
○ a brush stroke
○ a layer of paint

38 of 39   Look at the four squares [■] that indicate where the following sentence could be added to the passage.

> **This play of light can be seen in Claude Monet's paintings *Water Lilies, Green Harmony,* and *The Bridge at Argenteuil.***

The Impressionists delighted in painting landscapes (except for Edgar Degas, who preferred painting indoor scenes, and Mary Cassatt, who painted portraits of mothers and children). ■ Traditional painters, too, painted landscapes, but their landscapes tended to be somber and dark. ■ The Impressionists' landscapes sparkle with light. ■ Impressionists insisted that their works be "true to nature." ■ When they painted landscapes, they carried their paints and canvases outdoors in order to capture the ever-changing light. Traditional painters generally made preliminary sketches outside but worked on the paintings themselves in their studios.

Circle the square [■] that indicates the best place to add the sentence.

39 of 39   DIRECTIONS: Select phrases from the answer choices and match them to the category to which they relate. Two answer choices will not be used. ***This question is worth 4 points.***

Answer Choices	Impressionist Painters
A. Their classic pieces are very distinctive because of the methods they used to create them.	• _____
	• _____
B. They often painted serious scenes from history and mythology	• _____
	• _____
C. Their works were considered unusual at the time but are prized today.	
D. They used darker colors when painting landscapes.	*Traditional Painters*
E. They celebrated middle-class people enjoying their leisure time.	• _____
F. They seldom completely finished their paintings.	• _____
G. They concentrated on details.	• _____
H. They painted abstract scenes with no recognizable figures in them.	
I. Their landscape paintings were filled with light.	

This is the end of the Reading Review Test.

Reading Tutorial: Vocabulary Building

This section of the text provides synonyms for more than 500 words, together with practice exercises designed to improve your ability to use context to choose the word that best fits into a sentence.

Vocabulary Exercise 1

abandon *v.* desert, leave behind

able *adj.* capable, qualified, fit

abolish *v.* end, eliminate

abrupt *adj.* sudden, hasty, unexpected

acclaim *v.* applaud, praise, honor; *n.* applause, praise, honor

accommodating *adj.* helpful, welcoming, cooperative

acrid *adj.* bitter, sharp, biting

adapt *v.* adjust, modify

adept *adj.* skillful, expert

adhere *v.* stick, cling

admonish *v.* warn, caution, advise

adorn *v.* decorate, ornament

advent *n.* coming, arrival

adverse *adj.* hostile, negative, contrary

affluent *adj.* rich, wealthy, prosperous, well-to-do, thriving

aggravate *v.* (1) annoy, irritate; (2) intensify, worsen

aggregate *adj.* entire, total, combined

agile *adj.* graceful, nimble, lively

ailment *n.* sickness, illness, disease

allot *v.* divide, distribute

amazing *adj.* astonishing, astounding, surprising, startling

amiable *adj.* agreeable, congenial, pleasant, friendly

anticipate *v.* foresee, expect, predict

anxious *adj.* (1) worried, nervous, apprehensive; (2) eager, avid

appraise *v.* evaluate, estimate, assess

apt *adj.* (1) appropriate, suitable, correct, relevant, proper; (2) likely, prone

arduous *adj.* difficult, strenuous, exhausting

arid *adj.* dry, barren

aroma *n.* fragrance, smell, odor, scent

artificial *adj.* synthetic, imitation, man-made

astonishing *adj.* surprising, amazing, astounding

astute *adj.* intelligent, clever, perceptive

attain *v.* accomplish, achieve

augment *v.* supplement, increase, strengthen, expand

austere *adj.* strict, harsh, severe, stern

authentic *adj.* genuine, true

averse *adj.* opposed to, against, hostile to

aversion *n.* dislike, hostility, fear

awkward *adj.* clumsy

DIRECTIONS: Complete the following sentences by filling in the blanks with vocabulary items (A), (B), or (C), according to the context of the sentences. The first one is done for you as an example.

1. Penicillin can have an ___A___ effect on a person who is allergic to it.

    (A) adverse   (B) anxious   (C) awkward

2. Burning rubber produces an _____ smoke.

    (A) adept   (B) arid   (C) acrid

3. Rationing is a system for _____ scarce resources.

    (A) allotting   (B) adapting   (C) appraising

4. Anthrax is generally an _____ of sheep and cattle, but it can also be transmitted to humans.

    (A) ailment   (B) aroma   (C) aversion

5. Lawrence Gilman is admired for his _____, scholarly musical criticism.

    (A) austere   (B) astute   (C) abrupt

6. Mountain climbing is an _____ sport.

    (A) austere   (B) arduous   (C) anxious

7. Turtles _____ their eggs after they lay them and never see their young.

    (A) abandon   (B) appraise   (C) adorn

8. Scholarships allow some students from less _____ families to attend college.

    (A) artificial   (B) affluent   (C) amiable

9. Jewelers are sometimes asked to _____ jewelry for insurance purposes.

    (A) attain   (B) abandon   (C) appraise

10. Acrobats must be extremely _____ .

    (A) awkward   (B) affluent   (C) agile

11. Southern Arizona has an _____ climate.

    (A) arid   (B) astute   (C) acrid

12. A person suffering from claustrophobia has an _____ to confined spaces.

    (A) ailment   (B) aversion   (C) acclaim

13. Perhaps the most _____ evolutionary development in penguins is a gland that can remove salt from seawater.

    (A) arid   (B) astonishing   (C) amiable

14. Readers in the eighteenth century found Thomas Paine's pamphlet *Common Sense* extremely persuasive, in part because it contained many _____ quotations.

    (A) apt   (B) anxious   (C) awkward

15. Some lakes are natural, but others are _____, formed by damming rivers or streams.

    (A) acrid   (B) aggregate   (C) artificial

16. I was told that the librarians here were not very helpful, but I found them quite _____.

    (A) accommodating   (B) averse   (C) austere

Vocabulary Exercise 2

baffle *v.* confuse, puzzle, mystify

balmy *adj.* mild, warm

ban *v.* prohibit, forbid

bar *v.* prevent, obstruct, block

barren *adj.* sterile, unproductive, bleak, lifeless

barter *v.* trade, exchange

beckon *v.* summon, call, signal

belligerent *adj.* hostile, aggressive

beneficial *adj.* helpful, useful, advantageous

benevolent *adj.* benign, kind, compassionate, good

bias *n.* prejudice

blanched *adj.* whitened, bleached, pale

bland *adj.* mild, tasteless, dull

blatant *adj.* flagrant, obvious, overt

blend *v.* mix, mingle, combine; *n.* mixture, combination

bloom *v.* blossom, flower, flourish

blow up *v.* (1) explode; (2) become angry; (3) magnify, expand

blunder *v.* make a mistake; *n.* error, mistake

blunt *adj.* (1) unsharpened, dull; (2) rude, abrupt, curt

blurry *adj.* unfocused, unclear, indistinct

bold *adj.* brave, courageous

bolster *v.* support, sustain, boost, buttress

bond *v.* join, connect; *n.* tie, link, connection

boom *v.* expand, prosper; *n.* expansion, prosperity, growth

brace *v.* support, reinforce

brilliant *adj.* (1) bright, shiny, radiant, dazzling; (2) talented, gifted, intelligent

brisk *adj.* (1) lively, quick, vigorous; (2) cool, chilly, invigorating

brittle *adj.* fragile, breakable, weak

bulky *adj.* huge, large, clumsy

bully *v.* torment, bother, force others to do things; *n.* a person who torments others

buttress *v.* support, bolster, boost

DIRECTIONS: Complete the following sentences by filling in the blanks with vocabulary items (A), (B), or (C), according to the context of the sentences.

1. Many flowers _____ in the spring.
   (A) blend   (B) brace   (C) bloom

2. The Virgin Islands, located in the Caribbean, have a _____ climate.
   (A) blurry   (B) brittle   (C) balmy

3. Before currency came into use, people used the _____ system.
   (A) barter   (B) blunder   (C) bias

4. The airline _____. It sent me to Atlanta but my luggage to Montreal.
   (A) buttressed   (B) baffled   (C) blundered

5. People with ulcers should eat _____ foods.
   (A) bold   (B) bland   (C) bulky

6. Steel is not as _____ as cast iron; it doesn't break as easily.
   (A) brisk   (B) brittle   (C) brilliant

7. At one time, the city of Boston _____ Walt Whitman's poetry because it was considered immoral.
   (A) banned   (B) boomed   (C) braced

8. Many people think of deserts as _____ regions, but many species of plants and animals have adapted to life there.
   (A) bland   (B) barren   (C) balmy

9. An autocratic ruler who serves his people well is sometimes called a _____ dictator.
   (A) blatant   (B) belligerent   (C) benevolent

10. If you _____ this little photo of the team, you will be able to see the players' faces more clearly.

    (A) bloom   (B) boom   (C) blow up

11. Robert Goddard was a _____ pioneer in the field of rocketry.

    (A) brilliant   (B) balmy   (C) brisk

12. I enjoy taking walks on _____ autumn mornings.

    (A) barren   (B) brisk   (C) blurry

13. The victim was apparently struck by a club or some other _____ object.

    (A) bland   (B) brittle   (C) blunt

14. Some geese are _____ , attacking anyone who comes near them.

    (A) beneficial   (B) biased   (C) belligerent

15. The glass factories of Toledo, Ohio, _____ after Michael Owens invented a process that could turn out bottles by the thousands.

    (A) barred   (B) bolstered   (C) boomed

VOCABULARY EXERCISE 3

calamity *n.* disaster, catastrophe

candid *adj.* honest, truthful, realistic

capable *adj.* competent, able, efficient, skillful

carve *v.* cut, sculpt, slice

casual *adj.* (1) informal, relaxed; (2) accidental, chance

categorize *v.* classify, sort

caustic *adj.* biting, harsh, sarcastic

cautious *adj.* careful, alert, prudent

celebrated *adj.* distinguished, famous, prominent

charming *adj.* delightful, lovely, attractive

cherish *v.* appreciate, esteem, treasure

choice *n.* selection, option; *adj.* exceptional, superior

cite *v.* quote, mention, refer to, list

clash *v.* argue, dispute, quarrel; *n.* argument, conflict, dispute

classify *v.* categorize

clever *adj.* smart, sharp, witty, bright

cling *v.* stick, adhere, hold

clog *v.* block, obstruct

clumsy *adj.* awkward, inept

clue *n.* hint, suggestion, sign, piece of evidence

cluster *n.* group, bunch, collection

coax *v.* persuade, urge

colossal *adj.* huge, enormous, gigantic

commence *v.* begin, initiate, start

commerce *n.* trade, business

commodity *n.* product, good, merchandise

compel *v.* force, require, coerce

competent *adj.* adept, skillful, capable, able

DIRECTIONS: Complete the following sentences by filling in the blanks with vocabulary items (A), (B), or (C), according to the context of the sentences.

1. The Red Cross and the Red Crescent provide relief in case of _____ such as floods, earthquakes, and hurricanes.

   (A) clashes   (B) commodities   (C) calamities

2. Spoken language is generally more _____ than written language.

   (A) casual   (B) capable   (C) cautious

3. When writing research papers, writers must _____ the sources they use.

   (A) coax   (B) cite   (C) clog

4. Monkeys are _____ as primates.

   (A) compelled   (B) classified   (C) cherished

5. _____ remarks can offend people.

   (A) Charming   (B) Caustic   (C) Clever

6. Sculptors use hammers and chisels to _____ statues from stone.

   (A) cherish   (B) compel   (C) carve

7. The Space Age _____ in October, 1957, when Sputnik, the first artificial satellite, was launched by the Soviet Union.

   (A) commenced   (B) coaxed   (C) cited

8. Workers must be very _____ when dealing with toxic substances.

   (A) caustic   (B) clumsy   (C) cautious

9. Some fruit such as grapes grow in _____.

   (A) clashes   (B) choices   (C) clusters

10. Microorganisms on the surface of separate particles of soil _____ together, making the particles themselves cohere.

    (A) cling   (B) clash   (C) compel

11. With the growth of international _____, the economies of the world have become more interdependent.

    (A) commodity   (B) commerce   (C) choice

12. The Lincoln Memorial in Washington, D.C., features a _____ statue of the six-teenth president created by Daniel Chester French.

    (A) colossal   (B) caustic   (C) casual

13. Corn, cotton, sugar, and many other goods are bought and sold in _____ markets.

    (A) choice   (B) commerce   (C) commodity

14. Artists of the so-called "Ashcan School" of art portrayed their subjects in a _____ fashion that concealed none of their flaws.

    (A) candid   (B) choice   (C) charming

15. Water hyacinths grow so profusely that they may _____ waterways.

    (A) clog   (B) cling   (C) carve

16. The police detectives searched the scene of the crime looking for _____.

    (A) clashes   (B) clues   (C) clusters

VOCABULARY EXERCISE 4

complement *v.* supplement, complete; *n.* supplement, addition

compliment *v.* praise, flatter, commend; *n.* praise, flattery

comprehensive *adj.* complete, thorough, exhaustive

compulsory *adj.* necessary, obligatory, mandatory

concede *v.* admit, acknowledge, recognize

concise *adj.* brief, short, abbreviated

concrete *adj.* tangible, specific, real

conflict *n.* (1) disagreement, argument; (2) battle, war

congregate *v.* assemble, gather

conspicuous *adj.* noticeable, obvious, prominent

constant *adj.* continuous, steady

contemplate *v.* think about, ponder, speculate

controversial *adj.* disputable, debatable

convenient *adj.* accessible, available, handy

conventional *adj.* standard, ordinary, normal

cope with *v.* deal with, manage, handle

copious *adj.* abundant, ample, plentiful

cordial *adj.* congenial, warm, friendly

cosmopolitan *adj.* (1) sophisticated, worldly, urbane, well traveled; (2) international, worldwide, universal

courteous *adj.* polite, refined, gracious

covert *adj.* secret, hidden

cozy *adj.* (1) comfortable, warm; (2) friendly, intimate, close

crave *v.* desire, long for, hope for

craving *n.* desire, need,

craze *n.* fad, popular (but short-lived) fashion

critical *adj.* (1) unfavorable, fault-finding, disapproving; (2) important, crucial, vital, key; (3) serious, grave, dangerous; (4) analytical, judgmental

crooked *adj.* (1) curved, twisted, zigzag; (2) dishonest, corrupt

crucial *adj.* critical, decisive, key

crude *adj.* (1) rude, impolite, vulgar; (2) unprocessed, raw, unrefined

cruel *adj.* brutal, vicious, ruthless

cryptic *adj.* secret, mysterious

curb *v.* restrict, limit, control

curious *adj.* (1) inquisitive, fascinated; (2) odd, strange, unusual

curt *adj.* abrupt, blunt, impolite

DIRECTIONS: Complete the following sentences by filling in the blanks with vocabulary items (A), (B), or (C), according to the context of the sentences.

1. The use of seat belts is _____ in many states; failure to wear them may result in fines.

   (A) constant   (B) cruel   (C) compulsory

2. Every summer, black bears from all over southern Alaska _____ along the McNeil River to fish for salmon.

   (A) crave   (B) curb   (C) congregate

3. An abstract is a _____ form of an academic article. Many journals publish abstracts so readers can decide if it is worthwhile to read the full version of the article.

   (A) concise   (B) comprehensive   (C) concrete

4. Before 1754, Britain and the North American colonies had a _____ relationship, but after that, their relationship became strained.

   (A) conspicuous   (B) cozy   (C) curt

5. Automated teller machines provide a _____ means of banking twenty-four hours a day.

   (A) cordial   (B) crooked   (C) convenient

6. Lombard Street in San Francisco, which zigzags up Nob Hill, is known as the world's most _____ street.

   (A) controversial   (B) crooked   (C) cryptic

7. Alice had such a strong _____ for her favorite kind of ice cream that she drove across town at rush hour to get some.

   (A) craze   (B) craving   (C) conflict

8. A good writer supports generalizations with _____ examples.

   (A) concrete   (B) curious   (C) crude

9. Many hunters wear orange and other bright colors in order to be as _____ as possible, and therefore avoid being shot by other hunters by mistake.

   (A) covert   (B) crucial   (C) conspicuous

10. Movie directors use music to _____ the action on the screen.

    (A) contemplate   (B) complement   (C) compliment

11. Workers in the service sector should be trained to act as _____ as possible.

    (A) crudely   (B) courteously   (C) curtly

12. Trouble-shooting is the process of identifying and _____ problems.

    (A) conceding   (B) coping with   (C) craving

13. Spies often engage in _____ activities.

    (A) covert   (B) concrete   (C) cordial

14. The Hurricane 3000 appears to be a very _____ automobile, but it has a very unusual engine.

    (A) conventional   (B) copious   (C) cryptic

15. Professor Davenport is a very _____ person. He has lived and taught in France, Italy, Japan, and Australia.

    (A) conspicuous   (B) cosmopolitan   (C) covert

16. Everyone in the audience expected the governor's speech to be very _____ of his opponent, but in fact the governor was rather complimentary.

    (A) crucial   (B) comprehensive (C) critical

17. World War I was the first major _____ of the twentieth century.

    (A) conflict   (B) craze   (C) complement

18. The Earth is ____ being bombarded by cosmic rays.

    (A) curiously   (B) conspicuously (C) constantly

VOCABULARY EXERCISE 5

damp *adj.* moist, wet, humid
daring *adj.* bold, courageous, brave
dazzling *adj.* shining, sparkling, blinding, bright
debris *n.* wreckage, ruins, broken pieces
declare *v.* announce, proclaim
defective *adj.* flawed, faulty, broken, malfunctioning
defiant *adj.* rebellious, insubordinate

delicate *adj.* exquisite, fragile

delightful *adj.* charming, attractive, enchanting

delusion *n.* illusion, dream, fantasy

demolish *v.* tear down, destroy, wreck

dense *adj.* thick, solid, packed

desist *v.* stop, cease, discontinue

detect *v.* observe, spot, sense, perceive

determine *v.* (1) decide, agree on; (2) control, shape, govern

device *n.* instrument, tool, mechanism

devise *v.* invent, plan, figure out

dim *adj.* unclear, faint, indistinct

din *n.* noise, clamor, commotion

dire *adj.* desperate, grievous, serious

discard *v.* abandon, leave behind

dismal *adj.* gloomy, depressing, dreary

disperse *v.* scatter, distribute, spread

dispute *n.* argument, quarrel, debate, clash, feud, conflict

distinct *adj.* discrete, separate, different

distinguished *adj.* celebrated, notable, famous, well known

diversity *n.* variety, assortment

divulge *v.* reveal, admit, disclose

dogged *adj.* stubborn, determined, persistent

domestic *adj.* (1) home, household, residential; (2) national

dominate *v.* rule, control, govern

dominant *adj.* strongest, main, ruling, leading

dot *v.* are located in, are scattered around; *n.* spot, point

downfall *n.* collapse, defeat

doze *v.* sleep, nap

drab *adj.* dull, plain, uninteresting, dreary

draw *v.* (1) sketch, make a picture; (2) pull, attract

drawback *n.* disadvantage, weakness, flaw

dreary *adj.* dismal, gloomy, bleak, drab

drench *v.* wet, soak

drowsy *adj.* sleepy, tired

dubious *adj.* doubtful, skeptical, uncertain

durable *adj.* lasting, enduring, resistant

dusk *n.* evening, sunset, twilight

dwell *v.* live, reside, inhabit

dwelling *n.* house, home, residence

dwindle *v.* decrease, diminish

dynamic *adj.* energetic, forceful, active, vibrant

DIRECTIONS: Complete the following sentences by filling in the blanks with vocabulary items (A), (B), or (C), according to the context of the sentences.

1. The snow on the mountaintop was _____ in the bright morning sun.

   (A) dazzling   (B) dogged   (C) dim

2. A person who has been accused of a crime cannot be forced to _____ any information that is self-incriminating.

   (A) divulge   (B) desist   (C) disperse

3. Roses have a _____ beauty.

   (A) dense   (B) delicate   (C) dire

4. An odometer is a _____ for measuring distance.

   (A) device   (B) delusion   (C) dwelling

5. The amount of open space has _____ as more and more land has been developed.

   (A) dominated   (B) dwindled   (C) dispersed

6. Hermit crabs live in shells that have been _____ by other animals.

   (A) declared   (B) divulged   (C) discarded

7. Richard Byrd and his pilot Floyd Bennett undertook a _____ flight to the North Pole in May of 1926.

   (A) daring   (B) defiant   (C) distinct

8. Steep, round hills called knobs _____ southern Indiana.

   (A) demolish   (B) dot   (C) dwell

9. Artists Nathaniel Currier and James Merritt Ives produced some _____ prints of nineteenth-century New England scenes that are prized for their charm.

   (A) dreary   (B) dim   (C) delightful

10. Economists define _____ goods as ones intended to last more than four months.

    (A) durable   (B) dense   (C) delicate

11. One cause of the American Revolution was a _____ over taxation.

    (A) drawback   (B) din   (C) dispute

12. Florida has a humid climate. Summers there are particularly hot and _____.

    (A) dynamic   (B) damp   (C) dogged

13. All bookkeeping systems have certain advantages and certain _____.

    (A) drawbacks   (B) delusions   (C) downfalls

14. A person suffering from hypothermia, the extreme loss of body heat, may first feel _____ .

    (A) dogged   (B) distinguished   (C) drowsy

15. Handwriting experts try to compare a _____ signature against at least three genuine specimens before judging its authenticity.

    (A) dubious   (B) dismal   (C) dim

16. Bats help _____ seeds in tropical forests.

    (A) devise   (B) disperse   (C) drench

17. A carburetor _____ air into an engine and mixes it with fuel.

    (A) desists   (B) draws   (C) dots

18. Most nocturnal animals become active at _____ and go to sleep at dawn.

    (A) dusk   (B) dwelling   (C) dot

19. Seoul has two airports, one for international flights and one for _____ flights.

    (A) domestic   (B) dominant   (C) distinguished

20. When drivers begin to feel _____, they should pull off the road and get some rest.

    (A) dogged   (B) dim   (C) drowsy

21. It was impossible to drive across the island after the hurricane because the roads were blocked with _____.

    (A) downfall   (B) dwelling   (C) debris

VOCABULARY EXERCISE 6

eerie *adj.* strange, odd, unusual, mysterious, frightening

elderly *adj.* old, aged

electrify *v.* excite, thrill, exhilarate

elegant *adj.* sophisticated, polished, stylish

eligible *adj.* suitable, qualified, acceptable

elude *v.* escape, avoid, evade, stay away from

eminent *adj.* celebrated, distinguished, famous

emit *v.* send out, discharge

enchanting *adj.* delightful, charming, captivating

encounter *v.* meet, find, come across; *n.* meeting, confrontation

endeavor *n.* attempt, venture

endorse *v.* authorize, approve, support

enhance *v.* intensify, amplify, strengthen

ensue *v.* follow, result

entice *v.* lure, attract, tempt

era *n.* period, age, stage

essential *adj.* critical, vital, crucial, key

esteem *v.* cherish, honor, admire

evade *v.* escape, avoid, elude

exhaustive *adj.* thorough, complete, comprehensive

exhilarating *adj.* exciting, thrilling, stimulating, electrifying

extravagant *adj.* excessive, lavish

fable *n.* mythical story, tale

fabled *adj.* legendary, mythical, famous

facet *n.* aspect, point, feature

faint *adj.* dim, pale, faded, indistinct

falter *v.* hesitate, waver

fancy *adj.* decorative, ornate, elaborate

fasten *v.* attach, secure

fatal *adj.* mortal, lethal, deadly

fatigue *v.* tire, exhaust; *n.* exhaustion, weariness

faulty *adj.* flawed, inferior

feasible *adj.* possible

fee *n.* payment, fare

feeble *adj.* weak, fragile, frail

ferocious *adj.* fierce, savage, violent

feverish *adj.* (1) running a temperature, having a fever, hot; (2) intense, busy

fiery *adj.* (1) blazing, burning; (2) passionate, fervent

fitting *adj.* suitable, proper, apt, appropriate

flagrant *adj.* blatant, obvious

flaw *n.* defect, imperfection, fault

flee *v.* escape, go away, elude

fleeting *adj.* short-lived, quick

flimsy *adj.* fragile, frail, weak, feeble

foe *n.* enemy, opponent

forage *v.* hunt, look for, search

forego *v.* abandon, give up, do without

foremost *adj.* chief, principal, leading, dominant

forge *v.* (1) create, form, make; (2) falsify, fake, copy improperly

fragment *n.* particle, piece, bit

fragrant *adj.* aromatic, scented

fraudulent *adj.* false, deceptive, deceitful

fundamental *adj.* basic, integral, elemental

fuse *v.* join, combine, unite

fusion *n.* blend, merger, union

futile *adj.* useless, pointless, vain

fuzzy *adj.* (1) furry, hairy; (2) unclear, blurry, unfocused, hazy; (3) uncertain, indefinite

DIRECTIONS: Complete the following sentences by filling in the blanks with vocabulary items (A), (B), or (C), according to the context of the sentences.

1. In 1906 much of San Francisco was destroyed by an earthquake and the fires that _____.

   (A) evaded   (B) ensued   (C) encountered

2. The writer H. P. Lovecraft wrote many _____ stories about the supernatural.

   (A) essential   (B) eerie   (C) extravagant

3. A new _____ of aviation began in 1947 when Chuck Yeager became the first pilot to fly faster than the speed of sound.

   (A) fable   (B) endeavor   (C) era

4. Vance Packard's book *The Hidden Persuaders* deals with the tactics advertisers use to _____ consumers.

   (A) endorse   (B) entice   (C) enhance

5. Riding a roller coaster is _____ experience.

   (A) an exhilarating (B) a fancy   (C) a feeble

6. Riveting is a means of _____ metal plates together with hot metal bolts.

   (A) enhancing   (B) fleeing   (C) fastening

7. In the United States, citizens are _____ to vote at the age of eighteen.

   (A) fitting   (B) elderly   (C) eligible

8. Barracudas are _____ predators, sometimes called the "tigers" of tropical waters.

   (A) faulty   (B) futile   (C) ferocious

9. Certain gases such as neon _____ light when exposed to an electrical current.

   (A) emit   (B) evade   (C) esteem

10. People make more mistakes when they are _____ than when they are fresh.

    (A) exhaustive   (B) eminent   (C) fatigued

11. A _____ in a jewel makes it less valuable.

    (A) fragment   (B) facet   (C) flaw

12. Honeysuckle is a plant that has _____ white or yellowish blossoms.

    (A) elderly   (B) fragrant   (C) fiery

13. Some insects can detect the ultrasonic pulses that bats use to detect their prey and can therefore _____ the bats.

    (A) evade   (B) forego   (C) electrify

14. The snowy egret builds _____ nest from a few twigs and pieces of grass.

    (A) a faint   (B) an extravagant (C) a flimsy

15. When lightning strikes sand, the intense heat sometimes _____ the grains of sand into thin glass tubes called fulgurites.

    (A) falters   (B) fastens   (C) fuses

16. A common carrier is a company that provides public transportation for a _____ .

    (A) fee   (B) fable   (C) flaw

17. Someone stole Robert's checkbook from his car and then _____ his name on his checks.

    (A) forged   (B) fastened   (C) evaded

18. The escaped prisoner was able to _____ police for several weeks before he was finally caught.

    (A) elude   (B) forego   (C) falter

19. During the hunter-gatherer stage of human development, people had to _____ for their food.

    (A) forage   (B) fuse   (C) forge

20. I didn't focus the camera properly, so this photo of you is a little _____.

    (A) futile   (B) fuzzy   (C) feverish

VOCABULARY EXERCISE 7

gag *n.* (1) joke, trick; (2) something that prevents someone from speaking; *v.* (1) choke for a moment, feel momentarily sick; (2) prevent someone from speaking

gala *adj.* festive, happy, joyous

gap *n.* break, breach, opening

garrulous *adj.* talkative, chatty

gaudy *adj.* showy, flashy, conspicuous

genial *adj.* pleasant, cordial, agreeable

gentle *adj.* mild, kind, considerate, nice

genuine *adj.* authentic, real, valid

glitter *v.* sparkle, shine, glisten

glory *n.* grandeur, majesty, fame

gorgeous *adj.* attractive, beautiful

grade *n.* quality, value, worth

graphic *adj.* (1) related to visual images; (2) clear, explicit, vivid

grasp *v.* (1) grab, seize, grip; (2) understand

grave *adj.* serious, grievous

gregarious *adj.* sociable, friendly

grim *adj.* severe, dreary, bleak, somber

grip *v.* hold, grasp, seize; *n.* hold, grasp, possession

grueling *adj.* exhausting, difficult, arduous

gullible *adj.* innocent, naive, trusting, credulous

hamper *v.* delay, obstruct, hinder, block

handful *n.* not many, only a few

haphazard *adj.* random, chance, aimless, unplanned

hardly *adv.* barely, scarcely

hardship *n.* difficulty, trouble

harm *v.* injure, damage

harmful *adj.* hurtful, destructive

harmony *n.* accord, agreement, peace

harmonious *adj.* agreeable, friendly, peaceful

harness *v.* control, utilize

harsh *adj.* severe, rough, strict

hasty *adj.* quick, rushed, hurried

hazardous *adj.* dangerous, risky

hazy *adj.* (1) misty, cloudy, foggy; (2) unclear, fuzzy, obscure

heed *v.* obey, listen to, mind, follow

hinder *v.* block, obstruct, hamper

hitherto *adv.* up to now, previously, so far

hoist *v.* lift, raise, pick up

hue *n.* color, tint, shade

huge *adj.* enormous, giant, colossal, immense

hurl *v.* pitch, throw, fling

DIRECTIONS: Complete the following sentences by filling in the blanks with vocabulary items (A), (B), or (C), according to the context of the sentences.

1. During the construction of skyscrapers, cranes are used to _____ building materials to the upper floors.

   (A) hurl   (B) harness   (C) hoist

2. The 26-mile long Boston Marathon is a _____ foot race.

   (A) gorgeous   (B) grueling   (C) hasty

3. Dams can _____ the power of rivers, but they may also destroy their beauty.

   (A) heed   (B) harness   (C) hurl

4. The more facets a diamond has, the more it _____ .

   (A) glitters   (B) harms   (C) hinders

5. Many people celebrate the New Year with _____ parties.

   (A) gala   (B) grueling   (C) haphazard

6. Think it over for a while; don't make a _____ decision.

   (A) genuine   (B) gullible   (C) hasty

7. Bad weather _____ the rescue crews trying to locate the life rafts.

   (A) hampered   (B) grasped   (C) harnessed

8. Gorillas look ferocious but are actually quite _____ creatures.

   (A) hazardous   (B) gentle   (C) gorgeous

9. I just got an e-mail from a stranger asking me to supply details about my bank account. I can't believe that some people are _____ enough to respond to that kind of request.

   (A) garrulous   (B) grim   (C) gullible

10. Commercial fishing is one of the most _____ occupations.

    (A) hazardous   (B) genial   (C) haphazard

11. At Harper's Ferry, West Virginia, the Potomac River has cut a picturesque _____ through the Blue Ridge Mountains.

    (A) grip   (B) gag   (C) gap

12. Wool from different sheep, or even wool from different parts of the same sheep, is not all of the same _____ .

    (A) harmony   (B) hardship   (C) grade

13. "Attack ads" are political commercials that say negative things about a candidate's political _____.

    (A) foes   (B) gaps   (C) hues

14. It was hard to see the mountains today because the sky was so _____.

    (A) gaudy   (B) hazy   (C) grueling

15. The interior of Alaska has brief summers and long, _____ winters.

    (A) grave   (B) harsh   (C) huge

16. Animals that live in herds or packs are considered _____.

    (A) hasty   (B) gregarious   (C) gullible

VOCABULARY EXERCISE 8

idea *n.* concept, notion, thought

ideal *n.* model, standard; *adj.* perfect, model

idle *adj.* (1) inactive, unused, inert; (2) lazy

illusion *n.* (1) fantasy, delusion; (2) an erroneous perception or concept

illustration *n.* picture, drawing, description

imaginary *adj.* unreal, fantastic, fictitious

imaginative *adj.* creative, original, clever

immense *adj.* huge, enormous, massive, colossal

impair *v.* damage, injure, spoil, interfere with

impartial *adj.* fair, unbiased, neutral

implement *v.* realize, achieve, put into practice, execute; *n.* tool, utensil, instrument

incessant *adj.* constant, ceaseless, continuous

increment *n.* increase, amount

incursion *n.* raid, attack, small-scale invasion

indifferent *adj.* uncaring, apathetic, unconcerned

indigenous *adj.* native

indispensable *adj.* necessary, essential, vital, critical

indistinct *adj.* unclear, blurry, hazy, fuzzy

induce *v.* persuade, convince, coax

inept *adj.* incompetent, awkward, clumsy

inexorable *adj.* unstoppable

infamous *adj.* notorious, shocking

infinite *adj.* limitless, endless, boundless

infinitesimal *adj.* tiny, minute, minuscule

ingenious *adj.* brilliant, imaginative, clever, inventive

ingenuous *adj.* naive, trusting, gullible

inhabit *v.* live, dwell, reside, populate

inhibit *v.* control, limit, restrain

initial *adj.* original, first, beginning, introductory

innate *adj.* natural, inborn

innocuous *adj.* harmless, inoffensive

intense *adj.* powerful, heightened, concentrated

intricate *adj.* complicated, complex, involved

involved *adj.* complicated, intricate, complex, elaborate

irate *adj.* angry, annoyed, upset

jagged *adj.* rough, rugged, uneven, irregular

jeopardy *n.* danger, hazard, risk, threat

jolly *adj.* joyful, happy, cheerful

jolt *v.* shock, jar, shake up, surprise; *n.* blow, surprise, shock

keen *adj.* (1) sharp; (2) shrewd, clever, bright; (3) eager, enthusiastic

key *adj.* crucial, important, critical

knack *n.* skill, ability, aptitude, talent

DIRECTIONS: Complete the following sentences by filling in the blanks with vocabulary items (A), (B), or (C), according to the context of the sentences.

1. Many people feel that Hawaii has an almost _____ climate.
   (A) idle   (B) impartial   (C) ideal

2. A plow is a farm _____ used to break up soil and prepare the land for planting.
   (A) increment   (B) knack   (C) implement

3. A laser uses a synthetic ruby to concentrate light into an extremely _____ high-energy beam.
   (A) intense   (B) indistinct   (C) incessant

4. Jesse James was an _____ outlaw, well known as a bank robber and gun fighter.
   (A) inept   (B) ingenuous   (C) infamous

5. Antibiotics _____ the growth of bacteria.
   (A) inhabit   (B) jolt   (C) inhibit

6. Line A appears to be slightly longer than line B, but this is an optical _____.
   (A) illusion   (B) incursion   (C) illustration

7. Stockholders may be too _____ to vote in corporate elections, so they let management vote for them by proxy.
   (A) infamous   (B) indifferent   (C) ingenious

8. The states of Ohio, Michigan, Pennsylvania, and Florida are _____ states for any candidate in a presidential election.
   (A) initial   (B) impartial   (C) key

9. A virus is so _____ that it can be seen only with an electron microscope.
   (A) infinite   (B) intricate   (C) infinitesimal

10. The _____ character Falstaff is one of Shakespeare's finest comic creations.
    (A) keen   (B) jolly   (C) irate

11. Anyone can learn basic cooking skills; you don't need a special _____ .
    (A) knack   (B) idea   (C) implement

12. Alcohol _____ one's ability to drive.
    (A) jolts   (B) impairs   (C) induces

13. The _____ people of New Zealand are known as the Maori.

(A) indigenous (B) ingenuous (C) innate

14. The rhinoceros has a poor sense of sight but _____ sense of smell.

(A) an immense (B) an inept (C) a keen

15. The equator is _____ line running around the center of the earth.

(A) an imaginative (B) a jagged (C) an imaginary

16. A glacier's progress is slow but _____.

(A) indispensable (B) inexorable (C) involved

17. The _____ garter snake, often spotted in yards, parks, and gardens, is sometimes mistaken for a venomous snake.

(A) irate (B) ingenuous (C) innocuous

Vocabulary Exercise 9

lack *v.* need, require, not have; *n.* shortage, absence, scarcity

lag *v.* fall behind, go slowly

lavish *adj.* luxurious, plentiful, abundant

lax *adj.* careless, negligent, loose

legendary *adj.* mythical, fabled, famous

legitimate *adj.* proper, authentic, valid

leisure *n.* free time, spare time, nonworking hours

leisurely *adj.* slow, relaxed

lethargic *adj.* slow, listless, sluggish, lazy

liable *adj.* (legally) responsible

likely *adj.* probable, plausible, credible

linger *v.* remain, stay

link *v.* join, connect, fasten, bind; *n.* connection, tie

long *v.* desire, wish for

lucid *adj.* clear, plain, understandable

lucrative *adj.* profitable, money-making

lull *v.* soothe, calm, quiet; *n.* pause, break

luminous *adj.* bright, shining, glowing

lure *v.* attract, tempt, entice

lurid *adj.* shocking, sensational, graphic

lurk *v.* prowl, sneak, hide

luster *n.* shine, radiance, brightness

luxurious *adj.* lavish, elegant, plush

magnificent *adj.* majestic, impressive, splendid

magnitude *n.* size, extent, amount

mandatory *adj.* necessary, obligatory, compulsory

manipulate *v.* control, influence

mar *v.* damage, ruin, deface, spoil

massive *adj.* huge, giant, colossal, immense

memorable *adj.* unforgettable, impressive, striking

mend *v.* fix, repair

mild *adj.* gentle, moderate, calm, temperate

mingle *v.* blend, combine, mix

minute *adj.* tiny, minuscule, infinitesimal

mist *n.* fog, haze

monitor *v.* observe, watch

moral *adj.* honorable, ethical

morale *n.* spirit, confidence, attitude

mourn *v.* lament, cry, show sorrow

murky *adj.* unclear, cloudy, foggy, dark

mushroom *v.* expand rapidly, grow quickly

mysterious *adj.* puzzling, strange

mythical *adj.* legendary, imaginary, fictional

DIRECTIONS: Complete the following sentences by filling in the blanks with vocabulary items (A), (B), or (C), according to the context of the sentences.

1. Medieval books called bestiaries contained pictures and descriptions of _____ creatures such as unicorns and dragons.

   (A) mandatory   (B) lax   (C) mythical

2. In Colonial times, fishing off the coast of New England was a _____ occupation.

   (A) luxurious   (B) lethargic   (C) lucrative

3. Parents often sing to children to _____ them to sleep.

   (A) mourn   (B) lure   (C) lull

4. Julius Caesar is known not only for his military and political skills but also for his _____, informative writing.

   (A) lucid   (B) lurid   (C) lavish

5. A cobbler _____ damaged shoes.

   (A) mars   (B) mends   (C) lacks

6. One of the _____ exhibits of Impressionist art is found at the Art Institute of Chicago.

   (A) mildest   (B) most memorable   (C) most lucid

7. Quarks are _____ particles that are believed to be the fundamental unit of matter.

   (A) massive   (B) minute   (C) mythical

8. Paperback novels in the 1940's and 1950's often had _____ covers to attract readers' attention, even when their content was quite mild.

   (A) lurid   (B) murky   (C) legitimate

9. One problem caused by a rising crime rate is a _____ of space in prisons.

   (A) lag   (B) lack   (C) link

10. The _____ lumberjack Paul Bunyan and his giant blue ox Babe are two of the most famous figures in American folklore.

    (A) legendary   (B) moral   (C) likely

11. The transcontinental railroad, _____ the East Coast with the West Coast, was completed at Promontory Point, Utah, in 1869.

    (A) linking   (B) monitoring   (C) mingling

12. All over the world, urban populations have _____ in recent decades.

    (A) mushroomed   (B) lurked   (C) lingered

13. Compared to basketball or soccer, baseball is played at a _____ pace.

    (A) memorable   (B) leisurely   (C) luxurious

VOCABULARY EXERCISE 10

negligible *adj.* unimportant, trivial

nightmarish *adj.* frightening, terrifying, horrible

nimble *adj.* graceful, agile

notable *adj.* remarkable, conspicuous, striking

notify *v.* inform, tell

notion *n.* idea, concept, thought

notorious *adj.* infamous, disreputable

novel *adj.* new, innovative

objective *adj.* fair, impartial, unbiased, neutral; *n.* goal, purpose, aim

oblong *adj.* oval

obscure *adj.* unfamiliar, ambiguous, little-known

obsolete *adj.* antiquated, out of date, outmoded

odd *adj.* strange, unusual, peculiar, curious

offspring *n.* young, children, descendants

ominous *adj.* threatening, menacing, dangerous

opulent *adj.* luxurious, plush, affluent

ornamental *adj.* ornate, decorative, elaborate, showy

outgoing *adj.* (1) open, friendly; (2) departing, leaving

outlook *n.* (1) opinion, view; (2) prospect, forecast

outstanding *adj.* excellent, exceptional, notable, well known

overall *adj.* general, comprehensive

overcast *adj.* cloudy, gloomy

overcome *v.* subdue, defeat, overwhelm

overlook *v.* ignore, disregard, neglect

oversee *v.* supervise, manage, direct

oversight *n.* error, mistake, omission

overt *adj.* open, obvious, conspicuous

overtake *v.* catch up with, reach

overwhelm *v.* (1) astonish, astound, shock; (2) conquer, defeat, overcome, overpower

DIRECTIONS: Complete the following sentences by filling in the blanks with vocabulary items (A), (B), or (C), according to the context of the sentences.

1. The black clouds of a gathering thunderstorm look quite _____.

   (A) ominous   (B) negligible   (C) outgoing

2. Pulitzer Prizes are awarded to _____ journalists, novelists, poets, and other writers.

   (A) objective   (B) outstanding   (C) notorious

3. An _____ plant is cultivated chiefly for its beauty.

   (A) opulent   (B) obscure   (C) ornamental

4. Franklin D. Roosevelt was able to _____ his physical handicaps; he didn't permit them to interfere with his living a vigorous life.

   (A) oversee   (B) overcome   (C) overtake

5. The poetry of T. S. Eliot is sometimes difficult to understand because it contains so many _____ references.

   (A) notable   (B) obscure   (C) objective

6. The Bessemer process was once the most common method of making steel, but today this process is considered _____.

   (A) odd   (B) novel   (C) obsolete

7. Dolley Payne Madison, the wife of President James Madison, impressed the city of Washington with her stylish clothes and warm, _____ manner.

   (A) nimble   (B) ominous   (C) outgoing

8. The town planning commission said that their financial _____ for the next fiscal year was optimistic; they expect increased tax revenues.

   (A) outlook   (B) oversight   (C) notion

9. The new play was so successful that the demand for tickets was _____ .

    (A) odd   (B) overwhelming   (C) negligible

10. A book's table of contents provides readers with an _____ idea of what the book is about.

    (A) outgoing   (B) overt   (C) overall

11. Snails go out to feed only on rainy or ____ days.

    (A) obscure   (B) overcast   (C) overt

12. Although the accident appeared serious, only a _____ amount of damage was actually done.

    (A) novel   (B) notable   (C) negligible

13. The Austrian writer Franz Kafka wrote a _____ story called "Metamorphosis" in which a man turns into a gigantic insect.

    (A) nightmarish   (B) nimble   (C) outgoing

14. I made a few errors on my essay exam, but fortunately, my teacher decided to _____ them.

    (A) oversee   (B) overwhelm   (C) overlook

VOCABULARY EXERCISE 11

pace *n.* rate, speed

painstaking *adj.* careful, conscientious, thorough

pale *adj.* white, colorless, faded

paltry *adj.* unimportant, minor, trivial

paramount *adj.* chief, top, vital, supreme

particle *n.* piece, bit, fragment

path *n.* trail, track, way, route

peculiar *adj.* (1) strange, odd, puzzling; (2) distinctive, characteristic, unique, special

penetrate *v.* enter, go through, go into, pierce, puncture

perceive *v.* observe, sense, notice

peril *n.* danger, hazard, risk, threat

perilous *adj.* dangerous, risky, ominous, hazardous

perpetual *adj.* constant, endless, eternal

perplexing *adj.* puzzling, mystifying, confusing

pierce *v.* penetrate, puncture, stab, go into

pivotal *adj.* important, key, crucial

plague *n.* epidemic; *v.* trouble, bother, harass, vex

plausible *adj.* likely, credible, believable

plead *v.* appeal, beg

plush *adj.* luxurious, opulent, rich, elegant

ponder *v.* consider, think about, reflect on

portion *n.* share, part, section, segment

postpone *v.* delay, put off, defer

potent *adj.* strong, powerful, effective

pounce *v.* jump, leap, spring

precious *adj.* expensive, costly, rare, desirable

precise *adj.* accurate, exact, definite

premier *adj.* (1) first, opening, earliest, initial; (2) chief, leading, foremost

prescribed *adj.* arranged, set, agreed on

pressing *adj.* urgent, crucial, compelling

pretext *n.* excuse, pretense, justification

prevail *v.* succeed, win, triumph

prevalent *adj.* common, widespread, popular

prior *adj.* earlier, preceding, former

probe *v.* investigate, inquire into

procure *v.* obtain, acquire, secure

profound *adj.* important, significant, deep

profuse *adj.* plentiful, abundant, copious

prompt *adj.* punctual, timely

prosper *v.* flourish, thrive, succeed

provoke *v.* (1) irritate, anger, annoy; (2) cause, trigger

prudent *adj.* careful, sensible, cautious

pulverize *v.* crush, grind, powder

pungent *adj.* bitter, harsh, biting, sharp

pursue *v.* chase, follow, seek

puzzling *adj.* mystifying, confusing, baffling

DIRECTIONS: Complete the following sentences by filling in the blanks with vocabulary items (A), (B), or (C), according to the context of the sentences.

1. Turquoise is not valuable enough to be classified as a _____ stone.

   (A) perpetual   (B) pale   (C) precious

2. The invention of the lever was of_____ importance.

   (A) potent   (B) profound   (C) profuse

3. Hospitals define *urgent care* as medical care given to somewhat less_____ medical problems than emergency care.

   (A) perplexing   (B) pressing   (C) prudent

4. Tool makers must have the ability to work very _____ in order to meet exact specifications.

   (A) precisely   (B) profoundly   (C) plausibly

5. _____ of dust in the air may trigger allergies in some people.

   (A) Portions   (B) Pretexts   (C) Particles

6. When a tiger spots its prey, it crouches down and then_____ .

   (A) pleads   (B) ponders   (C) pounces

7. X-rays cannot _____ lead.

   (A) provoke   (B) penetrate   (C) pursue

8. Sherlock Holmes, a fictional detective, solved many _____ crimes.

   (A) puzzling   (B) prevalent   (C) prompt

9. Mallows are plants that grow_____ in prairies, woods, and marshes.

   (A) profusely   (B) profoundly   (C) preciously

10. Certain spices give foods a _____ taste.

    (A) painstaking   (B) pungent   (C) pale

11. Trade with Britain and the West Indies allowed colonial seaports such as Boston and Norfolk to_____ .

    (A) postpone   (B) provoke   (C) prosper

12. Alicia doesn't like to go camping when she travels. She'd rather stay at a _____ five-star hotel.

    (A) plush   (B) perilous   (C) profuse

13. A _____ investor never takes unnecessary financial risks.

    (A) perplexing   (B) prudent   (C) premier

14. To make cement, limestone is first_____ , and the resulting powder is then mixed with clay and water at high temperatures.

    (A) probed   (B) pulverized   (C) pierced

15. Outbreaks of cholera and other diseases were _____ in mining camps during the California gold rush because of the crowded, unsanitary conditions.

    (A) peculiar   (B) plausible   (C) prevalent

16. Only a small _____ of Carlsbad Cavern in New Mexico has been lighted and opened to visitors.

    (A) peril   (B) portion   (C) pace

17. Acting teacher Stella Adler played a _____ role in the development of the Method school of acting.

    (A) pivotal   (B) precious   (C) plush

18. It is of _____ importance that you finish this project by the deadline.

    (A) prescribed   (B) prevalent   (C) paramount

VOCABULARY EXERCISE 12

quaint *adj.* charming in an old fashioned way, picturesque, curious

quake *v.* shiver, shake, tremble

quandary *n.* problem, dilemma, predicament

quarrel *n.* argument, dispute, disagreement

quest *n.* search, journey, venture

radiant *adj.* bright, shiny, glowing

ragged *adj.* torn, tattered, worn

range *v.* (1) extend, vary, fluctuate; (2) roam, wander; *n.* scope, extent, spectrum

rash *adj.* thoughtless, careless, reckless

raw *adj.* (1) uncooked; (2) unprocessed, unrefined, crude; (3) sore, tender

raze *v.* demolish, level, knock down

real estate *n.* property such as buildings and land

rebuke *v.* scold, reprimand

recede *v.* retreat, go back, subside, withdraw

reckless *adj.* careless, rash

recollect *v.* recall, remember

recount *v.* narrate, tell

refine *v.* improve, process, purify

refuge *n.* shelter, haven, retreat

refuse *v.* reject, turn down, tell someone "no"; *n.* waste, garbage, trash

rehearse *v.* practice, train, go over

reliable *adj.* dependable, trustworthy

relish *v.* enjoy, savor, like

remarkable *adj.* incredible, amazing, extraordinary, noteworthy

remedy *n.* treatment, cure

remnant *n.* remainder, balance, fragment

remote *adj.* isolated, distant

renowned *adj.* famous, celebrated, notable

resent *v.* dislike, take offense at

retract *v.* withdraw, pull back

riddle *n.* puzzle, mystery

rigid *adj.* (1) stiff, unbending; (2) harsh, severe, strict

rip *v.* tear, cut, slash

ripe *adj.* mature, developed

risky *adj.* dangerous, hazardous, treacherous

roam *v.* travel, wander, range

rough *adj.* (1) uneven, jagged, rugged; (2) difficult; (3) impolite

route *n.* way, course, path, road

routine *n.* custom, habit, daily schedule; *adj.* ordinary, typical, regular, normal

rudimentary *adj.* elementary, fundamental, primitive

rugged *adj.* (1) jagged, rough, uneven; (2) strong, sturdy

rumor *n.* gossip, story

rural *adj.* agricultural

ruthless *adj.* cruel, brutal, vicious

DIRECTIONS: Complete the following sentences by filling in the blanks with vocabulary items (A), (B), or (C), according to the context of the sentences.

1. Motorists can be fined for driving _____ .
   (A) recklessly   (B) reliably   (C) rigidly

2. Musicians have to _____ before performing.
   (A) rehearse   (B) resent   (C) recollect

3. At the end of the Ice Ages, most glaciers began to _____ .
   (A) quake   (B) raze   (C) recede

4. Big Sur, a wild section of California's coastline, is known for its _____ beauty.
   (A) ragged   (B) rash   (C) rugged

5. Wetlands provide _____ for many species of birds, reptiles, mammals, and amphibians.
   (A) riddles   (B) refuge   (C) rumors

6. Wrecking balls are used to _____ buildings.
   (A) recede   (B) quake   (C) raze

7. The northernmost section of the Rocky Mountains, the Brooks Range, is located in a _____ section of Alaska.
   (A) remote   (B) ruthless   (C) routine

8. Dogs can hear a greater _____ of sounds than humans.
   (A) remnant   (B) quandary   (C) range

9. Visitors to Vermont delight in the beautiful scenery and picturesque villages and enjoy staying in some of the _____ country inns there.
   (A) rough   (B) ragged   (C) quaint

10. _____ materials have less economic value than processed materials.
    (A) Raw   (B) Rash   (C) Renowned

READING

11. Many legends and myths are stories about _____ , in which the hero must undertake a dangerous journey to find some significant or precious object.

    (A) quarrel   (B) quandaries   (C) quests

12. As we were walking along the beach, we saw a _____ beautiful sunset.

    (A) remarkably   (B) recklessly   (C) relentlessly

13. The Tennessee Valley Authority helped bring cheap electricity to farmers in the _____ South.

    (A) reliable   (B) rural   (C) rugged

14. Bobsledding is a fast, _____ sport.

    (A) risky   (B) quaint   (C) ripe

15. Quite logically, early roads in North America tended to follow the _____ of rivers.

    (A) remedies   (B) routes   (C) quandaries

16. Alex Haley's novel *Roots* _____ the history of an American family beginning in the mid-1700's in Africa.

    (A) recounts   (B) refines   (C) relishes

VOCABULARY EXERCISE 13

salvage *v.* save, rescue, recover, retrieve

savage *adj.* fierce, wild, aggressive, ferocious, belligerent

scale *v.* climb; *n.* (1) range, spectrum; (2) proportion

scarce *adj.* rare, sparse

scatter *v.* disperse, spread

scent *n.* aroma, fragrance, odor, smell

scorn *n.* mockery, derision, contempt, ridicule

scrap *v.* abandon, get rid of; *n.* piece, fragment

seasoned *adj.* experienced, veteran

secluded *adj.* hidden, isolated, secret

secrete *v.* produce (a liquid), squirt

sensational *adj.* thrilling, exciting, shocking

serene *adj.* quiet, peaceful, calm, tranquil

sever *v.* cut, slice off

severe *adj.* (1) harsh, strict, austere; (2) undecorated, plain

shatter *v.* break, smash, fragment

sheer *adj.* (1) steep, sharp, abrupt; (2) transparent, thin, filmy

shimmer *v.* shine, glow, glisten, gleam

shred *v.* rip up, tear up

shrewd *adj.* clever, sly

shrill *adj.* piercing, high-pitched

shun *v.* avoid, stay away from

shy *adj.* timid, reserved, easily frightened

significant *adj.* important, vital, major

signify *v.* symbolize, stand for, indicate, represent

simulate *v.* imitate, reproduce

sketch *v.* draw; *n.* drawing, picture, diagram

slender *adj.* thin, slim, slight; (2) unlikely

slim *adj.* (1) slender, thin, slight, trim; (2) unlikely

slice *n.* thin piece; *v.* cut, carve, divide

sluggish *adj.* slow, listless, lazy, lethargic

sly *adj.* cunning, clever, shrewd

soak *v.* wet, drench, saturate

solace *n.* comfort, consolation, relief

solitary *adj.* alone, single, solo, isolated

somber *adj.* serious, grave, solemn

sort *v.* classify, categorize; *n.* type, kind, variety

sound *adj.* safe, solid, secure; *n.* noise

DIRECTIONS: Complete the following sentences by filling in the blanks with vocabulary items (A), (B), or (C), according to the context of the sentences.

1. One of the most popular peaks for mountain climbers to _____ is El Capitan in Yosemite National Park.

   (A) scale   (B) soak   (C) shun

2. Gray foxes are not particularly rare animals, but they are seldom seen because they are so _____.

   (A) sluggish   (B) somber   (C) shy

3. _____ workers are more valuable to employers than beginners.

   (A) Shrill   (B) Seasoned   (C) Sluggish

4. The Shakers were a strict religious group that _____worldly pleasure.

   (A) scrapped   (B) shunned   (C) sketched

5. The city of Denver's plan to build a subway system was _____ in the 1970's.

   (A) scattered   (B) sorted   (C) scrapped

6. Even after a ship has sunk, its cargo can often be _____ .

   (A) severed   (B) shattered   (C) salvaged

7. Some economists believe that the best way to get a _____ economy moving again is to cut taxes.

   (A) sensational   (B) sluggish   (C) shrewd

8. Government bonds and blue-chip stocks are _____ investments.

   (A) sound   (B) shy   (C) scarce

9. If a person's spinal cord is _____, paralysis results.

   (A) soaked   (B) severed   (C) salvaged

10. Silk is a _____ fabric.

    (A) sheer   (B) shrewd   (C) shrill

11. A green flag _____ the beginning of an automobile race.

    (A) scatters   (B) simulates   (C) signifies

12. The raw materials of paper—wood pulp, rags, or old paper—must be _____ and cleaned before the paper-making process begins.

    (A) severed   (B) shredded   (C) sketched

13. A home aquarium should _____ a fish's natural habitat as closely as possible.

    (A) soak   (B) simulate   (C) salvage

14. Foxfire is an eerie, _____ blue light, often seen in swamps, that is caused by the bioluminescence of a fungus that lives on some decaying plants.

    (A) serene   (B) somber   (C) shimmering

15. He put ham, turkey, tomato, lettuce, mustard, and a thick _____ of onion on his sandwich.

    (A) scent   (B) slice   (C) scrap

VOCABULARY EXERCISE 14

sow *v.* plant

span *v.* extend, bridge, connect; *n.* length, extent, range

spawn *v.* generate, create, produce; *n.* offspring, descendants

specific *adj.* definite, particular, exact

specimen *n.* example, sample

spectacular *adj.* dramatic, sensational, impressive

spell *n.* interval, period, time

spirited *adj.* lively, energetic, vigorous

splendid *adj.* excellent, superb, wonderful

spoil *v.* (1) ruin, mar; (2) decay, deteriorate, decompose, rot

spot *v.* locate, find, see, identify; *n.* (1) location, site; (2) mark, stain, speck

spur *v.* stimulate, impel, encourage, provoke; *n.* inducement, stimulus

stable *adj.* steady, secure, stationary, fixed

stage *v.* present, put on; *n.* grade, step, level, phase

stain *v.* color, tint, discolor, dye; *n.* spot, mark, blemish

stale *adj.* (1) old, dry; (2) dull, trite, uninteresting

stall *v.* halt, delay, put off

standard *n.* pattern, ideal, norm; *adj.* normal, typical, ordinary, regular, stock

stately *adj.* dignified, grand, magnificent, elegant

steep *adj.* sheer, perpendicular

stern *adj.* firm, severe, strict, harsh

stock *n.* (1) supply, collection; (2) goods, merchandise; *v.* have a supply of, carry; *adj.* standard, routine, ordinary, typical

stray *adj.* wandering, undirected, lost, uncontrolled

strenuous *adj.* difficult, arduous

strident *adj.* loud, insistent

strife *n.* conflict, dispute, struggle

striking *adj.* prominent, remarkable, unusual, conspicuous, noteworthy, dramatic

strive *v.* attempt, try

struggle *v.* fight, argue, dispute; *n.* conflict, strife, battle, effort

stubborn *adj.* rigid, uncompromising, obstinate

stunning *adj.* (1) surprising, shocking; (2) attractive, beautiful

sturdy *adj.* strong, rugged, well built

subsequent *adj.* later, succeeding, following, ensuing

subtle *adj.* indirect, suggestive, implied

suitable *adj.* appropriate, correct, apt

summit *n.* peak, apex, zenith

sundry *adj.* miscellaneous, diverse, various

superb *adj.* excellent, splendid

supplant *v.* replace, substitute for

supple *adj.* pliable, flexible, bendable

sway *v.* (1) wave, rock, swing, bend; (2) persuade, influence

sweeping *adj.* complete, exhaustive, general, comprehensive

swift *adj.* fast, quick, rapid

swivel *v.* rotate, spin, turn

symbolize *v.* represent, stand for

DIRECTIONS: Complete the following sentences by filling in the blanks with vocabulary items (A), (B), or (C), according to the context of the sentences.

1. High-pressure cells may bring brief warm _____ even in the middle of winter.

   (A) struggles   (B) spells   (C) spans

2. The _____ cliffs of the Na Pali coast on the Hawaiian island of Kauai rise over 4,000 feet from the sea.

   (A) swift   (B) steep   (C) subtle

3. The process of refining oil involves a number of _____ .

   (A) specimens   (B) spots   (C) stages

4. In high winds, skyscrapers will _____ slightly.

   (A) swivel   (B) sway   (C) stall

5. Severe thunderstorms may _____ tornadoes.

   (A) spoil   (B) strive   (C) spawn

6. The snow-covered _____ of Mount Hood is the highest point in the state of Oregon.

   (A) spur   (B) summit   (C) span

7. D. W. Griffith was the first director of _____ films. These were movies made on a colossal scale.

   (A) stately   (B) suitable   (C) spectacular

8. Cheetahs are the _____ of all land mammals, with top speeds of up to 70 miles per hour.

   (A) stalest   (B) subtlest   (C) swiftest

9. Salt can be used to keep meat from _____ .

   (A) struggling   (B) spoiling   (C) stalling

10. Because they must be able to break a path through icebound waters, icebreakers have to be very _____ boats.

    (A) stately   (B) sturdy   (C) supple

11. According to studies, most people who divorce _____ remarry.

    (A) specifically   (B) subsequently   (C) stubbornly

12. A roadbed supplies a _____ base for a highway.

    (A) stable   (B) stock   (C) sweeping

13. Every year, the Folger Shakespeare Library in Washington, D.C., _____ a number of plays.

    (A) stalls   (B) stages   (C) spans

14. Farmers sometimes _____ crops such as timothy or clover and then plow them under the soil to increase its fertility.

    (A) supplant   (B) spur   (C) sow

15. The geographical center of the North American continent is a _____ near Drake, North Dakota.

    (A) spot   (B) stage   (C) summit

16. Many medical tests require a blood _____ .

    (A) spell   (B) specimen   (C) stain

17. Because of their pale color, ghost crabs blend in with the sand and are hard
    to _____ .
    (A) spur   (B) spawn   (C) spot

18. The Virginia reel is a _____ dance mainly performed by children.
    (A) stale   (B) spirited   (C) supple

19. A _____ piano has eighty-eight keys.
    (A) standard   (B) spectacular   (C) sundry

20. I found the _____ tone of his remarks particularly annoying.
    (A) stunning   (B) striking   (C) strident

21. A general store is a small store, often in a rural area, that sells food, clothing,
    supplies, and other _____ goods.
    (A) stale   (B) sundry   (C) sturdy

VOCABULARY EXERCISE 15

tact *n.* diplomacy, discretion, poise

tale *n.* story, legend

tame *v.* domesticate, master; *adj.* docile, domesticated, gentle

tamper (with) *v.* interfere (with)

tangled *adj.* knotted, twisted

tart *adj.* sour, tangy, piquant

taunt *v.* insult, mock, torment

tedious *adj.* boring, dull, tiresome

telling *adj.* effective, convincing, forceful

temperate *adj.* mild, moderate

tempting *adj.* alluring, attractive, enticing

tender *adj.* (1) delicate, soft; (2) gentle, loving; (3) sore, painful, raw

terminate *v.* end, finish, cease

thaw *v.* melt, warm up

thorough *adj.* complete, comprehensive

thoroughfare *n.* avenue, street

thrifty *adj.* economical, inexpensive

thrilling *adj.* exciting, stimulating, stirring, electrifying

thrive *v.* prosper, flourish

thwart *v.* prevent, impede, obstruct

tidings *n.* news, message

tilt *v.* incline, slope

timid *adj.* fearful, shy, retiring

tint *n.* color, hue, shade, tone; *v.* color, stain, dye

tiresome *adj.* tedious, dull, boring

toil *v.* labor, work; *n.* exertion, labor, work

tolerant *adj.* patient, impartial, open-minded

topple *v.* knock over, knock down, bring down, uproot

torment *v.* taunt, abuse, bully

torrent *n.* flood, deluge

tough *adj.* durable, strong

tow *v.* haul, draw, pull, drag

toxic *adj.* poisonous, noxious

trait *n.* characteristic, feature, quality

tranquil *adj.* quiet, peaceful, relaxing

transient *adj.* temporary, momentary, passing

transparent *adj.* clear, see-through

treacherous *adj.* dangerous, hazardous

trickle *n.* drip, leak

triumph *n.* victory, success, achievement; *v.* win, succeed, prevail

trivial *adj.* unimportant, minor

trying *adj.* demanding, difficult, troublesome

tug *v.* pull, draw; *n.* pull

twilight *n.* evening, dusk

DIRECTIONS: Complete the following sentences by filling in the blanks with vocabulary items (A), (B), or (C), according to the context of the sentences.

1. Citric acid gives lemons and limes their _____ taste.
   (A) temperate   (B) toxic   (C) tart

2. The use of robots has eliminated certain _____ factory jobs.
   (A) tedious   (B) thrilling   (C) transient

3. One should never buy food or medicine if the packaging has obviously been

   _____ .

   (A) tangled   (B) thwarted   (C) tampered with

4. Alfred Hitchcock directed a number of _____ psychological dramas; among the most exciting were *Psycho* and *North by Northwest*.
   (A) transparent   (B) trivial   (C) thrilling

5. Tides are caused by the _____ of the moon's gravity.
   (A) tangle   (B) torrent   (C) tug

6. Many people find chocolate _____ .
   (A) tempting   (B) tender   (C) telling

7. Peachtree Street is the main _____ in Atlanta.

(A) triumph   (B) thoroughfare   (C) tale

8. In her book *Silent Spring,* Rachel Carson wrote about insecticides and their _____ effects on animal life.

(A) tiresome   (B) tender   (C) toxic

9. In the desert, dry creek beds may turn into raging _____ after heavy rainstorms.

(A) trickles   (B) torrents   (C) toils

10. Colonial coral _____ mainly in warm, tropical waters.

(A) thrives   (B) terminates   (C) tows

11. _____ such as hair color and eye color are inherited genetically from one's parents.

(A) Traits   (B) Tangles   (C) Tints

12. Washington Irving collected and interpreted many famous old _____ , including the legends of Rip Van Winkle and the Headless Horseman.

(A) tales   (B) tidings   (C) traits

13. Wild rabbits are _____ creatures that mainly rely on their keen senses of hearing and smell to evade danger.

(A) thrilling   (B) timid   (C) treacherous

14. The dura mater is a _____ , protective fibrous membrane that covers the spinal cord and brain.

(A) tender   (B) tough   (C) temperate

15. Behind my desk is a _____ mass of electrical cords from my computer, monitor, printer, scanner, radio, and desk lamp.

(A) tangled   (B) transparent   (C) treacherous

16. The tropical storm _____ many palm trees in the coastal towns.

(A) toppled   (B) tugged   (C) triumphed

17. Most scientists believe that global warming is beginning to _____ the world's glaciers.

(A) thwart   (B) tint   (C) thaw

18. In 1880, Los Angeles was a _____ little town with a population of only 11,000, but it would not remain quiet for long.

(A) thrilling   (B) tranquil   (C) transient

VOCABULARY EXERCISE 16

ultimate *adj.* (1) conclusive, definite, final; (2) maximum, highest, best

unbearable *adj.* intolerable, agonizing

uncouth *adj.* impolite, rude, vulgar

underlying *adj.* fundamental, basic

undertake *v.* try, attempt

ungainly *adj.* awkward, unskillful

uniform *adj.* consistent, regular

unique *adj.* singular, one of a kind, special

unravel *v.* solve, explain

unruly *adj.* unmanageable, disorganized, disorderly

unsound *adj.* defective, faulty, unsafe

upheaval *n.* disturbance, disorder

uphold *v.* support, sustain

upkeep *n.* maintenance

uproar *n.* disorder, disturbance, commotion

urbane *adj.* sophisticated, cultured, elegant

urge *v.* encourage, advise, implore

urgent *adj.* pressing, compelling

utensil *n.* tool, implement, device

utter *v.* say, speak; *adj.* total, absolute, complete

vacant *adj.* empty, unoccupied

vague *adj.* unclear, uncertain, ambiguous

vain *adj.* (1) useless, pointless, unsuccessful, futile; (2) conceited, arrogant

valid *adj.* genuine, authentic, legitimate

vanish *v.* disappear, go away

variable *adj.* changeable, shifting

vast *adj.* huge, enormous, extensive, immense

venomous *adj.* poisonous

verbose *adj.* talkative, wordy

verge *n.* brink, edge, threshold

verve *n.* enthusiasm, energy

vessel *n.* (1) container, bottle; (2) ship, craft

vex *v.* irritate, anger, annoy

viable *adj.* (1) alive, living; (2) feasible, practical, possible

vicinity *n.* area, proximity, zone

vie (with) *v.* compete (with), rival

vigorous *adj.* dynamic, energetic, spirited

virtual *adj.* almost, nearly, not quite

vital *adj.* critical, crucial, key, essential

vivacious *adj.* lively, cheerful

vivid *adj.* clear, distinct, graphic

vow *v.* promise, pledge, swear; *n.* oath, promise, pledge

DIRECTIONS: Complete the following sentences by filling in the blanks with vocabulary items (A), (B), or (C), according to the context of the sentences.

1. To be fair, laws must be applied to all persons _____.

   (A) urgently   (B) vaguely   (C) uniformly

2. Rattlesnakes are the most common _____ snakes in the United States.

   (A) ungainly   (B) venomous   (C) variable

3. The League of Women Voters _____ all citizens to vote.

   (A) urges   (B) vexes   (C) upholds

4. In his novel *The Red Badge of Courage,* Steven Crane_____ describes a Civil War battle.

   (A) vividly   (B) uniformly   (C) vitally

5. An Erlenmeyer flask is a glass _____ used in chemistry labs.

   (A) vessel   (B) vow   (C) verge

6. Aerobics is _____ form of exercise.

   (A) a viable   (B) an uncouth   (C) a vigorous

7. A metropolitan area consists of a central city and any suburban areas in its _____.

   (A) vicinity   (B) vessel   (C) upkeep

8. Medical scientists still do not fully understand the _____ causes of migraine headaches.

   (A) unruly   (B) underlying   (C) viable

9. The kidneys play a _____ role in maintaining health by removing impurities from the bloodstream.

   (A) valid   (B) viable   (C) vital

10. The myth of Narcissus tells the story of a handsome but _____ young man who stares at his reflection in a pool of water for so long that he turns into a flower.

    (A) vain   (B) unbearable   (C) verbose

11. The fork has been used as an eating _____ at least since the twelfth century.

    (A) vessel   (B) utensil   (C) urge

12. Siberia covers _____ area in northeastern Asia.

    (A) a vast   (B) a viable   (C) an ultimate

13. A city's park and recreation budget must include funds for the _____ on buildings and grounds.

    (A) uproar   (B) verge   (C) upkeep

14. Mary Munsfeldt _____ some of the puzzles involving insects and the pollination of plants.

    (A) undertook   (B) upheld   (C) unraveled

15. Linguists say that hundreds of the world's languages may _____ in the next few decades because the number of speakers of these languages is dwindling rapidly.

    (A) vanish   (B) utter   (C) urge

16. A lack of parking spaces is a _____ problem in most cities.

    (A) unique   (B) vacant   (C) vexing

17. Under a policy of protectionism, domestic companies do not have to _____ international corporations.

    (A) vie with   (B) vow   (C) vex

VOCABULARY EXERCISE 17

wage *n.* salary, pay, earnings

waive *v.* to surrender (rights, privileges)

wake *n.* the track of a ship in water

wander *v.* roam, travel, range

wane *v.* shrink, decrease, decline

ware *n.* goods, merchandise

warn *v.* alert, caution, advise

warning *n.* alarm, alert

warp *v.* deform, bend, twist

wary *adj.* careful, cautious, alert

weary *adj.* tired, exhausted, fatigued

weird *adj.* strange, eerie, unusual

well-to-do *adj.* rich, wealthy, affluent

whiff *n.* a slight smell

wholesome *adj.* healthy, nutritious, beneficial

wicked *adj.* evil, corrupt, immoral

widespread *adj.* extensive, prevalent, sweeping

wily *adj.* crafty, cunning, shrewd

wise *adj.* astute, prudent, intelligent

withdraw *v.* retreat, pull out, remove

wither *v.* dry, shrivel, wilt

withhold *v.* reserve, retain, hold back

witty *adj.* comic, clever, amusing

woe *n.* trouble, distress, sorrow

wonder *v.* think about, speculate, ponder; *n.* marvel, miracle

wound *v.* injure, hurt; *n.* injury

wrinkle *n.* line, crease (in clothing, skin, etc.); *v.* to put lines or creases in something; to have lines or creases

yearn *v.* desire, crave, want

yield *v.* (1) give up, surrender; (2) produce, supply; *n.* production, output, crop

zealous *adj.* enthusiastic, eager

zenith *n.* peak, tip, apex, summit

zone *n.* area, vicinity, region

DIRECTIONS: Complete the following sentences by filling in the blanks with vocabulary items (A), (B), or (C), according to the context of the sentences.

1. If boards become wet, they may _____ .
   (A) wither   (B) yield   (C) warp

2. Whole grains and fresh fruit and vegetables are _____ foods.
   (A) weird   (B) wholesome   (C) well-to-do

3. The Green Revolution was a system of farming that depended on new varieties of seeds and the increased use of irrigation and fertilizers. It greatly increased farmers' _____ .
   (A) wonders   (B) yields   (C) woes

4. You must be _____ when buying a used car; be sure the engine is in good condition.
   (A) weary   (B) zealous   (C) wary

5. In the past, many salesmen tried to sell their _____ door-to-door.
   (A) wares   (B) woes   (C) wages

6. Humorist Will Rogers wrote many _____ newspaper columns.
   (A) wily   (B) weary   (C) witty

7. Congress sets the minimum _____ , which is the lowest amount of money workers may be paid per hour.
   (A) wage   (B) yield   (C) zone

8. Intelligent policies are needed so that public funds are used _____ .
   (A) wholesomely   (B) zealously   (C) wisely

9. Our small sailboat almost overturned when we passed through the _____ of the huge cruise ship.
   (A) wake   (B) zone   (C) wrinkle

10. As we drove past the bakery, I got a _____ of fresh bread.
    (A) wound   (B) whiff   (C) wake

11. Linen is a cool, comfortable fabric, but it _____ easily.

    (A) warps   (B) withholds   (C) wrinkles

12. Some superstitions are familiar to many cultures. For example, there is a _____ belief that black cats bring bad luck.

    (A) widespread   (B) wily   (C) wicked

13. A green belt is a park-like _____ around a city in which development is not permitted.

    (A) zenith   (B) wound   (C) zone

14. George Ropes painted portraits of sea captains, prosperous merchants, and other _____ citizens of eighteenth-century Massachusetts.

    (A) zealous   (B) well-to-do   (C) wicked

15. In his 1961 book *Night Comes to the Cumberlands,* Harry M. Caudil painted a grim picture of the _____ of the Appalachian region.

    (A) woes   (B) wares   (C) yields

Communicative Activities for Reading

The Reading section of the TOEFL iBT does not test your ability to communicate. However, communicative activities will help you practice using academic vocabulary and will help you prepare for the Writing and especially the Speaking sections of the test. These games and activities can also make your preparation for the test livelier and more fun. They are divided into activities for vocabulary and for reading comprehension.

Internet activities are marked with this icon: ⌐○⌐

Vocabulary Activities

You can use the "Vocabulary Building" tutorial in this book (pp. 188–228) to get vocabulary words for the activities in this section.

Activity 1

Vocabulary Search   ***Class Activity***

Your instructor/coordinator will give you cards of two different colors. Cards of one color have vocabulary items. Cards of the other color have definitions of the vocabulary. You will receive one card of each color. You will then need to find another student who has the definition that goes with your word, as well as the student who has the word that goes with your definition. The first person to find both of the matching cards is the winner.

Activity 2

Vocabulary Concentration   ***Pairs Activity***

This game is based on an old television quiz show. It tests your memory and helps you learn vocabulary at the same time. Your teacher or coordinator will create a set of twenty cards (the backs of all the cards will be identical). Half the cards will have a vocabulary item, and the other half will have definitions of the vocabulary items. You and another player will place the cards face down in rows so that you cannot see the words or definitions. Arrange the rows of cards into a rectangular shape. You and the other player will then take turns. One player turns over two cards. If the word and definition match, that player wins those two cards and removes them from the rectangle. If there is not a match, it's the other player's turn. The player who has collected the most cards by the end of the game wins. The game ends when all the cards have been removed from the rectangle.

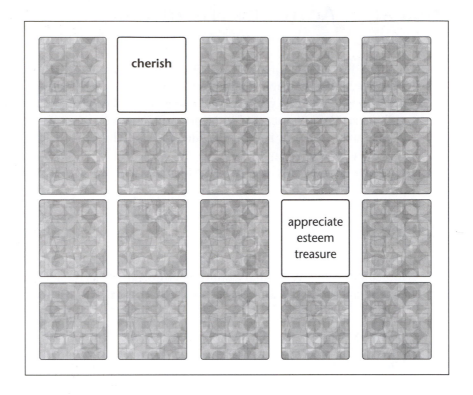

Activity 3

Crossword Puzzle Making   ***Small-Group Activity***

Type the phrase "Free Crossword Puzzle Maker" into a search engine such as Google. There are a number of sites that will let you create your own puzzles by first typing in words and then typing in definitions. After you have created a puzzle, print it out. Then exchange puzzles with another group and complete the puzzle.

Activity 4

Word Family Race   ***Small-Group Activity***

Your instructor/coordinator will give each group several categories of words (same categories for every group). These categories should have quite a few words that belong to them, for example: *words that describe emotions; words that are related to the weather; words that name kitchen utensils; words that are used in sports.* Within a set amount of time (one to two minutes per category) you will write as many words as possible. The team with the greatest number of "correct" words wins.

Activity 5

Vocabulary Bee   **Class Activity**

Your whole class will stand up. The instructor/coordinator will in turn give each player a word to define and act as referee, deciding if the definition/synonym is "close enough." If a player is unable to give a correct definition, he or she must sit down and the next player will be given the same word to define until a correct definition is given. The last player standing wins.

This game can also be played with teams. The last team with a member or members still standing wins.

READING ACTIVITIES

For most of these activities, you need to work with reading passages. You can find passages from newspapers or magazines, such as *Time Magazine, Newsweek,* and *National Geographic.* If the articles in these magazines are too long, you can use part of an article. If you have access to a computer connected to the Internet, you can also find appropriate passages online. You can find hundreds of readings by typing "ESL Readings" into your browser and visiting one of these sites. You can also visit news organizations such as CNN, NPR, or the BBC to look for readings about current events.

Activity 6

Scrambled Paragraphs   **Small-Group Activity**

This activity will help you answer sentence addition items on the test. Choose a paragraph from an appropriate passage. Write out each sentence from the paragraph on a strip of paper. First, see if your group can put the paragraph back together in the original order. You may have to add some transition words or other hints to make it easier to reassemble the paragraph. Afterwards, exchange your scrambled paragraph with another group. See if they can reassemble your group's paragraph by putting the sentences in the proper order while you do the same with the other group's paragraph.

Activity 7

Write Your Own TOEFL Items   **Small-Group Activity**

Find a suitable passage. Write five TOEFL-like multiple choice questions about this article. Next, exchange articles and questions with another group. After you have answered the questions, check with the group that wrote the test and see if your group has answered the questions correctly.

Activity 8

Scanning Race   *Small-Group Activity*

Your instructor/coordinator will find a suitable reading and then make up ten to twelve questions about it. (These do not have to be multiple-choice questions.) Your group will be given a copy of the reading and of the questions. Don't look at the article or questions until all the groups have received their copies. When your instructor/coordinator says "Go!" try to find the necessary information and answer the questions as quickly as possible. The first group to finish correctly wins. Everyone stops while the instructor or coordinator checks the answers. Making more than one mistake disqualifies a team, and other teams can continue until there is a winner.

Activity 9

Idea Auction   *Small-Group Activity*

This activity provides practice for complete-the-summary items. Your instructor/coordinator will find a passage and write out a list of ideas found in the passage. Half of the ideas will be main ideas that would be included in a passage summary. Half should be minor details or ideas not found in the passage. Each group will receive $100 in play money or credit. After you have read the article, an auction will be held. Your instructor/coordinator will read one of the sentences and offer it for sale. Groups can bid part of their money to "buy" the sentence. The highest bid wins the sentence. The group with the greatest number of correct main ideas at the end of the auction wins.

Activity 10

Student Teacher   *Individual Activity*

Your instructor/coordinator will choose several students to teach one of the eight reading lessons in this text. Each student who is selected will go back and study the lesson in detail, write out a lesson plan, and give a five- to ten-minute presentation on the lesson.

GUIDE TO LISTENING

ABOUT LISTENING

The second section of the TOEFL® iBT tests your understanding of spoken material and your ability to answer questions about the conversations and lectures that you hear. It contains two conversations and four lectures that take place in a university setting. (Some tests may also include an extra unscored conversation or lecture. You as the test-taker will not know which will be unscored, so it is important to do well on all of the conversations or lectures.) After each conversation or lecture, there is a set of questions asking about the information that was presented.

Skills that are tested in this section include the abilities to

▶ understand the main idea or topic of the conversation or lecture
▶ understand supporting ideas and details of the conversation or lecture
▶ draw inferences
▶ identify the speaker's purpose, method, and attitude
▶ recognize the relationship between parts of a lecture (cause and effect, comparison/contrast, chronological order, and so on)
▶ understand how the speaker's intonation affects meaning
▶ analyze and categorize information in order to complete summaries and charts

When you begin the Listening Section, you will see a computer screen with a photograph of a test-taker wearing headphones. This screen will tell you to put on your headphones.

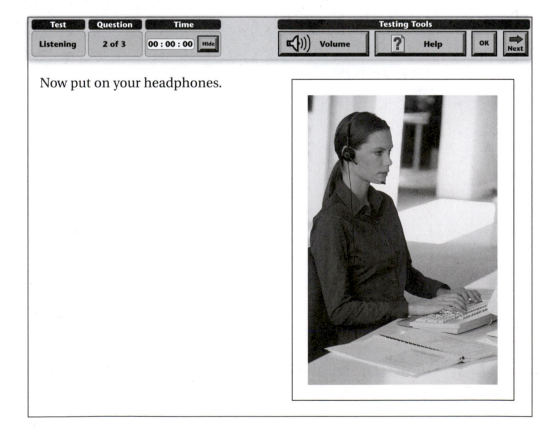

The next screen tells you how to change the volume by clicking on the volume icon on the toolbar. Subsequently, you will see the directions screen. After you click on the Dismiss Directions button on the toolbar, the Listening Section begins immediately.

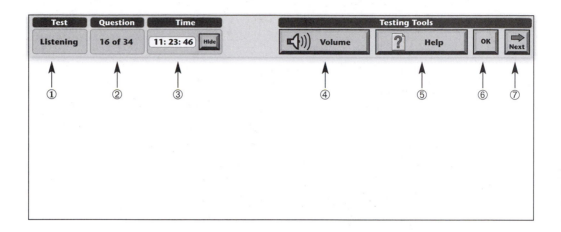

Toolbar button #1 tells you that you are taking the Listening Section. (You should already know this!) Button #2 tells you the question number that you are working on as well as the total number of questions you must answer in this section. Button #3 is a clock that keeps track of the amount of time you have to work on the Listening Section.

On the right side of the toolbar are the "Testing Tools." The volume button (#4) allows you to change the volume at any time during the test. The Help button (#5) gives you the directions for the Listening Section—however, it won't give you any real help! After you have answered a question, you need to click on the OK button (#6) to confirm your answer, and then on Next (#7) to move to the next question. You cannot go back to a previous question after you have confirmed your answer or listen to a talk a second time.

The Listening Section of the TOEFL iBT is *not* computer-adaptive. In other words, the level of difficulty will not change according to your ability to answer the previous question.

TIMING

You have twenty minutes in which to answer the questions. This does *not* include the time you spend listening to conversations and lectures. Individual questions have no time limit. You can take as long as you want to answer a question, as long as you finish the entire section within the time limit. The entire Listening Section (including time spent listening) will probably take you about sixty minutes to complete.

Note: *Although the TOEFL iBT gives you an indefinite amount of time to answer individual Listening questions, the multiple-choice questions on the Audio Program (tape or CD) for* The Guide *are separated by a ten-second pause. You will have a little more time to answer matching, ordering, and complete-the-chart questions. If you prefer, you can pause the Audio Program and take a little more time to answer questions.*

THE CONVERSATIONS

Conversations are dialogues between two people. One person is always a student. The other person may be another student, a professor, a teaching assistant, a librarian, a university administrator, and so on. These conversations take place on a college campus—in a dormitory, cafeteria, classroom building, or a professor's office. They deal with situations related to university life. They often deal with solving a problem that one of the two people is having.

You will first see a photograph that shows the speakers and sets the scene for you. However, the picture will not help you answer the questions.

At the same time that the picture appears, you will hear the narrator say, "Listen to a conversation between _____ and _____." The photograph will remain on the screen while you listen to the conversation. Conversations last two to three minutes, and there are from twelve to twenty-five exchanges between the two speakers. Conversations are followed by a set of five questions. You will *not* see the questions until after the conversation is over.

Below the photograph on your computer screen you will see a time bar that tells you approximately how much longer the conversation will last. A line in the time bar moves from left to right as the conversation progresses. The time bar on the screen shown on the previous page, for example, indicates that the conversation is about halfway over.

THE LECTURES

Lectures take place in a classroom and are usually given by a professor. Lectures may be monologues (one speaker), a monologue with one or two questions or comments from students, or academic discussions involving the professor and several students. They involve a wide variety of academic subjects: anthropology, biology, history, literature, chemistry, psychology, and so on. Lectures last five to six minutes and are about 500 to 800 words long.

You will first see a screen that identifies the type of class in which the lecture is given.

BIOLOGY

You will then see a photograph of a professor lecturing or having a discussion with a class. The narrator will say, "Listen to a lecture in a biology class" or "Listen to a discussion in a psychology class." Again there is a time bar below the photo that tells you approximately how much longer the lecture will last.

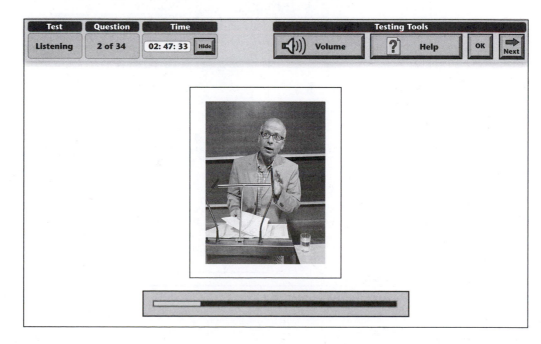

In many of the lectures you will see a "blackboard screen" that presents specialized vocabulary from the lecture—the kinds of terms a professor might write on a board during a class. Test questions are not about the information on the blackboards, so try not to get too distracted by the words.

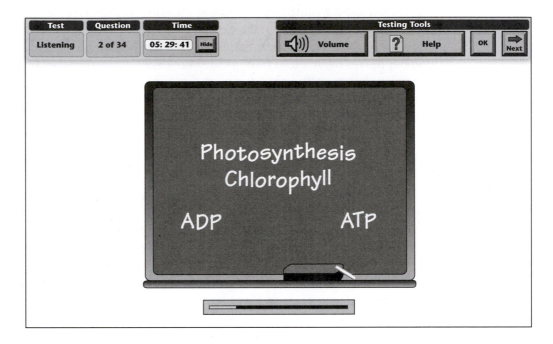

Sometimes you will also see a photograph, drawing, map, or chart related to the lecture.

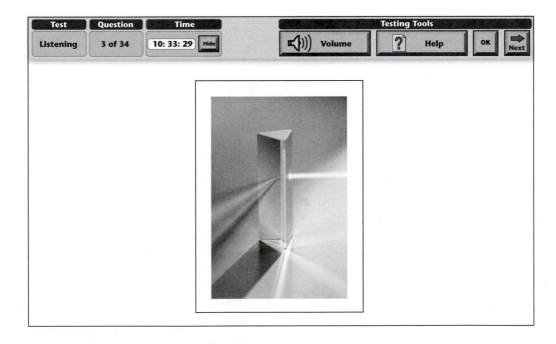

AUTHENTIC LANGUAGE

In the Listening Section of the TOEFL iBT, conversations and lectures do not sound as if they are being read aloud by actors. The speakers sound "authentic"—like people actually having conversations or giving lectures. This authentic language may include the following features:

▶ Polite interruptions

Professor
Okay, let's move on to the topic of . . .
Student
Excuse me, Professor Wade, but could we go over that last point one more time?

▶ Mistakes and corrections
Professor
Unlike most drums, tympani produce a definite pitch when struck. It was in the sixteenth century that they became a common feature of the classical orchestra. Wait. No, it was in the . . . uh, 1600's, in the seventeenth century, I should have said.

▶ Hesitations and repetitions
Student
Professor Jackson, excuse me, let me get this straight. You said that in the Canadian parliament, that the . . . umm, Senate was the upper house but . . . uh, that the House of Commons . . . . uhhh *(pause)* that the House of Commons, the lower house, actually has more power?
Professor
That's right. In practice, the House of Commons is the dominant branch of Parliament.

▶ Digressions
Professor
There are plenty of good reasons why New York City became the financial center of the country. Of course, it's not just finance. New York is a cultural center, an artistic center. I mean, if you want to see a good play, if you want to go to a good museum, then you go to New York, right?
   But anyway, one reason it became a financial center is that . . .

▶ Reduced speech
Student A
So are you *gonna* sign up for Professor Kimble's sociology class?
Student B
I guess. I've *gotta* take at least one more social science class.
   (*Gonna* is the reduced form of "going to." *Gotta* is the reduced form of "got to.")

▶ Sentence fragments
   Professor
   William Blake. A great poet. At least in my opinion.

Most of the speakers will have standard American accents. However, some speakers may have a regional U.S. accent (southern U.S. or New England, for example) or an accent from another English-speaking country (the U.K., Canada, Australia, India, or New Zealand, for example).

THE QUESTIONS

The chart below shows you the kinds of questions that are typically asked about the conversations and the lectures. The chart also shows you in which lesson in *The Guide* you will find more information and practice for this type of question.

Standard Multiple-Choice Listening Questions				
Type of question	*Explanation*	*Example*	*Probable number per test*	*Lesson*
Main-Topic Questions	These ask you what subject the conversation or lecture is generally about.	What is the main topic of this conversation? What is the primary topic of this lecture?	1 or 2	9
Main-Purpose Questions	These ask you why, in general, the speakers are having the conversation or why the lecture is being given.	Why is the man/woman talking to the professor? What is the main point of this lecture?	1 or 2	9
Factual Questions	These ask you about supporting ideas or details mentioned in the conversation or lecture.	What does the speaker say about _____? According to the professor, where does _____? According to the lecture, why does _____?	12 to 18	10

Type of question	Explanation	Example	Probable number per test	Lesson
Negative Factual Questions	These ask which of the answer choices is *not* true, according to information given in the conversation or lecture, or what information is *not* mentioned in the passage.	According to the lecture, which of the following is NOT true? Which of the following is NOT mentioned in the lecture?	2 to 4	10
Inference Questions	These ask you to draw conclusions based on information given in the conversations or lectures.	What does the man/woman imply about _____? What can be inferred about _____ from the lecture?	3 to 5	10
Purpose Questions	These ask you why a speaker mentions some point in the conversation or lecture.	Why does the professor mention _____ ?	2 to 4	11
Method Questions	These ask you to explain how the speaker explains or accomplishes something in the passage.	How does the speaker explain the concept of _____? How does the professor introduce the idea of _____?	1 to 2	11
Attitude Questions	These ask you how the speaker feels or thinks about a certain issue, idea, or person.	What does the speaker say about _____? What is the professor's opinion of _____?	1 to 2	11

To answer standard multiple-choice questions, you simply click on the oval next to the answer choice that you believe is correct, or on the choice itself. This will make the oval appear dark. You then click OK, followed by Next.

Other Types of Listening Questions

Some Listening questions have special directions, as described as follows:

Questions with Multiple Answers

Some factual and negative factual questions have two or even three (out of five) answers. You must click on two or three answers before you continue. These questions have boxes rather than ovals next to the answer choices, and when you click on each choice, the box is not completely blackened. Instead, an X appears in the box. You have to mark two (or three) choices before you can continue to the next question.

Which of the following are the most likely sites for active volcanoes?
Choose two answers.

- ☒ The Pacific Rim
- ☐ The Atlantic Basin
- ☒ The Mediterranean Belt
- ☐ Central Asia

According to the professor, which of the following persons became presidents of the United States?
Choose three answers.

- ☒ Thomas Jefferson
- ☐ Samuel Adams
- ☒ James Madison
- ☒ John Quincy Adams
- ☐ Benjamin Franklin

There will probably be three to five questions with multiple answers in each Listening Section.

You can find more information and practice questions in Lesson 9.

Replay Questions

Some questions first replay a short portion of the conversation and lecture and then ask you a question about what you hear. These questions usually ask you what the speaker meant or why that speaker made a comment. Replay questions require you to go beyond the literal meaning of statements in the talk. The meaning of the expression may depend on the speaker's intonation or tone of voice. These questions are marked with a headphones icon.

You see a screen on your computer that says:

> Listen again to part of the conversation/lecture.
> Then answer the question.

Professor

So, I don't have to go over that again, do I?

What does the professor mean when she says this? 🎧
- ● She thinks the students understand the point.
- ○ She doesn't think this is an important point.
- ○ She doesn't have enough time to review the point now.
- ○ She thinks this point is especially difficult to explain.

There will probably be four to six replay questions in each Listening Section. For more information and practice questions, see Lesson 12.

Matching Questions

Matching questions ask you to match characteristics or specific information with general categories.

Match the animal with the appropriate category:

A. Bear   **B. Frog**   **C. Snake**

Amphibian	Reptile	Mammal
B. Frog		

To answer this type of question, you simply click on each answer choice and then drag and drop it into the appropriate box.

There will probably be one or two matching questions per Listening Section. For more information and practice questions, see Lesson 13.

Ordering Questions

Ordering questions ask you to put four (or sometimes three) events or steps into the correct order.

The professor describes the process by which a tornado forms. Put these steps of the process in the correct order.
- A. Warm air rises quickly, pulling more warm air behind it.
- B. Masses of cool air meet warm, humid air.
- C. In-rushing air begins to rotate, forming a funnel cloud.
- D. A zone of thunderstorm clouds develops.

1. **B. Masses of cool air meet warm, humid air.**
2.
3.
4.

To answer these questions, you first click on the A, B, C, or D answer choice, then on the box where you think it belongs.

There will probably be one or two ordering questions per Listening Section. For more information and practice questions, see Lesson 13.

Complete-the-Chart Questions

Complete-the-chart questions test your ability to classify information or to determine whether or not points are made in a lecture. They ask you to complete charts that summarize all or part of a lecture.

In this lecture, the professor describes mature soil. Indicate whether each of the following is a characteristic of mature soil.

	Yes	**No**
Contains more microscopic life than immature soil	✓	
Consists of three layers		
Consists mostly of broken rock fragments		
Is darker in color than immature soil		

To answer these questions, you first click on the A, B, C, or D answer choice, then drag and drop the letter into the box where you think it belongs.

There will probably be one or two complete-the-chart questions in each Listening Section. There is more information and practice for this type of question in Lesson 14.

NOTE TAKING

Note taking is encouraged on the TOEFL iBT, and the notes you take can be very helpful when you are answering the questions. To help you improve your note-taking skills, the Listening Tutorial (pages 381–393) contains information and exercises to help you develop this ability. You may want to begin work on this section *before* you start working on the Listening lessons in this book.

Tactics for Listening

- As with all sections of the test, be familiar with the directions. When the directions appear, click on the Dismiss Directions button and begin the Listening section right away.

- Take notes and use your notes when you answer the questions. Try to record as much information as possible in your notes.

- Time management is important. Remember, you have as long as you like to answer each question, but you must complete the section within the time limit. Keep your eye on the clock and on the icon that tells you which question number you are working on.

- Always answer promptly after the answer choices appear, not only to save time but also to keep the listening material fresh in your mind. Refer to your notes as necessary to help you answer the questions.

- Don't spend too much time on any one question.

- Use your "power of prediction." As you are listening to the conversation or lecture, try to guess what questions will be asked.

- If you are not sure of an answer, try to eliminate unlikely choices. If you have no idea which answer is correct, guess and then go on to the next question.

- Concentration is very important in this part of the test. Once you have answered a question, don't think about it anymore—start thinking about the next question. Focus your attention on the voices you hear and the words on the screen.

LISTENING

LISTENING PREVIEW TEST
DIRECTIONS

▶ Now start the Audio Program. 🎧

This section tests your understanding of conversations and lectures. You will hear each conversation or lecture only once. Your answers should be based on what is stated or implied in the conversations and lectures.

You are allowed to take notes as you listen, and you can use these notes to help you answer the questions.

In some questions, you will see a headphones icon: 🎧. This icon tells you that you will hear, but not read, part of the lecture again. Then you will answer a question about the part of the lecture that you heard.

Some questions have special directions that are highlighted.

During an actual test, you may not skip questions and come back to them later, so try to answer every question that you hear on this test.

On an actual test, there are two conversations and four lectures. You have twenty minutes (not counting the time spent listening) in which to complete this section of the test.

On this Preview Test, there is one conversation and three lectures. Most questions are separated by a ten-second pause.

▶ Listen to a conversation between a student and a professor. 🎧

Now get ready to answer the questions.
You may use your notes to help you.

1 of 23   What is this conversation mainly about?
- ○ The student's grade in her geology class
- ○ The topic of a research paper that the student must write
- ○ A class assignment that the student did not hand in
- ○ The reason the student did not attend class

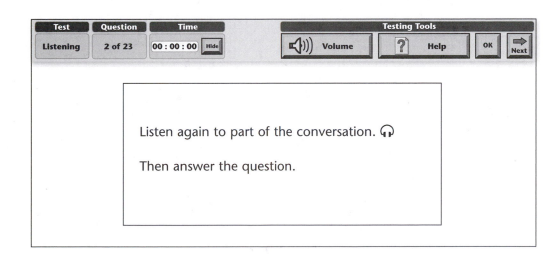

2 of 23   What can be inferred about the student?

○ She has never attended the professor's class.
○ She is not sure what course the professor teaches.
○ She is not sure that the professor knows who she is.
○ She is not certain that the professor's name is Dixon.

3 of 23   What assumption does the professor make about the student?

○ That she got up too late to attend his class yesterday
○ That she missed class because she had to go to the airport
○ That she is coming to his office to apologize for missing class
○ That she is unhappy about the research paper assignment

4 of 23   How did the student first get information about the topic she wants to write about?

○ From a magazine article
○ From the Internet
○ From the professor
○ From a television show

5 of 23   What is the professor's attitude towards the topic that the student wants to write about?

○ He does not think it is a proper topic for a research paper.
○ He thinks it might be a good topic if the student researches it carefully.
○ He believes students should not write about theories that have not been proved.
○ He thinks it is much too narrow a topic for her research paper.

▶ Now listen to a lecture in a biology class. 🎧

BIOLOGY

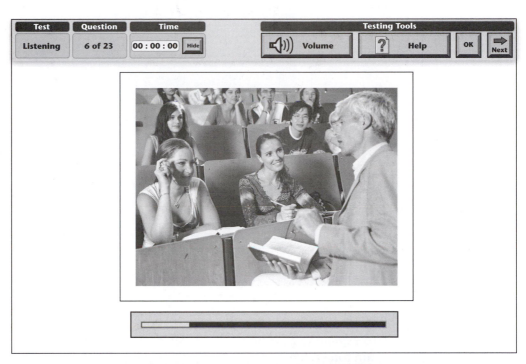

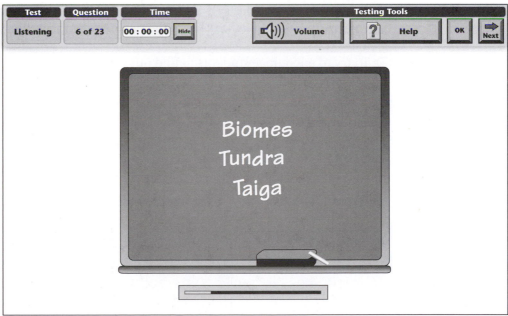

**Now get ready to answer the questions.
You may use your notes to help you.**

6 of 23   What does the professor say about the word *taiga?*

⃝ It is no longer commonly used.
⃝ It refers only to certain forests in Russia.
⃝ It was recently invented by biologists.
⃝ It has the same meaning as the term *boreal forest.*

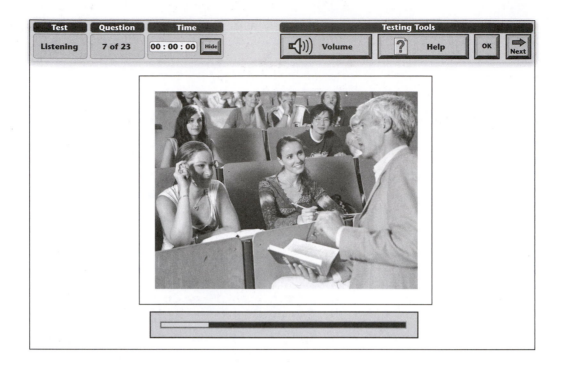

7 of 23   Why does the speaker say this? 🎧
- ○ To explain why he finds the taiga a less interesting biome than tropical rain forest
- ○ To emphasize that this sub-zone is far less varied than tropical rain forest
- ○ To explain to students why he is talking about the taiga today, not in a few days
- ○ To try to encourage students to find out more about different types of biomes

8 of 23   The professor discussed three sub-zones of the taiga. Match each sub-zone with its characteristic.

Write the letter of the answer choice in the appropriate box. Use each answer only once.

A. Open forest	B. Closed forest	C. Mixed forest
Larger needle-leaf trees grow closer together.	Some broad-leaf trees grow here, especially near water.	Widely spaced, small needle-leaf trees grow here.

9 of 23   When discussing needle-leaf trees, which of these adaptations to cold weather does the professor mention?

Mark three answers.

☐ Their thick bark
☐ Their dark green color
☐ Their deep root system
☐ Their conical shape
☐ The fact that they are "evergreen"

10 of 23   What characteristic do all of the predators of the taiga have in common?

○ They all migrate during the winter.
○ They all have thick, warm fur.
○ They all turn white in the winter.
○ They all hibernate in the winter.

11 of 23   What does the professor imply about moose?

○ They are more dangerous to humans than predators.
○ They have almost vanished from the taiga.
○ When fully grown, they are in little danger from predators.
○ Because of the value of their hides, they are often hunted.

▶ Listen to a discussion in the first class of a business course. 🎧

BUSINESS

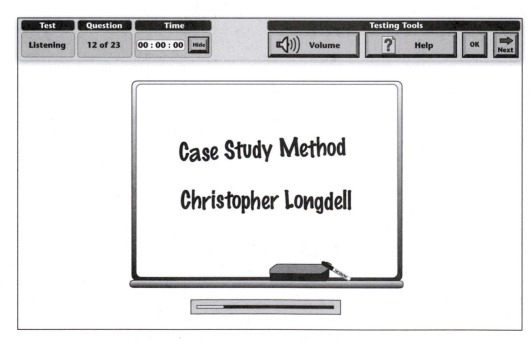

Now get ready to answer the questions.
You may use your notes to help you.

12 of 23   Professor Speed mentions several stages in the history of the case method. Put these steps in the proper order.

Place the letters in the proper boxes.

A. **Harvard University School of Business begins to use the case method.**
B. **Columbia University Law School begins to use the case method.**
C. **Chinese philosophers use a similar method.**
D. **Harvard University School of Law begins to use the case method.**

1.
2.
3.
4.

13 of 23   What does Professor Speed say about *exhibits?*

    ◯ They are the center of every case.
    ◯ They consist of ten to twenty pages of text describing a business situation.
    ◯ They are generally obtained from the Internet.
    ◯ They consist of statistical information about a company.

14 of 23   What does the professor mean when he says this? ⌒

    ◯ He wants to know if the class can answer his question.
    ◯ He's not sure exactly when the case study method was first used at a business school.
    ◯ He wants the students to express their opinion about when cases were first used.
    ◯ He's not sure where the case study method was first used.

15 of 23   Why does Professor Speed mention his wife?
- She uses case study in another type of class.
- She also teaches in the business school.
- She studied law by using the case study method.
- She disagrees with the professor's opinion of cases.

16 of 23   In this lecture, the professor describes the process of the case study method. Indicate whether each of the following is a step in the process.

Put a check mark (✓) in the proper box for each phrase.

	Yes	No
Analyze the business situation and exhibits		
Role-play		
Run a computer simulation		
Give a presentation and write a report		
Visit a real business and attend a meeting		

17 of 23   Which of the following reasons does the professor give for using the case study method?

Choose two answers.
- ☐ It builds a spirit of cooperation and teamwork among students.
- ☐ It allows students to study more than one discipline at the same time.
- ☐ It enables students to design and write their own cases.
- ☐ It develops students' decision-making and problem-solving skills.

▶ Listen to a student giving a presentation in an astronomy class. 🎧

ASTRONOMY

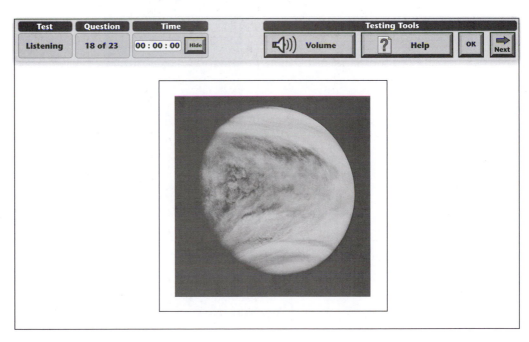

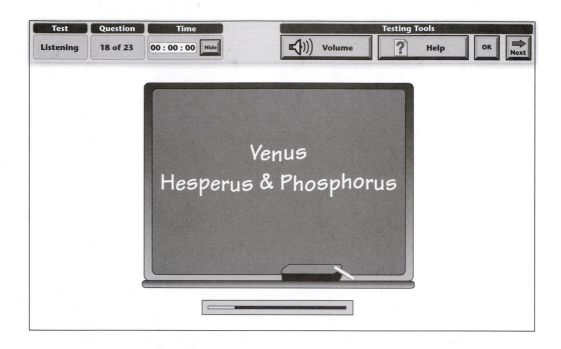

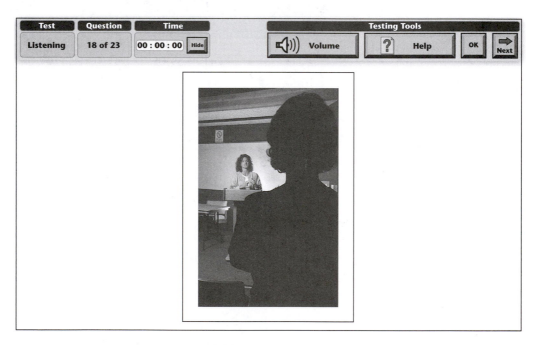

> **Now get ready to answer the questions.**
> **You may use your notes to help you.**

18 of 23   How does the speaker introduce the topic of Venus?

- ○ By comparing Venus with the eight other planets
- ○ By discussing what people in the past thought of the planet
- ○ By asking the class what they already know about Venus
- ○ By listing all of the space probes that have been sent to Venus

19 of 23   According to the speaker, which of the following were once common beliefs about Venus?

Choose two answers.

☐ That it was not a single object but two objects
☐ That it was actually much colder than the earth
☐ That it had two moons, Phosphorus and Hesperus
☐ That a superior form of life lived under its clouds

20 of 23   In this presentation, the speaker discusses some similarities between Earth and Venus and some of the differences between the two planets. Indicate which of the following is a similarity and which is a difference.

Put a check mark (✓) in the proper box for each phrase.

	Similarity	Difference
Their ages		
The directions in which they spin around their axes		
Their atmospheric pressures		
The presence of volcanoes		
Their sizes		

21 of 23   Which of the following is NOT true about the length of a day on Venus?

○ It is longer than an Earth day.
○ It is longer than an Earth year.
○ It is longer than a Venus year.
○ It is longer than a day on Jupiter.

22 of 23   In what order were these space probes sent to Venus?

Place the letters in the proper boxes.

A. **Mariner 2**
B. **Magellan**
C. **Venus Pioneer 2**
D. **Venera 4**

1. _____
2. _____
3. _____
4. _____

23 of 23   It can be inferred that the topic of the next student presentation will be about which of the following?

○ The Moon
○ The Sun
○ Earth
○ Mars

This is the end of the Listening Preview Test.

MAIN-TOPIC AND MAIN-PURPOSE QUESTIONS

After each conversation or lecture in the Listening Section, there is a set of questions. The first question of each set is often a **main-topic** question or a **main-purpose** question. To answer these questions, you need to understand the whole conversation or lecture. These questions can be phrased in a number of ways:

<u>Conversations</u>

What are these people mainly talking about?

What is the main topic of this conversation?

What is this conversation primarily about?

Why is the man/woman talking to the professor?

What is the purpose of this conversation?

<u>Lectures and Class Discussions</u>

What is the primary topic of this lecture?

What is the main point of this lecture?

What is the purpose of this lecture?

What is the topic of the class discussion?

What is the main subject of this discussion?

What are the students and the professor discussing?

The answer to main-topic/main-purpose questions must correctly summarize the conversation or lecture. Incorrect answers have one of these characteristics:

▶ They are too general.

▶ They are too specific, focusing on a detail in the conversation or lecture.

▶ They are incorrect according to information in the conversation or lecture.

▶ They are not mentioned in the conversation or lecture.

Although answering these questions will require an overall understanding of the conversations or lectures, the first few sentences often "set the scene" and give you a general idea of what the conversation or lecture will be about. In fact, in some lectures the speaker will actually announce the main topic at the beginning of the talk:

"In our last class, we discussed _____ , but today we're going to move on to _____ ."

"In this class, we're going to focus on _____ ."

"Today I'd like to introduce the topic of _____ ."

When you are taking notes, as soon as you become aware of the main topic of the conversation or lecture, you should write it down and underline or circle it.

Pay attention to the "blackboard screens" that are shown before these lectures begin—copy down the information shown on these screens on your note paper. The words that are written on the blackboard are often related to the main idea.

Here is conversation from the Listening Preview Test and a main-topic question about it.

Sample Item

▶ Listen to a conversation from the Listening Preview test and a main-topic question about it. Sample notes on this conversation are also provided. (You can see a script of this conversation in the Answer Key/Audioscript book or online at http://elt.heinle.com/toefl.)

▶ Now start the Audio Program. 🎧

Sample Notes:

	Prof. Dixon / student *(Brenda Pierce)*
S:	In Geol 210 class
P:	Big class + overslp? 8 a.m.
S:	To a'port traffic + need info re rshch paper
P:	no <12 pp no> 25 pp Biblio: 10 ref srces
	Topic up to stu.
S:	Earthquakes?
P:	Too broad . . .
S:	Using animals predict quakes . . .
P:	Maybe connections animals/quakes? But studies not promising
S:	Saw TV show. In China, animals predicted quake
P:	Haecheng Quake, 30 yrs ago snakes, horses, etc. evac. save 1,000s lives
	But: not able duplic. many quakes not predicted + many false alarms
	(evac. but no quake)
S:	So not good topic?
P:	Maybe OK . . . need look @ serious studies in j'nals, not pop-sci in
	papers or on TV
S:	Will go library, look . . .
P:	Need do formal prop., prelim biblio, due in 1 wk.

Sample Question:

What is this conversation mainly about?
- ◯ The student's grade in her geology class
- ◯ The topic of a research paper that the student must write
- ◯ A class assignment that the student did not hand in
- ◯ The reason that the student did not attend class

The subject of the student's grade (choice 1) was barely mentioned in the conversation. The professor simply says that the paper will account for 30% of the student's grade. The conversation does deal with a class assignment (a research paper) but it is an assignment that the student must do in the future, not one that she did not hand in, so choice 3 is not correct. The professor does mention the fact that the student did not attend class yesterday morning (choice 4), but this is only a detail in the conversation. The student and professor are mainly talking about the research paper that the student must complete and about a possible topic for this paper: predicting earthquakes by observing animals' behavior (choice 2).

EXERCISE 9.1

FOCUS: Answering main-topic/main-purpose questions about conversations.

DIRECTIONS: Listen to the conversations and the main-topic/main-purpose questions about them. Then mark the answer choices that correctly answer the questions. You may take notes on the conversations in the space allowed in the book or on another sheet of paper. As you take notes, try to decide what the main topic/main purpose of the conversation is and underline it in your notes. You may use your notes to help you answer the questions.

▶ Now start the Audio Program. 🎧

▶ Listen to a conversation between a student and a librarian. 🎧

Notes:

_____

_____

_____

_____

_____

_____

_____

_____

_____

_____

> **Now get ready to answer the question.**
> **You may use your notes to help you.**

1. What is the main topic of this conversation?
   - ○ Professor Quinn's approach to teaching
   - ○ The process of getting a student identification card
   - ○ Procedures for checking out reserve materials
   - ○ Several recent articles in political science journals

▶ Listen to a conversation between two students. ⌒

Notes:

_____

_____

_____

_____

_____

_____

_____

_____

_____

_____

**Now get ready to answer the question.
You may use your notes to help you.**

2. What is the main subject of the speakers' conversation?
   ○ Tina's plan for the coming school year
   ○ Tina's volunteer work for Professor Grant
   ○ Tina's vacation in Europe
   ○ An archaeology class that they both took

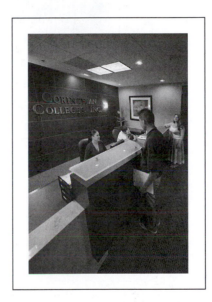

▶ Listen to a conversation between a student and an administrator. 🎧

Notes:

_____

_____

_____

_____

_____

_____

_____

_____

**Now get ready to answer the question.
You may use your notes to help you.**

3. Why does Mark Covelli want to speak to Ms. Kirchner?
   ○ He wants to pay for a meal plan that his parents signed him up for.
   ○ He doesn't want to eat in the dormitory at all.
   ○ He wants to change from Meal Plan 1 to Meal Plan 2.
   ○ He wants to eat three meals a day at the dormitory.

▶ Listen to a conversation between two students. 🎧

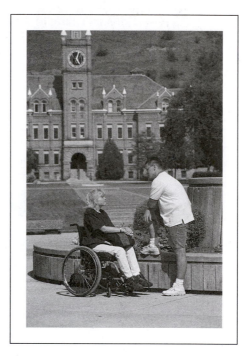

Notes:

_____

_____

_____

_____

_____

_____

_____

_____

_____

> **Now get ready to answer the question.**
> **You may use your notes to help you.**

4. What are these two people mainly discussing?
   ○ A race that the man and his friends will enter
   ○ Some problems that the man has with his car
   ○ A famous race held in Australia
   ○ Difficulties involved in using solar-powered cars

► Listen to a conversation between two students. 🎧

Notes:

_____

_____

_____

_____

_____

_____

_____

_____

_____

_____

_____

> **Now get ready to answer the question.**
> **You may use your notes to help you.**

5. What is the main topic of this conversation?
   ○ The requirements for getting into a photography class
   ○ The steps required to put together an art portfolio
   ○ Professor Lyle's style of photography
   ○ The difference between color and black-and-white photography

EXERCISE 9.2

FOCUS: Answering main-topic/main-purpose questions about lectures and discussions.

DIRECTIONS: Listen to the lectures/discussions and the main-topic/main-purpose questions about them. Then mark the answer choices that correctly answer the questions. You may take notes on the lectures/discussions in the space allowed in the book or on another sheet of paper. As you take notes, try to decide what the main topic/main purpose of the lecture/discussion is and underline it in your notes. You may use your notes to help you answer the questions.

▶ Listen to a lecture in a dance class. 🎧

DANCE

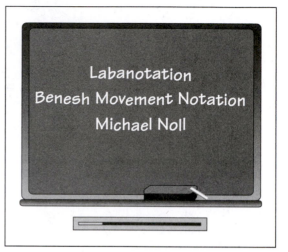

Labanotation
Benesh Movement Notation
Michael Noll

Notes:

_____
_____
_____
_____
_____
_____
_____
_____
_____
_____

> **Now get ready to answer the question.**
> **You may use your notes to help you.**

1. What is the main point of this lecture?
   ○ To contrast classical ballet and modern ballet
   ○ To compare two common systems of written dance notation
   ○ To talk about the space program's contribution to computer choreography
   ○ To discuss a problem once faced by choreographers and the means of solving it

▶ Listen to a discussion in a psychology class. 🎧

PSYCHOLOGY

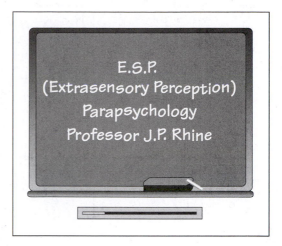

E.S.P.
(Extrasensory Perception)
Parapsychology
Professor J.P. Rhine

LISTENING

Notes:

_____

_____

_____

_____

_____

_____

_____

_____

_____

_____

| Now get ready to answer the question. |
| You may use your notes to help you. |

2. What are the speakers mainly discussing?
   ○ Reading experiments at Duke University
   ○ Reasons why scientists don't believe ESP is valid
   ○ The accomplishments of Professor Rhine
   ○ The failure of recent experiments in parapsychology

▶ Listen to a lecture in an archaeology class. 🎧

ARCHAEOLOGY

Notes:

_____

_____

_____

_____

_____

_____

_____

_____

_____

_____

> **Now get ready to answer the question.**
> **You may use your notes to help you.**

3. What does this lecture mainly concern?
   - ⃝ The archaeological record found in New England shipwrecks
   - ⃝ The rules for a game that the students are going to play
   - ⃝ The leading causes of shipwrecks off the coast of New England
   - ⃝ The role of the State Archaeological Society

▶ Listen to a discussion in an economics class. 🎧

ECONOMICS

Notes:

_____

_____

_____

_____

_____

_____

_____

_____

_____

> **Now get ready to answer the question.**
> **You may use your notes to help you.**

4. What is the main purpose of this discussion?
   ○ To compare regressive and progressive taxes
   ○ To explain the need for a new sales tax
   ○ To discuss the concept of income tax
   ○ To contrast direct and indirect taxation

▶ Listen to a discussion in an art class. 🎧

ART

Edward Hopper
Nighthawks
    The House by the Railroad
Film Noir

Notes:

_____

_____

_____

_____

_____

_____

_____

_____

_____

**Now get ready to answer the question.
You may use your notes to help you.**

5. What is the main topic of this discussion?
   ○ Edward Hopper's early career as a commercial artist
   ○ A style of moviemaking called *film noir*
   ○ Edward Hopper's realistic, bleak style of painting
   ○ Edward Hopper's influence on other painters

► Listen to a discussion in an advertising class. 🎧

ADVERTISING

Notes:

_____

_____

_____

_____

_____

_____

_____

_____

_____

_____

> **Now get ready to answer the question.**
> **You may use your notes to help you.**

6. What is the class mainly discussing?
   - ○ Government regulation and self-regulation in the advertising industry
   - ○ A court decision that affected advertising for children in Sweden
   - ○ The problems that a ban on advertising caused the tobacco industry
   - ○ A negative advertising campaign designed to prevent people from smoking

▶ Listen to a lecture in a world literature class. 🎧

WORLD LITERATURE

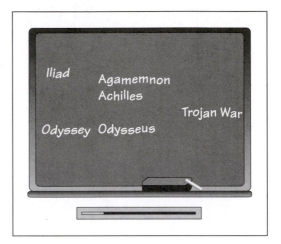

Notes:

_____

_____

_____

_____

_____

_____

_____

_____

_____

_____

| Now get ready to answer the question. |
| You may use your notes to help you. |

7. What is the main point of this lecture?
   ○ To compare the characters of Greek epic poetry and those of modern novels
   ○ To discuss why the professor enjoys the *Iliad* more than the *Odyssey*
   ○ To contrast the main characters of the *Iliad* and the main character of the *Odyssey*
   ○ To explain why the professor is going to have to change the syllabus

► Listen to a lecture in a modern history class. 🎧

MODERN HISTORY

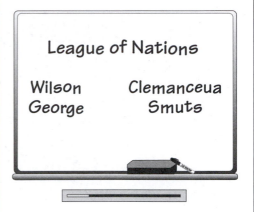

League of Nations

Wilson   Clemanceua
George   Smuts

Notes:

_____
_____
_____
_____
_____
_____
_____
_____
_____
_____
_____

> **Now get ready to answer the question.**
> **You may use your notes to help you.**

8. What is the main subject of this lecture?
   ○ The failures of the United Nations
   ○ The historical role of the League of Nations
   ○ The origins of World War II
   ○ The forgotten successes of the League of Nations

▶ Listen to a lecture in an environmental studies class. 🎧

ENVIRONMENTAL STUDIES

Notes:

_____

_____

_____

_____

_____

_____

_____

_____

_____

_____

_____

> **Now get ready to answer the question.**
> **You may use your notes to help you.**

9. What is the main idea of this lecture?
   - ○ Despite certain advantages, there are many problems involved in the use of hot dry rock technology.
   - ○ Hot dry rock technology is too expensive to ever be used as a practical energy source.
   - ○ The main purpose of hot dry rock technology is to provide pure, clean water.
   - ○ Hot dry rock is a potentially important alternative source of energy.

LESSON 10
FACTUAL, NEGATIVE FACTUAL, AND INFERENCE QUESTIONS

The three types of Listening questions—factual, negative factual, and inference—are very similar to those that are asked about in the readings in Section 1.

The best way to answer these three types of questions is to take complete, accurate notes on the conversations and lectures. If you are not sure that you remember the answer from the conversation or lecture, refer to your notes for more information. (See the Listening Tutorial on Note Taking, pages 381–393, for more information and practice.) Remember, just as in Reading, the order of these three types of questions follows the order of presentation. In other words, answers for the first few questions will be found in the first part of your notes, answers for the next few will be in the middle, and answers for the last few will be at the end. (To answer some questions, however, such as main-idea or complete-the-chart questions, you must have an understanding of the complete lecture rather than be able to find individual points in your notes.)

(A) Factual Questions

Factual questions ask about supporting ideas and details that are given in the conversation or lecture. These questions ask what, where, when, why, how much, and so on. Another common type of question is "What does the professor say about _____?" Many factual questions begin with one of these phrases:

Conversations

According to the man/woman, . . .

Lectures

According to the professor, . . .

According to the speaker, . . .

To answer these factual questions, you need an understanding of specific points.

If anything in a conversation is repeated or emphasized, it will likely be asked about, as in this portion of a conversation:

Student A

My project for my filmmaking class took me six weeks to finish.

Student B

Six weeks! I can hardly believe it. Doesn't your teacher realize you have other classes too?

You can be fairly sure that there will be a question like this: "How long did the man's project take to complete?"

Here is part of a lecture from the Listening Preview Test and a factual question about it.

Sample Item 1

▶ Listen to a discussion from the Listening Preview Test and a factual question about it. Sample notes on this lecture are also provided. (You can see a script of this lecture in the Answer Key/Audioscript book or online at http://elt.heinle.com/toefl.)

▶ Now start the Audio Program. 🎧

Sample Notes:

Cases = actual bus. sits.
   10-20 pp. of text describing real bus prob
      + 5-10 pp. of exhibits
Exhibits = statist. docs (e.g. spreadshts
                 sales reports
                 mktg. proj'tions)
  @ center of case: problem
    analyze data
    sometimes collect more data (from Int'net, etc.)
      Then, make decision

Sample Question:

What does the professor say about *exhibits?*

○ They are the center of every case.
○ They consist of ten to twenty pages of text describing a business situation.
○ They are generally obtained from the Internet.
○ They consist of statistical information about a company.

The first choice is not correct. The professor says that at the center of every case is the problem to be solved, not the exhibits. The second choice is not correct. The professor says that there are typically ten to twenty pages of text describing the problem, but that exhibits consist of five to ten pages of statistics. The third choice is not correct. The professor mentions that sometimes it will be necessary to go to the Internet to get more information about a case, but he does not say that the exhibits themselves are taken from the Internet. The best answer is the last one. The professor says that exhibits are "documents . . . statistical documents, really, that explain the situation. They might be oh, spreadsheets, sales reports . . . umm, marketing projections, anything like that."

Some questions will have two correct answers, and a few questions will have five answer choices, three of which will be correct.

Here is an example of a multiple-answer question based on part of a lecture from the Listening Preview Test.

Sample Item 2

▶ Listen to a lecture from the Listening Preview test and a multiple-answer question about it. Sample notes on this lecture are also provided. (You can see a script of this lecture in the Answer Key/Audioscript book or online at http://elt.heinle.com/toefl.)

▶ Now start the Audio Program. 🎧

Sample Notes:

Conditions in Taiga:

       Very cold   summer shrt

                  winter lng

  Organisms must adopt cold

      Trees: 1) Don't lse lves   evergrn   photosynth right away in

             spng   not need grow new lves

           2) Conical shpe   snow not accum.   slide off, brnches not

             break

           3) Dark grn color absorbs heat

Sample Question:

When discussing needle-leaf trees, which of these adaptations to cold weather does the professor mention?

Mark three answers.

- ☐ Their thick bark
- ☒ Their dark green color
- ☐ Their deep root system
- ☒ Their conical shape
- ☒ The fact that they are "evergreen"

The professor does not mention the fact that needle-leaf trees have thick bark that protects them from cold, so choice 1 is not correct. The professor *does* mention the dark green color (2). He says, "And even their color—that dark, dark green—it's useful because it absorbs the sun's heat," so you should mark the second choice as correct. There is no mention of the trees' root system, so choice 3 is not correct. However, choice 4 is correct because he does mention the trees' shape (". . . these trees are conical—shaped like cones—aren't they? This means that snow doesn't accumulate too much on the branches; it just slides off, and so, well, that means their branches don't break under the weight of the snow.). He also mentions the fact that these trees are evergreen (choice 5) (". . . they never lose their leaves—they're "evergreen," right, always green, so in the spring, they don't have to waste time—don't have to waste energy—growing new leaves. They're ready to start photosynthesizing right away.")

Factual questions are the most common type of question in Listening. There are usually two or three factual questions in each set of questions (about twelve to eighteen per Listening Section.) There will probably be three or four multiple-answer factual questions per Listening Section.

(B) Negative Factual Questions

Negative factual questions, ask you which answer choice is *not* true according to the conversation or lecture or is *not* mentioned in the conversation or lecture.

Here is part of one of the lectures from the Listening Preview Test and a negative factual question about it.

Sample Item 3

▷ Listen to part of a student presentation from the Listening Preview Test and a negative factual question about it. Sample notes on this lecture are also provided. (You can see a script of this lecture in the Answer Key/Audioscript book or online at http://elt.heinle.com/toefl.)

▷ Now start the Audio Program. 🎧

Sample Notes:

Strange fact: Ven. takes 225 E. days to go arnd Sun / E. takes 365 days (= 1 yr.)

Ven. turns on axis <u>very</u> slowly   243 days to turn completely

E. in 24 hrs.

∴ Venus day > Venus yr.

"   "   > days of all planets in sol. sys.

All planets in sol. sys. turn same direct EXCPT Ven.

(retrgrade spin)

Sample Question:

Which of the following is NOT true about the length of a day on Venus?

- ○ It is longer than an Earth day.
- ⊘ It is longer than an Earth year.
- ○ It is longer than a Venus year.
- ○ It is longer than a day on Jupiter.

Choice 1 *is* true, and so is not the best answer. An Earth day lasts 24 hours while a day on Venus lasts 243 Earth days. Choice 2 is the best answer because it is *not* true. An Earth year lasts 365 days, but a day on Venus lasts 243 days. Choice 3 *is* true. A year on Venus lasts 225 Earth days, but a day on Venus lasts 243 Earth days. Choice 4 is also true. The speaker says, "In fact, a day on Venus is . . . longer even than on those big gas planets like Jupiter."

There will probably be two or three negative questions per Listening Section.

(C) Inference Questions

Inference questions ask you to make a conclusion based on information in the conversation or lecture. These questions can be phrased in a number of ways:

<u>Conversations</u>

What does the man/woman imply about _____?

What can be inferred from the man's/woman's comment about _____?

What does the man/woman suggest about _____?

<u>Lectures</u>

What does the professor imply about _____?

What can be inferred from this lecture about _____?

What conclusion can be drawn from the lecture about _____?

Here is a part of a lecture from the Listening Preview Test and an inference question about it.

Sample Item 4

▶ Listen to a lecture from the Listening Preview Test and an inference question about it. Sample notes on this conversation are also provided. (You can see a script of this conversation in the Answer Key/Audioscript book or online at http://elt.heinle.com/toefl.)

▶ Now start the Audio Program. 🎧

Sample Notes:

Many Taiga animals migrate in wint, but some stay all yr.
Predators: Arct. foxes, wolves, bears, etc.
          All have thick warm coats (keep wrm, but make desirable to
          hunters)
          Some preds hibernate
          "   " change color (e.g. ermine)
Herbivores: Moose   only yng attacked
          Adlt moose biggest, strongest animal of taiga: preds have to be
             desperate to attack
          Preds mostly eat smaller prey: rabbits, voles, etc.

Sample Question:

What does the speaker imply about moose?

- ○ They are more dangerous to humans than predators.
- ○ When fully grown, they are in little danger from predators.
- ○ They have almost vanished from the taiga.
- ○ Because of the value of their hides, they are often hunted.

There is no information in the lecture to indicate whether or not moose are dangerous to humans, so choice 1 is not correct. The best answer is choice 2. The speaker says, ". . . only young moose are at risk of being attacked. The adult moose is the biggest, strongest animal found in the taiga, so a predator would have to be feeling pretty desperate to take on one of these . . ." This indicates that adult moose are not in much danger from predators. There is no information to support the idea in choice 3, that the moose is endangered in the taiga. The speaker says that the thick fur of predators is prized, but the moose is an herbivore, not a predator, and there is no indication that moose hide is especially valuable to hunters, so choice 4 is not correct.

There will probably be three to five inference questions per Listening Section.

EXERCISE 10.1

FOCUS: Answering factual, negative factual, and inference questions about conversations.

DIRECTIONS: Listen to the conversations and the questions about them. Then mark the answer choices that correctly answer the questions. You may take notes on the conversations in the space allowed in the book or on another sheet of paper. As you take notes, try to decide what factual, negative factual, and inference questions might be asked about the conversations. You may use your notes to help you answer the questions.

▶ Now start the Audio Program. 🎧

▶ Listen to a conversation between two students. 🎧

Notes:

_____

_____

_____

_____

_____

_____

_____

_____

_____

_____

1. What is Cindy's major?

   ○ Education
   ○ Physics
   ○ Mathematics
   ○ Literature

2. What decision about her future has Cindy recently made?

   ○ To change her major
   ○ To try to find a job in a field outside of teaching
   ○ To teach mathematics instead of science
   ○ To look for a job at a middle school

3. What was Cindy's main reason for coming to campus today?

   ○ To apply for a job
   ○ To attend a class
   ○ To arrange her schedule
   ○ To meet with some friends

4. What will Cindy be doing next semester?

   ○ Teaching at a high school
   ○ Taking university classes
   ○ Studying science
   ○ Taking some time off

▶ Listen to a conversation between a student and a visitor to the campus 🎧.

LISTENING

Notes:

_____

_____

_____

_____

_____

_____

_____

_____

_____

_____

**Now get ready to answer the questions.
You may use your notes to help you.**

5. Why was the woman confused at first when the man asked her for directions?

   ○ She didn't know where the art building was located.
   ○ She didn't know about the graduate student art show.
   ○ She was not very familiar with the name "the Reynolds Building."
   ○ She had never been to this campus before.

6. According to the woman, what is directly in front of the art building?

   ○ The library
   ○ A service road
   ○ The chemistry building
   ○ A metal sculpture

7. What was the woman's favorite exhibit at the art show?

   ○ Sculptures made of neon lights
   ○ Abstract paintings
   ○ A large metal sculpture
   ○ The painting of the purple lion

8. What can be inferred from the conversation about the man's sister?

   Choose two answers.

   ☐ She works at the gallery in the art building.
   ☐ She is a graduate student.
   ☐ She paints colorful, child-like paintings.
   ☐ She is an old friend of the woman.

▶ Listen to a conversation between two students. 🎧

Notes:

_____

_____

_____

_____

_____

_____

_____

_____

_____

> **Now get ready to answer the questions.**
> **You may use your notes to help you.**

9. Which of these courses is required for students in the Semester Abroad program in Greece?
   - ◯ Greek history
   - ◯ Ancient Greek language
   - ◯ Greek drama
   - ◯ Modern Greek language

10. Which of these is characteristic of the "island plan" Paul will take part in?
    - ◯ He will live and study on one of the Greek islands.
    - ◯ His travel and living arrangements will be made by the program.
    - ◯ He will live in an apartment surrounded by local people.
    - ◯ He will stay with a Greek family.

11. Why did Paul decide NOT to take part in the independent plan?
    ○ It was too expensive.
    ○ He thought he would be too isolated.
    ○ It would require too much of his time.
    ○ The academic program was too difficult.

12. What does Paul say about Professor Carmichael?
    Choose two answers.

    ☐ She once taught in a Semester Abroad program in France.
    ☐ She has taught in the program in Athens many times.
    ☐ She is no longer his advisor.
    ☐ She advised him to take part in the program in Greece.

▶ Listen to a conversation between two students. ⌒

Notes:

_____

_____

_____

_____

_____

_____

_____

_____

_____

_____

**Now get ready to answer the questions.
You may use your notes to help you.**

13. Why does Steve look tired?
    - ○ He stayed up most of the night.
    - ○ He had a test last night.
    - ○ He's been studying all morning.
    - ○ He's been too nervous to sleep lately.

14. How does Steve feel about the grade that he received on the chemistry test?
    - ○ It was an improvement.
    - ○ It was disappointing.
    - ○ It was completely unfair.
    - ○ It was a surprise.

15. Who teaches the seminars at the Study Skills Center?

    Choose two answers.

    - ☐ Undergraduate students
    - ☐ Junior professors
    - ☐ Librarians
    - ☐ Graduate students

16. Which of the courses at the Study Skills Center will Steve probably be most interested in?
    - ○ Basic Internet research methods
    - ○ Chemistry
    - ○ Business management
    - ○ Test-taking skills

17. Where is the Study Skills Center?
    - ○ In the library
    - ○ In the physics tower
    - ○ In a dormitory
    - ○ In Staunton Hall

18. What does the woman suggest Steve do now?
    - ○ Study for his next exam
    - ○ Go directly to the Study Skills Center
    - ○ Talk to his chemistry professor
    - ○ Get some sleep

▶ Listen to a conversation between a student and a campus housing administrator. 🎧

Notes:

_____

_____

_____

_____

_____

_____

_____

_____

_____

_____

_____

_____

> **Now get ready to answer the questions.**
> **You may use your notes to help you.**

19. Why does Jeff have to move out of his apartment?
   ○ The building was sold to a new owner.
   ○ He can't find a roommate to share with him.
   ○ The university will not allow him to live off-campus.
   ○ He has not paid his rent for several months.

20. How did Jeff find out about the Resident Advisor position?
   ○ From an ad in the newspaper
   ○ From his landlord
   ○ From another administrator in the housing authority
   ○ From a Resident Advisor

21. What will Jeff receive if he becomes a Resident Advisor?

    Choose two answers.

    ☐ A free room in the dormitory
    ☐ Free meals at a cafeteria
    ☐ Free college tuition
    ☐ A monthly salary

22. What does Ms. Delfino suggest Jeff do to get more information about the position?

    ○ Ask Mr. Collingswood for a brochure
    ○ Visit a dormitory and talk to some Resident Advisors
    ○ Take the position on a temporary basis
    ○ E-mail some Resident Advisors and get information from them

EXERCISE 10.2

FOCUS: Answering factual, negative factual, and inference questions about lectures and academic discussions.

DIRECTIONS: Listen to the lectures and discussions and the questions about them. Then mark the answer choices that correctly answer the questions. You may take notes on the lectures/discussions in the space allowed in the book or on another sheet of paper. As you take notes, try to decide what factual, negative factual, and inference questions might be asked about the lectures and discussions. You may use your notes to help you answer the questions.

▶ Now start the Audio Program. 🎧

▶ Listen to a discussion in an anthropology class. 🎧

ANTHROPOLOGY

Notes:

_____

_____

_____

_____

_____

_____

_____

_____

_____

_____

_____

**Now get ready to answer the questions.
You may use your notes to help you.**

1. What does the professor say about the word *potlatch*?

Choose two answers.

☐ It became part of the vocabulary of the Chinook Trade Jargon.

☐ According to some linguists, it originally came from the English word *potluck*.

☐ It was used not just by the Chinooks but by all the Northwestern tribes.

☐ It was originally a word in the language of the Kwakiutl tribe.

2. What was the most common gift at a potlatch?
   - ○ Wooden masks
   - ○ Fish packed in decorative boxes
   - ○ Fishing canoes
   - ○ Goat-hair blankets

3. What purpose did seal oil serve at a potlatch?
   - ○ It was burned in ceremonial lamps.
   - ○ It was used to burn up the host's possessions.
   - ○ It was used to flavor foods.
   - ○ It heated the building where the potlatch was held.

4. What does Professor Burke imply about the photograph of a potlatch taken in 1900?
   - ○ It showed one of the last legal potlatch ceremonies.
   - ○ It pictured a gift that the professor considered unusual.
   - ○ It indicated that Europeans sometimes attended the ceremony.
   - ○ It portrayed typical gifts that would be given away at a potlatch.

5. What does Professor Burke say about the Kwakiutl tribe?

   Choose two answers.

   - ☐ They held the most elaborate potlatch ceremonies.
   - ☐ They were the first tribe to hold potlatches.
   - ☐ They held potlatches but did not give away gifts.
   - ☐ They used the potlatch to bankrupt their enemies.

6. What does Professor Burke say about potlatch ceremonies held today?
   - ○ They are legal in Canada but not in the United States.
   - ○ They are illegal but are still held in secret.
   - ○ They are still held but are no longer called potlatches.
   - ○ They are again an important part of the tribes' culture.

LISTENING

▶ Listen to a lecture in a space science class. 🎧

SPACE SCIENCE

Notes:

_____

_____

_____

_____

_____

_____

_____

_____

_____

_____

_____

> **Now get ready to answer the questions.**
> **You may use your notes to help you.**

7. What happens to most pieces of orbital debris?
   ○ They burn up in the atmosphere.
   ○ They fly off into deep space.
   ○ They remain in orbit forever.
   ○ They collide with meteors.

8. How many orbital bodies are being monitored today?
   ○ Two hundred
   ○ Three to four hundred
   ○ About thirteen thousand
   ○ Half a million

9. Why is it impossible to monitor most pieces of orbital debris?
   - ○ They are too small.
   - ○ They are moving too fast.
   - ○ They are too far away.
   - ○ They are made of reflective material.

10. Which of the following types of orbital debris would NOT be particularly dangerous to astronauts on a spacecraft?

    Choose three answers.

    - ☐ A large booster rocket
    - ☐ A broken piece of a satellite antenna
    - ☐ A lost tool
    - ☐ A piece of metal the size of a grain of sand
    - ☐ A fleck of paint

11. The professor describes a collision in space between which of the following objects?
    - ○ A space shuttle and a space station
    - ○ Two rocket parts
    - ○ Two surveillance satellites
    - ○ A satellite and a rocket

12. What can be inferred about the collector described in this portion of the talk?
    - ○ It has been tested on Earth but not in space.
    - ○ It is no longer commonly being used.
    - ○ It has already been installed on some spacecraft.
    - ○ It has not been built yet.

LISTENING

► Listen to a discussion in a pharmacy class. 🎧

PHARMACY

Notes:

_____

_____

_____

_____

_____

_____

_____

_____

_____

_____

| **Now get ready to answer the questions.**
You may use your notes to help you. |

13. What point does Professor Findlay make about the drugs aspirin and digitalis?
   ○ They are both derived from herbal sources.
   ○ They are much more effective than herbal medicines.
   ○ They can be replaced by safer herbal medicines.
   ○ They should never be taken in combination with herbal medicines.

14. According to Professor Findlay, why do people generally take the herbal remedy Echinacea?
    ○ To prevent colds and the flu
    ○ To treat mild depression
    ○ To improve memory
    ○ To relieve stress

15. Which of the following is the best description of St. John's Wort?
    ○ A fan-shaped leaf
    ○ A yellow flower with five petals
    ○ Small white berries
    ○ Purple flowers that resemble daisies

16. What can be inferred from the professor's remarks about how most herbal medicines are used?
    ○ They are often taken in combination with pharmaceutical drugs.
    ○ They are often taken before people become sick to prevent illnesses.
    ○ They are most often used to treat symptoms of diseases, not their causes.
    ○ They are usually used because a doctor recommends them.

17. In what form are herbal remedies most often taken?
    Choose two answers.

    ☐ In capsules
    ☐ Sprinkled on food
    ☐ Brewed in tea
    ☐ In cold drinks

18. According to the professor, why has research on herbal drugs been limited?
    ○ It requires a very large initial investment.
    ○ It does not interest most research scientists.
    ○ It does not bring drug companies much profit.
    ○ It involves too many variables.

LISTENING

▶ Listen to a lecture in a U.S. history class. 🎧

U.S. History

Notes:

_____

_____

_____

_____

_____

_____

_____

_____

_____

_____

| **Now get ready to answer the questions.** |
| **You may use your notes to help you.** |

19. Which of the following caused the decline of roads in the United States in the nineteenth century?

   ◯ The effects of the Civil War
   ◯ The damage done by horses, carts, and carriages
   ◯ The lack of funds caused by economic crises
   ◯ The dominance of the railroads

20. How long did it take Dwight David Eisenhower to drive across the United States in 1919?

    ○ Three days
    ○ Sixty-two days
    ○ Seventy-two days
    ○ Almost a year

21. According to the speaker, which of these influenced the way President Eisenhower thought about highways?

    Choose two answers.

    ☐ His experience as a highway engineer
    ☐ His wartime experience with German superhighways
    ☐ His election as president
    ☐ His trip across the United States in 1919

22. When was the Interstate Highway System ORIGINALLY supposed to have been completed?

    ○ 1956
    ○ 1966
    ○ 1972
    ○ 1993

23. Which of the following is NOT given as an effect of the Interstate Highway System?

    ○ Job growth
    ○ Increased safety for motorists
    ○ The decline of the railroads
    ○ The establishment of the first suburb

24. In which of these cities were Interstate highway projects blocked by protests?

    Choose two answers.

    ☐ San Francisco
    ☐ Seattle
    ☐ Washington, D.C.
    ☐ Boston

LISTENING

▶ Listen to a discussion among students preparing a presentation for an architecture class. 🎧

ARCHITECTURE

Notes:

_____

_____

_____

_____

_____

_____

_____

_____

_____

_____

> **Now get ready to answer the questions.**
> **You may use your notes to help you.**

25. How did Joyce get most of her information about earthships?
    ○ From an Internet website
    ○ From her uncle
    ○ From a book
    ○ From her teacher

26. Which of these are NOT one of the main building materials used to construct earthships?

   ○ Wood
   ○ Old tires
   ○ Dirt
   ○ Aluminum cans

27. Which of the walls of an earthship is made of glass?

   ○ The north wall
   ○ The south wall
   ○ The east wall
   ○ The west wall

28. What is meant by the term *nest*?

   ○ A group of earthships
   ○ A large, expensive earthship
   ○ A kind of house similar to an earthship
   ○ A small, basic earthship

29. Why does Joyce call earthships "a real bargain"?

   Choose two answers.

   ☐ Earthships are built in factories, so little construction is necessary.
   ☐ Because earthships are small, owners do not have to purchase much land.
   ☐ Many owners save money by working on the houses themselves.
   ☐ Most of the materials used to build earthships are free or cheap.

30. What will the students probably bring to the presentation?

   ○ A model of an earthship
   ○ A video of an earthship
   ○ A detailed plan for an earthship
   ○ A photograph of earthships

LISTENING

▶ Listen to a lecture in a political science class. 🎧

POLITICAL SCIENCE

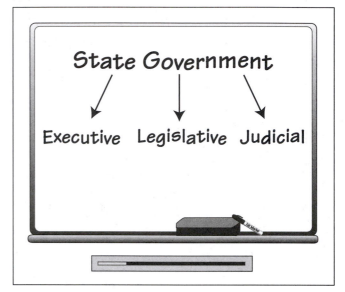

Notes:

_____

_____

_____

_____

_____

_____

_____

_____

_____

_____

> **Now get ready to answer the questions.**
> **You may use your notes to help you.**

31. What does the professor say about the unitary system of government?
    ○ It involves a single, powerful leader.
    ○ It features a government with only one branch.
    ○ It involves a powerful central government.
    ○ It features a legislature with one house, not two houses.

32. What does the professor say about Switzerland?
    - ○ Like Britain and France, it has a unitary form of government.
    - ○ Its government served as a model for the government of the United States.
    - ○ It has the oldest federalist system of government in the world.
    - ○ Like the United States and Canada, it has a federalist system.

33. According to the professor, which of the following is mainly responsible for primary and secondary education in the United States?
    - ○ The federal government
    - ○ State governments
    - ○ Local governments
    - ○ Private, nongovernmental agencies

34. Which of these states has the oldest constitution?
    - ○ Virginia
    - ○ Massachusetts
    - ○ Rhode Island
    - ○ Oregon

35. What is the maximum time that a governor of Virginia can serve?
    - ○ Two years
    - ○ Four years
    - ○ Eight years
    - ○ As many years as he or she wants

36. What is unique about the state legislature of Nebraska?
    - ○ It has a single house, not two houses.
    - ○ It lacks the power to impeach the governor.
    - ○ It is the only legislature that appoints supreme court justices.
    - ○ It is appointed, not elected.

▶ Listen to a discussion in a dance class. 🎧

DANCE

hula auane   hula kahiko

olapa   h'oa-paa   ukulele

Notes:

_____

_____

_____

_____

_____

_____

_____

_____

_____

_____

Now get ready to answer the questions. You may use your notes to help you.

37. What does the word *hula* mean in the Hawaiian language?
    ○ "Jumping flea"
    ○ "Dance"
    ○ "Graceful ones"
    ○ "Grass skirt"

38. What fact about the hula does the professor particularly emphasize?
    ○ That it is not as old as it was once believed to be
    ○ That it was introduced to the world by visitors from New England
    ○ That it is not as popular with tourists as it once was
    ○ That the current form of the dance differs greatly from the traditional form

39. What roles did the *h'oa-paa,* or "steady ones," play in the performance of the hula?

    Choose two answers.

    ☐ To perform the dance
    ☐ To sing and chant
    ☐ To play musical instruments
    ☐ To direct the dance

40. What did the New England missionaries first do when they arrived in 1820?
    ○ They had the hula completely banned.
    ○ They suggested new themes for the hula.
    ○ They proposed that the hula be performed for visitors.
    ○ They made the hula more conservative.

41. Which of the following would be the most likely theme of a modern hula?
    ○ A tale of a big military victory
    ○ A legend of Laki, goddess of the hula
    ○ The story of a great Hawaiian king
    ○ A description of fish swimming through the sea

42. What will the members of the class do next?
    ○ Attend a live dance performance
    ○ Study another type of traditional dance
    ○ Watch a video of a traditional hula
    ○ Learn to perform the modern hula

LISTENING

LESSON 11
PURPOSE, METHOD, AND ATTITUDE QUESTIONS

These three question types are very similar to purpose, method, and attitude questions in the Reading Section.

(A) Purpose Questions

Purpose questions ask *why* a speaker says something or what motivates a speaker to mention something in a conversation or lecture. They may ask you why a speaker presents certain information or gives a certain example.

Here is an example of a purpose question based on part of a lecture from the Listening Preview Test.

Sample Item 1

▶ Listen to part of a discussion from the Listening Preview Test and a purpose question about it. Sample notes on this conversation are also provided.
(You can see a script of this conversation in the Answer Key/Audioscript book or online at http:/elt.heinle.com/toefl.)

▶ Now start the Audio Program. 🎧

Sample Notes:

Prof Longdell: taught law @ Hvrd, not bus.

Case Meth 1st used for law stu.

Cple yrs later, used at Columb. U. Law School

± 1910, 1912 Hvrd Bus School

Used in other fields as well: e.g. education (Prof. Speed's wife)

Sample Question:

Why does Professor Speed mention his wife?
- ○ She uses case studies in another type of class.
- ○ She also teaches in the business school.
- ○ She studied law by using the case method.
- ○ She disagrees with the professor's opinion of cases.

The student asks if the case method can also be used in fields other than law and business. The professor first gives her a general answer ("it's been used in all sorts of disciplines"). He then gives her a specific example: he mentions his wife, who teaches in the School of Education, and says that she uses cases to train teachers. Choice 1 is therefore best. He does not say that she teaches in the business school (2); he says that she teaches in the School of Education. He does not say that she studied law (3). He also does not say that she disagrees with his own opinion of cases (4); in fact, since she uses cases herself, she probably agrees with his opinion.

You will probably see two to four purpose questions in each Listening Section.

(B) Method Questions

Method questions ask you *how* a speaker introduces an idea, emphasizes an idea, or explains an idea in a conversation or lecture. A speaker may, for instance, indicate cause/effect, contrast two concepts, give reasons, provide statistics, compare an unfamiliar concept with a familiar one, or provide examples to support a general concept.

Here is a portion of a presentation from the Listening Preview Test and a method question about it.

Sample Item 2

▶ Listen to part of a student presentation from the Listening Preview Test and a method question about it. Sample notes on this conversation are also provided. (You can see a script of this conversation in the Answer Key/Audioscript book or online at http://elt.heinle.com/toefl.)

▶ Now start the Audio Program. 🎧

Sample Notes:

Don: Sun

Lisa: Merc.

Presenter: Venus

1st: What people thght of Venus in past

    Thght Ven. = star

   actually 2 stars: Phosphorus, mrng star

                        Hesperus, eve.

   Named after goddess of love (Why?)

Sample Question:

How does the speaker introduce the topic of Venus?

○ By comparing Venus with the eight other planets
○ By discussing what people in the past thought of the planet
○ By asking the class what they already know about Venus
○ By listing all of the space probes that have been sent to Venus

The presenter does not compare Venus with the other planets in the first part of his presentation (although later he does compare specific aspects of Venus with those of certain other planets), so 1 is not correct. The best answer is 2. The student begins by talking about people's ideas of Venus in ancient times ("First off, back in the really . . . in the really ancient days, people thought Venus was a star, not a planet and . . ."). The presenter does *not* ask the other students what they already know about Venus, so choice 3 is not correct. Later in the lecture, he *does* mention a few of the space probes that were sent to Venus, but this is not part of the introduction. Therefore, 4 is not a good answer.

You will probably see one or two method questions per Listening Section.

(C) Attitude Questions

Attitude questions ask you about the speaker's attitude toward something mentioned in the conversation or lecture. What is the speaker's opinion of some concept, person, or thing? The answer to these questions is never given directly in the conversation or lecture. You must infer the answer from the speaker's vocabulary and tone of voice.

Here is a portion of a lecture from the Listening Preview Test and an attitude question about it.

Sample Item 3

▶ Listen to part of a conversation from the Listening Preview Test and an attitude question about it. Sample notes on this conversation are also provided. (You can see a script of this conversation in the Answer Key/Audioscript book or online at http://elt.heinle.com/toefl.)

▶ Now start the Audio Program. 🎧

Sample Notes:

○
S. So not good topic?
Prof. Maybe OK . . . need look at serious studies in j'nals, not pop-sci in
    papers or on TV

Sample Question:

What is the professor's attitude toward the topic that the student wants to write
about?
- ○ He does not think it is an interesting topic for a research paper.
- ○ He thinks it might be a good topic if the woman researches it carefully.
- ○ He believes students should not write about theories that have not been
  proved.
- ○ He thinks it is much too narrow a topic for her research paper.

Choice 1 is not correct. After discussing the topic with the student, he says, "It
could be a pretty interesting topic." Choice 2 best answers the question. The professor says "just because this theory hasn't been proven doesn't mean you couldn't
write a perfectly good paper about this topic . . . on the notion that animals can
predict earthquakes. Why not? It could be pretty interesting. But to do a good job,
you . . . you'll need to look at some serious studies in the scientific journals . . . ."
Choice 3 is not correct. The professor says that the woman *can* "write a perfectly
good paper" on a theory that has not been proved. Choice 4 is also incorrect.
Earlier in the conversation, the professor seems to think that the woman's topic is
too general. However, she then tells him that she is planning to write about a narrower topic, and his response is more positive.

You will probably see one or two attitude questions in each Listening Section.

EXERCISE 11.1

FOCUS: Answering purpose, method, and attitude questions about conversations.

DIRECTIONS: Listen to the conversations and the questions about them. Then mark
the answer choices that correctly answer the questions. You may take notes on the
conversations in the space allowed in the book or on another sheet of paper. As you
take notes, try to decide what purpose, method, or attitude questions might be
asked about the conversations. You may use your notes to help you answer the
questions.

▶ Now start the Audio Program. 🎧

▶ Listen to a conversation between two students. 🎧

Notes:

_____

_____

_____

_____

_____

_____

_____

_____

_____

_____

_____

> **Now get ready to answer the questions.**
> **You may use your notes to help you.**

1. Why does the woman mention her father?
   - ○ He may help solve the debate team's financial problem.
   - ○ Because he went to school in England, he suggested that the woman go there too.
   - ○ He advised his daughter to discuss the problem with Dean Metzger.
   - ○ Because of his own experience, he persuaded his daughter to join the debate team.

2. How does the man feel about the woman's appointment with Dean Metzger?

○ He doesn't think it will be as useful as a meeting with President Fisher would be.

○ He thinks it will probably hurt the woman's chances of getting what she wants.

○ He thinks it will be useless because he's heard that the dean is unfair.

○ He thinks it is a great idea as long as President Fisher does not attend the meeting.

▶ Listen to a conversation between two students. 🎧

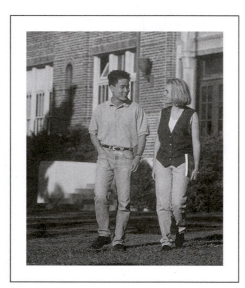

Notes:

_____

_____

_____

_____

_____

_____

_____

_____

_____

_____

Now get ready to answer the questions.
You may use your notes to help you.

3. How does the man explain his geology mid-term exam to the woman?

   ○ By comparing it with the exams she has taken in math class
   ○ By giving examples of tests that are used to identify minerals
   ○ By comparing it with both multiple-choice and essay exams
   ○ By showing her materials that his professor has prepared

4. What is the woman's attitude toward the taste test?

   ○ She finds it disgusting.
   ○ She realizes it is necessary.
   ○ She thinks it is amusing.
   ○ She doesn't understand it.

5. Why does the man mention quartz?

   ○ It is an example of a mineral that he has previously identified.
   ○ It is an example of a mineral that is softer than gypsum.
   ○ It is an example of a mineral that can be found in various colors.
   ○ It is an example of a mineral with a shiny metallic luster.

6. What is the man's attitude towards his geology mid-term?

   ○ He is hopeful and confident that he will do well.
   ○ He is sure of his abilities but not of his partner's.
   ○ He thinks it will be almost impossible to pass.
   ○ He thinks he needs more time to prepare for it.

LISTENING

EXERCISE 11.2

FOCUS: Answering purpose, method, and attitude questions about lectures and discussions.

DIRECTIONS: Listen to the lectures and discussions and the questions about them. Then mark the answer choices that correctly answer the questions. You may take notes on the lectures/discussions in the space allowed in the book or on another sheet of paper. As you take notes, try to decide what purpose, method, and attitude questions might be asked about the lectures and discussions. You may use your notes to help you answer the questions.

▶ Now start the Audio Program. 🎧

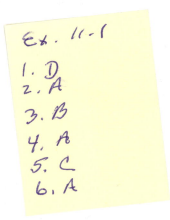

Ex. 11-1

1. D
2. A
3. B
4. A
5. C
6. A

► Listen to a discussion in a U.S. history class. 🎧

U.S. HISTORY

Notes:

_____

_____

_____

_____

_____

_____

_____

_____

_____

_____

**Now get ready to answer the questions.
You may use your notes to help you.**

1. Why does Ms. Adams mention the battle of Ivy Station?
   ○ It is not well known, but it was important to the outcome of the war.
   ○ It is an example of a battlefield that has already been lost to development.
   ○ It is a nearby battlefield that is in danger of being developed.
   ○ It is an example of a battlefield that has been adequately protected.

2. How does Ms. Adams make the class aware of the current condition of the Salt Run battlefield?
   - ○ She describes the battlefield in detail and urges students to visit it.
   - ○ She reads a description of the battle that took place there.
   - ○ She asks students to look at a photograph of the site.
   - ○ She draws a map of the site on the blackboard.

3. What is Ms. Adams's attitude toward re-enactors?
   - ○ She thinks they actually damage the battlefields.
   - ○ She disagrees with the methods they use but likes their goals.
   - ○ She would like to take part in a re-enactment herself.
   - ○ She appreciates the way they help her organization reach its goals.

4. What is David's attitude toward the preservation of Civil War battlefields?
   - ○ He doesn't think it is necessary to preserve the sites of unimportant battles.
   - ○ He thinks that the only good reason to save battlefields is for re-enactment.
   - ○ He doesn't agree that the government needs to protect big, important battlefields.
   - ○ He thinks that laws are needed to control further development of battlefields.

LISTENING

▶ Listen to a lecture in an American literature class. 🎧

AMERICAN LITERATURE

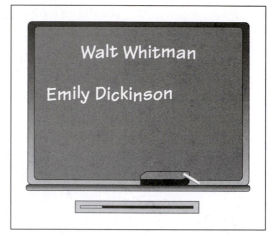

Notes:

_____

_____

_____

_____

_____

_____

_____

_____

_____

_____

> **Now get ready to answer the questions.**
> **You may use your notes to help you.**

5. Why does the professor mention the poet Walt Whitman?
   ○ He had a strong influence on Dickinson's poetry.
   ○ He and Dickinson became close friends.
   ○ He criticized Dickinson's lifestyle as well as her poetry.
   ○ He and Dickinson were both influential poets.

6. Why does the professor mention Harvard University?
   ○ Emily Dickinson attended Harvard for one year before her isolation at home.
   ○ Harvard owns the rights to Dickinson's poems and published her complete works.
   ○ Her first poem was published in a Harvard literary magazine.
   ○ A professor at Harvard was the first person to edit one of her poems.

7. Which of the following best summarizes the professor's attitude toward Emily Dickinson?
   ○ She thinks that Dickinson's isolation led her to choose unimportant topics for her poems.
   ○ She agrees with those scholars who say that Dickinson was not at all isolated.
   ○ She thinks Dickinson had a rather strange life but was a major poet.
   ○ She believes scholars pay too much attention to Dickenson's poems and not enough to her lifestyle.

8. How does the professor conclude her discussion of Emily Dickinson?
   ○ By reading part of one of her poems
   ○ By showing the class a picture of her
   ○ By reading what a critic said about her
   ○ By showing the class one of the "fascicles"

▶ Listen to a lecture in an art history class. 🎧

ART HISTORY

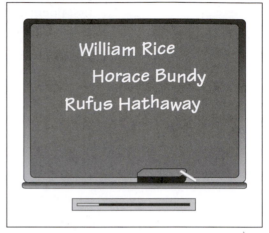

William Rice
Horace Bundy
Rufus Hathaway

Notes:

_____

_____

_____

_____

_____

_____

_____

_____

_____

_____

> **Now get ready to answer the questions.**
> **You may use your notes to help you.**

9. How does the professor introduce his discussion of folk art?
   - ○ He compares European folk art and American folk art.
   - ○ He compares folk art of the seventeenth century with that of the eighteenth century.
   - ○ He compares the views of European folklorists with those of American folklorists.
   - ○ He compares folk art created for commercial reasons to that created for artistic reasons.

10. Why does the professor mention wooden carousel horses?
    - ○ They were made in factories by groups of workers.
    - ○ The Hotchkiss Museum does not consider them to be folk art.
    - ○ They were all made by artists from a distinct group.
    - ○ European folklorists consider them a fine example of folk art.

11. How does the professor explain the concept of "visual literacy"?
    - ○ By contrasting it with other kinds of literacy
    - ○ By mentioning examples from the past as well as one from the present
    - ○ By giving the definition that appeared in an essay in the catalog
    - ○ By showing examples of it that appear in the catalog

12. Why does the professor mention the sign for the King's Inn?
    - ○ It is an example of a sign with a shape that indicated a certain type of business.
    - ○ It is an example of a trade sign that was used as a landmark in Philadelphia.
    - ○ It is an example of a sign used to honor the King of England, George III.
    - ○ It is an example of a trade sign with a political message.

13. Why does the professor mention the sign painter William Rice?
    - ○ He was once a famous artist but today is almost unknown.
    - ○ He painted the only signs in the exhibit that were signed by the artist.
    - ○ He is best known for painting portraits, not for painting signs.
    - ○ His signs were charming but were not part of the exhibit at the Hotchkiss.

LISTENING

Replay questions ask you to focus on a short portion of a conversation or lecture that you just listened to. You see the photograph of the speaker(s) again, and you hear (but you don't read) a few lines of the conversation or lecture a second time. An icon of headphones 🎧 tells you when you will hear the replayed section.

Replay questions can be phrased in a number of ways:

Why does _____ say this? 🎧

What does _____ mean when s/he says this? 🎧

What does _____ imply when s/he says this? 🎧

Replay questions ask for various types of information.

- Some of these questions ask you about the speaker's motivation for mentioning certain information in the lecture. The answers usually begin with an infinitive explaining possible purposes, such as "To explain . . ." or "To summarize . . ." or "To indicate . . . ," and so on.

- Some of these questions ask you about language "functions": Is the speaker apologizing? Changing the subject? Complaining? Clarifying? Asking for more information? Making a suggestion? Expressing doubt or uncertainty? Interrupting? Showing impatience?

- Some of these questions ask you what the speaker means or implies when s/he says something. These questions often ask you about an idiom or some other set expression that the speaker uses.

Example:

Student A

I'm going to ask Michael if he'll help me with these problems.

Student B

Save your breath. He's way too busy this week.

The idiom "Save your breath" means "Don't waste your time."

- Some of these questions ask you about language that can have different meanings in different circumstances. The context of the conversation or lecture as well as the speaker's tone of voice, stress on a certain word or phrase, or intonation, tells you which meaning the speaker intends.

  Here are four short conversations that all use the phrase "I'm sorry," but in each of the four sentences, the speaker's intention is different.

▶ Listen to these four conversations in the Audio Program. 🎧

- In the first conversation, the student is apologizing for turning in his assignment late and saying that he will not do so again in the future.

- In the second conversation, the student does not understand the phrase "the Krebs cycle" and is asking the professor to repeat the phrase.

- In the third conversation, the woman is turning down an invitation to go skiing.
- In the fourth conversation, the woman is explaining to the man the reason he cannot reserve a tennis court at that time (because the facility isn't open then).

There are two slightly different formats for replay questions.

Replay Question Type 1	In the first type, the narrator asks a question first. You then hear one line of the conversation or lecture and answer the question.
Replay Question Type 2	In the second type, the narrator tells you to listen again. You hear a short portion (several lines) of the conversation or lecture. After that, the narrator asks, "What does the speaker mean when s/he says this?" Then you hear one line from the conversation or lecture one more time.

LISTENING

Replay questions require close, word-for-word listening. And remember: you can (and you should!) take notes during the replay. In fact, you should try to write down as much as possible of what the speakers say during the replay.

Here is an example of a replay question based on part of a lecture from the Listening Preview Test.

Sample Item

▶ Listen to a replay question from the Listening Preview Test. Sample notes are also provided. (You can see a script of this part of the lecture in the Answer Key/Audioscript book or online at http://elt.heinle.com/toef1.)

▶ Now start the Audio Program. 🎧

Sample Notes:

○	This sub-zone: If like var'ty, not happy here— 　see only ½ doz. tree spec. for miles In few days, talk abt. trop rn forest lot of var'ty there

Why does the professor say this? 🎧

○ To explain why he finds the taiga a less interesting biome than the tropical rain forest

○ To emphasize that this sub-zone is far less varied than the tropical rain forest.

○ To explain to students why he is talking about the taiga today, not in a few days

○ To try to encourage students to find out more about different types of biomes

The best choice is 2. The professor is emphasizing that there are very few species of trees in this sub-zone (the closed forest) by comparing it with a tropical rain forest, where there are many species. He does this by saying that a person who likes a variety of trees would be unhappy in this sub-zone. Choice 1 is not correct because the professor does not say he himself thinks the taiga is less interesting than the tropical rain forest. He does not explain why he is discussing the taiga today (choice 3), he simply says that the class will begin to discuss tropical rain forests in a couple of days. He does not, in this part of the lecture, urge students to learn more about different types of biomes (choice 4).

There will probably be four or five replay questions in each Listening Section.

EXERCISE 12.1

FOCUS: Understanding the language and intonation of replay questions.

DIRECTIONS: Listen to some short conversations and statements followed by replay questions. Then mark the statements below **T** (true) or **F** (false) depending on the information that you hear.

▶ Now start the Audio Program. 🎧

T / F   1. Neither student enjoyed the statistics course.

T / F   2. The woman thinks her lab partner had a good excuse.

T / F   3. Professor White seldom changes his grade.

T / F   4. Greg has already changed his major several times.

T / F   5. The woman thinks the man should move out of his apartment quickly.

T / F   6. Doctor Stansfield does not think Mark should drop the physiology class.

T / F   7. The professor doesn't think he can translate the poem.

T / F   8. The man is already familiar with these terms.

T / F   9. The professor is explaining why the class will be continuing their study of imaginary numbers.

T / F 10. The student is certain that his answer is correct.

T / F 11. The professor is now returning to the main topic.

T / F 12. Most of the students' essays were too short.

EXERCISE 12.2

FOCUS: Answering replay questions about conversations.

DIRECTIONS: Listen to short portions of conversations and the questions about them. Then mark the answer choices that correctly answer the questions. You may take notes on the conversations in the space allowed in the book or on another sheet of paper. You may use your notes to help you answer the questions.

Note: *These short portions of conversations are taken from conversations that you heard in Lessons 9 through 11.*

▶ Now start the Audio Program. 🎧

(Question 1 is from the conversation in Lesson 9 about checking out reserve materials from the library.)

▶ Listen again to part of the conversation. Then answer the question.

Notes:

_____

_____

_____

_____

_____

1. What does the woman mean when she says this?
   ○ That she is willing to risk not seeing the reserve material this evening
   ○ That she is concerned about reading the material before another student checks it out
   ○ That she doesn't plan to eat dinner at her dorm this evening
   ○ That she's certain no other student will check out the reserve material this evening

(Question 2 is from the conversation in Lesson 9 about an archaeological dig.)

▶ Listen again to part of the conversation. Then answer the question.

Notes:

_____

_____

_____

_____

_____

2. What does the woman mean when she says this? 🎧
   ○ Absolutely no artifacts were found.
   ○ The trip was not fun or interesting.
   ○ All the artifacts that they found were broken.
   ○ The expedition was extremely successful.

(Questions 3 and 4 are from the conversation in Lesson 10 about the graduate art exhibit.)

▶ Listen again to part of the conversation. Then answer the question.

Notes:

_____

_____

_____

_____

_____

3. What does the woman imply when she says this?
   - ○ The sculpture is not really very abstract.
   - ○ She doesn't like the metal object.
   - ○ She wants to know what the man thinks of the object.
   - ○ She doesn't know the name of the work of art.

▶ Listen again to part of the conversation. Then answer the question.

Notes:

_____

_____

_____

_____

_____

4. What does the man mean when he says this?
   - ○ His sister gets paint on her clothing when she teaches art classes to children.
   - ○ The children who are in his sister's class have affected the way she paints.
   - ○ His sister has had a strong influence on the way that the children paint.
   - ○ He thinks his sister would rather teach art than paint pictures herself.

(Question 5 is from the conversation in Lesson 10 about the Study Skills Center.)

▶ Listen again to part of the conversation. Then answer the question.

Notes:

_____

_____

_____

_____

_____

5. What does the man mean when he says this? 🎧
   ○ He's pleased that the class is at a convenient location.
   ○ He doesn't care for the woman's suggestion.
   ○ He doesn't have enough time to take another class.
   ○ He thinks this class sounds perfect for him.

(Question 6 is from the conversation in Lesson 10 about the Resident Advisor position.)

▶ Listen again to part of the conversation. Then answer the question.

Notes:

_____

_____

_____

_____

_____

6. What does the man imply when he says this? 🎧
   ○ He is interested in the position but has not definitely decided to apply.
   ○ He is probably not going to apply, but he does not want to be impolite to Ms. Delfino.
   ○ He has definitely decided that he can't accept the position.
   ○ He assumes that he will not be offered the position even though he would like to have it.

(Questions 7 through 9 are from the conversation in Lesson 11 about the problems of the debate team.)

▶ Listen again to part of the conversation. Then answer the question.

Notes:

_____

_____

_____

_____

_____

7. What does the man mean when he says this? 🎧
   ○ He doesn't want to discuss the budget cuts.
   ○ He doesn't have any solution to the woman's problem.
   ○ He agrees with the woman's ideas but not with her methods.
   ○ He's afraid the woman will be offended by his opinion.

▶ Listen again to part of the conversation. Then answer the question.

Notes:

_____

_____

_____

_____

_____

8. What does the woman mean when she says this? 🎧
   ○ She doesn't know how to respond to the man's question.
   ○ What the man is asking her is not really clear.
   ○ There are many reasons why the debate team is worthwhile.
   ○ She does not wish to begin another discussion with the man.

▶ Listen again to part of the conversation. Then answer the question.

Notes:

_____

_____

_____

_____

_____

9. What does the man mean when he says this? ⌒

  ○ He's already convinced by the woman's arguments.
  ○ He would like to contribute to the debate team.
  ○ He wants to hear some more reasons.
  ○ He thinks the woman should quit the debate team.

(Questions 10 through 13 are from the conversation in Lesson 11 about the geology mid-term.)

▶ Listen again to part of the conversation. Then answer the question.

Notes:

_____

_____

_____

_____

_____

10. Why does the woman say this? 🎧
    - ○ To complain about the fact that the man's test will be so difficult
    - ○ To explain similar experiments on mineral samples that she has done herself
    - ○ To indicate surprise that one can identify minerals through tests
    - ○ To ask about the difference between minerals and rocks

▶ Listen again to part of the conversation. Then answer the question.

Notes:

_____

_____

_____

_____

_____

11. What does the woman mean when she says this? 🎧
    - ○ She wants to know what other types of tests the man must take.
    - ○ She wants to see the scale.
    - ○ She doesn't think the man is using the correct name for the scale.
    - ○ She's unfamiliar with the Mohs scale.

▶ Listen again to part of the conversation. Then answer the question.

Notes:

_____

_____

_____

_____

_____

12. What does the man mean when he says this? 🎧
    - ○ He's completely contradicting what he said before.
    - ○ He's explaining why he made a mistake earlier.
    - ○ He's clarifying what he said earlier with new information.
    - ○ He's apologizing for confusing the woman earlier.

▶ Listen again to part of the conversation. Then answer the question.

Notes:

_____

_____

_____

_____

_____

13. Why does the woman say this?
    - ○ To indicate that she does not wish to see any more photos of minerals
    - ○ To express satisfaction with the man's explanation
    - ○ To indicate confusion about the information the man just gave her
    - ○ To request more specific examples

EXERCISE 12.3

FOCUS: Answering replay questions about lectures and discussions.

DIRECTIONS: Listen to short portions of lectures and discussions and questions about them. Then mark the answer choices that correctly answer the questions. You may take notes on the lectures in the space allowed in the book or on another sheet of paper. You may use your notes to help you answer the questions.

Note: *These short portions of lectures and discussions are taken from lectures that you previously heard in the Listening Preview Test and in Lessons 9 through 11.*

▶ Now start the Audio Program. 🎧

(Question 1 is from the student presentation about Venus in the Preview Test.)

▶ Listen again to the professor's comment. Then answer the question.

Notes:

_____

_____

_____

_____

_____

LISTENING

1. Why does the professor say this? 🎧
   - ○ To explain to the class why Venus was the goddess of love
   - ○ To contradict what Charlie said about why the planet is named *Venus*
   - ○ To urge students to look at Venus both in the morning and in the evening
   - ○ To supply some information that was missing from Charlie's presentation

(Question 2 is from the lecture in Lesson 9 about computerized choreography.)

▶ Listen again to part of the lecture. Then answer the question.

Notes:

_____

_____

_____

_____

_____

2. What does the woman mean when she says this? 🎧
   - ○ Computers used children's pictures to choreograph dance.
   - ○ The first choreography programs used very simple graphic images.
   - ○ Computers have been used to choreograph dances for children.
   - ○ The dancers used as models for the figures were not very talented.

(Questions 3 and 4 are from the discussion in Lesson 9 about extra-sensory perception [ESP].)

▶ Listen **again** to part of the discussion. Then answer the question.

Notes:

_____

_____

_____

_____

_____

3. What does the professor mean when he says this? 🎧
   ○ He is not sure what most researchers think of the results of Rhine's experiments.
   ○ He thinks the language Rhine used to describe his own experiments was confusing.
   ○ He does not agree with the opinion of most scientists about Rhine's experiments.
   ○ He could use much stronger language to attack Rhine's conclusions.

▶ Listen **again** to part of the discussion. Then answer the question.

Notes:

_____

_____

_____

_____

_____

4. Why does the professor say this? 🎧
   - ○ To summarize his opinion on the validity of ESP
   - ○ To explain why many people believe in ESP
   - ○ To contradict what he said earlier about ESP
   - ○ To admit that he has never carefully examined the proof for ESP

(Question 5 is from the discussion in Lesson 9 about the painter Edward Hopper.)

▶ Listen again to part of the discussion. Then answer the question.

Notes:

_____

_____

_____

_____

_____

5. What does the professor mean when she says this? 🎧
   - ○ She agrees that the man has given the correct name for the painting but prefers to use the shorter name in class.
   - ○ She wants the students to know that the painter himself preferred the title *Nighthawks at the Diner.*
   - ○ She is pointing out that the man has made a common mistake about the title of the painting.
   - ○ She is indicating that she is not sure which of the two titles for the painting is correct.

(Questions 6 and 7 are from the lecture in Lesson 9 about the *Iliad* and the *Odyssey.*)

▶ Listen again to part of the lecture. Then answer the question.

Notes:

_____

_____

_____

_____

_____

6. What does the professor mean when she says this? 🎧
   - ⃝ The point that she makes about epic poems is not important to the lecture.
   - ⃝ The students are probably familiar with the concept of epic poems.
   - ⃝ The class has probably already read the epic poems she is discussing.
   - ⃝ She doesn't have time to discuss the concept of epic poems today.

▶ Listen again to part of the lecture. Then answer the question.

Notes:

_____

_____

_____

_____

_____

7. What does the professor mean when she says this? 🎧
   - ⃝ She is giving a reason why Odysseus is considered a strong warrior.
   - ⃝ She's telling the class why the Trojan War lasted so long.
   - ⃝ She's explaining why she prefers the characters in the *Iliad* to Odysseus.
   - ⃝ She is giving an example of how clever Odysseus could be.

(Question 8 is from the lecture in Lesson 9 about Hot Dry Rocks [HDR].)

▶ Listen again to part of the lecture. Then answer the question.

Notes:

_____

_____

_____

_____

_____

8. Why does the professor say this? 🎧
   ○ To indicate that, in reality, it is not possible to get energy from HDR
   ○ To stress that the process of obtaining energy from HDR is quite simple
   ○ To suggest that, in practice, getting energy from HDR might not be easy
   ○ To indicate that the theory of getting energy from HDR is not hard to understand

(Question 9 is from the discussion in Lesson 10 about potlatches.)

▶ Listen again to part of the discussion. Then answer the question.

Notes:

_____

_____

_____

_____

_____

9. What does the student mean when he says this?
   ○ He still doesn't understand the concept of a potlatch.
   ○ He didn't hear the last thing that the professor said.
   ○ He wants to apologize for making a mistake.
   ○ He thinks the professor must be mistaken.

(Questions 10 and 11 are from the discussion in Lesson 10 about the hula.)

▶ Listen again to part of the discussion. Then answer the question.

LISTENING

Notes:

_____

_____

_____

_____

_____

10. What does the student mean when she says this? 🎧
    ○ She thinks that the hula must be an easy dance to perform.
    ○ She finds the professor's question simple to answer.
    ○ She is sure that the topic of traditional dance is easily understood.
    ○ She believes that the professor's explanation is too simplistic.

▶ Listen again to part of the discussion. Then answer the question.

Notes:

_____

_____

_____

_____

_____

11. What does the professor mean when she says this? 🎧
    ○ She has absolutely no idea why the ukulele was given its name.
    ○ No one knows why the name "jumping flea" was given to the ukulele.
    ○ She is not sure if *ukulele* really means "jumping flea."
    ○ She is explaining why she has not been telling the truth.

(Questions 12 and 13 are from the discussion in Lesson 11 about Civil War battle sites.)

▶ Listen again to part of the discussion. Then answer the question.

Notes:

_____

_____

_____

_____

12. What does the speaker mean when she says this? 🎧
   - ○ She is describing the fighting during a Civil War battle.
   - ○ She is describing the re-enactment of a Civil War battle.
   - ○ She is describing the lack of interest in learning history.
   - ○ She is describing the difficulty of saving Civil War battlefields.

▶ Listen again to part of the discussion. Then answer the question.

Notes:

_____

_____

_____

_____

_____

13. What does Professor Nugent mean when he says this? 🎧
   - ○ He disagrees with Ms. Adams's viewpoint and wants to express his own.
   - ○ He wants to respond to what David said before Ms. Adams does.
   - ○ He agrees with what David said and wants to add his own comment.
   - ○ He wants David to clarify his comment before Ms. Adams responds.

(Questions 14 and 15 are from the lecture in Lesson 11 about Emily Dickinson.)

▶ Listen again to part of the lecture. Then answer the question.

Notes:

_____

_____

_____

_____

_____

14. What does the professor mean when she says this? ⌒
   ○ She has talked about Whitman's life, now she wants to discuss his poetry.
   ○ She now wants to talk about the other great voice in nineteenth-century American poetry.
   ○ She is now going to continue her discussion of Walt Whitman.
   ○ She momentarily forgot what she was going to say about nineteenth-century poetry.

▶ Listen again to part of the lecture. Then answer the question.

   Notes:

_____

_____

_____

_____

_____

15. What does the professor mean when she says this? ⌒
   ○ The poems are difficult to understand.
   ○ The students don't have to read all of the poems.
   ○ The poems are not very long.
   ○ The students have already read the poems.

LESSON 13
ORDERING AND MATCHING QUESTIONS

Ordering questions and **matching questions** require a general understanding of the lecture or at least a major section of the lecture. These two types of questions are asked only about the lectures and academic discussions, not about conversations.

(A) Ordering Questions

Ordering questions require you to put four (sometimes three) events or steps in a process into the correct order. Anytime a speaker presents events in chronological order (the order in which they occurred), a biography of a person, the steps of a process, or a ranking of things according to their importance, there will probably be an ordering question. Listen for time words (years, dates) and words that signal a sequence.

Common Sequence Words		
before that	afterwards	first
earlier than	next	second
previously	after that	third
prior to	later	fourth
sooner than	subsequent	following that

As you take notes, use numbers to keep track of the order of events or steps in the sequence. You can circle these numbers to make them easier to find.

Remember: The order in which the speaker *mentions* events or steps is not necessarily the order in which they happened.

To answer ordering questions on the computer, first click on one of the four words, phrases, or sentences in the top half of the screen and then drag and drop it into the appropriate box (labeled 1, 2, 3, and 4) in the lower half of the screen. The expression from the top will then appear in the box that you dropped it into. Do this for all four boxes. If you change your mind, click on the answer that you wish to change and your original choice will disappear from the box.

You need to figure out the correct positions for only three answers because the fourth answer must go in the remaining blank.

Sample Item 1

Here is a section of a presentation from the Listening Preview Test and an ordering question about it. Sample notes on this section of the lecture are also provided. (You can see a script of this lecture in the Answer Key/Audioscript book or online at http://elt.heinle.com/toefl.)

▶ Now start the Audio Program. 🎧

Sample Notes:

Important Space Probes:
   ④ Magellan—'90—4 years—radar, maps—volcanoes
   ① Mariner 2—'62—1st — (Mariner 1 blew up)
   ② Venera 4—'67—Sov. Union—dropped instrum—showed how hot—
     lasted only few secs.
   ③ Ven. Pioneer 2—'78—discovered CO_2
     + many others

Sample Question:

In what order were these space probes sent to Venus?

Place the letters in the proper boxes.

A. **Mariner 2**
B. **Venus Pioneer 2**
C. **Magellan**
D. **Venera 4**

1.
2.
3.
4.

The speaker mentions the space probe Magellan first. This was launched in 1990. He then goes on to mention the first probe sent to Venus, which was launched in 1962. He next discusses the Soviet Union's probe Venera 4, which was launched in 1967. The last probe he mentions is the Venus Pioneer, launched in 1978. Except for the first probe, Magellan, the speaker lists the probes in chronological order. Magellan is actually the most recent. Therefore, the correct order is A. Mariner 2, D. Venera 4, B. Venus Pioneer 2, and C. Magellan.

You will probably see one or two ordering questions in each Listening Section.

(B) Matching Questions

Matching questions require you to connect three words, phrases, or sentences with three categories somehow related to them. If the lecturer or speaker lists three or more general concepts and then gives definitions, examples, characteristics, or uses of those concepts, you will probably see a matching question.

As you take notes, you should normally list specific characteristics of a general concept under that concept. You can then use your notes to answer the questions.

To answer a matching question on the computer, click on one of the three expressions in the top half of the screen and then drag and drop it into the box below the expression that you think is related to it. That word or phrase will then appear in the box you dropped it into. Do this for all three boxes. If you change your mind, click on the item again and the choice will disappear.

For these questions, you really need to find only two correct choices because the third choice must obviously go in the remaining empty box.

Sample Item 2

Here is a section of a lecture from the Listening Preview Test and a matching question about it. Sample notes are also provided. (You can see a script of this conversation in the Answer Key/Audioscript book or online at http://elt.heinle.com/toefl.)

▶ Now start the Audio Program. 🎧

▶ Listen to part of a lecture in a biology class. 🎧

LISTENING

Sample Notes:

Taiga: 3 sub-zones
1. open forest—needle-leaf (= evergrn = connif.)
small, far apart sim. to tundra w/ few sm. trees
2. closed forest—bigger needle-leaf, closer together
feels like real forest not much var'ty _ doz. spec.
3. mixed zone—even bigger trees some broadlf (=decid.) trees esp. by
rivers, etc.
e.g. larch, aspen
more like temperate forests

Sample Question:

The professor discussed three sub-zones of the taiga. Match each sub-zone with its characteristic.

Write the letter of the answer choice in the appropriate box. Use each answer only once.

A. Open forest   **B. Closed forest**   **C. Mixed forest**

Larger needle-leaf trees grow closer together.	Some broad-leaf trees grow here, especially near water.	Widely spaced, small needle-leaf trees grow here.

    The professor describes open forest as having only needle-leaf trees that grow far apart, so choice A should be placed in the third box. He describes closed forest as having needle-leaf trees larger than those in an open forest. He says it feels more like a real forest and lacks variety. Choice B should therefore be placed in the first box. The professor says that mixed forest contains even bigger trees and some broad-leaf trees, especially along rivers and creeks. Therefore, you should place C in the second box. (Besides, this is the only empty box, so you have to put choice C here!)

    You will probably see one or two matching questions per Listening Section.

B   C   A

Exercise **13.1**

Focus: Answering ordering and matching questions about lectures and academic discussions.

Directions: Listen to the lectures and discussions and the questions about them. You may take notes on the lectures in the space allowed in the book or on another sheet of paper. As you take notes, try to decide what ordering and matching questions might be asked about the lectures. You may use your notes to help you answer the questions.

▶ Now start the Audio Program. 🎧

▶ Listen to a lecture in a chemistry class. 🎧

CHEMISTRY

Notes:

_____

_____

_____

_____

_____

_____

_____

_____

_____

_____

> **Now get ready to answer the questions.**
> **You may use your notes to help you.**

1. The lecturer discusses the steps involved in the creation of coal. Summarize this process by putting the steps in the proper order.

Place the letters in the proper boxes.

   A. During the decomposition process, plants lose oxygen and hydrogen.
   B. Layers of sand and mud put pressure on the peat.
   C. Plants grow in swampy areas.
   D. Plants die and fall into swampy waters.

1.	
2.	
3.	
4.	

2. Match the form of coal with the type of industry that primarily uses it.

Put the letters in the proper boxes.

   A. Coal tar   **B. Bituminous coal**   **C. Coke**

Electric utilities	Plastic manufacturers	Steel makers

▶ Listen to a discussion in an accounting seminar. 🎧

ACCOUNTING

Notes:

_____

_____

_____

_____

_____

_____

_____

_____

_____

_____

_____

**Now get ready to answer the questions.
You may use your notes to help you.**

3.   Match the accounting principle with the appropriate description of it.
       Place the letters in the proper boxes.

A. Matching principle	B. Cost principle	C. Business entity principle
Owner's and business's accounts must be separate.	Firm must record sales in period when they are made.	Expenses must be recorded at their original price.

▶ Listen to a guest lecture in an agricultural economics class. 🎧

AGRICULTURAL ECONOMICS

Notes:

_____

_____

_____

_____

_____

_____

_____

_____

_____

> **Now get ready to answer the questions.**
> **You may use your notes to help you.**

4. The lecturer mentions four types of crops that are grown in Harrison County. Rank these four types of crops in their order of economic importance, beginning with the *most* important.

Place the letters in the proper boxes.

A. **Heirloom crops**
B. **Wheat**
C. **Corn**
D. **Soybeans**

1.	
2.	
3.	
4.	

5. Match the type of wheat with the product that is most often made from it.

Place the letters in the proper boxes.

A. **Soft white wheat**   B. **Hard red wheat**   C. **Durum wheat**

Pasta	Bread flour	Breakfast cereals

▶ Listen to a discussion in a modern history class. 🎧

MODERN HISTORY

Notes:

_____

_____

_____

_____

_____

_____

_____

_____

_____

_____

> **Now get ready to answer the questions.**
> **You may use your notes to help you.**

6. The professor discusses some of the history of Antarctic exploration. Summarize this history by putting these events in the correct chronological order.

Place the letters in the proper boxes.

A. **Shackleton's expedition approaches the South Pole.**
B. **Scott's party reaches the South Pole.**
C. **Byrd flies over the South Pole.**
D. **Amundsen's party reaches the South Pole.**

1.
2.
3.
4.

7. Match these Antarctic explorers with the countries from which they came.

Place the letters in the proper boxes.

A. Byrd   **B. Scott**   **C. Amundsen**

United States	Norway	Britain

▶ Listen to a lecture in a musical acoustics class. 🎧

MUSICAL ACOUSTICS

 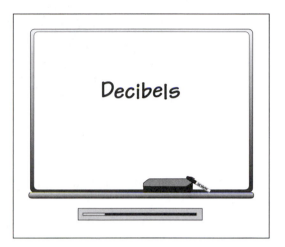

Notes:

_____

_____

_____

_____

_____

_____

_____

_____

_____

_____

**Now get ready to answer the questions.
You may use your notes to help you.**

8. The professor mentions several conditions caused by excessively loud music. Match the condition to the correct description of it.

Place the letters in the proper boxes.

A. Tinnitus   **B. NIHL**   **C. TTS**

Permanent loss of hearing from loud sounds	Ringing in the ears	Temporary loss of the ability to hear low-volume sounds

9. The professor lists several musical events at which her students recorded sound levels. List these events in the correct order based on volume, beginning with the highest volume.

Place the letters in the proper boxes.

A. **Amplified rock music concert at the stadium**
B. **Recorded music at Club 1010**
C. **Symphony concert**
D. **Automotive sound system**

1.
2.
3.
4.

▶ Listen to a lecture in a U.S. literature class. 🎧

U.S. LITERATURE

Notes:

_____

_____

_____

_____

_____

_____

_____

_____

_____

_____

**Now get ready to answer the questions.
You may use your notes to help you.**

10. The professor gives a brief biography of the writer Edgar Allan Poe. List these events from his life in the order in which they occurred.

Place the letters in the proper boxes.

A. **Published his first book of poems**
B. **Entered the U.S. military academy**
C. **Worked as a clerk**
D. **Traveled to England**

1. [ ]
2. [ ]
3. [ ]
4. [ ]

11. Match these works by Edgar Allan Poe with the type of writing that they represent.

Place the letters in the proper boxes.

A. **"The Gold Bug"**   B. **"The Raven"**   C. **"The Fall of the House of Usher"**

Poem	Horror Story	Detective Story

► Listen to a lecture in an anthropology class. 🎧

ANTHROPOLOGY

Notes:

_____

_____

_____

_____

_____

_____

_____

_____

_____

_____

> **Now get ready to answer the questions.**
> **You may use your notes to help you.**

12. The professor mentions a number of archaeological finds that were related to the domestication of dogs. Match these finds with their locations.

Place the letters in the proper boxes.

A. A fragment of a dog's bone	B. A rock painting showing hunting dogs	C. A rock painting showing herding dogs

A cave in Germany	The mountains of Iraq	The desert of Algeria

13. The professor mentions a number of roles that dogs have played since they were first domesticated. List these roles in chronological order, beginning with the earliest role that ~~dogs played~~ [oxes.]

A. Hunter
B. Companion
C. Guard
D. Herder

1. _____
2. _____
3. _____
4. _____

[Handwritten note:]
12. A, B C
13. C, A, D, B

LESSON 14
COMPLETING CHARTS

Complete-the-chart questions require an understanding of all or a major part of a lecture. (Chart questions will not be asked about conversations.)

The chart consists of a grid. There are actually several types of grids. One type lists steps in a process. You have to decide if the steps in the grid are actually given in the lecture and then mark each step "Yes" or "No." Another type of grid lists specific characteristics. You have to decide if these characteristics are associated with a certain idea or some general concept, and indicate whether this information was included in the lecture by placing check marks in the appropriate boxes.

Your notes can be very helpful when you answer complete-the-chart questions. During the lecture, listen for the speaker to mention steps in a process or characteristics related to a topic, and then write them down.

Sample Item

Here is a section of a discussion from the Listening Preview Test and complete-the-chart question about it. Sample notes are also provided. (You can see a script of this part of the lecture in the Answer Key/Audioscript book or online at http://elt.heinle.com/toefl.)

▶ Now start the Audio Program. 🎧

Sample Notes:

Cases are real business sits: 10-20 pp. of text describing a prob.
+ 5-10 pp. exhibits"
(Exhib. = statistic. info: spreadshts, etc.)
1. Analyze prob and data (get more if needed)
2. Make decisions about data
3. Usu. involves role-play (e.g., roleplay CEO, CFO)
4. Work in grps (4-5 Stu); builds teamwork
5. Give presentation/write report (group grade based on this)
Not all classes use cases; some lectures, some combin. lect + cases Some
use computer simulations (e.g. World Mktplace)

Sample Question:

In this lecture, the professor describes the process of the case study method.
Indicate whether each of the following is a step in the process.

Put a check mark (✓) in the proper box for each phrase.

	Yes	No
Analyze the business situation and exhibits		
Role-play		
Run a computer simulation		
Give a presentation and write a report		
Visit a real business and attend a meeting		

As you can see from the sample notes, the professor did mention the need to analyze the business problem and the data provided in the exhibits. You should therefore check **Yes** for the first step. The professor said that "solving the problem usually involves role-playing," so you should also click on **Yes** for the second step in the list. The professor said that some business classes involve computer simulations, but he was not talking about classes based on case study, so you should click on **No** for the third step. The professor said that a group grade was given for an oral presentation and a written report, so the fourth step should be marked **Yes.** There is no mention in the discussion that visiting a real business and attending a meeting was part of the case study process, so you should click **No** for the fifth step.

You will probably see one or two complete-the-chart questions in each Listening section.

EXERCISE 14.1

FOCUS: Answering complete-the-chart questions about lectures and academic discussions.

DIRECTIONS: Listen to the lectures and discussions and the questions about them. Then complete the chart by placing check marks (✓) in the appropriate boxes. You may take notes on the lectures in the space allowed in the book or on another sheet of paper. As you take notes, try to decide what complete-the-chart questions might be asked. You may use your notes to help you answer the questions.

Note: *You will not see more than one complete-the-chart question per lecture on actual tests. However, some of the lectures in this text feature more than one to give you more practice answering this type of question.*

▶ Now start the Audio Program. 🎧

▶ Listen to a discussion in an urban studies class. 🎧

URBAN STUDIES

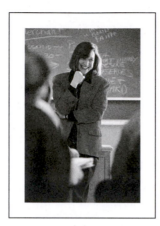

Notes:

_____
_____
_____
_____
_____
_____
_____
_____
_____

Now get ready to answer the questions.
You may use your notes to help you.

1. In this lecture, the professor describes the New Urbanism Movement. Indicate whether each of the following is a principle of this movement.

   Put a check mark (✓) in the proper box for each sentence.

	Yes	No
Plentiful parking is provided in large parking lots.		
Residents can walk easily to work or shopping areas.		
Residences, shops, and offices are all found on the same block.		
Communities are located only in large urban centers.		
Streets are generally laid out in a grid pattern.		

2. In this lecture, the professor mentions benefits associated with the New Urbanism Movement. Indicate whether each of the following is a benefit mentioned in the lecture.

   Put a check mark (✓) in the proper box for each sentence.

	Yes	No
Housing is less expensive in New Urban communities than in typical suburbs.		
There is less crime in New Urban communities.		
Most New Urban communities are conveniently located close to large suburban shopping malls.		
Residents of New Urban communities get more exercise.		
Most houses in New Urban communities feature garages that allow direct access to the house.		
There is less air pollution in New Urban communities.		

LISTENING

▶ Listen to a lecture in a British history class. 🎧

BRITISH HISTORY

Notes:

_____

_____

_____

_____

_____

_____

_____

_____

_____

_____

> **Now get ready to answer the question.**
> **You may use your notes to help you.**

3. In this lecture, the professor mentions myths (false stories) and realities (true stories) associated with the Magna Carta. Indicate whether each of the following is considered a myth or a reality.

Put a check mark (✓) in the proper box for each sentence.

	Myth	Reality
It created the first democratic society in England.		
It confirmed the rights of the English barons.		
It established the "model Parliament."		
It established courts in which citizens were tried by their peers.		
It was signed by King John himself.		

LISTENING

► Listen to a lecture in a paleontology class. 🎧

PALEONTOLOGY

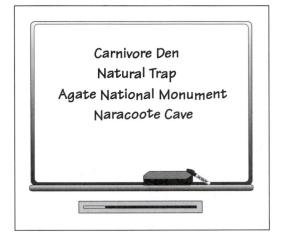

Carnivore Den
Natural Trap
Agate National Monument
Naracoote Cave

Notes:

_____

_____

_____

_____

_____

_____

_____

_____

_____

_____

**Now get ready to answer the questions.
You may use your notes to help you.**

4. In this lecture, the professor describes carnivore dens. Decide if the following are characteristics of carnivore dens.

Put a check mark (✓) in the proper box for each phrase.

	Yes	No
Tend to be found in horizontal caves with small entrances		
Contain only herbivore fossils		
May have had both herbivores and carnivores living in them		
Usually have a greater variety of fossils than natural traps		
Generally contain well-preserved fossils		

5. In this lecture, the professor describes important fossil finds at Naricoote Cave, a natural trap. Decide if the following are characteristics of Naricoote Cave.

Put a check mark (✓) in the proper box for each sentence.

	Yes	No
It was discovered by professional palaeontologists.		
Animals that fell in here died from the impact of the fall.		
Its entrance was covered by plants.		
It features the fossil bones of a previously unknown giant cat.		
It contains a greater variety of fossils than most natural traps.		

LISTENING

▶ Listen to a lecture in an astronomy class. 🎧

ASTRONOMY

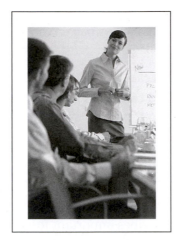

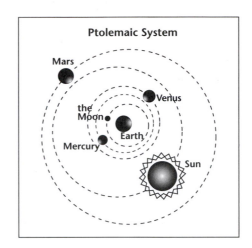

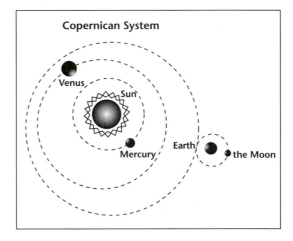

Notes:

_____

_____

_____

_____

_____

_____

_____

_____

_____

_____

**Now get ready to answer the question.
You may use your notes to help you.**

6. In this lecture, the professor describes two ways to look at the universe: the Ptolemaic model and the Copernican model. Decide if the following are characteristics of the Ptolemaic model or the Copernican model.

Put a check mark (✓) in the proper box for each sentence.

	Ptolemaic Model	Copernican Model
This model is also known as the "heliocentric model."		
"Epicycles" were used to help explain this model.		
This model became part of the medieval system of belief.		
This model was disproved by Galileo's discovery of the phases of Venus.		
This model provided a good picture of the solar system but not of the universe.		
Music was generated by the movement of crystal spheres.		

▶ Listen to a lecture in a marketing class. 🎧

MARKETING

Notes:

_____

_____

_____

_____

_____

_____

_____

_____

_____

_____

**Now get ready to answer the questions.
You may use your notes to help you.**

7. The lecturer describes the ABC approach to viewing consumer attitudes. Decide if the following are more closely related to the A component, the B component, or the C component of the ABC approach.

Put a check mark (✓) in the proper box for each sentence.

	A component	B component	C component
A consumer visits an Internet site to get more information about tires.			
A man feels a bicycle will make his daughter happy.			
A customer buys groceries at the store.			
An investor studies the market for art before buying a painting.			
A woman orders a sandwich and a drink at a fast-food restaurant.			

8. In this lecture, the professor describes the Katz system of attitude functions. Decide which of the following characteristics is related to which function.

Put a check mark (✓) in the proper box for each phrase.

	Value-expressive function	Ego-defensive function
May involve a product that protects a consumer from some threat		
May involve a product that consumers believe will make them more popular		
May involve a product that consumers believe will make people dislike them		
May involve a product that is harmful to the consumer who buys it		

LISTENING

LISTENING REVIEW TEST
DIRECTIONS

▶ Now start the Audio Program. 🎧

This section tests your understanding of conversations and lectures. You will hear each conversation or lecture only once. Your answers should be based on what is stated or implied in the conversations and lectures.

You are allowed to take notes as you listen, and you can use these notes to help you answer the questions.

In some questions, you will see a headphones icon: 🎧. This icon tells you that you will hear, but not read, part of the lecture again. Then you will answer a question about the part of the lecture that you heard.

Some questions have special directions that are highlighted.

During an actual test, you will not be allowed to skip questions and come back to them later, so try to answer every question that you hear on this test.

There are two conversations and four lectures. Most questions are separated by a ten-second pause.

▶ Listen to a conversation between a student and a professor. 🎧

> **Now get ready to answer the questions.**
> **You may use your notes to help you.**

1 of 34   What course does Scott want to drop?

　　○ Mathematics
　　○ Biochemistry
　　○ Medicine
　　○ Music

▶ Listen again to part of the conversation. 🎧

2 of 34   What does Professor Calhoun mean when she says this? 🎧

　　○ She respects Dr. Delaney's academic research.
　　○ She thinks that Dr. Delaney's advice should be respected.
　　○ She thinks that Scott should have more respect for Dr. Delaney.
　　○ She completely disagrees with Dr. Delaney's advice.

3 of 34   What does Professor Calhoun say about her class?

　　○ The most difficult part of it is already over.
　　○ It will be ending in a few days.
　　○ It is not required for students who plan to study medicine.
　　○ She will not be teaching it next year.

4 of 34   What does Professor Calhoun suggest that Scott do?

　　○ Wait a few days before he drops her class
　　○ Speak to Dr. Delaney again
　　○ Concentrate on his four other classes
　　○ Work with her teaching assistant

5 of 34   Which of the following best describes Professor Calhoun's attitude towards Scott?

　　○ Condescending
　　○ Angry
　　○ Encouraging
　　○ Disappointed

▶ Listen to a conversation between two students. 🎧

> **Now get ready to answer the questions.**
> **You may use your notes to help you.**

6 of 34   Why did Martha come to the library?
   ○ To look up some terms
   ○ To meet Stanley
   ○ To get some coffee
   ○ To prepare for a test

7 of 34   What did Stanley misplace?
   ○ His backpack
   ○ A notebook
   ○ Some index cards
   ○ A library book

▶ Listen again to part of the conversation. 🎧

8 of 34   What does Martha mean when she says this? 🎧
   ○ She thinks that Stanley had better hurry up.
   ○ She's surprised he is working on his papers so early.
   ○ She thinks she should do some research as well.
   ○ She's surprised that Stanley enjoys doing research.

9 of 34   According to Stanley, what does the term *stacks* refer to?
   ○ The section of the library where journals are stored
   ○ Piles of note cards
   ○ The part of the library where books are shelved
   ○ A place to get something to eat in the library

10 of 34   Where will Stanley go next?
   ○ To the periodicals room
   ○ To talk with a librarian
   ○ To the snack bar in the basement
   ○ To Williams Street

▶ Listen to part of a lecture in an elementary education class. 🎧

ELEMENTARY EDUCATION

My sister likes to ride her bike.

Pzol2tx
mssrlkrdrbk
mi ster like to rid hir bik
my sistre like to ride her bike.

**Now get ready to answer the questions.
You may use your notes to help you.**

11 of 34   Which of the following activities are signs of "writing readiness" in children?

Choose three answers.

☐ Asking to play with scissors and modeling clay
☐ Making marks on a page that look like writing
☐ Asking adults to guide their hands as they write something
☐ Writing numbers and simple words
☐ Using "invented letters"

12 of 34   What does the speaker imply about the system mentioned in the article that the students read, which was used to describe the development of writing skills?

○ It is no longer considered valid by most experts.
○ She does not agree with it at all.
○ It has fewer stages than some other systems.
○ It is the only one in common use today.

13 of 34   The speaker mentions four stages in the development of writing skills. Put these stages in the correct order, beginning with the earliest stage.

Put the letters of the stages in the proper boxes.

A. **Phonemic**
B. **Symbolic**
C. **Conventional**
D. **Transitional**

1.	
2.	
3.	
4.	

14 of 34   Why does the speaker mention Spanish and Finnish?

○ She thinks that children should learn to write several languages.

○ These languages are easier for young writers because they are phonetic languages.

○ She has learned to write in these languages herself.

○ Children often learn to write these languages without studying the rules of phonics.

15 of 34   Which of the following is the best example of writing done by a child in the transitional stage?

○ ꙗ ℧ℨ ꧒ ✕⊤⋔⊤ⵔ

○ ilketetpzaiskrmevda

○ I lik eat pissa an ise krim ever dae.

○ I'd like to eat piza and ice creem every day.

16 of 34   Which of these statements about writing assignments for young children would the professor probably agree with?

Choose two answers.

☐ They should be designed to increase accuracy and speed of writing.

☐ They should be as enjoyable as possible.

☐ They should emphasize communication skills.

☐ They should be carefully graded by teachers.

▶ Listen to a lecture in an astronomy class. 🎧

ASTRONOMY

> **Now get ready to answer the questions.**
> **You may use your notes to help you.**

17 of 34   What is the main purpose of this lecture?

- ○ To describe some recent research in astronomy
- ○ To discuss the first discovery of double stars
- ○ To give students an assignment to do in the observatory
- ○ To present a basic description of double stars

18 of 34   According to *most* astronomers, about what percentage of all stars are double stars?

- ○ 3% to 4%
- ○ 10%
- ○ 25%
- ○ 75%

19 of 34   According to the speaker, what does the term *comes* mean in astronomy?

- ○ It is the dimmer star in a binary pair.
- ○ It is one of the stars in a line-of-sight double.
- ○ It is a system having three or more stars.
- ○ In an eclipsing binary, it is the star that is eclipsed.

20 of 34   How many stars make up Mizar-Alcor?

- ○ Two
- ○ Three
- ○ Four
- ○ Eight

21 of 34   How does the speaker describe double stars of contrasting colors?

○ By comparing them to optical pairs
○ By comparing them to familiar objects found on Earth
○ By imagining what a space alien would think of them
○ By providing statistics about their relative ages

22 of 34   The speaker mentions a number of different double-star systems. Match these systems with their descriptions.

Place the letters of the choices in the proper boxes.

A. Mizar-Alcor   **B. Algol**   **C. Albireo**

Two stars of contrasting colors	An eclipsing binary	An optical pair

▶ Listen to a lecture in a marketing class. 🎧

MARKETING

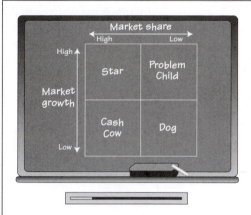

**Now get ready to answer the questions.
You may use your notes to help you.**

23 of 34   Which of the following is NOT one of the terms for the method the speaker
uses for classifying SBUs?

○ The BCG Method
○ The Boston Box
○ The General Electric/Shell Method
○ The Growth-Share Matrix

24 of 34   How does the speaker classify the SBU that makes athletic shoes?

○ As a star
○ As a dog
○ As a problem child
○ As a cash cow

25 of 34   Why is the term *cash cow* used to describe some SBUs?

○ Like actual dairy cows, they require a lot of care and daily attention.
○ They provide nourishment for "problem children."
○ They are often bought and sold as cows are sold at rural markets.
○ They produce a flow of profits as cows produce a flow of milk.

26 of 34   Which of these classification changes would probably most please the marketing manager of the firm that owns this SBU?

○ From star to problem child
○ From dog to cash cow
○ From cash cow to dog
○ From star to dog

27 of 34   In this lecture, the professor describes the marketing strategies of Langfield-Smith. Indicate whether each of the following is a strategy that Smith lists.

Put a check mark (✓) in the proper box for each phrase.

	Yes	No
Increase market share in an SBU and turn a cash cow into a star		
Reduce investment in an SBU and collect short-term profits		
Buy a well-performing SBU from another company, creating a new star		
Sell a poorly performing SBU and get rid of a dog		
Raise prices on an SBU's product and change a problem child to a cash cow		

28 of 34   What is the speaker's opinion of SBUs known as "dogs"?

○ Their products may be a useful part of a product portfolio.
○ They should be traded to other companies as soon as possible.
○ Their products should be aggressively promoted and advertised.
○ They should be "harvested" to increase short-term profits.

▶ Listen to a discussion in a marine biology class. 🎧

MARINE BIOLOGY

| Now get ready to answer the questions. |
| You may use your notes to help you. |

29 of 34 What is NOT known about the songs of the humpback whale?

Choose two answers.

- ☐ When humans first became aware of them
- ☐ Exactly how the whales produce them
- ☐ What they mean
- ☐ Who first heard them

30 of 34 In this lecture, the speaker describes two types of calls made by the humpback whale. Indicate whether each of the following is a characteristic of the low-frequency call or of the high-frequency call.

Put a check mark (✓) in the proper box for each phrase.

	Low-Frequency Sound	High-Frequency Sound
Travels a long distance		
Probably carries a lot of information		
Has a simple structure		
Is generally considered the "song" of the humpback whale		

31 of 34   The speaker analyzes the music of the humpback whale by breaking it down into its component parts. Arrange this list of the parts of the humpback's music, beginning with the simplest and shortest part and moving to the longest and most complex.

A. **Theme**
B. **Song**
C. **Element**
D. **Phrase**

Place the letters of the choices in the proper boxes.

1.
2.
3.
4.

32 of 34   How long does a humpback whale take to sing a complete song?

○ Three or four minutes
○ Seven or eight minutes
○ Ten to twenty minutes
○ Up to ten hours

33 of 34   When do humpback whales sing the most?

○ During the daytime when they are in warm waters
○ At night when they are feeding
○ During the day when they are migrating
○ On winter nights

▶   Listen again to part of the lecture. 🎧

34 of 34   What does the professor mean when she says this? 🎧

○ She agrees that the humpback songs are a form of oral history.
○ Because no one knows what humpback songs mean, the student's idea might be right.
○ She believes that the student's theory about the humpback songs is better than those of researchers.
○ Although it is not known what the humpback's songs mean, she is sure that they are not singing about their history.

This is the end of the Listening Review Test.

LISTENING TUTORIAL: NOTE TAKING

On the TOEFL iBT, note taking is not only allowed but encouraged. You will be given paper to use for taking notes. After the test, you will have to give your notes to the testing supervisor, but your notes will not be graded.

It certainly makes sense to allow note taking during the test, because the ability to take good lecture notes is an important academic skill. It's not common to take notes on conversations, except sometimes at meetings, but you will have to take notes on both conversations and lectures during this test.

Without notes, the Listening Section of the test is basically a test of memory, and few people have the memory skills to remember all the facts and ideas contained in a lecture lasting five to eight minutes. Research has shown that after twenty minutes has passed, people remember only about 50% of what they hear, and that about 20% of what they hear is remembered incorrectly.

Note taking is a complicated skill, especially note taking in another language. However, note-taking skills can definitely be improved by practice. The more you take notes, the faster and more accurate you will become. During all of the exercises in the Listening Section, you should take notes and use those notes to answer the questions.

TOEFL NOTE TAKING VS. UNIVERSITY NOTE TAKING

The lectures you hear in the Listening Section simulate (imitate) classroom lectures, but they are not the same. There are two important differences:

1. TOEFL iBT lectures are much *denser* than authentic lectures. From an hour-long classroom lecture, there may be one or two points that will be asked about on tests. On the other hand, there are six questions after a five- to eight-minute TOEFL iBT lecture. Therefore, TOEFL iBT lectures have more facts and information that can be asked about. As a result, your note taking must be more detailed and intensive for the TOEFL iBT than the notes you would take in a lecture class.

2. You may not need to use your notes for a few weeks or even for a few months after you hear a lecture in a classroom. After that much time has passed, you may have forgotten much of the lecture. However, you will use your TOEFL notes immediately after the lecture (and then never again!). Therefore, you can use more abbreviations and omit more words when you take notes on TOEFL lectures. And you don't have to worry too much about writing legibly.

SOME HINTS ON TAKING NOTES

1. Take notes throughout the lecture. Try to write down as much information as you possibly can.

2. Always write down any terms that are new to you, definitions, specific facts, lists of items, and statistics.

3. Speakers will sometimes give clues telling you which points in a lecture are especially important and will be asked about. Some of the most common clues:

   A. Repetition of a point

   B. Emphasis from tone of voice or from pauses before or after making a point

   C. The amount of time spent on a point

4. Pay attention to the use of signal words or phrases in the lecture, especially ones that indicate the structure of the lecture or a change of topic.

Common Signal Words
Words and Phrases Indicating the Structure of the Lecture
There are three kinds of . . .
We'll be looking at a couple of ways to . . .
First, . . .
Then , . . .
That brings us to . . .
There are two points of view . . .
Next I want to mention . . .
First, let's look at . . .
Next, let's consider . . .
Okay, now let's talk about . . .
Now, what about _____?
Finally, . . .

Words and Phrases Indicating a Change of Direction

On the other hand,
However,
But . . .

Words and Phrases Showing Emphasis or Importance

Most importantly,
One important point/issue/problem/question/concept is . . .
Especially
Significantly,
Be sure to note that . . .
Pay special attention to . . .

Words and Phrases Used to Give Examples

For example,
Take _____ , for example . . .
For instance,
Let's consider the case of . . .
Specifically,

5. In academic discussions, important information may be in comments that students make (particularly if the professor agrees with the student).

6. When taking notes on conversations, pay attention to who is saying what. For example, if a professor is speaking to a student, you may want to put the initial **P** before notes on what the professor says and **S** before what the student says.

7. Take notes during replay questions. In fact, try to write down as many words as possible when listening for the second time.

8. Organize your lecture notes according to order of importance. The most important ideas should be on the left side of the page. Indent to the right to show that an idea is subordinate to or supports the more important idea. In other words, ideas on the left side of the page are general divisions of the lecture. As you move to the right, ideas become more specific. You should also skip lines between important parts of the lecture. Writing notes in this way helps you analyze the material that you are listening to and organize your notes in a logical way.

    Main idea

        Supporting idea

        Supporting idea

            Minor point, example, detail, etc.

    Main idea

        Supporting idea

            Minor point, example, detail, etc.

            Minor point, example, detail, etc.

You can indicate ideas that you think are especially important with a box, a circle, an underline, or an exclamation point (!).

Leave plenty of white space around your notes so that, if the speaker returns to a point later, you can add new notes.

9. The average lecturer speaks about 125 to 150 words per minute. The average note taker can write only about 20 to 25 words per minute. Therefore, you need to use abbreviations and other shortcuts to help you get down as much information as possible.

A. Don't write your notes in complete sentences. Write in phrases.

B. Omit unimportant words and words that do not carry information. Suppose the lecturer says this:

The taiga is the largest of all the world's biomes.

Your note might read:

Taiga largest biome.

Common words that you can generally eliminate:

Be verbs *(is, are, was, were)*, articles *(a, an, the)*, pronouns *(they, his, them)*, determiners *(this, that, these)*, prepositions *(of, with, from)*

C. Use standard symbols and abbreviations:

+ or &	and
=	is, equals, is the same as
≠	isn't, doesn't equal, is not the same as
≈	is not quite the same as, is similar to
±	more or less, about, approximately
↑	increases, goes up
↓	decreases, goes down
/	per
%	percent
#	number
x	times
>	more than, bigger than, greater than
<	less than, smaller than, fewer than
→	causes, leads to, produces
$	money

♂	man, male
♀	woman, female
@	at
w/	with
w/o	without
p.	page
pp.	pages
re	regarding, about, concerning
etc.	and so on, and other things
e.g.	for example
i.e.	in other words
∴	therefore
∵	because

For example, if the speaker says this:

"The earth is about four times bigger than the moon."

You may take this note:

Earth ± 4 x bigger Moon

Another useful symbol is the ditto mark ("). This repeats the words that you wrote on a previous line.

Suppose a professor in a biology class says this:

"There are many types of crustaceans, and they live in many different habitats. Most of them are marine animals—they live in the sea. Some are fresh water animals, and a few types of crustaceans live on the land."

You might take these notes:

Many types of crustaceans
  "   environs.

Most crustac. live in sea

Some   "   " " freshwater

A few   "   " on land

D. Besides standard abbreviations and symbols, you often need to create your own abbreviations. There are two common ways to abbreviate words. You can use the first few letters of a word.

information	info
presentation	pres
definition	def
recommendation	rec

Another way to abbreviate words is to leave out letters from the middle of words.

large	lge
international	internat'l
market	mkt
manager	mgr

Remember, you will be using your notes as soon as the lecture is over. You can probably remember what your abbreviations mean for a few minutes, so abbreviate as much as possible.

10. If you miss a point, don't worry. Just keep taking notes.

11. Don't worry about spelling, punctuation, or correct grammar. Don't worry if your notes are messy.

12. Remember that there are no "perfect" notes. Everyone has his or her own style of taking notes. There are only three important issues in taking notes for the TOEFL test:

    A. Are they accurate?

    B. Do they help you answer the questions?

    C. Can you understand them?

    The sample notes that are provided in the *The Complete Guide to the TOEFL Test, iBT Edition* are examples of good note taking, but another person could take good notes in a completely different way.

NOTE-TAKING EXERCISE 1

▶ Now start the Audio Program. 🎧

DIRECTIONS: Listen to a list of words and phrases. Write down your own abbreviations of these words in the spaces below. (This vocabulary comes from a lecture on business organizations that you will be listening to in order to improve your note-taking skills.) When you have finished, compare your notes with those of a classmate. Check for similarities and differences in what you wrote. You can also compare your notes with those in the Answer Key.

Sample abbreviations appear in the Answer Key.

1. _____   11. _____

2. _____   12. _____

3. _____   13. _____

4. _____   14. _____

5. _____   15. _____

6. _____   16. _____

7. _____   17. _____

8. _____   18. _____

9. _____   19. _____

10. _____   20. _____

NOTE-TAKING EXERCISE 2

DIRECTIONS: Working by yourself or with a partner, use the list of abbreviations that you wrote in Exercise 1 to "reconstruct" the full forms of the words and phrases that you heard. Then discuss the meaning of these terms.

1. _____   11. _____

2. _____   12. _____

3. _____   13. _____

4. _____   14. _____

5. _____   15. _____

6. _____   16. _____

7. _____   17. _____

8. _____   18. _____

9. _____   19. _____

10. _____   20. _____

NOTE-TAKING EXERCISE 3

▶ Now start the Audio Program. 🎧

DIRECTIONS: Listen to the following sentences. Take notes on these sentences using abbreviations and symbols and omitting unimportant words. (These sentences come from a lecture on business organizations that you will be listening to in order to improve your note-taking skills.)

When you have finished taking notes, compare your notes with those of a classmate. Check for similarities and differences in what you wrote. You can also compare your notes with the sample notes in the Answer Key.

1. _____

2. _____

3. _____

4. _____

5. _____

6. _____

7. _____

8. _____

9. _____

NOTE-TAKING EXERCISE 4

DIRECTIONS: Working by yourself or with a partner, use the notes that you took in Exercise 3 to "reconstruct" the full forms of the sentences that you heard.

1. _____
2. _____
3. _____
4. _____
5. _____
6. _____
7. _____
8. _____
9. _____

NOTE-TAKING EXERCISE 5

▶ Now start the Audio Program. 🎧

DIRECTIONS: Listen to a lecture on business organizations. The lecture will be given in short sections. Take notes on each section. After each section, answer the questions **Yes** or **No** to find out if you are taking notes on the important points in the lecture. (The more **Yes** answers you have, the more complete your notes are.)

When you have finished taking notes, compare your notes with those of a classmate. Check for similarities and differences in what you wrote. You can also compare your notes with the sample notes in the Answer Key.

Section 1

_____

_____

_____

_____

_____

1. Did you note that there were once three main types of business organizations but that now there are four? Yes _____ No _____

2. Did you note the names of the four main types of business organizations? (sole proprietorship, partnership, corporation, and limited liability corporation)? Yes _____ No _____

3. Did you abbreviate the names of the four types? Yes _____ No _____

Section 2

_____

_____

_____

_____

_____

4. Did you note that one person is in complete control of a sole proprietorship? Yes _____ No _____

5. Did you note that a sole proprietorship begins when the owner makes the decision to start a business? Yes _____ No _____

6. Did you write down Paul Samuelson's example of when a sole proprietorship begins? Yes _____ No _____
(This is "extra" information that the speaker uses to clarify how sole proprietorships get started. You probably would not take notes on this during a classroom lecture. However, sometimes TOEFL asks questions such as "Why does the speaker mention Paul Samuelson?" so you may want to make a quick note of this example.)

7. Did you write down the main advantage of a sole proprietorship (that there is no separate tax on it)? Yes _____ No _____

8. Did you write down the main disadvantage of a sole proprietorship (that the owner is legally liable for all the company's debts)? Yes _____ No _____

LISTENING

Section 3

_____

_____

_____

_____

_____

9. Did you note that a partnership is similar to a sole proprietorship except that a partnership has more than one owner? Yes _____ No _____

10. Did you note that a partnership has the same tax advantage as a sole proprietorship? Yes _____ No _____

11. Did you note the example the author gave of the problem the two partners had because they were both sole agents? Yes _____ No _____
(This is not a very important point, and in a lecture class you would probably not note this at all. However, the TOEFL iBT sometimes asks you questions such as "Why does the speaker mention the two partners' problem?" Therefore, you may want to make a quick note of this example.)

12. Did you note that some partnerships have _silent partners_ who contribute money but do not take part in management decisions? Yes _____ No _____

Section 4

_____

_____

_____

_____

_____

13. Did you write down that the corporation is the most complex and the most expensive business organization? Yes _____ No _____

14. Did you note that the most important feature of a corporation is limited liability and that corporations are distinct legal entities? Yes _____ No _____

15. Did you note in some way (by underlining, circling, etc.) that the professor emphasized the point that corporations are distinct legal entities? Yes _____ No _____

16. Did you note that double taxation is a disadvantage to corporations and did you define double taxation? Yes _____ No _____

17. Did you write down that there are three important elements in the structure of the corporation (stockholders, the board of directors, and executive officers)? Yes _____ No _____

18. Did you note that shareholders have ultimate control but usually give their votes to the corporate officers (voting by proxy)? Yes _____ No _____

19. Did you write down that the board of directors makes major decisions and sets company policy? Yes _____ No _____

20. Did you note that day-to-day operations of corporations are performed by the executive officers and the corporate bureaucracy? Yes _____ No _____

21. Did you note that the CEO is often the chairman of the board? Yes _____ No _____

Section 5

_____

_____

_____

_____

_____

22. Did you note that the limited liability company (LLC) is becoming more popular with smaller businesses? Yes _____ No _____

23. Did you note that an LLC is a hybrid organization with features of both a partnership and a corporation? Yes _____ No _____

24. Did you note that the LLC eliminates double taxation? Yes _____ No _____

NOTE-TAKING EXERCISE 6

▶ Now start the Audio Program. 🎧

DIRECTIONS: Listen again to the lecture on business organizations and take notes. 🎧
After you have listened to the lecture, use your notes to answer the True/False
(T / F) questions and the fill-in-the-blank questions at the end of the lecture.
Sample lecture notes appear in the Answer Key.

_____

_____

_____

_____

_____

_____

_____

_____

_____

_____

_____

_____

_____

_____

_____

_____

_____

_____

_____

_____

_____

_____

_____

_____

_____

_____

_____

_____

T / F 1. The lecturer says that he has now added a new form of business organization to his lecture.

2. _____ is a relatively new form of business organization.

T / F 3. The speaker mentions Paul Samuelson in the lecture because Samuelson is an expert on corporate taxes.

4. The chief advantage of a sole proprietorship is that _____

_____.

5. The chief disadvantage of a sole proprietorship is that _____

_____.

6. Partnerships and sole proprietorships are similar except for the fact

that _____.

T / F 7. The speaker gives the example of the two partners who both buy 500 widgets* in order to explain how partners divide up their workload.

T / F 8. A silent partner does not invest money in a partnership.

T / F 9. Corporations cost more than sole proprietorships and partnerships to establish.

10. Corporations are distinct legal entities, so they are sometime called

_____ .

T / F 11. In theory, stockholders have ultimate control over a corporation, but they actually have little to do with routine operations.

T / F 12. Board members are appointed by the top executive officers.

T / F 13. Top executive officers are not allowed to serve on the board of directors.

T / F 14. "Double taxation" is a reason for the growing popularity of limited liability corporations.

15. An LLC has features of both a _____ and a _____ .

_____

*Widgets do not really exist. A widget is a term used by economists and business experts to mean "an unidentified product."

LISTENING

COMMUNICATIVE ACTIVITIES FOR LISTENING

Internet activities are marked with this icon: ⌒

Activity 1

Guess Who's Talking?   *Pairs Activity*

The instructor/coordinator writes paired relationships on a slip of paper as well as on the board. S/he gives one slip of paper to each pair of students. Here are some examples of relationships you can choose from (or you can create your own):

student/teacher   motorist/police officer   doctor/patient   journalist/news maker

student/advisor   customer/mechanic   lawyer/client   banker/customer

waiter/customer   librarian/library user   passenger/flight attendant

Together you and your partner will write out a short dialogue (with each person writing half of the dialogue). The dialogue should involve a problem that one of the two people is having and possible solutions for the problem. You and your partner will then perform the dialogue. The rest of the class will take notes on each of the dialogues and answer the following questions:

Who is speaking?

What is the problem?

How are these people trying to solve the problem?

What attitude did the two people take toward each other?

Activity 2

Following Directions   *Small-Group Activity*

As a group, create a series of directions for things to do on a piece of paper. Here are some examples:

1. In the left-hand bottom part of the page, write your mother's name.
2. Right above that, write your father's place of birth.
3. In the middle of the page, draw a circle.
4. Find out what movie the person on your left likes best. Write the name of the movie inside the circle.
5. To the right of the circle, draw a diamond.
6. Find out what color the person on your right likes best. Write the color in the diamond.
7. Draw three squares across the top of the page.
8. In the leftmost square, write the name of your favorite food.

After you have completed your directions, read them to the class and have the class follow your directions. After completing the task, exchange your sheet of paper with another student to see if s/he successfully followed all of the directions.

Activity 3

Fill-in-the-Lyric   *Small-Group Activity*

Record a song that you like from the radio, a CD, or the Internet. As a group, listen to the song and write down the lyrics that you hear. Next, take out one word from each line. Now make copies of the lyrics (words of the song) and give them to all the students in the class. Play the song and have everyone fill in the missing words. The winner is the student who correctly fills in the greatest number of missing words.

Activity 4

Storytelling   *Individual Activity/Class Activity*

On the Internet, find a suitable folk tale. Look for one from a country or culture other than your own. You can find many sites featuring folk tales from various countries by typing *folk tales* into your browser, or you can type in the name of a specific type of folk tale (Chinese folk tales, Moroccan folk tales, Navajo folk tales, for example). Bring the story to class and read it aloud. Your classmates will listen and take notes on your folk tale and then guess where the folk tale came from. Afterwards, your class will discuss the meaning of the folk tale.

Activity 5

Outside Interview   *Small-Group/Individual Activity*

As a group, write out a questionnaire that includes at least five questions about note taking. Then interview a university student, a professor, or anyone else who is familiar with academic lectures. Take notes on this person's responses. Report to the class what you learned from the interview.

Activity 6

Half a Class   *Pairs Activity*

To do this activity, you will need to live in a community where there is a university or college in which English is the language of instruction. With a partner, decide what type of class you would like to visit. Then call the department (art, economics, biology, etc.) and try to get permission to visit a class. You or your partner will attend the first half of the class and take notes, and then the other person will attend the second half. Afterwards, use your notes to tell your partner what happened in the half of the class that your partner missed.

Activity 7

Write Your Own TOEFL Items   *Small-Group Activity*

Find a suitable lecture and record it. There are many Web sites that feature lectures. One of the best is voanews.com. Listen to the lecture as a group and take notes. Then write five TOEFL-like multiple-choice questions about the lecture. Next, exchange lectures and questions with another group. After you've answered the other group's questions, check with the group that wrote the "test" and see if your group has answered the questions correctly.

Activity 8

Who Are They and What Are They Talking About?   *Individual/Pairs Activity*

Your instructor or coordinator will record a conversation from a television show or a movie and play it in class. Take notes. Then answer these basic questions about the conversation:

1. Who was speaking?
2. Where were they?
3. What were they talking about?
4. What were their attitudes toward each other?

　　Compare your answers with those of your partner. Then watch the show again and take further notes. Now you and your partner will write a paraphrase of the conversation. (In other words, you are to rewrite the conversation in your own words.) Perform your paraphrase for the class. The class can then vote on whose paraphrase was closest in meaning and feeling to the original.

Activity 9

Say It with Feeling   *Class Activity*

One student acts as "scribe" (writer). On the board, this student writes as many adverbs (words ending with -*ly*) as possible that describe emotions or attitudes, based on suggestions from the class (*angrily, proudly, nervously,* for example). Next, each student will write a series of sentences, such as the following:

1. Write a sentence about your family.
2. Write a sentence about a trip.
3. Write a sentence about the TOEFL test.

and so on.

Students then read their sentences in a way that demonstrates one of the adverbs written on the board. For example, a student might say "My brother is a good football player" *proudly*. Other students in class then try to guess what feeling/attitude the speaker is expressing.

Activity 10

Reduced-Forms Contest   *Pairs Activity*

Your instructor or coordinator will give you a list of sentences that are missing certain phrases. He or she will then read you a list of sentences with reduced forms. (Reduced forms are two or more words that are pronounced as if they were one word.)

1. <u>Wouldja c'mere</u> for a minute?   _____ for a minute?
2. <u>Howzee</u> doing in that class?   _____ doing in that class?
3. <u>Couldja</u> get me a <u>cuppa</u> tea, please?   _____ get me a
                                                _____ tea, please?

With your partner, decide which words are missing and write the full form of each reduced phrase.

> <u>Would you come here</u> for a minute?
>
> <u>How is he</u> doing in that class?
>
> <u>Could you</u> get me a <u>cup of</u> tea, please?

The pair that correctly writes down the most missing phrases wins.

Activity 11

Student Teacher   *Individual Activity*

Your instructor/coordinator will choose several students to teach one of the five Listening lessons in this text. Students who are selected will go back and study those lessons in detail, write out a lesson plan, and give a five- to ten-minute presentation on the lesson.

GUIDE TO SPEAKING

ABOUT SPEAKING

The third section of the TOEFL® iBT tests your ability to speak clearly and intelligibly. The entire Speaking Section takes about twenty minutes to complete. There are two main types of tasks: Independent Speaking Tasks and Integrated Speaking Tasks.

Speaking Section		
	Based on	*Timing per task*
Two Independent Tasks	Your own knowledge and experience	Preparation: 15 seconds Response: 45 seconds
Four Integrated Tasks:		
Two Listening/Reading/Speaking Tasks	Reading passage and related lecture or conversation	Reading: 45 seconds Lecture: 60 to 80 seconds Preparation: 30 seconds Response: 60 seconds
Two Listening/Speaking Tasks	Lecture or conversation	Lecture: 60 to 90 seconds Preparation: 20 seconds Response: 60 seconds

Skills that are tested in both parts of this section include the abilities to

- ▶ produce fluent, clear, and intelligible speech
- ▶ organize and deliver a spoken presentation of up to one minute in length
- ▶ connect parts of your speech by using transition words and phrases
- ▶ pronounce words properly
- ▶ use stress and intonation correctly
- ▶ use appropriate grammar
- ▶ use vocabulary accurately
- ▶ use idioms appropriately
- ▶ understand written and spoken information and prompts

INDEPENDENT VERSUS INTEGRATED TASKS

For the two Independent Speaking Tasks, you are given a specific topic and are asked to speak on the topic using your personal knowledge and experience.

For two of the four Integrated Tasks, you read short passages on the screen and then listen to lectures or conversations through your headphones. The lectures or conversations are about the same subjects as the passages that you read. You're allowed to take notes on both the reading and the lecture/conversation. For the other two tasks, you hear lectures and conversations, and again you may take notes on them. Your responses for the Integrated tasks are based on information from the lectures/conversations and the passages. The Integrated Task asks you only to summarize and paraphrase the information that you read and hear. You should *not* express your own opinion of the issues and you should *not* bring in any information from outside the passage or the lectures/conversations (just as in the Integrated Writing Tasks in Section IV).

Preparing Your Response

For all of the Speaking tasks, you have a short period of preparation time, from fifteen to thirty seconds depending on the task. A clock on the screen tells you how much time you have left to prepare your response. When the preparation time is up, you will hear a beep that tells you it is time to begin speaking.

During your preparation time, you should first analyze the question for the task to make sure that you know what the question is asking you to do. Then you should write notes or a very simple outline to look at when you are speaking. You will only have time to write down a few words. For the Independent tasks, write down a quick summary of your opinion or preference. For the Integrated tasks, you can use the notes that you took when you were reading the passages and listening to the lectures. Mark the points that you think are important and write a few words that will remind you, what you want to say.

Don't try to write out a complete response during your preparation time, and don't read from your notes. You will lose points if you seem to be reading your response.

Delivering Your Response

In this section, you will speak into a microphone and a digital recording of your voice will be made by the computer. At the same time you are speaking, other test-takers will be recording their responses as well. The headphones you are wearing will block most of the sounds of other people speaking, but you may hear them anyway. You need to focus on your own task and ignore any sounds around you.

Here are some hints for delivering your responses:

▶ Speak clearly and directly into the microphone.
▶ Don't speak too quickly or too slowly.
▶ Avoid long pauses and saying "um" or "uh" too many times.
▶ Try to pronounce words carefully.
▶ Pay attention to the on-screen clock and use it to adjust your timing.

Practicing Your Response

It is important that you practice taking this section by speaking into a microphone and recording yourself. One way to do this is to use a computer microphone and a computer equipped with a sound card and with the Windows® operating system. Plug the microphone into the microphone jack on the computer itself or on one of the speakers. Then follow these steps:

SPEAKING

▶ Click on Start.

▶ Click on Accessories.

▶ Click on Entertainment.

▶ Click on Sound Recording and you will see this window.

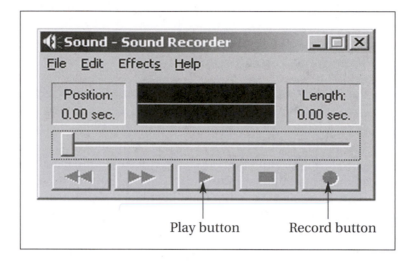

Play button   Record button

▶ Now click on the red Record button in the lower right-hand corner of this window and record your response. Time yourself carefully.

To hear your recording, click on the Play button. You can adjust the volume by clicking on Effects and then on Increase Volume by 25%. If you like, you can save your recording by clicking on File and then Save As.

You can, of course, also use a tape recorder or a digital recorder to record your voice.

Tactics for Speaking

- As with all sections of the test, familiarize yourself with the directions. When the directions appear, click on the Dismiss Directions button and begin the Speaking Section right away.

- Read the questions carefully to be sure you know what you are being asked to speak about.

- During the preparation time, plan what you are going to say and write a short, informal outline.

- Follow the outline as you speak.

- Use transition words and phrases to connect the parts of your response.

- Keep track of how much time you have by checking the on-screen clock.

- Know the types of questions you are likely to be asked and practice some typical phrases you might use in your answers.

About the Independent Speaking Tasks

The Speaking Section begins with two Independent Speaking Tasks. Both of these tasks are based on your personal knowledge and experience. In other words, the questions ask you to talk about topics that you are familiar with. There are no right or wrong answers.

Skills that are required to do well on the Independent Speaking Tasks include the abilities to

▶ understand the prompts (questions) and what they ask you to do

▶ "brainstorm" ideas and take notes on the ideas that you come up with

▶ write notes or a simple outline to help guide you as you speak

▶ clearly state and explain your opinion or preference

▶ support your ideas with examples, reasons, and details

▶ deliver a clear, well-reasoned response based on the prompt in forty-five seconds

You will first see a photograph of a person wearing headphones and you will be instructed to put on your headphones and listen carefully.

You will then see the directions screen for Speaking. After you have clicked on the Dismiss Directions button you will see and hear the prompt for the first Independent Speaking Task. After this, you have fifteen seconds to prepare your response. After fifteen seconds have passed, you will hear a beep and you will then have forty-five seconds to deliver your first response. An on-screen clock keeps track of time. A second beep tells you that you should stop speaking. After that, you will see the prompt for the second task, and you will again have fifteen seconds to prepare and forty-five seconds to deliver your second response.

You will not be penalized if you have not finished your response when the time is up as long as you have completed most of the task as given in the prompt.

Describe the most important day in your life and explain why it was important to you. Include details and examples to support your explanation.

Preparation Time: 15 Seconds
Response Time: 45 Seconds

PREPARATION TIME
00 : 00 : 00

THE TWO TYPES OF INDEPENDENT TASKS

SPEAKING

Task	Description	Example	Timing
Task 1: Personal Preference	Involves a single prompt (question) that asks you to express a personal choice from a category that is given in the prompt.	"Describe the most important day in your life and explain why it was important to you. Include details and examples to support your explanation."	Preparation time: 15 seconds Response time: 45 seconds
Task 2: Paired Choice	Involves a single prompt that asks you to express a personal preference from two choices that are given in the prompt.	"Some people prefer to work for a company and receive a salary. Other people prefer to own their own business. Which of these do you prefer, and why? Include details and examples in your explanation."	Preparation time: 15 seconds Response time: 45 seconds

In order to do well on Task 1, you need to be able to

- ▶ give descriptions of people, places, and things that you are familiar with
- ▶ narrate an event or action
- ▶ express your preference and support it with reasons and examples
- ▶ quickly decide on an answer and think of supporting information
- ▶ produce intelligible speech (use stress, intonation, and pauses to convey meaning)

In order to do well on Task 2, you need to be able to

- ▶ express your opinion and provide reasons and examples that support your opinion
- ▶ make recommendations and defend your recommendations
- ▶ take a position and provide justifications for it
- ▶ produce intelligible speech (use stress, intonation, and pauses to convey meaning)

SCORING THE INDEPENDENT SPEAKING RESPONSES

Each task is scored by a different human (not computer) rater. Raters give a score of 0 to 4 using a rubric (set of guidelines) similar to the one below.

Score	Overall Description of Response	Delivery of the Response	Use of Language (Grammar/Vocabulary)	Development of the Topic
4	**The response to the prompt is thorough and complete. The response is clear and fluent and demonstrates all three of the characteristics described in the columns on the right.**	The response is fluent, smooth, and highly comprehensible. There may be minor problems involving pronunciation, stress, and intonation but these do not affect the speaker's intelligibility (the ability to make oneself understood).	The response shows that the speaker has an effective command of high-level grammatical structures and uses sophisticated vocabulary and idiomatic expressions. There may be some minor grammatical or vocabulary errors but this does not interfere with the speaker's overall intelligibility.	The response is coherent and unified. The speaker clearly provides a topic statement and adequately supports this statement with specific reasons and examples. The speaker uses transitional words to connect parts of the response.
3	**The response adequately answers the prompt but may not be completely developed. The response is generally clear and fluent but may show weaknesses in the speaker's ability to communicate ideas. The response demonstrates at least two of the characteristics described in the columns on the right.**	The response is generally smooth, fluent, idiomatic, and comprehensible but there are noticeable problems with pronunciation, stress, and intonation. These problems, however, generally do not affect the speaker's overall intelligibility.	The response shows that the speaker can use intermediate-level grammatical structures and vocabulary. There will be some grammatical errors and problems with vocabulary. These problems, however, generally do not affect the speaker's overall intelligibility.	The response addresses the question and is generally coherent and unified. Development, however, is limited and the speaker's main ideas may not be adequately supported with the use of concrete examples. The connection between parts of the response may not be perfectly clear.

continued

SPEAKING

Score	Overall Description of Response	Delivery of the Response	Use of Language (Grammar/Vocabulary)	Development of the Topic
2	**The response attempts to address the prompt but lacks adequate development. Speech is generally clear but problems with the speaker's delivery and language use may make the response difficult to fully understand. The response demonstrates at least two of the characteristics described in the columns on the right.**	The response is comprehensible but problems with pronunciation, stress, and intonation may make the speaker's speech seem fragmented and unnatural. In places, problems with delivery will interfere with the listener's ability to understand the speaker's message.	The response shows the speaker has command of spoken grammar and vocabulary use at the basic level. Errors may make at least parts of the response difficult to understand.	The response is related to the prompt, but the number or appropriateness of the ideas presented is limited. The response may seem incomplete, vague, or repetitious. Connections between parts of the response may not be clear.
1	**The response is not closely related to the prompt or the speech is generally incomprehensible. The response demonstrates at least two of the characteristics described in the columns on the right.**	Serious problems with pronunciation, stress, and intonation make it difficult to understand the speaker's ideas. There may be many pauses and hesitations. Listeners may not be able to understand much of the response and then only with great effort.	Frequent errors in grammar and vocabulary use greatly limit or completely prevent the communication of the speaker's ideas.	Response may not be connected to the prompt. There is little or no development of the topic. Few, if any, comprehensible ideas are expressed and these ideas may not be connected. Speaker may not finish the task.
0	Test-taker does not give a response or the response is not related to the prompt.			

SAMPLE RESPONSES

Following are four responses to a Personal Preference Task, each illustrating one of the four scores. They were given in response to the following prompt:

> Describe the most important day in your life and explain why it was important to you. Include details and examples to support your explanation.

▶ While you are listening to the responses, follow along with these transcriptions. ∩

Sample Response 1

"When I was young, I used to play rugby. I was a member of the . . . of our national team . . . the junior team from my republic in the Soviet Union. My team . . . uh, we became the junior champions of rugby of the Soviet Union. It was the most important and happiest time in my life. I . . . it was most important event in my life because I made my first big steps in rugby. Also, because at that time I was only fourteen years and it was . . . well, you could say the biggest success in my life. I was happy and I was proud of my success . . . of our team success. These events will . . . uh, always be a pleasure to remember in my life as the best time I ever had. Even the success I have had in science and business cannot compare to this moment."

Score: ___4___

Comments: The speaker's answer is generally quite clear and coherent. His pronunciation and intonation are excellent, and he provides an explanation complete with details. The speaker has good control and use of vocabulary and structure. Although there are some grammatical mistakes and there is some repetition in the response, the answer is easy to understand.

Sample Response 2

"For me the most important day in my love, in my life was a day when I . . . um . . . got accepted to Simmons College. Um . . . um . . . I got accepted to the . . . um . . . teaching program and it was very exciting . . . um . . . during the symposium important for me because it took almost two years for me . . . um . . . to get accepted to the program and during this two years I had to take the tests and I had challenges because I had to take the tests two times . . . um . . . because of various reasons . . . um . . . so . . . um having seen that I got this . . . um . . . test (posital?) and I got accepted it was worthwhile and on top of that . . . ah . . . during this two years I worked hard on getting a job and I was eligible enough to be offered the job and the great thing also for financial reason is . . . um . . . to be eligible for . . . um . . . scholarship, which was a rare scholarship offered to . . . ah (foreigner?). So it was . . . um . . . all over . . . um . . . a great day for me."

Score: ___3___

Comments: The speech is generally intelligible and the topic is sufficiently developed and explained. There are a few minor problems with grammar and usage. The articulation and slow pace sometimes make the answer a bit difficult to understand.

Sample Response 3

"The most important day in my life . . . um . . . I think . . . um . . . the day I . . . *(pause)* I got married to my wife. Um . . . because . . . um before I met her I was thinking a lot a thing about how different between us and . . . um . . . um . . . I was thinking about . . . ah . . . culture, country, religions . . . uh . . . a lot of thing even though indi . . . indication and . . . ah . . . made me think just . . . um . . . like a . . . what a . . . was gonna happen . . . um . . . just don't expect too much about . . . about life and . . . um . . . the first time that I have trying to move to the university . . . to the U.S., I . . . ah . . . changed my mind a little bit about . . . ahmmm . . . how to expect something about between us and finally I had a chance to married to her and made me more . . . um . . . happy and I think the day that most important days in my . . . ah . . . my marriage day to her and . . . um . . . make me so happy . . . and . . . and . . ."

Score: 2

Comments: Some basic ideas are stated but are not clearly delivered. The response is not fluent. It is choppy and hesitant. There are some delays. Listener effort is required to understand the speaker. Vocabulary usage is at the basic level.

Sample Response 4

"Most important day I . . . especially . . . when have my first baby borned. It was . . . amazed. *(long pause)* For the, uh . . . is, um, beginning for . . . the . . . uh . . . for big . . . promise? Many time ago, uh, several more or less important day of the, of the life, uhhhh *(long pause)* . . . other day I go my, uhhh, my first work, I was . . . *(very long pause)* And uh, most important . . . for example, as holiday . . . holiday? . . . the people go . . . the people umm . . . to, to the house . . ."

Score: 1

Comments: There are problems with pronunciation and intonation. This speaker is not very clear and the response is choppy and fragmented. Even listening carefully, it is difficult to understand. The speaker may not have understood the prompt because her response mentions three important events (the birth of her first child, her first job, and holidays) rather than the single most important event. The use of vocabulary and verb tenses is limited, and the response lacks any substance.

EXERCISE: SCORING THE RESPONSE

DIRECTIONS: Here are three responses based on the prompt on page 405. Listen to the responses. Then, using the scoring rubric on pages 407–408, decide what score (0 to 4) that you would give each response.

This exercise will help you develop the ability to score your own responses.

Response 1 🎧

Score: _____

Comments:

Response 2 🎧

Score: _____

Comments:

Response 3 🎧

Score: _____

Comments:

Tactics for Independent Speaking Tasks

- When the directions for the Independent Task appear, click on the Dismiss Directions button and begin working right away.
- Read the prompts carefully. You must speak on the topics exactly as they are given.
- Plan your response by taking notes and writing a simple outline.
- The prompts for the Independent Tasks ask you to state your preference or to give your opinion. Make it clear in the introduction to your response what your preference is or what your opinion is.
- Support your preference or your opinion with specific reasons and concrete examples.

INDEPENDENT SPEAKING PREVIEW TEST
DIRECTIONS

▶ Now start the Audio Program and listen carefully. 🎧

The first two tasks in the Speaking Section are Independent Speaking Tasks. You have fifteen seconds in which to prepare your responses. When you hear a beep on the Audio Program, you will have forty-five seconds in which to answer the questions.

During actual tests, a clock on the screen will tell you how much preparation time or how much response time (speaking time) remains for each question. It is important that you time yourself accurately when you take this preview test. If possible, speak into a microphone and record your response. On an actual test your responses will be recorded and evaluated by trained raters.

Task 1

Describe the person who has had the greatest influence on your life. Explain why this person has had such an important influence on you. Give specific details and examples to support your explanation.

Preparation Time: 15 Seconds
Response Time: 45 Seconds

Notes:

_____

_____

_____

Task 2

In some university classes, students are graded according to a Pass/Fail system. In other words, the only possible grades that you may receive are P (Pass) or F (Fail). In most classes, however, students are graded according to a more traditional system in which many letter grades can be given (A+, A, A–, B+, etc.) Explain which of these two systems you prefer and why. Include details and examples in your explanation.

Preparation Time: 15 Seconds
Response Time: 45 Seconds

Notes:

_____

_____

_____

This is the end of the Independent Speaking Preview Test.

LESSON 15
PERSONAL PREFERENCE TASK

The first Independent Speaking Task consists of one prompt (question). The prompt asks you to state your preference or interest. It asks you to describe the best, the most important, the most interesting *something* in a given category. You have fifteen seconds in which to prepare your response. You can take notes during this preparation period. You have forty-five seconds in which to give your response.

You will see the prompt on the screen and hear it in your headphones. The prompt will remain on the screen during the task.

Here's a sample Personal Preference Task from the Speaking Preview Test and a sample response to it. You can listen to the prompt and the response as you read along.

▶ Now start the Audio Program 🎧

Sample

> Describe the person who has had the greatest influence on your life. Explain why this person has had such an important influence on you. Give specific details and examples to support your explanation.

"I think the person who has influenced me the most is my brother, my older brother. He's six years older than me and has always been . . . a kind of model. Everyone in my family—actually, everyone who has met my brother—thinks he's the . . . ah, the kindest person they know.

"Why I say that my brother is my most influential person? *(short pause)* Well, he's had a big role in . . . in shaping my life. For example, my brother is very good golfer, and when I was quite young, he started taking me to the golf course. He taught me to play. Today, playing golf and watching is the way . . . ah, how I relax. Also, after he . . . ah, finished university, my brother studied international law in the United States. Because of him, I've . . . ah, decided to go to university in the United States too."

This response would receive a high score. The speaker responds to the prompt in a complete and organized way. She says that her brother is the most influential person in her life. She offers a brief description of her brother (he is six years older, a role model, and a kind person). She also provides specific details that explain why her brother is such an influential person: He taught her to play golf, which is an important part of her life, and he decided to study in the United States, which led to her decision to study there as well.

The response is delivered clearly. The pronunciation and intonation pattern do not in any way interfere with our understanding the response. The vocabulary and the grammar are advanced. The speaker uses transitions *(For example . . . Also, . . .)*. She is fluent and confident, and there are no long pauses or hesitations.

(A) Pre-Speaking

Your preparation time is quite short, but it is an important time. Here's what you need to do during this fifteen-second period:

▶ Read and analyze the prompt.

▶ Decide on your answer.

▶ Take notes about what you will say and prepare a simple outline.

Reading and analyzing the prompts is one of the most important steps in the Independent Speaking Task. If you do not speak about the topic that is given to you, you will not receive a top score, no matter how well you speak.

The prompts are short and are written in simple English. You need to analyze the prompt—to put it into your own words and to tell yourself what the task is asking you to do. (You don't need to do this analysis in writing or aloud, only in your head.)

▶ Look at this analysis of the Sample Task.

Analysis

This prompt is asking me to name the most influential person in my life, and then to give a general description of this person. It also asks me to give reasons for my choice, to explain why I consider this person so influential. I could talk about a relative, a teacher, a friend, or anyone who has changed my life.

Remember: There is no "correct" answer for this task. Your choice doesn't even have to be your own real preference. Any answer that you can support is a good one. Besides reading and analyzing the task, you should take some brief notes during the preparation period and write a very simple outline. Follow this outline as you speak. When you took notes for Listening lectures, you used abbreviations and wrote down only important information. You should do the same when you take notes and prepare an outline for this task.

Your outline should include the following:

▶ Your preference

▶ A *brief* description of your preference

▶ At least one or two reasons for your preference

An outline for the sample item might look like this:

My older brother
6 years older—-kind, thnks of others
    made me interested in golf
        & studying in U.S.

(B) The Language of Personal Preference

Specific vocabulary and grammatical structures are often used to express personal preference.

Opinion

When you give your preference, you are really giving your opinion about a topic. When you begin your response, you should clearly state what your preference is. The following expressions can sometimes be used for your opening statement:

▶   *I think that* my older brother is the kindest person I know.

▶   *In my opinion,* Florence is the most beautiful city in the world.

▶   *I believe that* the Louvre is the most interesting museum in the world.

Superlatives

When you give your preference, you will often use superlative adjectives (the kindest, the most important, the most interesting). Keep in mind these simple rules for forming superlatives.

Rule	Examples	
Add *-est* to one-syllable adjectives and two-syllable adjectives that end in *-y*.	great funny	the greatest the funniest
Use the word *most* before two-syllable adjectives that do *not* end in *-y* and adjectives of three or more syllables.	common impressive	the most common the most impressive
The adjectives *good* and *bad* have irregular superlative forms.	good bad	the best the worst

In my opinion, *the greatest* leader of all time was Mahatma Gandhi.

I think air pollution is *the most common* problem.

The most important development of science was the discovery of electricity.

The best place to take a vacation, in my opinion, is Tahiti.

Favorite

Some Personal Preference prompts ask you to describe your favorite *something*. The word *favorite* is not used as a superlative, and is not used with the phrase *In my opinion . . .*

My favorite book is *Don Quixote.* (CORRECT)

There have been many great movies, but my favorite is *Seven Samurai.* (CORRECT)

In my opinion, my favorite book is *Don Quixote.* (INCORRECT)

My most favorite movie is *Seven Samurai.* (INCORRECT)

Reasons and Examples

Personal Preference prompts ask you not only to state your preference or interest but also to give several specific reasons why you prefer something or are interested by something. There are various ways to list reasons.

> *There are several reasons why* tennis is my favorite sport. *One* is that it is a fast-paced game and provides a lot of exercise. *Another* is that it is a game that requires quick thinking and decision-making.
>
> *One reason why* Tahiti is my favorite place for a vacation is that it is an amazingly beautiful place. *Another* is that the people there are very friendly and hospitable.
>
> *Why* is tennis my favorite sport? *One reason* is that it is a fast-paced game and provides a lot of exercise. *A second reason* is that it is a game that requires quick thinking and decision-making.
>
> Tennis is my favorite sport because it is a fast-paced game and provides a lot of exercise, and also because it requires quick thinking and decision-making.

You may also need to give specific examples in your response.

> There are several ways that Mr. Santos was helpful to me. *For example,* he would meet with me and other students after class to make sure that we understood his lessons. Also, he helped students who were interested in attending the university fill out their applications.
>
> My favorite kind of music is jazz. I especially like jazz from the 1940's and 1950's, *such as* the music of Miles Davis and Charlie Parker.

(C) Giving the Personal Preference Response

In the Personal Preference response, you need to clearly state what your preference is. You need to give a quick description of your choice and support your choice with specific reasons.

One important element of your response is timing. There is an on-screen clock that will let you know how much time is left.

Forty-five seconds is not much time. Don't "pad" your presentation with unimportant information because you might not have time to support your answer. Practice giving responses so that you finish in about forty-five seconds.

On the day of the test, if you find that you finish very early (with more than fifteen seconds remaining) you should probably take advantage of that extra time to give some additional information. However, if you finish with less time that that, just stop and go on to the next task.

Don't worry too much about running out of time just before you finish the task. As long as you have completed most of the task, you will not be penalized for not finishing on time.

When you give your response, you should also keep the following points in mind:

▶ State your preference in the first sentence of your response.

▶ Follow the simple outline that you made during the preparation time.

▶ Give at least two specific reasons to support your choice.

▶ Speak clearly and directly into the microphone.

▶ Don't speak too slowly or too fast.

▶ Keep your response flowing; avoid long pauses.

▶ Pay attention to your pronunciation and intonation.

▶ Keep it simple! Use familiar vocabulary and grammar.

EXERCISE 15.1

FOCUS: Using the language of Personal Preference.

DIRECTIONS: Orally complete each group of sentences according to the directions given. The first sentence in each group is done for you as an example.

Use one of these phrases below to give your opinion about . . .

> I believe . . .
>
> I think . . .
>
> In my opinion . . .

1. the best car in the world

   Example: "I think a Mercedes Benz is the best car in the world."

2. the most interesting discussion you've ever heard

3. the finest restaurant you've ever eaten at

4. the most important leader in history

5. the best known monument in your country

Use the superlative form of an adjective to give your opinion about . . .

6. bad traffic

   Example: "Of all the cities I've ever visited, I think the traffic in Los Angeles is the worst."

7. a good idea

8. an important invention

9. a difficult problem in your country

Use the word *favorite* to describe . . .

10. national holiday

    Example: "My favorite national holiday is Independence Day, which is celebrated in Greece on March 26."

11. place to study

12. food

13. singer

Give reasons for the following . . .

14. Why _____ is your favorite place to shop

> Example: "There are several reasons why I like to shop for food at the farmer's market in my neighborhood. For one, the fruit and vegetables are always fresh. Also, I just enjoy shopping at the market because I often see my friends there."

15. Why _____ is an interesting Web site

16. Why _____ was my favorite activity when I was a child

17. Why _____ was the most interesting class that I ever took

EXERCISE 15.2

FOCUS: Understanding Personal Preference prompts.

DIRECTIONS: Read the following prompts. Then give a brief oral (spoken) analysis of each of the prompts. The first one is done for you as an example.

1. | Describe the most interesting trip you have ever taken. Explain why it was the most interesting. Include details and examples to support your explanation.

> Example: "This prompt is asking me to decide which trip I have taken was the most interesting. It's also asking me why this trip was so important to me, so I have to give reasons why this trip was important. I guess I could talk about a vacation, or a business trip, or an educational trip I took when I was in school."

2. | Describe the type of food that you think is most representative of your country and explain why you think that it is representative. Include details and example to support your explanation.

3. | What do you think is your most important skill? Explain why you think so. Include details and examples to support your explanation.

EXERCISE 15.3

FOCUS: Writing simple outlines for Personal Preference responses.

DIRECTIONS: Using the prompts from Exercise 15.2, prepare a *brief* written outline of your response. The first one is done for you as an example.

1. | Describe the most interesting trip you have ever taken. Explain why it was the most interesting. Include details and examples to support your explanation.

Trip to Italy 2 yrs ago

    2 wks, went to Rome, Florence, Ital. Alps

    Most interest. because of Renais. art

             beautiful scenery, esp. mtns

             food

2. Describe the type of food that you think is most representative of your country and explain why you think that it is representative. Include details and examples to support your explanation.

_____

_____

_____

_____

_____

3. What do you think is your most important skill? Explain why you think so. Include details and examples to support your explanation.

_____

_____

_____

_____

_____

SPEAKING

EXERCISE 15.4

FOCUS: Giving Personal Preference responses.

DIRECTIONS: Using the outlines that you wrote for the previous exercise, give forty-five second responses based on the prompts in Exercise 15.2 and 15.3. The first one is done for you as an example.

▶ Now start the Audio Program and listen to the example while you read along. 🎧

1. "I'd say that the . . . the most important trip I've ever taken was a trip to Italy. It was a two-week trip, and it was sponsored by my university. We went to Rome, to . . . uh . . . Florence, and then to the Italian Alps, the mountains in the north of Italy. I enjoyed this trip because I have always been interested in Renaissance art, and Florence has some of the best examples of this kind of art, such as Michelangelo's statue David. I also enjoyed this trip because of the beautiful scenery, especially the mountain scenery. Oh, and . . . uh, another reason why this was a great trip was the food. I love Italian food!"

EXERCISE 15.5

FOCUS: More practice preparing and giving Personal Preference responses.

DIRECTIONS: Listen and read along with the following prompts. You will have fifteen seconds to prepare your response, and then you will hear a beep on the audio program. You will have forty-five seconds to give your response, and then you will hear another beep. Ideally, you should record your responses and then play them back.

▶ Now start the Audio Program. 🎧

1. | You are going to give a gift to a friend and you want it to be symbolic of your country. Describe the gift that you would give. Include details and examples to support your explanation.

2. | Describe your ideal job. Explain why you would like to have this job. Include details and examples to support your explanation.

3. | Imagine that you have the ability to solve any one problem in the world. Describe which problem you would choose to solve, and explain how you would solve it. Include details and examples to support your explanation.

LESSON 16
PAIRED CHOICE TASK

Task 2, the second Independent Speaking Task, also consists of a single prompt. The prompt presents two points of view on one issue or two alternative methods of doing something. Your job is to decide which of these two points of view you agree with and then to give specific reasons why you agree with it. You will have fifteen seconds to get ready to give your response and forty-five seconds to give it.

You will be able to see the prompt on the screen and listen to it. While you are preparing and giving your response, the prompt will be on the screen.

Here's a sample Paired Choice Task from the Speaking Preview Test and a sample response to it. Listen to the prompt and then to the response, and read along as you listen.

▶ Now start the Audio Program. 🎧

Sample

> In some university classes, students are graded according to a Pass/Fail system. In other words, the only possible grades that you may receive are P (Pass) or F (Fail). In most classes, however, students are graded according to a more traditional system in which many letter grades can be given (A+, A, A−, B+, etc.). Explain which of these two systems you prefer and why. Include details and examples in your explanation.

"In my opinion, the letter grades system is the better. I see some advantage in the Pass/Fail system. For example, there is less stress on students, less pressure to try to get good grades. But . . . uh, personally I *like* the challenge of grades, of working to get grades. A grade of A+ or A is . . . it's something to aim for, like a goal. Also, uh, grades are a way to compare students, uh . . . to compare their performances. This can be important in ranking students and later, when students are . . . are looking out for jobs. For example, some businesses and . . . uh, some government agencies only hire people who are in the tops of their class—if everyone had a Pass grade, they couldn't make good decisions about who to hire. So, all in all, I like the letter grades system."

This response is successful because it responds to the prompt in a well-organized and complete way. The speaker states his opinion in the first sentence. He mentions a reason why the Pass/Fail system might be useful (it reduces stress on students) but says that he prefers the traditional system of letter grades. The speaker then goes on to give two specific reasons why he prefers letter grades: (1) A good grade gives him a goal to aim for, and (2) Grades are a way to classify students according to ability. For the second reason, he gives the example of companies and agencies that only hire students with the best grades.

The response is given fluently and is easy to understand. Pronunciation, intonation, and phrasing are all good. There are only a few, very minor grammatical problems. The speaker uses a number of transition signals *(In my opinion, for example, personally, but, also, all in all)* to make it easy for listeners to follow his ideas. The speed of the response is good—neither too fast nor too slow.

(A) Pre-Speaking

In the short period in which you are allowed to prepare to speak, you need to do the same basic things you did before the first Independent Task:

▶ Read and analyze the prompt.

▶ Decide which of the two points of view to support.

▶ Take notes about what you will say and prepare a simple outline.

Again, it is important to read and analyze the prompt so that you understand what you are being asked to do. (You don't need to analyze the prompt in your notes, only mentally.) Remember: all of the prompts for this task have two points of view. You have to understand what these two points of view are.

Look at the analysis of the Sample Task.

Analysis

This prompt talks about two systems of grading. In one system, the only possible grades are Pass and Fail. In the other system, teachers can give a whole range of letter grades to students. The prompt asks me which of these two systems I prefer. If I choose to support the Pass/Fail system, I'll need to support the idea that this system benefits students in some way—that it reduces stress and competition, for example. If I choose to support the letter-grade system, I need to support the idea that this system is beneficial—that it provides a challenge to students, for example.

Once you understand what the prompt is asking, you need to take a position. You can choose either side of the issue. As in the first task, there is no correct answer. You should choose the side that is easier for you to support.

You should write a very simple outline to help you focus as you give your presentation.

An outline for a Paired Choice Task should include the following:

▶ Your choice

▶ Why the other choice might be a good choice*

▶ Two or three reasons why your choice is an even better choice

---

*It's not necessary to give a reason why the other point of view is valid, but this technique—called "admitting the opposition"—can actually make your response stronger.

Here is a simple outline based on the Sample Task:

Prefer ltr grades
P/F system reduces strss
    BUT . . .
            I like challenge
            Useful for ranking stu.

(B) The Language of Paired Choices

Some vocabulary and grammatical structures are often used when discussing paired choices.

Opinion

When you choose one of the options in a Paired Choice question you are expressing your opinion. The following expressions can be used to express opinions.

> *I think* that advertising serves some useful purposes.
> *I feel* that a small town is a better place to raise children than a big city.
> *I believe* that most celebrities make too much money.

You can add the word *personally* to the statements of opinion given above.

> *Personally, I think* that advertising serves some useful purposes.
> *Personally, I feel* that a small town is a better place to raise children than a big city.
> *Personally, I believe* that most celebrities make too much money.

You can use the phrase *in my opinion* or *It's my opinion that* . . .

> *In my opinion,* advertising does more harm than good.
> *It's my opinion that* a big city is a better place to raise a child than a small town.

SPEAKING

Preference

In paired choice questions, you must usually express your preference for one of the two choices.

The verb *enjoy* is used with a gerund (verb + *ing*).

> *I enjoy living* alone, so I would not want to have a roommate.

The verb *prefer* can be used with either an infinitive (*to* + base form) or a gerund (verb + *ing*).

> I *prefer to live* in an apartment.
> I *prefer living* in an apartment.

However, when you use the verb *prefer* to talk about two actions, you must use gerunds:

> I *prefer living* in an apartment to *living* in a dorm.

The verb *would rather* is used with the base form (the infinitive without *to*).

> *I'd rather open* my own business *than work* for a big company.

Agreement

You may need to agree or disagree with an idea or with what "some people" think when you respond to Paired Choice prompts.

> *I agree* (or *disagree*) *with the idea that* first impressions are important.
> *I agree* (or *disagree*) with those people who think that celebrities are generally overpaid.
> *I agree* that the Olympics should be held in the same location every four years.

Notice that the phrase *agree with* is used before nouns: *I agree with the idea; I agree with those people.* The verb *agree* is used with *that* + a clause: *I agree that* the Olympics. . .
A common mistake is to use the verb *agree* with the verb *to be*:

> *I am agree* with the idea that . . . (INCORRECT)
> *I am agreed* that the Olympics . . . (INCORRECT)

Generality

You may often want to agree in general with an idea rather than to agree with it in all situations.

> *In general,* I think that celebrities such as pop stars and actors are overpaid.
> I believe that first impressions are *generally* quite valuable.
> *On the whole,* I enjoy traveling by train rather than *by plane.*

Contrasting Ideas

If you "admit the opposition"—in other words, if you give a reason why the other side of the issue may be valid—you need to use a transition word before you begin to speak about "your side" of the issue.

> Many people like the idea of having the Olympics at locations all over the world. *However,* I think that the Olympics should be held at a single location, such as Athens.

> First impressions are important, *but* you should never be afraid to change your mind.

Reasons and Examples

When you respond to a Paired Choice prompt, you should try to give at least two reasons for your choice. There are several ways that you could do this (very similar to the way you provided reasons in Personal Preference responses).

> *There are several good reasons why* I would usually rather travel by train than by plane. *One* is cost. Train fare is less expensive for me than plane fare. *Another* is convenience. I live near the train station in my home town, and generally when I travel, I need to go to downtown locations that are also near train stations.

> *Why* do I like to travel by train rather than by plane? *One reason* is cost. Train fare is less expensive for me than plane fare. *A second reason* is convenience. I live near the train station in my hometown, and generally when I travel, I need to go to downtown locations that are also near train stations.

> I think that the Olympics should be moved to a single location *because* it would reduce the cost of holding the Olympics and also *because* the Olympic Committee would no longer have to choose Olympic sites for "political" reasons.

You may also give examples during your presentation.

> I think the Olympics should be held at the same site, *such as* Athens, every year.

> Sometimes my first impressions of people have been entirely wrong. *For example,* when I first met my academic advisor, I thought he was cold and unfriendly. However, over the next year, I gradually came to realize that he was a very warm and caring man when I got to know him.

Conclusion

In a forty-five second response, you do not really need to have a formal conclusion. However, you can add a summary or concluding sentence at the end if you have time.

> For *these reasons,* I think that the government should support high-tech development rather than heavy industry.

In conclusion, I am against the idea of moving the Olympics to a permanent site.

All in all, I would rather live in a dormitory than in an apartment.

(C) Giving the Paired Choice Response

When you give the Paired Choice response, you should begin by clearly stating which of the two choices you agree with and briefly explain or describe your choice. You may "admit the opposition"—give one reason why the other choice is valid—and then go on to give two or three reasons why your choice is the better of the two. If you have time, you can give a quick summary statement at the end.

Keep track of time by looking now and then at the on-screen clock. When giving practice responses, work on your timing so that you can give a response in about forty-five seconds.

If you find that you finish very early (with more than fifteen seconds remaining) take advantage of your extra time to give a summary or add an additional reason. However, if you finish with less than fifteen seconds remaining, just stop and go on to the next Speaking task.

When you give the Paired Choice response, keep the following points in mind:

▶ State your choice clearly in the first sentence of your response.

▶ Follow the simple outline that you made during the preparation time.

▶ If you want, give one reason why the opposite choice might be a good choice.

▶ If you admit the opposition, make a clear transition to the part of the response in which you support your own choice by using a transition of contrast, such as *however* or *but.*

▶ Give at least two specific reasons to support your choice.

▶ Speak clearly and directly into the microphone.

▶ Don't speak too slowly or too fast.

▶ Keep your response flowing; avoid long pauses.

▶ Pay attention to your pronunciation and intonation.

▶ Keep it simple by using familiar vocabulary and grammar.

EXERCISE 16.1

FOCUS: Using the language of Paired Choices.

DIRECTIONS: Orally complete each group of sentences according to the directions given. The first sentence in each group is done for you as an example.

Use the phrases below to give your opinion about the choices.

I believe . . .	Personally, I feel . . .
I think . . .	It's my opinion that . . .
In my opinion . . .	

Which is better?

1. learning in class/learning by experience

    Example: "I believe it is better to learn by experience."

2. driving your own car/taking public transportation

3. having dinner at a friend's house/eating out at a restaurant

4. showering/taking a bath

5. attending school abroad/attending school in your own country

Use the verbs below to give your preference about the choices.

    enjoy

    prefer

    would rather

6. getting up early/staying up late

    Example: "I enjoy staying up late more than getting up early."

7. being rich/being famous

8. studying at the library/studying at home

9. working out at a gym/jogging

SPEAKING

Use the expressions below to agree or disagree with one of the viewpoints.

    agree/disagree with the idea that

    agree/disagree with the people who think

    agree that

10. Money should be/should not be the most important factor in choosing a career.

    Example: "I disagree with the idea that money should be the most important factor in choosing a career."

11. Cell phones have made it more difficult/easier to communicate with people.

12. Nurses should /should not make as much money as doctors.

Use the expressions below to generally agree or disagree with the opinions.

    in general

    generally

    on the whole

13. Money should be the most important factor in choosing a career.

    Example: "In general, I disagree with the idea that money should be the most important factor in choosing a career."

14. Some people think that a library is the most important feature of a university. Other people think it is the quality of the faculty.

15. Some people prefer to watch a movie at a cinema. Other people would rather watch a video at home.

Use the expressions below to disagree with the opinions.

> however
>
> but

16. Some people think children should not be encouraged to use a calculator in their math classes.

> Example: "Some people think children should not be encouraged to use a calculator in math classes because they won't learn how to do basic arithmetic on their own. However, I think that using a calculator is itself a very important skill."

17. Some people like to travel with large groups of people. Other people prefer to travel alone.

18. Some people enjoy living in a small town. Some people prefer big city life. There are several good reasons . . .

Use the expressions below to support the statements.

> why . . .
>
> because

19. Some people prefer to get in touch with people by telephone. Others prefer to use e-mail.

> Example: "There are several reasons why I prefer to communicate with people via e-mail. One is that it is faster. I don't have to spend time finding someone or making small talk. Another is that there is always a record of my e-mails."

20. Students should/shouldn't be required to perform community service.

21. It is/isn't always important to make decisions quickly.

Use the expressions below to give examples based on the sentence.

> for example
>
> such as

22. Some people like to shop at big discount stores. Other people prefer to shop at small shops.

> Example: "I shop at big discount stores because the prices are low. For example, clothing is much cheaper in big discount stores than in small shops or boutiques."

23. Some people think watching television is a waste of time. Other people think it is a worthwhile activity.

24. There are advantages to using a credit card. There are also disadvantages.

EXERCISE 16.2

FOCUS: Understanding Paired Choice prompts.

DIRECTIONS: Read the following prompts. Then give a brief oral (spoken) analysis of each of the prompts. The first one is done for you as an example.

1. Some students like to do research on the Internet. Other students prefer to use their university library. Explain which of these you prefer and why. Include details and examples in your explanation.

> This prompt is asking me to explain which method of doing research I prefer. It also wants me to give reasons why I prefer one over the other. If I choose the first option, I have to give reasons why I like doing research on the Internet, such as convenience and speed. If I choose the second option, I have to show why it is preferable to use a library. I could say, for example, that many scholarly journals and books are still not available on the Internet, especially not for free.

2. Some people say that anyone who possesses a skill or knowledge can teach that skill or knowledge. Other people say that only certified teachers who have studied the principles of education should be teachers. Tell which view you agree with and why. Include details and examples in your explanation.

3. Some high schools and elementary schools require their students to wear school uniforms. Other schools let their students wear whatever clothing they like. Which of these two policies do you agree with, and why? Include details and examples in your explanation.

EXERCISE 16.3

FOCUS: Writing simple outlines for Paired Choice responses.

DIRECTIONS: Using the prompts from Exercise 16.2, prepare a *brief* written outline of your response. The first one is done for you as an example.

1. Some students like to do research on the Internet. Other students prefer to use their university library. Explain which of these you prefer and why. Include details and examples in your explanation.

○

Prefer library
　　Internet is convenient, work at home
　　But, Libr more acad. materials
　　　　free use of jnals, bks, etc.
　　　　　& more social

2. Some people say that anyone who possesses a skill or knowledge can teach that skill or knowledge. Other people say that only certified teachers who have studied the principles of education should be teachers. Tell which view you agree with and why. Include details and examples in your explanation.

_____

_____

_____

_____

_____

_____

3. Some high schools and elementary schools require their students to wear school uniforms. Other schools let their students wear whatever clothing they like. Which of these two policies do you agree with, and why? Include details and examples in your explanation.

_____

_____

_____

_____

_____

_____

EXERCISE 16.4

FOCUS: Giving Paired Choice responses.

DIRECTIONS: Using the outlines that you wrote for the previous exercise, give forty-five second responses based on the prompts in Exercise 16.2. The first one is done for you as an example.

▶ Now start the Audio Program and listen to the example while you read along. 🎧

1. I think I'd rather work in the . . . uh, in the library than in the . . . . than on the Internet. Why do I say this? Well, it's pretty convenient to work at home, on a home computer, and find information on the Web. However, from my experience, not all academic books and journals are available online now, at least not for free, not in my field, anyway—you might have to pay to use some of these journals, subscribe, you know. Also, a lot of the information that is online, it is not really appropriate for university research, it's not really academic. Finally, I just like to go to the library because I see a lot of people that I know there, it's, you know, just more social.

2.

3.

EXERCISE 16.5

FOCUS: More practice preparing and giving Paired Choice responses.

DIRECTIONS: Listen and read along with the following prompts. You have fifteen seconds to prepare your response, and then you will hear a beep on the Audio Program. You have forty-five seconds to give your response, and then you will hear another beep. Ideally, you should record your responses and then play them back.

▶ Now start the Audio Program. 🎧

1. Some students prefer to go to a small college or university, while others prefer to go to a large university. Explain which view you prefer, and why. Include details and examples in your explanation.

2. Some people believe that technology has improved life, while other people believe it has not. Explain which view you prefer, and why. Include details and examples in your explanation.

3. Because of computers and telephones, it is now possible for many people to work at home. Some people enjoy this, while others would rather work in an office. Explain which of these you prefer. Include details and examples in your explanation.

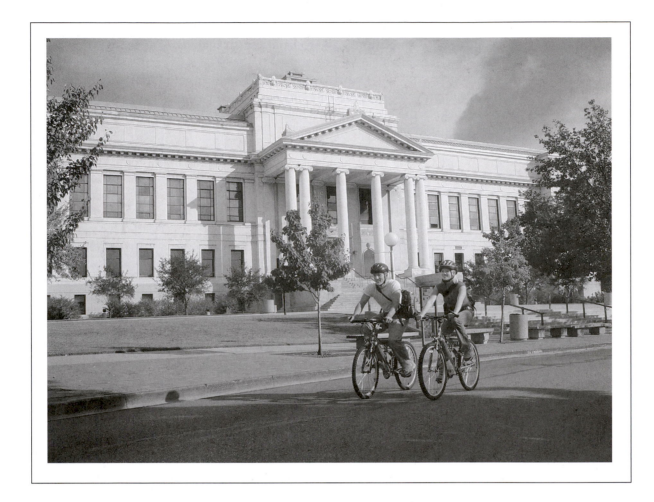

ABOUT THE INTEGRATED SPEAKING TASKS

Tasks 3, 4, 5, and 6 of the Speaking Section are Integrated Tasks. These tasks integrate (combine) two or three language skills. Tasks 3 and 4 integrate reading, listening, and speaking. Tasks 5 and 6 integrate listening and speaking.

Tasks 3 and 5 are based on "campus situations." In other words, the sources for these tasks come from events that take place at a university, but not in a classroom. Tasks 4 and 6 are based on academic situations. They are based on academic readings and/or lectures or discussions.

In your responses to Integrated Tasks, you should simply *report* what you read and hear. Unlike Independent Tasks, Integrated Tasks generally do *not* ask you to give your opinion of a topic or issue. (The exception is Task 5, which asks you to decide which of two solutions to a problem you think is best.)

Skills that are required to do well on the Integrated Speaking Tasks include the abilities to

▶ understand and take notes on readings (Tasks 3 and 4) and lectures/conversations (Tasks 3 through 6)

▶ understand the questions and what they ask you to do

▶ "brainstorm" ideas and take notes on the ideas that you come up with during the preparation time

▶ write notes or a simple outline to help guide you as you speak

▶ summarize and report key ideas from the readings and lectures/conversations

▶ support your ideas with examples, reasons, and details from the readings and lectures/conversations

▶ deliver a clear, well-organized response based on the information in the readings and lectures/conversations

For many test-takers, the integrated section of the Speaking Section may be the most challenging part of the TOEFL® iBT. Most of the topics that you have to talk about will be unfamiliar to you, and talking about unfamiliar topics is difficult, even for native speakers. Besides, you may not have had much practice with this type of task in the past. The practice that you will get in this part of the book, however, will prepare you to do your best on this part of the test.

The Four Types of Integrated Speaking Tasks			
Task and Type	*Description*	*Example Question*	*Timing*
Task 3: Announcement/ Discussion Reading/Listening/ Speaking Campus-based situation	You read a notice or announcement related to some aspect of university life and then hear two students discuss the written notice. You then report what was in the notice and what one of the students thought about it.	"The man expresses his opinion of the notice. State his opinion and explain the reasons he gives for having that opinion."	Reading: 45 seconds Lecture: 60 to 80 seconds Preparation: 30 seconds Response: 60 seconds
Task 4: General/ Specific Reading/Listening/ Speaking Academic situation	You read a passage from a textbook or academic article about a general concept or theory. Next you hear a lecture about a specific example of this concept or application of this theory. You then summarize the reading and lecture and discuss the relationship between the two.	"The professor describes A (a specific point). Explain how A is related to X (a general idea)."	Reading: 45 seconds Lecture: 60 to 90 seconds Preparation: 30 seconds Response: 60 seconds
Task 5: Problem/Solution Listening/Speaking Campus-based situation	You hear two students discussing a problem that one of them has and two possible solutions to this problem. You must summarize the problem and explain which of the two solutions you prefer.	"The students discuss a problem that the man is having. Describe the problem. Then explain which of the two solutions you think is better and give reasons why."	Conversation: 60 to 90 seconds Preparation: 20 seconds Response: 60 seconds
Task 6: Summary Listening/Speaking Academic situation	You hear a lecture or a classroom discussion. You must summarize the main points of the lecture/discussion.	"Using specific points and examples from the lecture, explain how the process of Z (the topic of the lecture) occurs."	Lecture/Discussion: 90 to 120 seconds Preparation: 20 seconds Response: 60 seconds

More about Tasks 3 and 4

After the two Independent Speaking Tasks, you will immediately begin the four Integrated Speaking Tasks. For Tasks 3 and 4, you will see short readings on the screen. You have forty-five seconds to read the material and to make notes. You will then see a photograph on the screen and you will hear a conversation (Task 3) or a lecture or classroom discussion (Task 4) in your headphones.

You may take notes while you listen. After this, you see a message on the screen telling you to get ready, and then you will see a question based on the reading and the lecture. You have thirty seconds in which to prepare your response. In thirty seconds, you will hear a beep and you have one minute in which to give your response. An on-screen clock keeps track of time. Another beep tells you that your time is up.

SPEAKING

> The man expresses his opinion of the notice. State his opinion and explain the reasons he gives for having that opinion.
>
> ---
>
> | Preparation Time: | 30 Seconds |
> |---|---|
> | Response Time: | 1 Minute |
>
> **PREPARATION TIME**
> 00 : 00 : 00

More about Tasks 5 and 6

For Tasks 5 and 6, you see photographs that set the scene. For Task 5, you will see a photograph of two students talking. For Task 6, you will see a professor lecturing a class or leading a discussion. You will hear a conversation (Task 5) or a lecture/discussion (Task 6) that lasts from sixty to ninety seconds. Once you have listened to the conversation or classroom talk, you will see a screen that tells you to get ready to answer the question and then a question about the listening material will appear. You have twenty seconds to get ready to respond. At the end of this twenty-second preparation time, you will hear a beep and you have one minute in which to give your response. A second beep tells you when you must stop speaking.

Note Taking

It's important to take accurate notes on both the readings and the listening material. The readings do *not* appear on the screen when you give your response, so you have to use your notes.

You use the same process in taking notes for the Speaking Task as you used in the Listening Section. Write down only the key ideas and use short forms and abbreviations whenever possible.

Summarizing, Paraphrasing, Citing, and Synthesizing

You do not have enough time to give a complete report on the lectures and readings. You must give a shortened version of the information that you read and hear. In other words, you must **summarize.** By taking good notes you will automatically be creating a summary, because the basic idea of note taking is to write down only the most important information.

You should avoid using exactly the same language that you read and hear. You must report information from the reading and lectures in your own words. In other words, you must **paraphrase** the language of the sources. Again, by using your notes you will automatically be paraphrasing because you probably will not copy down information in your notes word for word.

It is also important that you **cite** information that you are reporting: "The author informs us that . . . "; "The male student says that . . ."; "According to the lecture, . . .". Especially in Tasks 3 and 4, the "language of citation" is needed to tell your listeners if an idea comes from the written material or the spoken material.

In Tasks 3 and 4, you need to connect the readings and the lecture/conversations. In other words, you need to **synthesize** information from the two sources. There should be a balance between ideas that you take from the reading and ideas that you take from the lecture/conversation. You must also show the relationship between the ideas from the two sources: "The announcement says that students must now do X. However, Marie does not agree with this policy."

SCORING THE INTEGRATED SPEAKING RESPONSES

Each task is scored by a different human (not computer) rater. Raters give a score of 0 to 4 using a rubric (set of guidelines) similar to the following.

Score	Overall Description of Response	Delivery of the Response	Use of Language (Grammar/Vocabulary)	Development of the Topic
4	**The response addresses the task in a complete and well-organized way. The entire response is clear and fluent and demonstrates all three of the characteristics described in the columns on the right.**	The response is fluent, smooth, and intelligible. There may be minor problems involving pronunciation, stress, and intonation, but these do not affect the speaker's intelligibility.	The response shows that the speaker has an effective command of high-level grammatical structures and uses sophisticated vocabulary and idiomatic expressions. There may be some minor grammatical or vocabulary errors, but these problems do not interfere with the speaker's overall intelligibility.	The response is coherent and unified. The speaker clearly reports information from the lecture/reading. The speaker supports general statements with specific reasons and examples. The speaker uses transitional words to connect parts of the response.
3	**The response adequately addresses the task but may not be completely developed. The response is generally clear and fluent but may show weaknesses in the speaker's ability to communicate ideas. The response demonstrates at least two of the characteristics described in the columns on the right.**	The response is generally smooth, fluent, idiomatic, and intelligible, but there are noticeable problems with pronunciation, stress, and intonation. These problems, however, generally do not affect the speaker's overall intelligibility.	The response shows that the speaker can use intermediate-level grammatical structures and vocabulary. There are some grammatical errors and problems with vocabulary and usage. These problems, however, generally do not affect the speaker's overall intelligibility.	The response addresses the task and is generally coherent and unified. Development, however, is limited and the speaker's main ideas may not be adequately supported with the use of concrete examples. The connection between parts of the response may not be perfectly clear.

continued

SPEAKING

Score	Overall Description of Response	Delivery of the Response	Use of Language (Grammar/Vocabulary)	Development of the Topic
2	**The response attempts to address the prompt but lacks adequate development. Speech is generally clear but problems with the speaker's delivery and language use may make the response difficult to fully understand. The response demonstrates at least two of the characteristics described in the columns on the right.**	The response is intelligible but there are noticeable problems with pronunciation, stress, and intonation that may make the speaker's speech seem fragmented and unnatural. In places, problems with delivery will interfere with the listener's ability to understand the speaker's message.	The response shows the speaker has command of grammar and vocabulary use at the basic level. Errors may make at least parts of the response difficult to understand.	The response is related to the task, but the number or appropriateness of the ideas presented is limited. The response may seem incomplete, vague, or repetitious. Connections between parts of the response may not be clear.
1	**The response is not closely related to the task or the speech is generally incomprehensible. The response demonstrates at least two of the characteristics described in the columns on the right.**	Serious problems with pronunciation, stress, and intonation make it difficult to understand the speaker's ideas. There may be many pauses and hesitations. Listeners may not be able to understand much of the response and then only with great effort.	Frequent errors in grammar and vocabulary use greatly limit or completely prevent the communication of the speaker's ideas.	Response may not be connected to the prompt. There is little or no development of the topic. Few, if any, comprehensible ideas are expressed, and these ideas may not be connected. Speaker may not finish the task.
0	Test-taker does not give a response or the response is not related to the prompt.			

Following are four responses to an Announcement/Discussion task (Task 4). Each response illustrates one of the four scores. These were given in response to the following task:

Western Minnesota State University is instituting a new policy regarding parking requirements. Read the following notice from the Parking Office. You will have forty-five seconds in which to read the notice. You may take notes as you read. Begin reading now.

Western Minnesota State University
Changes in Parking Regulations

To help finance the new parking structure on campus, WMSU has approved the following parking policy:

1. Beginning in the Spring Semester, all people parking on university property must register their vehicle with the Parking Office and pay a $10 registration fee.
2. There will no longer be "free parking" at the Stadium parking lot.
3. Students living off-campus who wish to park on campus have two permit options:
   (a) Purchase a Student A permit, which allows parking in the central campus parking lots ($75 per semester).
   (b) Purchase a Student B permit, which allows parking in outlying lots, including the Stadium lot ($25 per semester).

Students with unpaid parking tickets must pay their outstanding tickets at the Campus Police Department before registering their vehicles.

▶ Now start the Audio Program and listen to two students discussing the new parking policy.

Now get ready to answer the question.

SPEAKING

> The woman expresses her opinion of the new parking policy. State her opinion and explain the reasons she gives for having that opinion.

▶ While you are listening to the responses, follow along with these transcriptions. 🎧

Sample Response 1

"The man is upset because of the parking rules, the . . . uh . . . new parking rules. He . . . he always parks at the stadium but now, uh, he must pay $25. Also, he must register his car and . . . um, pay his parking tickets. He doesn't think that the new rules are fair.

The woman doesn't . . . she doesn't think . . . she doesn't agree with what the man says. She . . . uh, she thinks that this is not . . . not so much money to pay for parking. The university will use the money for repairing the parking lot, for plowing the snow, for painting the lines in the parking lot. They will also use it for building new parking structure. So . . . uh, unlike the man, she doesn't think . . . she thinks that the policy is fair."

Score: __4__

Comments: The intonation and the pronunciation are clear and the use of vocabulary and grammar is fairly advanced. The response is fluent and easily understood. The speaker at first concentrates on the man's opinion (although the question asks about the woman's opinion). However, he then contrasts the man's opinion with the woman's and nicely summarizes the woman's reasons for not disagreeing with the new parking policies.

Sample Response 2

"The woman . . . eh, um . . . usually parks her car at the stadium and for her . . . eh . . . the new . . . eh . . . Minnesota policy about parking is not . . . ah, so bad and she just will have another . . . eh . . . eh . . . opinion and . . . eh . . . for . . . for the man . . . eh . . . it this is not a good . . . eh . . . policy . . . eh . . . because . . . eh . . . twenty-five dollar per semesters and more, ten dollars . . . eh . . . for just . . . registering the car. It's too much and the . . . maybe people . . . eh . . . will park . . . eh . . . their car in the . . . um . . . neighborhood around the university and . . . eh . . . eh . . . so . . . eh . . . the two people have different opinions . . . eh . . . the woman agrees with day . . . eh . . . university's policy while the man don't."

Score: __3__

Comments: The speech and pronunciation are generally clear and fluent although there are many hesitations. There is some inaccurate use of vocabulary and grammar, but it doesn't affect the overall intelligibility of the response.

Sample Response 3

"First, uh, she's not . . . uh . . . she's not upset to university decision because . . . uh . . . she felt that the fee for parking and the registration is not expensive, only twenty-five dollars for semester and she thought university also have to pay to maintain the parking area it costs . . . it costs . . . mmmmm . . . it, it may cost high, the cost for . . . mmmmm . . . paving or painting and clean snow during the winter so she, she thought that it fair that university . . . uh . . . made a rule for parking."

Score: __2__

Comments: Although the response is connected to the task, the examples and development of the ideas are very limited. The pace of the response is slow and not fluid, making it generally difficult to understand.

Sample Response 4

"The ladies seemed like a . . . um . . . she more agree with the new policy because she realized she didn't have, she doesn't have the problem with the parking, the new parking rules . . . um . . . she really seem like she ready to pay twenty-five dollars, personally there, but the guy Brad he's kinda like a little bit upset and . . . um . . . upset and he have some money situation and . . . um . . . he doesn't really want to . . . to pay more money . . . um. (pause) The lady, she . . . um . . . she gave a good reason about why the university have to . . . um, ah . . . cause the money for the parking and . . . um . . . she also . . . ah . . . say that if the . . . they collect the money for fixing the stadium . . ."

Score: __1__

Comments: The response is very fragmented, and the speaker has problems with pronunciation and word choice. The speaker does not provide a complete answer to the question, and the amount of details provided is not sufficient. There are also rather long pauses. Some of the speaker's ideas—such as the fact that the money for parking will be used to repair the stadium—are incorrect. This response requires considerable listener effort.

EXERCISE: SCORING THE RESPONSE

DIRECTIONS: Here are three responses based on the task on page 440. Listen to the responses. Then, using the scoring rubric on pages 437–438, decide what score (1 to 4) you would give each response.

This exercise will help you develop the ability to score your own responses.

Response 1 ⌒

Score: _____

Comments:

Response 2 ⌒

Score: _____

Comments:

Response 3 ⌒

Score: _____

Comments:

Tactics for Integrated Speaking Tasks

- Take careful, accurate notes on both the readings and the lectures/conversations.

- Read the question carefully, and make sure you understand what it is asking you to do.

- Plan your response by using your notes and writing a simple outline.

- Paraphrase and summarize the information in the reading and/or in the lectures/conversations.

- Use the "language of citation" (*"According to the article, . . ."; "The lecturer says . . ."*) to indicate when an idea comes from a reading or a lecture.

- For Tasks 3 and 4, explain the relationship between the information in the reading and that in the lecture.

- The Integrated questions ask you to explain what you learn from the readings and/or the lectures, and to give reasons for the response. In other words, you need to integrate both the key ideas and the important examples or details from the material you read and/or listen to.

- Use transition words and phrases to separate the parts of your responses.

INTEGRATED SPEAKING PREVIEW TEST
DIRECTIONS

▶ Now start the Audio Program and listen carefully. 🎧

The last four tasks of the Speaking Section are Integrated Speaking Tasks. The third and fourth questions involve a reading text and a listening passage. You will have forty-five seconds in which to read a short text. You will then hear a short conversation or part of a lecture on the same topic. You may take notes on both the reading and listening passage. You will then see a question on the screen asking about the information that you have just read and heard, and you will have thirty seconds in which to plan a response. When you hear a beep on the Audio Program, you will have sixty seconds in which to answer the question.

The fifth and sixth questions involve a short listening passage. You may take notes as you listen. After listening to the conversation or lecture, you will see a question, and you will have twenty seconds in which to plan your response. When you hear a beep on the Audio Program, you will have sixty seconds in which to answer the question.

During actual tests, a clock on the screen will tell you how much preparation time or how much response time (speaking time) remains for each question. It is important that you time yourself accurately when you take this practice test. If possible, record your response. On an actual test your responses will be recorded and evaluated by trained raters.

Task 3

Beginning this semester, all faculty members at Monroe University are required to hand out copies of the university's plagiarism policy. You will have forty-five seconds in which to read the policy. Begin reading now.

Monroe University

Plagiarism Policy

Plagiarism is considered intellectually dishonest and will not be tolerated at Monroe University.

Plagiarism is defined as the offering of the words or ideas of others as your own. It may be a single sentence, whole paragraphs, or an entire paper, whether from an Internet Web site, a book, a journal, or papers written by other students.

Also forbidden is the submission of your own research papers as original work in more than one course without the written permission of both professors. The Monroe University policy for dealing with instances of plagiarism is as follows:

(A) A warning will be given to first-year students.
(B) A reduction in grades will be given to second-year students.
(C) A failure for the course will be given to upperclassmen (third- and fourth-year students) and for honors students.

Faculty members will use anti-plagiarism software to assist in detecting plagiarism.

Notes:

_____

_____

_____

_____

▸ Now listen to two students discussing this notice. 🎧

Notes:

_____

_____

_____

_____

Now get ready to answer the question.

The man expresses his opinion of the policy. State his opinion and explain the reasons he gives for having that opinion.

Preparation Time: 30 Seconds
Response Time: 60 Seconds

Task 4

Read these paragraphs from a textbook describing animal camouflage.
    Reading time: 45 seconds

Reading

Animals are always in danger of being eaten by predators. They have therefore developed methods of avoiding these predators. One effective means that animals use to protect themselves is _camouflage._ What is meant by camouflage? Camouflage refers to the coloration or general appearance of an animal that makes it difficult to see when it is in its own environment. An animal employing camouflage blends in with its environment so that it is invisible, or it looks to its predators like an inanimate or inedible object.

   Now, when we think of camouflage, we often think of animals that appear dull and colorless in order to go unnoticed. This is sometimes true, but not always. Some animals may not look camouflaged to human eyes. In fact, they are easy for us to spot, especially out of their normal environments. However, to their predators, they are quite difficult to see.

Notes:

_____

_____

_____

_____

▶ Now listen to a lecture in a zoology class. 🎧

Notes:

_____

_____

_____

Now get ready to answer the question.

> The professor describes how camouflage protects two types of animals. Explain how this is related to the concepts of camouflage described in the reading.

Preparation Time: 30 Seconds
Response Time: 60 Seconds

Task 5

▶ Listen to a conversation between two students. 🎧

Notes:

_____

_____

_____

_____

_____

| Now get ready to answer the question. |

The man offers Lucy two possible solutions to her problem. Discuss her problem and then explain which of the two solutions you think is better and why you think so.

Preparation Time: 20 Seconds
Response Time: 60 Seconds

Task 6

▶ Listen to part of a lecture in a linguistics class. 🎧

Notes:

_____

_____

_____

_____

_____

| Now get ready to answer the question. |

Using specific examples and points from the lecture, explain the professor's concept of dialects and languages.

Preparation Time: 20 Seconds
Response Time: 60 Seconds

This is the end of the Integrated Speaking Preview Test.

SPEAKING

LESSON 17

ANNOUNCEMENT/DISCUSSION TASK

Task 3 involves getting ideas and details from two sources of information. First, you will be asked to read a short written announcement directed at students and related to university life. It might be a notice in a campus newspaper, part of a letter, a memo, an e-mail sent to students, or a sign on a bulletin board. These notices are often about new regulations or policies or changes in existing regulations or policies. You will have forty-five seconds in which to read the passage, and you may take notes.

After you have read this announcement, you will hear a conversation in which two students discuss the announcement. This conversation lasts from sixty to eighty seconds. You will be asked what *one* student thinks of the announcement. Again, you may take notes on what is said. You will then have thirty seconds to prepare your response and sixty seconds to give it.

While you are preparing and giving your response, you will see the question, but you will not see the reading. However, you can refer to your notes.

Here's a sample Announcement/Discussion Task from the Integrated Speaking Preview Test and a sample response to it. Read the announcement, then read along as you listen to the conversation, the question, and the sample response.

Sample

Reading time: 45 seconds

Beginning this semester, all faculty members at Monroe University are required to hand out copies of the university's plagiarism policy. You will have forty-five seconds in which to read the policy. Begin reading now.

Monroe University

Plagiarism Policy

Plagiarism is considered intellectually dishonest and will not be tolerated at Monroe University.

Plagiarism is defined as the offering of the words or ideas of others as your own. It may be a single sentence, whole paragraphs, or an entire paper, whether from an Internet Web site, a book, a journal, or papers written by other students.

Also forbidden is the submission of your own research papers as original work in more than one course without the written permission of both professors. The Monroe University policy for dealing with instances of plagiarism is as follows:

(A) A warning will be given to first-year students.
(B) A reduction in grades will be given to second-year students.
(C) A failure for the course will be given to upperclassmen (third- and fourth-year students) and for honors students.

Faculty members will use anti-plagiarism software to assist in detecting plagiarism.

▶ Now start the Audio Program and listen to two students discussing this notice. 🎧

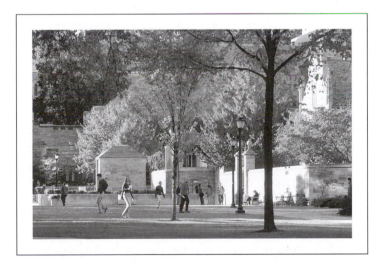

Student A

So it looks like they're serious about stopping plagiarism. I've gotten a copy of this in every class.

Student B

Yeah, well, in general, I don't have any argument with the policy . . . I'm just glad they're finally making this policy . . . making it a little more public, passing it out in every class. If I'd known about this policy a coupla years ago, I wouldn't have gotten in trouble . . .

Student A

Wait a minute, *you* got in trouble for plagiarism?

Student B

It . . . uh, well, it wasn't *exactly* plagiarism . . . . at least, *I* didn't consider it plagiarism, but it did . . . uh, violate the policy. See that part about using the same research paper for more than one class? Well, I was writing a paper for a geology class and one for a chemistry class. They were both about hydrocarbon compounds, and I used one section of my geology paper in my chemistry paper. I didn't know I couldn't do that. I'll tell you one thing—that software for detecting plagiarism really works. Or at least it did for my paper!

Student A

So, what happened? Did you just get a warning?

Student B

No, at the time, I was in my second year here, and so the grade on both my papers was lowered by a whole letter grade. That's another thing about this policy . . . I don't understand why a first-year student gets a warning and a second-year student gets a lower grade. That doesn't seem right to me.

Student A

Yeah, I know, that seems strange to me, too. I suppose the idea is, the longer you've been a student here, the more aware of the policy you should be. I guess you should be glad that it didn't happen when you were an upperclassman or you would have failed both classes.

Narrator

> The man expresses his opinion of the policy. State his opinion and explain the reasons he gives for having that opinion.

Sample Response

"The notice tells about the plagiarism policy and . . . uh, defines plagiarisms. It says a plagiarism is using someone else's words, um, like your own words. It can be a little bit, just a sentence, or a whole paper. It can be from other students or from books, Web sites, it doesn't matter where. It can also be that you use the same paper for more than one class, um, you hand in one paper for more than one class. The announcement also lists the . . . uh, punishments for plagiarism. These are worse for the older students than for the new students. It says that they, that there is software used to find a plagiarism.

"The man says that he, uh, generally agrees with the plagiarism policy. But he says that he just wishes that they published it more in the past, because he didn't know about it. The reason for that is . . . he, uh, violated the policy by using part of one paper in two classes, for geology and chemistry. His grades were lowered for his two classes. He also says he doesn't understand why there are different punishments for different students. The woman says it's maybe because students who have been at Monroe University for longer times, they should know this policy."

This response would be scored high because it clearly summarizes the key points of the university's plagiarism policy, defines plagiarism, and talks about the system of punishments. The response also explains how the man feels about the policy (he agrees with it but wishes it had been publicized more in the past) and it gives the reasons for the man's opinion (he unknowingly violated the policy by using part of one paper for two classes). The response also notes that the man doesn't know why there are different penalties for plagiarism based on what year a student is in, and that the woman thinks this is because students who have spent more time at the university should be more familiar with the policies.

The response is logically organized into a summary of the announcement and the man's reaction to the announcement. It is fluent and although there are a few minor errors in grammar and usage, it is highly intelligible. (In other words, it is easy to understand). Pronunciation and intonation are good. The speed of the response is fine, not too fast nor too slow.

(A) Pre-Speaking

Your first job is to read the announcement carefully looking for key ideas and supporting information. Take notes on the reading *while* you are reading it, not after.

Remember: You will not see the reading again while you are giving the response.

Sample notes on the reading:

Plagiarism: intel dishonest not tolerated
Def: words or ideas of others as yr own
sentce, paragr, paper
Int'nt, bk, jnal, other stu
+ submitting own paper for >1 course w/out permiss. also forbid.
Punishment: warning for 1st yr stu
reduc. grde 2nd " "
fail course 3rd 4th & honors stu
Will use softwre to find plag'ism

Next you will hear a male and a female student reacting to the announcement. The question asks you about the opinion of *one* of the students, so you should keep track of *who* is speaking in your notes.

Sample notes on the conversation:

F: Univ serious abt plag'ism   Got copy every clss
M: No argu w/ policy   glad making public   got in trble cple yr ago
F: (surprised)
M: used 1 sect of paper abt hydrocarbs for geol & chem cls
      softwre for plag'ism works!
F: ask if warning
M: No becse 2nd yr stu: ↓ grade on both papers
      not understnd why 1st yr stu gets warning 2nd yr ↓ grade
F: maybe longer been stu, more shld know policy ∴ shld be glad not
      up'clssman:
      fail clsses

Next, the question will appear on the screen. Be sure you understand what the question is asking you to do. And pay attention to which student's opinion is being asked about.

"What is the man's opinion of . . . ?"

"What is the woman's opinion of . . . ?"

"What is Paul's opinion of . . . ?"

"What is Lisa's opinion of . . . ?"

Instead of writing a separate outline during the thirty-second preparation time, you can use your notes to decide what to talk about. Just underline or circle the points you want to make in your response.

Here are notes a test-taker took during the reading and lecture. They are underlined to show what he will discuss:

Rdg.

Plagiarism: intel dishonest   not tolerated   (Topic)

   Def: words or ideas of others as yr own

      sentce, paragr, paper

      Int'nt, bk, jnal, other stu

  + submitting own paper for >1 course w/out permiss. also forbid.

  Punishment: warning for 1st yr stu

         reduc. grde 2nd "   "

         fail course 3rd 4th & honors stu

Will use softwre to find plag'ism

Conver.

F: Univ serious abt plag'ism   Got copy every clss

M: No argu w/ policy   glad making public   got in trble cple yr ago

(Man's opinion) &

reason for opin

F: (surprised)

M: used 1 sect of paper abt hydrocarbs for geol & chem cls

  software for plag'ism works!

F: ask if warning

M: No becse 2nd yr stu: ↓ grade on both papers

  not understnd why 1st yr stu gets warning 2nd yr ↓ grade

F: maybe longer been stu, more shld know policy ∴ shld be glad not

  up'clssman:

  fail clsses

(B) The Language of Announcement/Discussion

Some vocabulary and grammatical structures are often used when giving your announcement/discussion response. Being familiar with them will make it easier to focus on the details of the topic.

Topic

You will first need to quickly state the overall topic of the announcement. Here are some easy ways to do that.

> *The announcement is* about the plagiarism policy at Monroe University.
>
> *The topic of the announcement is* a new smoking policy.
>
> *The main point of the announcement is* to explain the campus newspaper's new policy about publishing letters to the editors.

SPEAKING

Citation

In the Announcement/Discussion task, and in all of the Integrated Speaking tasks, you need to clearly state who says what. In other words, you need to clearly say if an idea comes from the announcement, from the student you are being asked about, or (possibly) from the other student. The easiest way to do this is with the verb *say* (in the present tense) and the phrase *according to.*

> *According to the announcement,* smoking will no longer be permitted around the doorways of university buildings.
>
> *According to the man,* students should be able to publish letters at least once a week.
>
> *The man says that* smokers must have some place to go.
>
> *The woman says that* when she leaves some classroom buildings, she has to walk through a thick cloud of smoke.
>
> *The notice in the campus newspaper says that* all letters must be signed. The paper will no longer publish anonymous letters. *It also says that* letters must be under 250 words and that it will only publish one letter a month from each student.
>
> *The man tells the woman* that you can't fully explain some issues in a short letter.
>
> *The woman asks the man* if he is a smoker.
>
> *The man asks the woman* how many letters she has written to the editor.

Agreement/Opinion

In the Announcement/Discussion task, you do not give your own opinion, but you do report what one of the students thinks of the announcement.

> *The man thinks* the university's new policy on smoking is *unfair.*
>
> *The woman approves of* the new smoking policy.
>
> The professor's memo about cell phones in class *makes the woman angry.*
>
> *The man agrees with* the professor's ideas about cell phones.

A student may agree in general with the announcement but not with one or more points.

> *The woman agrees in general with* the newspaper's policy, *but she doesn't like* the limit on the number of words per letter.

Contrast

There may be contrast between the information in the announcement and the ideas of the students. There may be contrast between the ideas of the two students. One student may present contrasting ideas. The easiest way to show contrast is with the conjunction *but* (to join two parts of one sentence) or the conjunction *however* (to join two sentences).

The professor believes cell phones should be turned off entirely during class. *However,* the woman feels that this policy is too strict. She thinks that students should be allowed to set their phones on "vibrate."

The man thinks the new smoking policy is unfair, *but* the woman thinks the current situation is unhealthy for non-smokers.

The man agrees that all letters to the editor should be signed. *However,* he thinks the newspaper should publish some letters longer than 250 words.

Reasons and Examples

You must not only explain the student's opinion of the announcement, you must also give the reasons why he or she has that opinion.

The woman is in favor of the smoking policy *because* she thinks it is unhealthy to be exposed to secondhand smoke.

The reason why the man supports the professor's policy is that he thinks cell phones are distracting.

There are two reasons why the man does not like the campus newspaper's new policy. *One is that* he thinks students should be allowed to write longer letters if they want. *The other is that* he thinks students should be able to publish at least one letter a week.

You may also have to report examples that students give to support their opinion.

The woman believes that there are good reasons to leave phones on during class time. *For example,* there may be a family emergency.

The man says that some issues, *such as* the issue of tuition increases, cannot be fully discussed in a short letter.

(C) Giving the Announcement/Discussion Response

There are different ways to organize an Announcement/Discussion Response, but the easiest way is like this:

▶ State the topic of the announcement and a summary of the key points.

▶ Give a summary of the student's opinion.

▶ Identify reasons for the student's opinion.

You should begin by clearly stating what the announcement is about and give a couple of main points from the announcement. You should then summarize the opinion of the student that the question asks about. Then give the reasons why the student holds this opinion. You may also want to mention points made by the other student during the conversation.

Remember, you need to *summarize*. This means that you only want to report the main ideas of the announcement and the conversation. You also need to *paraphrase.* You must use your own words to talk about the announcement and the conversation. You should use different grammatical structures and synonyms whenever possible.

SPEAKING

Look now and then at the on-screen clock. When giving responses during exercises, practice your timing so that you can give a response in about forty-five seconds.

When you give the Announcement/Discussion response, keep the following points in mind:

▶ State the topic of the announcement clearly in the first sentence of your response.

▶ Follow the notes that you made during the preparation time.

▶ Clearly state the student's opinion and give one or two reasons why the student feels this way.

▶ Use transition words to show contrast, to give reasons, and to present examples.

▶ Use the language of citation ("According to the announcement, . . ."; "The man says that . . .").

▶ Speak clearly and directly into the microphone.

▶ Don't speak too slowly or too fast.

▶ Keep your response flowing; avoid long pauses.

▶ Pay attention to your pronunciation and intonation.

▶ Keep it simple by using familiar vocabulary and grammar.

EXERCISE 17.1

FOCUS: Taking notes on readings and conversations and using the language of announcement/discussion.

DIRECTIONS: For each item, read the announcement and then listen to the discussion. You may take notes as you listen and read. You will then see a number of questions and incomplete sentences about the announcement and the conversation. Answer these questions and complete these sentences orally. When you answer the questions, try to use only your notes, not the announcement itself. When possible, use the "language of announcement/discussion" as explained in Part B of this lesson in your responses. Use complete sentences. The first set of notes and the first question are done for you as examples.

Task A

Read the following announcement. (45 seconds)

Memo to All Students in Journalism 223

Effective today (Oct. 10) all cell phones must be turned off before entering the classroom. The sound of ringing phones and musical tones is extremely distracting both to me and to other students. Even vibrating phones are a distraction when students pull them out to determine who is calling. So please . . . be considerate to all: turn your phone off or leave it at home!

Thanks,
Professor Ribaudo, Ph.D.

Sample notes on the reading:

Oct. 10—turn off cell phs
distracting   even vibrating phs
be considerate

▶ Now start the Audio Program. Listen to two students discuss the announcement. 🎧

Sample notes on the conversation:

F: Prof Rib. upset abt cell phs
M: 4 X?
F: Maybe 5 X—thghtless
M: Rude
F: But harsh not to allow stu to turn off ring & set to vibrate—maybe a fam emerg
M: Not agree. Stu can go hr w/out phones. And prof right: distracting

Now orally answer the questions or complete the sentences about the announcement and the discussion.

1. What is the announcement about?

    Example: The announcement is about the use of cell phones in class.

2. The professor says that the sound of ringing phones _____.

3. Students must either _____ or _____.

4. According to the conversation, why did the professor write this memo?

5. What does the woman think of students whose cell phones ring in class? Does the man agree with her?

6. The woman thinks that students should be allowed to _____ because _____.

7. Does the man agree with her? Why or why not?

Task B

Read the following announcement. (45 seconds)

Library Amnesty Program

During the week of Nov. 28–Dec. 2, students may return overdue books and other overdue library materials to the main branch of Norton Library as well as to the Science Library, the Law Library, the Music Library, or the Business Library. For this week only, there will be NO fees charged and NO questions asked. Take advantage of this popular program to return materials without penalty and help us restore our valuable collections, which are needed by the entire university community.

Notes on the reading:

_____

_____

_____

_____

_____

▶ Now start the Audio Program. Listen to two students discuss the announcement. 🎧

Notes on the conversation:

_____

_____

_____

_____

_____

Now orally answer the questions or complete the sentences about the announcement and the discussion.

8. What is the topic of the announcement?

9. If students return library materials this week, they _____ and _____ .

10. How does this program help the library?

11. What is the man's opinion of the announcement?

12. Why does he feel this way?

13. What is the man going to do this evening?

Task C

Read the following announcement. (45 seconds)

Attention

As of Monday Jan. 9, the bulletin board in the hallway outside of the Computer Science Department is now reserved for official Department notices and for notices approved by the Department. All messages currently on the board will be removed on that date. In the future, all messages must be stamped by the executive secretary of the Department before being posted.

Notes on the reading:

_____

_____

_____

_____

_____

▶ Now start the Audio Program. Listen to two students discuss the announcement. 🎧

Notes on the conversation:

_____

_____

_____

_____

_____

Now orally answer the questions or complete the sentences about the announcement and the discussion.

14. What is this announcement mainly about? _____

15. What messages can go on the bulletin board in the future? _____

16. What will happen to all messages on the board on January 9? _____

17. In the future, all messages on the board _____.

18. What is the man's opinion of the announcement? _____

19. Why does he feel that way? _____

20. The woman tells the man that he should _____ or
_____.

21. Why does the man particularly want to use this bulletin board? _____

22. The man and the woman agree that _____.

Task D

Read the following announcement. (45 seconds)

FALL FILM FESTIVAL

The second annual Fall Film Festival will be held on the weekend of Oct. 21–23. Films will be shown at the Curtiss Theater in the Student Union Building and at the Uptown Cinema on College Hill Road. The festival features 24 top independent and local films. Local filmmakers will be in attendance and will give presentations and workshops. Tickets are available at the Curtiss Theater. For more information and a complete schedule, see Monday's edition of the campus newspaper or go to fallfilmfest.curtis.edu/arts/film.

Notes on the reading:

_____

_____

_____

▶ Now start the Audio Program. Listen to two students discuss the announcement. 🎧

Notes on the conversation:

_____

_____

_____

_____

_____

Now orally answer the questions or complete the sentences about the announcement and the discussion.

23. What is the announcement about?
24. The festival will feature _____. Also, local filmmakers will

    _____ .

25. How does the woman feel about the announcement?
26. Why does she feel this way?
27. What is the man's opinion of independent films?

EXERCISE 17.2

FOCUS: Taking notes on announcements and conversations.

DIRECTIONS: Read the announcements and listen to the conversations. Take notes as you read and listen.

Task A

Read the announcement. (45 seconds)

A professor in the psychology department is conducting a psychology experiment. Read the following advertisement recruiting subjects for this experiment.

Experimental Participants Needed

Are you interested in taking part in a psychology experiment regarding sleep difficulties? Twenty females, twenty males needed. Please check the eligibility requirements below before applying:

- Must be a student at Hambleton University from 18 to 24 years old
- Must have difficulty falling asleep at least one night a week
- Must not be taking sleeping aids or other medication
- Must be willing to spend one night a week in the Psychology Department's Sleep Lab for four weeks
- Must be non-smoker in good health

Participants must also complete a questionnaire and be interviewed before beginning the experiment.

Participants will receive $150, and psychology students will receive one credit hour for their time. Participants may also learn techniques that will help them sleep better in the future. Contact Dr. Jack Wagner at 313-555-8371, Ex. 32, or at jwagner@Hambleton.edu.

SPEAKING

Notes on the reading:

_____

_____

_____

_____

_____

▶ Now start the Audio Program. Listen to two students discuss the announcement. 🎧

Notes on the conversation:

_____

_____

_____

_____

_____

Task B

Read the announcement. (45 seconds)

Summer Internship Fair

Date
Saturday, May 11, 11:00 A.M. – 5:00 P.M.
Location
Ballroom A
Leroy P. Dodd Student Center
Lakeway University
Overview
The purpose of the fair is to provide an opportunity to meet with representatives of over 40 companies, private foundations, and government agencies that are seeking students to fill positions including internships as well as volunteer and community service positions during the summer break.

Notes on the reading:

_____

_____

_____

_____

_____

▶ Now start the Audio Program. Listen to two students discuss the announcement. 🎧

Notes on the conversation:

_____

_____

_____

_____

_____

Task C

Read the announcement. (45 seconds)

Call for Auditions

Peabody University's Department of Theater Arts will hold public auditions for the George Bernard Shaw comedy _Heartbreak House. Heartbreak House_ is considered one of Shaw's finest plays. Auditions are scheduled for Sunday and Monday, Feb. 21–22, in the Peabody University Theater. Auditions are at 7 P.M. each night and are open to everyone.

   Roles are available for actors of all ages, and no prior acting experience is required.

Notes on the reading:

_____

_____

_____

_____

_____

► Now start the Audio Program. Listen to two students discuss the announcement. 🎧

Notes on the conversation:

_____

_____

_____

_____

_____

Task D

Read the announcement. (45 seconds)

Stress Management Workshops

Final exam week is coming! Finals week can be a stressful period. Exams, essays, and catch-up reading often wear students down. Stress can cause fatigue and lower your resistance to minor illnesses. During an exam, anxiety can cause you to perform poorly. The University Counseling Center offers workshops that teach you to handle the stress of final exam week so that it does not interfere with your academic performance. We'll discuss how exercise and eating right can help relieve stress. Participants will also learn how to monitor their stress levels, practice relaxation techniques, and generally stay cool and calm during finals week.

▶ Now start the Audio Program. Listen to two students discuss the announcement. 🎧

Notes on the reading:

_____

_____

_____

_____

_____

Notes on the conversation:

_____

_____

_____

_____

_____

EXERCISE 17.3

FOCUS: Preparing and giving responses for Announcement/Discussion Tasks.

DIRECTIONS: Listen and read along to the questions about Tasks A-D in Exercise 17.2. Then, using the notes that you took for Exercise 17.2, give responses for these four Tasks. (Try to use only your notes, not the announcement itself.) You will have thirty seconds to prepare your response, and then you will hear a beep on the audio program. You will then have sixty seconds to give your response, and then you will hear another beep. Ideally, you should record your responses and then play them back.

▶ Now start the Audio Program. 🎧

Task A

The woman expresses her opinion of the announcement about the psychology experiment. State her opinion, and explain the reasons she gives for having that opinion.

Task B

The man expresses his opinion of the Summer Internship Fair. State his opinion, and explain the reasons he gives for having that opinion.

Task C

The woman expresses her opinion of the announcement about the audition. State her opinion and explain the reasons she gives for having that opinion.

Task D

The man expresses his opinion of the Stress Management Workshop. State his opinion and explain the reasons he gives for having that opinion.

LESSON 18
GENERAL/SPECIFIC TASK

Like Task 3, Task 4 involves taking ideas and details from two sources of information. You will first see a short reading that comes from a textbook or an article in any academic field: art, science, humanities, and so on. You will have forty-five seconds to read the passage, and you may take notes.

After you see the reading, you will hear part of a classroom lecture or a discussion between students and a professor on the same topic as the reading. Again, note taking is permitted. The lecture/discussion lasts from sixty to eighty seconds.

The reading deals with a *general* topic: a general theory or phenomenon. The reading gives two or three important characteristics or two or three categories within the general concept.

However, the lecture/discussion is about a *specific* topic. The professor presents one or two specific applications of the theory or examples of the phenomenon.

After listening to the lecture/discussion, you will see a question that asks you about the relationship between the general information in the reading and the specific information in the lecture/discussion. Your response to this question must show how the specific example(s) show the general characteristics and fit into the general categories given in the reading.

You will have thirty seconds to prepare your response and sixty seconds to give it. While you are preparing and giving your response, you will see the question, but you will not see the reading.

Here's a sample General/Specific Task from the Integrated Speaking Preview Test and a sample response to it. Read the passage, then read along as you listen to the lecture, the question, and the sample response.

Sample

Reading time: 45 seconds

Animals are always in danger of being eaten by predators. They have therefore developed methods of avoiding these predators. One effective means that animals use to protect themselves is *camouflage*. What is meant by camouflage? Camouflage refers to the coloration or general appearance of an animal that makes it difficult to see when it is in its own environment. An animal employing camouflage blends in with its environment so that it is invisible, or it looks to its predators like an inanimate or inedible object.

Now, when we think of camouflage, we often think of animals that appear dull and colorless in order to go unnoticed. This is sometimes true, but not always. Some animals may not look camouflaged to human eyes. In fact, they are easy for us to spot, especially out of their normal environments. However, to their predators, they are quite difficult to see.

▶ Now start the Audio Program. Listen and read along as you hear a lecture in a zoology class. 🎧

Professor

So . . . um, we're been talking about ways animals avoid predators, especially how animals use camouflage to stay safe, to hide from their predators. Let's consider an animal called the sloth. The sloth is a mammal that lives in the forests of Central America, South America. They hang from trees and they're lazy, very slow-moving, they sleep fifteen hours a day. Anyway, sloths are a very dull color, their fur is a dull brown and it has dull green streaks in it. Know what these green steaks are? They're algae—a kind of plant. This animal moves around so slowly that plants grow on it! Anyway, this dull green and brown color camouflages the sloth when it's hanging from trees.

Then there's a butterfly, you may have heard of it, it's called the blue morpho. It also lives in Central and South America. It has beautiful, shiny blue wings. It's so pretty its nickname is "the living jewel." You look at a blue morpho, you think, "Now this creature is not camouflaged!" But in fact it is. Blue morphos' wings are only bright blue when viewed from the top. The bottoms of its wings are dark brown. When it flaps its wings and flies, there are alternating flashes of bright blue and brown. When birds see this, they think they're seeing flashes of blue sky between trees. So, although blue morphos sure don't seem camouflaged to us, they are basically invisible to predators.

Narrator

The professor describes how camouflage protects two types of animals. Explain how this is related to the concepts of camouflage described in the reading.

Sample Response

"The reading discusses, uh *(pause)* it says that all animals are in danger, that they can be eaten by predators. And, uh, one way animals can be safe from predators is with camouflage. Camouflage—this means that an animal is hard to see by other animals. This animal doesn't look visible. The reading says some animals that use camouflage, they look dull and it's hard to notice them. But . . . uh, some don't look that way, they are easy to see. I mean, ummm *(pause)* it is easy for *us* to see them, but not for the predators to see them."

"The professor talks about two examples of animals that use camouflage. One example of these is the sloth. Sloth is a lazy animal. It is brown and has green color from an algae plant that grows in its fur because it moves so slow. So the sloth is an example of an animal that is hard to see because its colors are dull. The other example is the blue morpho butterfly. Like the reading said, some animals, umm *(pause)* they don't look camouflage because they are bright colors—the blue morpho is really bright blue. But, uh, when birds see this flying butterfly, they see flashes of the sky through trees, that's *(pause)* that's what the butterfly looks like to them. So . . . blue morphos are camouflage too."

This response would get the speaker a good score. It completely fulfills the demands of the question. He summarizes and paraphrases the ideas in the reading and the lecture and explains the relationship between them. The response begins by explaining the topic of the reading (animals that use camouflage as protection). It explains two categories of camouflage (those that seem drab and dull to us and those that look bright and uncamouflaged). The response then discusses the lecture. It summarizes the professor's comments about two specific animals that use camouflage. The response mentions an example of an animal that appears drab and blends into its environment (the sloth). It also mentions an animal (the blue morpho butterfly) that does not appear to be camouflaged to us, but that is camouflaged from predators.

There are minor problems with grammar, but the level of language is high and the response is mostly clear and intelligible. The response is spoken at a good speed and the delivery is generally smooth, although there are a few pauses. There are very minor pronunciation errors, but these do not interfere with communication at all.

(A) Pre-Speaking

You must first read the passage and take notes. You should take notes on the reading *while* you are reading it, not after. Look for key characteristics and categories in the reading. As in Task 3, the reading will not appear on the screen when you are giving your response, so you need to take good notes.

Sample notes on the reading:

Anims danger from predators
Camouflage a method of protecting
    Def: color, appearance of anim. that makes it hard to see in own environ
        looks like inanim. or ined. object
    Often think of camoufl. anim. as dull, colorless anims   true, but not always
    Some not look camoufl to humans   easy to see, esp. out of environ.
        BUT   not easy for predators to see

SPEAKING

Next, you will hear the classroom lecture or discussion. You must also take good notes on the listening material.

Sample notes on the lecture:

Topic: how anims stay safe from pred. thru camoufl.
 Sloth—hang from trees, lazy, slow
      Dull brown   grn streaks (algae)
      Colors + slow moving = difficult to see

Blue morpho bttrfly—pretty, "lvng jewel"
      bright blue: not LOOK camouflaged to people
      When fly, birds see flash of blue + brown—think seeing sky betwn
   trees
         —invis. to birds

The question appears on the screen after you have heard the lecture/discussion. Before you make your response, you need to carefully analyze the question:

> The professor describes how camouflage protects two types of animals. Explain how this is related to the concepts of camouflage given in the reading.

The question asks you to summarize the main points of the lecture and of the reading and explain how the specific information in the lecture is related to the general information in the reading.

Instead of writing a separate outline during the thirty-second preparation time, you can use your notes to decide what to talk about. Just underline what points you want to make, and add notes as needed.

Here are notes a test-taker took during the reading and lecture. They are underlined to show what he plans to discuss:

Rdg.

Anims danger" from predators

Camouflage a method of protecting

   Def: color, apprnce of anim. that makes it hard to see in own environ

       looks like inanim. or ined. object

1) Often think of camoufl. anim. as dull, colorless animas   true, but not

   always

2) Some not look camoufl to humans   easy to see, esp. out of environs.

   BUT   not easy for predators to see

Lect.

Topic: how anims stay safe from pred. thru camoufl.

   1) Sloth—hang from trees, lazy, slow

      Dull brown grn streaks (algae)

         Colors + slow moving = difficult to see

   2) Blue morpho bttrfly—pretty, "lvng jewel"

      bright blue: not LOOK camouflaged to people

      When fly, birds see flash of blue + brown—think seeing sky

        betwn trees—invis. to birds

(B) The Language of General/Specific

Some vocabulary and grammatical structures are often used when giving General/Specific topics. Being familiar with them will make it easier for you to focus on the details of the topic.

Reading Topic: General Concepts

You need to introduce your response by giving the overall topic of the reading. Because the reading is always about a general concept, you should mention this topic in the introductory sentence. Here are some easy ways to do that:

> *The reading is about* the general concept of camouflage.
> *The passage discusses* the general characteristics of numeral systems.
> *The reading gives an overall view* of local government.

Lecture Topic: Specific Points

Next, you need to mention specific points made by the speaker.

> *The professor talks specifically about* the system of government used in one city.
>
> *The speaker gives two specific examples of* numeral systems.

Citation

You need to clearly indicate whether you are talking about information from the reading or from the lecture/discussion.

> *The reading says that* we often think of camouflaged animals as being dull and colorless.
>
> *The professor says that* San Diego is a good example of a city that uses the council-manager form of government.

Definition and Description

The reading generally provides a basic description of the topic. You need to include this information in your summary of the reading.

> *According to the reading,* local government refers to the government of towns, cities, and counties.
>
> *The reading defines* a numeral system as a group of numerical symbols that can be used for counting and doing calculations.
>
> *Camouflage* refers to the coloration that makes it difficult to see an animal.

Characteristics and Categories

Generally, the main point of the reading is to provide two or three characteristics of the topic, or to break the topic down into a number of categories.

> According to the lecture, *there are two main types of* city government. *One is . . . The other is . . .*
>
> *There are three characteristics* that make numeral systems useful. *The first one is . . . The second characteristic is . . . The third characteristic is . . .*

Relating Specific and General Information

Your most important job when you are giving this response is to show the general/specific relationship between the information in the reading and the information in the lecture. In other words, you need to explain how the specific information in the lecture is typical of the general information in the reading and give the *reasons* why.

> The government of San Diego *is pretty typical of* a council-manager form of government *because* it has a council that creates policy and a city manager that implements policy . . .

The numeral system used by the Sumerians *is an example of* a system that is not base 10.

The sloth is a good example of an animal that appears to humans to be camouflaged.

Like many types of metamorphic rock, marble is a good building material.

(C) Giving the General/Specific Response

There are different ways to organize a General/Specific response. You can, for example, begin by discussing specific information in the lecture/discussion and then go on talk about general information in the reading. However, it is easier to follow the order in which you receive the information: talk about the reading first and then talk about the lecture/discussion and how it relates to the reading. You should include the following in your response:

▶ The general topic of the reading

▶ Two or three key characteristics or classifications of the general topic

▶ The specific topic of the lecture/discussion

▶ Information about how the specific points in the lecture/discussion relate to the reading. (How is the information that you hear a specific example or application of the information that you read?)

As in all Integrated Tasks, you need to *summarize.* Focus on the main ideas and supporting information in both the reading and lecture/discussion. You also need to *paraphrase.* Use your own words to report the information from the two sources.

Look now and then at the on-screen clock as you are speaking. Practice your timing during exercises so that you can give a response in about forty-five seconds.

Keep these points in mind when you give your response:

▶ Be sure to show the relationship between the two sources of information.

▶ Balance information from the passage and the lecture/discussion.

▶ Use transition words to divide parts of your presentation and to show contrast, to give reasons, and to present examples.

▶ Use the language of citation *("According to the reading, . . .";* *"The professor says that . . .").*

▶ Follow the notes that you made during the preparation time.

▶ Speak clearly and directly into the microphone.

▶ Don't speak too quickly or too slowly.

▶ Keep your response flowing; avoid long pauses.

▶ Pay attention to pronunciation and intonation.

▶ Keep it simple by using familiar vocabulary and grammar.

SPEAKING

EXERCISE 18.1

FOCUS: Taking notes on readings and lectures/discussions and using the language of General/Specific Tasks.

DIRECTIONS: For each item, read the passage and then listen to the lecture/discussion. Take notes as you listen and read. You will then see a number of questions and incomplete sentences about the reading and the lecture/discussion. Answer these questions and complete these sentences orally. Try to use your notes to answer questions about the passage rather than looking at the reading. When possible, use the "language of General/Specific responses" in your responses as explained in Part B of this lesson. The first set of notes and the first question are done for you as examples.

Task A

Read the following passage. (45 seconds)

> There are dozens, perhaps hundreds, of known numeral systems. By *numeral system,* we mean a set of symbols used to represent quantities. Most numeral systems are decimal systems, also called base-10 systems. This includes the numeral system we use, which is called the Arabic system, although it actually comes from India. One reason why base 10 is used is that humans have ten fingers, and we first used our fingers to count on. Another reason is that decimal systems tend to be easy to use for counting and calculations. For one thing, only ten different symbols are needed to represent any whole number.

Sample notes on the reading:

100's of numeral sys.
Def: set of symbs that rep, quants.
Most are decimal: base 10   Arabic sys (actu. India) = base 10
Why? 1) 10 fingers
2) easy to use for counting & calcs
only need 10 symbols

▶ Now start the Audio Program. Listen to a lecture in a mathematics class. 🎧

Sample notes on the lecture:

Most num sys base 10   but not all
    Yukis (Calif) base 8   count spaces betwn fingers
    Sumerians (W. Asia) base 60   60 symbols
        still have impact: 60 secs = min.
                    60 min = hr
            but calc very difficult w/ base 60

1. What is the reading mainly about?
    Example: "The reading is mainly about numeral systems."
2. What is a numeral system?
3. Most numeral systems are _____ , also known as _____ .
4. What does the reading say about the Arabic system?
5. One reason decimal systems are used is that _____ . Another reason is that _____ .
6. What is the main topic of the lecture?
7. The two primary examples that the professor mentions are _____ and _____ .
8. The Yukis used a base-8 system because _____ .
9. How did the Sumerian system have an impact on us?
10. According to the professor, the Sumerian system isn't used in other situations today because _____ .

Task B

Read the following passage. (45 seconds)

> Dolls are a useful way to learn about a society. Doll makers draw on their knowledge of their culture, and they often use traditional materials and traditional skills to create dolls. This is certainly true of Native American dolls. Some Native American dolls are simply toys. They are used to amuse children, to entertain them, to calm them when they are unhappy. However, other dolls are meant to educate children. There are two main types of these. Some dolls model adult activities, roles, and costumes. You might see dolls that hunt, dance, or carry babies on their backs. Other dolls represent spiritual figures. They are meant to educate Native American children about religious matters.

Notes on the reading:

_____

_____

_____

_____

_____

▶ Now start the Audio Program. Listen to a lecture in an anthropology class. 🎧

Notes on the discussion:

_____

_____

_____

_____

_____

11. What is the topic of the reading? _____

12. Why are dolls a good way to learn about a society? _____

13. Some dolls are used to amuse children, but _____ .

14. The two types of educational dolls are _____ and _____ .

15. What is the discussion about? _____

16. The kachina dolls are an example of _____ , because they teach Hopi
    children _____ and _____ .

17. Why do Hopi children need dolls to learn about spirits? _____

Task C

Read the following passage. (45 seconds)

The process of oxidation occurs when metals are exposed to air in the presence of a liquid. Oxygen molecules combine with the molecules of the metal and form an oxide layer on the surface of the metal. The process requires a liquid called an electrolyte that helps electrons move. Oxidation may simply be a cosmetic problem, a discoloration on the surface of otherwise shiny metal. In other cases, the process of oxidation may cause structural weakness in the metal, a process called corrosion.

SPEAKING

Notes on the reading:

_____

_____

_____

_____

_____

▶ Now start the Audio Program. Listen to a lecture in a chemistry class. 🎧

Notes on the lecture:

_____

_____

_____

18. What is the main point of the reading? _____

19. How does the formation of rust occur? _____

20. According to the reading, oxidation may be _____ or it may

_____ .

21. The professor says that rust is _____ .

22. What three things are needed to get rust? _____

23. According to the reading, the liquid that causes rust is called an _____ .

24. Rust is an example of _____ because it damages metal. _____

25. What are some examples of things that are affected by rust? _____

26. Rust costs a lot of money. People spend money on _____ and

_____ .

Task D

Read the following passage. (45 seconds)

Ever since the late nineteenth century, scientists have used identical twins in studies and experiments. Twins are particularly interesting to scientists who are investigating the concept of "nature versus nurture"—in other words, scientists who want to know if people are shaped more by their genetic inheritance or their environment. The most useful identical twins are those who have been raised apart from the time of infancy. That is because these twins have exactly the same genetic makeup but they have been raised in different environments.

Although many experiments have been done with separated identical twins in the past, there will not be many more in the future. After about 1970, couples were no longer allowed to adopt a twin unless they were willing to take both twins. After that date, adopted twins were seldom if ever separated.

Notes on the reading:

_____

_____

_____

▶ Now start the Audio Program. Listen to a lecture in a psychology class. 🎧

Notes on the lecture:

_____

_____

_____

27. What is the reading passage about? _____

28. Scientists are interested in twins to learn about _____.

29. Why will there not be many more experiments with separated twins? _____

30. What do the professor and the students mainly discuss? _____

31. The experiment on happiness was probably done on identical twins because

_____.

32. Many psychologists don't like twin research because _____.

EXERCISE 18.2

FOCUS: Taking notes on reading passages and lectures or discussions for General/Specific tasks.

DIRECTIONS: Read the passages and listen to the lectures/discussions. Take notes as you read and listen.

Task A

Read the following passage. (45 seconds)

More than any other animal except for humans, birds are known for their ability to build. Birds build nests in which to lay their eggs. For some birds, nests provide shelter from rain and cold. Bird nests vary greatly in complexity. Some birds build no nests at all, while others build simple nests of twigs or leaves. Perhaps

SPEAKING

the most familiar type of nest is the cup-shaped nest built in trees by many species of birds. The most complex type is the enclosed nest. Basically, the enclosed nest is a cup-shaped nest covered by a dome-shaped roof. Enclosed nests are solidly built and intricate. They have multiple chambers, and several generations of birds may live there for years. Even after the builders of these nests abandon them, they may be used by other birds or other types of animals.

Notes on the passage:

_____

_____

_____

_____

▶ Now start the Audio Program. Listen to a lecture in a zoology class. 🎧

Notes on the lecture:

_____

_____

_____

_____

Task B

Read the following passage. (45 seconds)

Metamorphic rocks are rocks that have changed from one type of rock to another type. (The word *metamorphosis* is Greek for "change of form.") The original rocks—called "parent rocks"—are other kinds of rocks—usually sedimentary rocks. Parent rocks change because of intense heat and pressure when they are buried deep in the earth for a very long period of time. The parent rocks change their mineral composition and texture. The process of metamorphism does not melt the rocks, but instead changes them into denser, stronger rocks. Metamorphic rocks often contain impurities, different kinds of minerals that are mixed in with the parent rock. Because they're strong, some metamorphic rocks are used as building materials.

▶   Now start the Audio Program. Listen to a lecture in a geology class. 🎧

Notes on the lecture:

_____

_____

_____

_____

Task C

Read the following passage. (45 seconds)

Investigative journalists don't just report the news. They spend months, sometimes years of research, interviewing, and fact-finding to uncover hidden information and to expose abuses. Investigative journalism became a popular form of journalism in the first decade of the twentieth century. At that time, there was a group of journalists called the "muckrakers." These reporters exposed many types of abuse: political corruption, child labor, conditions in slums, prisons, and mental hospitals, unsanitary conditions in food processing plants, and similar topics. One of their favorite targets was the abuse of power by large, monopolistic corporations called "trusts." The muckrakers helped bring about some important reforms.

Notes on the passage:

_____

_____

_____

_____

_____

▶ Now start the Audio Program. Listen to a lecture in a journalism class. 🎧

Notes on the lecture:

_____

_____

_____

_____

_____

Task D

Read the following passage. (45 seconds)

In the early years of photography, all photographs were monochromatic photographs—what we sometimes call "black-and-white" photographs. Some photographers—especially artistic photographers—still prefer monochromatic photos to color photos.

There are actually two types of monochromatic photos. One type is a gray-scale photograph, which is truly black and white. In a gray-scale photo, all you see is black, white, and shades of gray. Gray-scale photos tend to have a stark, cold look to them. The other type is sepia. Sepia photographs use shades of brown in place of shades of gray. Photographers started using the sepia process to give their photos warmer tones.

Some people think that sepia photographs are just gray-scale photos that have "aged," that have changed color over the years, but this isn't true. Sepia photos use silver sulphide in the developing process in place of silver iodide. This gives them their brownish tones. But there's a good reason why people think sepia photographs are old. Silver sulphide is more stable than silver iodide and can last 150 years with proper storage. Therefore, most old photographs that you see are sepia photographs because gray-scale photographs from the same era generally didn't survive.

Notes on the passage:

_____

_____

_____

_____

_____

▶ Now start the Audio Program. Listen to a discussion in a photography class. 🎧

Notes on the discussion:

_____

_____

_____

_____

_____

EXERCISE 18.3

FOCUS: Preparing and giving responses for General/Specific Tasks.

DIRECTIONS: Listen and read along to the questions about tasks A through D in Exercise 18.2. Then, using the notes that you took for Exercise 18.2, prepare and give responses for these four tasks. (Try to use only your notes, not the reading passage itself.) You will have thirty seconds to prepare your response, and then you will hear a beep on the Audio Program. You will have sixty seconds to give your response, and then you will hear another beep. Ideally, you should record your responses and then play them back.

▶ Now start the Audio Program. 🎧

Task A

> The professor's lecture is about the nest of the *hamerkop* bird. Describe the hamerkop's nest, and explain why it is a good example of an enclosed nest.

Task B

> The professor lectures about marble. Describe this type of rock, and explain why it is a typical metamorphic rock.

Task C

> The professor lectures about the journalist Ida Tarbell. Describe her accomplishments, and explain why she is considered a "muckraker."

Task D

> The professor and the students discuss two photographs. Describe the photographs using information from the discussion and the reading passage.

For Task 5, you will hear a conversation between two speakers that lasts from sixty to ninety seconds. Usually the speakers are two students, but there might be a student and a professor, a student and an advisor, or a student and an administrator. One of the two speakers has a problem related to university life. The speakers discuss two possible solutions to this problem. You are allowed to take notes as you listen to the conversation.

Your job is to summarize the problem and the two possible solutions. Then you must make a recommendation explaining which of the two solutions you think is best and the reasons why.

Remember: This is the *only* one of the four integrated tasks in which you should give your own opinion.

After you have heard the lecture, you will have twenty seconds of preparation time, and then you will have sixty seconds in which to give your response.

Here's a sample Problem/Solution Task from the Integrated Speaking Preview Test and a sample response to it. Read along as you listen to the conversation, the question, and the sample response.

Sample

▶ Listen to a conversation between two students. 🎧

Student A

Hey, Lucy, how are things?

Student B

Hi, Rick. Oh, I don't know. Okay, I suppose . . . I'm just . . . I'm just exhausted!

Student A

Yeah, you do look kinda tired . . . how come?

Student B

Well, I just never get enough sleep . . . my classes are really hard this term, especially my physiology class, so I'm in the library until it closes at eleven, and then I study for a couple of hours or so when I get back to my dorm room.

Student A

Yeah, I've had a couple of semesters like that myself . . .

Student B

I feel especially dead in the afternoon, and I have a one o'clock and a three o'clock class. Yesterday, the most incredibly embarrassing thing happened in my physiology class—I actually fell asleep! I've *never* done that before . . . And Doctor Daniels was like, "Am I boring you, Ms. Jenkins?"

Student A

That *is* embarrassing! Hey, you should do what I do . . . just get yourself some coffee.

Student B

Yeah, I bought a cup of coffee from the vending machine the other day—it was terrible!

Student A

Vending machine coffee's usually pretty awful. You could walk up to College Avenue—there are a coupla coffee shops up there.

Student B

Yeah, but their coffee's pretty expensive, and . . . I don't know, sometimes coffee just makes me really nervous . . . I don't feel that awake, I just feel nervous!

Student A

Hey, here's an idea. What buildings are your afternoon classes in?

Student A

One's in Old Main and one's in Castleton.

Student A

Those aren't far from your dorm. Here's what you should do. Go by your dorm and lie down for fifteen or twenty minutes between your two classes.

Student B

I don't know . . . I haven't taken a nap during the day . . . probably since I was in kindergarten.

Student A

Yeah, but, you don't have to sleep. Just lie down and completely relax. If you sleep, that's fine, if not . . . I still think you'll find yourself refreshed.

▶ Now listen to a question about the conversation:

> The man offers Lucy two possible solutions to her problem. Discuss her problem and then explain which of the two solutions you think is better and why you think so.

Sample Response

"Well, this conversation about a problem that this woman, mmm, Lucy, that she have. Her main problem is with not so much sleep. She has very difficult class and has to study too much, for eleven hours at library. Mmmm, so she is exhausting, and feel asleep in her class.

"The man tell her drink some coffee, but she doesn't like the taste of coffee, especially from vending machine. He suggest she get coffee from the people who sell on the street, but she say is too expensive. She say coffee sometime make her nervous.

"Then he suggest she go to her dormitory and sleep a short time. Lucy say not sleep during day for long time, since she a kid, but he tell her not have to feel asleep. Just relaxing.

"Mmmmm . . . I suggest she, Lucy, get a nap too, I think is better for her than coffee, because coffee make her nervous, but if she rest in her bed maybe feel not so tired, feel refreshing. Sometimes in afternoon I take a little rest, I feel much more awake, so I think she should go to her dormitory and take it easy."

This response would get the test-taker a good score, although perhaps not a 4. He summarizes and paraphrases the conversation about the woman's problem. There are, however, one or two minor factual errors. For example, the test-taker says that Lucy must study eleven hours a day. In fact, she says she studies at the library until 11:00 P.M.

The test-taker clearly chooses the solution that he thinks best and supports this choice with some personal information. There are a few grammatical and word usage problems (one that is repeated is the phrase *feel asleep* instead of the correct phrase, *fall asleep*). However, despite the problems, it is easy to follow the test-taker's ideas. The response is well organized and generally clear. The speed of delivery is a little bit fast, but this does not interfere with our ability to understand it. There are minor pronunciation errors, but these do not interfere with the student's communication of ideas.

(A) Pre-Speaking

You need to take notes as you listen to the conversation. Because you will be quoting and taking information from the speakers, you need to mark who says what in your notes. Since the speakers will always be male and female, you can abbreviate them *F* and *M*. You don't need to take a note on every line that the speakers say. As always when taking notes, write down only ideas that you think are important.

Sample notes on the reading:

F: exhausted   classes hard, esp. physiol.   library 11   study in dorm
rm cple hrs
    sleep during physiology class. never happen before
M: Embarrassing   should try coffee
F: cof from vend mach not so nice, make her nervous
M: Where class?
F: Old Main & Castle
M: Go dorm, lie down
F: Not take nap since kindergtn.
M: Just relax

The question appears on the screen after the conversation. Before you make your response, you need to analyze the question:

The man offers Lucy two possible solutions to her problem. Discuss her problem and then explain which of the two solutions you think is better and why you think so.

The question asks you to summarize the conversation about the problem and then to discuss the two solutions. You then need to recommend the solution that you think is best.

During the twenty seconds you have to prepare a response, you need to decide what you are going to say. Instead of writing a separate outline, use your notes to decide what to talk about. Just underline the points you want to make and add notes as needed.

Here are notes a test-taker took during the conversation. They are marked to show what he plans to discuss:

F: exhausted   classes hard,   esp. physiol.   library 11   study in dorm
rm cple hrs
sleep during physiology class. never happen before   (Problem)
M: Embarrassing   should try coffee   (SOL #1) F: cof from vend mach not
so nice, make her nervous
M: Where class?

```
F:  Old Main & Castle
M:  Go dorm, lie down   (SOL #2)
F:  Not take nap since kindergtn.
M:  Just relax   (I agree she shd take nap)
```

(B) The Language of Problem/Solution

Specific vocabulary and grammatical structures are often used when giving responses for Problem/Solution Tasks.

Stating the Problem

You need to begin your response by stating and explaining the problem that one of the speakers has. Here are some simple ways to do this:

> *Lucy's problem is* a lack of sleep.
>
> *The problem is that* Peter is not allowed to keep a pet in his dorm room.
>
> *The man has a problem with* cooking.

Solutions

The speakers will bring up and discuss two solutions to the problem. When you are listening to the conversation, you may hear speakers make suggestions in the following ways:

"Why don't you . . . ?"	"Why not . . . ?"
"Here's what you can do."	"I have an idea."
"Here's what I think: . . ."	"Here's my suggestion: . . ."
"You should . . ."	"Shouldn't you . . ."
"Maybe you could . . ."	"You could always . . ."
"I guess you could . . ."	"If I were in your shoes, . . ."
"If I were you . . ."	"Try . . ."
"You should give ____ a try."	

There are different ways you can report these solutions. However, you need to be careful of the grammatical rules with different verbs. Here is just a small guideline to help you.

Advise and Suggest

Some verbs used to make suggestions—*advise* and *suggest,* for example—take a special verb form called the present subjunctive. This is a base form of the verb (infinitive without *to*). Look at these examples:

> The man *advises that* Lucy *drink* some coffee.
>
> The woman *suggests that* the man *buy* a good cookbook.

Notice that the base form (the infinitive without *to*) is used in the *that* clause. The third person singular form with *-s* is NOT correct in this sentence.

> The man *advises that* Lucy *drinks* some coffee. (INCORRECT)
>
> The woman *suggests that* the man *buys* a good cookbook. (INCORRECT)

However, you use an infinitive (*to* + base form) with the verb *advise* (but not *suggest*) if you do not use *that*.

> The man *advises* Lucy *to drink* some coffee. (CORRECT)
>
> The man *advises that* Lucy *to drink* some coffee. (INCORRECT)

> The woman *suggests* the man *to buy* a good cookbook. (INCORRECT)
>
> The woman *suggests* the man *buy* a good cookbook. (CORRECT)

Think and Say

The verbs *think* and *say* can be used to report suggestions. These verbs do NOT use the present subjective in the *that* clause.

> The woman *thinks that* Peter *reads* the paper every day.
>
> The woman *says that* Peter *reads* the paper every day.

When reporting suggestions, the verbs *think* and *say* often use a modal verb such as *should* or phrase *ought to* in the *that* clause.

> The woman *says that* Peter *should keep* his pet bird at a friend's apartment.
>
> The man *thinks that* Lucy *ought to drink* some strong coffee.

Tell and Urge

The verbs *tell* and *urge* usually use the infinitive form in the second verb.

> The woman *tells* the man *to get* a cookbook.
>
> The woman *urges* the man *to clean up* his apartment before his parents arrive.

Remember that an object must follow the verbs *tell* and *urge*. (An object can NOT be used after *say*).

> He *tells her* to buy a bicycle. (CORRECT)
>
> He *tells* buy a bicycle. (INCORRECT)
>
> He *urges her* to buy a bicycle (CORRECT)
>
> He *urges* to buy a bicycle. (INCORRECT)
>
> He *says her* that she should buy a bicycle. (INCORRECT)

It is possible to use *that* <u>after the object</u> with *tell*. Use a modal verb or regular verb (not an infinitive or base).

> He *tells her that she needs* a bicycle for work.
>
> He *tells her that she should buy* a bicycle.

Compare:

He *tells* her that she should buy a bicycle. (CORRECT)

He *says* her that she should buy a bicycle. (INCORRECT)

He *advises* her that she should buy a bicycle. (CORRECT)

He *tells* that she should buy a bicycle. (INCORRECT)

He *says* that she should buy a bicycle. (CORRECT)

He *advises* that she should buy a bicycle. (INCORRECT)

She *tells* him that Lucy drinks coffee. (CORRECT)

She *says* that Lucy drinks coffee. (CORRECT)

She *advises* that Lucy drink coffee. (CORRECT)

Second Solutions

Often the same speaker will propose two solutions. You can report the second solution as follows:

The man then suggests that Lucy take a nap in her dorm room.

The woman also tells Peter that he ought to return the bird to the pet store.

The woman then urges John to clean up his apartment before his parents arrive.

The woman's second suggestion is that the man take his parents to a good restaurant rather than cook at home.

Notice that when the noun *suggestion* is followed by a *that* clause, the base form verb *(take)* is again used in the *that* clause.

Reactions to Suggestions and Reasons for the Reactions

As you listen to the conversation, you will hear one speaker make a suggestion. The other speaker will usually react to the suggestion. This speaker may think the suggestion is a good idea or a bad one. The speaker may like the idea but thinks it is not possible for some reason. The speaker may not like the suggestion but may consider it anyway. The speakers will often give their reasons for their reactions as well. Here are some ways to report reactions:

The man thinks the woman's idea is a good one but that it isn't practical.

The man likes this suggestion because . . .

Lucy isn't sure if this is a good idea because . . .

Peter doesn't want to follow the woman's advice because . . .

He doesn't know if he can afford to follow this advice.

The woman doesn't really want to buy a bicycle but thinks it may be necessary.

Recommendations and Reasons for Them

At the end of your response, you need to explain which of the two solutions you think is best.

In my opinion, Lucy ought to go to her dorm and rest between classes. *Why? Because* she . . .

I think Lucy should follow the man's first suggestion because . . .

I agree with the woman's suggestion that Peter ask a friend to take care of his pet bird. *The reason I think so is that* . . .

I like the woman's first idea because . . .

I believe that the man should do as the woman originally suggested. I think so because . . .

I think the man's second suggestion is better. Why? Because . . .

I also recommend that the man take his parents to a restaurant when they come to visit him *because* . . .

I think that the suggestion that the woman get a bus pass *is a good one because* . . .

Note: *The verb* recommend, *like* suggest *and* advise, *takes a base form (present subjunctive) in the* that *clause.*

It's also possible to reject both of the solutions mentioned in the conversation and to propose your own:

I wouldn't follow either of these two suggestions. Instead, I would . . .

I don't like either of these two plans. Here's what I would do. I would . . .

(C) Giving the Problem/Solution Response

You should include the following when you give your response to a Problem/Solution:

▶ A statement about the problem and a description of it

▶ The first possible solution and the other speaker's reaction to it

▶ The second possible solution and the other speaker's reaction to it

▶ Your recommendation and the reason you make that recommendation

You do *not* need to report everything that is said in the conversation. Focus on the problem and possible solutions. As much as possible, *paraphrase.* Explain the problem and the solutions in your own words.

Keep your eye on the on-screen clock as you are speaking. You do *not* want time to run out before you can give your recommendation because the recommendation is a key part of this task. Work on your timing as you do exercises so that you can give a response in about forty-five seconds.

Keep these points in mind when you give your response:

▶ You need to state the problem and the solutions clearly.

▶ Remember: Which solution you choose is not important. Choose the one that is easier to support.

▶ Use transition words to divide parts of your presentation, to give reasons, and to present examples.

▶ Use the language of giving advice correctly *("The woman suggests that the man go . . .").*

▶ Follow the notes that you made during the preparation time.

▶ Speak clearly and directly into the microphone.

▶ Don't speak too quickly or too slowly.

▶ Keep your response flowing; avoid long pauses.

▶ Pay attention to pronunciation and intonation.

▶ Keep it simple by using familiar vocabulary and grammar.

EXERCISE 19.1

FOCUS: Using the language of giving advice correctly.

DIRECTIONS: Use the words provided to report a suggestion. The first one is done for you as an example. Use different ways of reporting suggestions.

1. Doctor/woman/get more exercise

    Example: "The doctor tells the woman to get more exercise."

2. Man/Kathy/get new tires

3. Advisor/student/add another class

4. David/the woman/not sign lease

5. Woman/man/professor to change his grade

6. Diane/her friend/find a summer job

7. Thomas/the woman/not make quick decision

8. The dean/Robert/stay out of trouble in the future

9. The man/his friend/some tennis lessons

10. Professor/the student/a little more research

EXERCISE 19.2

FOCUS: Using the language of giving recommendations correctly.

DIRECTIONS: Use the words provided to give your recommendation. The first one is done for you as an example. Use different ways of giving recommendations.

1. The man/the woman's first suggestion

    Example: "I think that the man should follow the woman's first suggestion."

2. Elizabeth/the man's second suggestion

3. The woman/her doctor's original advice

4. The student/what the dean suggested first

5. Fred/get a good lawyer

6. Dana/the advice that her roommate gave her

7. The man/rewrite his paper

8. The woman/study early in the morning

9. The man/try out for the swim team

10. Tim/not drop out of school

SPEAKING

EXERCISE 19.3

FOCUS: Taking notes on conversations and using the language of Problem/Solution Tasks.

DIRECTIONS: For each conversation, take notes as you listen. You will then see a number of questions and incomplete sentences about the conversation. Answer these questions and complete these sentences orally. Use the "language of Problem/Solution" in your responses as explained in Part B of this lesson. The first set of notes and the first question are done for you as examples.

Task A

▶ Now start the Audio Program. Listen to a conversation between a nurse and a student. 🎧

Sample notes on the conversation:

M: smoker: pack a day—interested in speed skating   out of breath easily
   tried quit before, not able
F: 95% of people who quit w/out a program return to smoking
M: Asks about hypnosis . . . heard was best way to quit
F: Hypnosis not as simple & painless as man say. The clinics' program not use hypno . . .
   uses "nico. repl'mnt sys": gum, etc.
   + techniques for first few wks + support grp
M: Wants to try hypno . . .
F: says can try but expensive   Hlth Center's programs are free

1. What is the man's problem?

    Example: "He is a heavy smoker, and he wants to quit."

2. He is trying to solve this problem now because _____.

3. How has he tried to solve this problem in the past? _____

4. What does the nurse say about trying to solve this problem alone? _____

    _____

5. What solution does he want to try? Why? _____

    _____

6. What solution does the nurse suggest? _____

7. What is one advantage of the nurse's solution? _____

8. Which of these two solutions do you recommend? Why? _____

Task B

▶ Now start the Audio Program. Listen to a conversation between two students. 🎧

Notes on the conversation:

_____

_____

_____

_____

_____

9. The man's problem is that _____.

10. He is having this problem because _____.

11. What does the woman first suggest? _____

12. If he follows this advice, there are two advantages: _____

    and _____.

13. The woman's second suggestion is _____.

14. What is the advantage of following her second suggestion? _____

    _____

15. Which of these two suggestions would you follow? Why? _____

    _____

Task C

▶ Now start the Audio Program. Listen to a conversation between a student and her chemistry professor. 🎧

Notes on the conversation:

_____

_____

_____

16. The student is having a problem with _____.

17. Why is she having a problem? _____

18. The worst problem, according to the student, is that _____.

19. To solve her problem, the student proposes _____.

20. How does the professor react to this proposal? _____

21. What offer does the professor make? _____

22. What would you do in this situation? _____

_____

Task D

▶ Now start the Audio Program. Listen to a conversation between two students. 🎧

Notes on the conversation:

_____

_____

_____

23. What problem is the man having? _____

24. How did he get into this situation? _____

25. What solution does the man propose to solve his own problem? _____

_____

26. Karen thinks that the man's plan _____ .

27. What does Karen advise the man to do? _____

28. How does the man react to her suggestion? _____

29. Which of these two suggestions would you follow? _____

30. Can you think of another solution to this problem? What is it? _____

_____

EXERCISE 19.4

FOCUS: Taking notes on Problems/Solution conversations.

DIRECTIONS: Listen to the following conversations about problems and solutions. Take notes as you listen.

Task A

▶ Now start the Audio Program. Listen to a conversation between a student and his advisor. 🎧

Notes on the conversation:

_____

_____

_____

_____

_____

Task B

▶ Now start the Audio Program. 🎧

Notes on the conversation:

_____

_____

_____

_____

_____

Task C

▶ Now start the Audio Program. 🎧

Notes on the conversation:

_____

_____

_____

_____

_____

Task D

▶ Now start the Audio Program. 🎧

Notes on the conversation:

_____

_____

_____

_____

_____

Exercise 19.5

Focus: Preparing and giving responses for Problem/Solution Tasks.

Directions: Listen and read along to the questions about Tasks A through D in Exercise 19.4. Then, using the notes that you took for Exercise 19.4, give responses for these four Tasks.

You will have twenty seconds to prepare your response, and then you will hear a beep on the Audio Program. You will have sixty seconds to give your response, and then you will hear another beep. Ideally, you should record your responses and then play them back.

▶ Now start the Audio Program. 🎧

Task A

> Stan's advisor offers him two possible solutions to his problem. Discuss his problem, and then explain which of the two solutions you think is better and why.

Task B

> The man offers Margaret two possible solutions to her problem. Explain her problem, and then explain which of the two solutions you think is better and why.

Task C

> The clerk offers the student two possible solutions to his problem. Explain his problem, and then explain which of the two solutions you think is better and why.

Task D

> The woman offers Jim two possible solutions to his problem. Discuss his problem, and then explain which of the two solutions you think is better and why.

Task 6 involves a lecture on an academic subject that lasts sixty to ninety seconds. As usual, you may take notes. You have twenty seconds in which to prepare your response and sixty seconds in which to give it.

Your job in Task 6 is to give the main idea of the lecture that you hear and then to summarize the supporting ideas and give specific details from the lecture.

Here's a sample Summary Task from the Integrated Speaking Preview Test and a sample response to it. Read along as you listen to the lecture, the question, and the sample response.

Sample

▶ Listen to a lecture in a linguistics class. 🎧

Professor

You know, Wednesday after class, a student came up to me and said, "Professor, you're constantly using the terms *language* and *dialect* in class, but you've never really defined these words." Fair enough; I guess I haven't. And there's a good reason why not—I'm afraid to. Because, in my opinion, there's no good way to distinguish between these two terms. The standard definition of dialects is this . . . they're forms of one language that are mutually intelligible to speakers of other forms of the same language. If you have someone from Jamaica, say, and uh, someone from India, and they're seated next to each other on an airplane, they'll be able to have a conversation, they'll more or less understand each other, even though those are two very different dialects of English. But consider the various forms of Chinese. A person from southern China can't understand a person from Beijing. Yet these forms of Chinese are usually considered *dialects*, not separate languages. Now, people who speak different languages are *not* supposed to be intelligible to those who cannot speak that language. But what about Danish and Norwegian? Danish speakers and Norwegian speakers can understand each other perfectly well, but Danish and

Norwegian are considered separate languages, not dialects of the same language. Why? Who knows. I suppose part of it is national pride—countries are proud of "owning" a language. In fact, there's an old joke among linguists that a language is a dialect with an army and a navy. Anyway, these questions—What is a language? What is a dialect?—they're difficult to answer, and . . . uh, I guess that's why I've avoided them up until now.

▶ Now listen to a question about the lecture:

> Using specific examples and points from the lecture, explain the professor's concept of dialects and languages.

Sample Response

"This lecture is about the difference, um, the difference between dialect and language. It, uh, the main idea is that this difference is difficult to define. The professor says basically . . . the basic definition of dialect is a form of the language that, uh, that other people can understand—that other people who speak the language can understand each other. For example, people from Jamaica and India. These people speak different dialect but they understand each another. But, sometimes this definition is not true. For example, dialect of Chinese language. These are called as dialects but, um, very difficult to under-stand. In the other hand, people who speak other languages, they can't understand each another, but then, uh, some languages, different languages, the people can understand them. For example, Denmark people and Norway people. They have different languages but can understand each another. Maybe because of national pride—some people want their own country to have its own language. So—very difficult to answer this question about dialect and language."

This is a successful response to the question. The speaker provides a coherent summary of the lecture. She accurately states the topic and defines it. She mentions a specific example that supports the definition as well as an example that does not fit into the definition.

The response is clear and fluently delivered. The errors are mostly minor grammatical mistakes. The speaker maintains a steady pace with little or no hesitation. She does a good job forming sentences and expressing her ideas. Pronunciation and intonation are generally good.

(A) Pre-Speaking

One key to a high score on Task 6 is to take complete and accurate notes. You need to write down the main idea, a description or definition of the main idea, and supporting information: specific details, examples, or reasons that the professor gives.

You should, of course, use abbreviations and short forms whenever possible.

Sample notes on the reading:

```
○

 Dialects   /   Languages
 Dial.    def: form of lang mutually intel. to spkrs of other forms of same lang
    e.g. Jamaican, Indian people on a plane
 But some dialects NOT mutu. intel: e.g. Chinese dialects so. China & Beijing
 Lang.    def: not intel to people who don't speak that lang
    But some lang ARE mutu intel: e.g. Dan, Norw
 Nat'l pride?    ("Lang a dialect w/ army & navy")
 Difficult ques!

○
```

The question appears on the screen after the lecture:

> Using specific examples and points from the lecture, explain the professor's concept of dialects and languages.

Questions for Task 6 may be worded in different ways, but they will essentially all ask you to do the same thing: to give the main points of the lecture and to provide specific supporting information.

During the twenty seconds you have to prepare a response, you need to decide what points you want to emphasize and what you are going to say. Once again, you will not have enough time to write a separate, detailed outline for your response. Instead, underline main points in your notes and then add additional notes as needed.

Here are sample notes taken during the lecture. They are marked to show what the test-taker plans to discuss:

Sample notes on the lecture:

```
○

 Dialects   /   Languages   (main topic)
 Dial.    def: form of lang mutually intel. to spkrs of other forms of same lang
    e.g. Jamaican, Indian people on a plane
    But some dialects NOT mutu. intel:   e.g. Chinese dialects
 Lang.    def: not intelligible to people who don't speak that lang
    But some lang ARE mutu intel:   e.g. Dan, Norw
       Nat'l pride? ("Lang a dialect w/ army & navy")
    Difficult ques to answer!   (Prof's main point)

○
```

(B) The Language of Summaries

Specific vocabulary and grammatical structures are often used when giving responses for Summary Tasks.

Topics

You should begin your response by giving the topic of the lecture.

> *The lecture is about* dialects and languages.
> *The topic of the lecture is* the 1900 National Auto Show.
> *The professor mainly talks about* the building of canals.

Citation

You need to indicate that you are taking information from the lecture.

> *The professor says that* people who speak Danish can also understand Norwegian.
> *According to the lecture,* canals were a very efficient means of moving goods.

You can use these patterns to give additional information:

> *He goes on to say that* some countries claim a dialect is a language because of national pride.
> *The professor also says that* most people who attended the Auto Show thought of it as a social event rather than as a sales event.

Lists

You can use transition words to make a list of key parts of the lecture, of points that the professor makes, or of historical events.

> *First,* the professor gives some examples of dialects. *Second,* he talks about dialects that are not mutually intelligible. *Third,* he discusses languages that are mutually intelligible.
> *The first* attempt to build the Erie Canal was made by private companies. *Next,* the federal government provided some funds, but this help was ended by the War of 1812. Finally, the project was finished by the state of New York.
> *Some* of the cars at the Auto Show were steam-powered. People worried about explosions with steam-powered cars, however. *Others* were gasoline-powered, but these were noisy and smelly. *Still others* were powered by electricity. These were the most popular because they were quiet and safe.

Examples

The question for Task 6 tells you to use specific examples and points from the lecture. Here are some of the patterns that you can use for reporting examples:

The Erie Canal affected the United States in several ways. *For example,* it took a lot of traffic away from the Mississippi River.

According to the professor, many of the cars at the 1900 auto show did not have steering wheels. *He gives as an example* the Gasmobile, which was steered with a tiller like a boat.

Contrast and Reasons

You will often have to report contrasting ideas in the lecture:

Yue and Mandarin are considered dialects of the same language. *However,* Danish and Norwegian are considered separate languages.

The automobile was invented in Germany, *but* the United States pioneered the marketing of automobiles.

You may also have to give reasons and explain cause and effect in your response.

The Erie Canal permitted trade between the Great Lakes and New York City. *Therefore,* Boston and Philadelphia declined in importance.

Some dialects are considered languages *because of* national pride.

Visitors to the auto show liked electric cars better than gas-powered cars *because* they were quieter.

Notice that the word *because* is followed by a clause *(because they were quieter),* while the phrase *because of* is followed by a noun phrase without a verb *(because of national pride).*

Conclusions

If you have time, you should make a short concluding statement that wraps up the ideas of the lecture. You can use these sentence patterns:

All in all, canals had a huge impact on the U.S. in the early nineteenth century.

In conclusion, it's difficult to define the terms *dialect* and *language.*

In short, the auto show was established as a good way to introduce new cars to the public.

(C) Giving the Summary Response

You should include the following when you give your response to a Summary Task:

▶ A statement about the topic of the lecture
▶ A general definition or description of the topic
▶ Supporting information: specific examples, details, and reasons from the lecture
▶ A brief concluding sentence summing up the lecture

Remember: You do *not* need to report everything from the lecture. Focus on the main idea, but be sure to give specific examples. As much as possible, *paraphrase*. Explain the ideas of the lecture in your own words.

Keep your eye on the on-screen clock as you are speaking. Practice your timing as you do exercises.

Keep these points in mind when you give your response:

▶ State the main point of the lecture clearly in your opening sentence.

▶ Use transition words to divide parts of your presentation, to show contrast, to give reasons, and to present examples.

▶ Use the language of quotation: "The professor says . . ."; "According to the lecture, . . ."

▶ Follow your notes; pay particular attention to the notes that you marked during the preparation period.

▶ Speak clearly and directly into the microphone.

▶ Don't speak too quickly or too slowly.

▶ Keep your response flowing; avoid long pauses.

▶ Pay attention to pronunciation and intonation.

▶ Keep it simple by using familiar vocabulary and grammar.

EXERCISE 20.1

Focus: Taking notes on lectures; using the language of Summary Tasks.

Directions: For each item, listen to the lecture and take notes as you listen. You will then see a number of questions and incomplete sentences about the conversation. Answer these questions and complete these sentences orally. Use the "language of summaries" in your responses as explained in Part B of this lesson. The first set of notes and the first question are done for you as examples.

Task A

▶ Now start the Audio Program. Listen to a lecture in a business class. 🎧

Sample notes on the lecture:

Supermarkets

appr in 30's   take off in 50's

Before: small neighbor. stores, fam-owned

   After suprmkts: small stores disappeared   cldn't compete

Why? 1) ↓ Cost

   suprmkts part of region. chains: buy so much ∴ econ. of scale = ↓ prices

   + low person. costs: self service: take goods from shelves, put in carts,

take to cashier   Today: also self-service cashiers

    2) ↑ Variety

       Suprmkts carry more types of foods: fruit, veg, meat etc.)

         + non-food items: (e.g. hlth & beauty)

Challenge: "hypermarkets," "megamarts"

 nat'l chns: suprmkts + disc. dept. stores

   Have food, clothes, furniture etc. etc.

     ↓ Cost, ↑ Variety than suprmrkts

1. What is the main topic of the lecture?

    Example: "The lecture is about a familiar form of retailing, supermarkets."

2. When did supermarkets first appear? When were they first successful? _____

    _____

3. Where did most people shop in the days before supermarkets? _____

    _____

4. After supermarkets appeared, _____.

5. There are two reasons why supermarkets were successful: _____

    and _____.

6. "Economy of scale" means _____.

7. Supermarkets today are facing _____.

8. How is the situation faced by supermarkets today similar to the situation faced by small grocery stores in the 1950's? _____

    _____

Task B

▶ Now start the Audio Program. Listen to a lecture in an astronomy class. 🎧

Notes on the lecture:

_____

_____

_____

_____

_____

9. This lecture is mostly about _____.

10. The Sun consists of _____.

11. Why doesn't the Sun fly apart? _____

12. The Sun doesn't collapse because _____.

13. In 5 billion years, the Sun's center will _____ and the Sun will

_____ .

14. What will conditions be like on the Earth in 5 billion years? _____

_____

15. When the Sun uses up most of its fuel, _____.

16. After the Sun burns up all of its fuel, it _____ and the Earth

_____ .

17. The four stages that the Sun will pass through are _____,

_____, _____, and _____.

Task C

▶ Now start the Audio Program. Listen to a lecture in a telecommunications class. 🎧

Notes on the lecture:

_____

_____

_____

_____

_____

18. The professor mainly discusses three types of media: _____,
    _____, and _____.

19. When did television first become popular? _____

20. What prediction about television did people make at that time? _____

21. Was the prediction correct? _____

22. After the introduction of television, people did not listen to
    _____ on the radio but they listened to _____.
    They listened to radio when they couldn't _____.

23. How did people's moviegoing habits change after the introduction of television?

24. According to the lecture, many people enjoy going to the movies rather than
    watching television because _____ and because
    _____.

25. What prediction about the future of entertainment and communication tech-
    nology does the professor make? _____

Task D

▶ Now start the Audio Program. Listen to a lecture in a biology class. 🎧

Notes on the lecture:

_____

_____

_____

_____

_____

26. The main topic of this lecture is _____.

27. Why does the professor call this event a "murder mystery"? _____

28. This event happened _____ years ago. It should not be confused with
    _____, which happened _____ years ago.

29. One probable cause of this event was _____.

30. Scientists have found recently found two pieces of evidence indicating this
    event was caused by a collision: _____ and
    _____.

31. What was another possible cause of the event? _____

32. The direct cause of the event was probably _____.

33. The oxygen level at the time of the Great Dying was similar to _____
    _____.

34. Are scientists sure that this is the cause of this event? Give reasons for your
    answer. _____
    _____

SPEAKING

EXERCISE 20.2

FOCUS: Taking notes on lectures.

DIRECTIONS: Listen to the following lectures. Take notes as you listen.

Task A

▶ Now start the Audio Program. Listen to a lecture in a psychology class. 🎧

Notes on the lecture:

_____

_____

_____

_____

_____

Task B

▶ Now start the Audio Program. Listen to a lecture in a chemistry class. 🎧

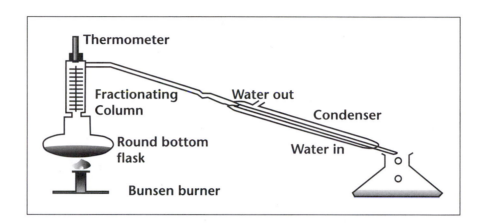

Notes on the lecture:

_____

_____

_____

_____

_____

Task C

▶ Now start the Audio Program. Listen to a lecture in a history class. 🎧

Notes on the lecture:

_____

_____

_____

_____

_____

Task D

▶ Now start the Audio Program. Listen to a lecture in a statistics class. 🎧

Notes on the lecture:

_____

_____

_____

_____

_____

EXERCISE 20.3

FOCUS: Planning and giving responses for Summary Tasks.

DIRECTIONS: Listen and read along to the questions about Tasks A through D in Exercise 20.2. Then, using the notes that you took for Exercise 20.2, plan and give responses for these four tasks. You will have twenty seconds to prepare your response, and then you will hear a beep on the audio program. You will have sixty seconds to give your response, and then you will hear another beep. Ideally, you should record your responses and then play them back.

▶ Now start the Audio Program. 🎧

SPEAKING

Task A

Using specific examples and points from the lecture, explain Seasonal Affective Disorder (SAD) and its treatment.

Task B

Using specific examples and points from the lecture, explain the process of fractional distillation and its importance.

Task C

Using specific examples and points from the lecture, describe the 1900 National Automobile Show and discuss its importance.

Task D

Using specific examples and points from the lecture, explain the Infinite Monkey Theorem and discuss its importance.

SPEAKING REVIEW TEST
DIRECTIONS

▶ Now start the Audio Program. 🎧

This section tests your ability to speak about various subjects. There are six tasks in this section. Listen carefully to the directions, and read the questions on the screen. The first two tasks are Independent Speaking Tasks. You will have fifteen seconds in which to prepare your response. When you hear a beep on the Audio Program, you will have forty-five seconds in which to answer the question.

The last four tasks are Integrated Speaking Tasks. The third and fourth questions involve a reading text and a listening passage. You will have forty-five seconds in which to read a short text. You will then hear a short conversation or part of a lecture on the same topic. You may take notes on both the reading and listening passage. You will then see a question on the screen asking about the information that you have just read and heard, and you will have thirty seconds in which to plan a response. When you hear a beep on the Audio Program, you will have sixty seconds in which to answer the question.

The fifth and sixth questions involve a short listening passage. You may take notes as you listen. After listening to the conversation or lecture, you will see a question, and you will have twenty seconds in which to plan your response. When you hear a beep on the Audio Program, you will have sixty seconds in which to answer the question.

During actual tests, a clock on the screen will tell you how much preparation time or how much response time (speaking time) remains for each question. It is important that you time yourself accurately when you take this practice test. On an actual test your responses will be recorded and evaluated by trained raters.

▶ Now start the Audio Program and listen carefully. 🎧

Task 1

> Describe an event in the history of your country and explain why you think it is important. Include details and examples to support your explanation.

> **Preparation Time: 15 Seconds**
> **Response Time: 45 Seconds**

Notes:

_____

_____

_____

_____

_____

Task 2

> Imagine that you have a time machine and can take one trip through time. Would you visit the past or the future? Explain your choice. Include details and examples in your explanation.

> **Preparation Time: 15 Seconds**
> **Response Time: 45 Seconds**

Notes:

_____

_____

_____

_____

_____

SPEAKING

Task 3

Colton College gives an annual prize to a member of the faculty. Read the following announcement in the campus newspaper about this prize. You will have forty-five seconds in which to read the announcement. Begin reading now.

Microbiology Professor Wins Outstanding Faculty Award

The dean of faculty announced yesterday that the winner of this year's Paulson-Davies Award for outstanding faculty member was Professor Grace Weng of the Department of Life Sciences. Winners of the Paulson-Davies Award are paid for a year of "pure research," during which the faculty member is paid to engage in the research project of his or her choice without classroom teaching or other faculty duties. The award also includes a research grant of $5,000.

Professor Weng has been teaching at Colton College for five years. She has focused her research on diseases spread by mosquitoes such as malaria, dengue fever, and West Nile disease.

The Paulson-Davies Award, named for two nineteenth-century professors at Colton College, is given for excellence in teaching, scholarship, and service to the college.

Runner-up for this year's award was Professor Christopher Pottinger of the Department of History, who won the award in 1979, 1992, and 2004.

Notes:

_____

_____

_____

▶ Now listen to two students discussing this announcement. 🎧

Notes:

_____

_____

_____

_____

| Now get ready to answer the question. |

The woman expresses her opinion of the announcement. State her opinion, and explain the reasons she gives for having that opinion.

Preparation Time: 30 Seconds
Response Time: 60 Seconds

Task 4

Read this passage about a type of American film. You will have forty-five seconds in which to read the passage. Begin reading now.

One of the most important types of American film is *film noir,* made in the 1940's and 50's. The word *noir* is French for "black"; films of this type show the dark side of life, in contrast to happy comedies or musicals. The emphasis is on the *atmosphere. Film noir* movies are all shot in black and white. They feature stark contrast between light and inky black shadows. There is often lonely, jazzy music on the soundtrack. *Noir* films are usually shot in streets and alleys, hotel rooms and apartments in the worst neighborhoods of big cities such as New York or San Francisco.

Crime—usually murder—is at the heart of these movies. The leading male character is often a private detective, a strong but lonely, cynical character. The primary female character is usually called a "femme fatale," a woman who is attractive, independent, and very dangerous. In the end, the male character must make a decision between good and evil.

Notes:

_____

_____

_____

_____

▶ Now listen to a lecture on two movies, *The Maltese Falcon* and *Chinatown.* 🎧

Notes:

_____

_____

_____

_____

_____

| Now get ready to answer the question. |

The professor's lecture is about two movies: _The Maltese Falcon_ and _Chinatown_. Describe these movies, and explain why they are considered examples of film noir.

Preparation Time: 30 Seconds
Response Time: 60 Seconds

Task 5

▶ Listen to a conversation between two students. 🎧

Notes:

_____

_____

_____

_____

| Now get ready to answer the question. |

The man discusses two possible solutions to Michelle's problem. Discuss her problem, and then explain which of the two solutions you think is better and why you think so.

Preparation Time: 20 Seconds
Response Time: 60 Seconds

Task 6

▶ Listen to part of a lecture in an economics class. 🎧

Notes:

_____

_____

_____

_____

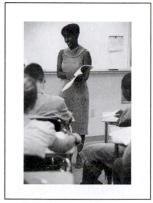

| Now get ready to answer the question. |

Using specific examples and points from the lecture, explain the concept of externalities.

Preparation Time: 20 Seconds
Response Time: 60 Seconds

This is the end of the Speaking Review Test.

SPEAKING

SPEAKING TUTORIAL: BUILDING PRONUNCIATION SKILLS

According to ETS, your "ability to speak clearly and fluently" will affect your speaking score. Clear, fluent speech involves vocabulary, grammar, and pronunciation. This section will help you with your pronunciation. You will review key features that have the most impact on clarity and fluency. These features include stress, intonation, phrasing, and word endings as well as select consonant and vowel sounds.

How should I use this review section?

▶ It is helpful, but not necessary, to have equipment to record your own speech as you do the exercises in this section. That way you can hear your progress.

▶ Perhaps you have studied pronunciation, and you know your pronunciation needs. If so, skip to those sections. Otherwise, move through the sections in order. If you want more practice than this review provides, refer to the additional resources at the end.

▶ Improving pronunciation is like learning to drive, ride a bicycle, or shoot a basketball. You have to practice until it becomes automatic, and that takes time. Ideally, begin this tutorial several months before taking the TOEFL iBT so that you have adequate time for some of the features to become automatic.

▶ If you truly want to improve your intelligibility, commit yourself to doing more than reading through this tutorial or memorizing rules. Rather, practice out loud. Repeat the same word, sentence, or paragraph over and over until you are comfortable with the rhythm, intonation, pauses, sounds, and timing.

▶ The most effective way to use this section is in segments of about thirty minutes. After working for thirty minutes, take a break and come back to it later.

▶ During your practice sessions, imagine that you are an actor rehearsing lines for a play—you want to be sure that you learn your lines well and that the audience will understand you without effort. As you work on different features in your speech, notice how English speakers in your daily life use those same features.

This tutorial contains a lot of material. Don't let it overwhelm you. Some of what you learn will help you to be a better *listener.* Some of what you learn will help you to be a better *speaker.* You will not learn everything, but that's all right. You don't need perfect or native-like speech in order to speak clearly and effectively.

Are there general pronunciation tips that will help my test performance?

1. Take your time when you are speaking. Do not speak rapidly in an effort to sound more fluent. You will just be harder to understand.

2. Make the more important words in your response stand out.
   Example: "The dePARTment isn't going to EXIST after this TERM."

3. Put in pauses when you speak. Pausing at appropriate places makes you sound more fluent. (/ = pause)
   Example: "She talked to her neighbors/ three or four times,/ but the next day/ it was noisy again."

4. When you listen to the announcements, lectures, and conversations, do not worry if you do not catch every word. Listen for the stressed words and you will get the essential points.

> *Example:* "TODAY we're going to talk about a form of RETAILING, a form we're all FAMILIAR with, the SUPERMARKET."

What are the most important pronunciation features?

These eight pronunciation basics contribute the most to intelligibility:

(A) **Word Stress:** In words of two or more syllables, one syllable is stronger than the others.

> *Example:* "HIStory"

If you misplace the stress, listeners might hear *"his story."*

(B) **Rhythm:** Listeners expect what is relatively more important to be stressed and what is less important to be weak or reduced.

> *Example:* "The anNOUNCEment was about a CHANGE in the orienTAtion."

(C) **Thought Groups and Pausing:** Speech is divided into meaningful phrases or thought groups. The thought groups are often followed by a brief pause. Words within the thought groups are linked to make speech sound smooth.

> *Example:* "The anNOUNCEment / was about a CHANGE/ in the orienTAtion. / The LIbrary tour at TWO/ has been MOVED to FIVE."

(D) **Thought Groups and Rising and Falling Intonation:** The end of each thought group has a rise or fall in intonation.

> *Example:* The LIbrary tour at TWO⬀/ has been MOVED to FIVE⬂."/

(E) **Thought Groups and Focus:** Every thought group has a focus—a word or syllable with the most emphasis—signaled by a pitch change. (Focus words are in boldface.)

> *Example:* The LIbrary tour at **TWO**/ has been MOVED to **FIVE.**"/

(F) **Grammatical Endings:** Grammatical endings on nouns or verbs can change the meaning of a sentence.

> *Examples:*
> They stole the new computers from my office. (*computers* is plural)
> I worked as a lab assistant. (*worked* is past tense)

(G) **Consonant Sounds:** Final consonant sounds (e.g., five), consonants in clusters (e.g., science; play), and word endings (e.g., plans; worked) are vital to meaning.

> *Example:* "If you park in the faculty zone, you will be fined." *(fine or fined?)*
> If you don't pronounce the final d, listeners will hear "fine."

(H) **Vowel Sounds:** Vowel sounds in stressed syllables are full and clear. Vowel sounds in unstressed syllables are often pronounced like schwa (i.e., /ə/ as in _about_).

Example: CAMpus = / ˈkæm pəs/

(A) Word Stress

Syllables: Words in English have one or more syllables, beats, or pulses.

Examples:	_1 syllable_	_2 syllables_	_3 syllables_	_4 syllables_
	sent	pre sent	pre sen ted	pre sen ta tion
	act	act tive	ac tive ly	ac ti vi ty

EXERCISE 1: NUMBER OF SYLLABLES

How many beats (syllables) are in these words? First say the words below. Then listen to the Audio Program and write the number of syllables that you hear. Then say the words again. You can tap your hand on the desk as you say each syllable.

▶ After you have said the words the first time, start the Audio Program. ⌒

1. basic	_2_	6. understand	_____
2. home	_____	7. authority	_____
3. Brazil	_____	8. Korea	_____
4. decide	_____	9. president	_____
5. decided	_____	10. information	_____

Listen again as the speakers "tap out" the syllables.

WORD STRESS: In words with two or more syllables, one syllable has primary stress.

The syllable with primary stress is

▶ louder
▶ higher in pitch
▶ clearer
▶ longer

The most important signals of stress are clarity and l-e-n-g-t-h.

Example: PRE si dent

EXERCISE 2: SYLLABLE STRESS

Say the words in the list below. Then listen to the words read on the Audio Program and underline the syllable with the longest, clearest vowel. Then say the words once more. Start with a closed fist. You can open your fist *as you say* the stressed syllable. This will help you lengthen the stressed syllable.

| Example: | so | **LU** | tion |

▶ After you read the words the first time, start the Audio Program. 🎧

1. <u>lec</u> ture
2. prob lem
3. dis cuss
4. so lu tion

5. pos si bi li ty
6. im por tant
7. com pare
8. si tu a tion

Multisyllable words sometimes have secondary stresses. Primary and secondary stresses have clear vowels. Unstressed syllables have reduced vowels like /ə/ in <u>a</u>bout.

Examples:	possibility	→	‚pos si 'bi li ty
			/ə/ /ə/
	announcement	→	ə n 'nounce ment
			/ə/ /ə/

Reduce unstressed vowels, or they may sound stressed and the listener might not understand the word.

EXERCISE 3: STRESS IN ACADEMIC VOCABULARY

Do you know where the stress is? First say the words. Then listen to the words being pronounced. Underline the stressed syllable in both words. Then say the words again. Stretch a rubber band as you say the stressed syllables.

MI   nor   mi   NOR   i   ty

▶ After you have read the words the first time, start the Audio Program. 🎧

1. minor   minority
2. valid   validity
3. stable   stability
4. strategy   strategic
5. philosophy   philosophical
6. economy   economic
7. distribute   distribution
8. apply   application

Most rules for word stress are too numerous and complicated to be helpful. However, here are a few simple guidelines to help you predict stress in academic words. These are simply guidelines, and there will be exceptions!

Guideline 1: Most (90%) two-syllable nouns have first-syllable stress.

LECture   PROBlem   STUdent

Guideline 2: Many two-syllable academic verbs have second-syllable stress.

exPLAIN   ocCUR   reQUIRE

Guideline 3: Many two-syllable noun-verb pairs differ according to stress. Nouns have first-syllable stress and verbs have second-syllable stress.

Noun	Verb	Noun	Verb
OBject	obJECT	CONtract	conTRACT
PROject	proJECT	PERmit	perMIT

Where's your PERmit to park?

Does the school perMIT free parking on weekends?

Guideline 4: Most compound nouns (and compounds made up of two nouns) have primary stress on the first noun.

CLASSroom   HOMEwork   DISK drive

EXERCISE 4: FIND THE STRESSED SYLLABLE

The words in each column have similar stress patterns. First say the words. Then listen to the words being pronounced. Underline the stressed syllable as you listen. Then say the words again.

After you have said the words the first time, start the Audio Program. 🎧

Verbs	Compound Nouns	Nouns	Nouns	Verbs
de fine	air port	cred it	pro duce	pro duce
ob tain	soft ware	out come	pro gress	pro gress
pre fer	math test	con cept	con duct	con duct
se lect	health care	of fice	in sult	in sult
com pare	stock market	fac tor	rec ord	rec ord
as sume	su per mar ket	in put	pres ent	pres ent

Guideline 5: These common suffixes beginning with -i shift the stress to the syllable before the suffix.

-ity   MAjor   maJORity

-ic(al)   eCOnomy   ecoNOMic

-ion   apPLY   appliCAtion

Guideline 6: The suffixes -*logy* and -*graphy* also shift the stress to the syllable before the suffix.

psyCHOlogy, biOlogy, techNOlogy

phoTOgraphy, biOgraphy, geOgraphy

Guideline 7: Notice the important differences between these numbers

THIRty	thirTEEN or THIR-TEEN
FIFty	fifTEEN or FIF-TEEN

It's a FORty-mile commute.   *(Stress in first syllable; /t/ = /d/: FORdy)*

It's a FOURTEEN-mile commute.   *(Stress in both syllables; /t/ is clear)*

EXERCISE 5: IDENTIFY THE STRESS

First say the words. Then listen to the words being pronounced. Underline the stressed syllable as you listen. Then say the words again.

▶ After you have said the words the first time, start the Audio Program. 🎧

1. se cure	se cur i ty	11. class ic	class i cal
2. le gal	le gal i ty	12. dem oc ra cy	dem o crat ic
3. di verse	di vers i ty	13. his to ry	his tor ic
4. e lec tric	e lec tric i ty	14. ge ol o gy	ge o log i cal
5. per son al	per son al i ty	15. pho to gra phy	pho to graph ic
6. no ti fy	no ti fi ca tion	16. four teen	for ty
7. gra du ate	gra du a tion	17. eigh teen	eigh ty
8. de fine	de fi ni tion	18. nine teen	nine ty
9. re gis ter	re gis tra tion	19. se ven teen	se ven ty
10. con gra tu late	con gra tu la tion	20. fif teen	fif ty

EXERCISE 6: PRODUCING WORD STRESS IN CONTEXT

First read the response. Then listen to the Audio Program. Underline the stressed syllables in the italicized words. Then read the paragraph aloud once more. Record if possible.

▶ After you have read the response the first time, start the Audio Program. 🎧

Well, *education* is important to my family and me so . . . I guess . . . the most important day in my life . . . . . was my *graduation* from Seoul *National University.* I'd always dreamed . . . uh . . . of becoming a *medical* doctor and my degree in *biology* was my first step toward that . . . that goal. On my *graduation,* it was a hot day and the *humidity* was high but nobody seemed to . . . notice. Everybody was so excited that they paid no *attention* to the weather . . . even though it took hours to call everyone's name. When the ceremony was over, my family and friends from my *community* . . . we all went to a restaurant for a *celebration.*

Listen to your recording. Evaluate your use of stressed syllables. Were they longer and clearer than the others? If not, record again. You may want to stretch a rubber band or open your fist on the stressed syllables. If you do something physical, it will help you internalize the learning.

When giving a lecture, professors may especially emphasize content words that they are introducing for the first time or that they consider especially important to an understanding of the lecture. They may even repeat these words to give added emphasis.

In the Integrated Speaking Tasks, these are words that you will probably "recycle." In other words, you will use them yourself in your response.

EXERCISE 7: LISTENING TO WORD STRESS IN A LECTURE

Listen to this Task 4 lecture prompt for a General/Specific Task. Which key terms from the lecture will you probably "recycle" in your response? Write them below. Underline the stressed syllables. Then say the words.

▶ Now start the Audio Program. 🎧

_____

_____

_____

_____

You should have written *marble, metamorphic, limestone,* and *sedimentary,* although you may have written a few other terms. Note that both *metamorphic* and *limestone* follow guidelines for word stress given previously. (*Metamorphic* is stressed on the syllable before -*ic*; *limestone* is a compound noun.)

> **Test-Taking Tip:** As you listen to the announcements, lectures, and conversations, note the stress patterns in the key words that you will recycle in your response.

(B) Rhythm

All languages have their own rhythm or beat. English rhythm is the alternation of strong stresses and weak stresses. In English, important content words—or the stressed syllables of the content words—usually have the strong stresses.

> *Example:* I don't know WHY the uniVERsity should SUDdenly start CHARging us to PARK there.

Content words (stressed) = nouns, verbs, adjectives, adverbs, *wh*-question words
Function words (unstressed) = articles, pronouns, prepositions, auxiliary verbs
Function words are usually reduced or weakened.

EXERCISE 8: IDENTIFYING STRESSED AND UNSTRESSED WORDS

Say the sentences below. Then listen as the sentences are read. Underline the words (or syllables) that you think should be strong. Then say the sentences once more. 🎧

1. The <u>prob</u>lem is her <u>neigh</u>bors are <u>noi</u>sy.
2. Participants can earn credit and also make money.
3. I prefer to work for a company.
4. The announcement is about regulations for parking at the university.
5. Her choices are to talk to her neighbors or to move.

> **Test-Taking Tip:** When taking notes, pay attention to the rhythm. If you write the important stressed words and omit the unstressed words that do not carry information, you will have the essence of the message.

EXERCISE 9: MATCHING ENGLISH RHYTHM

Read the following response. Then listen as it is read. Underline the words (or the syllable of the words) that the speaker stresses. You may need to listen more than once. Then read it one more time. After you have read the response the first time, start the Audio Program. 🎧

> Stan's trying to make a decision about college . . . about where to attend his last semester of college. The problem is . . . that . . . well, his major is classical languages . . . and his university is going to close that department at the end of the term.

EXERCISE 10: ENGLISH RHYTHM IN CONTEXT

Listen to the conversation. Discuss Lucy's problem in a few sentences. Record your response and listen to it. Did you make the content words (or the stressed syllables of the content words) stand out? 🎧

Many non-native speakers think that native speakers of English speak too fast. The problem isn't just speed, however. Native speakers weaken function words. As speech gets more casual, function words get harder to hear.

		Casual
He could have paid him.	*sounds like*	He couldə paid əm.

Using reductions is not poor or improper English. It is a part of English rhythm. You will hear some reductions on the test.

EXERCISE 11: REDUCED FORMS

Here are some common reductions you can expect to hear on the test. First listen to the sentences and write the word(s) in normal written English. Now say the sentences with the reduced words. (You do not need to use reduced forms in your spoken English, but if you practice saying them, you will be quicker to identify them in the speech of others.) 🎧

1. I thought _____ calling the cops.
2. She'll pay the fees _____keep parking at the stadium.
3. Stan, _____ you decided what classes you're taking?
4. He should _____ listened to the nurse's advice
5. They more _____ less understand each other.
6. We _____ register our cars.
7. He's _____ get another form of ID.
8. He's not _____ change his major.
9. She doesn't _____ call the police on her neighbors.
10. The man has a _____ solutions for Lucy's problem.
11. Tina _____ talk to her lab partner.

Pronunciation and Listening Tip: The words *can* and *can't* are often confused. The word *can* is weak and has a reduced vowel: /kən/ or /kn/. The word *can't* is stressed and has a clear vowel: /kænt/.

I kn underSTAND that.   (1 stress)

I CAN'T underSTAND that.   (2 stresses)

EXERCISE 12: CAN OR CAN'T?

Listen to the sentence. Underline the word (*can* or *can't*) that you hear. Then read the sentences aloud. ⌒

1. You (can / can't) park there with a student permit.
2. She (can / can't) study in her building.
3. Letter grades (can / can't) be used to rank students.
4. Today, couples (can / can't) adopt twin babies separately.
5. English speakers from Jamaica and India (can / can't) understand each other.
6. I (can / can't) believe some students don't turn off their phones in class.
7. You (can / can't) always use another bulletin board on campus.
8. The blue morpho is brightly colored, but its predators (can / can't) hardly see it.

(C) Thought Groups and Pausing

Fluent speakers speak in thought groups. They speak thought by thought, not word by word, and not long sentence by long sentence.

Long sentences need to be divided into thought groups.

Example: Nancy's problem is that everybody in her building makes so much noise that she can't study very well.

Read the example aloud. Pause briefly at the end of each thought group.

Nancy's problem is /

that everybody in her building /

makes so much noise /

that she can't study very well./

A thought group is a group of words that go together. Thought groups include the following:

▶ Short sentences

Example: She can't study. / Her building is just too noisy. /

▶ Phrases and clauses

Example: It's so noisy / that she can't study./

▶ Transition words and phrases that make your organization clear *(first, on the other hand, for example, in fact, the reason is, the problem is)*

Example: On the other hand, / her building is so noisy, / that she can't study./

Did you notice that the pauses are very brief? Pauses marked by commas are a little longer, and pauses at the end of a sentence (marked by periods or question marks) are longer still, but none of these pauses are very long. Avoid long pauses.

EXERCISE 13: PREDICTING THOUGHT GROUPS

Where do you pause for clarity and effect? First, read the two responses, pausing at the end of each thought group. Put a slash (/) at the end of each thought group where you paused.

1. To describe marble, first you have to define metamorphic rock. Metamorphic rock is rock that's, uh, changed, from one kind of rock to another. Ummm, marble comes from a softer rock that's called limestone, which is a sedimentary rock. Marble is a hard rock. Marble comes in various colors. Like other metamorphic rocks, it is so strong that it is often used for building.

2. Supermarkets have been successful for two main reasons. The first reason is that costs are low. One reason the costs are low is . . . uh, supermarkets buy in huge quantities. This is called . . .uh, let's see . . . economy of scale.

Now, listen to the speaker give the response, and put in a slash where you hear a pause. Are the slashes in the same place? Then give the response one more time. 🎧

1. To describe marble, first you have to define metamorphic rock. Metamorphic rock is rock that's, uh, changed, from one kind of rock to another. Ummm, marble comes from a softer rock that's called limestone, which is a sedimentary rock. Marble is a hard rock. Marble comes in various colors. Like other metamorphic rocks, it is so strong that it is often used for building.

2. Supermarkets have been successful for two main reasons. The first reason is that costs are low. One reason the costs are low is . . . uh, supermarkets buy in huge quantities. This is called . . .uh, let's see . . . economy of scale.

Note: *Different speakers pause at different places. There is more than one way to phrase the response above. Thought groups differ from speaker to speaker, but it is important to break long sentences into phrases and to keep phrases together.*

> **Pronunciation Tip:** If you are asked to describe or to define a term, it is a good idea to pause briefly after you give the term.
> *Example:* "Metamorphic rock (*pause*) is rock that has changed . . .″

(D) Thought Groups and Rising and Falling Intonation

How do speakers indicate the end of a thought group? They use a brief pause. They also use a falling or rising intonation. In the TOEFL iBT speaking tasks you will generally be giving information, so you will use these two primary patterns:

Rising   ↗   = more to come

Falling   ↘   = end of statement

NANcy's PROBlem is ↗ /

that EVerybody in her BUILDing↗ /

makes SO much NOISE↗ /

that she CAN'T STUDY very well↘./

Sometimes you will ask "rhetorical questions" in your response. (These are questions that you will answer yourself.) These questions end with rising intonation.

Rising   ↗   = end of rhetorical question

WHAT should the MAN DO↗
about the MISSing MOUSE? ↗

EXERCISE 14: LISTENING FOR THOUGHT GROUPS

Following are parts of Speaking responses. First say the responses. Use a rising intonation at the end of a thought group when there is more to come, or at the end of a rhetorical question. Use a falling intonation at the end of a statement.

> She wants to take part in the experiment. One reason is that she can make some extra money. Another reason is that she has lots of problems going to sleep at night.

> His sister got a position as an intern at an advertising agency in New York City. The pay was pretty good. And besides, it was good experience for her. It looks good on her résumé.

> There was a numeral system that was used by the Yuki Indians of California that was base 8. The Yukis counted the spaces between their fingers rather than their fingers themselves.

> The announcement is about plagiarism. What is plagiarism? According to the announcement, it is using someone else's words or ideas as your own without crediting the other person.

Now, listen to the responses on the Audio Program. Put an arrow at the end of each thought group indicating whether the intonation should rise or fall. Then say the responses one more time. 🎧

She wants to take part ↗
in the experiment.
One reason is
that she can make some extra money.
Another reason is
that she has lots of problems
going to sleep at night.

His sister
got a position as an intern
at an advertising agency.
The pay was pretty good,
and besides,
it was good experience for her.
It looks good
on her résumé.

There was a numeral system
that was used
by the Yuki Indians
of California
that was base 8.
The Yukis counted the spaces
between their fingers
rather than their fingers themselves.↘

The announcement is about plagiarism.
What is plagiarism?
According to the announcement,
it is using someone else's words or ideas
as your own
without crediting the other person.

(E) Thought Groups and Focus

Each thought group has one key word (or syllable) that gets the most emphasis.
These are often called focus words.

The focus words (or syllables) are in bold.

NANcy's **PROB**lem is ↗ /

that EVerybody in her **BUILD**ing↗ /

makes SO much **NOISE**↗ /

that she CAN'T **STUDY** very well↘./

What makes listeners notice the focus word? Focus words are louder, lo-o-o-nger,
and clearer. Most important, however, they have a major pitch change. They usually jump up in pitch.

NANcy's **PROB**lem is /

that EVerybody in her **BUILD**ing /

makes SO much **NOISE** /

that she CAN'T **STUDY** very well./

EXERCISE 15: LISTENING FOR THE FOCUS WORDS

Say the sentences, stressing the focus word in each thought group. Then listen to the response as it is read on the Audio Program. Underline the focus word (or stressed syllable of the focus words) in each thought group. Then say the responses again. 🎧

She wants to take part ↗
in the experiment. ↘
One reason is ↗
that she can make some extra money. ↘
Another reason is ↗
that she has lots of problems ↗
going to sleep at night. ↘

His sister ↗
got a position as an intern ↗
at an advertising agency. ↘
The pay was pretty good, ↗
and besides, ↗
it was good experience for her. ↘
It looks good↗
on her résumé. ↘

There was a numeral system ↗
that was used ↗
by the Yuki Indians ↗
of California ↗
that was base 8. ↘
The Yukis counted the spaces ↗
between their fingers ↗
rather than their fingers themselves. ↘

The announcement is about plagiarism. ↘
What is plagiarism? ↗
According to the announcement, ↗
it is using someone else's words or ideas ↗
as your own ↗
without crediting the other person. ↘

Why do we call attention to certain words and not others? That sometimes depends on what is in the mind of the speaker, but here are some general guidelines:

▶ Focus is often the last content word in the thought group (or the stressed syllable of the last content word).

Example: My MAjor's engiNEERing.

But the focus can shift to other words in thought groups.

▶ To highlight new information.

> *Example:* My MAjor's engi**NEER**ing, / **CIV**il engineering./

▶ To highlight contrasts

> *Example:* If you WORK for a **COM**pany,/ the **COM**pany might pay for health insurance./
>
> If you OWN your own **BUS**iness, /**YOU** pay for health insurance./

Did you notice that after the focus, the rest of the phrase—*pay for health insurance*—is de-emphasized? There are no more major pitch changes. That helps the listener know what is important—the contrast between who pays!

EXERCISE 16: FINDING THE FOCUS

What is the key word or focus is in each thought group? Underline it. 🎧

My sister—
my older sister—
got a job with an ad agency.
It was a New York ad agency.

He got in trouble for plagiarism.
Well, it wasn't exactly plagiarism.
At least, he didn't consider it plagiarism.

The nest of the hamerkop
has at least three rooms.
The highest room
is the sleeping room
where the female lays her eggs
When the babies grow up
they move to the middle room.

Did you notice in the exercise that when some focus words were new information (such as *sister, ad agency, plagiarism, room*), they were emphasized, but in the next thought group, the words became old information and were de-emphasized?

EXERCISE 17: PUTTING THOUGHT GROUPS, INTONATION, AND FOCUS TOGETHER

Read the response. Mark the thought groups (/). Underline the focus words or syllables. Then show rising ➚ or falling ➘ intonation at the ends of the thought groups. You may need to listen to the response more than once. After marking the passage, read it aloud. 🎧

I think I'd prefer living in a dorm to living in an apartment. It's true that many apartments are roomy and that most dorm rooms are kind of cramped, but there are other reasons why dorm rooms are better. The first is transportation. If I lived off campus, I'd have to drive and owning a car is expensive. So is parking. I've heard that it can cost $100 a semester. Another reason living in a dorm is better is that it is easier to make friends. In apartment buildings, people may say hello, but they aren't very friendly. In dorms, people stop and talk and are much more sociable. Finally, what about meals? If I lived in an apartment, I'd have to cook. On the other hand, in a dorm, meals are provided. And that's a relief, because frankly, I'm a terrible cook.

Pronunciation Reminder: In Exercise 17, you were reading. Don't expect your responses on the speaking test to be this fluent. On the test, you will have to do a lot of planning *while* you are speaking. That makes a big difference in the fluency of any speaker! There will be some pauses and "umms" and "ahs." Just remember to deliver your ideas in thought groups and to emphasize your key words.

SPEAKING

EXERCISE 18: THOUGHT GROUPS, INTONATION, AND FOCUS IN CONTEXT

Complete the prompt in your *own* words with your *own* ideas. Use the lines to make notes. Record a brief response.

If I had to choose between attending a school in a big city or in a small town, I would choose . . .

Notes:

_____

_____

_____

_____

If possible, share your response with a partner, and then answer these questions, first about your own response and then about your partner's:

1. I delivered most of my response in
   ☐ short, meaningful phrases   ☐ long sentences   ☐ single words

2. I could easily hear the important key words (or the stressed syllables of the key words) in my response
   ☐ most of the time   ☐ about half the time   ☐ rarely

3. My intonation made it clear when I was continuing and when I was finishing a sentence.

   ☐ most of the time   ☐ about half the time   ☐ rarely

4. I would make the following changes if I responded to this prompt again:

   _____

   _____

1. My partner delivered most of his/her response in

   ☐ short, meaningful phrases   ☐ long sentences   ☐ single words

2. I could easily hear the important key words (or the stressed syllables of the key words) in my partner's response

   ☐ most of the time   ☐ about half the time   ☐ rarely

3. My partner's intonation made it clear when he/she was continuing and when he/she was finishing a sentence.

   ☐ most of the time   ☐ about half the time   ☐ rarely

4. I would suggest the following changes in my partner's response if he/she gave it again:

   _____

   _____

   _____

(F) Grammatical Endings

Using grammatical endings is important in academic English. However, the –ed and –s endings are pronounced rapidly, and they blend in with subsequent words, so they may be hard for you to hear. They also create consonant clusters that may be difficult for you to say.

Examples: see<u>ms</u> /mz/   work<u>ed</u> /rkt/

Past Tense –ed Endings: Usually the past tense –ed ending is an added sound; sometimes it is an extra syllable.

Examples: <u>Added Sound:</u>	*1 syllable*	*1 syllable*
	move	mov<u>ed</u>
	miss	miss<u>ed</u>
<u>Added Syllable</u>	*1 syllable*	*2 syllables*
	start	start-ed
	need	need-ed

EXERCISE 19: ADDED SOUND OR ADDED SYLLABLE?

Listen to each verb in the present and past tenses. Is the *–ed* ending an added sound or syllable? 🎧

		Added Sound	*Added Syllable*
1. add	added		✓
2. park	parked	✓	
3. plan	planned		
4. wait	waited		
5. intend	intended		
6. apply	applied		
7. decide	decided		
8. believe	believed		

Guidelines for pronouncing *–ed*:

▶ When the last sound of the verb is /t/ or /d/ (e.g., *add, wait, intend*), add a syllable: *add-ed, wait-ed, intend-ed.*

▶ Otherwise, just add a sound: *parked, planned, believed.*

Fluency Tip: Speakers link words in a phrase or thought group. That makes some final consonant clusters easier to say. Link *–ed* endings to the next word in the phrase. If the next word starts with a vowel, move the last consonant sound to the next word.

Example:	/vd/ I lived in Beijing.	*sounds like*	I live din Beijing.
	/zd/ We caused it.	*sounds like*	We cause dit.

If the next word starts with the same or a similar consonant, the past tense ending will *not* be as clear to the listener.

Example: They talked to her neighbors. *sounds like* They talk to her neighbors.

EXERCISE 20: LISTENING TO PRESENT AND PAST TENSE

Listen. Do you hear the present or past tense? Underline A (present) or B (past). Afterwards, read both sentences aloud. 🎧

1. A. A lot of students park at the stadium.

   B. A lot of students parked at the stadium.

2. A. People believe that hamerkops carry snakes to their nests.

   B. People believed that hamerkops carried snakes to their nests.

3. A. They want to have control of their time.

   B. They wanted to have control of their time.

4. A. The students appreciate her assistance.

   B. The students appreciated her assistance.

5. A. Those two individuals cause all of the problems in the department.

   B. Those two individuals caused all of the problems in the department.

6. A. Not enough students major in classical languages.

   B. Not enough students majored in classical languages.

Were any *–ed* endings difficult to hear?

EXERCISE 21: PRONOUNCING THE PAST TENSE IN CONTEXT

Describe the funniest thing that has ever happened to you. Take some time to make some notes before you begin. If possible, record your response. Give yourself one minute to respond.

Notes:

_____

_____

_____

_____

Listen to the recording. Write every verb that you said with an *–ed* ending. Check your pronunciation of regular past-tense verbs.

The –s Ending

In the Speaking Section, you will use *–s* endings primarily in these three contexts:

PLURALS:	<u>Megamarts</u> can offer cheaper <u>prices</u>.
PRESENT TENSE:	They can't understand a person who <u>speaks</u> that dialect.
POSSESSIVES:	The <u>woman's</u> neighbors are in a band.

The *–s* ending is usually an added sound:

Examples:	ticket<u>s</u>, rock<u>s</u>, work<u>s</u>	= /s/
	believe<u>s</u>, give<u>s</u>, mile<u>s</u>	= /z/

Sometimes the *–s* ending is an added syllable:
Examples: pass-es, chang-es, pric-es   = /iz/

EXERCISE 22: SAYING THE –S ENDING

Repeat the list of words. When do you think *–es* is pronounced as a separate syllable? ⌒

	Added Sound	Added Syllable
1. takes	✓	
2. causes		
3. credits		
4. expresses		
5. dislikes		
6. explains		
7. fixes		
8. thinks		
9. Nancy's		
10. discusses		
11. reasons		
12. changes		
13. gives		

Guidelines for pronouncing *–s*:

If the original word ends in one of these sounds, add the syllable /iz/:

/s/ as in *miss*	= misses
/z/ as in *freeze*	= freezes
/ʃ/ as in *wish*	= wishes
/tʃ/ as in *watch*	= watches
/dʒ/ as in *percentage*	= percentages

Otherwise, add the sound /s/ or /z/.

SPEAKING

Exercise 23: Listening to –s Endings in Context

Listen and underline the word you hear. Then read the response. Pay attention to –s endings and linking. 🎧

The two (student / students) are discussing (preference / preferences) in housing. They both (prefer / prefers) living in a (dorm / dorms) to living in an (apartment/apartments). They (agree / agrees) that many (apartment / apartments) are roomy, and most dorm (room / rooms) are kind of cramped, but they (give / gives) some uh, good (reason / reasons) why they (think / thinks) that dorm (room / rooms) are better. The first (one / ones) is that it is easier to make (friend / friends). People are more sociable. Also, a dorm usually (provide / provides) meals. This is good, because they are both awful (cook / cooks).

(G) Consonant Sounds

Many speakers of other languages confuse English voiced and voiceless sounds.

	Voiceless	Voiced
Examples:		
	He likes his <u>c</u>lasses.	vs. He likes his <u>g</u>lasses.
	He <u>p</u>arks on campus.	vs. He <u>b</u>arks on campus.
	She gets a credit hour for her <u>t</u>ime.	vs. She gets a credit hour for her <u>d</u>ime.

Voiced and Voiceless Consonant Sounds

Some consonant sounds are made without the voice. They are voiceless. The vocal cords do not vibrate. Put your hand on your throat. Make a snake-like, hissing sound: s-s-s-s-s-s. There is no vibration.

Other consonant sounds are made with the voice. They are voiced. The vocal cords vibrate. Put your hand on your throat. Male a bee-like buzzing sound: z-z-z-z-z-z. Feel the vibration. See the complete chart of voiced and voiceless consonant sounds below.

	Pair Sounds	Others
Voiceless Consonants	/ p t k f θ s ʃ tʃ /	/h/
Voiced Consonants	/ b d g v ð z ʒ dʒ /	/m n ŋ l r w y /

Some consonant pairs are almost alike except that one is voiceless and the other is voiced. These initial voiced and voiceless consonants are often confused. Listen to the Audio Program, and then say the words.

▶ Start the Audio Program. 🎧

Voiceless	Voiced
1. /p/ <u>p</u>ay	/b/ <u>b</u>ay
2. /t/ <u>t</u>ime	/d/ <u>d</u>ime
3. /k/ <u>c</u>old	/g/ gold
4. /f/ <u>f</u>ew	/v/ <u>v</u>iew
5. /s/ <u>s</u>ip	/z/ <u>z</u>ip
6. /tʃ/ <u>ch</u>eap	/dʒ/ <u>j</u>eep

When you pronounce the voiceless consonants, hold your hand in front of your mouth. You should feel (and hear) a much stronger *puff* of air (aspiration) on the voiceless /p/, /t/, and /k/ than on voiced /b/, /d/, and /g/. You should feel (and hear) a much stronger *rush* of air on the voiceless /f/, /s/, and /g/ than on voiced /v/, /z/, and /dʒ/.

These final voiced and voiceless consonants are also confused. Listen to the difference, and then say the words.

▶ Start the Audio Program. ⌒

Voiceless	Voiced
1. /p/ co<u>p</u>	/b/ co<u>b</u>
2. /t/ nea<u>t</u>	/d/ nee<u>d</u>
3. /k/ bac<u>k</u>	/g/ bag
4. /f/ proo<u>f</u>	/v/ pro<u>v</u>e
5. /s/ pri<u>c</u>e	/z/ pri<u>z</u>e
6. /tʃ/ ri<u>ch</u>	/dʒ/ ri<u>dg</u>e

Vowels in the second column are longer. That is the most important difference. Listen to and repeat the word pairs. Make the vowels before final voiced consonants longer.

EXERCISE 24: IDENTIFYING VOICED AND VOICELESS CONSONANTS

Listen to the sentences. Underline the word that you hear. Then read the sentences aloud. ⌒

1. The audience was *cheering/jeering* the actors.
2. This is a *vast/fast* network.
3. She gave her son a little *pat/bat*.
4. There was a *mop/mob* in the lobby.
5. Don't you hear that *buzz/bus*?
6. Eugene's acting a little *tense/dense* this morning.
7. You have a lot of *fans/vans*.
8. What a nice *pear/bear*.
9. She has lovely little *girls/curls*.

10. Sam, who put that *dent/tent* in your car?

11. What was the *prize/price?*

12. He burned his *bridges/britches* behind him.

Practice aspiration (producing a puff of air) on these initial voiceless sounds: *professor, talked, took off, couldn't, cost, compete, prices.* Practice lengthening the vowel before these final voiced sounds: *food, good.* Now practice the words in the context of the response below. First listen to the response being read, then read it yourself. ⌒⌒

The professor talked about the success of supermarkets. They took off in the '50's for several reasons. One was a good selection of products—food, beauty products, magazines, and so on. Another reason was cost. Neighborhood groceries couldn't compete with their low prices.

Notes:

_____

_____

Difficulties with specific consonant sounds depend on the individual and the first language. Practices with a few of the more problematic sounds are given below. This little Listening Test will help you identify the sounds you need to practice.

Listening Test: Is it easy or hard to hear a difference? If hard, go to the exercise indicated below.

1. it's through – it's true   ☐ Easy   ☐ Hard   ☞ Exercise 29

2. a lot of math – a lot of mass   ☐ Easy   ☐ Hard   ☞ Exercise 29

3. pilot software – pirate software   ☐ Easy   ☐ Hard   ☞ Exercise 28

4. copy machine – coffee machine   ☐ Easy   ☐ Hard   ☞ Exercise 25

5. cash it – catch it   ☐ Easy   ☐ Hard   ☞ Exercise 26

6. in a vial – in a while   ☐ Easy   ☐ Hard   ☞ Exercise 27

Practice Hint: Refer to this Web site for animations and video about how to produce the sounds. Go to http://www.uiowa.edu/~acadtech/phonetics/about.html# and launch English Library. Use a mirror so you can imitate the speaker on the video.

EXERCISE 25: /p/ AS IN PAST VS. /f/ AS IN FAST

A. First, just listen to the speaker pronounce the pairs of words in the box. Then listen to the speaker say two words. If the speaker says the same two words (*peel-peel*), write S (same) in the blank. If the speaker says two different words (*peel-feel*), write D (different) in the blank. The first one is done for you as an example.

B. Next, underline the words that you hear in the sentences. The first one is done for you as an example.

C. Afterwards, go back and pronounce the words in the box and read all the sentences aloud.

► Now start the Audio Program. 🎧

A. | peel – feel   copy – coffee   pin – fin   pact – fact |

    1. _S_   2. ____   3. ____ 4. ____

B. 1. Can we agree on this *pact* / *fact*?

    2. Sometimes you have to *pace* / *face* yourself.

    3. I saw Amy driving *past* / *fast*.

    4. Where's the new *copy* / *coffee* machine?

    5. He *peels pine* / *feels fine*.

    6. Toss that letter in this *pile* / *file*.

    7. This is a new *pad* / *fad*.

    8. He had to face his *peers* / *fears*.

EXERCISE 26: /ʃ/ AS IN WA<u>SH</u> VS. /tʃ/ AS IN WAT<u>CH</u>

A. First, just listen to the speaker pronounce the pairs of words in the box. Then listen to the speaker say two words. If the speaker says the same two words (*wish-wish*), write S (same) in the blank. If the speaker says two different words (*wish-which*), write D (different) in the blank.

B. Then underline the words that you hear in the sentences.

C. Afterwards, go back and pronounce the words in the box and read all the sentences aloud.

► Now start the Audio Program. 🎧

A. | shop – chop   shoes – choose   wish – which   mush – much |

    1. ____   2. ____   3. ____   4. ____

B. 1. This is a good block for *shopping* / *chopping*.

    2. Don't *wash* / *watch* that pot.

    3. He tried to *cash* / *catch* it.

    4. He *shows* / *chose* his paintings.

    5. He just wants his proper *chair* / *share*.

    6. Hey! There's a *chip* / *ship* in that bottle!

SPEAKING

7. My dog hates *leashes / leaches.*

8. She bumped her *shin / chin.*

9. There were so many toppings that there wasn't *much room / mushroom* on the pizza.

10. I had a dream about three *wishes / witches.*

EXERCISE 27: /v/ AS IN <u>V</u>ERSE VS. /w/ AS IN <u>W</u>ORSE

A. First, just listen to the speaker pronounce the pairs of words in the box. Then listen to the speaker say two words. If the speaker says the same two words (*worse-worse*), write S (same) in the blank. If the speaker says two different words (*verse-worse*), write D (different) in the blank.

B. Next, underline the words that you hear in the sentences.

C. Afterwards, go back and pronounce the words in the box and read all the sentences aloud.

▶ Now start the Audio Program. 🎧

A.

verse – worse	vial – while	vest – west	very – wary

1. _____   2. _____   3. _____   4. _____

B. 1. This type of *vine / wine* was brought to California from Italy.

2. You call this *verse / worse*?

3. He'll bring the money *in a while / in a vial.*

4. He was pointing to the *vest / west.*

5. I was talking with my cousin *Vinnie / Winnie.*

EXERCISE 28: /l/ AS IN <u>L</u>IGHT VS. /r/ AS IN <u>R</u>IGHT

A. First, just listen to the speaker pronounce the pairs of words in the box. Then listen to the speaker say two words. If the speaker says the same two words (*late-late*), write S (same) in the blank. If the speaker says two different words (*late-rate*), write D (different) in the blank.

B. Next, underline the words that you hear in the sentences.

C. Afterwards, go back and pronounce the words in the box and read all the sentences aloud.

▶ Now start the Audio Program. 🎧

A.

late – rate	locks – rocks	long – wrong	collect – correct

1. _____   2. _____   3. _____   4. _____

B. 1. The teaching assistant was *collecting / correcting* the tests.

2. He wants to make the *light / right* choice, not the *long / wrong* one.

3. The lecture was about the *locks / rocks* in Panama.

4. In the late afternoon, *clouds / crowds* began to form.

5. The huge nests have three *looms / rooms.*

6. She put the *clock / crock* on the shelf.

7. They tried to *flee / free* the wild animals.

8. Can you *fly / fry* this?

Remember: *The tip of the tongue touches the roof of the mouth with /l/; the tongue tip does not touch with /r/.*

EXERCISE 29: /t/ AS IN THIN VS. /s/ IN SIN, /f/ IN FIN, AND /t/ IN TIN

A. First, just listen to the speaker pronounce the pairs of words in the box. Then listen to the speaker say two words. If the speaker says the same two words (*math-math*), write S (same) in the blank. If the speaker says two different words (*math-mass*), write D (different) in the blank.

B. Next, underline the words that you hear in the sentences.

C. Afterwards, go back and pronounce the words in the box and read all the sentences aloud.

▶ Now start the Audio Program. 🎧

A. | think – sink   math – mass   three – tree   both – boat   thought – fought |

1. ____   2. ____   3. ____   4. ____   5. ____

B. 1. Suddenly, Tony started to *think / sink.*

2. The council *thought / fought* about that issue all afternoon.

3. They found the *pass / path* through the mountains.

4. They had to call in *three / tree* surgeons to solve the problem.

5. A physicist must understand *math / mass.*

6. The general offered his *thanks / tanks.*

7. That's a nice *boot / booth.*

8. He didn't pick the right *theme / team.*

9. That's a *thick / sick* tree.

10. Will Dorothy be *free / three* on Saturday?

(H) Vowel Sounds

1	2	3	4	5	6	7	8	9	10	11	12	13	14	15
he	hit	may	get	mad	bird	cup	hot	too	good	no	law	fine	now	boy
/iʸ/	/ɪ/	/eʸ/	/ɛ/	/æ/	/ɜr/	/ʌ/	/ɑ/	/uʷ/	/ʊ/	/oʷ/	/ɔ/	/aɪ/	/aw/	/ɔɪ/

It is common to confuse "glided" and simple vowels.

▶ Glided vowels—the tongue moves toward the second sound; the second sound is represented by second symbol /ʸ/ or /ʷ/

▶ Simple vowels—tongue is motionless; one sound is represented by one symbol

Listen to the difference between glided and simple vowels, and then say the words.

▷ Now start the Audio Program. 🎧

Glided Vowels		*Simple Vowels*
/iʸ/ She's l<u>ea</u>ving there.	*vs.*	/ɪ/ She's l<u>i</u>ving there.
/eʸ/ He's worried about the d<u>a</u>te.	*vs.*	/ɛ/ He's worried about the d<u>e</u>bt.
/uʷ/ They p<u>oo</u>led it.	*vs.*	/ʊ/ They p<u>u</u>lled it.

Difficulties with specific vowel sounds depend on the individual and the first language. Practices with a few of the more problematic sounds are given below. The practices contrast glided and simple vowel sounds. This Listening Test will help you choose the sounds you need to practice.

Listening Test: Is it easy or hard to hear a difference? If hard, go to the exercise indicated below.

1. don't hit it – don't heat it ☐ Easy ☐ Hard ☞ Exercise 30

2. test it – taste it ☐ Easy ☐ Hard ☞ Exercise 31

Practice Hint: Refer to this Web site for animations and video about how to produce the sounds below: http://www.uiowa.edu/~acadtech/phonetics/about.html# and launch English Library. Use a mirror so you can imitate the speaker on the video.

EXERCISE 30: /iʸ/ AS IN HEAT VS. /ɪ/ AS IN H<u>I</u>T

A. First, just listen to the speaker pronounce the pairs of words in the box. Then listen to the speaker say two words. If the speaker says the same two words (*seen-seen*), write S (same) in the blank. If the speaker says two different words (*seen-sin*), write D (different) in the blank.

B. Next, underline the words that you hear in the sentences.

C. Afterwards, go back and pronounce the words in the box and read all the sentences aloud.

▷ Now start the Audio Program. 🎧

A.

seen – sin	leave – live	steal – still	feel – fill

   1.   2.   3.   4.

B. 1. That was a *cheap / chip* shot.

     2. I keep trying to *feel / fill* the empty space.

     3. The students want to *leave / live* here.

     4. They need better *heaters / hitters.*

     5. When the men came around the bend, they saw the *sheep / ship.*

EXERCISE 31: /eʸ/ AS IN LATE VS. /ɛ/ AS IN LET

A. First, just listen to the speaker pronounce the pairs of words in the box. Then listen to the speaker say two words. If the speaker says the same two words (*men-men*), write S (same) in the blank. If the speaker says two different words (*main-men*), write D (different) in the blank.

B. Next, underline the words that you hear in the sentences.

C. Afterwards, go back and pronounce the words in the box and read all the sentences aloud.

▶ Now start the Audio Program. 🎧

A.

wait – wet	late – let	main – men	date – debt

   1.   2.   3.   4.

B. 1. She sure has a lot of *dates / debts.*

     2. Don't you think that there's too much *paper / pepper?*

     3. Gus had a *pain / pen* behind his ear.

     4. Give that sauce a *test taste / taste test* to see if it needs more salt.

     5. Cynthia likes to wear *lace / less* in the summer.

Remember: *The front of the tongue moves up with /eʸ/; it is motionless with /ɛ/.*

Pronunciation Resources

If you want additional pronunciation help, see these pronunciation text/audio packages also published by Heinle/Cengage:

▶ *Well Said Intro* by Linda Grant (for high-beginning to mid-intermediate proficiency)

▶ *Well Said: Pronunciation for Clear Communication,* 2nd ed., by Linda Grant (for high-intermediate to advanced proficiency)

COMMUNICATIVE ACTIVITIES FOR SPEAKING

Activity 1

Interview Bingo   **_Individual Activity_**

Bingo is a game of chance. A "caller" selects numbers at random and calls them out. Players see if that number matches the numbers on a card such as this one (each player has a unique card) and if it does, they mark that square.

B	I	N	G	O
1	24	37	48	61
9	17	42	53	68
6	28	Free Space	60	75
13	25	36	59	74
7	18	31	56	70

The first player who marks all the squares in a vertical, horizontal, or diagonal line wins and calls out "Bingo!" For example, if the caller selected B1, I 17, G59, and O70, the player with the card above would win the game. (The center space on the card is a "free space.")

Interview Bingo is played in much the same way but with slightly different rules. You must find a classmate or another person in your school who can answer "Yes" to a certain question. When you do, you mark the corresponding square with the person's name. As in regular Bingo, the first player who marks all the squares in a vertical, horizontal or diagonal line wins.

Here is an Interview Bingo card with some of the questions filled in.

B	I	N	G	O
_____ can speak three languages.	_____ owns a pet that is not a dog or a cat.	_____ doesn't drink coffee.	_____ reads the newspaper every day.	_____ doesn't own a car.
_____ has visited at least five countries.				
_____ has been skiing.		FREE SPACE		
_____ is an only child (no brothers or sisters).				
_____'s favorite color is red.				

SPEAKING

You can begin your game by thinking up additional categories based on what people have done, what they like, what they can do, etc. The coordinator can write these on the board or type them on a computer. You can then use a word processor to create unique cards for each student.

Begin by asking questions of your classmates. For example, you might turn to the person behind you and ask, "Can you speak three languages?" You can use one name only one time per card. You can also ask questions of students in other classes as well as people who work at your school.

As in regular Bingo, the first player who marks all the squares in a vertical, horizontal, or diagonal line wins and shouts "BINGO."

Activity 2

Travel Agents   *Class/Small-Group Activity*

As a class, decide on an "ideal vacation." You may want to go to a resort destination such as Tahiti or Bermuda, an international city such as Paris or London, or a place of natural beauty such as the Grand Canyon or the Swiss Alps.

Next, meet in small groups and plan your trip. Each person in each group has $3,000 to spend on a one-week trip. Using the Internet, find the best (not necessarily the cheapest!) airfares, hotels, tours, and so on. Then plan a day-by-day schedule for your trip. (Don't forget to leave some time to relax—it's a vacation, after all.)

After you have prepared a budget and a schedule, groups will report back to the class about the trip they have planned. The class will vote on which group has planned the best vacation.

Activity 3

Newscast   *Small-Group Activity*

If possible, watch some local news broadcasts on television at home. Pay attention to the format of news programs.

For this activity, the class will divide into groups of four. Each group should bring a local or a campus newspaper. Read a number of news stories as well as sports stories and the weather forecast for the next few days.

Two students from each group will act as news "anchors" (reporters) and give brief summaries of three or four news stories. These can be international, national, local, or school news stories. One student should also report on sports events and one should give a weather report.

If possible, videotape these newscasts. (You may want to do only one group per day so that groups will have different stories to report.)

After all the groups have given their newscasts, discuss as a class which group gave the most interesting, informative, and polished report.

Activity 4

Investment Group   *Class/Small-Group Activity*

Divide into small groups. One person from each class should bring a copy of the financial section of a newspaper to class (or you can visit a site on the Internet that lists stock prices). Each group has $10,000 to spend. Decide on a portfolio of stocks. Which companies should your group invest in and how many shares of stock should you buy?

Every week for the next four weeks, check your stocks as a group. See if they have gone up or down and if your group is making money or losing money. If some of your stocks are not performing well, you can sell some stocks and buy new ones, but there is a $25 "broker's fee" for each buy-sell transaction.

At the end of four weeks, each group reports to the class on what investments they made and why, and on how much money they made or lost. The group with the most profits wins.

Activity 5

Great Debates   *Small-Group Activity*

Debate is a great way to prepare for both of the Independent Speaking Tasks. It enables you to practice the language of expressing opinions and making paired choices. When giving rebuttals, you practice planning and giving responses quickly.

A week or so before the debate, divide into groups of six students. Then each group of six should divide into two teams of three students each. The two teams should first meet together to decide on a "proposition" (a debate topic) and to decide which team will be the negative team and which will be the affirmative team. Propositions can be on any topic that has two arguable sides. They should be in the form of an affirmative statement. Some sample propositions:

▶ The TOEFL test is a good measure of a student's English ability.

▶ Our school should use pass/fail grades in place of letter grades.

▶ Violent or dangerous sports such as boxing should be banned.

▶ The Olympics should be held at a single permanent site every four years.

▶ The powers of the United Nations should be greatly increased in order to prevent war.

▶ Visas should not be required to enter any country; a valid passport should be sufficient.

Each team should then meet independently to research the proposition. You may need to use a library or the Internet. Then agree on roles for individual team members.

Debate Format	
Introduction of debaters and proposition (moderator)	
Affirmative (Yes) Team	*Negative (No) Team*
1. First constructive speech Student 1 (3 minutes) →	2. First rebuttal Student 1 (1 minute) ↓
4. First rebuttal Student 2 (1 minute) ↓	3. First constructive speech ← Student 2 (3 minutes)
5. Second constructive speech Student 2 (3 minutes) →	6. Second rebuttal Student 3 (1 minute) ↓
8. Second rebuttal Student 3 (1 minute) ↓	7. Second constructive speech ← Student 1 (3 minutes)
9. Summary and conclusion Student 3 (2 minutes) →	10. Summary and conclusion Student 3 (2 minutes)
Audience asks questions and votes	

During a *constructive speech,* a speaker gives points in favor of his side of the debate. For example, if the proposition is "the TOEFL test is a good measure of a student's English ability," the first affirmative constructive speech presents and develops two or three points that support the idea that the TOEFL test *is* a good measure of a student's English ability. During the first negative rebuttal, the debater for the negative team challenges the points that the speaker made in the first affirmative constructive speech. In the first negative constructive speech, the speaker presents and develops new ideas that suggest that the TOEFL test is *not* a good measure of a student's English ability.

A moderator introduces the members of each debate team and states the proposition. After the debate, the non-debating students in the audience should ask questions and vote on the winner of the debate.

Activity 6

Urban Legends Game   *Individual/Class Activity*

Urban legends are a kind of folklore consisting of stories about modern life. They are often thought to be true, according to the people that tell them. Many of them are frightening horror stories, but some are just funny. Storytellers often try to make these stories personal. They might say, "This really happened to a friend of mine" or "This is a true story. It happened to my cousin's boyfriend." Urban legends spread quickly all over the world, usually from person to person (often by e-mail). Not all urban legends are false (although most of them are), but even the true ones are often distorted or exaggerated.

There are a number of Internet sites that list urban legends. Generally the sites classify stories according to their truthfulness: Some are listed as true, some as false, some as possibly true. Here's a list of some of these sites.

www.snopes.com/

urbanlegends.about.com/

www.warphead.com/urbanlegends/

netsquirrel.com/combatkit/

science.howstuffworks.com/urban-legend.htm

www.bellaonline.com/site/urbanlegends/

Visit one of these urban-legend sites (Snopes is probably the largest and best known) and choose a legend that interests you. Take notes on the story (don't print it out). Report your story to the class. Each student in the class then writes down TRUE, FALSE, or POSSIBLY TRUE. The student with the greatest number of correct guesses wins.

Activity 7

Survivor Supplies   *Small-Group Activity*

Imagine that your group must spend a year on a deserted tropical island in the middle of the Pacific Ocean. Before you leave, you can buy supplies and equipment that you will need during the year. You have $10,000 to spend. Visit Internet sites that sell this type of merchandise and make a list of the items you would buy for your stay on the island.

Afterwards, report to the class what your group has decided to buy and why. The class votes on which group has best equipped themselves with their $10,000 purchase.

Activity 8

Talk Show   *Small-Group Activity*

If possible, watch some talk shows on television at home and pay attention to the format of these programs.

The class will divide into small groups. One student acts as the host or hostess. Other students are guests, and they play the role of some famous person they are familiar with: an actor, musician, athlete, politician, etc. The host/hostess asks the guests relevant questions, and the guests may chat among themselves.

If possible, videotape the talk shows. After all the groups have performed, discuss as a class which group's show was the most interesting.

Activity 9

Television Report   *Class/Pairs Activity*

The coordinator or instructor will record an English-language show from television: a comedy, a segment from a "news magazine" show, etc.

The class will divide into two groups, A and B. Group B leaves the room while Group A watches the first half of the show and takes notes. Group B then comes back and forms pairs with students from Group A. Using their notes, Group A students give their partners a summary of what they saw. Group A students then leave the room while Group B students watch the second half of the show and take notes on it. The Group A students then return to the room. Then Group B students tell their partners about the second half of the program. Afterwards, all the students can watch the program together.

Activity 10

Write Your Own Independent Speaking Items   *Individual Activity*

Using the items in Lessons 15 and 16 as models, write either a Personal Preference or a Paired Choice prompt. Try to make your prompt as realistic as possible. Afterwards, exchange your prompt with a partner. Your partner can prepare and give a brief response based on your prompt.

Activity 11

Student Teacher   *Individual Activity*

Your instructor/coordinator will choose several students to teach one of the six Speaking lessons in this text. Students who are selected will go back and study "their" lesson in detail, write out a lesson plan, and give a five- to ten-minute presentation on the lesson.

SPEAKING

GUIDE TO WRITING

ABOUT WRITING

The fourth section of the TOEFL iBT tests your ability to produce clear, well-organized academic writing. This section contains two writing tasks: an Integrated Writing Task and an Independent Writing Task.

Writing Section				
Task	Based on	Type of Task	Timing	Recommended Length
Integrated Writing Task	Reading passage and related lecture	Summarize and compare lecture and passage.	Reading: 3 minutes Lecture: 2 minutes Writing: 20 minutes	200 words
Independent Writing Task	Your own knowledge and experience	Give your opinion of an issue or express your personal preference	30 minutes	300 words

INTEGRATED VERSUS INDEPENDENT TASKS

For the **Integrated Writing Task,** you read a short passage, then listen to a short lecture on the same topic. You then write an essay summarizing the lecture and the reading passage and showing the relationship between them. You may take notes on both the reading passage and the lecture. The Integrated Task asks you only to summarize and paraphrase the information that you read and hear. You should *not* express your own opinion of the issues and you should *not* bring in any information from outside the passage and the lecture (just as in the Integrated Speaking Tasks).

The **Independent Writing Task** requires you to read a prompt (a topic) and express your opinion in your response. Your response is based entirely on your own knowledge and experience (just as in the Independent Speaking Tasks).

ENTERING AND EDITING THE WRITING TASKS ON THE COMPUTER

This is the only part of the test in which you will primarily use the keyboard rather than the mouse. You must type your responses on the computer. If you do not have much typing experience, or you are not used to typing in English, you will need to practice as much as possible. You can also download typing lessons from the Internet. Type "free typing tutorial" into your browser and take your pick.

The program for typing the essay is a simplified version of a standard word processing program. For the most part, all you need to do is type in the essay. Unfortunately, there are no "spell check" or "grammar check" tools! In fact, there are only the simplest editing tools: Cut, Paste, and Undo. If you are not familiar with how to use these commands, read the section below.

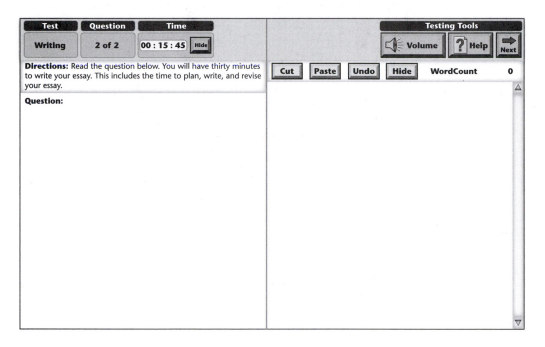

CUT AND PASTE

You can use Cut and Paste to move part of your essay to another place in the essay. To use these two commands, you must first highlight text (select something that you have written). To do this, use the mouse to position the blinking cursor at the beginning of the text that you want to select and then click once. Then, holding down the left-click button on the mouse, slowly move the cursor over the text that you want to select. This highlights the text. In other words, the selected text will appear in white letters on a black background.

Cut Paste Undo

This is sentence 1. This is sentence 2. This is sentence 3. This is sentence 4. This is sentence 5.

Now, click Cut. What happens? The highlighted text disappears.

Cut Paste Undo

This is sentence 2. This is sentence 3. This is sentence 4. This is sentence 5.

You can stop here if you just want to get rid of Sentence 1. But if you want to move it, use the mouse to position the blinking cursor where you want the text to go, and then click Paste. The text now magically reappears in the new location.

Cut Paste Undo

This is sentence 2. This is sentence 3. This is sentence 4. This is sentence 5. This is sentence 1.

UNDO

The Undo command will reverse any commands or typing you have just done. For example, if you cut and paste a sentence from one paragraph to another and then decide you want the sentence back where you first had it, click on Undo and the sentence will go back to where it was before you did the cut and paste. You can also undo the last sentence that you typed. If you decide that using the Undo command was a mistake, just click Undo again.

MOVING AROUND THE ESSAY

There are a number of commands you can use to move the cursor from one part of your essay to another.

- ▶ You can use the four arrow keys to move the cursor up, down, left, or right.
- ▶ You can move to the end of the line that you are working on by hitting the End key, or to the beginning of the line by hitting the Home key.
- ▶ You can move up and down through the essay quickly (one screen at a time) by hitting the PgUp or PgDn key.
- ▶ You can move to a new line (where you have not typed) by hitting the Enter key.

DELETING TEXT

There are a number of ways you can delete (erase) text.

- ▶ You can delete a character to the left by hitting the Backspace key.
- ▶ You can delete one character to the right by hitting the Del (delete) key.
- ▶ You can delete a large piece of text by highlighting it and clicking on the Cut icon. It will disappear.
- ▶ If you decide you didn't really want to delete something, you can click on the Undo icon.

Tactics for Writing

- As with all sections of the test, be familiar with the directions. When the general directions and the directions for each task appear, click on the Dismiss Directions button and begin working right away.

- Give yourself time to think about the question or the prompt and to plan your essay by taking notes and writing a simple outline.

- Time management is important. Keep your eye on the clock as you work on both tasks.

- Divide both responses into an introduction, body, and conclusion.

- Use signal words to indicate transitions. Signal words can be used to join paragraph to paragraph and sentence to sentence.

- Give yourself time to check your responses for problems with content, grammar, and mechanics.

- Don't exit either task early. Keep checking your response for problems until you run out of time.

WRITING

ABOUT THE INTEGRATED WRITING TASK

Skills that are required to write an effective Integrated Response include the abilities to

- ▶ understand and take notes on the spoken lecture and the reading passage
- ▶ find the main idea and key points of both the lecture and the passage
- ▶ understand what the question asks
- ▶ summarize the material in the lecture and the passage
- ▶ paraphrase the material in the lecture and the passage (rewrite it in your own words)
- ▶ synthesize (connect) the material in the lecture and the passage
- ▶ write a clear, well-organized, coherent response to the question
- ▶ use correct written grammar and appropriate vocabulary
- ▶ edit your response for content, grammar, and mechanics (spelling, punctuation, capitalization, etc.)
- ▶ word-process (type) your response

You will first see the general directions for the Writing Section, then the specific directions for the Integrated Task. You should dismiss both sets of directions immediately. (You will already be familiar with the directions because of your work in *The Guide*.) Next you will see the reading passage. You will then hear the lecture. After that, you will see the question and write a response to it.

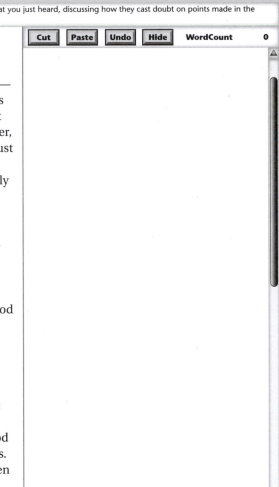

Directions: You have 20 minutes to plan and write your response. Your response will be judged on the basis of the quality of your writing and on how well your response presents the points in the lecture and their relationship to the reading passage. Typically, an effective response will be 150 to 225 words.

Question: Summarize the main points made in the lecture that you just heard, discussing how they cast doubt on points made in the reading. You can refer to the reading passage as you write.

Cut   Paste   Undo   Hide   WordCount   0

Recently, there have been protests and demonstrations here on our campus, as well as at many other places, about medical research performed on animals—what is sometimes called *vivisection*. It is natural that people are concerned about the ethical treatment of animals. However, most of us agree that our top priority must be the reduction of *human* suffering.

Of course, it is possible, and absolutely necessary, to keep animal suffering to a minimum. Animal researchers use anesthesia whenever possible to reduce pain and keep their animals clean, comfortable, and healthy. It *is* possible to conduct experiments using animals without inflicting cruelty on animals.

The problem is, there simply is no good substitute for animal experimentation. Other techniques can be used to test drugs, but none is as effective as testing them on animals. Humans and chimpanzees share about 99% of their genes. Other animals also share the same basic life functions as humans, and the reactions of these animals to drugs are a good guide to the reactions of human patients. The usefulness of animal testing has been shown over and over. For example, the

THE PASSAGES AND LECTURES

The reading passages in the Integrated Writing Section are 200 to 300 words long—about half as long as those in the Reading Section. The passage can be about any academic subject—the physical sciences, life sciences, social sciences, arts, humanities, etc. The passage typically describes a theory, a concept, a problem, an issue, a system of classification, or a process. You have three minutes in which to read the passage, and you may take notes as you read.

The lecture lasts about two minutes, and note taking is allowed. The lecture is on the same topic as the passage.

You hear the lecture only once; you may not go back to it. However, while you are working on the response to the question, you will be able to reread the passage and look at your notes.

The most common relationship between the passage and the lecture is one of opposition. The lecture refutes (contradicts) the ideas of the passage or takes a different view of the ideas in the passage. Typically, the passage presents three positive points, while the lecture presents three corresponding (related) negative points. Or the passage may give three negative points, while the lecture presents three corresponding positive points.

Passage	*Lecture*
Statement of the Concept	**Restatement of the Concept**
1. Positive point	1. Corresponding negative point
2. Positive point	2. Corresponding negative point
3. Positive point	3. Corresponding negative point

Passage	*Lecture*
Statement of the Concept	**Restatement of the Concept**
1. Negative point	1. Corresponding positive point
2. Negative point	2. Corresponding positive point
3. Negative point	3. Corresponding positive point

Here is an example of a typical passage and lecture. First read a passage from a textbook in a secondary education class.

WRITING

Two principal types of tests are used in secondary schools, and, in fact, in all types of schools. One type is the objective test. Different types of questions can be asked on objective tests: multiple choice, fill in the blanks, true-or-false, matching, and so on. The other type of test is the subjective test, or essay test. This type of test asks students to write essays on one or more topics.

Although objective tests continue to be used in many high school classrooms, today the essay test is most often used because it tests a higher level of understanding. Objective tests simply test a student's ability to memorize dates, names, and other facts. Essay tests, on the other hand, require students to organize and analyze, to see relationships, and to present information in a clear way. This is a much more realistic task than any presented in an objective test. In real life, of course, questions will not be presented in a multiple-choice format; instead, they require students to organize and communicate their thoughts in a logical way.

Essay exams emphasize to high school students the need to express themselves clearly and effectively in writing. Everyone agrees this is a necessary skill for all students at all levels and in all disciplines. And if teachers in history classes give essay exams, they encourage their students to apply themselves with more enthusiasm in their composition classes. Besides, as a bonus for the busy teacher, essay exams take far less time to construct than objective tests.

Now listen to a lecture in a secondary education class. You may read along with this lecture as you listen, but on actual tests, the lecture will not be written out.

▶ Now start the Audio Program. 🎧

Professor

"Now, as your textbook points out, there are two types of tests: objective and essay. Your textbook author takes a pretty strong stand in favor of essay tests, doesn't he? Well, I happen to agree with some of his ideas. I have nothing against essay tests, and they *do* get at different things than, uh, objective tests do. They test students' ability to think critically, to . . . uh, solve problems. That's why I generally include a couple of essay questions in every test *I* give. But I also use multiple-choice items.

It's true that, objective tests check your memorization skills—but what's wrong with that? Sometimes, in some classes at least, you need to memorize basic facts and information!

And it's also true that . . . that essay tests emphasize writing skills. It's true—and it's part of the problem! Good writers can get good grades on essay tests even if they don't know very much about the topic.

And as far as saving time—sure, it may take less time to write essay tests. But . . . it takes a *lot* more time to grade them. Not only that, but you really should grade *all* the essays at the same time, because . . . well, studies show that the same teacher will grade the same essay differently at different times. To be fair, you've got to grade all the tests at one sitting. Now, with a small class, this isn't a big problem, but if you have a large class . . . well, it's a lot easier to grade objective tests, and lots of times, you can have them machine graded.

So . . . when you start teaching, and giving tests yourself . . . by all means, use essay tests, but for some classes, for some material, for some situations . . . objective tests, or combinations of objective and essay tests, may be best."

Here's an outline of the sample passage and lecture:

Passage	*Lecture*
Statement of the Concept: There are two main types of tests, objective and essay. Essay tests are preferable.	**Restatement of the Concept: There are two types of tests, objective and essay. Essay tests are useful, but so are objective tests.**
1. Positive point: Essay tests test a higher type of understanding (objective tests assess only memorization skills.)	1. Corresponding negative point: Sometimes it is necessary to test memorization.
2. Positive point: Essay tests develop writing skills.	2. Corresponding negative point: Good writers can do well on essay tests without knowing content.
3. Positive point: Essay tests are easy to write.	3. Corresponding negative point: Essay tests take a long time to grade.

Although the relationship between the lecture and the passage is generally one of opposition, you may sometimes see other relationships. The passage may present a generalization and the lecture may give examples that support this generalization or counter-examples that weaken the generalization. Another possibility: The passage may present a problem and the lecture a solution that successfully (or unsuccessfully) deals with the problem. Still another possibility: The passage may describe a cause and the lecture may describe the effects (either expected or unexpected) of that cause.

NOTE TAKING

You are allowed to take notes on both the reading passage and the lecture. Since you will hear the lecture only once, it is important to take good notes on the lecture. You need to identify the main idea of the lecture and the three to four key points that support this main idea in order to compare and contrast these with the main idea and corresponding key points that are made in the reading passage.

For more information about note taking, see the Listening Tutorial on Note Taking (pp. 381–393).

THE QUESTIONS

The questions ask you to write about the relationship between the passage and the lecture. Because the most common relationship between the passage and the lecture is one of opposition, most questions ask you to show how the points in the lecture refute (contradict) those in the passage.

Question:

Summarize the main points made in the lecture that you just heard, discussing how they cast doubt on points made in the reading. You can refer to the reading passage as you write.

Note: Cast doubt on *means "show the weakness of" or "contradict."*

Question:

Summarize the main points made in the lecture that you just heard, explaining how they differ from the points made in the reading. You can refer to the reading passage as you write.

When the relationship between the passage and lecture is not one of opposition, you will see other types of questions.

Question:

Summarize the main points made in the lecture that you just heard, explaining how they illustrate the points made in the reading. You can refer to the reading passage as you write.

Question:

Summarize the main points made in the lecture that you just heard, explaining how they may solve the problem described in the reading. You can refer to the reading passage as you write.

Question:

Summarize the main points made in the lecture that you just heard, explaining how they are the results of the event described in the reading. You can refer to the reading passage as you write.

THE RESPONSE

Your response should be at least 200 words long.

The Integrated Writing Task does *not* ask you to give your opinion. It asks you only to report on the information in the passage and the lecture and to connect the information from the two sources.

When you write your response, you must **summarize** the information in both the reading passage and the lecture. The most important information to include is the main ideas and the key points of both passage and lecture. Sometimes you may want to include important examples that illustrate the key points, but you should not include unimportant details. Even when you are reporting the key points in the passage, you should shorten and simplify the information from the passage and lecture in your response.

You must **paraphrase** (*rewrite in your own words*) the information in the passage. Whenever possible, you need to use different vocabulary and different grammatical structures in your response.

You must **cite** information that you use in your response. In other words, you must indicate whether the information comes from the passage or the lecture. (*According to the lecture, . . . ; The passage says that . . .*).

You must **synthesize** *(connect)* the information from the passage and the lecture. The best way to do this is to first determine which key point from the passage corresponds to which key point in the lecture. Then explain the relationship between the key points. You will probably want to use one short paragraph to explain each point in the passage and contrast it with the corresponding point from the lecture. You'll need to use transitions and special language that shows comparison and contrast or other relationships.

Remember: It is important that you balance information from the passage and the lecture more or less equally.

An outline of a typical Integrated Writing Task might look like this:

Introduction
Paragraph 1
    Main topic of the passage and the lecture
    Main idea of the passage
    Main idea of the lecture, and how it relates to that of the passage

Body
Paragraph 2
    Key point 1 of the passage
    Important example or supporting information
    Corresponding key point of the lecture, and how it relates to that of the passage
    Important example or supporting information

Paragraph 3
    Key point 2 of the passage
    Important example or supporting information
    Corresponding key point of the lecture, and how it relates to that of the passage
    Important example or supporting information

Paragraph 4
    Key point 3 of the passage
    Important example or supporting information
    Corresponding key point of the lecture, and how it relates to that of the passage
    Important example or supporting information

Conclusion
Paragraph 5
    Brief summarizing sentence or two

THE WRITING PROCESS

You have twenty minutes in which to prepare the response for the Integrated Writing Task. You should divide your time more or less like this:

Pre-Writing

(two to three minutes)
    Read the question.
    Look over your notes and think about the passage and the lecture.
    Write notes.
    Make an informal outline.

Writing the Integrated Task

(about fifteen minutes)

Checking Your Writing

(two to three minutes)
    Look for and correct problems with content, grammar, and mechanics.

SCORING THE INTEGRATED WRITING TASK

Both writing tasks are scored by two human (not computer) raters who score them *holistically*. In other words, your responses are not judged according to individual mistakes that you make but by the overall effectiveness of your writing.

Your score on the Integrated Task depends not just on the quality of your writing but also on how well your essay demonstrates your understanding of the passage and the lecture and the relationship between the two.

Scores on the Integrated Writing Task range from 0 to 5. Each rater will give you a "whole number" score (0, 1, 2, 3, 4, 5). Your score will be the mean of the two ratings. If one rater gives you a 4, for example, and another rater gives you a 5, you will receive a score of 4.5. If the two raters give you scores that are quite different, a third rater will score the response.

The following **rubric** (set of guidelines or standards) is similar to the one used by ETS to score the Integrated Writing Task.

Score	Explanation of Score
5	Includes all of the important information from the passage and accurately relates it to the important information in the lecture. The response is clearly organized. A variety of sentence structures is used and a sophisticated vocabulary is employed. There may be infrequent grammatical and mechanical errors. These mistakes will not make it difficult to understand the ideas and relationships that the writer describes.
4	Includes most of the important information in the passage and relates it to the most important information in the lecture. Some information may be presented somewhat inaccurately or imprecisely. There may be some problems with vocabulary, grammar, or mechanics, but these problems generally do not interfere with an understanding of the writer's ideas or the relationships he or she describes.
3	Includes important information from the passage and relates it to information in the lecture. However, the response has one or more of the following problems: <ul><li>The relationship between key points in the passage and the lecture is not accurate or complete or is stated in very general terms.</li><li>One of the key points is not mentioned in the response.</li><li>Language mistakes may sometimes make it difficult to understand the writer's ideas or the relationships he or she describes.</li></ul>
2	The essay attempts to include some relevant information from the passage and the lecture but has one or both of the following problems: <ul><li>Omits or shows a complete misunderstanding of the points in the lecture or passage or the relationship between them.</li><li>Language mistakes make the writer's ideas or the relationships he or she describes generally difficult to understand.</li></ul>

continued

WRITING

1   Has one or both of the following problems:

- Provides little or no information from either the passage or the lecture.
- Language mistakes are so frequent that it is impossible to understand the writer's ideas.

---

0   Only repeats sentences from the reading passage, writes on an entirely different topic, writes in a language other than English, or does not write a response at all.

SAMPLE RESPONSES

Following are five responses for an Integrated Writing Task, each illustrating one of the five scores. They are based on the passage and lecture given on pages 568–569.

Response 1

The reading stated that there are two main types of tests used in secondary education. One type is objective tests. Objective test often consist of multiple choice, matching, fill in the blank and etc. The other is subjective test, namely the essay test.

The author of the reading emphasized subjective tests. The reading said objective tests mostly test memory, where as essays test problem solving skills. This was the first reason the author favors objective test. In the future, students will need the skills for subjective tests, not objective test. A second reason in favor of objective reasons is that they train students to write well. This skill, writing, is necessary, everyone agrees. And a third reason: it is easier for teachers to construct these tests.

The professor said that the author of textbook takes too stong position for subjective test. Objective tests test memorization, but this is not a problem. Sometimes you need good memorization. He also said that good writers can get good grades even though they don't know the information. Furthermore, he told that essay tests take less time to contruct, yet they take alot more time to grade, and its bettter for the teacher to grade all tests at the same time to be fair. It takes much less time to grade objective tests. You can even have them graded using technology such as a computer scanner.

He concluded that both types of test have their places in testing at schools. The best way depends on the purpose of the test. Sometimes, he said, use objective test, sometimes use subjective, sometimes blend the two.

Score: ___5___

Comments: This response accurately chooses three important points from the lecture and coherently contrasts these ideas with the relevant points presented in the reading. There are occasional grammatical or usage mistakes, but they do not make it difficult to understand the writer's ideas. The response is well organized, and signal words (*the first reason . . . a second reason . . . and a third reason . . . furthermore*) make it easy to follow the author's logic.

Response 2

In the speaker's opinion about the subjective test, he differs on the fact that those are not always the best option in secondary schools. He thinks that sometimes students need to memorize important information like dates in history or important facts given by the professor. In addition, the objective tests take less time to correct.

On the other hand, as the writing part says, subjective tests can be good to help students to solve problems,, learn multiple idioms, give them a higher level of understanding. Although the speaker says that if the students are good writers this can be easy for them eventhough they don't know enough about the subject. Also if the class is small the correction can be easy, but if not, it can be very hard for the professor. It actually should take one day to correct them.

In conclusion the speaker thinks that depending on the situation and times, they should use one of the other or the combination of both.

Score: __4__

Comments: This response integrates most of the important ideas from the reading and the lecture. However, a lack of organization makes it somewhat difficult to follow the writer's reasoning. This response also lacks the sophistication of vocabulary and grammar required for a score of 5.

Response 3

According the article, there is two principle type of test in secondery school. What they are? One type is objective test. This type have the multiple choice and true-false question. In objective test, there can only be one answer. They test your memorization and bassic facts.

Other type is subjective test (essey test). The lecture say that these are the most important type test. Essey test good for testing writing skills. Good writers can get good grades on essey test. Also essey test help you to think clear. But for teachers it take more time to grade them. On essey test there not just one good answer.

In my opinion, the best of these two types of test the essey test. When I was student in the secondery school my favorite type test taking is the essey. I think the article is right this type test help thinking skill and writing skill. However, also true as the presentre say that take a lot of time to grade the esseys for the teacher.

Score: __3__

Comments: The response contains quite a few grammatical mistakes, especially involving singular/plural noun use and subject/verb agreement. There are some spelling mistakes (*bassic* and *essey*, for example, should be *basic* and *essay*) and the range of vocabulary use is quite limited. There is some repetition of ideas and the writer offers an opinion about testing even though an opinion is not asked for in an Integrated Writing response. However, the errors do not generally obscure the writer's meaning, and the writer accurately reports some of the important ideas from both the article and the lecture.

Response 4

The reading passage is talking about two types of test:

1. the objective and
2. the subjective (essay)

Objective test apply different kind of questions like multiple choice, fill in the blank and so. One obsevation on the objective test is the continuation of the use in many high school. Subjective tests, or essay test, have more freedom to write essays on one of more topics. Actually the essay test is more frequently use because test a higher level of understanding. Another requirement is, the students have to be organize and analize. This is more realistic tesk than any presented in multiple choice format. Also require students to communicates their thoughts in very organized way.

Score: 2

Comments: This response focuses almost entirely on information in the reading. There is very little if any information taken from the lecture, and there is no effort to relate the two and no development of ideas. Significant parts of the response are taken directly from the reading. There are also problems with grammar, vocabulary, and spelling.

Response 5

Essay exam the teacher can use some class as writing or in small class is use too lot in school. now essay test use offen in the school about one or more topic.essay exam need writing in all disipline. as a bonus if teacher

Score: 1

Comments: The response does not provide any meaningful information from the lecture and little from the reading. The response is so short that there is no development of ideas and the writing itself is fragmentary, mainly consisting of phrases. In fact, the language level is so low that it is difficult to understand the writer's basic point.

EXERCISE: SCORING THE RESPONSE

DIRECTIONS: Here are three responses based on the passage and lecture on pages 568–569. Read each response and, using the scoring rubric on pages 573–574, decide what score (1 to 5) you would give each response.

This exercise will help you develop the ability to score your own responses.

Response 1

How can the teachers check the students' ability in high school? The so-called objective tests and the subjective test (essays) are the most popular tests used in high schools.

The article says that the subjective test verifies the ability to organize thoughts, analyze events in a logical way, and involves a greater participation. It teaches the student valuble skills in writing. The essay tests also easier to write and grade.

The presenter says that a good essay does not imply that the student knows the events that she is writing about. The same person can write different essays at different times. The objective test shows the persons' ability for memorization of facts, etc. It is especially suitable for a large class, and computers can be used to grade them.

Maybe the best way to verify the student's ability is to combine the two forms, testing both ther ability to express themselves in logical way and their knowlege of the events.

Score: _____

Comments: _____

_____

_____

_____

Response 2

Two type of test use in secondery school. These are first object test and second subject test. Object test multipe choice, true false, atc. Subject test best, students have to write assay in the topic. Object test used for tested student about memorized and abilty. assay test used for improve students about writing skill. is a necessary using for all student level because assay test improve student with writing contruct. Student write assay have to know and learn all of the english's grammars and vocabularies.

Score: _____

Comments: _____

_____

_____

_____

Response 3

The teacher agreed with idea that essay test are great way to express students ideas clearly and effectively. However, he is against the reading about objective tests.

He said that checking the memorization by objective tests is not useless. Getting facts and information is also an important base for education.

Further, he mentioned that if student is good at writing essays but not memorization, teachers cannot check his/her knowledge. Because such a student can write well witout enough information. Moreover, that may lead poor basics of education in his/her future.

He advocates that essay tests should be done at the same place and time because students should be in the same conditions for reading information. Besides he said its more ideal to measure students ability by the combination of both types of tests

Score: _____

Comments: _____

_____

_____

_____

Strategies for the Integrated Task

- Take notes on key points and important examples as you read the passage and listen to the lecture. Use your notes to connect the two sources of information and to write a brief, informal outline.
- Summarize and paraphrase the material from the lecture and the passage.
- Balance the amount of material that you take from the lecture and the amount that you take from the passage.
- Synthesize (connect) and cite the material from the lecture and the passage (*According to the passage, . . . ; The professor says that . . .*).

INTEGRATED WRITING PREVIEW TEST
DIRECTIONS

▶ Now start the Audio Program. 🎧

This Writing Section tests your ability to write academic English. It consists of two writing tasks.

   The first writing task is an "integrated" task. It involves reading a short passage and listening to a short lecture on the same topic. You will then have twenty minutes in which to write a response based on the information in the passage and the lecture.

   Now read the directions for the first writing task.

DIRECTIONS: Take three minutes to read the short passage on the following page. You may take notes as you read.

   After three minutes, start the Audio Program. You will hear a lecture on the same topic as the reading. Again, you may take notes as you listen.

   You will have twenty minutes to write your response. Your response should include information from both the reading and the lecture.

   Your essay will be rated on the completeness and accuracy of your response as well as on the correctness and quality of your writing. A typical response should be 150 to 225 words.

   You may use your notes and look at the reading passage as you write. (During the actual exam, you can view the reading passage on the computer screen after the lecture is over.)

   You will have twenty minutes in which to finish the Integrated Writing Task. If possible, you should write your response on a computer.

Recently, there have been protests and demonstrations here on our campus, as well as at many other places, about medical research performed on animals—what is sometimes called *vivisection.* It is natural that people are concerned about the ethical treatment of animals. However, most of us agree that our top priority must be the reduction of *human* suffering.

Of course, it is possible, and absolutely necessary, to keep animal suffering to a minimum. Animal researchers use anesthesia whenever possible to reduce pain and keep their animals clean, comfortable, and healthy. It *is* possible to conduct experiments using animals without inflicting cruelty on animals.

The problem is, there simply is no good substitute for animal experimentation. Other techniques can be used to test drugs, but none is as effective as testing them on animals. Humans and chimpanzees share about 99% of their genes. Other animals also share the same basic life functions as humans, and the reactions of these animals to drugs are a good guide to the reactions of human patients. The usefulness of animal testing has been shown over and over. For example, the very basis of modern medicine, the germ theory—the idea that diseases are caused by micro-organisms—was proven by the great French scientist Louis Pasteur by experimenting on chickens and pigs and other farm animals. The effectiveness of penicillin was tested on rabbits and mice, and insulin, which is used to treat diabetes, was tested on dogs. Animal testing remains a crucial tool today. It is simply immoral to risk the lives of humans when a drug or procedure can be tested on non-humans.

Notes on the reading:

_____

_____

_____

_____

▶ Now start the Audio Program. Now listen to part of a lecture in a biology class. 🎧

Notes on the lecture:

_____

_____

_____

_____

_____

_____

_____

> **Now get ready to answer the question.**
> **Remember, you may look back at the reading passage.**
> **You may also use your notes to help you.**
> **You have twenty minutes to prepare and write your response.**

Question:

> Summarize the main points made in the lecture that you just heard, discussing how they cast doubt on points made in the reading. You can refer to the reading passage as you write.

_____

_____

_____

_____

_____

_____

_____

_____

_____

_____

_____

_____

_____

_____

_____

_____

_____

LESSON 21
TAKING NOTES AND PLANNING THE INTEGRATED RESPONSE

To get a good score on the TOEFL iBT, you will need to take accurate notes on the lecture for the Integrated Writing Task. It's also a good idea to take notes on the reading passage even though you will be permitted to look at the passage as you are writing your response.

To write your response, you will need to take notes on the following information:

▶ The main idea of both the lecture and the passage
▶ Key supporting points from the lecture
▶ Corresponding key points from the passage
▶ Important examples or supporting ideas for these key points
▶ Conclusions (if any)

The principles for taking notes for the lecture in this section are the same as those for the Listening Section and the Speaking Section. You need to write down only important points, and you need to use abbreviations and symbols. For more information on note taking, review the Listening Tutorial on Note Taking at the end of the Listening Section (pp. 381–393).

Here are some sample notes based on the reading passage and lecture in the Integrated Writing Preview Test.

Sample reading passage:

> Recently, there have been protests and demonstrations here on our campus, as well as at many other places, about medical research performed on animals— what is sometimes called *vivisection.* It is natural that people are concerned about the ethical treatment of animals. However, most of us agree that our top priority must be the reduction of *human* suffering.
>
> Of course, it is possible, and absolutely necessary, to keep animal suffering to a minimum. Animal researchers use anesthesia whenever possible to reduce pain and keep their animals clean, comfortable, and healthy. It *is* possible to conduct experiments using animals without inflicting cruelty on animals.
>
> The problem is, there simply is no good substitute for animal experimenta-tion. Other techniques can be used to test drugs, but none is as effective as testing them on animals. Humans and chimpanzees share about 99% of their genes. Other animals also share the same basic life functions as humans, and the reactions of these animals to drugs are a good guide to the reactions of human patients. The usefulness of animal testing has been shown over and over. For example, the very basis of modern medicine, the germ theory—the idea that diseases are caused by micro-organisms—was proven by the great French scientist Louis Pasteur by experimenting on chickens and pigs and other farm animals. The effectiveness of penicillin was tested on rabbits and mice, and insulin, which is used to treat diabetes, was tested on dogs. Animal testing remains a crucial tool today. It is simply immoral to risk the lives of humans when a drug or procedure can be tested on non-humans.

You might take these notes on the passage:

Sample notes on the reading passage:

Protests, demonstrations agnst med. resch (= vivisection)

Top priority: reduc. human suffering

keep animal suffering to minum.

     anesthes.

       clean, comfortable, hlthy

can conduct anim. experiments w/out cruelty

Problem: no subs for anim. experim.
   humans/chimps share 99% genes other anim. share basic life functs.
   Usefulness shown over & over
      e.g., germ theory—Pasteur: chickens, pigs
                       penicillin: rabbits, mice
                       insulin: dogs
Immoral to risk human life when can test on non-hum.

Listening Lecture

▶ Now start the Audio Program. Now listen to part of a lecture in a biology class. 🎧

Sample notes on the listening lecture:

Prof. opposes anim. experim.
   Maybe import. drugs like penicillin used anim experi but . . . maybe would
   have been discovered anyway . . . and many drugs invented w/out anim
   experim.
                  e.g. quinine   ether   aspirin
   and if some drugs had been tested on anim, maybe never develop:
      e.g., morphine kills pain in humans but stimul. cats
   And there are substitutes for testing . . .

> *e.g. cultiv human tissue   clinic studies etc.*
> *Anim NOT treated well e.g. not enough anesthesia   abuse*
> *Anims can't give consent—therefore immoral*

After you have seen the passage and heard the lecture, you will have twenty minutes in which to complete the response. You should spend the first few minutes planning what you will write. Here are the most important things to do during this planning time:

1. Find the main idea, key points, and important examples in the lecture and in the passage. Underline these points in your notes.

2. Decide which of the points in the passage correspond with those in the lecture. You may want to mark these 1, 2, 3, etc., in your notes. (These points may not appear in the same order in the passage as they appear in the lecture.)

Here are the sample notes on the passage and the lecture from the Preview Test with the main points underlined and numbered:

Sample notes on the passage:

> *Protests, demonstrations agnst med. resch (= vivisection)*
> *Top priority: reduc. human suffering*
> *keep animal suffering to minum.   (1)*
> *   anethes*
> *   clean, comfortable, hlthy*
> *can conduct anim. experiments w/out cruelty*
> *Problem: no sub for anim. Experim.   (2)*
> *   humans/chimps share 99% genes other anim. share basic life functs.*
> *   Usefulness shown over & over   (3)*
> *   e.g., germ theory—Pasteur: chickens, pigs*
> *   penicillin: rabbits, mice*
> *   insulin: dogs*

Sample notes on the lecture:

Prof. opposes anim. experim.   uneth.
   Maybe import. drugs like penicillin used anim experi BUT . . . maybe
   would have
      been discovered anyway . . . and many drugs invented w/out anim
      experim.   (3)
                                    e.g. quinine   ether   aspirin
      and if some drugs had been tested on anim, maybe never develop:
                           e.g., morphine kills pain in humans but stimul. cats
      And there are substitutes for testing . . .   (2)
            e.g. cultiv human tissue   clinic studies etc.
      Anim NOT treated well e.g. not enough anesthesia   abuse   (1)
      Anims can't give consent—. . immoral

Sample Outlines

Next you will want to write an informal outline. Although there are several ways to organize your response, the most effective way is to make a "point-by-point" comparison of the three different points in the passage and in the lecture. You can begin with the first point of the passage or the first point of the lecture.

The following outline begins with the first point of the passage.

Introduction
Paragraph 1
   Main topic of the passage and the lecture
   Main idea of the passage
   Main idea of the lecture, and how it relates to that of the passage

Body
Paragraph 2
   Key point 1 of the passage
      Important example or supporting information
   Corresponding key point of the lecture, and how it relates to that of the passage
      Important example or supporting information

Paragraph 3
   Key point 2 of the passage
      Important example or supporting information
   Corresponding key point of the lecture, and how it relates to that of the passage
      Important example or supporting information

Paragraph 4
    Key point 3 of the passage
        Important example or supporting information
    Corresponding key point of the lecture, and how it relates to that of the passage
        Important example or supporting information

Conclusion
Paragraph 5
Brief summarizing sentences

The next outline begins with the first point of the lecture:

Introduction
Paragraph 1
    Main topic of the lecture and passage
    Main idea of the lecture
    Main idea of the lecture, and how it relates to that of the passage

Body
Paragraph 2
    Key point 1 of the lecture
        Important example or supporting information
    Corresponding key point of the passage, and how it relates to that of the lecture
        Important example or supporting information

Paragraph 3
    Key point 2 of the lecture
        Important example or supporting information
    Corresponding key point of the passage, and how it relates to that of the lecture
        Important example or supporting information

Paragraph 4
    Key point 3 of the lecture
        Important example or supporting information
    Corresponding key point of the passage, and how it relates to that of the lecture
        Important example or supporting information

Conclusion
Paragraph 5
Brief summarizing sentences

Here is an outline of the response for the Integrated Task in the Preview Test (beginning with the first point of the passage).

Sample Outline

Intro: Main Topic: Animal research
        Author of passage supports: reduce hum. suffering
        Speaker opposes; unethic.
1. Passage says important to minimize suffering
    Anesth.   clean conditions, etc.
    Lect says: in practice, NOT humane
    terrible diseases, chemicals   Inadeq anesth   abuse
2. Psge: no sub. for animal testing
        humans/chimps share most genes   other animals useful too
    Lect: many sub. for anim. testing
        growing tissue samples, etc.
3. Psge: Important theories, drugs devel. by anim. rsch.
        Pasteur, germ theory   penicillin etc.
    Lect: Maybe discover drugs, etc. anyway
        Many drugs devel. w/out anim. rsch.
                e.g. aspirin
        Some drugs, if tested on animals, might NOT have been devel.
                e.g. morphine
Conclu: Psge: Immoral to test humans when non-humans avail.
        Lect. Must give consent for rsch; anim can't consent

EXERCISE 21.1

FOCUS: Taking notes on passages and lectures for the Integrated Writing Task.

DIRECTIONS: Give yourself three minutes to read each passage. Take notes on the main idea, key points, and important examples. Then listen to the lecture and take notes on the main idea and corresponding key points and important examples. The first one is done for you as an example.

Task 1

Read the following passage (3 minutes).

In 1991, an international treaty (which was fully implemented in 1998) was signed by most of the world's nations regulating activities in Antarctica. The treaty designates Antarctica as a "natural reserve, devoted to peace and science." It bans all economic activity except for fishing and tourism. It also upholds the provisions of a 1959 treaty banning military activity of any kind.

Should some exploration and exploitation of Antarctic resources be permitted? Antarctica is a huge and almost completely unpopulated continent. Only the coastal areas support any kind of animal or plant life. Well-regulated oil and gas exploration and extraction should be allowed. Yes, the conditions would be extremely difficult. Yes, precautions must be put in place to avoid environmental problems. But remember: It was once believed that oil and gas from northern Alaska and from the North Sea could not be exploited safely, or indeed, at all. However, these two oil fields have proved to be extremely valuable sources of energy. With our current and future levels of technology, resources can be harvested from Antarctica with little or no danger.

And yes, it would be expensive to build and maintain the infrastructure needed to drill, pump, and transport oil and gas from Antarctica. Probably at present these operations would not pay for themselves. However, as fossil fuels become scarcer, and as demand for fossil fuels increases, it will become more and more economical.

At present, a small, elite group of scientists and environmentalists controls the future agenda for an entire continent, declaring it entirely off-limits for economic development. If Antarctica can provide necessary resources for a rapidly growing world population, then we should be able to have an intelligent debate about the costs and benefits involved.

WRITING

Notes on the reading passage:

1991: treaty regulating activ. in Antarctica

"nat'l reserve; peace & science" bans all but fishing, tour'm

Antarct. huge, unpop. only life in coastal areas

Gas. oil explor, extract shld be allowed w/ precautions

Alaska, N. Sea difficult too, but those were devel'd

W/ current, fut. technol, resources could be taken from Antarct.

Would be expensive but in future wld pay for self as prices ↑

At present elite grp scientists, environ'ists control Antarc—shld have debate

▶ Now start the Audio Program. Listen to part of a lecture in an ecology class. 🎧

Notes on the lecture:

○

Most of Antarct lifeless . . . but fragile

Only coast supports life—but oil & gas must be shipped from coasts

  danger of icebergs hitting supertanker   penguins, whales, etc.

Conditions in Antarct very harsh, much worse than Alas, N. Sea

  Spkr has personal exper.

  VERY expensive

better to invest in altern source, H fuel, e.g.

Treaty not just agrd to by scientists—also gov't reps from all over world,

  keeping Antarct safe from politicians, corps a good idea

○

Task 2

Read the following passage (3 minutes).

All of us have seen science fiction movies about space aliens coming to Earth in flying saucers. Sometimes these aliens are nice, but sometimes they are terrible creatures who want to invade us. Or we've seen movies about Earth astronauts who journey to other worlds and make contact with alien civilizations. Some science fiction movies would have you believe that we live in a very crowded universe, full of races similar to us. But you must remember that science fiction is *fiction,* based on imagination. In reality, I'm afraid, we live in a very lonely universe indeed. The only place where we are likely to find intelligent life forms is on Earth—and even here, they are pretty rare!

When we look up at the nighttime sky, we see thousands of stars. We all want to think that some must have planets like Earth and that one of those planets must have intelligent beings looking up at the stars from *their* world. However, astronomers tell us that most of those stars are very different from ours. They generate too much radiation or heat, or they are too big or too small to have planets with earth-like conditions. We've learned, in recent decades, that there are planets around other stars, but what are the odds of discovering a planet at *exactly* the right distance from its star? If our Earth were a little bit closer to its star, a little bit farther away, a little hotter, a little colder, if it didn't have water or just the right type of atmosphere, then humans could never have evolved here. And even if there are planets where life *has* evolved, why do we suppose it is intelligent life? There are millions of species of life on Earth, and yet only one of them can truly be considered intelligent.

If the universe really is full of intelligent alien species, why haven't we heard from them? We have been broadcasting radio signals into space for almost a hundred years and television signals for sixty years. These signals move at the speed of light. Surely, if the universe is populated, there should be an intelligent race within a hundred light years or so who has heard our radio or seen our television shows. Why haven't these aliens beamed us a message telling us to please send some better programming?

I'm afraid it's because no one is out there listening.

Notes on the reading passage:

_____

_____

_____

_____

_____

_____

_____

WRITING

▶ Now start the Audio Program. Listen to part of a lecture in an astronomy class. 🎧

Notes on the lecture:

_____

_____

_____

_____

_____

_____

Task 3

Read the following passage (3 minutes).

In the general Australian election of 1922, the percentage of Australian citizens who voted dropped to 59%. Australians became alarmed at this low voter turnout, and by 1924, a law was passed that made it compulsory for all adult Australians to vote. Today, about 94% of eligible voters in Australia vote, even though the penalty for not voting is mild. Voting has simply become a habit for Australians. Voting has been mandatory in Belgium since 1892, and in Argentina since 1914. It is mandatory in Greece, Luxembourg, Thailand—in fact, in about 20% of all democratic nations. All countries that have compulsory voting laws enjoy high voter turnout. However, in countries in which voting in non-compulsory, such as the United States and the United Kingdom, average voter turnout in national elections is what it was in Australia in 1922—about 60%.

Why should citizens of a country be required to vote? American president Thomas Jefferson, who was instrumental in writing the U.S. Declaration of Independence, said that government derives its authority from the consent of the governed. I believe that if you do not vote, you are not giving your active consent to be governed. In other words, if a nation's citizens don't vote, their government loses its legitimacy.

Voting, to me, is much like taxation. Both should be considered obligations, not privileges. A nation as a whole relies on all its citizens fulfilling their obligations to pay taxes, and cannot operate without tax revenue. Similarly, a nation depends on the consent of the citizens and should be able to rely on its citizens to vote

Notes on the reading passage:

_____

_____

_____

_____

_____

_____

▶ Now start the Audio Program. Listen to part of a lecture in a political science class. 🎧

Notes on the lecture:

_____

_____

_____

_____

WRITING

_____

_____

Task 4

Read the following passage (3 minutes).

Around 11,000 years ago, at the end of the last Ice Age, the mammoth elephants of North America had it pretty good. Food was plentiful, the herds were strong, the climate was favorable. However, something happened and in a short time, all the mammoths disappeared. What happened? These are the three main theories explaining their extinction.

The most likely theory involves "man vs. mammoths." Around 11,000 years ago, the first humans, a group called the Clovis People, came across the land bridge connecting Asia and North America. According to University of Arizona scientist Paul Martin, the Clovis People were clever hunters. They were accompanied by dogs and were armed with spears with sharp stone points. According to Professor Martin, the Clovis People hunted the mammoths to extinction.

A second theory is that climactic changes killed off the mammoths. During the Ice Age, humans may have found the climate harsh, but it was perfect for wooly mammoths. The weather seldom changed; it was cold and damp all year round, and there were no seasons. Little by little, however, the climate grew warmer, the glaciers receded, and the moist air became drier. Seasons emerged, plant life changed. Grassy plains became deserts, and the wooly mammoths died of starvation, according to this theory.

A third theory, advanced by Ross McPhee of the American Museum of Natural History, is that mammoths were destroyed by diseases brought by humans from the Old World. The microbes may have been carried by the lice in their hair or by the fleas on their dogs. The mammoths had no resistance. This plague may have passed from mammoth to mammoth and from herd to herd, destroying the species.

Notes on the reading passage:

_____

_____

_____

_____

_____

_____

▶ Now start the Audio Program. Listen to part of a lecture in a geo-science class. 🎧

Notes on the lecture:

_____

_____

_____

_____

_____

_____

Task 5

Read the following passage (3 minutes).

In 1965, President Lyndon B. Johnson said, "Art is a nation's most precious heritage. For it is in our works of art that we reveal to ourselves and to others the inner vision which guides us as a nation." These days, however, it is becoming more and more difficult for artists to support themselves financially. This is especially true for experimental artists, whose art does not have as much commercial potential as that of other artists. In Europe, there is broad governmental support for the arts. Here in the U.S., artists have been funded by a combination of private and governmental funds. However, government funding for the arts has remained stable or even dropped in recent years.

Throughout history, great artists from da Vinci to Tchaikovsky have been supported by patrons. Today, few people contribute directly to individual artists, but artists still need support. It takes time to create great art. What is required is funds in the form of government grants for artists to live on while they develop as artists or complete artistic projects.

Besides, when the government spends money on the arts, it is making a good investment. According to a study conducted by economists at the Georgia Institute of Technology, federal, state, and local governments spent about $3 billion dollars on the arts over a ten-year period. However, the arts generated $134 billion in economic revenue and $24 billion in taxes during those ten years. This is a tremendously good return on investment.

Notes on the reading passage:

_____

_____

_____

_____

_____

_____

▶ Now start the Audio Program. Listen to part of a lecture in an art class. 🎧

Notes on the lecture:

_____

_____

_____

_____

_____

_____

Task 6

Read the following passage (3 minutes).

According to a 2005 study by an association of pediatricians, the overall negative effects of television on children outweigh the positive effects. This comes as no surprise to those of us in the field of juvenile psychology who have seen the effects on children of more and more television watching.

The researchers analyzed standardized test results and television viewing habits of 1,700 children. Children aged 6 to 7 who watch more than three hours of TV a day score significantly lower on reading and short-term memory tests than children who watch little or no television.

Another study showed us that, on the average, children spend more time watching television than doing any other activity except sleeping. They spend more time watching television than at school! All television shows, even educational shows, replace activities in children's lives that parents value more, such as studying, reading, and playing sports.

Another problem is that kids who watch television are physically inactive. Not only are they inactive, but they tend to snack a lot. Advertisements for inappropriate foods encourage them. This leads to children being overweight and out of shape.

Studies such as this one simply confirm what most psychologists already know. As far as children are concerned, television viewing is harmful and should be severely limited or altogether eliminated from their lives.

Notes on the reading passage:

_____

_____

_____

_____

_____

_____

▶ Now start the Audio Program. Listen to part of a lecture in a psychology class. 🎧

Notes on the lecture:

_____

_____

_____

_____

_____

_____

EXERCISE **21.2**

FOCUS: Connecting corresponding key points and preparing a simple outline for the Integrated Writing task.

DIRECTIONS: Using the notes that you took on the passages and the lectures in Exercise 21.1, complete the outlines in this exercise. The first one is done for you as an example.

Outline for Task 1

Main topic:
Treaty regulating economic activity in Antarctic

Main idea of the lecture:
No developm't in Antarctica; continue following treaty

Main idea of the passage:
Change treaty; exploration, extraction of oil & gas should be considered.

Key Point 1 + supporting information from the lecture:
Oil & gas must be shipped from coast
Dangerous because of icebergs; great damage to environ. if oil tanker damaged
(penguins, whales, e.g.)

Key Point 1 + supporting information from the passage:
Antarct. a huge continent; only coast has life

Key Point 2 + supporting information from the lecture:
Conditions much worse than Alas, N. Sea
Spkr has personal experiences in Antarc.

Key Point 2 + supporting information from the passage:
Difficult conditions, but so were Alaska, North Sea
Today & in future have better technol. for extracting oil, etc.

Key Point 3 + supporting information from the lecture:
Too expensive, even if oil prices go up
Better to invest in alternate fuel (H fuel, e.g.)

Key Point 3 + supporting information from the passage:
Expensive, but in the future, gas prices will go up

Conclusion (if any):
Lecture:
Not only scientists, gov't reps from all over world agree to treaty—good idea to
protect Antarc from politicians, multi-nat'l corps
Passage:
Only scientific elite now control fut. of Antarct.—devel should be debated

WRITING

Outline for Task 2

Main topic:

_____

_____

Main idea of the passage:

_____

_____

Main idea of the lecture:

_____

_____

Key Point 1 + supporting information from the passage:

_____

_____

Key Point 1 + supporting information from the lecture:

_____

_____

Key Point 2 + supporting information from the passage:

_____

_____

Key Point 2 + supporting information from the lecture:

_____

_____

Key Point 3 + supporting information from the passage:

_____

_____

Key Point 3 + supporting information from the lecture:

_____

_____

Conclusion (if any):
   Passage:

_____

_____

_____

   Lecture:

_____

_____

_____

Outline for Task 3

Main topic:

_____

_____

Main idea of the passage:

_____

_____

Main idea of the lecture:

_____

_____

Key Point 1 + supporting information from the passage:

_____

_____

Key Point 1 + supporting information from the lecture:

_____

_____

Key Point 2 + supporting information from the passage:

_____

_____

Key Point 2 + supporting information from the lecture:

_____

_____

Key Point 3 + supporting information from the passage:

_____

_____

Key Point 3 + supporting information from the lecture:

_____

_____

Conclusion (if any):
    Passage:

_____

_____

_____

    Lecture:

_____

_____

_____

WRITING

Outline for Task 4

Main topic:

_____

_____

Main idea of the passage:

_____

_____

Main idea of the lecture:

_____

_____

Key Point 1 + supporting information from the passage:

_____

_____

Key Point 1 + supporting information from the lecture:

_____

_____

Key Point 2 + supporting information from the passage:

_____

_____

Key Point 2 + supporting information from the lecture:

_____

_____

Key Point 3 + supporting information from the passage:

_____

_____

Key Point 3 + supporting information from the lecture:

_____

_____

Conclusion (if any):
   Passage:

_____

_____

_____

   Lecture:

_____

_____

_____

Outline for Task 5

Main topic:

_____

_____

Main idea of the passage:

_____

_____

Main idea of the lecture:

_____

_____

Key Point 1 + supporting information from the passage:

_____

_____

Key Point 1 + supporting information from the lecture:

_____

_____

Key Point 2 + supporting information from the passage:

_____

_____

Key Point 2 + supporting information from the lecture:

_____

_____

Key Point 3 + supporting information from the passage:

_____

_____

Key Point 3 + supporting information from the lecture:

_____

_____

Conclusion (if any):
   Passage:

_____

_____

_____

   Lecture:

_____

_____

_____

WRITING

Outline for Task 6

Main topic:

_____

_____

Main idea of the passage:

_____

_____

Main idea of the lecture:

_____

_____

Key Point 1 + supporting information from the passage:

_____

_____

Key Point 1 + supporting information from the lecture:

_____

_____

Key Point 2 + supporting information from the passage:

_____

_____

Key Point 2 + supporting information from the lecture:

_____

_____

Key Point 3 + supporting information from the passage:

_____

_____

Key Point 3 + supporting information from the lecture:

_____

_____

Conclusion (if any):
   Passage:

_____

_____

_____

   Lecture:

_____

_____

_____

LESSON 22
SUMMARIZING, PARAPHRASING, CITING, AND SYNTHESIZING FOR THE INTEGRATED WRITING RESPONSE

(A) Summarizing

When you give your response for Integrated Speaking Tasks, you should not simply repeat words from the passage or from lectures (see Lesson 20). The same is true when you write your response for the Integrated Writing Task. You should shorten and simplify the material that you read and hear (summarize it) and write it in your own words (paraphrase it).

As mentioned in Lesson 21, it is a good idea to take notes on both the passage and the lecture. When you take notes, you automatically summarize the material that you take notes on because you are writing down only key ideas and important supporting information. Therefore, when writing your response, you should use your notes and look back at the passage only when necessary.

Remember: When you write your response, you do not have to use all the examples from the passage or the lecture. Try to simplify sentences and condense information from two or three sentences into one. Eliminate any sentences, phrases, or words that are not necessary to explain the important information in the passage or lecture.

(B) Paraphrasing

You must also **paraphrase** the information in the passage and the lecture. In other words, you must express the ideas in the passage in your own words and using your own sentence structures. When you paraphrase information, you are really "translating" the author's English into your own English.

Again, by using your notes rather than the passage itself, you are less likely to take information word for word from the passage.

Here are some techniques for paraphrasing information:

1. Change word forms.

You can change nouns to verbs, verbs to nouns, nouns to adjectives, and so on. This process usually involves making other changes in sentence structure as well.

Examples:

When we look at a comparison between A and B . . .

When we *compare* A and B . . .

The noun *comparison* is replaced with the verb *compare.*

There are a *variety* of solutions to problem C.

There are *various* solutions to problem C.

The noun *variety* is replaced with the adjective *various.*

2. **Replace words or phrases with synonyms.**

   X is not *allowed.*

   X is not *permitted.*

Permitted is a synonym for *allowed.*

   Project Y was *almost completed.*

   Project Y was *nearly finished.*

The phrase *nearly finished* is synonymous with *almost completed.*

Note: *It is not a good idea to use synonyms for concept words, technical terms, or "proper nouns" (words that begin with capital letters, such as names).*

   Example: The *International Science Foundation* is investigating the effects of *gamma rays.*

In the sentence above, you would *not* paraphrase International Science Foundation (proper noun) or *gamma rays* (technical term).

3. **Change the grammar.**

   Trained scientists *performed* this research.

   This research *was performed by* trained scientists.

The active verb *performed* is replaced by the passive verb *was performed by.* (For more information on verbs, see the Writing Tutorial on Grammar, Point 5, pp. 720–721.)

Note: *Try to avoid replacing too many active verbs with passive verbs; active verbs are preferable because they are stronger than passive verbs.*

   Several computer programs can be used to solve this problem.

   There are several computer programs that can be used to solve this problem.

A *there + to be . . .* pattern is used in place of a subject + verb pattern.

   It's easy *to use* A.

   Using A is easy.

The gerund *using* is substituted for the infinitive *to use.*

   This A, *which is one* of the most powerful Zs in the world, has . . .

   This A, *one* of the most powerful Zs in the world, has . . .

An appositive (noun phrase) is used in place of a relative clause.

   Study Y, *which was conducted* by sociologists in 2004, shows that . . .

   Study Y, *conducted* by sociologists in 2004, shows that . . .

A past participle is used to *reduce* (shorten) a relative clause. (For more information on participles, see the Writing Tutorial on Grammar, Point 6, pages 723–724.)

4. Reverse negatives.

A is *not as easy as* . . .

A is *harder than* . . . .

A comparative phrase (*harder than*) is used in place of a *not* + *as* . . . *as* . . . phrase.

It's not uncommon to see Z . . .

It's common to see Z . . .

A double-negative phrase such as (*not uncommon*) is replaced by a word with a positive meaning (*common*).

The *least expensive* B . . .

The *cheapest* B . . .

The negative superlative phrase *least expensive* is replaced by a superlative word with the same meaning, *cheapest.*

5. Change the word order.

For many years, people have believed A.

People have believed A *for many years.*

The prepositional phrase *for many years* is moved from the beginning of the sentence to the end of it.

After this problem has been solved, work on X can continue.

Work on X can continue *after this problem has been solved.*

The adverb clause *after this problem has been solved* is moved to the end of the sentence.

6. Change sentence connectors.

Although there is a lot of evidence to support theory Y, not all scientists believe it.

There is a lot if evidence to support theory Y; *however,* not all scientists believe it.

The transition word *however* is used in place of the adverb-clause marker *although.*

There are some dangers involved in B; *therefore,* researchers must be very cautious.

Because there are some dangers involved in B, researchers must be very cautious.

The adverb clause marker *because* is used in place of the transition word *therefore.*

Below are several sentences taken from the reading for the Preview Test and some notes from the lecture. Following this selection are sentences from sample responses that summarize and paraphrase the information in the reading and lecture.

WRITING

Sample

Read these sentences from the passage:

The usefulness of animal testing has been shown over and over. For example, the very basis of modern medicine, the germ theory—the idea that diseases are caused by micro-organisms—was proven by the great French scientist Louis Pasteur by experimenting on chickens and pigs and other farm animals. The effectiveness of penicillin was tested on rabbits and mice, and insulin, which is used to treat diabetes, was tested on dogs.

Sample notes:

Usefulness shown over & over
  e.g., germ theory—Pasteur: chickens, pigs
            penicillin: rabbits, mice
            insulin: dogs

▶ Now start the Audio Program. Listen to part of a lecture in a biology class. 🎧

Sample notes:

Maybe import. drugs like penicillin used anim experi <u>but</u> . . . maybe would have been discovered anyway . . . and many drugs invented w/out anim. experim.

e.g. quinine   ether   aspirin

<u>and</u> if some drugs had been tested on anim., maybe never develop:

e.g., morphine kills pain in humans but stimul. cats

Sample Summaries/Paraphrases

Passage:

Again and again, we've seen that animal testing is useful. Louis Pasteur developed the germ theory, a foundation of modern medicine, by means of animal testing. Important drugs such as penicillin and insulin were discovered by doing research on animals as well.

Lecture:

Although some important drugs were first tested on animals, it is possible that these drugs would have been developed anyway. And other useful drugs such as aspirin and quinine did not depend on animal research. If some drugs had first been tested on certain animals, they probably would never have been approved for humans. Consider morphine, for example. For humans, morphine is a pain-killer, but it has the opposite effect on cats.

WRITING

Notice that both summaries/paraphrases omit certain details and examples, and they are shorter than the original versions. Notice also that both responses use some of the methods given above to paraphrase the material: different word forms (*useful/usefulness*, for example); replacing words and phrases with synonyms (*over and over/again and again*); changing grammatical structures (*The germ theory . . . was proven by . . . Louis Pasteur/ Louis Pasteur developed the germ theory*).

(C) Citing

When writing your response, it is important for you to **cite** information. In other words, you need to clearly identify which information comes from the passage and which information comes from the lecture. A number of structures can be used to cite information.

Structures for Citing

According to + noun

> *According to the passage,* A is true.
>
> B, *according to the author,* is also true.
>
> *According to the lecture,* C is no longer generally accepted.
>
> Y is a better method of solving this problem, *according to the speaker.*
>
> The author's ideas may be correct, *according to the professor,* but they are misleading.

Subject + verbs of reporting + *that* clauses
Clause, subject + verb of reporting
> Many verbs, including those listed below, are used to report information. (Remember: You need to **paraphrase** the information in the *that* clause.)

tell*	report	suggest	explain	conclude
say	argue	state	quote	remind*
indicate	cite	claim	discuss	inform*
explain	point out	mention	admit	

> The author *tells* us that *that* A . . .
>
> The lecturer *says that* B is always . . .
>
> The article *indicates that* C should probably . . .
>
> The writer *reports that* X may not . . .
>
> Y is not necessarily true, the speaker *argues.*
>
> The speaker *concludes,* therefore, that Z . . .
>
> The speaker *admits* that the author has a good point, but he thinks that . . .
>
> In her lecture, the speaker *cites* a study about X done by Professor Y.
>
> The author *quotes* Doctor Z, who says in an article, " _____ ."

---

*These verbs must be used with personal objects (the writer tells *us* that . . . the professor informs *us* that . . . the speaker reminds *the class* that . . .).

Personal subject + verb of thinking (*think, believe, know*) + *that* clause

> The professor *thinks that* . . .
>
> The lecturer *believes that* . . .
>
> The author *knows that* . . .

The verbs *ask* and *wonder* are used with indirect questions, not statements beginning with *that*.

> The professor *wonders* if C can really be true.
>
> The author *asks* when Project X will be finished.

Some verbs can be used only for **counterarguments** (arguments against an original argument): *not agree; disagree; reject; contradict; challenge; take a different view; dispute the fact that/the idea that/the theory that.*

> The author does *not agree* with idea A.
>
> The speaker *disagrees* with point X. He says that . . .
>
> The speaker also *disputes* the idea that X causes Y.
>
> The writer of the passage *rejects* the idea that Z is true. In fact, the writer says that . . .
>
> The professor *challenges* the author's theory about A.
>
> The speaker *denies* that B is true.

(D) Synthesizing

When writing your response, you must **synthesize** key points in the passage and key points in the lecture. Because most of the passages and lectures contain opposing ideas, you will typically be bringing together and contrasting different points of view. There are various transition words, adverb clause markers, and other sentence patterns you can use to show contrast.

Transition Words Showing Contrast

however; on the other hand; in contrast

> According to the paragraph from the textbook, A should sometimes be considered a Y; *however,* the professor indicates that A should always be classified as an X.
>
> The journal article says that B makes things clear. The speaker, *on the other hand,* believes that B actually makes matters more confusing.
>
> The lecturer tells us that C is highly effective but very expensive; *in contrast,* the author says that C is a complete waste of money.

WRITING

Adverb Clause Markers Showing Contrast

although; even though; while

> *Although* the professor believes that A is a good idea, the author of the passage thinks that B is a better one.
>
> According to the speaker, *even though* many experts agree that A is the best solution, there is some evidence that B will work too.
>
> The lecturer supports the idea that A is true, *while* the author thinks B is true.

Because the passage and the lecture often provide more than one idea or example supporting a point, you may also need to use structures that show **addition.**

Transition Words Showing Addition

Transition Words

moreover; furthermore; in addition; besides

> The professor informs us that A is a problem; *moreover,* B is a problem as well.
>
> The article indicates that X can be shown to be true in an experiment. *Furthermore,* Y can also be shown to be true in a similar experiment.
>
> There are many examples of Z, according to the passage. *In addition,* there are a number of examples of A.

Adverbs

too; also; as well

> The lecturer states that B is a common occurrence, and that C is *too.*
>
> The passage points out one of the weaknesses of plan X. It *also* points out several strengths.
>
> According to the reading, there was a recent study on the subject of X done in Japan. There have been some European studies done on this subject *as well.*

Verbs

go on to say; add

> The speaker first tells us A. She *goes on to say* that . . .
>
> The author states that X is essential. The author then *adds* that . . .

Sample Synthesis and Citations

According to the author, we've seen again and again that animal testing is useful. Louis Pasteur developed the germ theory, a foundation of modern medicine, by means of animal testing. Furthermore, important drugs such as penicillin and insulin were discovered by doing research on animals. However, the lecturer takes quite a different view of animal testing. The lecturer says that, although some important drugs were first tested on animals, she believes it is possible that these drugs would have been developed anyway. She goes on to say that other useful drugs such as aspirin and quinine did NOT depend on animal research. Moreover, if some drugs had first been tested on certain animals, they probably would never have been approved for humans. Consider morphine, for example. According to the lecturer, morphine is a pain-killer for humans, but it has the opposite effect on cats.

Notice that the writer of this sample cites information from both the passage and the lecture. The writer also uses an appropriate transition to contrast the information from the passage and the lecture (*However, the lecturer takes quite a different view . . .*).

EXERCISE 22.1

FOCUS: Summarizing and paraphrasing key points from passages and lectures.

DIRECTIONS: First, read the points taken from the reading passage and take notes. Then listen to the corresponding point given in a lecture and take notes. Use your notes to summarize and paraphrase the information that you read and hear. The first one is done for you as an example.

Task 1

Asteroids pose a great danger to every human on Earth. It was almost certainly an asteroid crashing into the earth that made the dinosaurs extinct. There have been several near-misses in recent years. Right now, there are only a few programs designed to detect potentially dangerous asteroids, and they are almost all in the northern hemisphere. Therefore, we need a huge international program to watch the skies at all times and from both hemispheres.

WRITING

Notes on the passage:

Asteroids = great danger
   Aster → dinos. extinct
   In recent yrs, sev. near-misses
   Now only few programs   all in N. Hemi.
   ∴ need int'l prog; both hemis

Summary/Paraphrase of the passage:

Asteroids might be very dangerous to all the people living on our planet. Probably the dinosaurs were killed off when an asteroid smashed into the earth. Recently asteroids have come close to hitting the Earth. There are no major programs designed to observe asteroids. Because of the danger, we need a comprehensive international program.

▶ Now start the Audio Program. Listen to part of a lecture in an astronomy class. 🎧

Notes on the lecture:

Aster do pose prob – but how much?
  large aster, global prob: 1 per 100,000 yrs
  Can't see all aster.   e.g., ones from direct. of the sun
  No way to destroy

Summary/Paraphrase of the lecture:

Asteroids *do* pose a danger, but how serious is this danger? An asteroid capable of causing global damage strikes the earth only about once every 100,000 years. With our current technology, we can't see all asteroids. We can't see one, for example, coming from the direction of the Sun. Even if we do see one, there is no way to destroy it before it hits the Earth.

Task 2

Two common forms of democratic government are the parliamentary system and the presidential system. One way in which the parliamentary system differs from the presidential system is that, under this system, power is concentrated in the elected assembly—the parliament. The executive branch is not separate from the parliament. The prime minister and the other ministers—the cabinet, in other words—are members of the assembly, and must often meet with parliament.

Notes on the passage:

_____

_____

_____

_____

_____

WRITING

Summary/Paraphrase of the passage:

_____

_____

_____

▶ Now start the Audio Program. Listen to part of a lecture in a political science class. 🎧

Notes on the lecture:

_____

_____

_____

_____

_____

Summary/Paraphrase of the lecture:

_____

_____

_____

Task 3

> Today, it is estimated that there are about 6,000 languages spoken in the world. However, many of these languages are spoken by an increasingly small number of speakers. Nearly half of them are considered endangered. One of the principal causes of this is the rise of English as a global language. English is increasingly the language of international entertainment (movies, television, and music) as well as technology, especially information technology. Almost 75% of all Internet Web sites are in English. English is a "killer language" that is forcing out the use of smaller languages.

Notes on the passage:

_____

_____

_____

_____

_____

Summary/Paraphrase of the passage:

_____

_____

_____

▶ Now start the Audio Program. Listen to part of a lecture in a linguistics class. 🎧

Notes on the lecture:

_____

_____

_____

_____

_____

Summary/Paraphrase of the lecture:

_____

_____

_____

Task 4

Most environmentalists agree that the best way to reduce our dependence on fossil fuels is to increase the use of renewable sources of energy. According to many environmentalists, wind power is a promising method of producing energy. And it's true that when electricity is produced by wind, there is no air pollution, no toxic or radioactive wastes from wind power. However, right now, we just can't claim that wind energy technology causes *no* environmental damage. Some wind energy sites—they're called *wind farms*—are very harmful to birds. The worst offender is a huge wind farm in California at a place called Altamont Pass—it's actually the second largest wind farm in the United States. Over 5,000 birds a year are killed by the hundreds of spinning blades. These birds include golden eagles, red-tailed hawks, and other rare predators. No more wind farms should be built until we can protect birds from the dangers of wind-powered generators.

Notes on the passage:

_____

_____

_____

_____

_____

Summary/Paraphrase of the passage:

_____

_____

_____

▶ Now start the Audio Program. Listen to part of a lecture in an ecology class. 🎧

Notes on the lecture:

_____

_____

_____

_____

_____

Summary/Paraphrase of the lecture:

_____

_____

_____

Task 5

In the last few weeks, we've been seeing letters to the editors in the campus newspaper from some of the faculty of the astronomy department. It seems that some of the astronomers who work nights at the Hodgkins Observatory are upset because the surrounding campus, as well as our city streets, are too well lighted. This makes it difficult, the astronomers say, for them to observe the stars and conduct their experiments.

Well, I am sorry for these scientists. However, if you ask any of the professors in the department of criminology, I'm sure *they* will tell you that bright lights serve a useful purpose for all of the students and for all of the residents of our city. Studies show that good lighting stops crime. It's as simple as that. We need more nighttime light on our campus and on our streets, not less.

Notes on the passage:

_____

_____

_____

_____

_____

Summary/Paraphrase of the passage:

_____

_____

_____

▶ Now start the Audio Program. Listen to part of a lecture in an astronomy class. 🎧

Notes on the lecture:

_____

_____

_____

_____

_____

Summary/Paraphrase of the lecture:

_____

_____

_____

Task 6

Until the late 1950's, protozoa were considered the simplest forms of animals. (The name *protozoa* means "first animal.") In some ways they *do* resemble animals. Some protozoa move about freely and can be seen eating food. Other protozoa, however, have characteristics of plants. Some cannot move on their own. Some contain chlorophyll. This created a problem for biologists. Larger organisms can easily be classified into one of the two kingdoms, plant or animal. With micro-organisms such as protozoa, the system breaks down. However, since organisms had to be classified as either plants or animals, protozoa were considered animals.

Notes on the passage:

_____

_____

_____

_____

_____

WRITING

Summary/Paraphrase of the passage:

_____

_____

_____

▶ Now start the Audio Program. Listen to part of a lecture in a biology class. 🎧

Notes on the lecture:

_____

_____

_____

_____

_____

Summary/Paraphrase of the lecture:

_____

_____

_____

EXERCISE 22.2

FOCUS: Citing and synthesizing key points from passages and lectures.

DIRECTIONS: For this exercise you will be using the summaries/paraphrases that you wrote for both the passages and the lectures in Exercise 22.1. Rewrite the summary and the paraphrases into one paragraph. Using a variety of methods, **cite** information from the paragraph and lecture. (In other words, make it clear whether the information in your response comes from the lecture or the passage.) Then, using a variety of methods, **synthesize** the information from the two sources. The first one is done for you as an example.

Task 1

According to the passage, asteroids are extremely dangerous. The author points out that the dinosaurs were probably killed off when an asteroid smashed into the Earth. The author says that, recently, asteroids have come close to hitting the Earth. There are no major programs designed to observe asteroids. Because of the danger, we need a comprehensive international program. However, in the lecture, the professor indicates that the danger from asteroids might not be too serious because an asteroid capable of causing global damage only strikes the Earth about once every 100,000 years. She goes on to say that, given our current state of technology, we can't see all asteroids approaching the Earth. We can't see one, for example, coming from the direction of the Sun. Moreover, even if we can see an oncoming asteroid, she points out, there is no way to destroy it before it hits the Earth.

Task 2

_____

_____

_____

_____

_____

_____

_____

_____

_____

Task 3

_____

_____

_____

_____

_____

_____

_____

_____

Task 4

_____

_____

_____

_____

_____

_____

_____

_____

Task 5

_____

_____

_____

_____

_____

_____

_____

_____

Task 6

_____

_____

_____

_____

_____

_____

_____

_____

_____

_____

After taking notes and writing an informal outline, you will be ready to write the Integrated Writing Response. You should spend about fifteen minutes doing the actual writing, and you should try to produce at least a 200-word response.

Remember: You *must* type the response on the keyboard of a computer. You may *not* write your response with pen and paper.

Most of the Integrated Writing Tasks that you see will consist of a passage expressing the author's point of view and three key points that develop the author's point of view. These key points are supported by examples, details, or reasons. Then there is a lecture on the same topic, usually expressing an opposing point of view, with three points that correspond to the three in the passage. These points are also supported by details and reasons.

There are various ways to organize your response, but the clearest method is to follow the informal outline presented in Lesson 21 (pp. 582–604). This outline provides for a five-paragraph structure: an introduction, three body paragraphs (one per key point), and a conclusion.

Remember, you should work mainly from the informal outline that you make based on your notes. And remember that you need to summarize, paraphrase, cite, and synthesize the information from the passages and lectures (see Lesson 22).

(A) Writing the Introduction

Your introduction for the Integrated Response should be simple and straightforward. You should begin the introduction by clearly stating the *topic* (the subject) of both the lecture and the passage (which will always be the same.) If other important information is given in the introduction to the passage or the lecture, you may summarize that information as well. You should then give the point of view of the lecture and that of the passage. As mentioned before, these two points of view will generally be in *opposition*.

Here is a sample introductory paragraph based on an outline of the Preview Test from Lesson 21 (p. 588).

Sample Outline

Introduction

Intro: Main Topic: Anim. rsch
    Author of passage supports: reduce hum. suffering
    Spkr opposes; unethic

Sample Introduction

The article and the lecture are about the use of animals in medical experiments. The author of the article, Professor White, claims that although there have been protests and demonstrations, animal testing is needed to minimize people's suffering. However, the lecturer argues that this kind of research is just not ethical in any situation.

(B) Writing the Body of the Response

The organization of the body of your response should usually follow that of the lecture. Each of the three paragraphs of the body should focus on one of the points made in the passage and the corresponding point that is made in the lecture.

Remember that you should *not* use any "outside" information in the body or anywhere else. In other words, you should not bring in information about the topic that you may have read in a book, magazine, or Web site, or that you may have heard about in a class or on television or radio.

Below are three sample body paragraphs based on the Preview Test.

Sample Outline

Body Paragraphs

1. Passage says important to minimize suffering
Anesth   clean conditions, etc.
Lect says: in practice, NOT humane
terrible diseases, chemicals   Inadeq anesth, abuse
2. Psge: no substi. for animal testing
humans/chimps share most genes   other animals useful too
Lect: many subs for anim. testing
growing tissue samples, etc.
3. Psge: Important theories, drugs devel. by anim. rsch.
Pasteur, germ theory   penicillin etc.
Lect: Maybe discover drugs, etc. anyway
Many drugs devel. w/out anim. rsch.
e.g. aspirin
Some drugs, if tested on anims. might NOT have been devel.
e.g. morphine

Sample Body Paragraphs

The author states that laboratory animals should be protected from pain whenever possible and that that they should kept in sanitary, safe conditions. Experiments, the author claims, do not have to involve cruelty. The lecturer disputes this idea. She says that the actual treatment of experimental animals is generally not compassionate. Animals are deliberately infected with horrible sicknesses or treated with poisonous chemicals. She says that laboratory animals are not given sufficient amounts of anesthetics to prevent pain and that they are frequently abused.

The author of the article says that there really are no good substitutes for animal testing. The author goes on to say that we can get a good idea of how humans will react to drugs by observing how animals react. This is especially true of animals that are closely related to humans, such as chimpanzees. The lecturer argues that animal testing is unnecessary today because there now are, in fact, many alternative ways to do research. She mentions, for example, the use of human tissue samples.

According to the author, we've seen again and again that animal testing is useful. Louis Pasteur developed the germ theory, a foundation of modern medicine, by means of animal testing. Furthermore, important drugs such as penicillin and insulin were discovered by doing research on animals. However, the speaker takes quite a different view of animal testing. The lecturer says that, although some important drugs were first tested on animals, she believes it is possible that these drugs might have been developed anyway. She says that the discovery of other useful drugs such as aspirin and quinine did *not* depend on animal research. Moreover, if some drugs had first been tested on certain animals, they probably would never have been approved for humans. Consider morphine, for example. According to the lecturer, morphine is a pain-killer for humans, but it has the opposite effect on cats.

(C) Writing the Conclusion to the Response

The conclusion to the response should be brief—only a sentence or two. Often the passage or the lecture or both will end with conclusions of their own. This is true of the sample. If so, you only need to summarize and paraphrase what the writer and the speaker say. If not, you need to briefly summarize the main points of the passage and the lecture.

Remember: You should *not* give your own opinion of the issue in the conclusion (or anywhere else in the passage).

Here is a sample of a conclusion from the Preview Test.

Sample Outline

Conclusion

Conclu: Psge: Immoral to test humans when non-humans avail.

Lect. Must give consent for rsch; anim can't consent

Sample Conclusion

In conclusion, the author's opinion is that it is immoral to perform tests on humans when the same research can be done on non-humans, while the lecturer believes that it is unethical to perform research on any creature that cannot give its consent.

Exercise 23.1

Focus: Writing responses for Integrated Writing Tasks.

Directions: Write responses (five paragraphs each) based on **Tasks 1, 2,** and **3** that you read and heard in Exercise 21.1 (pp. 588–594). You can use the outlines that you wrote for these tasks in Exercise 21.2 to write these responses. You should give yourself about fifteen minutes to complete each of these responses.

Note: *Remember that you will need to write your response on the computer during an actual test. If it is possible, you should practice writing these responses on a computer as well. You can use any word processing program, but do not use the spell-check or grammar-check features. If you use MSWord®, go to Tools → Options → Spelling And Grammar and be sure that the Check Spelling As You Type feature is turned off (not checked).*

Task 1

_____

_____

_____

_____

_____

_____

_____

_____

_____

_____

_____

_____

_____

_____

_____

_____

_____

_____

_____

_____

_____

Task 2

_____

_____

_____

_____

_____

_____

_____

_____

_____

_____

_____

_____

_____
_____
_____
_____
_____
_____
_____
_____
_____
_____
_____

Task 3

_____
_____
_____
_____
_____
_____
_____
_____
_____
_____
_____
_____
_____
_____
_____
_____
_____
_____

WRITING

_____

_____

_____

_____

_____

EXERCISE 23.2

FOCUS: More practice writing responses for Integrated Writing Tasks.

DIRECTIONS: Write five-paragraph responses based on **Tasks 4, 5,** and **6** that you read and heard in Exercise 21.1 (pp. 594–598). You can use the outlines that you wrote for these tasks in Exercise 21.2 to write these responses. You should give yourself about fifteen minutes to complete each of these responses.

Note: _Remember that you will need to write your response on the computer during an actual test. If it is possible, you should practice writing these responses on a computer as well. You can use any word processing program, but do not use the spell-check or grammar-check features. If you use MSWord®, go to Tools → Options → Spelling And Grammar and be sure that the Check Spelling As You Type feature is turned off (not checked)._

Task 4

_____

_____

_____

_____

_____

_____

_____

_____

_____

_____

_____

_____

_____

_____

_____

Task 5

Task 6

LESSON 24
CHECKING AND EDITING THE INTEGRATED RESPONSE

You should give yourself three to four minutes after writing the Integrated Response to **check** your response (look for mistakes) and to **edit** it (correct the mistakes). Of course, because you are working on the computer, you can make changes easily and neatly. There are three main types of problems that you should be looking for.

(A) Checking and Editing Content and Organizational Errors

There will not be enough time to make any major changes in the organization of the responses. However, you should quickly check for problems.

1. **Problems in the Introduction**
   ▶ Does your introduction include the main topic of the passage and the lecture?
   ▶ Does it explain the author's point of view? The speaker's?

2. **Problems in the Body Paragraphs**
   ▶ Does the body of the passage compare the main points of the passage and the lecture?
   ▶ Does the response accurately restate the ideas of the passage and lecture?
   ▶ Is there a balance between ideas from the passage and the lecture?
   ▶ Are there unnecessary details or "outside information" in the body? (If so, delete them.)
   ▶ Is the language in the lecture paraphrased?

3. **Problems in the Conclusion**
   ▶ Does the conclusion summarize the main points of the lecture and passage?
   ▶ Did you state your own opinion in the conclusion or elsewhere in the passage? (If so, delete it.)

(B) Checking and Editing Grammatical Errors

When checking/editing the Integrated Task, you can look for many types of grammatical errors. Some of the more common ones are listed here. For explanations, examples, and exercises involving these and other written structures, see the Writing Tutorial on Grammar (pp. 706–729).

1. **Sentence Fragments and Run-on Sentences**

   Check for **sentence fragments** that do not contain a subject, a verb, or some other necessary element. Check for **run-on sentences** that go on "too long," joining clauses without connectors. Split these into two sentences or join them correctly. (See Grammar Point 1 in the Writing Tutorial, page 706).

2. **Verb Errors**

   These errors are so common that you should automatically check all the verbs in your response. Check for **tense errors, subject-verb agreement,** and **active/passive errors.** (See Grammar Point 5 in the Writing Tutorial, pp. 720–721).

3. **Pronoun Errors**

   Check for **pronoun agreement.** Make sure a singular pronoun refers to a singular noun and a plural pronoun refers to a plural noun. (See Grammar Point 7 in the Writing Tutorial, pp. 725–726).

4. **Singular and Plural Errors**

   Check nouns to make sure a **singular noun** is used when needed and a **plural noun** when needed.

5. **Word Forms**

   Be sure you are using the correct form (**adjective, adverb, noun,** or **verb**) of the word. (See Grammar Point 4 in the Writing Tutorial, pp. 716–718).

   There are, of course, many other types of grammatical errors. If you have ever taken a writing class, look at the corrections the teacher made on your papers to see what kinds of mistakes you commonly made, and look for those mistakes when you check your essay.

(C) Checking and Editing Mechanical Errors

1. **Spelling Errors**

   Look for words that you may have misspelled. Look especially for words that are similar in your language and English but have different spellings. However, don't spend too much time looking for spelling mistakes—the scorers will not subtract much for misspellings unless they are especially frequent or make it difficult for the scorers to understand your response.

2. **Punctuation Errors**

   The most important thing to check is that each sentence ends with a period or, in the case of questions, with a question mark. Also check for commas after initial adverb clauses, between cities and states or cities and countries, and between dates and years. Be sure to leave a space after every punctuation mark.

3. **Capitalization Errors**

   Be sure that you have capitalized the first word of every sentence, the names of people and places, and the word *I*.

4. **Paragraphing Problems**

   Make sure that you either indent paragraphs (begin the first line of each paragraph half an inch from the left margin) or skip a line (leave an empty line) between paragraphs.

EXERCISE 24.1

FOCUS: Checking and editing organizational/content errors, grammatical errors, and mechanical errors in paragraphs from Integrated Writing Responses.

DIRECTIONS: Each of the following paragraphs contains a number of mistakes. Find as many mistakes in the paragraph as possible. Correct the mistakes, writing in the space between the lines. Then use your corrections to rewrite the paragraph. The first sentence of paragraph 1 is done as an example.

Paragraph 1

to   should not be a
According ˄ the passage, there ~~no should be~~ ˄ mandatory retirement age. The author say that this practice takes valuable worker from the work force. Older worker has the most experience and making them to retire wastes theirs talent. Further more, the author tells that studies show that older worker can to do most jobs as well younger worker. I know this is true because my uncle was manager of a railroad station, but he have to retire at age of 65 because of the company policy. The lecture, however, say that if older worker stay on job, then no possible for young worker to get promotion or more responsible. Also say that, despite there are exceptions, many young workers have qualities that employer need, such as concentration, memmory, and energize.

<u>According to the passage, there should not be a mandatory retirement age.</u>

_____

_____

_____

_____

_____

_____

_____

_____

_____

Paragraph 2

The speaker says that no many animals can capture the attentions of both young or old people like a dinosaur. One of the most well known dinosaurs is the animal we used to call as the "brontosaur." Everyone familiar with this dinosaur. It has appearing in museums, movies, advertisements, even in cartons such like *The Flintstones.* But in recently, this animal has other name. It is now called as the "apatosaurus." The speaker believes that we should keep their name as the "brontosaur." The author of the article that we read is not agree with this concept. He says is not scientific or fair to name this creature as a brontosaur. In 1877 a scientist who's name was Marsh found the bones of a dinosaur and he named it as apatosaurus. In 1879 another scientist who's name was Cope found the bones of a dinosaur. He has believed it was a difference species and called it a brontosaur but later was learned that these two animals were same. A international commission for naming animals has rules that say the name given for the first animal to discover is name that should use. Therefore the name apatosaurus is really correct.

_____

_____

_____

_____

_____

_____

_____

_____

_____

_____

_____

_____

_____

_____

Paragraph 3

Both of the aurthor and the lecturor discuss about the same sociological study. The study about online education. The author takes the positive point of view. One of his points, he citing that in study statistics shows that high percent of students think online course very affective. The lecturor concentrates in negative point. He says even though students think affective, a higher percent of students in online course dropping out of class before finish then in "face-to-face" (f2f) class. He says students in online classes don't like study alone and feel isolation. But aurthor says maybe changes in technology in future will solve some of todays problems with online classes. I agree that there are more advantages to "f2f" classes and I would rather take this kind of class.

_____

_____

_____

_____

_____

_____

_____

_____

_____

WRITING

Paragraph 4

---

article—it say that vanishing languages because of english is a killer language most magazine television website etc are in english and this kills small languages

lecture—it say that english not main reson for killing "vanishing languages." it say true many magazine and news paper are in english but few comparing to those in language of country or region. and movie and television. it say english only penetrating big city and where tourist go, but national and regional language penetrating all part of country or region. he say english can often coexist with other language for example in singapore "singlish" spoken (singapore english) but not danger to other languages in singapore

---

_____

_____

_____

_____

_____

_____

_____

_____

_____

_____

EXERCISE 24.2

FOCUS: Checking and editing organizational/content errors, grammatical errors, and mechanical errors in your own Integrated Responses.

DIRECTIONS: Check and edit Tasks 1, 2, and 3 that you wrote for Exercise 23.1. If you wrote these responses on computer, check and edit on the computer as well. If not, you may use the spaces below to rewrite your responses.

Rewrite for Task 1

_____

_____

_____

_____

_____

_____

_____

_____

_____

_____

_____

_____

_____

_____

_____

_____

_____

_____

_____

_____

_____

Rewrite for Task 2

_____

_____

_____

_____

_____

_____

_____

_____

_____

_____

WRITING

Rewrite for Task 3

_____

_____

_____

_____

_____

_____

_____

EXERCISE 24.3

FOCUS: More practice checking and editing organizational/content errors, grammatical errors, and mechanical errors in your own Integrated Responses.

DIRECTIONS: Check and edit tasks 4, 5, and 6 that you wrote for Exercise 23.2. If you wrote these responses on the computer, check and edit on the computer as well. If not, you may use the spaces below to rewrite your responses.

Rewrite for Task 4

_____

_____

_____

_____

_____

_____

_____

_____

_____

_____

_____

_____

_____

_____

_____

_____

_____

_____

_____

_____

_____

_____

_____

Rewrite for Task 5

_____

_____

_____

_____

_____

_____

_____

_____

_____

_____

_____

_____

_____

_____

_____

_____

_____

_____

_____

_____

Rewrite for Task 6

_____

_____

_____

_____

_____

_____

_____

_____

_____

_____

_____

_____

_____

_____

_____

_____

_____

_____

_____

_____

_____

_____

_____

_____

WRITING

ABOUT THE INDEPENDENT WRITING TASK

Skills that are required to successfully complete the Independent Writing Task include the abilities to

- ▶ understand the prompt and what it asks you to do
- ▶ "brainstorm" ideas and take notes on the ideas that you come up with
- ▶ organize your ideas into an outline
- ▶ clearly state and explain your opinion or preference
- ▶ support your ideas with examples, reasons, and details
- ▶ write a unified, well-organized, and coherent response based on the prompt
- ▶ use correct grammar and sophisticated vocabulary
- ▶ use transitions so that one idea flows smoothly into another
- ▶ write a variety of sentence types
- ▶ edit your response for content, grammar, and mechanics (spelling, punctuation, capitalization, and so on)
- ▶ word-process (type) your response

After you have completed the Integrated Writing Task, you will see the directions for the Independent Writing Task. After you click on Dismiss Directions you will see the prompt (the topic you must write about). You will be able to see the prompt as you are working on the response.

THE PROMPT

The **prompt** provides you with the topic about which you must write. There is no choice of topic. All of the prompts are very general and do not require any special knowledge or experience. The prompts will never be about controversial topics such as drugs or international politics.

Here are some common contexts for prompts:

education	career
art and culture	friendship
technology	sports and games
famous people	travel
transportation	communication
business	entertainment (TV, movies, books)
the future	language

There are three common types of prompts:

1. **Defend an opinion.**

   This type of prompt presents two points of view and asks you to choose one side to support. The prompt usually follows this pattern: "Some people believe A, but other people believe B. Which do you believe?"

Sample

> Some people believe that money spent on space research benefits all of humanity. Other people take the opposite view and say that money spent on this type of research is wasted. Tell which point of view you agree with and explain why, using specific details and reasons.

2. **Agree or disagree with a statement.**

   This type of prompt presents a general statement and asks whether you agree or disagree with it.

Sample

> Do you agree or disagree with this statement?
>   It is much easier to learn in a small class than in a large one.
> Use specific examples and reasons to support your answer.

3. **Explain the importance of a development, invention, or phenomenon.**

   This type of prompt essentially says, "There are many important Xs in the world. What do you think is the most important?"

Sample

> Developments in transportation such as the automobile have had an enormous impact on modern society. Choose another development in transportation that you think is of great importance. Use specific examples and reasons for your choice.

THE RESPONSE

Your response on the Independent Writing Task should be about 300 words long.

The Independent Writing Task asks you to express your opinion about the issue in the prompt. Which side of the issue you choose to support is up to you; there is no "right" answer. You need to clearly state your opinion (usually in the introduction to your response). In the body of the response, you need to explain and support your opinion. In the conclusion, you need to restate or explain the significance of your opinion.

An outline of a typical Independent Writing Task might look like this:

Introduction
Paragraph 1
    Introduction to the general topic
    Statement of your opinion or preference (thesis statement)

Body
Paragraph 2
    Key point #1 of the passage
    Examples, reasons, and details that support your opinion or preference

Paragraph 3
    Key point #2 supporting your opinion or preference
    Examples, reasons, and details that support your opinion or preference

Paragraph 4
    Key point #3 supporting your opinion or preference
    Examples, reasons, and details that support your opinion or preference

Conclusion
Paragraph
    Summary or statement showing the significance of your opinion

Other possible ways to organize Independent Responses are given in Lessons 25 and 26.

WRITING

THE WRITING PROCESS

You have thirty minutes in which to write the response for the Independent Writing Task. You should divide your time more or less like this:

Pre-Writing

(two to five minutes)
> Read the prompt.
> Think about the prompt.
> Brainstorm and take notes.
> Make an informal outline.

Writing the Independent Task

(twenty to twenty-five minutes)

Checking Your Writing

(two to five minutes)
> Look for and correct problems with content, grammar, and mechanics.

SCORING THE INDEPENDENT WRITING TASKS

Like the Integrated Writing Task, the Independent Writing Task is scored by two raters who score it *holistically*.

Scores on the Independent Writing Task range from 0 to 5. Each rater assigns a "whole number" score to the response (0, 1, 2, 3, 4, 5). Your score will be the mean of the two ratings. If one rater gives you a 3, for example, and another rater gives you a 4, you will receive a score of 3.5. If the two raters give you scores that are quite different, a third rater will read the response.

The following **rubric** (set of guidelines or standards) is similar to the one used by ETS to score the Independent Writing Task.

Score	Explanation of Score
5	Strongly indicates the ability to write a well-organized, well-developed, and logical response. Specific examples and details support the main ideas. All of the elements of the response are unified and cohesive. A variety of sentence structures are used successfully, and sophisticated vocabulary is employed. Grammatical and mechanical errors are infrequent but a few minor mistakes may occur.

4   Indicates the ability to write an organized, developed, and logical response. The main ideas are adequately supported by examples and details. Sentence structure may be less varied than that of a level 5 response, and vocabulary less sophisticated. Grammatical and mechanical errors appear.

3   Indicates some ability to write an acceptable response, but involves weaknesses in organization and development. Sentence structure and vocabulary may lack sophistication, and there may be frequent grammatical and mechanical errors.

2   Indicates the inability to write an acceptable response. Organization and development are weak. May lack unity and cohesion. Few specific details are given in support of the writer's ideas. If details are given, they may seem inappropriate. Significant and frequent errors in grammar occur throughout the response, making it difficult to understand the writer's ideas. Writer may not have fully understood the response prompt.

1   Strongly indicates the inability to write an acceptable response. No apparent development or organization. Sentences may be brief and fragmentary and unrelated to each other. Very significant grammatical and mechanical errors occur throughout the response and make it very difficult to understand any of the author's ideas. Writer may have completely misunderstood the response prompt.

0   Did not write an response, did not write on the topic, or wrote in a language other than English.

SAMPLE RESPONSES

Following are five responses, each illustrating one of the five scores. They are written in response to the following prompt:

> Some people believe that money spent on space research benefits all of humanity. Other people take the opposite view and say that money spent on this type of research is wasted. Tell which point of view you agree with and explain why, using specific details and reasons.

Response 1

It has become quite a common proverb that "there is no free lunch." Another way to say this is that spending money always has it's "opportunity cost." In other words, money spent on some venture could have been used for financing some other alternative venture.

Some people believe that money spent on space research has a benefit for all people. Other people believe that there are better opportunities for spending this fund. The first group of people say that space research has helped all peoples' lives very much. They point out that research on space has informed us about many environmental damages which we have caused to our planet.

Similarly, they say that today's modern satelite system is due to the research done in the past on space. There are also many new materials and inventions that can be traced directly to space research. These people want to spend more money on research, visit all the planets, and build space colonies.

In the other hand, there are people who think that money spent on space is a complete wastage because it does not have enough direct benefit to all of the humanity. For example, billions of US$ were spent on the Project Apollo and they only brought back a bag of rocks. In the meanwhile, there is a sizeable portion of the humanity that does not have any access to food, education, sanitation, health care, and especially peace.

Personally, I find that I cannot allign myself completely with either group. I have some reservation about both positions. No one can deny that weather satelites and communication satelites are a good investment. But I think that "unrealistic" research like exploring Mars or Venus does not have any good bearing on most of humans' development at the present time. Some scientists may be interested in the composition of those planets, but the opportunity cost is too much. In my opinion, it is like the poor man who wants to buy diamond jewlry when his family does not have enough food to eat or clothes to wear.

Score: __5__

Comments: This writer clearly understands the assignment and gives supporting information for both arguments. The essay is well organized, and the writer shows that he or she can say things in more than one way, uses idioms and verb tenses appropriately, and chooses clear and concrete examples to support his or her position.

Response 2

Some people do really believe that space reseaches benefit all of humanity. And it's quite understandable because all the history of humanity development is connected with the space discovers. From the beginning people have been looking the sky and observing the star's movements and their influence. For example, everyone knows about astrology and how ancient people try to predict the future using knowledge of the stars.

The present space discovery started in 1957, when the sputnik was launched. The first person flew in the space in 1961, and after several years first Americans landed on moon.

Nowdays space researches can solve a lot of problems, For example, reseaches with new materials and technologies. Such materials can be used in medicine, chemistry, and etc. With the help of space satellites we can observe the atmosphere around the Earth and that's why we can try to predict storms and so on. Through such observation we can save people's lifes and decrease destructions, also we can solve problems with the different kinds of pollutions of ocean and atmosphere.

However, it is quite understandable the position of those who say that space researches are wasted. There are to many places where the main problem of life is to survive. My native country once was part of Soviet Union, where the big first steps in space were taken. I see people there who works hard and doesn't receive enough or any salary. I wonder if they approve the space researches?

But I'm sure that if we concentrate only on the question of how to survive, the humanity will lose the reason for development. If we refuse from space researches, or any kind of the scientific researches, we will stop moving forward. And the absence of moving forward means the death of the humanity's spirit. That's why I agree with the statement.

Score: ___4___

Comments: This essay shows that the writer has a good command of English vocabulary and grammar usage. While the essay is generally coherent and provides details, the writer sometimes digresses and provides unnecessary information. This essay would be more on track if the writer took a position in the opening paragraph and supported his or her position more clearly in the remaining paragraphs.

Response 3

Well, about the topic, I think that there are others subjects much more important to be researching. One of them, and to me the most important one, is the health. The cancer cure is not totally developed yet. The number of AIDs' victims multiplying at an incredibly way.

So, although I find in "space" a very fascinating and misterious subject, I agree with the opposite view that the money spend on it is wasted when are so many people dying around the world as a result of unknown diseases or not having answers or cures for the ones we already known, or because is not enough money for purification of the water, vaccines for the diseases, or training the doctors.

More money for the education is also very important. More schools and good teachers are needed.

I believe cientifics should focus "health" in the first place and then to extend the researches in other fields.

Score: ___3___

Comments: This writer understands the assignment yet answers it by telling the reader what other things are more important before stating his or her position on the topic. The writer shows that he or she has some knowledge of English vocabulary, but there are errors in sentence structure, grammatical usage, and overall clarity.

Response 4

At the first the research in any thing is very useful for people because without research we will not development our life, so that I believe the money spent in space research benefit the humanity.

Maybe the other side people think that the money which paid for these research is so much and if we paid it for poor people it well be help him in they life and help him for many thing like food or healthy or any way of they life.

But the people which agrees with have a lot of point for example: one of this is the life must be development. Other point, the rule materials become less and we must find a new one and must find new resource of power, so that they agree with a research in space.

Score: __2__

Comments: This writer's essay is very short and does not adequately take a position and give supporting information. The ideas are not fully developed. The writer's knowledge of sentence structures is limited, and word forms are not always used properly, making this essay difficult to follow.

Response 5

the peoples take the opposive view because we don't buy something one time and we don't see another things. that is a save way. the money is important things. for this reason to spent money the peoples need to be very cerfully ihave two opinion for spent money. the money important to spent all humanty, because this point very important. i'm not agree money wested. in the futurre very important

Score: __1__

Comments: This essay is very disorganized. The writer uses very limited vocabulary and provides no details, making this essay difficult to understand. There are significant errors in every sentence. The punctuation is incorrect, and verbs are not used correctly.

EXERCISE: SCORING THE RESPONSE

DIRECTIONS: Here are three responses based on the passage below. Read each response and, using the scoring rubric on pages 650–651, decide what score (1 to 5) that you would give each response.

This exercise will help you develop the ability to score your own responses.

> Some people believe that money spent on space research benefits all of humanity. Other people take the opposite view and say that money spent on this type of research is wasted. Tell which point of view you agree with and explain why, using specific details and reasons.

Response 1

When we think that mony spent space reserches, are two opinins. Some peoples beliefe that we can reserche benfits all of humanity, But on the othrt hand, people take opposite view say that this type research is wasted the mony and we have limitation this kinds reserches. In my opinin I agree last one.

We, humen, reserche our space all time until now and we .spending a lots mony this kinds reserches. Some peoples think if we use expansive machines and spent a lots money we can make all kinds reserches about humanity. In fact, we found many benfit from these reserches and recive benfits, For example, we could gone to moon. But, sometime, even although spent a lots money, we cant find results and spent a lots time, furthermore, some acident which we cant expect happen, such as Challenger acident. The reson why, space is not man-made but nature. It means we cant expect and investigate exactlty. Because, they are nature, therefore they change all the time. We, humen, have follow this changes.

In my opinin, we cant reserche whole things. Because, they are nature and change all the time.

Score: _____

Response 2

Space research is an integral part of the modern civilization. Certainly this kind of scientific research needs a huge amount of investment. And of course, there is a lot of competition for very rare intelectual and fiscal resources. In other words, there are a lot of alternative investment opportunities for these resources that could benefit humanity.

Space research is a long-run investment process. The benefits out of this kind of research, once implemented, have a tremendous positive influence on all of the world. I want to take a position in favour of this type of research.

Space research, particularly as related to developments of satelite technology, may bring many positive development in the area of eradicating the root causes of many problems prevailing in this world. The most important to consider is poverty. Following are the scope of satelite technology-related research:

a) remote sensing
b) weather forecasting
c) early warning of any calamaties
d) long-range forecasting of weather for the agriculture
e) impact assessment of el nino and la nina conditions

Development of Global Positioning System (GPS) using satellite-driven information may contribute in modern infra-structure planning. Another aspect of satelite technolgy is the Geographical Information System (GIS), now playing pioneering role in information technology having resource-saving opportunities for development, and the saved resources can always be used for betterment of humanity.

All and all, I can't help to believe that in the long-run, space research is one of the optimal investments that humanity can do.

Score: _____

Response 3

The use of money is very important. In the pre-historic period, the human person has not money. The products were only changed one against another. This is called the barter process. but one epoque of pre-history was called the "Homo faber" period. That means the human persons learned to devlop the human conditions of living. They learned to make objets. After this, the value of products could be determine with money. A widespread proverbe of the french people tells us that the money serves very well the people but the money also is the worst master for the people who become enclosed by money.

Aristote is the father of science. He begun the psychic and philosophic and scientific research. Then there is the invention of mendicaments, the invention of planes, the invention of computer, all these invention are the resultat of research in science.

Surely, the research is important but the resultat of research can be negative while it can also be positive. What about the research of the space? all of us saw the spectacular pictures of the earth from space and of international space station and shuttle. So are these pictures worth billion of dollars used annually around the world?

Some people say that expenditures on space research have no effect and is comletely useless. It does not enter the progress of the human people. it has no relation to our life and actually does not do us any good.

All of us benefit from the research of the space. It advances the theoretical body of many sciences, like physics, astronomie, chemistrie etc. It also has more tangible accompliments in the way it improve the technology we can use in our every day life. For example, we can all enjoy a diversity of TV chanels and the satellite predictions of the weather. There is also a positive influence on peoples health and natural disasters.

But the resultats of the space research not divided fairly among the human persons. Scientists recive the best effects of it. Also the rich nations benefit more than the poor ones such as our african nations.

In concluding, the money spent for space is very important and has a lot of benefits for all us. I think we should embrace it. But the resultats of that research should be divided fairly among all the persons of the world.

Score: _____

Tactics for the Independent Task

- When the directions for the Independent Task appear, click on the Dismiss Directions button and begin working right away.

- Read the prompt carefully. You must write on the topic exactly as it is given. Give yourself time to think about the prompt and to plan your response by taking notes and writing a simple outline.

- The prompt will ask to give your opinion, to support one side of an issue, or to give your personal preference. Make it clear what your opinion is or what you prefer and why. Remember, there is no "right answer." You should choose the side that is easier to support.

- Use concrete examples and specific reasons. Whenever you make a general statement, support it with specific examples. If you state an opinion, give reasons.

INDEPENDENT WRITING PREVIEW TEST

DIRECTIONS

The second writing task in the Writing Section is an "independent" task. It involves writing a response to a question using your own experience and background knowledge.

Now read the directions for the second writing task.

DIRECTIONS: Read the question below. You will have thirty minutes to write your essay. This includes the time to plan, write, and revise your essay. A typical response should be a minimum of 300 words. Your essay will be rated on the correctness and quality of your writing, including the way you organize your essay and develop and support your ideas. If possible, write your responses on a computer.

Some people believe that zoos serve useful functions. Other people believe that it is cruel and wrong to confine animals in zoos. Tell which point of view you agree with and explain why, using specific details and reasons.

You should spend about five minutes "pre-writing" your essay for the Independent Response. What should you do during this time? You have three main tasks:

1. Read the essay prompt (topic) carefully.
2. Brainstorm (think about) the prompt.
3. Plan your response.

During the second and third tasks, you should take notes to use as an outline when you write the response.

Try to spend no more than five minutes on pre-writing, but don't skip this stage altogether—it's a very important use of your time!

(A) Reading the Prompts

In some ways, carefully reading each prompt is the most important step of the entire process. If you don't understand the prompt, you can't properly respond to it. If you write an essay that does not fully respond to the prompt, you will receive a lower score, no matter how well you have written the response.

The prompts for the Independent Response tend to be written in very simple English. If any of the vocabulary is difficult, it is usually explained. Not only do you need to read the prompt carefully, you also need to understand what it is asking you to do. You need to analyze the prompt—to be able to **paraphrase** it (put it into your own words) and to explain to yourself what it asks you to do. (You don't need to do this analysis in writing, only mentally.)

Read the following analyses of the sample prompts given in the Preview Test and About the Independent Writing Task.

> Some people believe that zoos serve useful functions. Other people believe that it is cruel and wrong to confine animals in zoos. Tell which point of view you agree with and explain why, using specific details and reasons.

Analysis

This prompt says that there are two opinions about zoos. Some people believe that zoos have a positive purpose. Others think that zoos are harmful to animals. To respond to this prompt, I have to decide which of these positions I want to support. If I choose to defend zoos, I must think of some good purposes that zoos serve. On the other hand, if I choose to emphasize the negative aspects of zoos, I must think of ways in which zoos are damaging or unsafe for animals or are not useful for the humans who pay for these zoos through their taxes.

> Do you agree or disagree with this statement?
>   It is much easier to learn in a small class than in a large one.
> Use specific examples and reasons to support your answer.

Analysis

This prompt asks about my opinion of class size and whether I think it has an effect on learning. I can choose one of two positions. One position is that small class size *does* make it easier to learn, and I'll need to give examples of ways in which it does.

If I choose the other side, I have to say that size is *not* an important factor. I could say that a good teacher can make sure students learn in even a large class, and give examples of ways in which he or she could do that.

> Developments in transportation such as the invention of the automobile have had an enormous impact on modern society. Choose another development in transportation that you think is of great importance. Use specific examples and reasons for your choice.

Analysis

For this prompt, I have to choose some development in transportation that I think is equally important or almost as important as the development of the automobile. I can't choose the automobile because the prompt says to choose *another* development. I could, for example, choose the development of the railroad and talk about how this had an impact on the world in general or on one country in particular.

(B) Brainstorming

The process of brainstorming involves generating ideas on a topic. Just sit back for a moment and think about the topic and write down any ideas that come to you. These may be things you have read in newspapers and magazines, things you've heard in classes or on television, or personal experiences. These ideas may turn out to be useful or not—just write them all down.

Let's say that you are assigned the first prompt. You would try to think about anything—positive or negative—that you have read about or heard about in connection with zoos, and quickly write these ideas down. For the second topic, you would probably use your own experiences. Can you remember any positive experiences with either a large class or a small one? Any negative ones? Write them down.

WRITING

Your brainstorming notes for the first prompt might look like this:

Some endangered animals are found only in zoos; would be extinct without zoos

Costs a lot of money to maintain zoos properly

Some people think that zoos are unnatural

Take away animals dignity and put them on show

Like prisons for animals

But modern zoos give animals more space

duplicate natural environments

Zoos protect animals from predators

from development

from hunters

Zoos educate children, in fact, everyone

Most people would never see animals from far away places if they didn't see them in zoos

Zoos are a nice place to spend the day with family   good entertainment

(C) Planning the Essay

This stage of pre-writing actually overlaps with Step B; while you are brainstorming, you are beginning to plan your essay.

The first step in planning is to choose your basic **thesis.** A thesis is the central or controlling idea of an essay. For the first two types of prompts—defending an opinion and agreeing/disagreeing with a statement—choosing a thesis simply means choosing which side of the argument you are going to support. For example, for the first prompt your thesis might be "In my opinion, zoos serve several useful purposes." For the second, your thesis might be "With the right teacher, large class size has little effect on learning." For the third prompt, you have to choose what development you are going to discuss; for example, your thesis might be "I believe that the development of jet airliners was extremely important."

Remember that when you choose a thesis, there is no right or wrong answer. The readers at ETS don't care whether you are in favor of zoos or against them, whether you like small classes or big ones, or whether you think the development of rockets, railroads, or roller skates was most important. In fact, you should choose whatever side of the argument is easiest to support. It's possible, for example, that you have had generally good experiences in large classes, but that you can think of more reasons why small classes are better. It is not necessary to fully support either point of view. Sample Response 1 (p. 651) is an example of an essay that partially supports both points of view. Once you have chosen a thesis, you need to think of ways to support it. Look at the notes you took while brainstorming. Are there any concrete details or compelling reasons that support the thesis you have chosen? If not, think of some now.

Next, you need to write a simple outline. You don't have to write a formal outline with Roman numerals and letters, just a basic plan for your four or five paragraphs. You may be tempted to skip this step to save time, but writing an outline is very important. Following a simple outline is the best way to keep an essay organized, and good organization is one of the most important things readers look for in scoring your essay.

For the "opinion" prompts (types 1 and 2), there are two basic ways to organize the body of your essay. One is to write two or three paragraphs, each providing a reason why your opinion is the "correct" one.

Introduction
Paragraph 1
> Here is my opinion.

Body
Paragraph 2
> My opinion is right for this reason . . .

Paragraph 3
> A second reason why my opinion is right is that . . .

Paragraph 4
> A third reason why my opinion is right is that . . .

Conclusion
Paragraph 4 or 5
> As you can see, my opinion *is* right.

Another approach is to restate both sides of the argument—A and B—in your introduction. The introduction does not say which side of the argument is "correct." Then, in one paragraph of the body, you provide several reasons to support the side that you do *not* agree with—opinion A. This tactic is sometimes called **admitting the opposition.** Then, in the next paragraph or two of the body, you give even stronger reasons why the other point of view, opinion B, is the better or more logical one. The conclusion restates the idea that opinion B is the right one.

Introduction
Paragraph 1
> There are two possible opinions on this topic, opinions A and B. Which is better?

Body
Paragraph 2
> Here are some reasons to believe opinion A is right.

Paragraph 3
> But here are some even better reasons to believe opinion B is right.

Paragraph 4
> Here are more reasons why opinion B is right.

Conclusion
Paragraph 5
> As you can see, opinion B *is* right.

WRITING

Samples

Outlines for the three prompts given in this lesson might look like this:

Prompt A Outline

Introduction

Paragraph 1

If no zoos, some animals wouldn't even exist; that's why I support zoos

    But some people think zoos are unnat'l, inhumane

Body

Paragraph 2

Neg ideas abt zoos

People prefer to think of wild animals living in natural surroundings, free

    Zoos = prisons for anim.

  Cramped, dirty cages

(However, not true in mod. zoos: more space, more like nat'l environ)

Paragraph 3

Pos idea abt zoos

    keep some species alive; breeding programs; maybe re-introduce later

      protect animals from predators, humans

        (e.g., tigers)

Paragraph 4

Another pos. idea

    educate public about animals, problems

  provide opportun. to see animals from all over world

Conclusion

Paragraph 5

Opposition to zoos based mainly on outmoded ideas of zoos

    Zoos protect & educate & on the whole positive

Prompt B Outline

Introduction
Paragraph 1

Sometimes it's necessary to have big classes. Good tcher can make big
      classes as good a learning environ as small ones

Body
Paragraph 2

Intro classes, lecture the same no matter what size
     Sometimes lecturers more dynamic in large cl

Paragraph 2

Some people think not as much interaction in big classes
    But . . . teacher can break cl into small grps for discussion, projects, etc.
   teacher can use tching asst. to lead discus. grps

Conclusion
Paragraph 3

Many people think small is best, but big classes can be good places to
     learn too

Prompt C Outline

Introduction
Paragraph 1

One of most important develop is internat'l jet transport—since '60s—
 because of speed, convenience & low costs, has changed way people
 think abt travel

Body
Paragraph 2

Speed: 100 yrs ago, took weeks to cross ocean: today, few hrs—this has
 changed people's concept of space

Paragraph 3

 Convenience: can travel almost any day of year
  can depart or arrive at many cities, not just a cple of ports

Paragraph 4

Low costs: In past, only wealthy could travel comfortably; poor people had
  to save for years— today, more and more people can travel
 businesspeople
  students
   tourists

Conclusion
Paragraph 5

Because of jet travel, countries no longer so isolated; people think of world
 as own hometowns

EXERCISE 25.1

FOCUS: Reading and analyzing Independent Writing prompts.

DIRECTIONS: Read the six prompts for Independent Writing tasks given below, then write an analysis for each one similar to the analyses on pages 658–659.

Prompt for Task 1

Some people believe that schools should primarily teach students how to best compete with others. Other people believe that schools should primarily teach students how to cooperate with others. Which of these two approaches do you favor? Use specific reasons and examples to support your answer.

Analysis of Task 1

_____

_____

_____

_____

_____

_____

_____

Prompt for Task 2

Imagine that you can talk for one hour with any person who has lived at any time in history. Which person would you choose to meet? Use specific details and examples to explain your choice.

Analysis of Task 2

_____

_____

_____

_____

_____

_____

_____

WRITING

Prompt for Task 3

Do you agree or disagree with the following statement?
When people are traveling, they often behave differently from the way they behave at home.
Use specific details and examples to support your answer.

Analysis of Task 3

_____

_____

_____

_____

_____

_____

_____

Prompt for Task 4

Some university students prefer living in campus housing such as dormitories. Other students prefer living in off-campus housing such as apartments. If you were faced with this decision, which of these two options would you choose? Use specific reasons and details to explain your choice.

Analysis of Task 4

_____

_____

_____

_____

_____

_____

_____

Prompt for Task 5

Do you agree or disagree with the following statement?
> It is better for university students to first get a general education, taking classes in many fields, than it is for them to take classes only in their own field of study.

Use specific details and examples to support your answer.

Analysis of Task 5

_____

_____

_____

_____

_____

_____

_____

Prompt for Task 6

Your hometown has just received a grant from an international organization to fund a single improvement project. Which of the following would you recommend to receive the funding?

the city airport	the streets and roads
the police department	the fire department
the local schools	the city parks
the public transportation system	the local hospitals
the art museum	

Give specific examples and reasons to support your recommendation.

Analysis of Task 6

_____

_____

_____

_____

_____

_____

_____

_____

EXERCISE 25.2

FOCUS: Brainstorming and taking notes on Independent Writing prompts.

DIRECTIONS: Brainstorm the six prompts in Exercise 25.1 and take notes on any ideas that occur to you. Don't spend more than one or two minutes per prompt.

Notes for Task 1:

_____

_____

_____

_____

_____

_____

Notes for Task 2:

_____

_____

_____

_____

_____

_____

Notes for Task 3:

_____

_____

_____

_____

_____

_____

_____

_____

_____

Notes for Task 4:

_____

_____

_____

_____

_____

_____

_____

_____

_____

Notes for Task 5:

_____

_____

_____

_____

_____

_____

_____

_____

_____

_____

WRITING

Notes for Task 6:

_____

_____

_____

_____

_____

_____

_____

_____

EXERCISE 25.3

FOCUS: Writing informal outlines for Independent Writing Responses.

DIRECTIONS: Write short, informal outlines from the notes that you took on prompts 1, 2, and 3 in Exercise 25.2. Do not spend more than three or four minutes per outline.

Outline for Task 1:

_____

_____

_____

_____

_____

_____

_____

Outline for Task 2:

_____

_____

_____

_____

_____

_____

_____

_____

Outline for Task 3:

_____

_____

_____

_____

_____

_____

_____

EXERCISE 25.4

FOCUS: More practice writing informal outlines for Independent Writing Responses.

DIRECTIONS: Write short, informal outlines from the notes that you took for tasks 4, 5, and 6 in Exercise 25.2. Do not spend more than three or four minutes per outline.

Outline for Task 4:

_____

_____

_____

_____

_____

_____

_____

Outline for Task 5:

_____

_____

_____

_____

_____

_____

_____

_____

WRITING

Outline for Task 6:

_____

_____

_____

_____

_____

_____

_____

_____

_____

LESSON 26
GIVING OPINIONS AND CONNECTING IDEAS IN THE INDEPENDENT RESPONSE

(A) Giving Opinions

To write the Independent Response, you must give your **opinion** of issues and ideas. You may have to show your preference for one concept or another or **agree** or **disagree** with a statement. You then must **support** your opinions and ideas with valid arguments.

The following structures and sentence patterns can be used to express your opinion:

> *In my opinion,* A is the best choice.
>
> *It's my opinion that* B is an excellent idea.
>
> *I think that* X should be used.
>
> *I believe that* we should choose Y.
>
> *I feel that* A is correct.
>
> *It's my belief that* C is the best plan.
>
> *Personally, I think/feel/believe that* X should not be . . .

Expressing your **preference** for one concept over another is a way of giving your opinion, so the sentence patterns for showing your preferences are often combined with the patterns used to express your opinion.

> In my opinion, A *is a much better choice than* B.
>
> It's my opinion that C *should be used in place of* Y.
>
> I believe that X *is preferable to* Y.
>
> Personally, I feel that Z *is superior to* A.
>
> I *prefer* A *to* C.
>
> I *like* Y *more than* B.
>
> I *like* to do Y *more* than to do Z.
>
> I *like* doing Y *more* than doing Z.
>
> I *would rather* do X than Z.*
>
> I *would prefer* to see a B than a C.*
>
> I *would choose* to have X rather than to have Y.*
>
> I generally *enjoy* going to Z more than to A.*

Pay special attention to the examples marked with an asterisk (*). Notice that the verb phrase *would rather* is used with a base form (*would rather do*). The verb phrases *would prefer* and *would choose* take an infinitive (*would prefer to see; would choose to have*). The verb *enjoy* takes a gerund (*enjoy going*).

Showing **agreement** and **disagreement** with a person or an idea is also a way of expressing an opinion.

I *agree with* the statement that X is the best way to do Y.

I *disagree with* those people who believe that B is the best option.

I *agree that* people should generally do A before they do B.

Some people think C is the most important quality in a Z, *but I don't agree.*

Note that *agree/disagree with* is used with noun phrases, while *agree/disagree that* is used with clauses.

It is not enough, in the independent response, to simply give your opinion or preference or to just say that you agree or disagree. You must **support** your ideas with **reasons.** Here are some sentence patterns for giving reasons:

I agree with those people who say that X is true *because of* Y.

I disagree with those people who believe that B is the best option *because* A is true.

Note that *because of* is used with noun phrases, while *because* is used with clauses.

There are several reasons why I think X is better than Y.

I agree with the opinion of people who believe that X is true. *There are several reasons for this.*

You should also develop your ideas by providing **examples:**

I would rather visit city X than any other city in the world because it has so many cultural attractions. *For example,* Museum Y has one of the best collections of Z in the world.

There are many ways in which students can get higher grades in a class. *For instance,* students can ask their teachers how to do A.

What is the most useful subject I have ever studied? I believe Y is by far the most helpful. *Here are three examples* of how studying Y has helped me.

I chose to attend the University of X because it has many excellent teachers. *A good example of this is Professor Y.*

We have the use of many technological devices that were not available to our grandparents. The C *is a good example of this.*

In some countries, *such as Y,* this practice is quite common.

You should *not* use the phrase *for example* or *for instance* + noun as a complete sentence:

INCORRECT: I would rather visit city *X* than any other city in the world because it has so many cultural attractions. *For example, Museum Y.*

The phrase *For example, Museum Y* is a sentence fragment (not a complete sentence) because it does not include a verb.

CORRECT: I would rather visit city X than any other city in the world because it has so many cultural attractions. *Museum Y is a good example.*

CORRECT: I would rather visit city X than any other city in the world because it has so many cultural attractions. *For example,* Museum Y has a wonderful collection of modern art.

You can also support a general idea with **personal experiences.** Here are some sentence patterns used to give personal experiences.

Some people support the idea that we should generally do A before we do B. *In my experience,* this is not necessarily true.

The statement says that C is true. *Some experiences from my own life* support this idea.

How can we learn how to do Y? *For me,* there have been at least three ways.

(B) Connecting Ideas

Transition words (such as *therefore, however,* and *moreover*) and other expressions can be used to join paragraph to paragraph, sentence to sentence, and clause to clause. Some of these expressions are given below.

1. **Expressions used to list points, examples, or reasons**

   First example or reason:

   First, let's consider X.

   The first reason for this is that Y . . .

   One example of this is Y.

   Additional examples or reasons:

   Second, there is the example of Z.

   A second (third) good *example* of this phenomenon is A . . .

   Another example is B . . .

   Next, there is the example of Y . . .

   Another reason is that C is usually . . .

   Final example or reason:

   Finally, we have Z.

2. **Expressions that show addition**

   The transition words/phrases in *addition, furthermore,* and *moreover* can be used to join clauses or sentences.

   Clause 1; *furthermore,* clause 2.

   Sentence 1. *Furthermore,* sentence 2.

   One point is given in the first clause or sentence and another in the second clause or sentence.

   I like to use Y as a method of keeping in touch with my friends because it is fast; *furthermore,* it is efficient and simple.

I would never want to own a Y because it is so expensive. *In addition*, it often breaks down.

I predict that, in the future, people of all ages will use Ys. *Moreover*, Ys will be found in every country of the globe.

3. Expressions that show a result or conclusion

The conjunction *so* can be used to join two independent clauses. The first clause gives a reason, the second clause a result. (Clause 1, *so* clause 2).

I believe doing C is a waste of time, *so* I avoid C whenever possible.

The transition words *therefore, consequently*, and *thus* can be used to join clauses or sentences. The first clause or sentence gives a reason, the second clause or sentence a result.

Studying mathematics teaches you how to A; *therefore*, everyone should study mathematics.

A recent study showed that many high school graduates could not do Y. *Consequently*, Y should be part of the curriculum of all high schools.

In high school, I learned how to A, how to B, and how to C; *thus*, I was prepared for my studies at a university.

4. Expressions that show contrast

The conjunction *but* can be used to join two independent clauses that contain contrasting information. (Clause 1, *but* clause 2).

People who oppose Y may have some good points, *but* on the whole, I think Y serves a useful function.

The adverb clause markers *although* and *while* can be used to join an adverb clause and an independent clause with contrasting information.

Although most of the people in my country choose to study X as a second language, I wanted to learn how to speak Y first.

Some people believe that doing X is harmful, *while* others enjoy it.

These transition words/phrases can join clauses and sentences containing contrasting information.

Many people like to visit large cities such as X or Y; *however*, I prefer to see scenic natural places such as Z and A.

Many people think that the government should encourage people to do Y because it will help the economy. *On the other hand*, doing Y can have a number of negative results.

5. Expressions that show similarity

The transition words *likewise* and *similarly* can join clauses and sentences containing similar information.

I think it is useful for children to do X; *likewise*, I think it is helpful for adults to do the same.

There is too much violence in movies; *similarly*, many TV shows contain a lot of violence.

6. Expressions that introduce a concluding paragraph

These transition phrases can be used at the beginning of the last paragraph of your response.

In conclusion, for all these reasons, I think that X is a valid argument.

In summary, there is no doubt in my mind that Y is true.

All in all, I must agree with those people who support X.

Below are some additional examples of the vocabulary used for giving opinions and connecting ideas.

1. *I completely agree* with the idea of stricter gun control for a number of reasons. *First,* statistics show that guns are not very effective in preventing crime. *Moreover,* accidents involving guns frequently occur. *Finally,* guns can be stolen and later used in crimes.

2. *I believe* that a good salary is an important consideration when looking for a career. *However,* the nature of the work is more important to me. *Thus,* I would not accept a job that I did not find rewarding.

3. There are many reasons why I *would rather* live in an urban area *than* in a small town. *The first and most important reason* is that there are more professional opportunities for me in a big city than in a small town. *Another* is that the educational opportunities for my children are much better in a city. *Third,* a city offers cultural attractions *such as* museums, theaters, and good restaurants. *Personally, I think* that I would be bored living in a small town. *Therefore, I agree* with those people who prefer to live in big cities.

EXERCISE 26.1

FOCUS: Using transition words and other expressions to connect ideas.

DIRECTIONS: Complete each of the following sentences with one of the words or phrases below. Do not use any item more than once.

likewise	for example	personally	furthermore
however	therefore	on the other hand	similarly

1. I believe that women should have the right to serve in the military. _____, I don't believe that they should be assigned to combat roles.

2. Many actors, rock musicians, and sports stars receive huge amounts of money for the work that they do. _____, a baseball player was recently offered a contract worth over twelve million dollars. _____, I feel that this is far too much to pay a person who simply provides entertainment.

3. The development of the automobile has had a great impact on people everywhere. _____, the development of high-speed trains has had an impact on people in many countries, including my home country of France.

4. I used to work in a restaurant when I was in college. I realize what a difficult job restaurant work is. ＿＿＿＿＿＿＿＿＿＿, whenever I go out to eat, I try to leave a good tip for my waiter or waitress.

5. Many people would agree with the idea that the best use for the open space in our community is to build a shopping center. ＿＿＿＿＿＿＿＿＿＿, there are other people who feel we should turn this open space into a park.

6. In the United States, people celebrate their independence from Britain on July 4. ＿＿＿＿＿＿＿＿＿＿, we Mexicans celebrate our independence from Spain on September 16.

7. Corporations should do more to reduce air pollution. ＿＿＿＿＿＿＿＿＿＿, they should encourage recycling.

EXERCISE 26.2

FOCUS: Connecting ideas with transition words and other expressions.

DIRECTIONS: Complete the following sentences in your own words.

1. Young children have a special talent for language learning; therefore,

＿＿＿＿＿＿＿＿＿＿＿＿＿＿＿＿＿＿＿＿＿＿＿＿＿＿＿＿＿.

2. Some forms of advertising serve a useful purpose; however,

＿＿＿＿＿＿＿＿＿＿＿＿＿＿＿＿＿＿＿＿＿＿＿＿＿＿＿＿＿.

3. Small classes are the best environment for learning, but

＿＿＿＿＿＿＿＿＿＿＿＿＿＿＿＿＿＿＿＿＿＿＿＿＿＿＿＿＿.

4. Some people relax by watching television; personally,

＿＿＿＿＿＿＿＿＿＿＿＿＿＿＿＿＿＿＿＿＿＿＿＿＿＿＿＿＿.

5. Although there are many ways to learn a language,

＿＿＿＿＿＿＿＿＿＿＿＿＿＿＿＿＿＿＿＿＿＿＿＿＿＿＿＿＿.

6. The use of computers has had a major impact on the banking industry; likewise,

＿＿＿＿＿＿＿＿＿＿＿＿＿＿＿＿＿＿＿＿＿＿＿＿＿＿＿＿＿.

EXERCISE 26.3

FOCUS: Using the vocabulary of showing preference and connecting ideas.

DIRECTIONS: Complete the following Independent Response with transition words/phrases and with verbs that show preference. For this exercise, you may use words from the list more than one time. In some cases, more than one word or phrase may be correct.

Note: *You may have to change the form of the verb to fit the context of the sentence.*

Transition Words/Phrases

moreover	furthermore	on the other hand	while	personally
however	therefore	but	because	

Verbs of Preference

prefer	would rather	enjoy

> Some people like to go to the same place for their vacations. Other people like to take their vacations in different places. Which of these two choices do you prefer? Give specific reasons for your choice.

There are certain people who _____ to take their vacations in the same place. When they return from a vacation, they ask themselves, "When can I go back there again?" _____, there are people who _____ visit many places. _____, they _____ doing many different things on their vacations. When they return from a vacation, they ask themselves, "Where can I go next and what can I do there?"

My parents are perfect examples of the first kind of people. They always go to a lake in the mountains. They first went there on their honeymoon, and several years later they bought a vacation cabin there. They have gone there two or three times a year for over thirty years. They have made friends with the people who also own cabins there and often get together with them. My mother _____ sailing and swimming _____ my father _____ to go fishing. My parents like variety, _____ they say they can get variety by going to their cabin at different times of the year. They particularly like to go there in the autumn when the leaves are changing color.

_____, I feel it's important to visit different places. Of course, when I was a child, I went to my parents' cabin with them for my vacation, _____ when I got older, I began to want to travel to many different places. I _____ skiing; _____, the ski resorts in my country are very crowded and expensive. I _____ go skiing in Switzerland or in Canada. My favorite subject at the university was ancient history; _____, I like to visit historic places. Several years ago, I traveled to Angkor Wat in Cambodia with my uncle and aunt. I also want to visit the pyramids in Egypt; _____, I'd like to see Machu Picchu in Peru.

WRITING

My parents believe that you can never get to know a place too well. I understand their point of view. _____, I find that going to strange places is more exciting. I don't want to go to the same place twice _____ the world is so huge and exciting.

EXERCISE 26.4

FOCUS: Using the vocabulary of giving opinions and connecting ideas to write short paragraphs.

DIRECTIONS: Write one-paragraph answers to the following questions, using a number of the vocabulary words and phrases that are discussed in this lesson. The first one is done for you.

1. | What was the most important decision that you have ever made? Why was this decision important to you?

I believe that the most important decision I ever made was to major in economics as an undergraduate student at my university. There are several reasons why this was an important decision for me. One is that my studies at the university led to my job with the Ministry of Trade. Because of my position at the Ministry, I was chosen to travel to the United States to get a master's degree. Finally, this decision was important to me because I met my future wife in a micro-economics class at my university.

2. | If you could spend a year living in any city on the world, which city would you choose to live in? Give the reasons why you would want to live there.

_____

_____

_____

_____

_____

_____

_____

3. | What do you think of this statement?

   Failure often leads to success.

   Give an example of why you think this is sometimes true. Give another example of why you think this statement is sometimes NOT true. Then state your opinion of this statement.

_____

_____

_____

_____

_____

_____

4. | There are many types of television shows: comedies, news programs, dramas, reality series, and so on. What is your favorite type of television show? Why do you prefer this type of show? Give some examples from your own experiences watching television.

_____

_____

_____

_____

_____

5. | You have received a full scholarship to a good university in your country. You have also been offered a full scholarship to a top university in another country. Which of these two scholarships would you accept? Why?

_____

_____

_____

_____

_____

_____

After spending about five minutes on pre-writing, you are now ready to get down to the real task: writing the response. You have only about twenty minutes in which to write it, and you need to produce a 200- to 300-word response. That's about ten to fifteen words a minute. You can do this if you concentrate and keep working steadily.

According to ETS, quality is more important than quantity in the response, but typically only longer responses get top scores. A long response does not guarantee a good score on this section, but a short response almost guarantees a low one. This lesson will discuss writing all three parts of a typical response.

(A) Writing the Introduction

The introduction for an Independent Response can be fairly simple. It does not need to be more than two or three sentences long.

There are a number of functions that a good introduction can serve (but no introduction will serve all of these functions).

▶ To get the reader's attention
▶ To restate the ideas of the prompt
▶ To present some general background information about the topic
▶ To preview the main points that will appear in the response
▶ To present a clear statement of the main idea of the response. (This is called the **thesis statement;** it typically is the last sentence of the introduction, but sometimes it appears in the conclusion.)

Here are three sample introductory paragraphs, written in response to the three prompts presented in the Independent Writing Pretest and About the Independent Writing Task.

Samples

Prompt 1

> Some people believe that zoos serve useful functions. Other people believe that it is cruel and wrong to confine animals in zoos. Tell which point of view you agree with and explain why, using specific details and reasons.

Introduction 1

> If there were no zoos, some species of animals would not exist at all. That is one of several good reasons why I believe it is important to support zoos. Some people, however, have a negative view of zoos. They think zoos are unnatural and inhumane.

This introduction begins with a strong, rather startling statement about zoos that gets the reader's attention: "If there were no zoos, some species of animals would not exist at all." The writer goes on to say that she thinks it is important to support zoos for this and other reasons. However, the introduction also mentions the opposite point of view: that zoos do *not* serve good purposes.

Prompt 2

> Do you agree or disagree with this statement?
>   It is much easier to learn in a small class than in a large one.
> Use specific examples and reasons to support your answer.

Introduction 2

> Many students believe that small classes offer much better educational opportunities than large ones. However, in my experience, that is not necessarily true. I believe that, with a good teacher, a large class can provide as good a learning opportunity as a small one.

In the introduction, the writer paraphrases the prompt in the first sentence. However, in the second sentence the writer disagrees with the idea stated in the prompt. In the last sentence of the introduction, the writer gives his thesis statement: learning depends on good teaching, not class size.

Prompt 3

> Developments in transportation such as the automobile have had an enormous impact on modern society. Choose another development in transportation that you think is of great importance. Use specific examples and reasons for your choice.

WRITING

Introduction 3

I believe that one of the most important developments in transportation has been the development of international jet transport. Jet airliners first appeared in the early 1960's. Since then, planes have gotten bigger and faster and capable of flying longer distances. Jet transport has had some revolutionary effects. Because of the high speeds, the convenience, and the relatively low costs of this type of travel, it has changed the way people look at the world.

In the first sentence of the paragraph, the writer answers the question brought up in the prompt. The writer then goes on to provide a little background information about this development, and then provides a preview of the main points that the body of the response will discuss: speed, convenience, and low costs, and how these have changed people's view of the world.

(B) Writing the Body of the Response

The body of the paragraph makes up most of the response. It is in the body of the response that the writer **develops** the thesis statement. (That's why these paragraphs are sometimes called the **development paragraphs**.) In the body, the writer provides information to convince the reader that his or her opinion is correct or that his or her ideas are valid.

A typical body paragraph begins with a **topic sentence** that contains the main idea of that paragraph (just as the thesis statement contains the main idea of the response). It also contains several sentences that support this main idea. The writer should provide specific details, reasons, examples, and/or personal experiences to support these sentences.

> **Topic sentence**
> > **Supporting sentence**
> > > Detail/reason/example/personal experience
> > > Detail/reason/example/personal experience
> > **Supporting sentence**
> > > Detail/reason/example/personal experience
> > > Detail/reason/example/personal experience

Remember that the supporting sentences and the details must be directly relevant to the main idea of the paragraph; do not include irrelevant material.

Look at these sample paragraphs from the body of responses written in response to the prompts provided on pages 682–683.

Samples

Body 1

The idea that zoos are cruel to animals is somewhat understandable. People like to think of wild animals in their natural habitats, living free in the way they have done for thousands or millions of years. They think of zoos as prisons for animals. They think that displaying animals in cages for the benefit of visitors takes away from the animals' dignity and confines them in small, uncomfortable spaces. In part, however, these people's belief is based on a misconception. It's true that in the past, animals in zoos generally lived in cramped, dirty cages. Newer zoos, however, try to duplicate animals' natural habitats as much as possible and give animals a comfortable amount of space. Even many older zoos are upgrading their facilities for their animals.

There are a number of reasons why I think that zoos' functions are mainly positive. One reason is that zoos protect not only species of animals but also individual animals. Many species are endangered because of human development or other environmental problems. As mentioned, some species only exist in captivity. Zoos around the world have cooperative breeding programs to increase the number of endangered animals. In the future, it may be possible to re-introduce these species into the wild. Furthermore, some animals' native habitats have become dangerous for them, not just because of predators but because of humans. Tigers, for example, are often killed because parts of their bodies are used in very expensive "medicines." In zoos, at least these animals are protected.

Another reason to support zoos is that they provide an educational experience. How many of us would be able to see elephants from Africa, penguins from Antarctica, or koala bears from Australia if we did not see them in a zoo? Moreover, zoos provide information about which animals are endangered and tell us why these animals are in trouble.

In the first body paragraph, the writer "admits the opposition," giving reasons why the opinion that zoos are harmful places could be valid. The writer says that some people prefer to think of wild animals as living only in wild settings. These people find zoos undignified, and they think that animals are forced to live in small, uncomfortable cages. The writer here points out that this view of zoos is outmoded because new zoos and even some older zoos now provide more space and try to duplicate animals' natural habitats.

In the second body paragraph, the writer then gives her own reasons for supporting zoos. The writer says that zoos protect both endangered species and endangered individuals.

In the third paragraph, the writer explains an additional reason for supporting zoos. She says that zoos serve an educational function. They allow people to see animals from faraway places and learn about endangered species.

WRITING

Body 2

When I was an undergraduate student, most of the large classes I took were introductory classes for first- and second-year students. For example, I took classes in world history and economics that had over 100 students and met in large lecture halls. I think these classes were as good as some of the smaller classes I took later. At the introductory level, the lectures that the professors gave were basically the same no matter what size the class was. Moreover, the professors who taught these classes seemed more enthusiastic and energetic than the teachers I had in smaller classes. Personally, I think they enjoyed having a large audience!

One supposed advantage of small classes is that there is usually a lot more interaction among students and between the teacher and the students than in large ones. However, in the large classes I took, discussion sessions were held every week with a graduate teaching assistant in which there was a lot of interaction. Besides, the teachers for these classes had office hours, and they were always willing to answer questions and talk over problems.

The writer uses personal experiences with large and small classes in both paragraphs to support the thesis statement. In the first paragraph, he says that in introductory classes the teachers' lectures were basically the same no matter how many students there were. In fact, in his experience, teachers were more dynamic in larger classes.

The second paragraph says that people think there is more interaction in small classes than in large ones, but that, in fact, the writer found that there was a lot of interaction in the weekly discussion sessions held in conjunction with the large classes. He also says that the teachers held office hours in which to answer questions.

Body 3

The most obviously important characteristic of jet travel is the high speed involved. A hundred years ago, it took weeks to cross the Atlantic or Pacific oceans by ship. However, today, those same trips can be completed in a matter of hours. One can attend a meeting in Paris and have dinner in New York on the same day. These amazing speeds have changed people's concepts of space. Today the world is much smaller than it was in the past.

Convenience is another reason why international jet travel is so important. In the past, if someone wanted to travel between Europe and North America, he or she might have to wait days or even weeks before a ship sailed. Furthermore, there were only a few ports in Europe where one could board a large ship, and almost all of them went only to New York City. Today, however, there are probably several hundred flights a day connecting the two continents and one can board international flights in the airport of almost every large European city and fly to any large city in the United States or Canada.

Another important aspect of jet travel is its relatively low cost. An international journey one hundred years ago was extremely expensive. Only wealthy people could afford to travel comfortably, in first class. Poor people had to save for years to purchase a ticket, and the conditions in which they traveled were often miserable. Today, it is possible for more and more people in every country to travel in comfort. Thus, it is possible for business people to do business all over the world, for students to attend universities in other countries, and for tourists to take vacations anywhere in the world.

In its topic sentence, the first paragraph gives the first reason why jet transport is an important development: its speed. The writer compares the speed of jets with that of ships one hundred years ago, gives an example of the speed of jets (attending a meeting in Paris, having dinner in New York on the same day), and shows the effect of this speed on the way people view the world.

In the second paragraph, the writer mentions the convenience of travel by jet, explaining how passengers can fly on almost any day and leave from and arrive at any large city. In the past, ships left only every few weeks and from only a few ports.

The third paragraph begins by stating another important aspect of jet travel: its relatively low cost. The writer again compares travel today with travel in the past and shows how more and more people travel comfortably. He gives examples of specific types of people who have been affected by the affordability of jet travel: business people, students, and tourists.

(C) Writing the Conclusion

Like the introduction, the conclusion for a response can be fairly short and simple. It does not have to be more than a few sentences in length. The conclusion should give the reader the feeling of completion, not a feeling that the writer has simply run out of ideas or out of time.

Here are some of the functions a conclusion can serve:

▶ To present the thesis statement (if this is not presented in the introduction)
▶ To restate the thesis statement (if this is given in the introduction)
▶ To summarize the main points presented in the body
▶ To show the significance of the points made in the body
▶ To present one last compelling reason why the writer's opinion is the correct one

Look at these samples of concluding paragraphs:

WRITING

Conclusion 1

All in all, I agree with the concept that zoos are desirable institutions. Opposition to zoos, I think, is mainly based on outmoded ideas of zoos. Today's zoos protect animals and educate people about animals and the environmental dangers they face.

This conclusion begins with the thesis statement for the response—that the writer agrees with those that support zoos. The writer also summarizes key points from the body: that opposition to zoos is based on ideas about zoos that are no longer valid, and that modern zoos protect animals and provide educational experiences for visitors.

Conclusion 2

In conclusion, I don't think that the size of a class is very important. I think that learning depends more on the quality of the teaching than on the number of students in the class.

This is a very simple conclusion that restates the thesis statement from the introduction and summarizes the main point of the body paragraphs.

Conclusion 3

To summarize, the speed, the convenience, and the low cost of international jet travel have changed the world. Individual nations are not as isolated as they were in the past, and people now think of the whole planet as they once thought of their own hometowns.

This conclusion summarizes points made in the body paragraphs and shows the significance of these points.

EXERCISE **27.1**

FOCUS: Writing Independent Responses.

DIRECTIONS: Write responses for prompts 1, 2, and 3 below. Give yourself about twenty minutes per response. (*Note:* You may use the notes and informal outlines that you wrote for these prompts in Exercises 25.1 and 25.2, pp. 665–670.) If possible, write your responses on a computer. Otherwise, you may use the spaces provided below.

Prompt 1

> Some people believe that schools should primarily teach students how to best compete with others. Other people believe that schools should primarily teach students how to cooperate with others. Which of these approaches do you favor? Use specific reasons and examples to support your answer.

Response 1

_____

_____

_____

_____

_____

_____

_____

_____

_____

_____

_____

_____

_____

_____

_____

_____

_____

Prompt 2

Imagine that you can talk for one hour with any person who has lived at any time in history. Which person would you choose to meet? Use specific details and examples to explain your choice.

Response 2

_____

_____

_____

_____

_____

_____

_____

_____

_____

_____

_____

_____

_____

_____

_____

_____

_____

_____

_____

_____

_____

_____

_____

_____

_____

Prompt 3

Do you agree or disagree with the following statement?
When people are traveling, they often behave differently from the way they behave at home.
Use specific details and examples to support your answer.

Response 3

_____

_____

_____

_____

_____

_____

_____

_____

_____

_____

_____

_____

_____

_____

_____

_____

_____

_____

_____

_____

_____

WRITING

EXERCISE **27.2**

FOCUS: More practice writing Independent Writing Responses.

DIRECTIONS: Write responses for prompts 4, 5, and 6 below. Give yourself about twenty minutes per response. (*Note:* You may use the notes and informal outlines that you wrote for these prompts in Exercises 25.1 and 25.2, pp. 665–670). If possible, write your responses on a computer. Otherwise, you may use the spaces provided below.

Prompt 4

> Some university students prefer living in campus housing such as dormitories. Other students prefer living in off-campus housing such as apartments. If you were faced with this decision, which of these two options would you choose? Use specific reasons and details to explain your choice.

Response 4

_____

_____

_____

_____

_____

_____

_____

_____

_____

_____

_____

_____

_____

_____

_____

_____

_____

_____

_____

_____

Prompt 5

Do you agree or disagree with the following statement?

It is better for university students to first get a general education, taking classes in many fields, than it is for them to take classes only in their own field of study.

Use specific details and examples to support your answer.

Response 5

_____

_____

_____

_____

_____

_____

_____

_____

_____

_____

_____

_____

_____

_____

_____

_____

_____

_____

_____

_____

_____

Prompt 6

Your hometown has just received a grant from an international organization to fund a single improvement project. Which of the following would you recommend to receive the funding?

the city airport

the police department

the local schools

the public transportation system

the art museum

the streets and roads

the fire department

the city parks

the local hospitals

Give specific examples and reasons to support your recommendation.

Response 6

_____

_____

_____

_____

_____

_____

_____

_____

_____

_____

_____

_____

_____

_____

_____

_____

_____

_____

_____

_____

_____

LESSON 28
CHECKING AND EDITING THE INDEPENDENT RESPONSE

You should give yourself about five minutes after writing the essay to look for and correct mistakes. You will need to look for the same kinds of mistakes that you looked for when checking and editing the Integrated Writing Response.

(A) Checking and Editing Content and Organizational Errors

Again, there will not be enough time to make any major changes in the organization of your responses. However, you should quickly check for the following problems:

1. **Problems in the introduction**
   ▶ Does the introduction accurately restate the prompt?
   ▶ Is there a thesis statement that summarizes your opinion of the prompt? (In some responses, the thesis statement is given in the conclusion.)

2. **Problems in the body paragraphs**
   ▶ Does all the information in the body paragraphs develop and support your opinion as given in the thesis statement?
   ▶ Are there reasons, examples, details, or experiences from your own life that support general statements?
   ▶ Are there sentences in the body that are unrelated to the thesis statement? (If so, delete them.)
   ▶ Do the ideas flow clearly from sentence to sentence and paragraph to paragraph? If not, can you add transition words that improve the flow of ideas?

3. **Problems in the conclusion**
   ▶ Is there a conclusion that gives readers the feeling that the essay is complete?

(B) Checking and Editing Grammatical Errors

The grammatical errors that you will be checking for in the Independent Response are the same as those in the Integrated Response. The most common errors are listed here:

1. Sentence fragments and run-on sentences
2. Verb errors
3. Pronoun errors
4. Singular and plural errors
5. Incorrect word forms

   For more information, see Lesson 24 about editing the Integrated Response (pp. 635–636), and for explanations, examples, and exercises involving these and other written structures, see the Writing Tutorial on Grammar (pp. 706–729).

(C) Checking and Editing Mechanical Errors

You should check your response for the following mechanical problems:

1. Spelling errors
2. Punctuation errors
3. Capitalization errors
4. Paragraphing problems

Again, see Lesson 24 (pp. 635–636) for more information about editing these kinds of problems.

EXERCISE 28.1

FOCUS: Checking and editing organizational/content errors, grammatical errors, and mechanical errors in paragraphs taken from Independent Writing Responses.

DIRECTIONS: Each of the following paragraphs contains a number of mistakes. Find as many mistakes in the paragraph as possible. Correct the mistakes, writing in the space between the lines. Then use your corrections to rewrite the paragraph. The first sentence of paragraph 1 is done as an example.

Paragraph 1

~~The~~ Technology has had *a* major impact ~~in~~ *on* many field*s*. Nowadays we can't even suppose business, communication, or traveling without computers. I want to discuss about the impact of computers on the education. The modern technology has made live easy for students and professors. If a student want to contact with a professor, you haven't problem. It is enough only to send professor's an e-mail and you haven't to go to office. More over, many university created special network for students in order to make the studying process easy for its students. For such kind net you could enter only by using your pass word and identification number. There are many categories you can chose to enter, such as "student tools" or "assignment box" where you can know about your homeworks. Also is possible to access to the university library to make researches. Computers also give students opportunity to gather informations about various topic from the internet. It is one of most easiest ways of making research for student. One other way that computers can help students, especially those from another countries, to stay touch with their freinds and family at their home, personally I could not study in usa if not contact with my family, because I am both student as well as work as a manager in my families business so I must stay in touch with my assistents.

Technology has had a major impact on many fields.

_____

_____

_____

_____

_____

_____

_____

_____

_____

_____

_____

Paragraph 2

Some people are believing that is impossible falling in love with someone "at the first sight." In the other hand, there are others people who are believing that you recognition a person that you love immediately. I know its possible falling in love at first sight. Because this happened to my wife and I.

_____

_____

_____

_____

_____

_____

_____

Paragraph 3

If you are ever in thailand in month of may I suggest you to go to the Rocket Fetival. It held every year in a small town called yasothon about 500 kilometer bangkok. bangkok has many beautiful temples, including the temple of the dawn. This two day fetival is well known and famous in thailand. It mark the beginning of rice growing season. Fetival will open with a parate of women performing a Bang Fai Dance. They dance around villagers carrying colorful rockets in shape of river snakes. Villagers construct gigantic home made rockets and fire them into the sky to 'ensure' plentiful raining during the rice-planting season. The farmers believe if spirit pleased by their actions, he will deliver the raining necessary for good rice harvest. People from all over thailand and tourists from all over world join the local people in celebrate. First single rocket launched to forefell the next season's rains. The higher it goes, the better is raining. Then, the rocket competition begins with the same rule - the rocket that goes highest is the winner of the game. If a rocket fails take off or explores, the owner will be throw into the mud. The Rocket Festival is spectacular and provides a great opportunity to experience fun. However, if you go, you need being careful. Both villagers or tourists sometimes injure or even kill by rockets that goes out of control.

_____

_____

_____

_____

_____

_____

_____

_____

_____

_____

_____

_____

_____

_____

_____

_____

Paragraph 4

When I was small child I live in the town of Sendai, the biggest city in the north part of japan. My grandmother live in Tokyo. Which is in the center part of Japan. While I was live in Sendai, I often went to see my grandmother, but it takes five hours to get to tokyo by local train. Since about twenty-five years ago, the high speed express train called the "Shinkansen" (bullet train) built, and connected between Sendai and Tokyo. For me personally, this was most importent development in transportation. It now take only a hour and half to travel to Tokyo from Sendai. The trip become very easy. It also was a great impact on sendai. Economics development there increased. In the negative side, prices for housing and other things went up. In the whole, however, this development was very big benefit for the city.

_____

_____

_____

_____

_____

_____

_____

_____

_____

_____

_____

_____

Paragraph 5

I'm from Korea. Once, Koreans had large families. They lived three times families altogether (grandparents-parents-children). They were almost farmers, so they preferred large numbers of families. In present, Korea has develop and society change from agriculture to industrial. Many people has moved from rural areas to urban ones. Because their job in the city. For example my husband went to Seoul in 2000 for his college. He leaved his parents and lived alone. After his graduation, he got a job at Seoul. At that time we worked together. After we marriaged, we lived at

Seoul. Of course his parents want us to live together them as Koreans traditional do, but we have no jobs in parents area. For me, I think this changes of society are natural and reasonable.

_____

_____

_____

_____

_____

_____

_____

_____

_____

_____

_____

Paragraph 6

Today you can see very often people arguing about advantages of computer game. There are millions of computer games today. Millions different ones. Some time computer games so attractive that young people, and not just young, can spend ours and even days in front of computer. And of cors if you spend to much tim on playing computer games you can heart your eye, physical conditions, and you can isolade yourself from sosiety, may be have problem communicating with other people.

_____

_____

_____

_____

_____

_____

_____

_____

_____

Paragraph 7

When I first come to the united states I was only 17 years old and have never been away from my home. I come here for one year. I lived with a family american in suburban of new orleans. I went to high school there. Imagine how difficult is it for me on a first day of school. I didn't know where should I go or what should I do. I spoken only little english. But, I was very fortunate. The daughter of my host families neighbors recognizing me, and she did everything for helping me. Not only, she helped me talk with the principal of the school and she introduced me my teacher for my first class. She even eat her lunch with me. I am still remember her kindness!

_____

_____

_____

_____

_____

_____

_____

_____

_____

_____

_____

WRITING REVIEW TEST
DIRECTIONS

▶ Now start the Audio Program. 🎧

This Writing Section tests your ability to write academic English. It consists of two writing tasks.

The first writing task is an "integrated" task. It involves reading a short passage and listening to a short lecture on the same topic. You will then have twenty minutes in which to write a response based on the information in the passage and the lecture.

Now read the directions for the first writing task.

DIRECTIONS: Take three minutes to read the short passage on the following page. You may take notes as you read.

After three minutes have passed, turn the page and start the Audio Program. You will hear a lecture on the same topic as the reading. Again, you may take notes as you listen.

You will have twenty minutes to write your response. Your response should include information from both the reading and the lecture.

Your essay will be rated on the completeness and accuracy of your response as well as on the correctness and quality of your writing. A typical response should be 150 to 225 words.

You may use your notes and look at the reading passage as you write. (During the actual exam, you can view the reading passage on the left side of the computer screen after the lecture is over.)

You have twenty minutes in which to finish the Integrated Writing Task.

For three hundred years, there have been those who have been in favor of Free Trade. Allowing businesses from all over the world access to your country's markets, and having access to all the world's markets, supposedly helps the economies of both developing and developed countries. However, the theory that Free Trade has brought only blessings is simply not true.

Proponents of Free Trade claim that open trade policies lead to peaceful cooperation between nations on many levels and make war between trading partners impossible. Historically, this had not been the case. Most of the nations that fought each other in World War II had previously been trading partners. And even if trade disagreements do not lead to military conflicts, they may still poison the relationship between nations, even between "friendly" nations.

Free Trade brings global competition, and according to Free Trade advocates, competition brings lower prices. This may be true—at least at first. A giant international soft-drink company has what's called "economy of scale." The more soft drinks it produces, the cheaper it is to make them. Therefore, they can undersell local soft-drink producers. This international soft-drink maker also has a huge advertising budget, unlike local companies. By offering lower prices and filling the market with advertising, the giant company crowds out the local soft-drink companies. Many go bankrupt, and local workers lose their jobs. After the companies are gone, of course, there is little competition. Global companies can then charge whatever they want for their products.

Usually, governments that limit trade do so through "tariff barriers." In other words, they charge a tax on imported goods. This makes the cost of local goods more competitive with the cost of imported goods. And although it's a fact that is often forgotten, tariffs provide a useful source of income for governments—and at no cost to the taxpayers of their own countries.

Notes:

_____

_____

_____

_____

_____

_____

_____

_____

_____

_____

_____

_____

WRITING

▶ Now start the Audio Program. Listen to part of a lecture in an economics class. 🎧

Notes:

_____

_____

_____

_____

_____

> **Now get ready to answer the question. Remember, you may look back at the reading passage. You may also use your notes to help you. You have twenty minutes to prepare and write your response.**

Question:
Summarize the main points made in the lecture that you just heard, discussing how they differ from the points made in the reading. You can refer to the reading passage as you write.

_____

_____

_____

_____

_____

_____

_____

_____

_____

_____

_____

_____

► Now read the directions for the second writing task.

DIRECTIONS: Read the question below. You have thirty minutes to write your essay. This includes the time to plan, write, and revise your essay. A typical response should be a minimum of 300 words.

Your essay will be rated on the correctness and quality of your writing, including the way you organize your essay and develop and support your ideas.

> Do you agree or disagree with this statement?
>   The most important information does not come from books.
> Use specific reasons and examples to explain your choice.

_____

_____

_____

_____

_____

_____

_____

_____

_____

_____

_____

_____

_____

_____

_____

_____

_____

_____

_____

_____

_____

_____

_____

_____

WRITING

WRITING TUTORIAL: GRAMMAR

Grammar is not tested directly in the Writing section—there are no multiple-choice grammar items—but your ability to use written grammar correctly is an important part of your score on the Writing section. In this section of *The Guide,* some common grammar points are explained and exercises are provided.

GRAMMAR POINT 1: RUN-ON SENTENCES AND SENTENCE FRAGMENTS

When you are writing responses, it is easy to make two mistakes. The first is to write **run-on sentences.** These are not simply long sentences; they are sentences that consist of two or more clauses that are not correctly connected.

> RUN-ON SENTENCE: *Professional workers such as lawyers or accountants usually work longer hours than factory workers they have more freedom in planning their time.*

The sentence above has two independent clauses that are not correctly joined. You can repair run-on sentences by joining clauses correctly or by breaking the run-on sentences into two shorter sentences.

> CORRECTION A: *Professional workers such as lawyers or accountants usually work longer hours than factory workers; however, they have more freedom in planning their time.*
>
> CORRECTION B: *Professional workers such as lawyers or accountants usually work longer hours than factory workers. However, they have more freedom in planning their time.*

Another common mistake is to write a **sentence fragment:** an incomplete sentence that is missing some important sentence elements such as a verb or a subject. By themselves, adverb clauses, adjective clauses, and all kinds of phrases are fragments.

> FRAGMENT: Larry wasn't able to finish graduate school. *Because he didn't get a scholarship.*

Fragments can also be fixed in two ways: by joining the fragment to another sentence or by rewriting the fragment as a stand-alone sentence.

> CORRECTION A: Larry wasn't able to finish graduate school because he didn't get a scholarship.
>
> CORRECTION B: Larry wasn't able to finish graduate school. He didn't get a scholarship.

GRAMMAR EXERCISE 1

DIRECTIONS: Mark the following items **F** if they contain a fragment, **RU** if they are run-on sentences, and **C** if they are correct. Then write corrections eliminating fragments and run-ons. The first one is done for you as an example.

___F___   1. After its introduction in 1969. The float process became the world's principal method of manufacturing flat sheets of glass.

         After its introduction in 1969, the float process became the world's principal method of manufacturing flat sheets of glass.

_____   2. We heard a lecture by Professor Taylor. Who is the chairman of the history department.

_____   3. Thomas Edison invented the light bulb and the phonograph. But not the telephone.

_____   4. Arnold Palmer, a famous American golfer, is no longer playing professionally, but he is still respected by golf fans all over the world.

_____   5. Seals appear clumsy on the land, they are able to move short distances faster than most people can run.

_____   6. You can't get to the island from here. Without a boat.

_____   7. While all birds are alike in that they have feathers and lay eggs, there are great differences among them in terms of size, structure, and color.

_____   8. A barometer is a device it is used to measure atmospheric pressure.

WRITING

_____ 9. Sometimes cloth is made by blending natural fibers and synthetic fibers. Rayon and cotton, for example.

_____

_____

_____ 10. Professor Roberts bought a car in Rome. Then sold it in Amsterdam after her vacation.

_____

_____

_____ 11. Technical climbing means mountain climbing with special equipment, it shouldn't be attempted without training.

_____

_____

_____ 12. Almost 92% of people get married over one third of these marriages end in divorce half of all divorced people choose to get married a second time.

_____

_____

GRAMMAR POINT 2: ADJECTIVE CLAUSES

Adjective clauses—also called **relative clauses**—are a way of joining two sentences. However, test-takers sometimes use these clauses incorrectly.

In the joined sentence, the adjective clause modifies (describes) a noun in another clause of the sentence. An adjective clause begins with a word called an **adjective clause marker.**

I wanted the book. The book was already checked out.

The book _that I wanted_ was already checked out.

The adjective clause in this example begins with the marker _that_ and modifies the noun _book_.

Adjective clause markers are **relative pronouns** such as _who, that,_ or _which_ or the **relative adverbs** _when_ or _where_.

Adjective Clause Marker	Use	Example
who	Subject (people)	A neurologist is a doctor *who* specializes in the nervous system.
whom	Object (people)	This is the patient *whom* the doctor treated.
whose	Possessive (people/things)	Mr. Collins is the man *whose* house I rented.
which	Subject/Object (things)	The assignment, *which* was due last week, took me four hours to complete.
that	Subject/Object (people/things)	Art *that* is in public places can be enjoyed by everyone. (*that* as subject)
		The painting *that* Ms. Wallace bought was very expensive. (*that* as object)
where	Adverb (place)	That is the site *where* the bank plans to build its new headquarters.
when	Adverb (time)	This is the hour *when* the children usually go to bed.

Like all clauses, adjective clauses must have a subject and a verb. In some cases the adjective clause marker itself is the subject; in some cases, there is another subject.

The painting was very expensive. Ms. Wallace bought it.
The painting *that Ms. Wallace bought* was very expensive.

The adjective clause marker in the joined sentence replaces *it*, the object of the verb *bought*. In the joined sentence, the adjective clause keeps the subject—*Ms. Wallace*—that it had in the original sentence. Notice that the inclusion of the pronoun *it* in the joined sentence above would be an error. INCORRECT: The painting that Ms. Wallace bought *it* was very expensive.

The assignment took me four hours to complete. It was due last week.
The assignment, *which was due last week*, took me four hours to complete.

The adjective clause marker in the joined sentence replaces *it*, the subject of the second original sentence. In the joined sentence, the marker itself is the subject of the adjective clause.

WRITING

In some adjective clauses, the relative pronoun *that* may be used in place of *which* or *who*. These sentences are called **identifying adjective clauses** (also called **restrictive adjective clauses**). The information in the clause is needed to identify the noun. This type of clause is *not* set off by commas.

The island that we visited was beautiful.

The people that moved next door are very friendly.

In other adjective clauses (called **non-identifying** or **non-restrictive**), the clause provides "extra" information. It's not needed to identify the head noun. These clauses are always set off with commas.

Maui, which is one of the Hawaiian Islands, is quite beautiful.

The Smiths, who are our new neighbors, are very friendly.

The word *that* cannot be used to introduce this type of clause.

INCORRECT: Maui, that is one of the Hawaiian Islands, is quite beautiful.

INCORRECT: The Smiths, that are our new neighbors, are very friendly.

The adjective clause markers *which* and *whom* can also be used as objects of prepositions:

That is the topic. I will write on it.

That is the topic *on which* I will write.

Marie is the student. The teacher gave the special assignment to her.

Marie is the student *to whom* the teacher gave the special assignment.

You may also see sentences with adjective clauses used in this pattern:

quantifier* + *of* + relative clause

He met with two advisors. He had known both of them for years.

He met with two advisors, *both of whom* he had known for years.

I read a number of articles. Most of them were very useful.

I read a number of articles, *most of which* were very useful.

Grammar Exercise 2.1

DIRECTIONS: Join the two sentences below into a single sentence using adjective clause markers (*who, which, that, whom, whose,* and so on). The word in italics will be replaced. The first one is done for you as an example.

---

*Quantifiers are words that show numbers or amounts, such as *much, several, some, a few, both, many, most, all, each, one, two.*

1. Most folk songs are ballads. *They* have simple words and tell simple stories.

   Most folk songs are ballads that have simple words and tell simple stories.

2. A battery is a device. *It* provides electricity by chemical means.

   _____

3. In May, the university will finish building a new wing of the library. Rare books will be stored *there*.

   _____

4. The melting point is the temperature. At *this temperature,* a solid changes to a liquid.

   _____

5. A keystone species is a species of plant or animal. *Its* absence has a major effect on an ecological system.

   _____

6. Active stocks are stocks. *They* are frequently bought and sold.

   _____

7. There are many varieties of snakes. Most of *them* are harmless to humans.

   _____

8. Charlotte Gilman's best-known book is *Women and Economics.* In *this book* she urges women to become financially independent.

   _____

   _____

GRAMMAR EXERCISE 2.2

DIRECTIONS: Decide if the underlined word or phrase in the sentences below is used correctly. If the phrase is used correctly, mark the sentence **C**. If the sentence is used incorrectly, mark the sentence **X** and rewrite the underlined expression, correcting the mistake. The first one is done for you as an example.

__X__ 1. There are many species of plants and animals <u>that they</u> are peculiar to Hawaii.
   ____that____

_____ 2. Diamonds are often found in rock formations called pipes <u>that</u> resemble the throats of extinct volcanoes. _____

_____ 3. There are thousands of kinds of bacteria, many of <u>whom</u> are beneficial.
   _____

_____ 4. Today meteorologists obtain the information <u>that they</u> use to make weather predictions chiefly from satellites. _____

_____ 5. The Pritzker Prize is given every year to architects <u>their</u> work benefits humanity and the environment. _____

_____ 6. Pipettes are glass tubes, open at both ends, <u>which chemists use them</u> to transfer small volumes of liquid. _____

_____ 7. The size and shape of a nail depends primarily on the function <u>which for it was</u> intended. _____

_____ 8. Jakarta, <u>that</u> is the capital of Indonesia, is also the largest city. _____

GRAMMAR POINT 3: ADVERB CLAUSES

An **adverb clause** consists of a connecting word, called an **adverb-clause marker** (also called a **subordinate conjunction**) and at least a subject and a verb.

> The demand for economical cars increases *when gasoline becomes more expensive.*

In this example, the adverb-clause marker *when* joins the adverb clause to the main clause. The adverb clause contains a subject (*gasoline*) and a verb (*becomes*).
An adverb clause can precede the main clause or follow it. When the adverb clause comes first, it is separated from the main clause by a comma.

> *When gasoline becomes more expensive,* the demand for economical cars increases.

Adverb Clause Marker	Use	Example
because	cause	*Because* the speaker was sick, the program was canceled.
since	cause	*Since* credit cards are so convenient, many people use them.
although	opposition	*Although* Mr. Crane earns a good salary, he never saves any money.
even though	opposition	*Even though* Rosa was tired, she stayed up late.
while	contrast	Some people arrived in taxis *while* others took the subway.
if	condition	*If* the automobile had not been invented, what would people use for basic transportation?
unless	negative condition	I won't go *unless* you do.
when	time	Your heart rate increases *when* you exercise.

while	time	Some people like to listen to music *while* they are studying.
as	time	One train was arriving *as* another was departing.
since	time	We haven't seen Professor Hill *since* she returned from her trip.
until	time	Don't put off going to the dentist *until* you have a problem.
once	time	*Once* the dean arrives, the meeting can begin.
before	time	*Before* he left the country, Richard bought some traveler's checks.
after	time	Emily will give a short speech *after* she receives the award.

When the subject of the main clause and the subject of the adverb clause are the same person or thing, the adverb clause can be reduced (shortened). **Reduced adverb clauses** do not contain a verb or a subject. They consist of a marker and either a present or past participle. If the verb in the full adverb clause is active, the present participle is used. If the verb in the full adverb clause is passive, a past participle is used.

When astronauts are orbiting the earth, they don't feel the force of gravity.
(full adverb clause with an active verb)

When orbiting the earth, astronauts don't feel the force of gravity.
(reduced clause with present participle)

Although it had been damaged, the machine was still operational.
(full adverb clause with a passive verb)

Although damaged, the machine was still operational.
(reduced clause with a past participle)

You will most often see reduced adverb clauses with the markers *although, while, if, when, before, after,* and *until.* Reduced adverb clauses are NEVER used after *because.*

Don't use *because* in the expression *reason . . . because . . .* Use *reason . . . that.*

INCORRECT:	The reason Laura moved to Arizona is *because* she enjoys a warm, dry climate.
CORRECT:	The reason Laura moved to Arizona is *that* she enjoys a warm, dry climate.

There are certain **prepositions** that have essentially the same meaning as adverb clause markers but are used with noun phrases or pronouns, not with clauses.

WRITING

Preposition	Related Marker	Example
because of	*because/since*	Roberto chose that university *because of* its fine reputation.
due to	*because/since*	The accident was *due to* mechanical failure.
on account of	*because/since*	Visibility is poor today *on account of* air pollution.
in spite of	*although/even though*	He enjoys racing motorcycles *in spite of* the danger.
despite	*although/even though*	*Despite* its loss, the team is still in first place.

GRAMMAR EXERCISE 3.1

DIRECTIONS: Join the two sentences below into a single sentence using the adverb clause marker or other words in parentheses (   ). The first one is done for you as an example.

1. (if)
   Small sailboats can easily capsize. They are not handled carefully.
   <u>Small sailboats can easily capsize if they are not handled carefully.</u>

2. (although)
   Parrots are tropical birds. They can live in temperate or even cold climates.

   _____

3. (since)
   Advertising has had an enormous effect on American life. It is so widespread in the United States.

   _____

4. (as)
   A wave moves towards shore. Its shape is changed by its collision with the shallow sea bottom.

   _____

5. (when) *Use a reduced adverb clause.*
   It can be added to a liquid. Antifreeze lowers the freezing temperature of that liquid.

   _____

6. (while)
   Most bamboo blooms every year. There are some species that flower only two or three times a century.

   _____

7. (once) *Use a reduced adverb clause.*

It is granted by the Patent Office. A patent becomes the inventor's property.

GRAMMAR EXERCISE 3.2

DIRECTIONS: Decide if the underlined word or phrase in the sentences below is used correctly. If the phrase is used correctly, mark the sentence **C**. If the sentence is used incorrectly, mark the sentence **X** and rewrite the underlined expression, correcting the mistake.

_____ 1. <u>Although</u> their light weight, aluminum alloys can be very strong.

_____ 2. Snake birds were not given their names because they eat snakes but <u>because of</u> their long, thin necks resemble snakes. _____

_____ 3. <u>Although people</u> are increasingly linked over long distances by electronic means of communication, but many of them still prefer face-to-face encounters.

_____ 4. <u>In spite of</u> its frightening appearance, the octopus is shy and completely harmless. _____

_____ 5. The reason large bodies of water never freeze solid is <u>because</u> the sheet of ice on the surface protects the water below it from the cold air. _____

_____ 6. Natural silk is still highly prized <u>even though</u> similar artificial fabrics are available. _____

_____ 7. <u>Because of</u> cheese is essentially a concentrated form of milk, it contains the same nutrients as milk. _____

GRAMMAR POINT 4: WORD FORMS

One common problem in test-takers' writing is the incorrect use of one part of speech (a noun, verb, adjective, or adverb) in place of the correct part of speech. Parts of speech can often be identified by their suffixes (word endings).

Common Noun Endings

-tion	information	-ery	recovery
-sion	provision	-ship	scholarship
-ence	existence	-tude	multitude
-ance	acceptance	-ism	capitalism
-ity	creativity	-cracy	democracy
-hood	childhood	-logy	biology
-dom	wisdom	-ness	happiness
-th	health	-ment	experiment
-age	marriage		

Endings for Nouns That Refer to Persons

-er	explorer	-ee	employee
-or	sailor	-ic	comic
-ist	psychologist	-ian	technician
-ent	student	-ant	attendant

Common Verb Endings

-ize	realize	-ify	satisfy
-en	shorten	-ate	incorporate
-er	recover		

Common Adjective Endings

-ate	moderate	-y	sunny
-ous	dangerous	-ic	economic
-al	normal	-ical	logical
-ial	remedial	-ory	sensory
-able	comfortable	-less	hopeless
-ible	sensible	-ive	competitive
-ish	foolish	-ly	friendly
-ant	resistant	-ful	colorful
-ent	different	-ile	sterile

Adverb Endings

-ly	quickly	-ally	historically

The most common type of word form problem involves the use of an adverb in place of an adjective or an adjective in place of an adverb. A few points to keep in mind:

▶ **Adjectives** modify nouns, noun phrases, gerunds, and pronouns.

Hang up your *wet* clothes. (adjective modifying the noun *clothes*)

The two children were *kind.* (adjective modifying the noun phrase *the two children*)

We saw some *wonderful* acting in the play. (adjective modifying the gerund *acting*)

They were very *brave.* (adjective modifying the pronoun *they*)

- Adjectives often come before words they modify.

  an *important* test   a *quiet* evening   a *long* article

- Adjectives may also follow the verb *to be* and other linking verbs.

  The glass was *empty.*

  That song sounds *nice.*

  They look *upset.*

- They often answer the question *What kind?*

  She is a *brilliant* scholar. (What kind of a scholar is she? *A brilliant one.*)

▶ **Adverbs** modify many types of words, including verbs, participles, adjectives, and other adverbs.

Ann *eagerly* accepted the challenge. (adverb modifying the verb *accepted*)

It was a *rapidly* changing situation. (adverb modifying the present participle *changing*)

She wore a *brightly* colored scarf. (adverb modifying the past participle *colored*)

Ted seemed *extremely* curious about that topic. (adverb modifying the adjective *curious*)

The accident occurred *incredibly* quickly. (adverb modifying the adverb *quickly*)

- Sometimes adverbs are used at the beginning of sentences, usually followed by a comma. These adverbs modify the entire sentence rather than one word in the sentence.

  Generally, I like my classes.

  Usually Professor Fowles's lectures are more interesting than the one he gave today.

- Adverbs of manner are formed by adding the suffix -*ly* to an adjective (or -*ally* if the adjective ends with the letter -*c*).

  quick   quickly   comic   comically

  comfortable   comfortably   historic   historically

- Adverbs of manner answer the question *How?*

  Ms. Lang treats her employees *honestly.* (How does she treat her employees? *Honestly.*)

- A few adverbs (*fast, hard,* and *high,* for example) have the same form as adjectives.

  Charles bought a *fast* car. (adjective)

  He was driving so *fast* that he got a speeding ticket. (adverb)
- *Well* is the irregular adverb form of the adjective *good.*

  Juan is an exceptionally *good* student.

  He did very *well* on the last test.

Besides adjective/adverb problems, there are many other word form problems. Some examples are given here:

Corn played an important role in the *cultural* of the Indians of the Southwest.

(The noun *culture,* not the adjective *cultural,* is needed.)

The galaxy Andromeda is the most *distance* object visible to observers in the Northern Hemisphere.

(The adjective *distant* is needed in place of the noun *distance.*)

Scientists *belief* that the continents once formed a single continent surrounded by an enormous sea.

(The verb *believe* is needed in place of the noun *belief.*)

Bunsen burners are used to *hot* materials in a chemistry lab.

(The adjective *hot* is used incorrectly in place of the verb *heat.*)

Grammar Exercise 4.1

DIRECTIONS: Underline the form that correctly completes the sentence.

1. Floods cause billions of dollars worth of property damage (annual/annually).

2. Writer Ernest Hemingway is known for his (simple/simply) language and lively dialogue.

3. Most snails venture out to look for (feed/food) only after sunset or on (rain/rainy) days.

4. The Richter Scale measures the (severely/severity) of earthquakes.

5. (General/Generally), bauxite is found near the surface, so it is relatively (simple/simply) to mine.

6. By-products from chicken eggs are used by (industry/industrial) in manufacturing such (produces/products) as soap and paint.

7. Analgesics such as aspirin are used to (relieve/relief) pain and reduce fever.

8. Rose Han Lee wrote a number of (scholar/scholarly) accounts about the effects of (immigrant/immigration) on mining towns in the western United States.

9. A gap in the Coast Range of California provides (easy/easily) access to the San Francisco Bay area.

10. The Nassau grouper is a (tropics/tropical) fish that is noted for its (able/ability) to change color.

11. Some airplanes have an automatic pilot that is connected to the airplane's controls and (automatic/automatically) keeps the plane on course.

12. Alpha rays (loss/lose) energy (rapidity/rapidly) as they pass through matter.

13. The cherry is one of the only fruits that will not (ripe/ripen) if it is removed from the tree.

14. The tiny coral snake is (beautiful/beautifully) but deadly.

15. Colorado shares with Wyoming the (distinction/distinctly) of having four (perfect/perfectly) straight borders.

GRAMMAR EXERCISE 4.2

DIRECTIONS: Decide if the underlined word or phrase in the sentences below is used correctly. If the phrase is used correctly, mark the sentence **C**. If the phrase is used incorrectly, mark the sentence **X** and rewrite the underlined expression, correcting the mistake.

_____ 1. Liberal arts colleges cultivate general <u>intellectually</u> abilities rather than technical or professional skills. _____

_____ 2. Goats are extremely <u>destructive</u> to natural vegetation and are often responsible for soil erosion. _____

_____ 3. One important branch of linguistics is semantics, which <u>analysis</u> the meaning of words. _____

_____ 4. Unlike folk <u>dancers</u>, which are the product of a single culture, ballet is an international art form. _____

_____ 5. Bears can move rapidly when necessary and are skillful tree-climbers for their size and <u>weigh</u>. _____

_____ 6. Peach trees grow <u>good</u> in a variety of soil types but do best in sandy loam. _____

_____ 7. A chemical <u>react</u> that absorbs heat is called endothermic. _____

_____ 8. Some games rely mainly on skill and practice while others primarily involve <u>luck</u>. _____

_____ 9. To make candles, pioneers twisted string into wicks, dipped the wicks into hot fat, then hung the candles to cool and <u>hard</u>. _____

GRAMMAR POINT 5: VERBS

Errors with verbs are common in test-takers' writing. You should automatically check all your verbs when you edit your response.

Some points about verbs to keep in mind:

▶ A gerund, infinitive, or participle cannot be used alone as a sentence verb.

INCORRECT: The woman *going* to her office.

INCORRECT: The woman *to go* to her office.

INCORRECT: The woman *gone* to her office.

▶ If the subject of the sentence *performs* the action, the verb must be in the **active voice.**

The architect *designed* the building. (active verb)

▶ If the subject of the sentence *receives* the action, the verb must be in the **passive voice.**

The building *was designed* by the architect. (passive verb)

▶ The verb must **agree** with its subject. Singular subjects require singular verbs; plural subjects require plural verbs.

The class *is* . . .	The classes *are* . . .
The bicycle *was* . . .	The bicycles *were* . . .
The game *has* been . . .	The games *have* been . . .
The child *likes* . . .	The children *like* . . .

- A sentence with two subjects joined by *and* takes a plural verb.

  The chemistry lab and the physics lab *are* . . .

- Some words end in *-s* but are singular in form. Many of these words are the names of fields of study (*economics, physics,* and so on). *News* is another word of this kind.

  Economics *is* . . .

  The news *was* . . .

- Subjects with *each* and *every* take singular verbs. (This includes compound words like *everyone* and *everything.*)

  Each state *has* . . .

  Each of the representatives *was* . . .

  Every person *was* . . .

  Everyone *wants* . . .

- Singular subjects used with phrases such as *along with, accompanied by, together with, as well as,* and *in addition to* take singular verbs.

  The mayor, along with the city council, *is* . . .

  Together with his friends, Mark *has* . . .

- Quantities of time, money, distance, and so on, usually take a singular verb.

  Five hundred dollars *was* . . .

  Two years *has* . . .

  Ten miles *is* . . .

► The appropriate **tense** must be used according to the time-related words or ideas in the sentence.

The simple present tense is a general time tense. It usually indicates that a condition is always true or that an action always occurs. It may also indicate that an action regularly occurs.

The atmosphere *surrounds* the Earth.

Karen often *stays* at this hotel.

Generally, the lectures in this class *are* very interesting.

- The future tense is used for future time.

  Next semester I *will take* a chemistry class.

- The simple past tense indicates that an action took place at a specific time in the past.

  They *moved* to Phoenix five years ago.

  This house *was built* in the 1920's.

  Dinosaurs *lived* millions of years ago.

- The present perfect tense usually indicates that an action began at some time in the past and continues to the present. It may also indicate that an action took place at an unspecified time in the past.

  Mr. Graham *has worked* for this company since 2003.

  Steven *hasn't been* to a doctor for over a year.

  Jennifer *has* recently *returned* from Europe.

► The correct **form** of the main verb—base form, *-ing* form, past tense, past participle—must be used.

The base form follows all modal auxiliaries (verb forms such as *can, could,* and *might*).

might be	can remember	should study
must know	could go	may follow

- Certain similar auxiliary verbs require infinitives (*to* + base form of the verb).

ought to attend	used to play	have to hurry

- The past participle is used after a form of *have* in all perfect forms of the verb.

has done	had called	should have said
have run	will have read	could have made

- The *-ing* form is used after a form of *be* in all progressive forms of the verb.

is sleeping	has been writing	should have been wearing
was working	had been painting	will be waiting

- The past participle is used after a form of *be* in all passive forms of the verb.

is worn	has been shown	would have been lost
is being considered	had been promised	might have been canceled
were told	will have been missed	

GRAMMAR EXERCISE 5.1

DIRECTIONS: Complete the sentence with the correct form of the verb in parentheses ( ). The first one is done for you as an example.

1. Physician Alice Hamilton (know) __is known__ today for her research on industrial diseases.

2. The business school at our university (found) _____ almost 100 years ago.

3. For thousands of years, farmers (use) _____ scarecrows to protect their crops from hungry birds.

4. NASA's space probe New Horizon (fly) _____ by the planet Pluto in the year 2015.

5. Before the late eighteenth century, most textiles (make) _____ at home.

6. Sarah Knight (write) _____ a fascinating account of a journey she made from Boston to New York in 1704.

7. Each of the four types of human tooth (suit) _____ to a specific purpose.

8. Since about 1980, computers and new methods of communication (revolutionize) _____ office work.

GRAMMAR EXERCISE 5.2

DIRECTIONS: Decide if the underlined word or phrase in the sentences below is used correctly. If the phrase is used correctly, mark the sentence **C**. If the sentence is used incorrectly, mark the sentence **X** and rewrite the underlined expression, correcting the mistake. The first one is done for you as an example.

____ 1. Cans of paint must be <u>shaking</u> before use to mix the pigments with the medium in which they are suspended. __shaken__

____ 2. Each of the Ice Ages <u>were</u> more than a million years long. _____

____ 3. The white pine <u>is</u> the most commercially important forest tree in North America until the beginning of the twentieth century. _____

____ 4. The first bicycle race on record in the United States <u>taken</u> place in 1883. _____

____ 5. Teeth <u>are</u> covered with a hard substance called enamel. _____

____ 6. When scientists search a site for fossils, they begin by examining places where the soil has <u>wore</u> away from the rock. _____

_____   7. The first seven American astronauts <u>were chose</u> in 1959. _____

_____   8. Medical students must <u>to study</u> both the theory and practice of medicine. _____

_____   9. Ethics <u>is</u> the study of moral duties, principles, and values. _____

_____   10. In music, a chord is the sound of two or more notes that <u>are playing</u> together. _____

_____   11. Every one of the body's billions of cells <u>requires</u> a constant supply of food and oxygen. _____

_____   12. The more or less rhythmic succession of economic booms and busts <u>are</u> referred to as the business cycle. _____

_____   13. In the late nineteenth century, many important theories in both the biological and the physical sciences <u>have been produced</u>. _____

_____   14. Chromium <u>used</u> to make stainless steel. _____

GRAMMAR POINT 6: PARTICIPLES

Participles are verbal adjectives. There are two kinds of participles: present participles and past participles. The present participle always ends in *-ing*. The past participle of regular verbs ends in *-ed,* but many verbs have irregular past participles.

Participial phrases (a participle and related words) are often used after nouns. Participial phrases used this way are actually **reduced** (shortened) **adjective clauses.** Present participles are used to reduce adjective clauses that contain active verbs.

> Minnesota, *which joined the Union in 1858,* became the thirty-second state. (full adjective clause with an active verb)
>
> Minnesota, *joining the Union in 1858,* became the thirty-second state. (participial phrase with a present participle)

Past participles are used to reduce adjective clauses with passive verbs.

> The College of William and Mary, *which was founded in 1693,* is the second oldest college in the United States. (full adjective clause with a passive verb)
>
> The College of William and Mary, *founded in 1693,* is the second oldest college in the United States. (participial phrase with a past participle)

Participial phrases can also come before the subject of a sentence.

> *Joining the Union in 1858,* Minnesota became the thirty-second state.
>
> *Founded in 1693,* William and Mary College is the second oldest university in the United States.

WRITING

Participles can also be used before nouns as one-word adjectives. When used before a noun, present participles have an active meaning; past participles have a passive meaning.

It was an *exhausting* ten-kilometer race. (present participle)

The *exhausted* runners were too tired to move after the race. (past participle)

In the first sentence, the race exhausts the runners. The race "performs" the action. In the second sentence, the runners are exhausted by the race. They receive the action.

GRAMMAR EXERCISE 6.1

DIRECTIONS: In the following sentences, change the adjective clauses to reduced adjective clauses (participial phrases). The first one is done for you as an example.

1. Aerodynamics is the study of the forces that act on an object as it moves through the atmosphere.
   Aerodynamics is the study of the forces acting on an object as it moves through the atmosphere.

2. Anyone who works under conditions that cause a heavy loss of perspiration can suffer heat exhaustion.

   _____

   _____

3. A mosquito that is filled with blood is carrying twice its own body weight.

   _____

   _____

4. A delta is a more or less triangular area of sediments that is deposited at the mouth of a river.

   _____

   _____

5. Natural resources provide the raw materials that are used to produce finished goods.

   _____

   _____

6. In this part of the campus there are several buildings that date from the 1790's.

   _____

   _____

7. A filter that is placed in front of a camera lens changes the color of the light that reaches the film.

_____

_____

GRAMMAR EXERCISE 6.2

DIRECTIONS: Decide if the underlined word or phrase in the sentences below is used correctly. If the phrase is used correctly, mark the sentence **C**. If the sentence is used incorrectly, mark the sentence **X** and rewrite the underlined expression, correcting the mistake. The first one is done for you as an example.

_____ 1. An avalanche can race down a mountainside with great speed and <u>devastated</u> results. ___*devastating*___

_____ 2. Most candles are made of paraffin wax <u>mixing</u> with compounds that have higher melting points to keep them from melting in hot weather. _____

_____ 3. Plants <u>growing</u> for their strong fiber include flax and hemp. _____

_____ 4. <u>Produced</u> by the fermentation of organic matter, methane can be used as a fuel. _____

_____ 5. The Farallon Islands are a group of <u>uninhabited</u> islands lying about 40 miles west of San Francisco. _____

_____ 6. The <u>crushing</u> leaves of yarrow plants can serve as a traditional medicine for cleansing wounds. _____

_____ 7. Throughout his long career, Pete Seeger has been a <u>leading</u> figure in reviving folk music. _____

_____ 8. Geometry is the branch of mathematics <u>dealing</u> with the properties of lines, curves, shapes, and surfaces. _____

_____ 9. <u>Received</u> an average of 460 inches of rain a year, Mount Waialeale in Hawaii is the wettest spot in the world. _____

_____ 10. It has been known since at least the third century that coffee has a <u>stimulated</u> effect. _____

GRAMMAR POINT 7: PRONOUNS

A pronoun must agree with the noun to which it refers (the pronoun's **referent**).

INCORRECT: The best way for children to learn science is for them to perform experiments *himself.*

The referent is plural (*children*), so the reflexive pronouns must also be plural (*themselves*) to agree with it.

Sometimes writers make errors with the form of pronouns:

INCORRECT: This backpack is mine, and that one is *your.*

The word *your* should be changed to *yours.*

GRAMMAR EXERCISE 7

DIRECTIONS: If the underlined form is correct, mark the sentence **C**. If the underlined form is incorrect, mark the sentence **X** and write a correction for the underlined form in the blank at the end of the sentence.

_____   1. Investment banking is concerned with the sale of government bonds, and <u>they</u> also deals with corporate stocks and bonds. _____

_____   2. Compared to the fossil record of animals, <u>that</u> of plants is relatively skimpy. _____

_____   3. The emerald gets <u>their</u> beautiful green color from titanium and chromium impurities in the stone. _____

_____   4. Ducks make nests out of leaves and <u>its</u> own feathers. _____

_____   5. The molecules of a liquid are held together tighter than <u>that</u> of a gas. _____

_____   6. The clipper ship *Flying Cloud* was one of the fastest ships of <u>their</u> kind. _____

_____   7. There are between 100 and 400 billion stars in <u>ours</u> galaxy, the Milky Way. _____

_____   8. The arrangement of keys on the keyboard of a personal computer is almost the same as <u>those</u> on a standard typewriter. _____

_____   9. A beaver uses its strong front teeth to cut down trees and peel off <u>its</u> bark. _____

_____ 10. Savannah, Georgia, has preserved to a remarkable degree <u>its</u> historic houses and famous gardens. _____

_____ 11. Bees collect pollen, which furnishes protein for <u>its</u> diet. _____

_____ 12. People with myopia, or nearsightedness, have trouble focusing on distant objects, but <u>their</u> can see nearby objects clearly. _____

GRAMMAR POINT 8: SINGULAR AND PLURAL NOUNS

A common error in written responses is the use of singular nouns when plural nouns should be used and plural nouns that should be singular.

Certain determiners are used only before singular nouns while other determiners are used only before plural nouns.

Determiners Used with Singular Nouns	*Determiners Used with Plural Nouns*
a/an	two, three, four, *etc.*
one	dozens of, hundreds of, thousands of, *etc.*
a single	a few (of)
each	many (of)
every	a number of
this	the number of
that	a couple (of)
	several (of)
	every one of
	each one of
	each of
	one of
	these
	those

Each *contestant* won a prize.

Each of the *contestants* won a prize.

This *flower* is a yellow rose.

These *flowers* are yellow roses.

I only attended one *game* this season.

It was one of the most exciting *games* that I've ever attended.

Most plural nouns in English end in -*s*, but a few are irregular.

Common Irregular Plural Nouns

child	children
man	men
woman	women
foot	feet
mouse	mice
fish	fish
sheep	sheep
series	series

Sometimes writers incorrectly pluralize a non-count noun (such as *information, equipment, art, luggage,* and so on).

INCORRECT: I got some *informations* about this topic from an online encyclopedia.

Information is an uncountable noun and cannot be pluralized.

Compound nouns consist of two *nouns* used together to express a single idea: travel agent, house cat. Only the second noun of a compound noun is pluralized: travel agents, house cats.

INCORRECT: I enjoy reading biographies and *detectives stories.*

The correct plural form of this compound noun is *detective stories.*

Some errors involve numbers + measurements:

INCORRECT: They went for a *six-miles* hike.

There are two ways to say this correctly:

They went for a *six-mile* walk.
They walked *six miles.*

In the first sentence, the number + measurement is used as an adjective, and the measurement is singular. In the second, the measurement is a noun, and is therefore plural.

GRAMMAR EXERCISE 8.1

DIRECTIONS: Complete the sentences with the correct form of the noun in parentheses (singular or plural). The first one is done for you.

1. The major (source) __sources__ of air pollution vary from city to city.

2. Zoonoses are diseases that can be transmitted to (human) _____ beings by animals.

3. The Newbery Award is granted every year to the authors of outstanding books for (child) _____ .

4. Many championship (automobile) _____ and motorcycle races take place in Daytona Beach, Florida.

5. Russell Cave in northeastern Alabama was the home of cliff-dwelling Indians (thousand) _____ of years ago.

6. The electric toaster was one of the earliest (appliance) _____ to be developed for the kitchen.

GRAMMAR EXERCISE 8.2

DIRECTIONS: If the underlined form is correct, mark the sentence **C**. If the underlined form is incorrect, mark the sentence **X** and write a correction for the underlined form in the blank at the end of the sentence.

_____ 1. Tornadoes can pick up objects as heavy as automobiles and carry them for hundreds of <u>foots</u>. _____

_____ 2. Many <u>kind</u> of vegetables are grown in California's Imperial Valley. _____

_____ 3 In typical pioneer settlements, men, women, and children worked from morning until night at <u>farms</u> and household tasks. _____

_____ 4. Few of the doctors practicing in the thirteen North American colonies had formal training in <u>medicines</u>. _____

_____ 5. The pine tree is probably the most important lumber <u>tree</u> in the world. _____

_____ 6. Around seventy-five <u>percents</u> of the earth's surface is covered by water. _____

_____ 7. All colleges and universities get their <u>funds</u> from a variety of sources. _____

_____ 8. The Federalist Papers are a <u>500-pages</u> collection of eighteenth-century newspaper articles written to support the Constitution. _____

_____ 9. In 1821 Emma Willard founded Troy Female Seminary, the first institution of higher education for <u>woman</u> in the United States. _____

_____ 10. Phytoplankton is found only in the upper layers of the ocean, where <u>sunlights</u> can reach. _____

WRITING

COMMUNICATIVE ACTIVITIES FOR WRITING

Activity 1

News Report   *Individual Activity*

First, listen to a news broadcast on television or radio. If possible, record it. Take notes on a news story that interests you. Then, try to find information on the *same* story in an English-language newspaper or magazine or on a news Web site (such as the sites for National Public Radio, *The New York Times, USA Today,* CNN, or the BBC). Take notes on the information that you read.

   Now use your notes to write your own news report in English. Note how the information that you listened to differs from the information that you read. Mention these differences in the report that you write. After all the students have written news reports, you can put them together to create a newspaper.

Activity 2

Advice Column   *Individual and Class Activity*

First, find an advice column in a newspaper or online. (An advice column is a section of a newspaper or a Web site in which readers write letters about their personal problems and the columnist gives his or her advice. The *Dear Abby* column is one famous example of an American advice column, but there are many others.)

   After you are familiar with the format of advice columns, write a letter requesting advice. You can ask for advice to deal with a personal problem, an academic problem, or you can make up a problem! Your instructor/coordinator will distribute these requests so that each student has one, and then students will respond to the requests, giving suggestions on how to deal with the problems.

   Afterwards, each student will read aloud the letter requesting advice and the advice that he or she gave. The class can vote on who provided the best advice.

Activity 3

The Best of Everything   *Small-Group Activity*

Many newspapers publish "Best of" lists. These list the best shops, restaurants, and so on, for a community. You may first want to take a look at one or more of these lists. (Type *Best of* and the name of a city into your browser: *Best of Boston, Best of Toronto,* etc.) Next, meet in a small group and choose four or five categories for the best of *your* community (Best Shopping Mall, Best Coffee Shop, Best Ice Cream, Best Pizza). For each of the categories that you choose, select one place or product to be the best and write a short review. In other words, explain why you think this place or product is the best. Read your list to the class and discuss the choices.

Activity 4

Movie Review   *Individual/Pair Activity*

Choose a movie that you have seen recently and write a short review. In other words, give your opinion of the movie and explain why you did or did not enjoy it. Exchange your review with a partner. Next, find a review of the movie that your partner reviewed in a newspaper or magazine or on a Web site. Write a summary of the review that you find. Focus on how the reviewer's opinion was different from your partner's review. Read your partner's review and your summary to the class.

Activity 5

Letter to the Editor   *Individual Activity*

Read the "Letters to the Editor" section of a newspaper (usually found on the editorial page, which is often the last page of the first section). You can use a city newspaper or a university newspaper. Find a letter on a topic that interests you. Summarize the opinion of the letter writer, writing down his or her key arguments. Next, write a letter of your own, giving your own opinions and responding to the letter-writer's ideas. Read aloud the letter that you found and your response.

Activity 6

Editing Race   *Pairs or Small-Group Activity*

The instructor/coordinator will take a short passage from a newspaper, magazine, or Web site and rewrite it, adding a set number of grammatical or mechanical errors (say 10, 15, or 20). The coordinator will then give the passage with these mistakes to each pair or small group. As a group, try to find and mark these errors as quickly as possible. The first group to correctly identify all the errors wins.

Activity 7

Now You're Cooking   *Small-Group Activity*

Each student chooses a well-known international dish or a dish from his/her own country, then finds a recipe for that dish. Students can use a cookbook, visit an online cooking Web site, or e-mail someone who knows how to prepare the dish. The coordinator/instructor will choose several complicated dishes (from a cookbook or recipe) including the list of necessary ingredients and the directions for preparing the dish. Everyone takes notes. Afterwards, group members compare notes and try to recreate the recipes in writing.

Activity 8

Sentence Auction   *Small-Group/Class Activity*

The instructor/coordinator takes a number of sentences from a newspaper, magazine, or Web site and rewrites them. Some sentences will be correct, some will have one mistake, and some will have two.

Each group then receives $250.00 in play money or in an "account." The instructor/ coordinator will then auction off each sentence. In other words, each group makes a bid (an offer) and the highest offer wins the sentence.

A sentence with no mistakes is worth five points, one with one mistake is worth two points, and one with two mistakes is worth no points. The group with the greatest number of points at the end of the auction wins.

Activity 9

Write Your Own Prompts   *Pair Activity*

Look over some of the prompts for Independent Writing Tasks in this section of *The Guide.* With a partner, write one or more prompts of your own. Try to make these prompts as much as possible like the prompts that appear on actual tests. Afterwards, share the prompts that you wrote with the class. Decide which are the most accurate (most similar to those on real tests) and which ones would be the most interesting to write about. If you like, you can choose one of these prompts and, for more practice, write a response to it.

Activity 10

Student Teacher   *Individual Activity*

Your instructor/coordinator will choose several students to teach one of the eight Writing lessons in this text. Students who are selected will go back and study those lessons in detail, write out a lesson plan, and give a five- to ten-minute presentation on the lesson.

PRACTICE TESTS

ABOUT TAKING THE PRACTICE TESTS

One of the best ways to prepare for the TOEFL® iBT is to take realistic practice tests. The tests included with this program are up-to-date versions that include all the new item types found on the Internet-based test. As closely as possible, they duplicate the actual test in format, content, and level of difficulty.

If possible, take a test all at one time. If you are taking the tests at home, work away from distractions such as televisions or radios.

You can take these tests as paper-and-pencil tests or as computerized tests on the CD-ROM that accompanies *The Guide.*

If you take the tests in the book, for the Listening, Speaking, and Writing sections, you will need to use the Audio Program (the audio cassettes or CDs).

If you take the tests in the book, you should follow these guidelines:

Reading

Time yourself as you take this section (allow yourself 60 minutes). You can skip items in this section and go back to them later, and you can go back and change your answers if you want.

Listening

On the actual test, you will be able to control the speed at which you hear the questions. On the Audio Program, most questions are followed by a pause of 10 seconds. There is a 12-second pause after ordering and matching questions and a 15-second pause after complete-the-chart questions. However, you or your teacher can stop the tape or CD and give yourself more time. If possible, listen to the Audio Program through headphones.

While the conversations and lectures are being read, you should look only at the photos. Don't look at the questions or the answer choices until the question is read on the Audio Program. Don't skip questions, and don't go back to any questions after you have answered them.

Speaking

If possible, listen to the script for the Speaking Section using headphones and record your responses. A beep on the Audio Program tells you when your preparation time is over. Begin speaking then. A second beep tells you when your response time is over.

Writing

Time yourself carefully as you write both responses. If possible, write your responses on a computer.

Scoring the Practice Tests

You can use the charts on the following pages to calculate your approximate scores on the Practice Tests. Keep in mind that your scores on practice tests are not necessarily accurate predictors of what you will score on actual tests.

Reading

To calculate your score on the Reading Section, you must first find your raw score. Simply add up the number of correct answers in the Reading Section for all the questions except the last question in each set of questions (Questions 13, 26, and 39). In both tests, those questions are either summary questions or complete-the-chart questions. Here are the guidelines for scoring these questions:

Summary Questions

3 correct choices = 2 points

2 correct choices = 1 point

Fewer than 2 correct choices = 0 points

Complete-the-Chart Questions

Seven-answer chart

7 correct choices = 4 points

6 correct choices = 3 points

4 correct choices = 1 point

Fewer than 4 correct choices = 0 points

Five-answer chart

5 correct choices = 3 points

4 correct choices = 2 points

3 correct choices = 1 point

Fewer than 3 correct choices = 0 points

Your raw score on Reading will range from 0 to 46 (Practice Test 1) or 45 (Practice Test 2). Use this chart to convert your raw score to your scaled Reading Section score.

Reading			
Raw Section Score	Scaled Section Score	Raw Section Score	Scaled Section Score
46	30	22	15
45	30	21	14
44	29	20	13
43	29	19	13
42	28	18	12
41	27	17	11
40	27	16	11
39	26	15	10
38	25	14	9
37	25	13	9
36	24	12	8
35	23	11	7
34	23	10	7
33	22	9	6
32	21	8	5
31	21	7	5
30	20	6	4
29	19	5	3
28	19	4	3
27	18	3	2
26	17	2	1
25	17	1	1
24	16	0	0
23	15		

Listening

You must also determine your raw score (number of correct answers for the Listening Sections) in order to calculate your scaled section score. In the Listening section, one, two, and three-answer multiple choice items count as one point; test-takers must get all answers correct to get a point. Three-answer matching questions also count as one point; test-takers must get all answers correct to get a point. For Listening questions with four or five answers (ordering questions and complete the chart questions), use these guidelines:

> 5 correct answers = 3 points
> 4 correct answers = 2 points
> 2-3 correct answers = 1 point
> 0-1 correct answers = 0 points

In Practice Test 1, question 14 has four answers; questions 20, 28, and 34 have five answers. In Practice Test 2, questions 12 and 17 have four answers; questions 15, 21, and 25 have five answers.

Your raw score on the Listening Section will range from 0 to 41 (Practice Test 1) or 42 (Practice Test 2). Use this chart to convert your raw score to your scaled Listening score.

		Listening			
Raw Section Score	*Scaled Section Score*	*Raw Section Score*	*Scaled Section Score*	*Raw Section Score*	*Scaled Section Score*
42	30	27	21	13	10
41	30	26	21	12	9
40	29	25	20	11	8
39	29	24	19	10	7
38	28	23	18	9	6
37	27	22	18	8	6
36	27	21	17	7	5
35	26	20	16	6	4
34	25	19	16	5	3
33	25	18	15	4	3
32	24	17	14	3	2
31	24	16	13	2	1
30	23	15	12	1	0
29	23	14	11	0	0
28	22				

Speaking

For the Speaking Section, you (or your instructor, or your classmates) will need to estimate your score on each of the six speaking tasks. Use the rubrics in About Independent Speaking (pp. 407–408) and About Integrated Speaking (pp. 437–438). The range of scores is from 0 to 4 per task (0 to 24 for the Section). To get your raw score for Speaking, add the six scores. Then use the following chart to calculate your scaled Speaking Section score.

Speaking			
Raw Section Score	Scaled Section Score	Raw Section Score	Scaled Section Score
24	30	12	15
23	29	11	14
22	28	10	13
21	27	9	12
20	25	8	10
19	24	7	9
18	23	6	8
17	22	5	7
16	20	4	5
15	19	3	4
14	18	1	3
13	17	0	0

Writing

As in the Speaking Section, you must estimate your scores in the Writing Section (or your instructor or classmates can estimate them for you). Use the rubrics for About Independent Writing (pp. 650–651) and About Integrated Writing (pp. 573–574). Each of the two responses is worth 5 points, so the range of raw scores for the Writing Section is 0 to 10. To get your raw score, you simply add your two scores on the responses. Then use this chart to calculate your scaled Writing Section score.

Writing			
Raw Section Score	Scaled Section Score	Raw Section Score	Scaled Section Score
10	30	4	13
9	28	3	11
8	25	2	8
7	22	1	4
6	18	0	0
5	15		

To calculate your total score on the Practice Test, just add the four scaled Section scores.

Example

Let's say that your raw score on the Reading Section is 38. Your scaled score (from the chart) is 25.

Your raw score on the Listening Section is 26. Your scaled score for Listening is 23.

Your estimated scores on the six Speaking tasks are 3-4-2-2-3-3, for a raw score of 17. Using the chart, convert that to a scaled score of 22.

Your estimated scores on the two Writing tasks are 4 and 4, for a raw score of 8. Your scaled score is 25.

Reading Score	25
Listening Score	23
Speaking Score	22
Writing Score	25
Total Score	**95**

Personal Score Record

Record your scores on the two Practice Tests below.

Practice Test 1

Reading Score   ———

Listening Score   ———

Speaking Score   ———

Writing Score   ———

Total Score   ———

Practice Test 2

Reading Score   ———

Listening Score   ———

Speaking Score   ———

Writing Score   ———

Total Score   ———

To compare your score with equivalent scores on the computer-based test or the paper test, see the chart in Getting Started: Questions and Answers (pp. xiv–xv).

PRACTICE TEST 1

READING SECTION

DIRECTIONS

This section tests your ability to comprehend academic reading passages. It consists of three passages and a set of questions about each of them. All of the questions are worth one point except for the last question in each set. Special directions for the last question will tell you how many points it is worth.

You have sixty minutes in which to complete this section of the test.

In the passages, some words or phrases are underlined. Definitions or explanations for these words are provided at the end of the passage. On the actual test, these words will be underlined in blue and you can click on them to get the definition or explanation.

As soon as you have finished one question, you may move on to the next one. (On the actual test, you will click on Next to move to the next question.) You may skip questions and come back to them later, and you can change your answers if you wish. (On the actual test, you can click on Back to return to a previous question.)

As soon as you have read these directions, go on to the first reading.

Bioluminescence

1   Bioluminescence, or "living light," is produced by a number of organisms. It is most common among marine creatures, especially deep-sea fish. In fact, 90% of deep-sea marine life is estimated to produce bioluminescence in one form or another. Among land animals, the most familiar light-emitting organisms are certain adult insects known as fireflies and their <u>larval</u> forms, known as glowworms. Bacteria, protozoa, crustaceans, fungi, and mollusks all have species that emit light. The only groups that do not display bioluminescence are freshwater fish, mammals, birds, reptiles, amphibians, and leafy plants.

2   Bioluminescence is produced when a <u>pigment</u> called luciferin is combined with oxygen in the presence of an <u>enzyme</u> called lucifrase. When other chemicals take part in the reaction, the color of the light changes, ranging from yellow-green to blue, blue-green, green, violet, and red. Bioluminescence is often called "cold light" because almost no energy is lost as heat. It compares favorably in efficiency with fluorescent lighting.

3   Some organisms, such as fungi, emit a steady glow. Others, such as fireflies, blink on and off. Certain types of bacteria that grow on decomposing plants produce a shimmering luminescence. The popular name for this eerie light is "foxfire." Some organisms, such as dinoflagellates, emit light only when disturbed. When a ship plows through tropical waters at night (particularly in the Indian Ocean), millions of these single-cell algae light up, producing the "milky sea" phenomenon, a softly glowing streak in the wake of the ship.

4   In some species, the role of bioluminescence is obvious. Fireflies and marine fireworms use their light to attract mates. The anglerfish uses a dangling luminous organ to attract prey to come within striking distance. The cookie cutter shark utilizes a bioluminescent patch on its underbelly to appear as a small fish to lure large predatory fish such as tuna and mackerel, and when these fish try to consume the "small fish," they are attacked by the shark. The bobtail squid uses its bioluminescence as nighttime camouflage. When viewed from below, its spots of light blend in with the light of the stars and the moon. Some squids use luminous fluids to confuse and escape from predators in the same way that other squids use their dark ink. It is widely believed that many of the creatures that live in the dark depths of the ocean developed the ability to produce light simply as a way to see around them. Most deep-sea creatures produce blue and green light, and unsurprisingly, the light of those colors has the most powerful penetrating power in water. The only cave-dwelling creature capable of generating light is a New Zealand glowworm.

5   The reasons why fungi, bacteria, and protozoa are able to glow are more obscure. Perhaps, at one time, it was a way to use up oxygen. Millions of years ago, before green plants created oxygen, there was little of that gas in the atmosphere, and living creatures could not use it. Indeed, it may have been poisonous to some creatures. As more oxygen was created by green plants, new types of life developed that could breathe it. Some species died off, while other species developed techniques such as bioluminescence to reduce the amount of oxygen in their immediate environment and thus survive in the richer atmosphere. These organisms have since adapted and are no longer poisoned by oxygen, so their bioluminescence is no longer functional.

6 Through genetic engineering, scientists have been able to produce bioluminescence in species that do not naturally have it, such as tobacco plants. This ability was originally developed as a way to trace the movement of substances through a living plant, but other uses have been suggested. Some people have proposed lining highways with glowing trees to save electricity. Others have proposed producing luminous ornamental plants for the lawn or garden, or even pets such as goldfish, mice, and rabbits that glow in the dark. Scientists are also studying bioluminescent organisms in order to learn how to produce light chemically without producing heat. Someday homes may be lit with lamps based on a method of creating light suggested by bioluminescent creatures.

Glossary

larval: *related to the earliest stage of life of many types of insects; larvae are wingless and often wormlike*

pigment: *a chemical that produces color*

enzyme: *a natural chemical that helps chemical reactions take place in an animal or plant*

1 of 39 Which of the following groups do NOT have representatives that produce bioluminescence?

○ Adult insects and their larvae
○ Deep-sea fish and other ocean organisms
○ Bacteria and protozoa
○ Reptiles and birds

2 of 39 In paragraph 2, the author compares bioluminescence to fluorescent lighting because the two forms of lighting

○ produce about the same amount of light
○ are almost equally energy efficient
○ both require oxygen to produce light
○ are produced with similar chemicals

3 of 39 The word eerie in the passage is closest in meaning to

○ strange
○ dim
○ steady
○ greenish

4 of 39 What can be inferred about dinoflagellates from the information in paragraph 3?

○ They are found only in the Indian Ocean.
○ Their light blinks on and off like fireflies.
○ They are most common in warm waters.
○ Millions of them are destroyed by passing ships.

5 of 39   The phrase the wake of the ship in the passage is closest in meaning to the

    ○ interior of the ship
    ○ track left by the ship in the water
    ○ course that the ship will follow
    ○ water in the bottom of the ship

6 of 39   Which of the following sentences best expresses the essential information in the sentence below? (Incorrect answer choices omit important information or change the meaning of the original sentence in an important way.)

The cookie cutter shark utilizes a bioluminescent patch on its underbelly to appear as a small fish to lure large predatory fish such as tuna and mackerel, and when these fish try to consume the "small fish," they are attacked by the shark.

    ○ The bioluminescence of a cookie cutter shark attracts small fish, which in turn attract predators such as the tuna and mackerel, which the shark can then attack.
    ○ The glowing patch on a cookie cutter shark attracts large predatory fish that the shark can then prey on.
    ○ The cookie cutter shark uses its bioluminescence to frighten off large, dangerous predators such as the mackerel and the tuna.
    ○ Large, predatory fish such as sharks are attracted by the sight of small fish.

7 of 39   In paragraph 4, how does the author explain the way some squids use their bioluminescent secretions?

    ○ By comparing it to an everyday activity that most readers have experienced
    ○ By providing the example of the bobtail squid
    ○ By comparing it with the way some squids use another type of secretion
    ○ By explaining the chemical composition of this secretion

8 of 39   Why does the author mention the fact that deep-sea creatures mainly use blue and green light?

    ○ To support the idea that they use bioluminescence simply to light up their environment
    ○ To explain how they are different from the bioluminescent glowworms that live in caves
    ○ To show that they are unique in producing bioluminescence in these two colors
    ○ To provide an example of creatures that produce bioluminescence for no particular reason

9 of 39   The word obscure in the passage is closest in meaning to

    ○ misunderstood
    ○ interesting
    ○ complex
    ○ unclear

10 of 39   The phrase These organisms in paragraph 5 refers to species that

○ no longer use bioluminescence
○ became extinct millions of years ago
○ create their own oxygen
○ once used bioluminescence to use up oxygen

11 of 39   Which of the following is NOT one of the possible uses for artificial bioluminescent organisms mentioned by the author in paragraph 6?

○ To create glow-in-the-dark pets
○ To light houses in an efficient way
○ To provide light along highways
○ To produce glowing ornamental plants

12 of 39   Look at the four squares [■] that indicate where the following sentence could be added to the passage.

> **For some reason, however, bioluminescence is not common in the unending darkness of caves.**

In some species, the role of bioluminescence is obvious. Fireflies and marine fireworms use their light to attract mates. The anglerfish uses a dangling luminous organ to attract prey to come within striking distance. The cookie cutter shark utilizes a bioluminescent patch on its underbelly to appear as a small fish to lure predatory fish such as tuna and mackerel, and when these fish try to consume the "small fish," they are attacked by the shark. The bobtail squid uses its bioluminescence as nighttime camouflage. When viewed from below, its spots of light blend in with the light of the stars and the moon. Some squids use luminous fluids to confuse and escape from predators in the same way that other squids use their dark ink. ■ It is widely believed that many of the creatures that live in the dark depths of the ocean developed the ability to produce light simply as a way to see around them. ■ Most deep-sea creatures produce blue and green light, and unsurprisingly, the light of those colors has the most powerful penetrating power in water. ■ The only cave-dwelling creature capable of generating light is a New Zealand glowworm. ■

Circle the square [■] that indicates the best place to add the sentence.

13 of 39   DIRECTIONS: Below is an introductory sentence for a brief summary of the passage. Complete the summary by writing the letters of **three** of the answer choices that express the most important ideas of the passage. Some of the answer choices are incorrect because they express ideas that are not given in the passage or because they express only details from the passage. *This question is worth 3 points.*

Produced by chemical reactions, bioluminescence is seen in a wide variety of organisms.

- _____
- _____
- _____

Answer Choices

A. Genetic engineering has enabled scientists to create artificial bioluminescence, which could be used in a number of ways.

B. Fireflies and other creatures once used bioluminescence as a way to attract mates, but today, their bioluminescent abilities serve no particular function.

C. Some animals glow with a steady light, some blink on and off, some shimmer, and some light up only when disturbed.

D. At one time there was much less oxygen in the earth's atmosphere as a result of bioluminescent creatures.

E. The "milky sea" phenomenon is a large-scale display of bioluminescent activity.

F. Today, some species have developed a variety of uses for bioluminescence, but for some species, it may be related to the now-unneeded ability to reduce oxygen around them.

Modern Times

1   Probably Charlie Chaplin's most important film is his comic masterpiece *Modern Times,* made in 1936. Set in the Great Depression era, the film's main concerns are those of millions of people at the time: unemployment, poverty, and economic oppression. Chaplin was motivated to make the film by a journalist who, while interviewing him, happened to describe working conditions in industrial Detroit. Chaplin was told that healthy young men were attracted by promises of high wages to come to work on the assembly lines in the automobile factories there. The stress of long hours and endlessly repetitive work soon destroyed these young men's physical and mental health.

2   Chaplin not only starred in *Modern Times* but also wrote the script and the music and directed and produced it. It was the last movie in which Chaplin played the "Little Tramp," a popular character he had first created in 1915. The Little Tramp is a simple, kind wanderer with a

small mustache, a Derby hat, baggy pants, and a cane. He falls into many misfortunes but always maintains a sweet, sad optimism. *Modern Times* was also Chaplin's final silent movie. "Talkies" had appeared nine years earlier, but Chaplin's humor was mostly based on body language and visual gags. However, it is somewhat deceptive to call *Modern Times* a silent film. While there is no dialogue, there is music and sound effects, such as the roar of machinery and the scream of factory whistles. In *Modern Times,* the world of sound is the noisy world of technology, although the Tramp, a symbol of humanity, is silent.

3   Only about one-third of *Modern Times* takes place inside a futuristic factory (the Electro Steel Works), but these are the scenes viewers remember most vividly. The Tramp has one job, to tighten nuts and bolts on the machines in the factory with a large wrench. In one inventive scene, he is chosen to test an automatic feeding machine. The machine can be brought to the assembly line so that workers do not have to pause for lunch. The device suddenly malfunctions. It hurls food at the Tramp, who is strapped into his position on the assembly line and cannot escape. This illustrates people's utter helplessness in the face of machines that should be serving them. In another memorable scene, the owner orders that the speed of the assembly line be increased to its maximum level. No one who has seen the film can forget watching Chaplin vainly trying to keep pace with the conveyor belt. At one point in this scene, he is taken inside, literally "eaten" by the nightmarish machinery, and caught up in its whirring wheels, gears, and cogs. The Tramp loses his mind and rushes around trying to tighten anything that resembles a nut, including the buttons on a woman's dress. He is led from the factory by attendants in white coats and is taken away.

4   The Tramp recovers from his nervous breakdown and is released. The doctor tells him, "Take it easy and avoid excitement," but for the rest of this episodic film, the Tramp experiences one calamity after another. He unintentionally joins a labor strike and later is sent to jail. He becomes a roller-skating night watchman at a department store, an overstressed singing waiter, and a fugitive from the law. He meets an orphan (played by Chaplin's real-life wife, Paulette Goddard) and becomes her friend and protector. In the final scene, the Tramp walks down a country road into the sunset. This is a stock ending for Chaplin's films, but usually the tramp walks off alone. In his last film, the Tramp walks off arm-in-arm with the girl.

5   Clearly, *Modern Times* has its flaws, but it is the best film about the effects of technology on humanity ever made. It is as relevant now as it was when it was first made. It does not offer a radical social message, but it warns that standardization, mechanization, and misuse of authority rob men and women of their individuality. It also offers a reminder that, no matter how bad things seem, one can always smile.

Glossary

talkies: *films in which you can hear the actual voices of the actors, not just music*

14 of 39   In paragraph 1, how does the author explain the main themes of the film *Modern Times*?

○ By identifying them as the concerns of many people at the time
○ By contrasting them to those of another Chaplin movie
○ By explaining what movie critics of the time thought of them
○ By showing what a strong influence the movie had at the time

15 of 39   According to the passage, Chaplin got his idea for the film *Modern Times* from

○ a newspaper article
○ a scene in a movie
○ a conversation with a reporter
○ a job that he had once held

16 of 39   The word gags in the passage is closest in meaning to

○ messages
○ jokes
○ symbols
○ expressions

17 of 39   In paragraph 2, why does the author say that "it is somewhat deceptive to call *Modern Times* a silent film"?

○ Chaplin wanted to use dialogue in this film, but the technology was not available.
○ Chaplin's body language was so expressive that he communicated as well as if he were speaking.
○ Although there is little speaking in the film, there is music and noise.
○ It was originally made as a silent movie, but at a later time, dialogue was added.

18 of 39   It can be inferred from the information in paragraph 3 that two-thirds of the film *Modern Times*

○ is more entertaining than the other third
○ is not usually shown today
○ takes place outside of the factory
○ does not involve the Little Tramp

19 of 39   The word This in paragraph 3 refers to

○ the food that is thrown at the Tramp
○ the scene involving the feeding device
○ the Tramp's repetitive job
○ the assembly line

20 of 39   The word nightmarish in the passage is closest in meaning to

○ terrifying
○ efficient
○ powerful
○ malfunctioning

21 of 39   The author implies that when the Tramp is taken away from the factory (paragraph 3), he is taken to

○ a jail
○ a department store
○ his home
○ a mental hospital

22 of 39   The author probably includes the doctor's quote in paragraph 4 because

○ the doctor gives the Tramp the same advice that the author would give
○ it is in contrast with the difficulties that the Tramp faces in the rest of the film
○ the doctor is advising the Tramp to go back to his job at the factory
○ it indicates that the doctor thinks the Tramp should not leave

23 of 39   The word stock in the passage is closest in meaning to

○ unhappy
○ sudden
○ exciting
○ standard

24 of 39   In paragraph 5, what does the author find obvious about the movie?

○ That it is not a perfect film
○ That its message is, "Smile no matter how bad the situation appears"
○ That it is the best film about technology ever made
○ That it does not offer a revolutionary message

25 of 39   Look at the four squares [■] that indicate where the following sentence could be added to the passage.

> **The voice of the brutal factory owner is also heard coming through a giant two-way television screen (many years before television was actually invented).**

Chaplin not only starred in *Modern Times* but also wrote the script and the music and directed and produced it. It was the last movie in which Chaplin played the "Little Tramp", a popular character he had first created in 1915. The Little Tramp is a simple, kind wanderer with a small mustache, a Derby hat, baggy pants, and a cane. He falls into many misfortunes but always maintains a sweet, sad optimism. *Modern Times* was also Chaplin's final silent movie. "Talkies" had appeared nine years earlier, but Chaplin's humor was mostly based on body language and visual gags. ■ However, it is somewhat deceptive to call *Modern Times* a silent film. ■ While there is no dialogue, there is music and sound effects, such as the roar of machinery and the scream of factory whistles. ■ In *Modern Times*, the world of sound is the noisy world of technology, although the Tramp, a symbol of humanity, is silent. ■

Circle the square [■] that indicates the best place to add the sentence.

26 of 39   DIRECTIONS: Below is an introductory sentence for a brief summary of the passage. Complete the summary by writing the letters of **three** of the answer choices that express the most important ideas of the passage. Some of the answer choices are incorrect because they express ideas that are not given in the passage or because they express only details from the passage. ***This question is worth 3 points.***

Modern Times, which addressed the economic problems of the Great Depression era, may have been Charlie Chaplin's most important film.

┌─────────────────────────────────────┐
│ • _____ │
│ • _____ │
│ • _____ │
└─────────────────────────────────────┘

Answer Choices

A. *Modern Times* depicted healthy young men going to work in the automobile factories of Detroit because of the high wages that they could earn there.

B. In *Modern Times*, the Tramp faces many dehumanizing, difficult experiences while working in a factory and at other jobs.

C. *Modern Times* was the last silent movie Chaplin made, and it was the last one featuring the popular "Little Tramp."

D. Although the movie *Modern Times* contains dark, bleak scenes, it also contains some happy scenes such as the Tramp's marriage to the orphan.

E. Chaplin warns in *Modern Times* that technology and its effects endanger people's individuality.

F. Chaplin played the Little Tramp character from 1915 to 1936.

Balloon-Frame Houses

1   Until the 1830s, domestic architectural styles in North America were heavily influenced by European styles. The log cabin of the frontier came from Sweden, brought by settlers to the Swedish colony of Delaware in the 1630s. The typical residence in Colonial cities was greatly influenced by the standard British house of the time. No doubt there were some uniquely North American touches, but on the whole, the North American style of building houses was an adaptation of European construction methods.

2   Two factors made building different in North America. One was an abundance of wood. Wood was used at a rate impossible to match in a mostly deforested Europe. The other was the fact that labor was scarce in most communities. European houses built in the traditional timber-frame style used heavy cut stone. That took a huge toll in labor. Another key feature of European houses was the use of heavy timbers fitted with complex joints. Wooden pegs were used instead of iron nails. This type of home construction was time-consuming and required a team of expert carpenters and other workers with specialized tools. Fundamentally, it was the same method of building homes that had been used in Europe since medieval times.

3   In 1833, while constructing houses in Fort Dearborn, Illinois, Augustine Taylor, a builder from Hartford, Connecticut, invented a new method of building that utilized a framework of lightweight lumber. This was the birth of the "balloon-frame house." This type of house could be built in under a week by two or three careful workers who could saw in a straight line and hammer a nail. Almost overnight, home construction changed from a specialized craft into an industry.

4   Skeptics predicted that the first strong wind would send a balloon-frame house flying off its foundations and into the air, and at first, *balloon-frame* was a term of scorn. In fact, these houses were more like woven baskets than like balloons. They were light, flexible, and yet very sturdy.

5   Balloon-frame houses required huge amounts of machine-planed lumber. This demand was met by improved sawmill technology that could quickly cut boards to standard sizes. They also required enormous numbers of machine-made nails. These were provided by recently developed automated nail-making machines. After 1800, the cost of nails in the United States steadily dropped, and by 1830 one could buy a five-pound bag of nails for pennies, less than the tax alone on a bag of nails in Europe.

6   The balloon-frame design first caught on in Chicago, Illinois. In the 1830s, that city established itself as a new gateway to the West. And with a mushrooming population came a soaring demand for housing. Because they could be built so quickly, most new houses were balloon-frame houses. Another advantage of balloon-frame houses was their mobility. Today, houses are seldom moved, but Chicagoans in the 1830s, 1840s, and 1850s took advantage of the mobility of lightweight balloon-frame structures without utility connections. New arrivals could buy homes and then move them to more desirable locations. Chester Tupper, Chicago's first house mover, moved thousands of homes on rollers through Chicago's unpaved streets. The downside of balloon-frame houses was that they were made almost exclusively of flammable materials. Chicago rapidly became a city of wood. That fact came back to haunt the city on a hot, terrible night in 1871.

7   This building method spread from Chicago to the cities, towns, and farms of the American and Canadian West, where new settlers needed shelter in a hurry. Always ready to supply a new product, Chicago provided settlers with prefabricated kits for building balloon-frame structures. The Lyman-Bridges Company sold buildings of "any size or style, in any number, on short notice." Shipped by rail, the building kits contained milled lumber, roofing shingles, windows, doors, and building plans. The smallest house offered by the company was a one-room house measuring 10 by 12 feet (3.3 by 4.0 meters), while the largest had eight big rooms as well as a pantry, several hallways, and four closets. Prices ranged from $175 for the smallest model to $3,500 for the deluxe model. These reasonable prices allowed many workers the luxury of owning their own homes, in contrast to Europe where traditional construction techniques kept the rates of home ownership low for most of the nineteenth century. Balloon-frame housing remained the dominant style of home building in North America until the 1940s.

Glossary

sawmill: *a factory that cuts trees into lumber (boards) for building*

PRACTICE TEST 1

27 of 39   The word domestic in the passage is closest in meaning to

    ◯ residential
    ◯ ordinary
    ◯ international
    ◯ useful

28 of 39   The phrase The other in paragraph 2 refers to

    ◯ another factor
    ◯ a place outside of Europe
    ◯ a feature in building traditional homes
    ◯ another kind of material

29 of 39   Where was the first balloon-frame house built?

    ◯ Hartford, Connecticut
    ◯ Chicago, Illinois
    ◯ Delaware
    ◯ Fort Dearborn, Illinois

30 of 39   Builders of traditional homes did NOT require

    ◯ wood
    ◯ sophisticated tools
    ◯ nails
    ◯ cut stone

31 of 39   According to the passage, the term *balloon-frame* was applied to certain houses because

    ◯ like balloons, they could be easily moved from place to place
    ◯ their rounded frames made them slightly resemble balloons
    ◯ they resembled the baskets in which passengers ride below large balloons
    ◯ they were made of lightweight materials

32 of 39   The word scorn in the passage is closest in meaning to

    ◯ disapproval
    ◯ misunderstanding
    ◯ delight
    ◯ jealousy

33 of 39   Which of the following sentences best expresses the essential information in the sentence below? (Incorrect answer choices omit important information or change the meaning of the original sentence in an important way.)

After 1800, the cost of nails in the United States steadily dropped, and by 1830 one could buy a five-pound (2.2-kilogram) bag of nails for pennies, less than the tax alone on a bag of nails in Europe.

    ◯ In the nineteenth century, the tax on a five-pound bag of nails was actually higher than the cost of the nails themselves.
    ◯ European nails cost far more than American nails because after 1800, nails produced in Europe were so heavily taxed.
    ◯ By 1830, the price of a bag of nails in the United States had dropped below the cost of the tax on a bag of nails in Europe.
    ◯ The declining rate of taxes in the early nineteenth century encouraged U.S. nail-makers to drop their prices, while in Europe the opposite was true.

34 of 39   The word mushrooming in the passage is closest in meaning to
- ○ rapidly growing
- ○ mostly transient
- ○ generally poor
- ○ highly demanding

35 of 39   Which of these inferences can be made from the information in paragraph 6?
- ○ Chicago's unpaved roads led to a great disaster in the nineteenth century.
- ○ Balloon-frame houses could be built quickly but were not comfortable, especially in hot weather.
- ○ Chicago was damaged by a great fire in 1871.
- ○ Many of Chicago's balloon-frame houses had been brought there from other parts of the country.

36 of 39   What kind of business did the Lyman-Bridges Company engage in?
- ○ Building and then shipping balloon-frame houses to various parts of the country
- ○ Moving balloon-frame houses on rollers throughout Chicago
- ○ Supplying parts and directions for people to build their own houses
- ○ Training workers who could then build balloon-frame houses for other people

37 of 39   Why does the author supply information about two types of houses in paragraph 7?
- ○ To show that the smaller house was a bargain, but that the deluxe house was overpriced
- ○ To show the full range of houses available in terms of size and cost
- ○ To indicate how the size and price of balloon-frame houses changed over time
- ○ To demonstrate that balloon-frame houses were more economical than traditional houses

38 of 39   Look at the four squares [■] that indicate where the following sentence could be added to the passage.

> **In particular, there was a lack of trained artisans.**

Two factors made building different in North America. One was an abundance of wood. Wood was used at a rate impossible to match in a mostly deforested Europe. The other was the fact that labor was scarce in most communities. ■ European houses built in the traditional timber-frame style used heavy cut stone. ■ That took a huge toll in labor. ■ Another key feature of European houses was the use of heavy timbers fitted with complex joints. ■ Wooden pegs were used instead of iron nails. This type of home construction was time-consuming and required a team of expert carpenters and other workers with specialized tools. Fundamentally, it was the same method of building homes that had been used in Europe since medieval times.

Circle the square [■] that indicates the best place to add the sentence.

39 of 39   DIRECTIONS: Select phrases from the answer choices and match them to the category to which they relate. Two answer choices will not be used. ***This question is worth 4 points.***

Answer Choices	Timber-Frame Houses
A. Increased the percentage of working-class people who owned homes	• _____
B. Required only one or two skilled artisans with specialized tools	• _____
C. Were based on medieval building techniques	• _____
D. Were made possible by advances in technology	Balloon-Frame Houses
E. Transformed home building into an industry	
F. Took a lot of labor and time to build	• _____
G. Were built of both wood and stone	• _____
H. Were easy to move from place to place	• _____
I. Is the dominant style of building in use today	• _____

This is the end of the Reading Section. Go on to the Listening Section.

LISTENING SECTION

DIRECTIONS

▶ Now start the Audio Program. 🎧

This section tests your understanding of conversations and lectures. You will hear each conversation or lecture only once. Your answers should be based on what is stated or implied in the conversations and lectures.

You are allowed to take notes as you listen, and you can use these notes to help you answer the questions.

In some questions, you will see a headphones icon: 🎧. This icon tells you that you will hear, but not read, part of the lecture again. Then you will answer a question about the part of the lecture that you heard.

Some questions have special directions that are highlighted.

During an actual listening test, you will *not* be able to skip items and come back to them later, so try to answer every question that you hear on this practice test.

This test includes two conversations and four lectures. Most questions are separated by a ten-second pause.

▶ Listen to a conversation between a professor and a student. 🎧

Notes:

_____

_____

_____

> **Now get ready to answer some questions about the conversation. You may use your notes to help you.**

1 of 34   Why is Ted unable to meet with Professor Jacobs after class?

- ○ He wants to go to a poetry reading.
- ○ He has to attend a meeting.
- ○ He has another class.
- ○ He has to check his e-mail.

▶ Listen again to part of the conversation. Then answer the question.

2 of 34   What does Ted mean when he says this? 🎧

- ○ He is expressing surprise.
- ○ He's showing a lack of interest.
- ○ He's not sure what he is being asked to do.
- ○ He's confused and upset.

3 of 34   What is Ted most interested in reading aloud next Friday?

- ○ Part of a novel
- ○ A newspaper article
- ○ A collection of poems
- ○ A nonfiction guide to fishing

4 of 34   Which of the following can be inferred about Professor Jacobs?

- ○ He likes some of Ted's poems, but not the poem "Northern Lights."
- ○ He doesn't always express his feelings about his students' work in class.
- ○ He prefers teaching graduate students to teaching undergraduates.
- ○ He doesn't like poems in which the imagery is frightening.

5 of 34   Why does Professor Jacobs ask Ted to come to his office?

- ○ To discuss Ted's grade in the creative-writing class
- ○ To help Ted practice for the reading
- ○ To help Ted select some poems to read aloud
- ○ To give Ted a written invitation

▶ Listen to a conversation between a university administrator and a student. 🎧

Notes:

_____

_____

_____

> **Now get ready to answer some questions about the conversation. You may use your notes to help you.**

6 of 34   Why does Dana want a work-study position?

- ○ To pay for day-to-day expenses
- ○ To pay for her tuition
- ○ To pay back a bank loan
- ○ To pay for her room and board

7 of 34   What can be inferred about merit-based work-study jobs?

- ○ They are given only to students who receive financial aid.
- ○ They are not arranged by Ms. Fong's office.
- ○ They involve less pay than need-based work-study jobs.
- ○ They are not funded by the government.

8 of 34   Which of these work-study positions does Dana express the most enthusiasm for?

- ○ Cafeteria worker
- ○ Receptionist
- ○ Lab technician
- ○ Museum tour guide

9 of 34   What must Dana do first to apply for the position that she is interested in?

- ○ Arrange an interview with Dr. Ferrara
- ○ Mail an application to the museum
- ○ Fill out some forms
- ○ Meet with Ms. Fong in person

10 of 34   Why does Ms. Fong say this? 🎧

- ○ To encourage Dana to pursue the job.
- ○ To offer Dana an alternative job.
- ○ To suggest reasons for not taking the position.
- ○ To encourage Dana not to work.

▶ Listen to a lecture in an anthropology class. 🎧

ANTHROPOLOGY

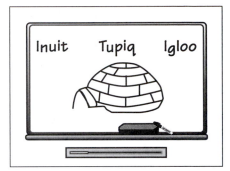

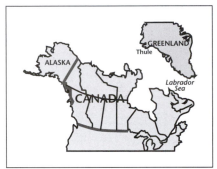

Notes:

_____

_____

_____

Now get ready to answer some questions about the lecture. You may use your notes to help you.

11 of 34   The professor mentions three types of winter houses used by the Inuit. Match these three types of houses with the locations where they were used.

    A. Snow houses
    B. Houses made of driftwood
    C. Houses made of stone, earth, and whalebone

Place the letters of the choices in the proper boxes.

Northern Alaska	North Central Canada and Greenland	Labrador (Northeastern Canada)

▶ Listen again to part of the lecture. Then answer the question.

12 of 34   Why does the professor say this? 🎧

    ○ To review part of a lecture he gave earlier
    ○ To give additional information about one group of Inuit
    ○ To explain why the Inuit in Greenland were isolated
    ○ To indicate where Thule is located

13 of 34   What can be inferred about the word *igloo*?

    ◯ Inuit might use this word to talk about a summer house.
    ◯ It is no longer used at all by the Inuit.
    ◯ In Inuit, it refers only to houses made from snow.
    ◯ It was used only in one small part of the Canadian Arctic.

14 of 34   In this lecture, the professor describes the process the Inuit used to build a simple igloo. Indicate whether each of the following is a step in the igloo-building process.

Put a check mark (✓) in the proper box for each phrase.

	Yes	No
Build a framework to support the igloo from inside		
Cut blocks of hardened snow with a knife		
Dig an entrance tunnel		
Stand on top of the igloo in order to compress the snow and make it stronger		
Melt snow on the interior surface of the igloo with lamps and then let the water refreeze		

15 of 34   The professor did NOT mention that larger igloos were used in which of these ways?

Choose two answers.

    ☐ As a place to dance
    ☐ As a home for five or more families
    ☐ As a place to hold wrestling matches
    ☐ As a location for singing contests
    ☐ As a storage space for food

16 of 34   According to the professor, what did the Inuit do in the early 1950s?

    ◯ They completely stopped building snow houses.
    ◯ They began making an entirely different type of snow house.
    ◯ They began connecting clusters of igloos with tunnels.
    ◯ They stopped using snow houses except as temporary shelters.

PRACTICE TEST 1

► Listen to a discussion in an astrophysics class. 🎧

ASTROPHYSICS

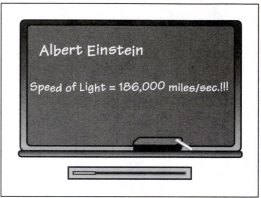

Notes:

_____

_____

_____

**Now get ready to answer some questions about the
discussion. You may use your notes to help you.**

17 of 34   What is Professor Fuller's opinion of Albert Einstein?

○ She feels he was mistaken about some key points.
○ She believes he predicted travel to other stars.
○ She thinks that his theories are no longer completely valid.
○ She agrees with him about traveling faster than light.

18 of 34   What powers the "sails" on the ship that the class discusses?

○ Laser light
○ Nuclear reactions
○ Sunlight
○ Wind

19 of 34   According to Professor Fuller, what must be developed before ships can travel
to the stars?

○ A deeper understanding of Einstein's theories
○ New materials from which to build spaceships
○ A new means of powering spaceships
○ Another method of calculating the speed of light

20 of 34   Professor Fuller discusses the process by which a new technology evolves. Summarize this discussion by putting these four steps in the proper order.

A. **Technology phase**
B. **Application phase**
C. **Speculation phase**
D. **Science phase**

Put the letters of the stages in the proper boxes.

1. _____
2. _____
3. _____
4. _____

21 of 34   What does Professor Fuller say about the planets that have so far been discovered around other stars?

Choose two answers.

☐ Most of them are gas giants.
☐ Some of them are similar to the earth.
☐ Many of them may be inhabited.
☐ A few of them are very close to their stars.

► Listen again to part of the discussion. Then answer the question. 🎧

22 of 34   What does Professor Fuller imply about travel to other stars when she says this? 🎧

○ It is strongly inadvisable.
○ It is unlikely in the foreseeable future.
○ It may begin sooner than people realize.
○ It is a complete impossibility.

▶ Listen to a lecture in an art class. 🎧

ART

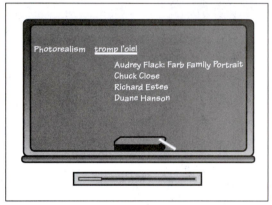

Notes:

_____

_____

_____

> **Now get ready to answer some questions about the lecture. You may use your notes to help you.**

23 of 34   What does the professor say about Minimalism and Conceptualism?

Choose two answers.

- ☐ They were the dominant schools of art when Photorealism began.
- ☐ They were very similar in their philosophy and style to Photorealism.
- ☐ They were abstract schools of art.
- ☐ They had been influenced by both the Dutch Masters and the *trompe l'oeil* school.

24 of 34   Which of the following did Audrey Flack NOT use when painting *The Farb Family Portrait*?

- ○ An airbrush
- ○ A computer
- ○ A slide projector
- ○ Acrylic paints

25 of 34   How does the professor explain the subjects that Photorealists painted?

Choose two answers.

☐ She quotes two Photorealistic painters on their choice of subjects.
☐ She gives specific examples of subjects that Photorealists have painted.
☐ She tells her students to read a paper about the topic of Photorealistic paintings.
☐ She compares the subjects of Photorealistic paintings to those of famous photographs.

26 of 34   Which of the following would Richard Estes most likely choose to paint?

○ A farmhouse and open fields
○ A woman examining her reflection in a mirror
○ A telephone booth reflected in a large store window
○ A broken window

27 of 34   According to the professor, why are the sculptures of Duane Hanson so remarkable?

○ They are very valuable.
○ They are quite large.
○ They are easy to create.
○ They are extremely lifelike.

28 of 34   In this lecture, the professor gives a number of characteristics of the Photorealistic school of painting. Indicate whether each of the following is a typical characteristic of paintings of that school of art.

Put a check mark (✓) in the proper box for each phrase.

	Yes	No
They feature three-dimensional optical illusions.		
Their subjects are ordinary people and scenes.		
They are often painted in bright colors.		
They may be either representational or non-representational.		
They show great attention to detail.		

▶ Listen to a discussion in a meteorology class. 🎧

METEOROLOGY

Notes:

_____

_____

_____

Now get ready to answer some questions about the discussion. You may use your notes to help you.

29 of 34   According to the professor, which of the following are most often damaged by hail?

Choose two answers.

☐ Rides at amusement parks
☐ Cars and other vehicles
☐ Farmers' crops
☐ Buildings

30 of 34   According to the professor, which of these methods of preventing damage from hail was used most recently?

○ Banging on pots and pans
○ Dancing
○ Shooting hail cannons
○ Ringing bells

▶ Listen again to part of the discussion. Then answer the question.

31 of 34   What does the professor mean when he says this? 🎧

○ He doesn't understand the student's question and wants her to clarify it.
○ He's unsure, but doesn't think it happens often.
○ He doesn't think there is any way to know the answer.
○ He doesn't think the question makes sense.

32 of 34   Why does the professor compare a hailstone to an onion?
  ○ Because of its size
  ○ Because of its structure
  ○ Because of its color
  ○ Because of its weight

33 of 34   At what time of year are hailstorms most common?
  ○ In the spring
  ○ In the summer
  ○ In the fall
  ○ In the winter

34 of 34   In this lecture, the professor describes the process by which hail is formed. Indicate whether each of the following is a step in that process.

Put a check mark (✓) in the proper box for each phrase.

	Yes	No
Hailstones become so heavy that they fall to the ground.		
Water droplets are lifted into the cold region of a thundercloud and freeze.		
Tornado clouds circulate ice crystals inside of thunderclouds.		
Droplets are lifted into the cloud again and again, adding more ice.		
A mass of fast-moving warm air hits a slower-moving mass of cold air.		

This is the end of the Listening Section of Practice Test 1. You may take a ten-minute break before beginning work on the Speaking Section.

PRACTICE TEST 1

SPEAKING SECTION
DIRECTIONS

▶ Now start the Audio Program and listen carefully. 🎧
This section tests your ability to speak about various subjects. There are six tasks in this section. Listen carefully to the directions and read the questions on the screen. The first two tasks are independent speaking tasks. You have fifteen seconds in which to prepare your response. When you hear a beep on the Audio Program, you will have forty-five seconds in which to answer the question.

The last four tasks are integrated speaking tasks. The third and fourth questions involve a reading text and a listening passage. You have forty-five seconds in which to read a short text. You will then hear a short conversation or part of a lecture on the same topic. You may take notes on both the reading and listening passage. You will then see a question on the screen asking about the information that you have just read and heard, and you will have thirty seconds in which to plan a response. When you hear a beep on the Audio Program, you have sixty seconds in which to answer the question.

The fifth and sixth questions involve a short listening passage. You may take notes as you listen. After listening to the conversation or lecture, you will see a question, and you have twenty seconds in which to plan your response. When you hear a beep on the Audio Program, you have sixty seconds in which to answer the question.

During actual tests, a clock on the screen will tell you how much preparation time or how much response time (speaking time) remains for each question. It is important that you time yourself accurately when you take this practice test. On an actual test your responses will be recorded and evaluated by trained raters.

Task 1

> What is the most important decision that you have ever made? Give specific
> details and examples to support your explanation.

Preparation Time: 15 Seconds
Response Time: 45 Seconds

Task 2

> In some university classes, grades depend mainly on tests, such as quizzes and
> final exams. In other classes, grades depend primarily on academic papers that
> the students write. Which type of class would you prefer to take? Give specific
> details and examples to support your explanation.

Preparation Time: 15 Seconds
Response Time: 45 Seconds

Task 3

Lincoln University is instituting a new policy regarding requirements for graduation. Read the following notice from the Dean of Education. You will have forty-five seconds in which to read the notice. Begin reading now.

Notice from the Dean of Education

Because our graduates will all be living in an increasingly globalized world, and because it is important that they know how to communicate in international settings, the Lincoln University Board of Regents has voted to require all students to satisfy a foreign-language requirement. You may satisfy this requirement with a successful completion of four terms (12 credit hours) of language instruction in the language program of choice. (Only students whose native language is not English may satisfy this requirement by taking English classes.)

Students with prior language training may demonstrate their proficiency by taking a placement test in the language in question. Students with scores of 85 or above are not required to take further foreign-language courses. However, we encourage students who have achieved a high level of language competency to continue their language study.

This ruling affects all incoming students and all currently enrolled first- and second-year students regardless of major.

Notes:

_____

_____

_____

▶ Now turn the page and listen to two students discussing this notice. 🎧

Notes:

_____

_____

_____

Now get ready to answer the question.

The woman gives her opinion of the notice written by the Dean of Education. Explain her opinion and discuss the reasons she gives for having this opinion.

Preparation Time: 35 Seconds
Response Time: 45 Seconds

Task 4

▶ Read the following passage about airships. You will have forty-five seconds in which to read the passage. Begin reading now.

Unlike helicopters and airplanes, lighter-than-air craft depend on buoyant gases—hydrogen and helium—to make them fly. Because of these gases, they rise into the air. Powered lighter-than-air craft have engines and fins and rudders—just like airplanes—so their pilots can control the speed and direction of their flight.

There are two main types of powered lighter-than-air craft: rigid airships and nonrigid airships. Rigid aircraft have internal frames made of aluminum—that's why they are called *rigid.* The first one of these was built in 1900 by a German engineer named Count Zeppelin. Rigid airships are therefore sometimes called *zeppelins.* These long, cigar-shaped ships were filled with hydrogen, which made them very dangerous. When hydrogen combines with oxygen, it can burn violently. The other type of lighter-than-air craft is the nonrigid airship. These airships are also called *blimps.* Blimps have no internal skeleton, no internal structure. They are merely fabric envelopes. It is the buoyant gas that gives them their shape. They are fatter and much, much shorter in length than the old zeppelins. Blimps are filled with helium, which is a nonflammable gas, and so they are much safer than rigid airships. Unlike rigid zeppelins, blimps are still a fairly common sight in our skies, especially during important sporting events.

▶ Now turn the page and listen to a discussion about airships. 🎧

Notes:

_____

_____

_____

Now get ready to answer the question.

The professor and the students discuss two airships, the blimp *Columbia* and the zeppelin *Hindenburg.* Using information from the passage and the discussion, compare these two airships.

Preparation Time: 30 Seconds
Response Time: 60 Seconds

Task 5

▶ Listen to a conversation between two students. 🎧

Notes:

_____

_____

_____

Now get ready to answer the question.

Mike offers Diane two possible solutions to her problem. Discuss her problem and then explain which of the two solutions you think is better and why you think so.

Preparation Time: 20 Seconds
Response Time: 60 Seconds

Task 6

▶ Listen to part of a lecture in a botany class. 🎧

Now get ready to answer the question.

Using specific examples and points from the lecture, explain the relationship between the lantana plants and insects and discuss how it benefits both of them.

Preparation Time: 20 Seconds
Response Time: 60 Seconds

This is the end of the Speaking Section. Go directly to the Writing Section.

WRITING SECTION
DIRECTIONS

This section tests your ability to write academic English. It consists of two writing tasks.

The first writing task is an "integrated" task. It involves reading a short passage and listening to a short lecture on the same topic. You will then have twenty minutes in which to write a response based on the information in the passage and the lecture.

The second writing task is an "independent" task. It involves writing a response to a question using your own experience and background knowledge.

Now read the directions for the first writing task.

INTEGRATED WRITING TASK
DIRECTIONS

▶ Now start the Audio Program.

Take three minutes to read the short passage that follows. You may take notes as you read.

After three minutes, turn the page and start the Audio Program. You will hear a lecture on the same topic as the reading. Again, you may take notes as you listen.

You will have twenty minutes to write your response. Your response should include information from both the reading and the lecture.

Your essay will be rated on the completeness and accuracy of your response as well as on the correctness and quality of your writing. A typical response should be 150 to 225 words.

You may use your notes and look at the reading passage as you write. (During the actual exam, you can view the reading passage on the computer screen after the lecture is over.)

If you finish this writing task in less than twenty minutes, you may start working on the second writing task if you want.

Another personality type is called the "universal risk-taking personality." People with this type of personality engage in risky activities in all aspects of their lives, endangering themselves, their families and friends, and their fortunes for little or no reason or reward. Since the need for safety is the most fundamental of all human needs, behaviors of this kind must be considered illogical and, in their most extreme forms, pathological. These extreme behaviors are indicative of suicidal tendencies, of what some psychologists call *thanatos,* the death wish.

Of course, there are those who *must* face risks. Soldiers may be called on to face the dangers of the battlefield. This is their duty, and we expect them to do their duty. Lumberjacks encounter daily dangers when chopping down trees in the forest. This is their job. In many other occupations, people face dangers willingly, but for good reason. However, young daredevils who drive their cars in street races do so for no reason. They endanger their lives and the lives of others for no reason except for the satisfaction they get from their selfish thrill-seeking.

Many people who engage in dangerous activities for no purpose do so to hide some sort of inadequacy. For example, a student whose grades are not good, who does not do well in school, may try to cover up his failure in this respect by taking needless chances. This may be somewhat understandable in the young, but there are plenty of adults who behave the same way. Some of our so-called "adventurers" are really just like schoolchildren themselves, showing off to get attention and to hide their feelings of inadequacy.

▶ Now start the Audio Program. Listen to part of a lecture in a psychology class on the same topic that you just read about. 🎧

> **Now get ready to answer the question. Remember, you may turn the page and look back at the reading passage. You may also use your notes to help you. You have twenty minutes to prepare and write your response.**

Summarize the main points made in the lecture that you just heard, discussing how they cast doubt on points made in the reading. You can refer to the reading passage as you write.

Notes:

_____

_____

_____

_____

_____

_____

Response:

_____

_____

_____

_____

_____

_____

_____

_____

_____

_____

_____

_____

_____

_____

_____

_____

_____

_____

INDEPENDENT WRITING TASK
DIRECTIONS

Read the question below. You have thirty minutes to write your essay. This includes the time to plan, write, and revise your essay. A typical response should be a minimum of 300 words.

Your essay will be rated on the correctness and quality of your writing, including the way you organize your essay and develop and support your ideas.

> Books can be divided into two main types: fiction (novels and stories) and non-fiction (histories, biographies, and self-help books, for example). Which of these two types of books do you generally prefer to read? Use specific reasons and details to support your answer.

Notes:

_____

_____

_____

_____

_____

_____

Response:

_____

_____

_____

_____

_____

_____

_____

_____

_____

_____

_____

_____

_____

_____

_____

_____

_____

This is the end of the Writing Section and of Practice Test 1.

PRACTICE TEST 2

This section tests your ability to comprehend academic reading passages. It consists of three passages and a set of questions about each of them. All of the questions are worth one point except for the last question in each set. Special directions for the last question will tell you how many points it is worth.

You have sixty minutes in which to complete this section of the test.

In the passages, some words or phrases are underlined. Definitions or explanations for these words are provided at the end of the passage. On the actual test, these words will be underlined in blue and you can click on them to get the definition or explanation.

As soon as you have finished one question, you may move on to the next one. (On the actual test, you will click on Next to move to the next question.) You may skip questions and come back to them later, and you can change your answers if you wish. (On the actual test, you can click on Back to return to a previous question.)

As soon as you have read these directions, go on to the first reading.

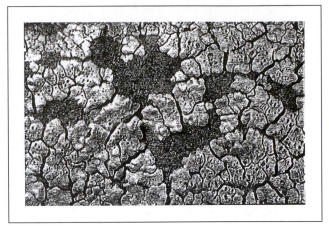

Lichens

1 Lichens look like splashes of paint left behind by a careless painter. Unlike many plants, they do not require soil to grow. They grow on the bark of trees in steaming tropical rain forests, on farmers' fenceposts, on the bricks of big-city buildings, and on old gravestones. Lichens can tolerate extremes of climate. They grow on rocks in hot springs, on wind-swept mountaintop boulders, and on stones in the driest deserts. In the Arctic, lichens, known as reindeer moss, are the principal source of food for caribou. Whole mountainsides in Antarctica appear green and orange because of the presence of lichens; they are one of the few plants that can survive there. They are among the oldest of known plants. Recently, scientists discovered lichen fossils on a rock in a phosphate mine in southwest China that date back 600 million years.

2   When conditions become harsh, lichens become dormant. If there is not enough moisture, they simply dry up, but a short rain or even a heavy dew gives them new life. When growing on rock surfaces, lichens secrete acids that dissolve the minerals, contributing to the process of weathering by which rocks are slowly turned to soil. This property enables lichens to be pioneers. They appear on barren rock scoured clean by glaciers, fires, lava flows, or floods, beginning the process of soil formation that allows mosses, ferns, and other plants to later take root. But, despite their hardiness, lichens are extremely sensitive to airborne particles. That's why they serve as an early warning system for air pollution.

3   It is the acids lichen produce that give them their distinctive colors. Lichens are often spoken of in the same breath as mosses, and some lichens are even called mosses, but true mosses are all distinctively green, whereas lichens appear in many vivid colors. At one time, before the invention of aniline dyes, acids from lichens were used to make dyes, such as the purple dye orchil, the blue dye litmus, and the red dye cudbear, and they are sometimes still used that way today. Some lichens, such as oak moss, contain oils that produce fragrant odors used in scented soaps, cosmetics, and perfumes. Some lichens are also known to have antibiotic properties.

4   Lichens are a partnership of two or more types of plants, a <u>fungus</u> and a type of <u>algae</u>. If you look at the lichen body through a magnifying glass, you

will see that it is made up of a tangled mass of fungal strands called hyphae. In the upper layer of these hyphae grow colonies of another type of plant. These are most commonly green algae but are sometimes blue-green algae.

5   The two types of organisms live together to the benefit of both, a relationship known as symbiosis. The fungus provides support for the algae and protects the tender algae from direct sunlight and dry air. The fungus provides moisture and minerals for the plant. The fungus also produces chemicals that, when combined with alcohol produced by the algae, form acid crystals. This acid carves tiny holes in rocks and other substances, and the fungus inserts threads (not true roots) into these holes to anchor the plant in place. The algae contain <u>chlorophyll</u> and synthesize sugars from carbon dioxide and sunlight, producing food for the lichen. A chemical secreted by the fungus softens the cell walls of the algae and allows nutrients to pass from the algae to the fungus.

6   There are many examples of symbiosis in nature, but lichens are unique because they look and behave differently from their components. The algal components of lichen can live independently and are recognizable as species that grow alone. The fungal components, on the other hand, cannot live apart from their partners. They can be placed in known families of fungi but are unlike any species that live independently.

7   So definite are the form, color, and characteristics of these double organisms that for hundreds of years lichens were classified as one. More than 15,000 species were named. If these organisms are classified as single species, it is difficult to fit them into the existing system of classification. But if they are classified as separate species, these fungal species that cannot live alone seem rather strange. Lichens, then, are a splendid example of the difficulties faced by taxonomists in classifying species.

Glossary

fungus: *a non-green, plant-like organism such as a mushroom that feeds on dead or living plants*

algae: *a simple plant that usually lives in water*

chlorophyll: *a chemical that enables plants to photosynthesize (use sunshine to create food)*

1 of 39   What point about lichens does the author emphasize in paragraph 1?
○ They live primarily in cold places.
○ They live only in remote locations far from human communities.
○ They have adapted to a wide variety of environments.
○ They grow only on rock surfaces.

2 of 39   The word secrete in the passage is closest in meaning to
○ conceal
○ produce
○ absorb
○ withstand

3 of 39   Why does the author refer to lichens as *pioneers* in paragraph 2?

○ Because they developed so early in the history of the planet
○ Because of their primitive structure
○ Because they grow in areas before other plants do
○ Because they are found in remote parts of the world

4 of 39   Which of the following sentences best expresses the essential information in the sentence below? (Incorrect answer choices omit important information or change the meaning of the original sentence in an important way.)

Lichens are often spoken of in the same breath as mosses, and some lichens are even called mosses, but true mosses are all distinctively green, whereas lichens appear in many vivid colors.

○ Lichens are associated in people's minds with mosses, but real mosses are always green, whereas lichens exhibit a variety of bright colors.
○ Many people know about green mosses, but only a few people are familiar with multicolored lichens.
○ It is widely believed that mosses and lichens are the same organism, but in fact only green lichens should be considered true mosses.
○ People speak of lichens and mosses as if they were the same, and they even call some lichens "mosses" because the two types of plants are difficult to distinguish.

5 of 39   Which of the following is NOT given in paragraph 3 as one of the ways humans use lichens?

○ As a means of coloring their clothing
○ As a type of medicine
○ As a source of food
○ As an ingredient in perfume

6 of 39   The word tangled in the passage is closest in meaning to

○ twisted
○ damp
○ solid
○ clear

7 of 39   Which of the following is an example of *symbiosis* as described in paragraph 5?

○ Mistletoe, a kind of plant, grows on oak trees and harms them by extracting water and nutrients.
○ Fish called remoras attach themselves to sharks and eat the scraps of the sharks' meals.
○ Certain types of tall grass conceal tigers because of the tigers' striped markings.
○ Protozoa that live in the intestines of termites digest the cellulose that the termites eat, and their waste products nourish the termites.

8 of 39   Which of the following can be inferred from the passage about the effects of direct sunlight on lichens?

○ It destroys the fungal component.
○ It is required for the fungus to carry on photosynthesis.
○ It causes lichens to become different colors.
○ It damages the algal component.

9 of 39   The word one in paragraph 7 refers to

⚪ one species
⚪ one organism
⚪ one year
⚪ one color

10 of 39   In paragraph 7, why does the author say that these species of fungi "seem rather strange"?

⚪ They are more complex than typical fungi.
⚪ Unlike other fungi, they can produce their own food.
⚪ They exist only as partners of algae.
⚪ They do not fit into any known class of fungi.

11 of 39   The word splendid in the passage is closest in meaning to

⚪ unique
⚪ excellent
⚪ famous
⚪ improbable

12 of 39   Look at the four squares [■] that indicate where the following sentence could be added to the passage.

A few enterprising lichens contain both.

Lichens are a partnership of two or more types of plants, a fungus and a type of algae. ■ If you look at the lichen body through a magnifying glass, you will see that it is made up of a tangled mass of fungal strands called hyphae. ■ In the upper layer of these hyphae grow colonies of another type of plant. ■ These are most commonly green algae but are sometimes blue-green algae. ■

Circle the square [■] that indicates the best place to add the sentence.

13 of 39   DIRECTIONS: Select phrases from the answer choices and match them to the category to which they relate. Two answer choices will not be used. ***This question is worth 3 points.***

Answer Choices	Fungi
A. Anchor the plant	• _____
B. Can be identified as species that live alone	• _____
C. Produce carbon dioxide	• _____
D. Provide the plant with water and minerals	
E. Cannot exist independently	*Algae*
F. Use sunlight to provide the plant with food	• _____
G. Tolerate air pollution well	• _____

The Rosetta Stone

1   Things were not going well for Ptolemy V, king of Egypt in the second century B.C. He was not one of the all-powerful Egyptian pharaohs who had ruled for many centuries. The young king was one of the Ptolemaic pharaohs who were of Greek heritage, descendants of a ruler put in place by Alexander the Great when he conquered Egypt in the fourth century B.C. The reign of Ptolemy V was a time of civil unrest and foreign incursions, and the king was unpopular. It was time for a public-relations campaign. The priests of the king wrote a short history of the king's family, described his accomplishments, and explained his future plans. This message was written on stone tablets in demotic Egyptian for the common people, in Egyptian hieroglyphs for the priests, and in Greek for the ruling class. Thus, it was written in two languages but in three scripts. These tablets were posted all over Egypt.

2   Almost two thousand years later, in 1799, the French army, led by Napoleon Bonaparte, was occupying Egypt. Several years earlier, Napoleon's army had defeated the British army near Cairo and had taken over the country. However, the British fleet had destroyed the French navy and there was no way for the French soldiers to return home. During this "extended vacation," French military engineers strengthened existing defensive positions. In the port town of Rosetta (now known as El-Rashid), the French were rebuilding an old fort when Captain Pierre-François Bouchard discovered an irregularly shaped slab made of dark granite (often misidentified as basalt) with three types of writings on it in three distinct bands. Besides military forces, Napoleon had also brought scientists and scholars with him. The Rosetta Stone, as it became known, was turned over to them. They quickly realized that the three scripts contained the same message. They translated the Greek quickly but could not understand the other two scripts.

3   In 1801, the French were forced to surrender. Under the terms of the Treaty of Alexandria, the British claimed the artifacts that the French had found during their occupation. The French tried to smuggle the Rosetta Stone out of Egypt in a small boat but failed. The stone was brought to London and presented to the British Museum. On the back of the stone is the painted message, "Captured by the British Army in Egypt in 1801."

4   It was through the Rosetta Stone that scholars learned how to read Egyptian hieroglyphs. The hieroglyphic alphabet, one of the earliest writing systems ever developed, had been used by the Egyptians for 3,500 years. However, it is far more complex than simple picture writing and contains thousands of symbols. After Egypt was conquered by the Romans, Latin became the dominant language, and by the fourth century A.D., no one could understand the symbols. Before the Rosetta Stone was discovered, some scholars even believed that hieroglyphs were not really an alphabet at all but were merely decorations.

5   Copies of the Rosetta Stone were sent by the British Museum to linguists all over Europe, but learning which Greek word represented which hieroglyph proved difficult. It was the brilliant French linguist Jean François Champollion who finally unlocked the mystery. He began studying the Rosetta Stone at the age of 18. After fourteen years, he deciphered the code. In a letter to the French Royal Academy of Inscriptions, he explained the three basic assumptions that led to a translation: (1) The Coptic Egyptian language, still spoken by a small group of Egyptians, was the final stage of the ancient Egyptian language. Champollion could consult with experts on Coptic Egyptian to learn about Ptolemaic Egyptian. (2) Hieroglyphs served not only as symbols of words and ideas (ideograms) but also as symbols of spoken sounds (phonograms). (3) Certain hieroglyphs enclosed in ovals were phonetic transcriptions of pharaohs' names. Once these hieroglyphs were understood, it was easier to decipher the rest. Armed with Champollion's translation, scholars all over the world took a new interest in Egypt and laid the foundation for our understanding of this ancient civilization.

6   The Rosetta Stone is still displayed at the British Museum and is one of the most popular exhibits there, but the Egyptian government wants it back. In 2003, Dr. Zahi Hawass, director of the Supreme Council of Antiquities in Cairo and a noted archaeologist himself, formally requested its return, saying, "The British . . . should volunteer to return the stone because it is the icon of our Egyptian identity."

Glossary

demotic: *describing a form of a language that is spoken by ordinary people*

hieroglyphs: *symbols used in ancient Egypt to represent words or sounds*

What was the original purpose of the Rosetta Stone?

○ To preserve the writing systems that were once used in ancient Egypt
○ To record the history of the all-powerful pharaohs of Egypt
○ To announce that a new king had been crowned
○ To present information about the then current ruler of Egypt, Ptolemy V

The word incursions in the passage is closest in meaning to

○ influences
○ travelers
○ invasions
○ adventures

16 of 39   It can be inferred from the information in paragraph 1 that the author believes that

○ demotic Egyptian and the form of Egyptian used by the priests were the same language

○ the priests of ancient Egypt were all members of the ruling class

○ demotic Egyptian was a spoken language that did not have a written form

○ ancient Greek and demotic Egyptian were different languages but used the same script

17 of 39   Why do you think the author put quotation marks (" ") around the phrase *extended vacation* in paragraph 2?

○ The French ruler Napoleon Bonaparte used this exact phrase to refer to the time his army spent in Egypt.

○ The French Army was in Egypt because their fleet had been destroyed, not because they were on vacation there.

○ The French were not really in Egypt for an extended period, but rather for a very short time.

○ Unlike the soldiers, the scientists and scholars who came with Napoleon's army were enjoying their time in Egypt.

18 of 39   What was Pierre-François Bouchard's probable occupation?

○ Captain of a warship

○ Archaeologist

○ Military engineer

○ Linguist

19 of 39   When writing about the Rosetta Stone, authors are sometimes mistaken about

○ the significance of the writing on it

○ its true shape

○ the name of the place where it was discovered

○ the material it is made of

20 of 39   The word bands in the passage is closest in meaning to

○ lines

○ areas

○ symbols

○ pieces

21 of 39   We can infer from the passage that the scholars mentioned in paragraph 4

○ did not think that the hieroglyphic alphabet could ever be translated

○ were experts on the decorations used by the ancient Egyptians

○ played an important role in deciphering the Rosetta Stone

○ did not believe that Latin was ever the dominant language in Egypt

22 of 39   Which of the following is NOT one of the assumptions that helped Champollion to translate the Rosetta Stone?

○ That hieroglyphs represented not only words and ideas but also sounds

○ That the three messages written on the stone did not have exactly the same meanings

○ That some of the hieroglyphs set off from the others represented the names of pharaohs

○ That one form of modern Egyptian was related to the ancient Egyptian language

23 of 39   The phrase the rest in paragraph 5 refers to

      ○ pharaohs' names
      ○ ovals
      ○ scholars
      ○ hieroglyphs

24 of 39   How does the author emphasize the point that is made in paragraph 6?

      ○ By making a comparison
      ○ By asking the reader a question
      ○ By quoting an expert
      ○ By summarizing the previous paragraph

25 of 39   Look at the four squares [■] that indicate where the following sentence could be added to the passage.

> **Hieroglyphic script is mostly pictorial, consisting of images of natural and man-made objects.**

It was through the Rosetta Stone that scholars learned how to read Egyptian hieroglyphs. The hieroglyphic alphabet, one of the earliest writing systems ever developed, had been used by the Egyptians for 3,500 years. ■ However, it is far more complex than simple picture writing and contains thousands of symbols. ■ After Egypt was conquered by the Romans, Latin became the dominant language, and by the fourth century A.D., no one could understand the symbols. ■ Before the Rosetta Stone was discovered, some scholars even believed that hieroglyphs were not really an alphabet but were merely decorations. ■

Circle the square [■] that indicates the best place to add the sentence.

26 of 39   DIRECTIONS: Below is an introductory sentence for a brief summary of the passage. Complete the summary by writing the letters of **three** of the answer choices that express the most important ideas of the passage. Some of the answer choices are incorrect because they express ideas that are not given in the passage or because they express only details from the passage. *This question is worth 3 points.*

The priests of Ptolemy V wrote a message in three scripts: Greek, demotic Egyptian, and hieroglyphic.

- _____
- _____
- _____

Answer Choices

A. Officials at the British Museum have so far refused to discuss the return of the Rosetta Stone to Egypt.

B. Through Champollion's brilliant work, the Rosetta Stone was translated and scholars were able to read hieroglyphs for the first time in many centuries.

C. Despite its name, the Rosetta Stone is not actually made of stone.

D. Napoleon's expedition to Egypt included not just soldiers but also scientific and scholarly experts.

E. The Rosetta Stone was discovered in Egypt by the French but was captured by the British and taken to the British Museum.

F. Egypt has requested the return of the Rosetta Stone.

Transient Lunar Phenomena

1   For many years, sky watchers have reported seeing mysterious sights known as *Transient Lunar Phenomena* (TLP) on the surface of the moon. These are of two main types: fleeting flashes of light and spreading clouds of mist. Most professional astronomers have tended to dismiss these phenomena as figments of the observers' imagination or as "observational errors": either optical illusions or problems with the observers' telescopes. One explanation put forth by professional astronomers blames the flashes on Earth satellites passing in front of the moon. Satellite surfaces can flash like a car's windshield in sunlight, simulating a lunar flash. It was this mechanism that astronomers R. R. Raste and P. Maley used to explain a large lunar flash observed on March 23, 1983, and other sightings as well.

2   One problem with the satellite theory is that TLP were reported long before the advent of artificial satellites. The earliest known account comes from the twelfth-century writer Gervase. On June 18, 1178, in Canterbury, England, Gervase was observing an eclipse of the moon. He was startled by what appeared to be "a flaming torch . . . that spewed out fire, hot coals, and sparks." Eighteenth-century astronomer Sir William Herschel, discoverer of the planet Uranus, also reported seeing both types of TLP. He described one TLP as looking like a piece of slowly burning charcoal. In 1830, Andrew Grant, studying the moon from an observatory in Cape Town, South Africa, also observed flashing lights. He told newspaper reporters that he believed the lights came from the sun flashing off clear glass domes that covered cities and forests on the otherwise dead moon. Grant claimed in an interview that he had seen flocks of red and white birds, herds of "diminutive bison," and strange beavers that walked on their hind legs. Not only that, but he claimed even to have seen people with batlike wings who had built towers and pyramids beneath the domes.

3   In more recent times, a record number of TLP were monitored from 1968 to 1972, during the Apollo missions to the moon. This fact is hardly surprising given that more telescopes were probably trained on the moon during these four years than had been in the entire 270-year history of telescopic observation preceding that time. Though many sightings were dubious, some were highly plausible because they were made by independent observers at different locations. Another notable TLP observation, and the only one confirmed by photographic evidence, took place on April 23, 1994. When over a hundred amateur astronomers reported seeing a dark red cloud spreading across a portion of the Aristachus crater, astronomer Bonnie Buratti of the Jet Propulsion Laboratory decided to investigate. She got access to photographs of the moon taken by the U.S. lunar mapping satellite *Clementine,* and indeed, these images confirmed the presence of a reddish cloud obscuring part of the crater.

4   Even those who believe in TLP cannot agree why the moon sporadically flashes and forms clouds, but many theories have been proposed. Another possibility is that, in some places on the moon, there are chemicals that glow when they are exposed to bursts of radiation from the sun during solar flares. There is, in fact, some evidence that TLP are observed more frequently during episodes of solar activity. After Project Apollo astronauts brought lunar rocks back to the earth, scientists determined that there are flammable gases inside some moon rocks. Perhaps these rocks crack open and are then ignited by a

stray spark, causing the flash. However, what causes these rocks to split open? One possibility is "thermal cracking." A rock heats up in the intense sunlight. Suddenly, when the sun sets, the temperature drops, and the stone cracks. The rocks might also be shattered by "moonquakes," seismic activity on the moon, or by meteors. Scientist R. Zito believes the flashes come not from gas trapped inside the rocks but from the crystals of the rocks themselves. If someone chews a sugar cube in a dark room, sparks appear to come from the person's mouth as the sugar crystals are crushed. Zito believes that this "sugar cube effect" occurs when meteors smash into lunar rocks, crushing the crystals.

5   And what about the billowing clouds? The most commonly held belief today is that they are caused by pockets of gas trapped beneath the lunar surface. The clouds may be caused by the rapid escape of these gases, which kicks up clouds of dust. The pockets of gas may be freed by moonquakes or the pockets may be punctured by meteors.

6   The true cause of TLP—if indeed they do exist—is still an unsolved mystery, however, and will probably remain that way at least until humans return to the moon.

27 of 39   Which of the following statements best summarizes the overall organization of the passage?

○ A popular idea is challenged, and this challenge is then refuted.
○ A generalization is made, and examples of it are examined.
○ Historical information is reviewed and then the current situation is presented.
○ A phenomenon is described and possible explanations for it are proposed.

28 of 39   The word fleeting in the passage is closest in meaning to

○ brightly glowing
○ amazing
○ short-lived
○ blinking

29 of 39   The phrase this mechanism in paragraph 1 refers to

○ the flashing of sunlight off a reflective surface
○ the windshield of an automobile
○ a satellite
○ an observer's telescope

30 of 39   Why does the author mention the writer Gervase in paragraph 2?

○ To weaken the satellite theory of Raste and Maley
○ To document the earliest sighting of a lunar eclipse by a scientist
○ To support the ideas of Herschel and Grant
○ To provide an early theory about the causes of TLP

31 of 39   Which of these sightings claimed to be made by Andrew Grant (paragraph 2) does the author apparently find most unbelievable?

○ The flocks of red and white birds
○ The bat-winged people who built towers and pyramids
○ The herds of tiny bison
○ The unusual beavers that walked on two legs

32 of 39   Which of the following sentences best expresses the essential information in the boldface sentence below? (Incorrect answer choices omit important information or change the meaning of the original sentence in an important way.)

> **In more recent times, a record number of TLP were monitored from 1968 to 1972, during the Apollo missions to the moon, a fact that is hardly surprising given that more telescopes were probably trained on the moon during these four years than had been in the entire 270-year history of telescopic observation preceding that time.**

○ Because far more people were looking at the moon through telescopes during the Apollo missions, more TLP were seen then than had been seen during any prior period.
○ From 1968 until 1972, not just amateur astronomers but also trained scientists saw more TLP than they had ever seen before.
○ More TLP occurred on the moon between 1968 and 1972 than had occurred during the previous 270 years of telescopic observation.
○ It is unsurprising that in the four years between 1968 and 1972 more people with telescopes were observing the moon than had observed it in the previous 270 years.

33 of 39   According to the author, an observation is more reliable when it is made by

○ a professional astronomer
○ a group of astronomers working together
○ a number of observers working separately in different locations
○ a person observing the same part of the moon night after night

34 of 39   How was astronomer Bonnie Buratti able to "confirm" the presence of a cloud on the moon?

○ By interviewing one hundred amateur astronomers
○ By examining satellite photography
○ By analyzing lunar rocks
○ By taking a picture through a telescope

35 of 39   The word stray in the passage is closest in meaning to

○ speeding
○ hot
○ spinning
○ undirected

36 of 39   Which of the following situations is an example of "thermal cracking" as it is described in paragraph 4?

○ A dam breaks when water rises behind it
○ Sparks appear when someone chews a candy mint in a dark room
○ A cool glass breaks when it is filled with boiling water
○ An ice cube melts in the heat of the sun

37 of 39   All of the following are given as possible reasons for the cracking of moon rocks EXCEPT

   ○ seismic activity
   ○ sudden temperature changes
   ○ the action of meteors
   ○ the pressure of gases

38 of 39   Look at the four squares [■] that indicate where the following sentence could be added to the passage.

> **Many observers once thought that they were caused by lunar volcanoes, but today the moon is believed to have been geologically inactive for billions of years.**

And what about the billowing clouds? ■ The most commonly held belief today is that they are caused by pockets of gas trapped beneath the lunar surface. ■ The clouds may be caused by the rapid escape of these gases, which kicks up clouds of dust. ■ The pockets of gas may be freed by moonquakes or the pockets may be punctured by meteors. ■

Circle the square [■] that indicates the best place to add the sentence.

39 of 39   DIRECTIONS: Select sentences from the answer choices and match them to the category to which they relate. Two answer choices will not be used. ***This question is worth 3 points.***

Answer Choices	*Theories that explain why TLP do not exist*
A. TLP are caused by the collision of two meteors.	• _____
B. TLP are caused by the reflection of sunlight off satellites.	• _____
C. TLP are caused by meteors crushing the crystals in lunar rocks.	*Theories that explain why TLP do exist*
D. TLP are caused by chemicals on the surface of the sun that are affected by solar activity.	• _____
E. TLP are caused by errors made by amateur astronomers.	• _____
F. TLP are caused by the reflection of the sun off glass domes.	• _____
G. TLP were caused by the actions of astronauts on the Moon.	

This is the end of the Reading Section. Go on to the Listening Section.

SECTION 2

▶ Now start the Audio Program. 🎧

This section tests your understanding of conversations and lectures. You will hear each conversation or lecture only once. Your answers should be based on what is stated or implied in the conversations and lectures.

You are allowed to take notes as you listen, and you can use these notes to help you answer the questions.

In some questions, you will see a headphones icon: 🎧. This icon tells you that you will hear, but not read, part of the lecture again. Then you will answer a question about the part of the lecture that you heard.

Some questions have special directions that are highlighted.

During an actual listening test, you will *not* be able to skip items and come back to them later, so try to answer every question that you hear on this practice test.

This test includes two conversations and four lectures. Most questions are separated by a ten-second pause.

▶ Listen to a conversation between two students. 🎧

Notes:

_____

_____

_____

> **Now get ready to answer some questions about the conversation. You may use your notes to help you.**

1 of 34   Why can't Allen vote for Janet?

   ○ Because he is no longer attending the university
   ○ Because she has decided to drop out of the election
   ○ Because they do not attend the same school at the university
   ○ Because she is running for president, not for the Student Council

2 of 34   How many candidates for office is each student allowed to vote for in this election?

   ○ One
   ○ Two
   ○ Three
   ○ Eleven

3 of 34   What is learned about Janet from this conversation?

Choose two answers.

   ☐ She is currently a member of the Student Council.
   ☐ She doesn't believe that she has a chance of getting elected.
   ☐ She doesn't think that the president should be directly elected.
   ☐ She may run for Student Council president next year.

4 of 34   According to Janet, what is the most important responsibility of the Student Council?

   ○ To determine how to spend student fees
   ○ To decide when and where to hold concerts
   ○ To attend meetings of the Board of Trustees
   ○ To change the student government charter

> ▶ Listen again to part of the conversation. 🎧

5 of 34   What does Allen imply when he says this? 🎧

   ○ He'll be too busy to vote tomorrow.
   ○ He won't attend tonight's debate.
   ○ He's already decided whom to vote for.
   ○ He hopes the woman gets elected.

▶ Listen to a conversation between two students. 🎧

Notes:

_____

_____

_____

> **Now get ready to answer some questions about the
> conversation. You may use your notes to help you.**

6 of 34   What subject does Professor Marquez probably teach?

○ Chemistry
○ Filmmaking
○ Drama
○ Marketing

7 of 34   What will Professor Marquez give the man if he comes to her class the next day?

○ Information about what role he will play
○ Several types of ice cream
○ A list of questions about the product
○ Money to pay him for his time

8 of 34   What does the woman imply about focus groups that test Hollywood films?

○ They are mainly exploratory focus groups.
○ They are used to help select directors for films.
○ They are mainly experiential focus groups.
○ They are usually used before work on films has begun.

9 of 34   What will Professor Marquez probably pay most attention to during the focus-group activity?

○ The knowledge that the moderators have about the product
○ The types of ice cream that are used
○ The opinions that the volunteers express
○ The interaction between focus groups and moderators

▶ Listen again to part of the conversation. 🎧

10 of 34   What does Tony imply when he says this? 🎧

○ He wants to take part in the focus-group activity, but he can't.
○ He likes mint chocolate-chip ice cream.
○ He's already formed his opinion about the product.
○ He would like to become a moderator of the focus group.

▶ Listen to a lecture in an American literature class. 🎧

AMERICAN LITERATURE

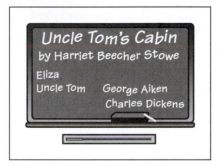

Notes:

_____

_____

_____

> **Now get ready to answer some questions about the lecture. You may use your notes to help you.**

11 of 34   Where did Harriet Stowe live when she wrote *Uncle Tom's Cabin?*

     ○ Cincinnati, Ohio
     ○ Kentucky
     ○ Brunswick, Maine
     ○ Connecticut

12 of 34   The professor mentions a number of versions of *Uncle Tom's Cabin.* List these in the order in which they were produced, beginning with the earliest.

     A. The book
     B. The movie
     C. The newspaper serial
     D. The plays

> Put the letters of the versions in the proper boxes.

1.	
2.	
3.	
4.	

PRACTICE
TEST 2

13 of 34   Why does the professor mention Charles Dickens?

○ He wrote a book on the same topic as that of Stowe's book.
○ Like Stowe, he wrote about some characters in a sentimental way.
○ His novel *The Old Curiosity Shop* strongly influenced Stowe's writing.
○ He strongly criticized Stowe's novel *Uncle Tom's Cabin*.

14 of 34   What does the professor say about the scene in which Eliza is chased across the icy river by men with dogs?

Choose two answers.

☐ It is considered the most frightening part of the book.
☐ It is one of the scenes that people remember best.
☐ It is a part of the book but not of the play.
☐ It does not appear in the book *Uncle Tom's Cabin*.

15 of 34   In this lecture, the professor mentions a number of criticisms of Harriet Beecher Stowe's novel *Uncle Tom's Cabin*. Indicate whether each of the following is a criticism that was mentioned in the lecture.

Put a check mark (✓) in the proper box for each phrase.

	Yes	No
It is not strong enough in its criticism of slavery.		
It treats its characters too sentimentally.		
It is not based on the author's first-hand experiences.		
It is difficult for modern readers to understand.		
It is far too long and repetitive.		

▶ Listen again to part of the lecture. Then answer the question. 🎧

16 of 34   What does the professor suggest to the students when she says this? 🎧

○ They should read the book several times.
○ They must read the entire textbook.
○ They should read short selections from the novel.
○ They should read all of *Uncle Tom's Cabin*.

▶ Listen to a lecture in a geology class. 🎧

GEOLOGY

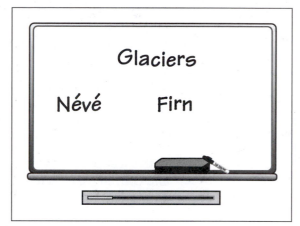

Notes:

_____

_____

_____

> **Now get ready to answer some questions about the lecture. You may use your notes to help you.**

17 of 34   The professor discusses four types of materials involved in the formation of a glacier.

Give the order in which these materials appear.

A. **Glacial ice**
B. **Névé**
C. **Firn**
D. **Ordinary snow**

Put the letters of the materials in the proper boxes.

1. _____
2. _____
3. _____
4. _____

18 of 34   Where can continental glaciers be found today?

Choose two answers.

☐ West Virginia
☐ Iceland
☐ Greenland
☐ Antarctica

19 of 34   Which of the following describe a valley formed by a valley glacier?

Choose two answers.

☐ Shaped like the letter V
☐ Gently curving
☐ Shaped like the letter U
☐ Having sharp angles

20 of 34   It can be inferred from the lecture that which of the following is the smallest type of glacier?

○ A tributary glacier
○ A piedmont glacier
○ A valley glacier
○ A continental glacier

21 of 34   In this lecture, the professor gives a number of characteristics of valley glaciers and continental glaciers. Indicate whether each characteristic is typical of valley glaciers or continental glaciers.

Put a check mark (✓) in the proper box for each phrase.

	Valley Glaciers	Continental Glaciers
Today cover about 10% of the world's landmass		
Flow together to form piedmont glaciers		
As they recede, seem to flow uphill		
About 11,000 years ago, covered 30% of the world's landmass		
As they grow, seem to flow outwards in all directions		

22 of 34   What danger does the professor mention?

○ The water from melting glaciers may cause sea levels to rise.
○ Melted ice from glaciers may cause the water in the oceans to cool off.
○ Global warming may cause damaging storms in the Indian Ocean.
○ Glaciers may form in places such as Africa where there are no glaciers today.

▶ Listen to a discussion in an economics class. 🎧

ECONOMICS

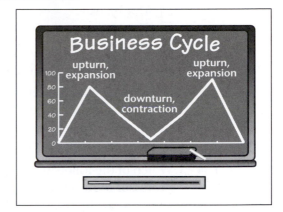

Notes:

_____

_____

_____

Now get ready to answer some questions about the discussion. You may use your notes to help you.

23 of 34   What is the main topic of this discussion?
○ The causes of the Great Depression
○ The effects of climate on business cycles
○ The stages of the business cycle
○ Government regulation of business

24 of 34   What does Professor Martin imply when he says this? 🎧
○ These terms are still used but are no longer common.
○ Other terms were more common in the past.
○ These are the correct terms, but they are not very descriptive.
○ He himself prefers to use other terms for the four stages.

25 of 34   In this lecture, the professor describes the business cycle. Indicate whether each of the following is a characteristic of the cycle mentioned by the professor.
   Put a check mark (✓) in the proper box for each phrase.

	Yes	No
They vary in length from cycle to cycle.		
They are measured from the peak of economic activity to the trough, the lowest point of economic activity.		
They vary in intensity from cycle to cycle.		
They have involved deeper recessions in recent years because of globalization.		
They are sometimes called _fluctuations_ because they are irregular.		

26 of 34   In which of these decades did economic depressions occur?

Choose two answers.

☐ The 1870s
☐ The 1930s
☐ The 1970s
☐ The 1990s

27 of 34   In what ways do governments usually try to affect business cycles?

○ By reforming the central bank
○ By hiring more government employees
○ By spending less money
○ By controlling the money supply

28 of 34   Which of the following statements about William Jevons's theory would Professor Martin probably agree with?

○ It's interesting but no longer generally accepted.
○ It may be valid, but there were never any statistics to support it.
○ As time has gone by, more and more economists have accepted it.
○ It was valid when it was first proposed but not today.

▶ Listen to a lecture in a film studies class. 🎧

FILM STUDIES

Notes:

_____

_____

_____

> **Now get ready to answer some questions about the
> lecture. You may use your notes to help you.**

29 of 34   Why does the professor mention the work of the French director Georges
Méliès?

○ To point out that one of the earliest movies was a science fiction movie
○ To give an example of a realistic science fiction movie
○ To discuss the very first use of special effects in any movie ever made
○ To compare the role of a magician with that of a film director

30 of 34   When does the action in the movie *Metropolis* supposedly take place?

○ In 1902
○ In 1926
○ In 1984
○ In 2026

31 of 34   What topic does the movie *Them!* and many other 1950s science-fiction
movies deal with?

○ An invasion from outer space
○ An attack by robots
○ The effects of radiation on insects
○ A nuclear war

32 of 34   Which of the following influenced the movie *Forbidden Planet?*
Choose two answers.

☐ The theories of Sigmund Freud
☐ A novel by the French author Jules Verne
☐ A play by William Shakespeare
☐ Movies about the American West

33 of 34   What does the professor think is remarkable about the movie *ET?*

○ That it's considered the most popular science fiction of all time
○ That it features a friendly alien rather than a hostile one
○ That it was popular with audiences but not with critics
○ That it is so similar to other movies about visitors from space

34 of 34   What does the professor imply when she says this? 🎧

○ She prefers recent movies to older movies such as *Forbidden Planet.*
○ She would like to be able to show more of the film *Forbidden Planet.*
○ She doesn't really want to show scenes from any 1950s movies.
○ She doesn't have time to show scenes from her favorite movie today.

***This is the end of the Listening Section of Practice Test 2. You may take a
ten-minute break before beginning work on the Speaking Section.***

SPEAKING SECTION
DIRECTIONS

▶ Now start the Audio Program and listen carefully. 🎧

This section tests your ability to speak about various subjects. There are six tasks in this section. Listen carefully to the directions and read the questions on the screen. The first two tasks are independent speaking tasks. You have fifteen seconds in which to prepare your response. When you hear a beep on the Audio Program, you will have forty-five seconds in which to answer the question.

The last four tasks are integrated speaking tasks. The third and fourth questions involve a reading text and a listening passage. You have forty-five seconds in which to read a short text. You will then hear a short conversation or part of a lecture on the same topic. You may take notes on both the reading and listening passage. You will then see a question on the screen asking about the information that you have just read and heard, and you will have thirty seconds in which to plan a response. When you hear a beep on the Audio Program, you have sixty seconds in which to answer the question.

The fifth and sixth questions involve a short listening passage. You may take notes as you listen. After listening to the conversation or lecture, you will see a question, and you have twenty seconds in which to plan your response. When you hear a beep on the Audio Program, you have sixty seconds in which to answer the question.

During actual tests, a clock on the screen will tell you how much preparation time or how much response time (speaking time) remains for each question. It is important that you time yourself accurately when you take this practice test. On an actual test your responses will be recorded and evaluated by trained raters.

Task 1

Describe the most interesting book that you have ever read. Explain why it was important to you. Include details and examples to support your explanation.

Preparation Time: 15 Seconds
Response Time: 45 Seconds

Task 2

Because of computers, telephones, and other technology, it is now possible for many people to work at home. Some people prefer working at home, while others would rather work in an office. Which of these do you prefer and why?

Preparation Time: 15 Seconds
Response Time: 45 Seconds

Linslade University has begun a new program involving free laptop computers. Read the following notice from the university. You will have forty-five seconds in which to read the notice. Begin reading now.

Frequently Asked Questions about the Linslade University Laptop Give-Away Program

Q: What is the Laptop Give-Away?
A: All full-time freshmen enrolling at Linslade University this fall will receive a laptop computer equipped with a comprehensive software package to use throughout their entire university career.

Q: Why is the university beginning this program?
A: As electronic technology becomes more and more a part of our lives, it is critical that students be provided with the latest tools. Making laptops available to all incoming freshmen ensures that everyone has equal access to technology.

Q: How can the computers be used?
A: However you like. You can, for example, take lecture notes, e-mail your professors and fellow students, do research on the Internet, and submit assignments electronically.

Q: Is this program available only to full-time incoming freshmen?
A: Yes. This is a pilot program launching this fall. Free laptops will be available, this year at least, only to full-time first-year students. As the program expands, Linslade University hopes to be able to offer free laptops to incoming transfer students as well. So that the rest of the student community will not be left behind, laptops will available for purchase at a discount.

▶ Now turn the page and listen to two students discussing this notice. ⌂

Notes:

_____

_____

_____

Now get ready to answer the question.

The man expresses his opinion of the new program. State his opinion and explain the reasons he gives for having that opinion. Please begin speaking after the beep.

Preparation Time: 30 Seconds
Response Time: 60 Seconds

Task 4

Read the following description of utopian communities.

Many nineteenth-century reformers hoped to reform society through education or by eliminating specific social problems, but some wanted to start over by founding *utopian* ("ideal") communities. These thinkers hoped that the success of these small, cooperative communities would lead to imitation, and that eventually communities free of crime and poverty would cover the land. Many such communities were founded. Most had some or all of the following characteristics: (1) They were isolated geographically and socially from surrounding communities. (2) They experimented socially and economically. (3) They lasted only a few years.

▶ Now turn the page and listen to a lecture on the utopian community Brook Farm. 🎧

Notes:

_____

_____

_____

_____

Now get ready to answer the question.

The professor's lecture is about the Brook Farm community. Describe this community and explain why it is a typical utopian community.

Preparation Time: 30 Seconds
Response Time: 60 Seconds

Task 5

▶ Now listen to a conversation between two students. 🎧

Online access code as well.

Niagara College Canada

English for Academic Preparation
FALL 2010
September –Dec 17th

Re: Textbook Rental

Dear 15 week students:

Welcome to ESL program at Niagara College! Since you are enrolled into 15 week EAP program, we have provided you a rental textbook DEC 17th, 2010

Please do not write anything on the books, and remember to return your books to Rasha, no later than DEC 17th, 2010. If the books are clean (no writing) and good conditions when you return all books, you will get your deposit back. If you fail to return the books in good conditions or failed to return the books, you must pay $50(per book) penalty without receiving your deposit back.

To borrow ESL textbooks, please see Rasha Abu Ramadan in S100 (Welland). You must pay $50 deposit cash and sign on a rental list. If you have any questions, please see Rasha.

Sincerely,

Carolyn Ambrose
International Department
Tel: 905-735-2211

ESL level: 3
Student Name: Valencia Elizabeth
Student Signature: [signature]
Date received: October 13, 2010.

problem. Discuss her prob-
think is better and why

Task 6

▶ Now listen to a lecture in a meteorology class. 🎧

Notes:

_____

_____

_____

Now get ready to answer the question.

Using specific examples and points from the lecture, explain the naming process for hurricanes.

Preparation Time: 20 Seconds
Response Time: 60 Seconds

This is the end of the Speaking Section. Go directly to the Writing Section.

INTEGRATED WRITING TASK
DIRECTIONS

Take three minutes to read the short passage that follows. You may take notes as you read.

After three minutes, turn the page and start the Audio Program. You will hear a lecture on the same topic as the reading. Again, you may take notes as you listen.

You will have twenty minutes to write your response. Your response should include information from both the reading and the lecture.

Your essay will be rated on the completeness and accuracy of your response as well as on the correctness and quality of your writing. A typical response should be 150 to 225 words.

You may use your notes and look at the reading passage as you write. (During the actual exam, you can view the reading passage on the computer screen after the lecture is over.)

If you finish this writing task in less than twenty minutes, you may start working on the second writing task.

These days, many tourists are tired of just sitting on the beach or looking at paintings in museums. Many enjoy getting back to nature in undeveloped parts of the globe. In fact, the most rapidly growing segment of the tourist industry is "eco-tourism," tourism in sites that have ecological significance such as national parks and nature preserves in rain forests, deserts, and mountainous regions.

Eco-tourism is having significant positive results on these previously remote areas. First and foremost, eco-tourism serves as a substitute for forms of development that would be much more damaging to the environment, such as logging, farming, and manufacturing. And eco-tourism encourages conservation. Let's say there is a rainforest in a country where several rare species of birds and mammals live. Now, the government could allow loggers to cut down this rain forest and sell the wood and could allow developers to build on this site. But suppose the government decides to preserve this national treasure and to instead develop this area for eco-tourism. There would then a steady stream of revenue from tourists. Local people could find jobs working at small hotels, lodges, and tour companies. Many of these natural wonders lie in areas that have previously been passed over by development of any kind. Eco-tourism provides jobs and better living conditions for people who need it the most. Both the government and the local people have a vested interest in preserving this sensitive wilderness site. And governments can use some of the funds from entry fees to parks and so on to help pay for preservation and protection. Eco-tourism, then, is one of those rare situations where all parties benefit—tourists, governments, the local people, and especially the animals and plants.

▶ Now start the Audio Program. Listen to part of a lecture in an economics class on the same topic that you just read about. 🎧

Now get ready to answer the question. Remember, you may look back at the reading passage. You may also use your notes to help you. You have twenty minutes to prepare and write your response.

Summarize the main points made in the lecture that you just heard, discussing how they cast doubt on points made in the reading. You can refer to the reading passage as you write.

Notes:

_____

_____

_____

_____

_____

_____

_____

Response:

_____

_____

_____

_____

_____

_____

_____

_____

_____

_____

_____

_____

_____

_____

_____

_____

_____

_____

INDEPENDENT WRITING TASK
DIRECTIONS

Read the question below. You have thirty minutes to write your essay. This includes the time to plan, write, and revise your essay. A typical response should be a minimum of 300 words.

Your essay will be rated on the correctness and quality of your writing, including the way you organize your essay and develop and support your ideas.

> A new acquaintance of yours is thinking about studying your native language. How would you convince him or her that this would be a good decision? Use specific reasons and details in your response.

Notes:

_____
_____
_____
_____
_____
_____
_____
_____
_____

Response:

_____
_____
_____
_____
_____
_____
_____
_____
_____
_____
_____
_____
_____
_____
_____

This is the end of the Writing Section and of Practice Test 2.

Photo Credits